An Atypical ASP.NET Core 5 Design Patterns Guide

A SOLID adventure into architectural principles, design patterns, .NET 5, and C#

Carl-Hugo Marcotte

BIRMINGHAM—MUMBAI

An Atypical ASP.NET Core 5 Design Patterns Guide

Group Product Manager: Ashwin Nair

Publishing Product Manager: Pavan Ramchandani

Commissioning Editor: Kunal Chaudhary

Acquisition Editor: Chaitanya Nair

Senior Editor: Keagan Carneiro

Content Development Editor: Rakhi Patel

Technical Editor: Shubham Sharma

Copy Editor: Safis Editing

Project Coordinator: Kinjal Bari

Proofreader: Safis Editing

Indexer: Tejal Daruwale Soni

Production Designer: Shankar Kalbhor

First published: December 2020

Production reference: 1301220

Published by Packt Publishing Ltd.

Livery Place

35 Livery Street

Birmingham

B3 2PB, UK.

ISBN 978-1-78934-609-1

www.packt.com

To everyone who has supported me in my life and my career
or from whom I learned something.

– Carl-Hugo Marcotte

Packt>

Packt.com

Subscribe to our online digital library for full access to over 7,000 books and videos, as well as industry leading tools to help you plan your personal development and advance your career. For more information, please visit our website.

Why subscribe?

- Spend less time learning and more time coding with practical eBooks and Videos from over 4,000 industry professionals

- Improve your learning with Skill Plans built especially for you

- Get a free eBook or video every month

- Fully searchable for easy access to vital information

- Copy and paste, print, and bookmark content

Did you know that Packt offers eBook versions of every book published, with PDF and ePub files available? You can upgrade to the eBook version at packt.com and as a print book customer, you are entitled to a discount on the eBook copy. Get in touch with us at customercare@packtpub.com for more details.

At www.packt.com, you can also read a collection of free technical articles, sign up for a range of free newsletters, and receive exclusive discounts and offers on Packt books and eBooks.

Foreword

After 10 years of abiding partnership with Carl-Hugo, I still remember the production support project that ushered this partnership in – the application's accuracy and reliability were the overriding factors, providing the final product's competitive edge. This project brought to light Carl-Hugo's talent and his solid grasp of the .NET programming platform, which spurred me to entrust him with more sensitive and crucial projects, laying the groundwork for our extended partnership.

We started tackling projects that had been on hold for a long time, requiring deep analysis, and more importantly, acute imagination to put them across using .NET programs. Once again, Carl-Hugo's knowledge and skills stood out, leading to robust and flexible .NET application designs.

Carl-Hugo has consolidated his expertise by spending several years teaching programming. His book *An Atypical ASP.NET Core 5 Design Patterns Guide* unites that experience with his long-term expertise in the field. Therefore, I highly recommend reading the book and putting it into practice as I've already had the opportunity to attend some of his training sessions and bear witness to this manual's consistency and practical features.

Abdelhamid Zebdi

IT Director – Nortek Air Solutions 2007-2017
IT OPS Management – House of Commons of Canada 2017 – present

Contributors

About the author

Carl-Hugo Marcotte has been developing, designing, and architecting web applications professionally since 2005. He wrote his first line of code at about 8 years old and has been a computer enthusiast since. He holds a Bachelor's degree in Computer Science from Université du Québec à Trois-Rivières.

After working at a firm for a few years, he became an independent consultant, where he developed projects of different sizes for SMEs and educational institutions. He is passionate about software architecture, C#, ASP.NET Core, and the web.

He loves to share his knowledge, which led him to teaching programming; blogging; and creating, maintaining, and contributing to multiple open source projects.

I want to thank everyone who supported me during my journey into the world of authoring, especially my other half and partner in life, Cathie, who is always there no matter the idea I pursue.

About the reviewers

Will Marcouiller is the founder and current CEO of Société Groupe Conseil WMI. Since its beginnings, WMI has partnered worldwide with clients of all sizes, from its initial focus on small-and medium-sized enterprises (SMEs) to international corporations, to optimize business processes through the application of continuous improvement concepts combined with the usage of cutting-edge technologies. WMI endeavors to deliver the highest quality integrated software to its clients in fields such as insurance, manufacturing, real estate, transportation, and ministries/governmental organizations. In addition to helping the clients of WMI achieve their objectives, Will has worked to educate the next generation of programmers by teaching in private colleges.

David Guida is a software engineer with more than 15 years of professional experience in different domains, including healthcare, finance, and large-scale e-commerce. He is a Microsoft MVP on Developer Technologies and a member of the .NET Foundation.

He regularly writes articles on his blog and on other platforms as well, such as DZone and Dev.to. When he is not busy coding or looking for the next book to read, you can find him in his kitchen baking cakes.

Packt is searching for authors like you

If you're interested in becoming an author for Packt, please visit `authors.packtpub.com` and apply today. We have worked with thousands of developers and tech professionals, just like you, to help them share their insight with the global tech community. You can make a general application, apply for a specific hot topic that we are recruiting an author for, or submit your own idea.

Table of Contents

3
Architectural Principles

Section 2: Designing for ASP.NET Core

4
The MVC Pattern using Razor

5
The MVC Pattern for Web APIs

6

Understanding the Strategy, Abstract Factory, and Singleton Design Patterns

7

Deep Dive into Dependency Injection

8
Options and Logging Patterns

Section 3: Designing at Component Scale

9
Structural Patterns

10

Behavioral Patterns

11

Understanding the Operation Result Design Pattern

Section 4:
Designing at Application Scale

12
Understanding Layering

13
Getting Started with Object Mappers

14
Mediator and CQRS Design Patterns

15

Getting Started with Vertical Slice Architecture

16

Introduction to Microservices Architecture

Section 5:
Designing the Client Side

17
ASP.NET Core User Interfaces

18
A Brief Look into Blazor

Assessment Answers

Acronyms Lexicon

Other Books You May Enjoy

Index

Preface

Design patterns are a set of solutions to many of the common problems occurring in software development. They are essential for any experienced developer and professionals crafting software solutions of any scale.

We start by exploring basic design patterns, architectural principles, dependency injection, and other ASP.NET Core mechanisms. Then we explore component-scale patterns oriented toward small chunks of software. Next, we move on to application-scale patterns and techniques, where we explore higher-level patterns and how to structure the application as a whole. The book covers many unavoidable GoF patterns, such as strategy, singleton, decorator, facade, and composite. The chapters are organized based on scale and topics, allowing you to start small with a strong base and build slowly on top of it, the same way that you would build a program. Many use cases in the book combine more than one design pattern to display alternate usage. It also shows that design patterns are tools to be used, not complex concepts to be feared. Finally, we tackle the client side to connect the dots and make ASP.NET Core a viable full-stack alternative.

By the end of the book, you will be able to mix and match design patterns and will have learned how to think about architecture. This book is a journey to learn the reasoning behind the craft.

Who this book is for

The book is intended for intermediate software and web developers with an understanding of .NET who want to write flexible, maintainable, and robust code for building scalable web applications. The book assumes knowledge of C# programming and an understanding of web concepts such as HTTP.

What this book covers

Section 1, Principles and Methodologies

This section contains the book's foundations: an overview of unit testing and xUnit, the SOLID principles, and some theory and examples on how to design software.

Chapter 1, Introduction to .NET, contains the prerequisites and an explanation of how the book works as well as a few important topics that will be useful to a software developer.

Chapter 2, Testing Your ASP.NET Core Application, introduces you to the basics of unit testing and the xUnit testing framework as well as to some good practices and methodologies to help write unit tests.

Chapter 3, Architectural Principles, lays the architectural ground with crucial principles used throughout the book and extremely important to any engineer trying to write "SOLID code."

Section 2, Designing for ASP.NET Core

This section introduces ASP.NET Core-specific subjects, including Model-View-Controller (MVC), View Models, DTOs, and a few classic design patterns. We also deep dive into dependency injection and explore the evolved usage of certain patterns in ASP.NET Core as pillars of modern software engineering.

Chapter 4, The MVC Pattern using Razor, introduces you to the Model-View-Controller and the View Model design patterns to render views using Razor and ASP.NET Core MVC.

Chapter 5, The MVC Pattern for Web APIs, takes you further on the ASP.NET Core MVC journey, focusing on web APIs. We explore the Data Transfer Object (DTO) pattern and API contracts.

Chapter 6, Understanding the Strategy, Abstract Factory, and Singleton Design Patterns, introduces you to the traditional implementation of three basic Gang of Four (GoF) design patterns: Strategy, Abstract Factory, and Singleton.

Chapter 7, Deep Dive into Dependency Injection, takes the ASP.NET Core dependency injection container for a ride, introducing you to one of the most important aspects of modern software development. This chapter connects ASP.NET Core and the SOLID principles. Once the basics of dependency injection are laid out, we review the previous three GoF design patterns and revisit them using dependency injection, opening the way to build testable, flexible, and reliable software.

Chapter 8, Options and Logging Patterns, takes ASP.NET Core-related subjects and digs into them. We cover different options patterns and the abstraction provided to us. We also explore how to leverage logging in .NET 5.

Section 3, Designing at Component Scale

This section focuses on component design, where we study how an individual piece of software can be crafted to achieve a particular goal. We explore a few more GoF patterns that should help us design SOLID data structures and components as well as simplifying the complexity of our code by encapsulating our logic in smaller units.

Chapter 9, Structural Patterns, introduces you to four new GoF structural design patterns and a few variants, such as transparent façades and opaque façades. It also introduces you to Scrutor, an open source project that adds support for the dependency injection of decorators.

Chapter 10, Behavioral Patterns, introduces two GoF behavioral design patterns and concludes by mixing them together as a final improvement on the code sample's design.

Chapter 11, Understanding the Operation Result Design Pattern, covers multiple variants of the Operation Result design pattern, structuring a result object to carry more than a simple result.

Section 4, Designing at Application Scale

This section takes a step forward, leading toward application design and introducing layering, vertical slices, and microservices. We overview each technique making sure you know how to get started. We also cover different component-level patterns that help put those architectural styles together.

Chapter 12, Understanding Layering, introduces you to layering and clean architecture, covering the primary objectives behind the presentation, domain, data (persistence) layers, and their clean architecture counterparts, which is the apogee of layering. It also highlights the evolution of application design that happened in the last few decades, helping you to understand where it started (the beginning of the chapter) and where it is headed (the end of the chapter).

Chapter 13, Getting Started with Object Mappers, covers object mapping (that is, copying an object into another), also known as the Translator pattern, the Mapper pattern, and Entity Translator. The chapter introduces AutoMapper at the end, an open source library, to help us cover the most common scenarios automatically.

Chapter 14, *Mediator and CQRS Design Patterns*, introduces the Command Query Responsibility Segregation (CQRS) and the Mediator patterns. After covering those two patterns, we explore an open source tool named MediatR that is foundational to many subsequent subjects.

Chapter 15, *Getting Started with Vertical Slice Architecture*, introduces Vertical Slice Architecture. It uses a number of the previous patterns and tools that we have explored to piece together a different way to see the design of an application. It also introduces FluentValidation, which gets added to MediatR and AutoMapper.

Chapter 16, *Introduction to Microservices Architecture*, introduces microservices, what they are, what they are not, and talks about a few related patterns. It is a theoretical chapter introducing many concepts, such as message queues, events, Publish-Subscribe, and Gateway patterns. We also revisit CQRS at cloud scale. At the end of the chapter, we explore the basics of containers.

Section 5, Designing the Client Side

This section introduces multiple UI patterns that we can use when developing ASP.NET Core 5 applications, such as Blazor, Razor Pages, and various types of components. It overviews what ASP.NET Core 5 offers in terms of user interfaces, leading to additional learning paths if you are interested.

Chapter 17, *ASP.NET Core User Interfaces*, explores most of the UI elements available to us in ASP.NET Core 5, such as Razor Pages, Partial Views, Tag Helpers, View Components, Display Templates, and Editor Templates. We also explore multiple C# 9 features, such as init-only properties and record classes.

Chapter 18, *A Brief Look into Blazor*, touches upon Blazor Server quickly, then explores Blazor WebAssembly (Wasm) to complete our journey and transform C#/.NET into a full-stack alternative to other JavaScript technologies. We explore Razor Components and the Model-View-Update design pattern. We end the chapter with a medley of possibilities you can start digging into.

To get the most out of this book

You must know C# and how to program. Boolean logic, loops, and other basic programming constructs should be mastered, including object-oriented programming basics. Some knowledge of ASP.NET will be beneficial. Knowing how to read UML class and sequence diagrams is an asset, but not required.

The code samples and resources are available on GitHub (`https://net5.link/code`). The `README.md` file at the root of the repository is filled with information to help you find the code and resources that you are looking for. If you don't find something, look at the `README.md` file – chances are you will find a pointer to the information that you seek.

Most links are shortened in the form of `https://net5.link/****` so readers of a physical copy can easily type URLs quickly.

In the book, I use a mix of Visual Studio 2019 (which has a free version) and Visual Studio Code (free). I recommend that you use one or both of those. The IDE is unrelated to most of the content. You could use Notepad if you are impetuous enough (I don't recommend that). Unless you install Visual Studio, which comes with the .NET SDK, you may need to install the .NET 5 SDK. The SDK comes with the `dotnet` CLI as well as the building tools for running and testing your programs. I develop on Windows, but you should be able to use another OS. OS-related topics are very limited, even inexistent. The code compiles on both Windows and Linux.

Software/Hardware covered in the book	OS Requirements
.NET 5	Windows, macOS, and Linux (any): well its any Linux that is supported by .NET 5
ASP.NET Core 5	
C# 9.0	
xUnit	
Multiple other .NET open source libraries	

Linux that is supported by .NET 5: `https://github.com/dotnet/core/blob/master/release-notes/5.0/5.0-supported-os.md`

If you are using the digital version of this book, we advise you to type the code yourself or access the code via the GitHub repository (link available in the next section). Doing so will help you avoid any potential errors related to the copying and pasting of code.

Download the example code files

You can download the example code files for this book from GitHub at `https://net5.link/code`. In case there's an update to the code, it will be updated on the existing GitHub repository.

We also have other code bundles from our rich catalog of books and videos available at https://github.com/PacktPublishing/. Check them out!

Conventions used

There are a number of text conventions used throughout this book.

Code in text: Indicates code words in text, database table names, folder names, filenames, file extensions, pathnames, dummy URLs, user input, and Twitter handles. Here is an example: "Mount the downloaded WebStorm-10*.dmg disk image file as another disk in your system."

A block of code is set as follows:

```
html, body, #map {
  height: 100%;
  margin: 0;
  padding: 0
}
```

When we wish to draw your attention to a particular part of a code block, the relevant lines or items are set in bold:

```
[default]
exten => s,1,Dial(Zap/1|30)
exten => s,2,Voicemail(u100)
exten => s,102,Voicemail(b100)
exten => i,1,Voicemail(s0)
```

Any command-line input or output is written as follows:

```
$ mkdir css
$ cd css
```

Bold: Indicates a new term, an important word, or words that you see onscreen. For example, words in menus or dialog boxes appear in the text like this. Here is an example: "Select **System info** from the **Administration** panel."

> **Tips or important notes**
> Appear like this.

Get in touch

Feedback from our readers is always welcome.

General feedback: If you have questions about any aspect of this book, mention the book title in the subject of your message and email us at customercare@packtpub.com.

Errata: Although we have taken every care to ensure the accuracy of our content, mistakes do happen. If you have found a mistake in this book, we would be grateful if you would report this to us. Please visit www.packtpub.com/support/errata, selecting your book, clicking on the Errata Submission Form link, and entering the details.

Piracy: If you come across any illegal copies of our works in any form on the Internet, we would be grateful if you would provide us with the location address or website name. Please contact us at copyright@packt.com with a link to the material.

If you are interested in becoming an author: If there is a topic that you have expertise in and you are interested in either writing or contributing to a book, please visit authors.packtpub.com.

Reviews

Please leave a review. Once you have read and used this book, why not leave a review on the site that you purchased it from? Potential readers can then see and use your unbiased opinion to make purchase decisions, we at Packt can understand what you think about our products, and our authors can see your feedback on their book. Thank you!

For more information about Packt, please visit packt.com.

Section 1: Principles and Methodologies

This section focuses on architectural principles and development methodologies that we use throughout the book. Those introductory chapters are essential in terms of progressing toward making great architectural decisions.

We first look at how to approach the book itself, explore prerequisites, and see a few helpful topics. Then, we cover automated testing and xUnit, to finally jump into the architectural principles, where we begin our study of the fundamentals of modern software engineering.

This section comprises the following chapters:

- *Chapter 1, Introduction to .NET*
- *Chapter 2, Testing Your ASP.NET Core Application*
- *Chapter 3, Architectural Principles*

1

Introduction to .NET

The goal behind this book is not to create yet another design pattern book, but instead, it organizes the chapters cohesively based on scale and topics, allowing you to start small with strong bases and build slowly on top, in just the same way that you would build a program.

Instead of writing a guide that covers a few ways of applying a design pattern, we explore the thinking process behind the systems that we are designing from a software engineer's point of view.

This is not a magic recipe book, and from experience, there is no magic recipe when designing software; there is only your logic, knowledge, experience, and analytical skills. From that last sentence, let's define experience according to *your past successes and failures*. And don't worry, you will fail during your career, but don't get discouraged by it. The faster you fail, the faster you can recover and learn, leading to successful products. Many techniques covered in this book should help you achieve that goal. Everyone has failed and made mistakes; you won't be the first, and you certainly won't be the last.

The high-level plan looks like this:

- We start by exploring basic patterns, architectural principles, and some crucial ASP.NET Core mechanisms.

- Then we move to the component scale, exploring patterns oriented toward small chunks of the software.

- Next, we move to application-scale patterns and techniques, where we explore higher-level patterns and how to structure the application as a whole.

- Afterward, we tackle the client side to connect the dots and make ASP.NET a viable full stack alternative.

Many subjects covered throughout the book could have a book of their own. Once you are done with this book, you should have plenty of ideas about where to continue your journey into software architecture.

Here are a few pointers that I believe are worth naming:

- The chapters are organized to start with small-scale patterns then get to higher-level ones, making the learning curve easier.

- Instead of giving you a recipe, the book focuses on the thinking aspect and shows evolutions of some techniques to help you understand why the evolution happened.

- Many use-cases combine more than one design pattern to illustrate alternate usage, aiming toward the understanding of the patterns and how to use them efficiently, as well as showing that a pattern is not a beast to tame but a tool to use, manipulate, and bend to your will.

- As in real life, no textbook solution can solve all of our problems, and real problems are always more complicated than as they are explained in textbooks. In this book, my goal is to show you how to mix and match patterns and how to think "architecture" instead of how to follow instructions.

The introduction introduces different concepts that we will be exploring throughout the book, including refreshers on a few notions. We are also covering .NET and its tooling, as well as the technical requirements, such as where the source code is located.

The following topics will be covered in this chapter:

- What is a design pattern?
- Anti-patterns and code smells

- Understanding the web – Request/Response
- Getting started with .NET

What is a design pattern?

Since you just purchased a book about design patterns, I guess that you have some idea of what they are, but let's just make sure that we are on the same page:

Abstract definition: A design pattern is a proven technique that can be used to solve a specific problem.

In this book, we apply different patterns to solve different problems and how to leverage some open source tools to go further, faster! Abstract definitions make people sound intelligent and all, but there is no better way to learn than by experimenting with something, and design patterns are no different.

If that definition does not make sense to you yet, don't worry. You should have enough information at the end of the book to correlate the multiple practical examples and explanations with that definition, making it clear enough.

I like to compare programming to playing with LEGO® because what you must do is mostly the same: snap small pieces together to create something. It could be a castle, a spaceship, or something else that you want to build. With that analogy in mind, a design pattern is a plan to assemble a solution that fits one or more scenarios; a tower or a reactor, for example. Therefore, if you lack imagination or skills in the case of LEGO®, possibly because you are too young, your castle might not look as good as someone else's that has more experience. Design patterns give you those tools, helping you build and glue beautiful and reliable pieces together to improve that masterpiece. However, instead of snapping LEGO® blocks together, you nest code blocks and interweave objects in a virtual environment!

Before going into more detail, well-thought-out applications of design patterns should improve your application designs. That is true when you design a small component or a whole system alike. However, be careful; throwing patterns into the mix just to use them can lead to the opposite. Aim to write readable code that solves the issue at hand, not at over-engineering systems with as many patterns as you can.

As we have briefly mentioned, there are design patterns applicable to multiple software engineering levels, and in this book, we start small and grow cloud-scale! We follow a smooth learning curve, starting with simpler patterns and code samples that bend good practices a little to focus on the patterns, and finally end with more advanced full stack topics, integrating multiple patterns and good practices.

Anti-patterns and code smells

Anti-patterns and code smells are architectural bad practices or tips about possible bad design. Learning about best practices is as important as learning about bad ones, which is where we start. Moreover, there are multiple anti-patterns and code smells throughout the book to help you get started.

Unfortunately, we can't cover every detail of every topic, so I encourage you to dig deeper into those fields as well as into design patterns and architectural principles.

Anti-patterns

An anti-pattern is the opposite of a design pattern: it is a proven flawed technique that will most likely cause you some trouble and cost you time and money (and probably give you a headache or two along the way).

A priori, an anti-pattern is a pattern that seems to be a good idea, and that seems to be the solution that you were looking for, but in the end, it will most likely cause more harm than good. Some anti-patterns started out as legitimate design patterns and got labeled anti-patterns later. Sometimes, it is a matter of opinion, and sometimes the classification can be influenced by the programming language.

Anti-pattern – God class

A *God class* is a class that handles way too many things. It is usually a central class that many other classes inherit from or use; it is the class that knows and manages everything in the system; **it is the class**. On the other hand, it is also the class that nobody wants to update, and the class that breaks the application every time somebody touches it; **it is an evil class**!

The best way to fix this is to separate responsibilities and distribute them to multiple classes instead of only one. We see how to split responsibilities throughout the book, which helps create more robust software at the same time.

If you have a personal project with a *God class* at its core, start by reading the book, and then try to apply the principles and patterns that you learned to divide that class into multiple smaller classes that interact together. Try to organize those new classes into cohesive units, modules, or assemblies.

We are getting into architectural principles very soon, which opens the way to concepts such as responsibility segregation.

Code smells

A code smell is an indicator of a possible problem. It points to some areas of your design that could benefit from a redesign. We could translate code smell to the code that stinks.

It is important to note that code smells only indicate the possibility of a problem; it does not mean that there is one; they usually are good indicators though, so it is worth taking the time to analyze that part of the software.

An excellent example of this is when many comments are explaining the logic of a method. That often means that the code could be split into smaller methods with proper names leading to more readable code, and allowing you to get rid of those pesky comments.

Another thing about comments is that they don't evolve, so what often happens is that the code described by the comments has changed, but the comment remained the same. That leaves a false or obsolete description of a block of code that can lead a developer astray.

Code smell – Control freak

An excellent example of an anti-pattern is when you use the new keyword. That is an indication of a hardcoded dependency where the creator controls the new object and its lifetime. That is also known as the *Control freak* anti-pattern. At this point, you may be wondering how it is possible not to use the new keyword in object-oriented programming, but rest assured, we cover that and expand on the *Control freak* code smell in *Chapter 7, Deep Dive into Dependency Injection*.

Code smell – Long methods

A follow-up example that could be represented by our previous over-commented example would be *long methods*. When a method starts to extend to more than 10 to 15 lines of code, it is a good indicator that you should think about that method differently.

Here are a few examples of what could have happened:

- The method contains complex logic intertwined in multiple conditional statements.
- The method contains a big switch block.
- The method does too many things.
- The method contains duplications of code.

To fix this, you could do the following:

- Extract one or more private methods.

- Extract some code to new classes.

- Reuse the code from external classes.

- If you have a lot of conditional statements or a huge switch block, you could leverage a design pattern such as the Chain of Responsibility, or CQRS, which you will learn in *Chapter 10, Behavioral Patterns* and *Chapter 14, Mediator and CQRS design patterns.*

Usually, each problem has one or more solutions, suffice to spot the problem then find, choose, and implement the solution. Let's be clear here; a method containing 16 lines does not necessarily need refactoring; it could be OK. Remember that a code smell is merely an indicator of a problem, and is not necessarily a problem; apply common sense.

Understanding the web – Request/Response

Before going any further, it is imperative to understand the basic concept of the web. The idea behind HTTP 1.X is that a client sends an HTTP request to a server, and then the server responds to that client. That can sound trivial if you have web development experience. However, it is one of the most important web programming concepts, irrespective of whether you are building web APIs, websites, or complex cloud applications.

Let's reduce an HTTP request lifetime to the following:

1. The communication starts.

2. The client sends a request to the server.

3. The server receives the request.

4. The server most likely does something (executes some code/logic).

5. The server responds to the client.

6. The communication ends.

After that cycle, the server is no longer aware of the client. Moreover, if the client sends another request, the server is not aware that it responded to a request earlier for that same client because **HTTP is stateless**.

There are mechanisms for creating a sense of persistence between requests in order for the server to become "aware" of its clients. The most well-known of these is probably cookies.

If we dig a little deeper, an HTTP request is composed of a header and an optional body. The most commonly used HTTP methods are GET and POST. Made popular by web APIs, we could also add PUT, DELETE, and PATCH to that list. Although not every HTTP method accepts a body, here is a list:

Method	Body allowed
GET	No
POST	Yes
PUT	Yes
PATCH	Yes
DELETE	No

Here is an example of a GET request (without a body since that's not allowed for GET requests):

```
GET http://www.forevolve.com/ HTTP/1.1
Host: www.forevolve.com
Connection: keep-alive
Upgrade-Insecure-Requests: 1
User-Agent: Mozilla/5.0 (Windows NT 10.0; Win64; x64)
AppleWebKit/537.36 (KHTML, like Gecko) Chrome/70.0.3538.110
Safari/537.36
Accept: text/html,application/xhtml+xml,application/
xml;q=0.9,image/webp,image/apng,*/*;q=0.8
Accept-Encoding: gzip, deflate
Accept-Language: en-US,en;q=0.9,fr-CA;q=0.8,fr;q=0.7
Cookie: ...
```

The HTTP header is composed of a list of key/value pairs representing metadata that a client wants to send to the server. In that case, I queried my blog using the GET method and Google Chrome attached some additional information to the request. I replaced the Cookie header's value with . . . because cookies can be quite large and are irrelevant to this sample. Nonetheless, cookies are passed back and forth like any other HTTP header.

> **Important note about cookies**
>
> The client sends cookies, and the server returns them for every request-response cycle. That could kill your bandwidth or slow down your application if you pass too much information back and forth. I'm thinking of the good old Web Forms ViewState here.

When the server decides to respond to the request, it returns a header and an optional body as well, following the same principles as the request does. The first line indicates the status of the request; whether it was successful. In our case, the status code was 200, which indicates success. Each server can add more or less information to their response, as do you in your code.

Here is the response from the previous request:

```
HTTP/1.1 200 OK
Server: GitHub.com
Content-Type: text/html; charset=utf-8
Last-Modified: Wed, 03 Oct 2018 21:35:40 GMT
ETag: W/"5bb5362c-f677"
Access-Control-Allow-Origin: *
Expires: Fri, 07 Dec 2018 02:11:07 GMT
Cache-Control: max-age=600
Content-Encoding: gzip
X-GitHub-Request-Id: 32CE:1953:F1022C:1350142:5C09D460
Content-Length: 10055
Accept-Ranges: bytes
Date: Fri, 07 Dec 2018 02:42:05 GMT
Via: 1.1 varnish
Age: 35
Connection: keep-alive
X-Served-By: cache-ord1737-ORD
X-Cache: HIT
X-Cache-Hits: 2
X-Timer: S1544150525.288285,VS0,VE0
Vary: Accept-Encoding
X-Fastly-Request-ID: 98a36fb1b5642c8041b88ceace73f25caaf07746

HERE WAS THE BODY THAT WAS WAY TOO LONG TO PASTE; LOTS OF HTML!
```

Now that the browser has received the server's response, in the case of HTML pages, it starts rendering it. Then, for each resource, it sends another HTTP call to its URI and loads it. A resource is an external asset, such as an image, a JavaScript file, a CSS file, or a font.

> **Note**
> There are a limited number of parallel requests that a browser can send, which could lead to increased load time depending on the number of assets to load, their size, and the order in which they are sent to the browser. You may want to look into optimizing this.

After the response, the server is no longer aware of the client; the communication has ended. It is essential to understand that in order to create a pseudo state between each request, we need to use an external mechanism. That mechanism could be the *session-state*, or we could create a stateless application. I recommend going stateless whenever you can.

To conclude this subject, HTTP/2 is more efficient and supports streaming multiple assets using the same TCP connection. It also allows "server push," leading to a more stateful World Wide Web. If you find HTTP interesting, HTTP/2 is an excellent place to start digging deeper as well as the newest experimental HTTP/3.

Getting started with .NET

A bit of history; the team did a magnificent job building ASP.NET Core from the ground up, cutting out compatibility with older versions. That brought its share of problems at first, but those interoperability issues got alleviated by the creation of .NET Standards. Now, with the reunification of most technologies into .NET 5 and the promise of a shared BCL, the name ASP.NET Core is (almost) no more, but became the future. Afterward, Microsoft is planning a major release of .NET every year, so 2021 should be .NET 6, and so on.

The good thing is that architectural principles and design patterns should remain relevant in the future and are not tightly coupled with the versions of .NET you are using. Minor changes to the code sample should be enough to migrate the knowledge and the code to the new versions.

Now, let's cover some key information surrounding .NET 5 and the .NET ecosystem.

.NET SDK versus runtime

You can install different binaries grouped under SDKs and runtimes. The SDK allows you to build and run .NET programs, while the runtime only allows you to run .NET programs.

As a developer, you want to install the SDK on your deployment environment. On the server, you want to install the runtime. The runtime is lighter, while the SDK contains more tools, including the runtime.

.NET 5 versus .NET Standard

When building .NET projects, there are multiple types of projects, but basically, we could separate them into two categories:

- Applications
- Libraries

Applications are targeting a version of .NET, such as net5.0. Examples of that would be an ASP.NET application or a console application.

Libraries are bundles of code compiled together, often distributed as a NuGet package over NuGet.org. .NET Standard class library projects allow code to be shared between .NET Core, .NET 5+, and .NET Framework projects. .NET Standards came into play to bridge the compatibility gap between .NET Core and .NET Framework, which eased the transition. It was not easy when .NET Core 1.0 first came out.

With .NET 5 unifying all of the platforms and becoming the future of that unified .NET ecosystem, .NET Standards is no longer required.

> **Note**
> I'm sure that we are going to see .NET Standard libraries stick around for
> a while though. All projects are not going to migrate from .NET Framework
> to .NET 5 magically, and people are likely to want to continue sharing code
> between the two.

Next versions of .NET should be built over .NET 5, while .NET Framework 4.X is going to stay where it is today, receiving only security patches and minor updates.

Visual Studio Code versus Visual Studio versus the command-line interface (CLI)

How can one of those projects be created? .NET Core comes with the `dotnet` CLI, which exposes multiple commands, including `new`. Running the `dotnet new` command in a terminal generates a new project.

To create an empty class library, we can run the following commands:

```
md MyProject
cd MyProject
dotnet new classlib
```

That would generate an empty class library in the newly created `MyProject` directory. The `-h` option can come in handy when discovering available commands and their options. You can use `dotnet -h` to find the available SDK commands, or `dotnet new -h` to find out about options and available templates.

Visual Studio Code is my favorite text editor. I don't use it much for .NET coding, but I still do to reorganize projects, when the CLI time comes, or for any other task that is easier to complete using a text editor, such as writing documentation using markdown, writing JavaScript or TypeScript, or managing JSON, YAML, or XML files. To create a project or solution, or to add a NuGet package using VS Code, open a terminal and use the CLI.

As for Visual Studio, my favorite IDE, it uses the CLI under the hood to create the same projects, making it consistent between tools. Visual Studio adds a user interface over the CLI.

You can also create and install additional `dotnet new` project templates to the CLI or even create global tools. Those topics are beyond the scope of this book.

An overview of project templates

Here is an example of the templates that are installed (`dotnet new`):

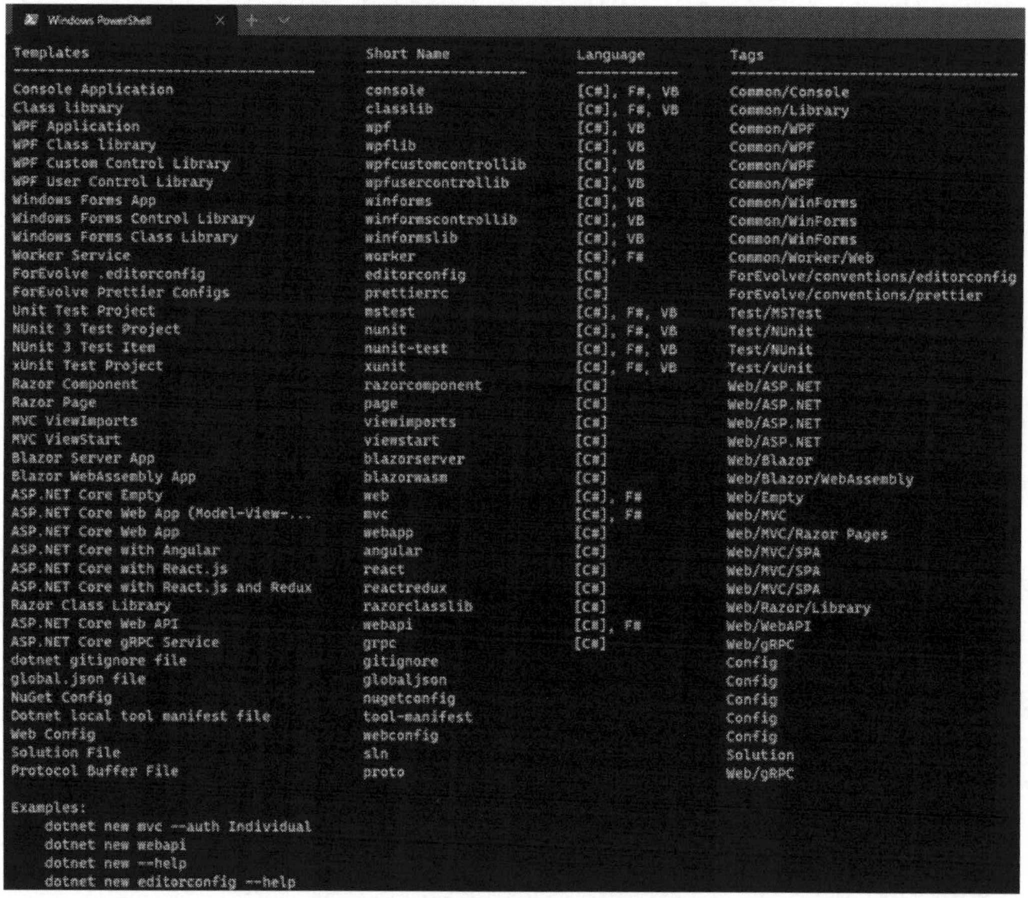

Templates	Short Name	Language	Tags
Console Application	console	[C#], F#, VB	Common/Console
Class library	classlib	[C#], F#, VB	Common/Library
WPF Application	wpf	[C#], VB	Common/WPF
WPF Class library	wpflib	[C#], VB	Common/WPF
WPF Custom Control Library	wpfcustomcontrollib	[C#], VB	Common/WPF
WPF User Control Library	wpfusercontrollib	[C#], VB	Common/WPF
Windows Forms App	winforms	[C#], VB	Common/WinForms
Windows Forms Control Library	winformscontrollib	[C#], VB	Common/WinForms
Windows Forms Class Library	winformslib	[C#], VB	Common/WinForms
Worker Service	worker	[C#], F#	Common/Worker/Web
ForEvolve .editorconfig	editorconfig	[C#]	ForEvolve/conventions/editorconfig
ForEvolve Prettier Configs	prettierrc	[C#]	ForEvolve/conventions/prettier
Unit Test Project	mstest	[C#], F#, VB	Test/MSTest
NUnit 3 Test Project	nunit	[C#], F#, VB	Test/NUnit
NUnit 3 Test Item	nunit-test	[C#], F#, VB	Test/NUnit
xUnit Test Project	xunit	[C#], F#, VB	Test/xUnit
Razor Component	razorcomponent	[C#]	Web/ASP.NET
Razor Page	page	[C#]	Web/ASP.NET
MVC ViewImports	viewimports	[C#]	Web/ASP.NET
MVC ViewStart	viewstart	[C#]	Web/ASP.NET
Blazor Server App	blazorserver	[C#]	Web/Blazor
Blazor WebAssembly App	blazorwasm	[C#]	Web/Blazor/WebAssembly
ASP.NET Core Empty	web	[C#], F#	Web/Empty
ASP.NET Core Web App (Model-View-...	mvc	[C#], F#	Web/MVC
ASP.NET Core Web App	webapp	[C#]	Web/MVC/Razor Pages
ASP.NET Core with Angular	angular	[C#]	Web/MVC/SPA
ASP.NET Core with React.js	react	[C#]	Web/MVC/SPA
ASP.NET Core with React.js and Redux	reactredux	[C#]	Web/MVC/SPA
Razor Class Library	razorclasslib	[C#]	Web/Razor/Library
ASP.NET Core Web API	webapi	[C#], F#	Web/WebAPI
ASP.NET Core gRPC Service	grpc	[C#]	Web/gRPC
dotnet gitignore file	gitignore		Config
global.json file	globaljson		Config
NuGet Config	nugetconfig		Config
Dotnet local tool manifest file	tool-manifest		Config
Web Config	webconfig		Config
Solution File	sln		Solution
Protocol Buffer File	proto		Web/gRPC

```
Examples:
    dotnet new mvc --auth Individual
    dotnet new webapi
    dotnet new --help
    dotnet new editorconfig --help
```

Figure 1.1 – Project templates

A study of all the templates is beyond the scope of this book, but I'd like to visit the few that are worth mentioning or because we will use them later:

- `dotnet new console` creates a console application.
- `dotnet new classlib` creates a class library.
- `dotnet new xunit` creates an xUnit test project.
- `dotnet new web` creates an empty web project.

- `dotnet new webapp` creates an empty web project with a preconfigured `Startup` class.

- `dotnet new mvc` scaffolds an MVC application.

- `dotnet new webapi` scaffolds a web API application.

Async main (C# 7.1)

From C# 7.1 onward, a console application can have an `async main` method, which is very convenient as more and more code is becoming async. This new feature allows the use of `await` directly in the `main()` method, without any quirks.

Previously, the signature of the `main` method had to fit one of the following:

```
public static void Main() { }
public static int Main() { }
public static void Main(string[] args) { }
public static int Main(string[] args) { }
```

Since C# 7.1, we can also use their `async` counterpart:

```
public static async Task Main() { }
public static async Task<int> Main() { }
public static async Task Main(string[] args) { }
public static async Task<int> Main(string[] args) { }
```

Now, we can create a console that looks like this:

```
class Program
{
    static async Task Main(string[] args)
    {
        Console.WriteLine("Entering Main");
        var myService = new MyService();
        await myService.ExecuteAsync();
        Console.WriteLine("Exiting Main");
    }
}

public class MyService
{
```

```
public Task ExecuteAsync()
{
    Console.WriteLine("Inside MyService.ExecuteAsync()");
    return Task.CompletedTask;
}
}
```

When executing the program, the result is as follows:

```
Entering Main
Inside MyService.ExecuteAsync()
Exiting Main
```

Nothing fancy, but it allows advantage to be taken of the await/async language feature.

Since .NET Core, all types of application start with a Main method (usually Program. Main), including ASP.NET Core 5 web applications.

Running and building your program

If you are using Visual Studio, you can always hit the play button, or *F5*, and run your app. If you are using the CLI, you can use one of the following commands (and more). Each of them also offers different options to control their behavior. Add the -h flag with any command to get help on that command, such as dotnet build -h:

Command	Description
`dotnet restore`	Restore the dependencies (a.k.a. NuGet packages) based on the `.csproj` or `.sln` file present in the current directory.
`dotnet build`	Build the application based on the `.csproj` or `.sln` file present in the current directory. It implicitly runs the `restore` command first.
`dotnet run`	Run the current application based on the `.csproj` file present in the current directory. It implicitly runs the `build` and `restore` commands first.
`dotnet watch run`	Watch for file changes. When a file has changed, the CLI rebuilds the application and then reruns it (equivalent to executing the `run` command again). If it is a web application, the page should refresh automatically.
`dotnet test`	Run the tests based on the `.csproj` or `.sln` file present in the current directory. It implicitly runs the `build` and `restore` commands first. We cover testing in the next chapter.
`dotnet watch test`	Watch for file changes. When a file has changed, the CLI reruns the tests (equivalent to executing the `test` command again).
`dotnet publish`	Publish the current application, based on the `.csproj` or `.sln` file present in the current directory, to a directory or remote location, such as a hosting provider. It implicitly runs the `build` and `restore` commands first.
`dotnet pack`	Create a NuGet package based on the `.csproj` or `.sln` file present in the current directory. It implicitly runs the `build` and `restore` commands first. You don't need a `.nuspec` file.
`dotnet clean`	Clean the build(s) output of a project or solution based on the `.csproj` or `.sln` file present in the current directory.

Technical requirements

Throughout the book, we explore and write code. I recommend that you install Visual Studio, Visual Studio Code, or both, to help out with that.

> **Note**
> You could also use Notepad or your favorite text editor if you prefer. I use VS and VS Code. Choose the tools that you prefer.

Unless you install Visual Studio, which comes with the .NET SDK, you may need to install the .NET 5 SDK. The SDK comes with the CLI that we explored earlier, as well as the building tools for running and testing your programs. Have a look at the `README.md` file of the GitHub repository for more information and links to those resources.

The source code of all chapters is available for download on GitHub at the following address: `https://net5.link/code`.

Summary

In this chapter, we peaked at design patterns, anti-patterns, and code smells. We also explored a few of those. We then moved to a reminder about the request/response cycle of a typical web application.

We continued by exploring .NET essentials, such as SDK versus runtime and app target versus .NET Standard. This sets us on the path to exploring the different possibilities that we have when it comes to building our .NET applications. We then dug a little more into the .NET CLI, where I laid down a list of essential commands, including `dotnet build` and `dotnet watch run`. We also covered how to create new projects.

In the next two chapters, we explore automated testing and architectural principles. These are foundational chapters for anyone wishing to build robust, flexible, and maintainable applications.

Questions

Let's take a look at a few practice questions:

1. Can we add a body to a GET request?
2. Why are **long methods** a code smell?
3. Is it true that .NET Standard should be your default target when creating libraries?
4. What is a code smell?

Further reading

Here are some links to consolidate what has been learned in the chapter:

- Overview of how .NET Core is versioned: `https://net5.link/n52L`
- .NET Core CLI overview: `https://net5.link/Lzx3`
- Custom templates for `dotnet new`: `https://net5.link/74i2`

2

Testing Your ASP.NET Core Application

This chapter focuses on automated testing and how helpful it can be for crafting better software. It also covers a few different types of tests as well as the foundation of **test-driven development (TDD)**. We also outline how testable ASP.NET Core is and how much easier it is to test ASP.NET Core applications compared to old ASP.NET MVC applications, for instance.

In this chapter, we will cover the following topics:

- Overview of automated testing and how it applies to ASP.NET Core
- Test-driven development (TDD)
- Testing made easy through ASP.NET Core

Overview of automated testing and how it applies to ASP.NET Core

Testing is an integral part of the development process, and automated testing becomes crucial in the long run. You can always run your ASP.NET website, open a browser, and click everywhere to test your features. That's legit, but it is harder to test individual units of code that way. Another downside is the lack of automation; when you first start with a small app containing a few pages, a few endpoints, or a few features, it may be fast to manually run those tests. However, as your app grows, it becomes more tedious, takes longer, and the likelihood of making a mistake as a tester increases. Don't get me wrong here, you will always need real users to test out your applications, but you may want those tests to focus on the UX, the features content, or on some experimental features that you are building instead of bug reports that automated tests could have caught early on.

There are multiple types of tests, and developers are very creative at finding new ways to test things. Here is a list of three broad categories that represent how we can divide automated testing; let's call these three families:

- Unit tests
- Integration tests
- Functional tests

Unit tests focus on individual units, like testing the outcome of a method. Unit tests should be fast and should not rely on any infrastructure such as a database. Those are the kind of tests that you want the most because they run fast, and each one should test a precise code path. They should also help you design your application better because you use your code in the tests, so you become its first consumer, leading to you finding some design flaws and making your classes better. If you don't like how you are using your system in your tests, that is a good indicator that nobody else will.

Integration tests focus on component interaction, such as what happens when a component queries the database or what happens when two components interact with each other. Integration tests often require some infrastructure to interact with, which makes them slower to run. You want integration tests, but you want fewer of them than unit tests.

> **Note**
>
> We are going to break this rule later on, so always be critical about rules and principles; sometimes, it can be better to break or bend them.

Functional tests focus on application-wide behaviors, such as what happens when a user clicks on a specific button, navigates to a specific page, posts a form, or sends a PUT request to some web API endpoint. Functional tests focus on testing the whole application, from the user's perspective, from a functional point of view, not just part of the code, as unit and integration tests do. Usually, functional tests should be run in-memory, using an in-memory database or any other resource; this helps to speed things up, but you could run **end-to-end** (**e2e**) tests on real infrastructure as well to test your application and your deployment.

There are other types of automated tests and some sub-genres, as we could call them. For example, we could do load testing, performance testing, **e2e** testing, regression testing, contract testing, penetration testing, and more. You can automate tests for almost anything that you want to validate, but some kinds of tests are harder to automate or more fragile than others, such as UI tests. That said, if you can automate a test, in a reasonable timeframe: do it! In the long run, it should pay off.

One more thing, don't blindly rely on metrics such as code coverage. Those metrics make for cute badges in your GitHub project's readme.md file, but can lead you off track writing useless tests. Don't get me wrong, code coverage is a great metric when used correctly, but remember that one good test can be better than a bad test suite covering 100% of your codebase.

Writing good tests is not easy and comes with practice.

> **Note**
> One piece of advice: keep your test suite healthy by adding missing test cases and removing obsolete or useless tests. Think in terms of use case coverage, not about how many lines of code are covered by your tests.

Now that we have explored automated testing, it is time to explore TDD, which is a way to apply those testing concepts, starting with the tests in mind.

Test-driven development (TDD)

TDD is a method of developing software that states that you should write a test before writing the actual code. So, you invert your development flow by following the **Red-Green-Refactor** technique.

What is **Red-Green-Refactor**?

It goes like this:

1. You write a failing test (red).

2. You write just enough code to make your test pass (green).

3. You refactor that code to improve the design by ensuring that all of the tests are still passing.

Okay, but what does **refactoring** mean?

I'd define refactoring as (continually) improving the code without changing its behavior.

Having an automated test suite should help you achieve that goal and should help you discover when you break something. No matter whether you do TDD or not, I do recommend refactoring as often as possible; this helps clean your codebase, and it should also help you get rid of some technical debt at the same time.

Okay, but what is **technical debt**?

Technical debt represents all of the corners that you cut short during the development of a feature or a system. That happens no matter how hard you try, because life is life, and there are delays, deadlines, budgets, and all sorts of antagonists such as managers, high-level execs, and external resources that drive the development of systems; not only developers. Okay, let's be honest, we should add developers to that list too – we create technical debt too.

First, you must understand that you cannot avoid technical debt completely, so it's better to embrace the fact and live with it than to fight it. From that point forward, you can then try to limit the amount of technical debt that is generated.

One way to limit the piling up of technical debt is to refactor often. So, factor the refactoring time into your feature evaluations.

Another way is to learn to cooperate with everyone and include the stakeholders in your projects' building process. Help them understand your reality and try to understand theirs. Everyone must work toward the same goal if you want your projects to succeed.

You may need to cut the usage of best practices short from time to time but come back later to fix them as soon as possible. You know, after that critical feature release on that important date the vendor told the client would happen before consulting the development team? Unfortunately, from my experience, that kind of situation does happen all the time. However, there are ways to limit the number of times those circumstances occur. For example, a high level of collaboration between actors, departments, and teams should help, while proper project management techniques and good governance should also help.

> **Tip**
> I realize that some of these things might be out of your control, so you may have to live with more technical debt than you had hoped for. You can also always work hard toward changing the enterprise's culture that you are working for and be a pioneer; I'll leave that up to you.

All of that said, if marketing cannot sell the software, it is pointless to develop it, and you may end up without a job, so let's live with the fact that compromises are mandatory. On the other hand, automated tests should help you refactor your code and get elegantly rid of that debt. However, don't let the technical debt pile up too high, or you may not be able to pay it back, and at some point, that's where a project begins to break and fail. Don't be mistaken; a project in production can be a failure. Delivering a product does not guarantee success, and I'm talking about the quality of the code here, not the amount of generated revenue (I'll leave that one to your accounting department).

There are other approaches, such as **behavior-driven development (BDD)** and **acceptance test-driven development (ATDD)**. DevOps brings a mindset to the table that focuses on embracing automated testing in its continuous integration and deployment ideas. However, instead of writing a book inside a book, I will leave you to it. I left a few references at the end of the chapter for more information about some of those subjects.

Testing made easy through ASP.NET Core

The ASP.NET Core team made our life easier by designing ASP.NET Core for testability; most of the testing is way easier than before the ASP.NET Core era. Internally, they use xUnit to test .NET Core and EF Core, and we use xUnit as well throughout the book. xUnit is my favorite testing framework; what a nice coincidence. We are not going full-TDD-mode for all samples as it would deviate our focus from the matter at stake, but I did my best to bring as much automated testing as possible to the table! Why? Because testability is usually the sign of a good design, which allows me to prove some concepts by using tests instead of words.

Moreover, in many code samples, the test cases are the consumers, making the program lighter without building a full user interface over it. That allows us to focus on the patterns that we are exploring instead of getting our focus scattered over some boilerplate code.

How do you create an xUnit test project?

To create a new xUnit test project, you can run the `dotnet new xunit` command, and the CLI does the job for you by creating a project containing a `UnitTest1` class. That command does the same as creating a new xUnit project from Visual Studio like this:

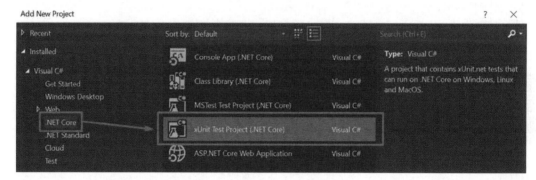

Figure 2.1 – Create a xUnit project

Basic features of xUnit

In xUnit, the `[Fact]` attribute is the way to create unique test cases, while the `[Theory]` attribute is the way to create data-driven test cases.

Any method with no parameter can become a test method by decorating it with a `[Fact]` attribute, like this:

```
public class FactTest
{

    [Fact]
    public void Should_be_equal()
    {
        var expectedValue = 2;
        var actualValue = 2;
        Assert.Equal(expectedValue, actualValue);

    }

}
```

From the Visual Studio Test Explorer, that test case looks like this:

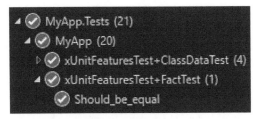

Figure 2.2 – Test results

Then, for more complex test cases, xUnit offers three options to define the data that a [Theory] should use: [InlineData], [MemberData], and [ClassData]. You are not limited to only one; you can use as many as suits you to feed a theory with data. You must make sure that the number of values matches the number of parameters defined in the test method.

[InlineData] is the most suitable for constant, literal values, like this:

```
public class InlineDataTest
{
    [Theory]
    [InlineData(1, 1)]
    [InlineData(2, 2)]
    [InlineData(5, 5)]
    public void Should_be_equal(int value1, int value2)
    {
        Assert.Equal(value1, value2);
    }
}
```

That yields three test cases in the Test Explorer, where each can pass or fail individually:

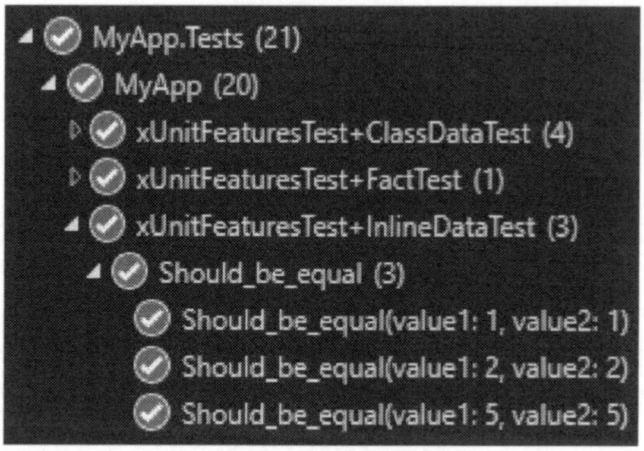

Figure 2.3 – Test results

[MemberData] and [ClassData] can be used to simplify the declaration of the test method, to reuse the data in multiple test methods, or to encapsulate the data away from the test class. Here are a few examples of [MemberData] usage:

```
public class MemberDataTest
{
    public static IEnumerable<object[]> Data => new[]
    {
        new object[] { 1, 2, false },
        new object[] { 2, 2, true },
        new object[] { 3, 3, true },
    };

    public static TheoryData<int, int, bool> TypedData =>
new TheoryData<int, int, bool>
    {
        { 3, 2, false },
        { 2, 3, false },
        { 5, 5, true },
    };

    [Theory]
    [MemberData(nameof(Data))]
    [MemberData(nameof(TypedData))]
```

```csharp
[MemberData(nameof(ExternalData.GetData), 10, MemberType =
typeof(ExternalData))]
[MemberData(nameof(ExternalData.TypedData), MemberType =
typeof(ExternalData))]
    public void Should_be_equal(int value1, int value2, bool
shouldBeEqual)
    {
        if (shouldBeEqual)
        {
            Assert.Equal(value1, value2);
        }
        else
        {
            Assert.NotEqual(value1, value2);
        }
    }

    public class ExternalData
    {
        public static IEnumerable<object[]> GetData(int start)
=> new[]
        {
            new object[] { start, start, true },
            new object[] { start, start + 1, false },
            new object[] { start + 1, start + 1, true },
        };

        public static TheoryData<int, int, bool> TypedData =>
new TheoryData<int, int, bool>
        {
            { 20, 30, false },
            { 40, 50, false },
            { 50, 50, true },
        };
    }
}
```

That test case should yield 12 results. If we break that down, the code start by loading three sets of data from the `IEnumerable<object[]> Data` property by decorating the test method with the **[MemberData(nameof(Data))]** attribute.

Then, to make it clearer, we replace `IEnumerable<object[]>` with a `TheoryData<...>` class, making it more readable, which is my preferred way of defining member data. We feed those three sets of data to the test method by decorating it with the **[MemberData(nameof(TypedData))]** attribute.

Then, three more sets of data are passed to the test method. Those originate from a method on an external type taking `10` as an argument (the `start` parameter). We specify the `MemberType` where the method is located, so xUnit knows where to look, which is represented by the [MemberData(nameof(ExternalData.GetData), 10, MemberType = typeof(ExternalData))] attribute.

Finally, we are doing the same for the `ExternalData.TypedData` property, which is represented by the [MemberData(nameof(ExternalData.TypedData), MemberType = typeof(ExternalData))] attribute.

When running the tests, those [MemberData] attributes yield the following result in the Test Explorer:

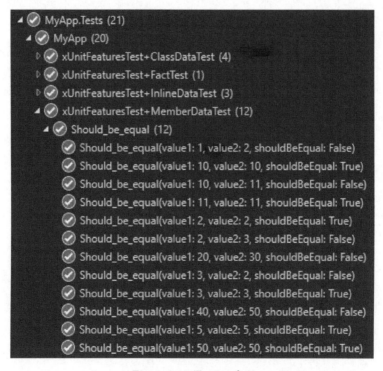

Figure 2.4 – Test results

These are only a few examples of what we can do with the `[MemberData]` attribute.

Now to the `[ClassData]` attribute. That one gets its data from a class implementing `IEnumerable<object[]>` or by inheriting from `TheoryData<...>`. Here is an example:

```csharp
public class ClassDataTest
{
    [Theory]
    [ClassData(typeof(TheoryDataClass))]
    [ClassData(typeof(TheoryTypedDataClass))]
    public void Should_be_equal(int value1, int value2, bool shouldBeEqual)
    {
        if (shouldBeEqual)
        {
            Assert.Equal(value1, value2);
        }
        else
        {
            Assert.NotEqual(value1, value2);
        }
    }

    public class TheoryDataClass : IEnumerable<object[]>
    {
        public IEnumerator<object[]> GetEnumerator()
        {
            yield return new object[] { 1, 2, false };
            yield return new object[] { 2, 2, true };
            yield return new object[] { 3, 3, true };
        }

        IEnumerator IEnumerable.GetEnumerator() =>
        GetEnumerator();
    }

    public class TheoryTypedDataClass : TheoryData<int, int,
```

```
bool>
    {
        public TheoryTypedDataClass()
        {
            Add(102, 104, false);
        }
    }
}
```

These are very similar to [MemberData], but instead of pointing to a member, we point to a type. Here is the result in the Test Explorer:

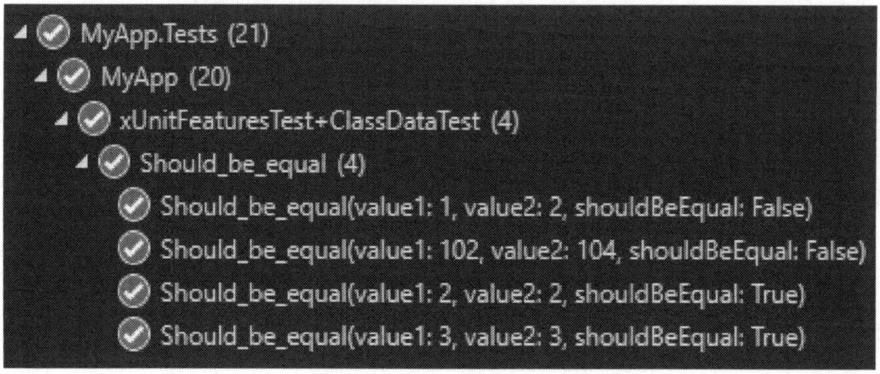

Figure 2.5 – Test Explorer

Now that [Fact] and [Theory] are out of the way, xUnit offers **test fixtures** to allow developers to inject dependencies into a test class constructor, as parameters. Fixtures allow those dependencies to be reused by all of the test methods of a test class by implementing the IClassFixture<T> interface. The last code sample of the chapter shows that in action. That is very helpful for costly dependencies like accessing a database; create once, use many times.

You can also share a fixture (a dependency) between multiple test classes by using ICollectionFixture<T>, [Collection], and [CollectionDefinition] instead. We won't get too deep into the details here, but you will know where to look if you ever need something similar.

Finally, if you worked with other testing frameworks, you might have encountered **setup** and **teardown** methods. In xUnit, there are no particular attributes or mechanisms to handle setup and teardown code. Instead, xUnit uses existing OOP concepts:

- To set up your tests, use the class constructor.

- To teardown (clean up) your tests, implement `IDisposable`, and dispose of your resources there.

That's it, xUnit is very simple, yet powerful, which is the main reason why I adopted it as my main testing framework several years ago, and why I chose it for this book. Let's see how to organize those tests now.

How to organize your tests

There are many ways of organizing test projects inside a solution. One that I like is to create a unit test project for each project in the solution, one or more integration test project(s), and a single functional test project. Since we, most of the time, have more unit tests and unit tests are directly related to single units of code, it makes sense to organize them into a one-on-one relationship. Then we should have fewer integration and functional tests, so a single project should be enough to keep our code organized.

> **Note**
>
> Some people may recommend creating a single unit test project per solution instead of one per project. This approach could save discovery time. I think that for most solutions, it is only a matter of preference. If you have a preferred way to organize yours, by all means, use that approach instead! That said, I find that one unit test project per assembly is more portable and easier to navigate.

Most of the time, at the solution level, I create my application and its related libraries in an `src` directory, and I create my test projects in a `test` directory, like this:

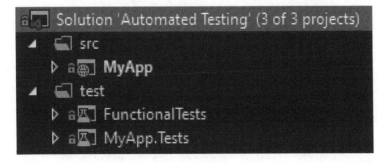

Figure 2.6 – The Automated Testing Solution Explorer, displaying how the projects are organized

In the *Automated Testing* solution, I don't have any integration tests, so I haven't created an integration test project. I could have named one *IntegrationTests* or *MyApp. IntegrationTests* depending on my approach.

One more detail that I found helps get tests and code aligned perfectly is to create unit tests in the same namespace as the subject under test. To make it easier in Visual Studio, you can change the default namespace used by Visual Studio when creating a new class in your test project by adding <RootNamespace>[Project under test namespace]</RootNamespace> to a PropertyGroup of the test project file (*.csproj), like this:

```
<PropertyGroup>
  <TargetFramework>net5.0</TargetFramework>
  <IsPackable>false</IsPackable>
  <RootNamespace>MyApp</RootNamespace>
</PropertyGroup>
```

Then I name my test classes [class under test]Test.cs and create them in the same directory as in the original project, like this:

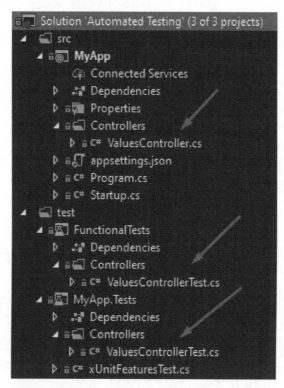

Figure 2.7 – The Automated Testing Solution Explorer, displaying how tests are organized

Finding tests is trivial when you follow that simple rule. Sometimes, it is not possible to do that for integration tests or functional tests; in those cases, use your specifications to help you create clear naming conventions that make sense for your tests. Remember, we are testing use cases.

Finally, for each class, I nest one test class per method that inherits from the nested class's parent class, then I create my test cases inside of it using [Fact] and [Theory] attributes. This helps organize tests efficiently by method, ending with a test hierarchy like this:

```csharp
namespace MyApp.Controllers
{
    public class ValuesControllerTest
    {
        public class Get : ValuesControllerTest
        {
            [Fact]
            public void Should_return_the_expected_strings()
            {
                // Arrange
                var sut = new ValuesController();

                // Act
                var result = sut.Get();

                // Assert
                Assert.Collection(result.Value,
                    x => Assert.Equal("value1", x),
                    x => Assert.Equal("value2", x)
                );
            }
        }
    }
}
```

That technique allows you to set up tests step by step. For example, you can create top-level private mocks; then, for each method, you can modify the setup or create other private test elements, then you can do the same per test case, inside of the test method. Don't go too hard on reusability though; it can make tests hard to follow to an external eye, such as a reviewer or another developer that needs to play there. Unit tests should remain clear, small, and easy to read.

How is it easier?

Microsoft built .NET Core (now .NET 5) from the ground up, so they fixed and improved so many things that I cannot enumerate them all here, including testability. Not everything is perfect, but it is way better than it ever was.

Let's start by talking about the `Program` and the `Startup` classes. Those two classes are the place to define how the application boots and its composition. Based on that model, the ASP.NET Core team created a test server class that allows you to run your application in memory.

They also added `WebApplicationFactory<TEntry>` in .NET Core 2.1 to make integration and functional testing even easier. With that class, you can boot up your ASP.NET Core application in-memory and query it with the supplied `HttpClient`. All of that in only a few lines of code. There are extension points to configure it, such as replacing implementations with mocks, stubs, or any other test-specific elements that you may require. The `TEntry` generic parameter should be the `Startup` or `Program` class of your project under test.

I created a few test cases in the `Automated Testing` project that exposes this functionality:

```
namespace FunctionalTests.Controllers
{
    public class ValuesControllerTest :
IClassFixture<WebApplicationFactory<Startup>>
    {
        private readonly HttpClient _httpClient;
        public
ValuesControllerTest(WebApplicationFactory<Startup>
webApplicationFactory)
        {
            _httpClient = webApplicationFactory.CreateClient();
        }
```

Here, we are injecting a `WebApplicationFactory<Startup>` object into the constructor by implementing the `IClassFixture<T>` interface. We could use the factory to configure the test server, but since it was not required here, we can only keep a reference on the `HttpClient` that is configured to connect to the in-memory test server running the application.

```
public class Get : ValuesControllerTest
{
    public Get(WebApplicationFactory<Startup>
webApplicationFactory) : base(webApplicationFactory) { }

    [Fact]
    public async Task Should_respond_a_status_200_OK()
    {
        // Act
        var result = await _httpClient.GetAsync("/api/
values");

        // Assert
        Assert.Equal(HttpStatusCode.OK, result.
StatusCode);
    }
```

In the preceding test case, we are using the test `HttpClient` to query the `http://localhost/api/values` URI, accessible through the in-memory server. Then we test the status code of the HTTP response to make sure it was a success (`200 OK`).

```
    [Fact]
    public async Task Should_respond_the_expected_
strings()
    {
        // Act
        var result = await _httpClient.GetAsync("/api/
values");

        // Assert
        var contentText = await result.Content.
ReadAsStringAsync();
        var content = JsonSerializer.
```

```
Deserialize<string[]> (contentText);
            Assert.Collection(content,
                x => Assert.Equal("value1", x),
                x => Assert.Equal("value2", x)
            );
        }
    }
}
}
```

This last test does the same but deserializes the body's content as a `string[]` to ensure the values are the same as what we were expecting. If you've worked with an `HttpClient` before, this should be very familiar to you.

When running those tests, an in-memory web server starts; then, HTTP requests are sent to that server, testing the full application. In that case, the tests are trivial, but you can create more complex test cases as well.

You can run .NET 5 tests within Visual Studio, or using the CLI by running the `dotnet test` command. In VS Code, you can use the CLI or find an extension to help you out with test runs.

Summary

In this chapter, we covered automated testing such as unit tests, integration tests, and functional tests. We took a quick look at xUnit, the testing framework that we use throughout the book, as well as a way of organizing tests. Then we saw how ASP.NET Core makes it easier than ever before to test our web applications by allowing us to mount and run our ASP.NET Core application in memory.

There are many xUnit tests in the book, so you will become more familiar along the way. I also suggest taking a deeper look at it if you feel the need to.

Now that we have talked about testing, we are ready to explore a few architectural principles that lead to unit testing and TDD while augmenting programs' testability. Those are a crucial part of modern software engineering that marries very well with automated testing.

Questions

Let's take a look at a few practice questions:

1. Is it true that in TDD, you write tests before the code to be tested?

2. What is the role of unit tests?

3. How big can a unit test be?

4. What type of tests is usually used when the subject under test must access a database?

5. Is doing TDD required?

Further reading

Here are some links to build upon what we learned in the chapter:

*   xUnit: `https://xunit.net/`

*   If you use Visual Studio, I have a few handy snippets to help improve productivity. They are available on GitHub: `https://net5.link/5TbY`

*   What is DevOps? `https://net5.link/BPcr`

*   The following book is a DevOps/DevSecOps resource that someone I trust recommended to me. I have not read it myself but have peeked at the content, and it seems like a good resource to get started: `https://net5.link/X6bW`.

3
Architectural Principles

This chapter focus on fundamental architectural principles instead of design patterns. The reason behind this is simple: those principles are the foundation of modern software engineering. Moreover, we apply these principles throughout the book to make sure that by the end, we write better code and make better software design decisions.

In this chapter, we will cover the following topics:

- The **SOLID** principles and their importance
- The **DRY** principle
- The separation of concerns principle

The SOLID principles

SOLID is an acronym representing five principles that extend the basic OOP concepts of Abstraction, Encapsulation, Inheritance, and Polymorphism. They add more details about what to do and how to do it, guiding developers toward more robust designs.

It is also important to note that they are principles, not rules to follow at all costs. Weigh the cost in the context of what you are building. If you are building a small tool, it may be OK to cut it short more than if you are designing a business-critical application. For the latter case, you may want to consider being stricter. However, following them is usually a good idea, irrespective of the size of your application, which is the main reason to cover them here, in the beginning, before digging into design patterns.

The SOLID acronym represents the following:

- **S**ingle responsibility principle
- **O**pen/Closed principle
- **L**iskov substitution principle
- **I**nterface segregation principle
- **D**ependency inversion principle

By following these principles, your systems should become easier to test and maintain.

Single responsibility principle (SRP)

Essentially, the SRP means that a single class should hold one, and only one, responsibility, leading me to the following quote:

> *"There should never be more than one reason for a class to change."*
>
> *– Robert C. Martin*

OK, but why? Before giving you the answer, I'd like you to think about each time that a specification was added, updated, or removed. Then, think about how easier it would have been if every single class in your system had only a single responsibility: one reason to change.

I don't know if you visualized that clearly or not, but I can think of a few projects off the top of my head that would have benefited from this principle. Software maintainability problems can be due to the programmers, the managers, or both. I think that nothing is black or white and that most situations are gray; sometimes, it is of a darker or lighter gray, but gray nonetheless. That lack of absoluteness is also true when designing software: do your best, learn from your mistakes, and be humble.

Let's review why that principle exists:

- Applications are born to change.
- To make our classes more reusable and create more flexible systems.

- To help maintain applications. Since you know the only thing a class does before updating it, you can quickly foresee the impact on the system, unlike with classes that hold many responsibilities, where updating one can break one or more other parts.

- To make our classes more readable. Fewer responsibilities lead to less code, and less code is simpler to visualize in a few seconds, leading to a quicker understanding of that piece of software.

Let's try this out in action. I have written some horrible code that violates a few principles, including the SRP. Let's start by analyzing the code to partially fix it, so that it no longer violates the SRP.

The following is an example of the poorly written code:

```
public class Book
{
    public int Id { get; set; }
    public string Title { get; set; }

    private static int _lastId = 0;

    public static List<Book> Books { get; }
    public static int NextId => ++_lastId;

    static Book()
    {
        Books = new List<Book>
        {
            new Book
            {
                Id = NextId,
                Title = "Some cool computer book"
            }
        };
    }

    public Book(int? id = null)
    {
```

```csharp
            Id = id ?? default(int);
    }

    public void Save()
    {
        // Create the book if it does not exist,
        // otherwise, find its index and replace it
        // by the current object.
        if (Books.Any(x => x.Id == Id))
        {
            var index = Books.FindIndex(x => x.Id == Id);
            Books[index] = this;
        }
        else
        {
            Books.Add(this);
        }
    }

    public void Load()
    {
        // Validate that an Id is set
        if (Id == default(int))
        {
            throw new Exception("You must set the Id to the
Book Id you want to load.");
        }

        // Get the book
        var book = Books.FirstOrDefault(x => x.Id == Id);

        // Make sure it exist
        if (book == null)
        {
            throw new Exception("This book does not exist");
        }
```

```
        // Copy the book properties to the current object
        Id = book.Id; // this should already be set
        Title = book.Title;
    }

    public void Display()
    {
        Console.WriteLine($"Book: {Title} ({Id})");
    }
}
```

That class contains all the responsibilities of that super small console application. There is also the Program class, which contains a quick and dirty user interface, the consumer of the Book class.

The program offers the following options:

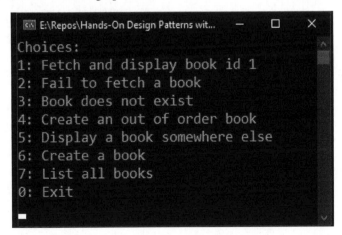

Figure 3.1 – The program's user interface

Let's look at the Program code:

```
class Program
{
    static void Main(string[] args)
    {
        // ...
    }
```

I omitted the `Main` method code because it is just a big `switch` with `Console.`
`WriteLine` calls. It dispatches the user input to the other methods (explained later)
when a user makes a choice. See `https://net5.link/jpxa` for more information
on the `Main` method. Next, the method called when a user chooses 1:

```
private static void FetchAndDisplayBook()
{
    var book = new Book(id: 1);
    book.Load();
    book.Display();
}
```

The `FetchAndDisplayBook()` method loads the `book` instance that has an `id` equal
to `1`, and then displays it in the console. Next, the method called when a user chooses 2:

```
private static void FailToFetchBook()
{
    var book = new Book();
    book.Load(); // Exception: You must set the Id to the
Book Id you want to load.
    book.Display();
}
```

The `FailToFetchBook()` method loads a `book` instance without specifying an `id`,
which results in an exception thrown when loading the data; refer to the `Book.Load()`
method (preceding code block, first highlight). Next, the method called when a user
chooses 3:

```
private static void BookDoesNotExist()
{
    var book = new Book(id: 999);
    book.Load();
    book.Display();
}
```

The `BookDoesNotExist()` method loads a book instance that does not exist, leading to an exception being thrown when loading the data; refer to the `Book.Load()` method (preceding code block, second highlight). Next, the method called when a user chooses 4:

```
private static void CreateOutOfOrderBook()
{
    var book = new Book
    {
        Id = 4, // this value is not enforced by anything
        and will be overriden at some point.
        Title = "Some out of order book"
    };
    book.Save();
    book.Display();
}
```

The `CreateOutOfOrderBook()` method creates a book instance specifying an `id` manually. That ID could be overridden by the auto-incremental mechanism of the `Book` class. These kinds of behaviors are good indicators of a problem in the design of a program. Next, the method called when a user chooses 5:

```
private static void DisplayTheBookSomewhereElse()
{
    Console.WriteLine("Oops! Can't do that, the Display
    method only write to the \"Console\".");
}
```

The `DisplayTheBookSomewhereElse()` method points to another problem with that design. We cannot display the books anywhere else other than in the console because the `Book` class owns the display mechanism; refer to the `Book.Display()` method. Next, the method called when a user chooses 6:

```
private static void CreateBook()
{
    Console.Clear();
    Console.WriteLine("Please enter the book title: ");
    var title = Console.ReadLine();
    var book = new Book { Id = Book.NextId, Title =
    title };
```

```
        book.Save();
    }
```

The `CreateBook()` method lets us create new books. It uses the `Book.NextId` static property, which increments the `Id`. That breaks encapsulation and leaks the creation logic out to the consumer, which is another problem associated with the design that we will be fixing later. Next, the method called when a user chooses 7:

```
    private static void ListAllBooks()
    {
        foreach (var book in Book.Books)
        {
            book.Display();
        }
    }
}
```

The `ListAllBooks()` method displays all of the books that we have created in the program.

Before going further, I'd like you to think about what is wrong in the `Book` class and how many responsibilities there are that violate the SRP. Once done, please continue reading.

OK, let's start by isolating features:

- The class is a data structure that represents a book (`Id`, `Title`).
- It saves and loads data, including keeping a list of all existing books (`Books`, `Save()`, `Load()`).
- It "manages" auto-incremented IDs by exposing the `NextId` property that hacks the feature into the program.
- It plays the presenter role, outputting a book in the console with its `Display()` method.

From those four points, what roles could we extract?

- It is a book.
- It does data access (manages the data).
- It presents the book to the user by outputting itself in the console.

These three elements are responsibilities, which is an excellent starting point for splitting the `Book` class. Let's look at those three classes:

- We can keep the `Book` class and make it a simple data structure that represents a book.

- We can create a `BookStore` class whose role is to access the data.

- We can create a `BookPresenter` class that outputs (presents) a book on the console.

Here are those three classes:

```csharp
public class Book
{
    public int Id { get; set; }
    public string Title { get; set; }
}

public class BookStore
{
    private static int _lastId = 0;

    private static List<Book> _books;
    public static int NextId => ++_lastId;

    static BookStore()
    {
        _books = new List<Book>
        {
            new Book
            {
                Id = NextId,
                Title = "Some cool computer book"
            }
        };
    }

    public IEnumerable<Book> Books => _books;
```

```csharp
    public void Save(Book book)
    {
        // Create the book when it does not exist,
        // otherwise, find its index and replace it
        // by the specified book.
        if (_books.Any(x => x.Id == book.Id))
        {
            var index = _books.FindIndex(x => x.Id == book.Id);
            _books[index] = book;
        }
        else
        {
            _books.Add(book);
        }
    }

    public Book Load(int bookId)
    {
        return _books.FirstOrDefault(x => x.Id == bookId);
    }
}

public class BookPresenter
{
    public void Display(Book book)
    {
        Console.WriteLine($"Book: {book.Title} ({book.Id})");
    }
}
```

That does not fix every problem yet, but at least it is a good start. By extracting the responsibilities, we have achieved the following:

- The FailToFetchBook() use case has been fixed (see the Load() method).

- Fetching a book is now more elegant and more intuitive.

- We also opened a possibility about the DisplayTheBookSomewhereElse() use case (to be revisited later).

From an SRP standpoint, we still have a problem or two:

- The auto-incremented ID is still exposed publicly, and `BookStore` is not managing it.
- The `Save()` method is handling the creation and the update of books, which seems like two responsibilities, not one.

For the next updates, we focus on those two problems that share a synergy, making them easier to fix independently than together (dividing responsibility between the methods).

What we are about to do is the following:

1. Hide the `BookStore.NextId` property to fix encapsulation (not the SRP, but it is essential nonetheless).

2. Split the `BookStore.Save()` method into two methods: `Create()` and `Replace()`.

3. Update our user interface: `Program.cs`.

After hiding the `NextId` property, we need to move that feature inside the `BookStore` class. The most logical place would be the `Save()` method (not yet split in two), since we want a new unique identifier for each new book. Here are the changes:

```csharp
public class BookStore
{
    ...
    private static int NextId => ++_lastId;
    ...
    public void Save(Book book)
    {
        ...
        else
        {
            book.Id = NextId;
            _books.Add(book);
        }
    }
}
```

The auto-incremented identifier is still a half-baked feature. To help improve it more, let's split the `Save()` method into two. By looking at the resulting code, we can imagine that handling both use cases was easier to write. It is also easier to read and clearer to use for any developer who may come into contact with that code in the future. See for yourself:

```csharp
public void Create(Book book)
{
    if (book.Id != default(int))
    {
        throw new Exception("A new book cannot be created with an id.");
    }
    book.Id = NextId;
    _books.Add(book);
}

public void Replace(Book book)
{
    if (_books.Any(x => x.Id == book.Id))
    {
        throw new Exception($"Book {book.Id} does not exist!");
    }
    var index = _books.FindIndex(x => x.Id == book.Id);
    _books[index] = book;
}
```

Now we are beginning to get somewhere. We have successfully split the responsibilities into three classes and also split the `Save()` method, such that both handle only a single operation.

The `Program` methods now looks like this:

```csharp
private static readonly BookStore _bookStore = new BookStore();
private static readonly BookPresenter _bookPresenter = new
BookPresenter();
//...
private static void FetchAndDisplayBook()
{
    var book = _bookStore.Load(1);
```

```csharp
        _bookPresenter.Display(book);
}

private static void FailToFetchBook()
{
    // This cannot happen anymore, this has been fixed
automatically.
}

private static void BookDoesNotExist()
{
    var book = _bookStore.Load(999);
    if (book == null)
    {
        // Book does not exist
    }
}

private static void CreateOutOfOrderBook()
{
    var book = new Book
    {
        Id = 4,
        Title = "Some out of order book"
    };
    _bookStore.Create(book); // Exception: A new book cannot be
created with an id.
    _bookPresenter.Display(book);
}

private static void DisplayTheBookSomewhereElse()
{
    Console.WriteLine("This is now possible, but we need a new
Presenter; not 100% there yet!");
}

private static void CreateBook()
```

```
{
    Console.Clear();
    Console.WriteLine("Please enter the book title: ");
    var title = Console.ReadLine();
    var book = new Book { Title = title };
    _bookStore.Create(book);
}


private static void ListAllBooks()
{
    foreach (var book in _bookStore.Books)
    {
        _bookPresenter.Display(book);
    }
}
```

Apart from automatically fixing the FailToFetchBook method, I found the code easier to read. Let's compare the FetchAndDisplayBook method:

```
// Old
private static void FetchAndDisplayBook()
{
    var book = new Book(id: 1);
    book.Load();
    book.Display();
}


// New
private static void FetchAndDisplayBook()
{
    var book = _bookStore.Load(1);
    _bookPresenter.Display(book);
}
```

Conclusion

One thing to be careful about when thinking about the SRP is not to over-separate classes. The more classes in a system, the more complex to assemble the system can become, the harder it can be to debug or to follow the execution paths. On the other hand, many well-separated responsibilities should lead to a better, more testable system.

How to describe "one reason" or "a single responsibility" is unfortunately impossible to define, and I don't have a hard guideline to give you here. When in doubt, with no one else to help you figure out your design dilemma, I'd say that you should split it.

A good indicator of the SRP violation is when you don't know how to name an element. That is often a good pointer that the element should not reside there, should be extracted, or should be split into multiple smaller pieces.

Another good indicator is when a method becomes too big, optionally with many `if` statements or loops. In that case, you should split that method into multiple smaller ones. That should make the code easier to read and make the initial method's body cleaner. It often also helps you get rid of useless comments. Please name your private methods clearly, or this won't aid readability (see the *Naming example* section).

How can you know when a class is getting too thin? Once again, you won't like it. I don't have any hard guidelines for this either. However, if you are looking at your system and all of your classes only have a single method in them, you might have abused the SRP. That said, I am not saying that a class with only one method is wrong.

Naming example

In this example, we extract methods to see how naming them well improves readability by applying the SRP to the following long method. Let's take a first look at the `RandomizeOneString` method of the `OneMethodExampleService` class:

```csharp
namespace ClearName
{
    public class OneMethodExampleService : IExampleService
    {
        private readonly IEnumerable<string> _data;
        private static readonly Random _random = new Random();

        public OneMethodExampleService(IEnumerable<string> data)
        {
            _data = data ?? throw new
```

```
ArgumentNullException(nameof(data));
        }


        public RandomResult RandomizeOneString()
        {
            // Find the upper bound
            var upperBound = _data.Count();

            // Randomly select the index of the string to
return
            var index = _random.Next(0, upperBound);

            // Shuffle the elements to add more randomness
            var shuffledList = _data
                .Select(value => new { Value = value, Order =
_random.NextDouble() })
                .OrderBy(x => x.Order)
                .Select(x => x.Value)
            ;

            // Return the randomly selected element
            var randomString = shuffledList.ElementAt(index);
            return new RandomResult(randomString, index,
shuffledList);
        }
    }
}
```

With all of the comments, we can isolate a few operations that need to happen in order to find that random string. Those operations are as follows:

- Finding the upper bound of the _data field (an IEnumerable<string>).
- Generating the next random index at which our item should be taken.
- Shuffling the list of items to add more randomness.
- Returning the results, including the index and the shuffled data, to make it easier to display later.

Once we isolated those operations, we can extract a method for each one.

> **Note**
>
> I do not recommend systematically extracting one-line methods as it creates lots of code that is not necessarily useful. That said, if you find that extracting a one-line method makes the code more readable, by all means do it.

By taking that into account, we could extract one method and make it easier to read, like the one from the `CleanExampleService` class. Doing that led to applying the SRP inside the class for improved readability, as we can see here:

```
public RandomResult RandomizeOneString()
{
    var upperBound = _data.Count();
    var index = _random.Next(0, upperBound);
    var shuffledData = ShuffleData();
    var randomString = shuffledData.ElementAt(index);
    return new RandomResult(randomString, index, shuffledData);
}
```

In that resulting method, we even removed the comments, so by extracting the shuffle responsibility away from the `RandomizeOneString` method, we made the code easier to read than before. Moreover, by using descriptive variable names, it becomes easier to follow the method, without the comments.

We only studied a small part of the code, but the full code sample is available on GitHub. In `Startup.cs`, you can comment out the first line, `#define USE_CLEAN_SERVICE`, to use the `OneMethodExampleService` class instead of `CleanExampleService`; they do the same thing.

The full sample also exhibits the ISP and the DIP in action; we cover those two principles soon. You should come back to this sample (the full source code) once you read the chapter.

Open/Closed principle (OCP)

Let's start this section with a quote from Bertrand Meyer:

> *"Software entities (classes, modules, functions, and so on) should be open for extension but closed for modification."*

OK, but what does this mean, you may ask yourself? It means that a class's behaviors should be updatable from the outside, a.k.a., from the caller code. Instead of manually rewriting the code of a method inside the class, you should be able to change the class behaviors from the outside, without altering the code itself.

The best way to pull that off is to assemble the application using multiple well-designed units of code, sewed together using dependency injection.

To illustrate that, let's play with a ninja, a sword, and a shuriken; be careful, that's dangerous ground here!

Here is the IAttackable interface used in all the examples:

```
public interface IAttackable { }
```

Let's start with an example that does not follow the OCP:

```
public class Ninja : IAttackable
{
    //...
    public AttackResult Attack(IAttackable target)
    {
        if (IsCloseRange(target))
        {
            return new AttackResult(new Sword(), this, target);
        }
        else
        {
            return new AttackResult(new Shuriken(), this, target);
        }
    }
    //...
}
```

In this example, we can see that the Ninja class selects a weapon depending on its target range. The idea behind that is not wrong, but what happens when we add new weapons to our ninja's arsenal? At that point, we would need to open the Ninja class and update its Attack method.

Let's rethink the Ninja class by setting the weapon externally and by abstracting the Attack method. We could manage the equipped weapon internally, but for simplicity, we are managing it from the consuming code.

Our empty shell now looks like this:

```csharp
public class Ninja : IAttackable
{
    public Weapon EquippedWeapon { get; set; }
    // ...
    public AttackResult Attack(IAttackable target)
    {
        throw new NotImplementedException();
    }
    // ...
}
```

Now, the ninja's attack is directly related to his equipped weapon; for example, a shuriken is thrown, while a sword is used to deliver a close-range blow. The OCP dictates that the attack should be handled elsewhere, allowing the modification of the ninja's behavior without altering its code.

What we want to do is called **composition**, and the best way of implementing this is the **Strategy pattern**, which we explore in more detail in *Chapter 6, Understanding the Strategy, Abstract Factory, and Singleton Design Patterns* and *Chapter 7, Deep Dive into Dependency Injection*. For now, let's forget about those details, and let's play with some code that follows the OCP.

The new `Attack` method goes like this:

```csharp
public AttackResult Attack(IAttackable target)
{
    return new AttackResult(EquippedWeapon, this, target);
}
```

It now does the same thing as initially, but we can add weapons, set the `EquippedWeapon` property, and the program should use the new weapon instead; no more need to change the `Ninja` class for that.

OK, let's be honest; that code does nothing. It only allows us to print out what is going on in our program and show how we can modify the behaviors without modifying the class itself. We could, however, start from there to create a small ninja game. We could manage the ninjas' positions to compute the actual distance between them and enforce minimum and maximum ranges for each weapon, but that is way beyond the scope of the current section.

Now, let's take a look at the `AttackResult` class. We can see that it is a small data structure containing no behavior. It is used by our program to output the result:

```
public class AttackResult
{
    public Weapon Weapon { get; }
    public IAttackable Attacker { get; }
    public IAttackable Target { get; }

    public AttackResult(Weapon weapon, IAttackable attacker,
IAttackable target)
    {
        Weapon = weapon;
        Attacker = attacker;
        Target = target;
    }
}
```

The program code, in the `Startup` class, appears as follows:

```
// Setup the response
context.Response.ContentType = "text/html";

// Create actors
var target = new Ninja("The Unseen Mirage");
var ninja = new Ninja("The Blue Phantom");

// First attack (Sword)
ninja.EquippedWeapon = new Sword();
var result = ninja.Attack(target);
await PrintAttackResult(result);

// Second attack (Shuriken)
ninja.EquippedWeapon = new Shuriken();
var result2 = ninja.Attack(target);
await PrintAttackResult(result2);

// Write the outcome of an AttackResult to the response stream
```

```
async Task PrintAttackResult(AttackResult attackResult)
{
    await context.Response.WriteAsync($"'{attackResult.
Attacker}' attacked '{attackResult.Target}'
using'{attackResult.Weapon}'!<br>");
}
```

When running the program, using the `dotnet run` command and browsing to `https://localhost:5001/`, we should have the following output:

```
'The Blue Phantom' attacked 'The Unseen Mirage' using 'Sword'!
'The Blue Phantom' attacked 'The Unseen Mirage' using
'Shuriken'!
```

In a more complex application, combining composition and dependency injection would allow the application of behavior changes to the whole program from a single place, called the composition root, without changing our existing code; "open for extension, but closed for modification." To add new weapons, we can create new classes and do not need to modify any existing ones.

All of those new terms could be overwhelming at first, but we cover them in more detail in subsequent chapters and use those techniques extensively throughout the book.

> **A bit of history**
>
> The first appearance of the OCP, in 1988, was referring to inheritance, and OOP has evolved a lot since then. You should, most of the time, opt for composition over inheritance. Inheritance is still a useful concept, but you should be careful when using it; it is a concept that is easy to misuse, creating direct coupling between classes.

Liskov substitution principle (LSP)

The LSP emanated from Barbara Liskov at the end of the '80s and was revisited during the '90s by both Liskov and Jeannette Wing to create the principle that we know and use today. It is also similar to *Design by contract*, by Bertrand Meyer.

The LSP focuses on preserving subtype behaviors, which leads to system stability. Before going any further, let's start with the formal definition introduced by Wing and Liskov:

> *Let $\varnothing(x)$ be a property provable about objects x of type T. Then, $\varnothing(y)$*
> *should be true for objects y of type S, where S is a subtype of T.*

This means that you should be able to swap an object of type T with an object of type S, where S is the subtype of T, without breaking your program's correctness.

Without putting up some effort, you can't violate the following rules in C#, but they are still worth mentioning:

- The contravariance of method arguments in the subtype.

- The covariance of return types in the subtype.

One way to break contravariance would be to test for a specific subtype, such as the following:

```
public void SomeMethod(SomeType input)
{
    if (input is SomeSubType)
    // ...
}
```

One way to break covariance would be to return a supertype as a subtype, which would require some work on the developer's side.

Then, to prove subtype correctness, we must follow a few more rules:

- Any precondition implemented in a supertype should yield the same outcome in its subtypes, but subtypes can be less strict about it, never more.

- Any postcondition implemented in a supertype should yield the same outcome in its subtypes, but subtypes can be more strict about it, never less.

- Subtypes must preserve the invariance of the supertype; in other words, the behaviors of the supertype must not change.

Finally, we must add the "history constraint" to that list of rules, which states that what happened in the supertype must still happen in the subtype. While subtypes can add new properties and methods (in other words, new behaviors), they must not modify the supertype state in any new way.

OK, at this point, you are right to feel that this is rather complex. Rest assured that this is the less important of those principles, yet the more complex, and we are moving as far as we can from inheritance, so this should not apply often.

That said, I'd resume all of that previous complexity by doing the following:

- In your subtypes, add new behaviors; don't change existing ones.

You should be able to swap a class by one of its subclasses without breaking anything.

It is important to note that "without breaking anything" includes not throwing new exceptions in subtypes. Subtyping exceptions thrown by the supertype is acceptable as the existing code should already handle those and catch the subtyped exceptions if they do.

As a side note, before even bothering with the LSP, start by applying the "is-a" rule from inheritance; if a subtype is not a supertype, don't use inheritance.

To make a LEGO® analogy: LSP is like swapping a 4x2 blue block with a 4x2 green block: neither the structural integrity of the structure nor the role of the block changed, just its color.

> **Tip**
> An excellent way of enforcing those behavioral constraints is automated testing. You could write a test suite and run it against all subclasses of a specific supertype to make sure that behaviors are preserved.

Let's jump into some code to visualize that out in practice.

Project – HallOfFame

Now, let's see what this looks like in code. For this one, we explore a hall of fame feature of a fictive game that we are working on.

Feature description: the game should accumulate the number of enemies killed during the game session, and if you killed at least 100 enemies, your ninja should reach the hall of fame. The hall of fame should be ordered from the best score to the worst.

We created the following automated tests to enforce those rules, with sut (subject under test) being of type HallOfFame. Here is the empty implementation of the HallOfFame class:

```
public class HallOfFame
{
    public virtual void Add(Ninja ninja)
        => throw new NotImplementedException();
    public virtual IEnumerable<Ninja> Members
        => throw new NotImplementedException();
}
```

> **Note**
>
> I'm not following the convention that I talked about in the previous chapter because I need inheritance to reuse my test suite for the three versions of the code. That could not have been done using nested classes.

The `Add()` method should add ninjas that killed more than 100 enemies:

```csharp
public static TheoryData<Ninja> NinjaWithAtLeast100Kills => new
TheoryData<Ninja>
{
    new Ninja { Kills = 100 },
    new Ninja { Kills = 101 },
    new Ninja { Kills = 200 },
};

[Theory]
[MemberData(nameof(NinjaWithAtLeast100Kills))]
public void Add_should_add_the_specified_ninja(Ninja
expectedNinja)
{
    // Act
    sut.Add(expectedNinja);

    // Assert
    Assert.Collection(sut.Members,
        ninja => Assert.Same(expectedNinja, ninja)
    );
}
```

The `Add()` method should not add a ninja more than once:

```csharp
[Fact]
public void Add_should_not_add_existing_ninja()
{
    // Arrange
    var expectedNinja = new Ninja { Kills = 200 };

    // Act
```

```
    sut.Add(expectedNinja);
    sut.Add(expectedNinja);

    // Assert
    Assert.Collection(sut.Members,
        ninja => Assert.Same(expectedNinja, ninja)
    );
}
```

The `Add()` method should validate that a ninja has at least 100 kills before adding it to the `Members` collection of the `HallOfFame` instance under test:

```
[Fact]
public void Add_should_not_add_ninja_with_less_than_100_kills()
{
    // Arrange
    var ninja = new Ninja { Kills = 99 };

    // Act
    sut.Add(ninja);

    // Assert
    Assert.Empty(sut.Members);
}
```

The `Members` property of the `HallOfFame` class should return its ninja ordered by their number of kills, from the most to the least:

```
[Fact]
public void Members_should_return_ninja_ordered_by_kills_desc()
{
    // Arrange
    sut.Add(new Ninja { Kills = 100 });
    sut.Add(new Ninja { Kills = 150 });
    sut.Add(new Ninja { Kills = 200 });

    // Act
    var result = sut.Members;
```

```
// Assert
Assert.Collection(result,
    ninja => Assert.Equal(200, ninja.Kills),
    ninja => Assert.Equal(150, ninja.Kills),
    ninja => Assert.Equal(100, ninja.Kills)
);
}
```

The implementation of the HallOfFame class looks like this:

```
public class HallOfFame
{
    protected HashSet<Ninja> InternalMembers { get; } = new
HashSet<Ninja>();

    public virtual void Add(Ninja ninja)
    {
        if (InternalMembers.Contains(ninja))
        {
            return;
        }
        if (ninja.Kills >= 100)
        {
            InternalMembers.Add(ninja);
        }
    }

    public virtual IEnumerable<Ninja> Members
        => new ReadOnlyCollection<Ninja>(
            InternalMembers
                .OrderByDescending(x => x.Kills)
                .ToArray()
        );
}
```

Now that we have completed our feature and pushed our changes, we demo the hall of fame to our client.

Update 1

After the demo, an idea arises: why not add a *hall of heroes* for players who do not qualify for the hall of fame? After deliberation, we decided that we should implement that feature.

Feature description: the game should accumulate the number of enemies killed during the game session (already done), and add all ninjas to the hall of heroes, no matter the score. The results should be ordered by the best score first, in descending order, and each ninja should only be present once.

The first idea that arises to implement this feature quickly is to reuse the hall of fame code. Step one, we decide to create a `HallOfHeroes` class that inherits the `HallOfFame` class and rewrite the `Add()` method to support the new specifications.

After thinking about it, do you think that change would break the LSP?

Before giving you the answer, let's take a look at that `HallOfHeroes` class:

```
namespace LSP.Examples.Update1
{
    public class HallOfHeroes : HallOfFame
    {
        public override void Add(Ninja ninja)
        {
            if (InternalMembers.Contains(ninja))
            {
                return;
            }
            InternalMembers.Add(ninja);
        }
    }
}
```

Since the LSP states that *subclasses can be less strict about preconditions*, removing the number of kill preconditions should be acceptable.

Now, if we run the tests built for `HallOfFame` by using `HallOfHeroes` instead, the only test that fails is the one related to our precondition, so the subclass changed no behavior, and all use cases are still valid.

To test our features more efficiently, we can encapsulate all shared tests into a base class but keep `Add_should_not_add_ninja_with_less_than_100_kills` only for the `HallOfFame` tests.

With that in place to validate our code, we can begin to explore the role of the LSP as we can use an instance of `HallOfHeroes` everywhere our program expects a `HallOfFame` instance, without breaking it.

Here is the complete `BaseLSPTest` class:

```csharp
namespace LSP.Examples
{
    public abstract class BaseLSPTest
    {
        protected abstract HallOfFame sut { get; }

        public static TheoryData<Ninja>
NinjaWithAtLeast100Kills => new TheoryData<Ninja>
        {
            new Ninja { Kills = 100 },
            new Ninja { Kills = 101 },
            new Ninja { Kills = 200 },
        };

        [Fact]
        public void Add_should_not_add_existing_ninja()
        {
            // Arrange
            var expectedNinja = new Ninja { Kills = 200 };

            // Act
            sut.Add(expectedNinja);
            sut.Add(expectedNinja);

            // Assert
            Assert.Collection(sut.Members,
                ninja => Assert.Same(expectedNinja, ninja)
            );
        }

        [Theory]
        [MemberData(nameof(NinjaWithAtLeast100Kills))]
```

```
        public void Add_should_add_the_specified_ninja(Ninja
expectedNinja)
        {
            // Act
            sut.Add(expectedNinja);

            // Assert
            Assert.Collection(sut.Members,
                ninja => Assert.Same(expectedNinja, ninja)
            );
        }

        [Fact]
        public void Members_should_return_ninja_ordered_by_
kills_desc()
        {
            // Arrange
            sut.Add(new Ninja { Kills = 100 });
            sut.Add(new Ninja { Kills = 150 });
            sut.Add(new Ninja { Kills = 200 });

            // Act
            var result = sut.Members;

            // Assert
            Assert.Collection(result,
                ninja => Assert.Equal(200, ninja.Kills),
                ninja => Assert.Equal(150, ninja.Kills),
                ninja => Assert.Equal(100, ninja.Kills)
            );
        }
    }
}
```

The `HallOfFameTest` class is way simpler and looks like the following:

```
using LSP.Models;
using Xunit;

namespace LSP.Examples
{
    public class HallOfFameTest : BaseLSPTest
    {
        protected override HallOfFame sut { get; } = new
HallOfFame();

        [Fact]
        public void Add_should_not_add_ninja_with_less_
than_100_kills()
        {
            // Arrange
            var ninja = new Ninja { Kills = 99 };

            // Act
            sut.Add(ninja);
            // Assert
            Assert.Empty(sut.Members);
        }
    }
}
```

Finally, the `HallOfHeroesTest` class is almost empty:

```
using LSP.Models;

namespace LSP.Examples.Update1
{
    public class HallOfHeroesTest : BaseLSPTest
    {
        protected override HallOfFame sut { get; } = new
HallOfHeroes();
```

```
        }
    }
```

That new feature is implemented, but we are not done yet.

Update 2

Later on, the game is using those classes. However, Joe, another developer, decides to use HallOfHeroes in a new feature, but he needs to know when duplicated ninjas are added, so he decides to replace the return; statement with throw new DuplicateNinjaException() instead. He is proud of his feature and shows that to the team.

Do you think Joe's update is breaking the LSP?

The class looks like this after the changes:

```csharp
using LSP.Models;
using System;

namespace LSP.Examples.Update2
{
    public class HallOfHeroes : HallOfFame
    {
        public override void Add(Ninja ninja)
        {
            if (InternalMembers.Contains(ninja))
            {
                throw new DuplicateNinjaException();
            }
            InternalMembers.Add(ninja);
        }
    }

    public class DuplicateNinjaException : Exception
    {
        public DuplicateNinjaException()
            : base("Cannot add the same ninja twice!") { }
    }
}
```

Yes, it is violating the LSP. Moreover, if our engineer had run the tests, it would have been clear that one test was failing!

What do you think is violating the LSP?

All of the existing code was not expecting a `DuplicateNinjaException` to be thrown anywhere by a `HallOfFame` instance, so that could have created runtime crashes, possibly breaking the game. Throwing new exceptions in subclasses is forbidden as per the LSP.

Update 3

To fix his mistake and conform to the LSP, our engineer decides to add an `AddingDuplicateNinja` event to the `HallOfHeroes` class and then subscribes to that event instead of catching the `DuplicateNinjaException`.

Would that fix the previous LSP violation?

The updated code looks like this:

```
using LSP.Models;
using System;

namespace LSP.Examples.Update3
{
    public class HallOfHeroes : HallOfFame
    {
        public event
EventHandler<AddingDuplicateNinjaEventArgs>
AddingDuplicateNinja;

        public override void Add(Ninja ninja)
        {
            if (InternalMembers.Contains(ninja))
            {
                OnAddingDuplicateNinja(new
AddingDuplicateNinjaEventArgs(ninja));
                return;
            }
            InternalMembers.Add(ninja);
        }
```

```
        protected virtual void
OnAddingDuplicateNinja(AddingDuplicateNinjaEventArgs e)
        {
            AddingDuplicateNinja?.Invoke(this, e);
        }
    }

    public class AddingDuplicateNinjaEventArgs : EventArgs
    {
        public Ninja DuplicatedNinja { get; }

        public AddingDuplicateNinjaEventArgs(Ninja ninja)
        {
            DuplicatedNinja = ninja ?? throw new
ArgumentNullException(nameof(ninja));
        }
    }
}
```

Yes, that fix allowed the existing code to run smoothly while adding the new feature that Joe required. Publishing an `event` instead of throwing an `Exception` was just one way to fix our fictional problem. In a real-life scenario, you should choose the solution that fits your problem best.

The important part of the previous example is that introducing a new exception type can seem harmless but can cause much harm. The same goes for other LSP violations.

Conclusion

Once again, this is only a principle, not a law. A good tip would be to see the violation of the LSP as a *code smell*. From there, perform some analysis to see whether you have a design problem and what could be the impact. Use your analytical skills on a case-by-case basis and conclude whether or not it would be acceptable to break the LSP in that specific case.

I think that we could also name this principle the *backward-compatibility principle*, because everything that worked in a way before should still work at least the same way after the substitution, which is why this principle is important.

The more we advance, the more we move away from inheritance, and the less we need this principle. Don't get me wrong here, if you use inheritance, do your best to apply the LSP, and you will most likely be rewarded by doing so.

Interface segregation principle (ISP)

Let's start with another famous quote, by Robert C. Martin:

> *"Many client-specific interfaces are better than one general-purpose interface."*

What does that mean? It means the following:

- You should create interfaces.

- You should value small interfaces more.

- You should not try to create a multipurpose interface as "an interface to rule them all."

An interface could refer to a class interface here (all exposed elements of a class), but I prefer to focus on C# interfaces instead, as we use them a lot throughout the book. If you know C++, you could see an interface as a header file.

What is an interface?

Interfaces are one of the most useful tools in the C# box to create flexible and maintainable software alike. I'll try to give you a clear definition of what an interface is, but don't worry; it is very hard to understand and grasp the power of interfaces from an explanation.

- The role of an interface is to define a cohesive contract (public methods, properties, and events); there is no code in an interface; it is only a contract.

- An interface should be small (ISP), and its members should align toward a common goal (cohesion) and share a single responsibility (SRP).

- In C#, a class can implement multiple interfaces, and by doing so, a class can expose multiples of those public contracts or, more accurately, be used as any of them (polymorphism).

Let's be honest, that definition is still a bit abstract, but rest assured, we use interfaces intensively throughout the book, so by the end, interfaces should not hold many secrets for you.

> **On another more fundamental note**
>
> A class does not inherit from an interface; it implements an interface. However, an interface can inherit from another interface.

Project – The door locks

One way to see a contract would be as a key and a lock. Each key fits one lock based on a specific contract defining how the key should be made to work. If we have multiple locks following the same contract, one key should fit all of those locks, while multiple keys could also fit the same lock as long as they are identical.

The idea behind an interface is the same; an interface describes what is available, and the implementation decides how it does it, leaving the consumer to expect a behavior (by following the contract) to happen while ignoring how it is done in the background (by the implementation).

Our key contract looks like this:

```
/// <summary>
/// Represents a key that can open zero or more locks.
/// </summary>
public interface IKey
{
    /// <summary>
    /// Gets the key's signature.
    /// This should be used by <see cref="ILock"/> to decide
    whether or not the key matches the lock.
    /// </summary>
    string Signature { get; }
}
```

And our lock contract appears like this:

```
/// <summary>
/// Represents a lock than can be opened by zero or more keys.
/// </summary>
public interface ILock
{
    /// <summary>
    /// Gets if the lock is locked or not.
```

```
///    </summary>
    bool IsLocked { get; }


    ///    <summary>
    ///    Locks the lock using the specified <see cref="IKey"/>.
    ///    </summary>
    ///    <param name="key">The <see cref="IKey"/> used to lock
the lock.</param>
    ///    <exception cref="KeyDoesNotMatchException">The <see
cref="Exception"/> that is thrown when the specified <see
cref="IKey"/> does not match the <see cref="ILock"/>.</
exception>
    void Lock(IKey key);


    ///    <summary>
    ///    Unlocks the lock using the specified <see
cref="IKey"/>.
    ///    </summary>
    ///    <param name="key">The <see cref="IKey"/> used to unlock
the lock.</param>
    ///    <exception cref="KeyDoesNotMatchException">The <see
cref="Exception"/> that is thrown when the specified <see
cref="IKey"/> does not match the <see cref="ILock"/>.</
exception>
    void Unlock(IKey key);


    ///    <summary>
    ///    Validate that the key's <see cref="IKey.Signature"/>
match the lock.
    ///    </summary>
    ///    <param name="key">The <see cref="IKey"/> to validate.</
param>
    ///    <returns><c>true</c> if the key's <see cref="IKey.
Signature"/> match the lock; otherwise <c>false</c>.</returns>
    bool DoesMatch(IKey key);
}
```

As you can see, the contract is clear, and a few details have been added to describe what is to be expected when using it or when implementing it.

> **Note**
>
> These specifications could help enforce an extended view of the LSP by validating that implementations respect their contract, allowing the consumer to use any implementation of the interfaces safely.
>
> Please note that it is rare that exceptions are defined at the interface level as I did. In our case, I felt that it made more sense to do that, making the description of the contract crystal clear, instead of returning a `bool` that could have been misleading. Moreover, returning a `bool` would have created a lack of feedback about the source of the failure. We could have returned an object or picked another solution, but it would have added unwanted complexity to the code sample. We are exploring alternatives to similar problems later in the book.

Let's take a look at a basic key and lock implementation.

Basic implementations

Physical keys and locks are easy to visualize. A key has notches and ridges, a length, a thickness, is made from particular materials giving it a color, and so on. A lock, on the other hand, is composed of pins and springs. When you insert the right key into the right lock, you can lock or unlock it.

In our case, to keep it simple, we use the `Signature` property of the `IKey` interface to represent the physical key's properties while the lock can handle keys as it wishes.

Our most basic key and lock implementation looks like this:

```
public class BasicKey : IKey
{
    public BasicKey(string signature)
    {
        Signature = signature ?? throw new
ArgumentNullException(nameof(signature));
    }

    public string Signature { get; }
}

public class BasicLock : ILock
{
    private readonly string _expectedSignature;
```

```csharp
    public BasicLock(string expectedSignature)
    {
        _expectedSignature = expectedSignature ?? throw new
ArgumentNullException(nameof(expectedSignature));
    }


    public bool IsLocked { get; private set; }


    public bool DoesMatch(IKey key)
    {
        return key.Signature.Equals(_expectedSignature);
    }
    public void Lock(IKey key)
    {
        if (!DoesMatch(key))
        {
            throw new KeyDoesNotMatchException(key);
        }
        IsLocked = true;
    }


    public void Unlock(IKey key)
    {
        if (!DoesMatch(key))
        {
            throw new KeyDoesNotMatchException(key);
        }
        IsLocked = false;
    }
}
```

As you can see, the implementations are doing what was described by the interface and
its /// comments, using a private field named _expectedSignature to validate the
key's signature.

For reasons of brevity, I'm not copying all the tests here, but most of the code of this sample is covered by unit tests that you can browse on GitHub or clone locally. Here is an example, covering the specifications of the DoesMatch method:

```csharp
using Xunit;

namespace DoorLock
{
    public class BasicLockTest
    {
        private readonly IKey _workingKey;
        private readonly IKey _invalidKey;

        private readonly BasicLock sut;
        public BasicLockTest()
        {
            sut = new BasicLock("WorkingKey");
            _invalidKey = new BasicKey("InvalidKey");
            _workingKey = new BasicKey("WorkingKey");
        }

        public class DoesMatch : BasicLockTest
        {
            [Fact]
            public void Should_return_true_when_the_key_matches_the_lock()
            {
                // Act
                var result = sut.DoesMatch(_workingKey);

                // Assert
                Assert.True(result, "The key should match the lock.");
            }

            [Fact]
            public void Should_return_false_when_the_key_does_
```

```
not_match_the_lock()
        {
                // Act
                var result = sut.DoesMatch(_invalidKey);

                // Assert
                Assert.False(result, "The key should not match
the lock.");
            }
        }
        //...
    }
}
```

We can see that the tests of `DoesMatch` are a direct representation of the interface `///` comments:

```
<returns><c>true</c> if the key's <see cref="IKey.Signature"/>
match the lock; otherwise <c>false</c>.</returns>.
```

Let's get into a few more implementations before going further into the ISP.

Multi-lock implementation

To prove that small, well-defined interfaces are important, let's implement a special type of lock: a lock that contains other locks, the `MultiLock` class:

```
public class MultiLock : ILock
{
    private readonly List<ILock> _locks;
    public MultiLock(List<ILock> locks)
    {
        _locks = locks ?? throw new
ArgumentNullException(nameof(locks));
    }
    public MultiLock(params ILock[] locks)
        : this(new List<ILock>(locks))
    {
        if (locks == null) { throw new
```

```
ArgumentNullException(nameof(locks)); }
    }

    public bool IsLocked => _locks.Any(@lock => @lock.
IsLocked);

    public bool DoesMatch(IKey key)
    {
        return _locks.Any(@lock => @lock.DoesMatch(key));
    }

    public void Lock(IKey key)
    {
        if (!DoesMatch(key))
        {
            throw new KeyDoesNotMatchException(key);
        }
        _locks
            .Where(@lock => @lock.DoesMatch(key))
            .ToList()
            .ForEach(@lock => @lock.Lock(key));
    }

    public void Unlock(IKey key)
    {
        if (!DoesMatch(key))
        {
            throw new KeyDoesNotMatchException(key);
        }
        _locks
            .Where(@lock => @lock.DoesMatch(key))
            .ToList()
            .ForEach(@lock => @lock.Unlock(key));
    }
}
```

That new class allows consumers to create a lock composed of other locks. MultiLock remains locked until all locks are unlocked and get locked as soon as any lock is locked.

> **As a side note**
>
> The MultiLock class implements the composite design pattern, discussed later in the book.

Picklock

Now that we have secure locks, someone needs to create a picklock, but how would we create that? Do you think that a picklock is an IKey?

In a different design, maybe; in ours, no, a picklock is not a key. So, instead of wrapping the use of the IKey interface, let's create an IPicklock interface that defines picklocks:

```
/// <summary>
/// Represent a tool that can be used to pick a lock.
/// </summary>
public interface IPicklock
{
    /// <summary>
    /// Create a key that fits the specified <see
cref="ILock"/>.
    /// </summary>
    /// <param name="lock">The lock to pick.</param>
    /// <returns>The key that fits the specified <see
cref="ILock"/>.</returns>
    /// <exception cref="ImpossibleToPickTheLockException">
    /// The <see cref="Exception"/> that is thrown
when a lock cannot be picked using the current <see
cref="IPicklock"/>.
    /// </exception>
    IKey CreateMatchingKeyFor(ILock @lock);

    /// <summary>
    /// Unlock the specified <see cref="ILock"/>.
    /// </summary>
    /// <param name="lock">The lock to pick.</param>
```

```
        /// <exception cref="ImpossibleToPickTheLockException">
        /// The <see cref="Exception"/> that is thrown when a
            lock cannot be picked using the current <see
            cref="IPicklock"/>.
        /// </exception>
        void Pick(ILock @lock);
}
```

Once again, I wrote the specifications using /// right on the interface, including the exceptions.

The initial implementation is based on a collection of IKey.Signature. That collection is injected into the constructor so we can reuse our picklock. We could regard it as a predefined collection of keys, a kind of keyring:

```
public class PredefinedPicklock : IPicklock
{
    private readonly string[] _signatures;

    public PredefinedPicklock(string[] signatures)
    {
        _signatures = signatures ?? throw new
ArgumentNullException(nameof(signatures));
    }

    public IKey CreateMatchingKeyFor(ILock @lock)
    {
        var key = new FakeKey();
        foreach (var signature in _signatures)
        {
            key.Signature = signature;
            if (@lock.DoesMatch(key))
            {
                return key;
            }
        }
        throw new ImpossibleToPickTheLockException(@lock);
    }
}
```

```
    public void Pick(ILock @lock)
    {
        var key = new FakeKey();
        foreach (var signature in _signatures)
        {
            key.Signature = signature;
            if (@lock.DoesMatch(key))
            {
                @lock.Unlock(key);
                if (!@lock.IsLocked)
                {
                    return;
                }
            }
        }
        throw new ImpossibleToPickTheLockException(@lock);
    }

    private class FakeKey : IKey
    {
        public string Signature { get; set; }
    }
}
```

From that sample, we can see a private implementation of IKey named FakeKey. We use that implementation inside the PredefinedPicklock class to simulate a key and send an IKey.Signature to the ILock instance that we are trying to pick. Unfortunately, PredefinedPicklock has very limited capabilities.

The strength of interfaces is starting to show from this sample. If we take a look at the Pick test method named Should_unlock_the_specified_ILock, we can see how we leveraged the use of the ILock interface by testing it against different types of lock without knowing it inside the test case:

```
using Xunit;

namespace DoorLock
```

```
{
    public class PredefinedPicklockTest
    {
        //...
        public class Pick : PredefinedPicklockTest
        {
            public static TheoryData<ILock> PickableLocks = new
TheoryData<ILock>
            {
                new BasicLock("key1", isLocked: true),
                new MultiLock(
                    new BasicLock("key2", isLocked: true),
                    new BasicLock("key3", isLocked: true)
                ),
                new MultiLock(
                    new BasicLock("key2", isLocked: true),
                    new MultiLock(
                        new BasicLock("key1", isLocked: true),
                        new BasicLock("key3", isLocked: true)
                    )
                )
            };

            [Theory]
            [MemberData(nameof(PickableLocks))]
            public void Should_unlock_the_specified_ILock(ILock
@lock)
            {
                // Arrange
                Assert.True(@lock.IsLocked, "The lock should
be locked.");
                var sut = new PredefinedPicklock(new[] {
"key1", "key2", "key3" });

                // Act
                sut.Pick(@lock);
```

```
                    // Assert
                    Assert.False(@lock.IsLocked, "The lock should
    be unlocked.");
                }
            //...
            }
        }
    }
```

That is just the beginning. By using interfaces, we can add flexibility without much effort. We could expand this example for quite some time, like creating a `BruteForcePickLock` implementation that tries to generate the `IKey` signature automatically. That last idea could be a helpful exercise for you to do.

Contract tests

Before moving forward, I'd like to take a look at the `ContractsTests` class. That class contains our initial assessments regarding a key and a door:

```
using System.Collections.Generic;
using Xunit;

namespace DoorLock
{
    public class ContractsTests
    {
        [Fact]
        public void A_single_key_should_fit_multiple_locks_
    expecting_the_same_signature()
        {
            IKey key = new BasicKey("key1");

            LockAndAssertResult(new BasicLock("key1"));
            LockAndAssertResult(new BasicLock("key1"));
            LockAndAssertResult(new MultiLock(new List<ILock> {
                new BasicLock("key1"),
                new BasicLock("key1")
            }));
```

```
        void LockAndAssertResult(ILock @lock)
        {
            var result = @lock.DoesMatch(key);
            Assert.True(result, $"The key '{key.Signature}'
should fit the lock");
        }
    }


    [Fact]
    public void Multiple_keys_with_the_same_signature_
should_fit_the_same_lock()
    {
        ILock @lock = new BasicLock("key1");

        var picklock = new PredefinedPicklock(new[] {
"key1" });
        var fakeKey = picklock.CreateMatchingKeyFor(@lock);

        LockAndAssertResult(new BasicKey("key1"));
        LockAndAssertResult(new BasicKey("key1"));
        LockAndAssertResult(fakeKey);

        void LockAndAssertResult(IKey key)
        {
            var result = @lock.DoesMatch(key);
            Assert.True(result, $"The key '{key.Signature}'
should fit the lock");
        }
    }
    }
}
```

In those two test methods, we can see the reusability and versatility of interfaces. No matter the lock, we can infer its usage from its interface and lower repetitive code.

In a program, as we explore throughout the book, we can leverage those interfaces for multiple reasons, including dependency injection.

> **Note**
>
> If you wonder how I can write methods inside methods, we will be talking about expression-bodied function members (C# 6) in *Chapter 4, The MVC Pattern using Razor.*

Conclusion of this example

Now that we have talked about all of that, why are smaller interfaces better? Let's start by merging all of our interfaces into one like this:

```
public interface IMixedInterface
{
    IKey CreateMatchingKeyFor(ILock @lock);
    void Pick(ILock @lock);
    string Signature { get; }
    bool IsLocked { get; }
    void Lock(IKey key);
    void Unlock(IKey key);
    bool DoesMatch(IKey key);
}
```

When you look at it, what does that interface tell you? Personally, it's telling me that there are way too many responsibilities in there and that I would have a hard time building a system around it.

The main problem with that interface is that every door would also be a key and a picklock, thus making no sense. By splitting the interfaces, it is easier to implement different, smaller parts of the system without compromise. If we want to have a key that is also a picklock, we can implement both the IKey and the IPicklock interfaces, but all keys would not be required to be a picklock too.

Let's jump to another example to add more perspective.

Project – Library

Context: We are building a web application where users have different roles; some are administrators, and some are just consuming the app. The administrators can read and write all of the data in the system while the normal users can only read. UI-wise, there are two distinct parts: the public UI and an admin panel.

Since users are not allowed to write data, we don't want to expose those methods there just in case certain developers, at some point in time, decide to use them. We don't want unused code to linger around in places where that code should not be used. On the other hand, we don't want to create two classes either, one that reads and one that writes; we prefer keeping only one data access class, which should be easier to maintain.

To do that, let's start by remodeling the earlier `BookStore` class by extracting an interface. To improve readability, let's rename the `Load()` method to `Find()`, and then let's add a `Remove()` method; which was missing before. The new interface looks like this:

```
public interface IBookStore
{
    IEnumerable<Book> Books { get; }
    Book Find(int bookId);
    void Create(Book book);
    void Replace(Book book);
    void Remove(Book book);
}
```

Then, to make sure that consumers cannot alter our `IBookStore` instances from the outside (encapsulation), let's also update the `Books` property of our `BookStore` class to return a type `ReadOnlyCollection<Book>` instead of the `_books` field directly. This does not affect the interface, just our implementation, but it also allows me to introduce that concept.

> **Note**
>
> The `System.Collections.ObjectModel` namespace contains a few read-only classes:
>
> a) `ReadOnlyCollection<T>`
>
> b) `ReadOnlyDictionary<TKey,TValue>`
>
> c) `ReadOnlyObservableCollection<T>`
>
> Those are very useful for exposing data to the clients without allowing them to modify it. In our example, the `IEnumerable<Book>` instance is of the `ReadOnlyCollection<Book>` type. We could have kept returning our internal `List<Book>`, but some clever developer could have figured this out, cast `IEnumerable<Book>` to a `List<Book>`, and added some books to it, thereby breaking encapsulation!

Now, let's look at that updated `BookStore` class:

```csharp
public class BookStore : IBookStore
{
    private static int _lastId = 0;
    private static List<Book> _books;
    private static int NextId => ++_lastId;

    static BookStore()
    {
        _books = new List<Book>
        {
            new Book
            {
                Id = NextId,
                Title = "Some cool computer book"
            }
        };
    }

    public IEnumerable<Book> Books => new
ReadOnlyCollection<Book>(_books);

    public Book Find(int bookId)
    {
        return _books.FirstOrDefault(x => x.Id == bookId);
    }

    public void Create(Book book)
    {
        if (book.Id != default(int))
        {
            throw new Exception("A new book cannot be created
with an id.");
        }
        book.Id = NextId;
        _books.Add(book);
```

```
    }

    public void Replace(Book book)
    {
        if (_books.Any(x => x.Id == book.Id))
        {
            throw new Exception($"Book {book.Id} does not
exist!");
        }
        var index = _books.FindIndex(x => x.Id == book.Id);
        _books[index] = book;
    }

    public void Remove(Book book)
    {
        if (_books.Any(x => x.Id == book.Id))
        {
            throw new Exception($"Book {book.Id} does not
exist!");
        }
        var index = _books.FindIndex(x => x.Id == book.Id);
        _books.RemoveAt(index);
    }
}
```

When looking at that code, if we expose the interface in the public UI, we expose the write interface as well, which is what we want to avoid.

To solve our design problem, we can use the ISP and start by splitting the `IBookStore` interface into two: `IBookReader` and `IBookWriter`:

```
public interface IBookReader
{
    IEnumerable<Book> Books { get; }
    Book Find(int bookId);
}
public interface IBookWriter
{
```

```
    void Create(Book book);
    void Replace(Book book);
    void Remove(Book book);
}
```

By following the ISP, we could even split `IBookWriter` into three interfaces:
`IBookCreator`, `IBookReplacer`, and `IBookRemover`. Word of warning, we must
be careful, because doing ultra-granular interface segregation like that could create quite
a mess in your system, but it could also be super beneficial, depending on the context
and your goals.

> **Tip**
>
> So, a word of advice. Be careful not to overuse this principle blindly and think
> about cohesion and about what you are trying to build, and not about how
> granular an interface can blindly become. The more granular your interfaces,
> the more flexible your system could be, but remember that flexibility has a cost,
> and that cost can become very high very quickly.

Now, we need to update our `BookStore` class. First, we have to implement our two new
interfaces:

```
public class BookStore : IBookReader, IBookWriter
{
    // ...
}
```

That was easy! With that new `BookStore` class, we can use `IBookReader` and
`IBookWriter` independently like this:

```
IBookReader reader = new BookStore();
IBookWriter writer = new BookStore();
// ...
var book3 = reader.Find(3);
// ...
writer.Create(new Book { Title = "Some nice new title!" });
// ...
```

Let's focus on the `reader` and `writer` variables. On the public side, we can now use
only the `IBookReader` interface, hiding the `BookStore` implementation behind the
interface. On the administrator side, we could use both interfaces to manage books.

Conclusion

To resume the idea behind the ISP, if you have multiple smaller interfaces, it is easier to reuse them and to expose only the features that you need instead of exposing APIs that are not needed. This is the goal: **only depend on interfaces that you consume**. Furthermore, with multiple specialized interfaces, it is easier to compose bigger pieces by implementing multiple interfaces if needed. If we compare that to the opposite, we cannot remove methods from a big interface if we don't need it in one of its implementation.

If you don't see all of the benefits yet, don't worry. All the pieces should come together once we cover the next principle, DIP, and dependency injection. With all of that, we can achieve adequate interface segregation in an elegant and manageable way.

Dependency inversion principle (DIP)

And yet another quote, from Robert C. Martin (including the implied context from Wikipedia):

One should "depend upon abstractions, [not] concretions."

In the previous section, I introduced you to interfaces with the SRP and the ISP. Interfaces are one of the pivotal elements of our SOLID arsenal! Moreover, using interfaces is the best way to approach the DIP. Of course, abstract classes are also abstractions, but as a rule of thumb, you should depend on interfaces whenever possible instead.

Why not use abstract classes, you might think? An `abstract class` is an abstraction, but is not 100% abstract, and if it is, you should replace it with an interface. Abstract classes are used to encapsulate default behaviors that you can then inherit in sub-classes. They are useful, but interfaces are more flexible, more powerful, and better suited to design contracts.

Moreover, using interfaces can save you countless hours of struggling and complex workaround when programming unit tests. That is even truer if you are building a framework or library that other people use. In that case, please be kind and provide your consumers with interfaces.

All of that talk about interfaces again is nice, but how can dependencies be inversed? Let's begin by comparing a direct dependency and an inverted dependency.

Direct dependency

If we have a `Ninja` class using a `Weapon` instance, the dependency graph should look like this because the `Ninja` directly depends on the `Weapon` class:

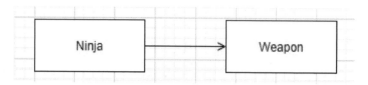

Figure 3.2 – Direct dependency schema

Inverted dependency

If we invert the dependency by introducing an abstraction, the `Ninja` class would depend only on that new `IWeapon` interface. Doing this gives us the flexibility to change the type of weapon without any impact on the system's stability and without altering the `Ninja` class, especially if we also followed the OCP. Indirectly, the `Ninja` still uses a `Weapon` class instance, thereby breaking the direct dependency.

Here is the updated schema:

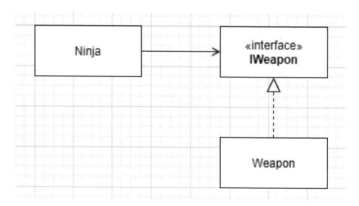

Figure 3.3 – Indirect dependency schema

Inverting subsystems using DIP

To go a little further, you can also isolate and decouple a complete subsystem this way by creating two or more assemblies:

1. An abstraction assembly containing only interfaces.

2. One or more other assemblies that contain the implementation of the contracts from that first assembly.

There are multiple examples of this in .NET, such as the `Microsoft.Extensions.DependencyInjection.Abstractions` and the `Microsoft.Extensions.DependencyInjection` assemblies. We are also exploring this concept in *Chapter 12, Understanding Layering*.

Before jumping into more code, let's take a look at another schema representing this idea. This time, it is related to abstracting data access from the database itself (we will also talk more about this later):

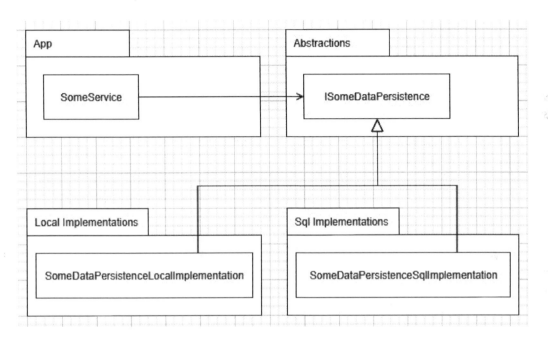

Figure 3.4 – Diagram representing how to break tight coupling by inverting dependencies

In the diagram, the `App` package directly depends on the `Abstractions` package while two implementations are available: `Local` and `Sql`. From there, we should be able to swap one implementation for the other without breaking our App. The reason is that we depend on the abstractions and coded the app using those abstractions. No matter what implementations are used, the program should run just fine.

Another example that I recently designed in a microservices-based application is a publish-subscribe (pub-sub) communication library. There are some abstractions that the microservices use, and there are one or more implementations that are swappable, so one microservice could use a provider, while another microservice could use another provider without directly depending on it. We discuss the Pub-Sub pattern and microservices architecture in *Chapter 16, Introduction to Microservices Architecture*. Until then, think of a microservice as an application.

> **Packages**
>
> The packages described here could be namespaces as well as assemblies.
> By dividing responsibilities around assemblies, it creates the possibility to load
> only the implementations that need to be loaded. For example, one app could
> load the "local" assembly and another app could load the "SQL" assembly, while
> a third app could load both.

Project – Dependency inversion

Context: We just learned about the DIP and want to apply it to our bookstore app.
Since we do not have any real user interface yet, we believe that it makes sense to create
multiple reusable assemblies that our ASP.NET Core app can use later, allowing us to swap
one GUI with another. Meanwhile, we are going to test our code using a little console
application.

There are three projects:

- GUI: the console app

- Core: the application logic

- Data: the data access

> **Layering**
>
> This concept is called layering. We will visit layering in more depth later. For
> now, you can think of it as splitting responsibilities into different assemblies.

Using a classical dependency hierarchy, we would end up with the following
dependency graph:

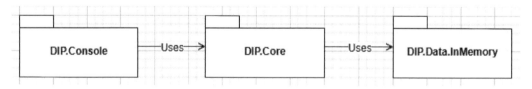

Figure 3.5 – Diagram representing assemblies that directly depend on the next assembly

This is not very flexible as all assemblies are directly linked to the next in line, creating
a strong, unbreakable bond between them. Let's now revisit this using the DIP.

> **Note**
>
> To keep it simple and to focus on only one portion of the code, I only abstracted the data portion of the program. We will explore dependency inversion in more depth further on in the book, along with dependency injection.
>
> For now, focus on `DIP.Data`, `DIP.Data.InMemory`, and the code sample of the chapter.

In the solution, there are four projects; three libraries and one console. Their goals are as follows:

- `DIP.Console` is the entry point, the program. Its role is to compose and run the application. It uses `DIP.Core` and defines what implementation should be used to cover the `DIP.Data` interfaces, in this case, `DIP.Data.InMemory`.

- `DIP.Core` is the program core, the shared logic. Its only dependency is on `DIP.Data`, abstracting away the implementation.

- `DIP.Data` contains persistence interfaces: `IBookReader` and `IBookWriter`. It also contains the data model (the `Book` class).

- `DIP.Data.InMemory` is a concrete implementation of `DIP.Data`.

To visualize the assemblies' relationships, let's take a look at the following diagram:

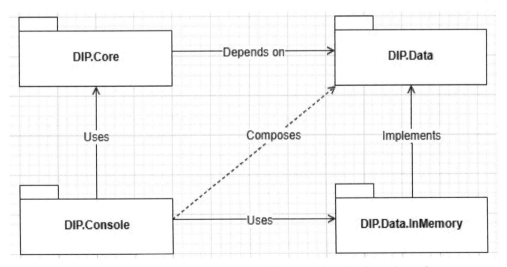

Figure 3.6 – Diagram representing assemblies that invert the dependency flow, breaking coupling between DIP.Core and DIP.Data.InMemory

If we start by looking at the `PublicService` class of the `Core` project, we can see that it only depends on the `Data` project's `IBookReader` interface:

```
public class PublicService
{
    public IBookReader _bookReader;

    public Task<IEnumerable<Book>> FindAllAsync()
    {
        return Task.FromResult(_bookReader.Books);
    }

    public Task<Book> FindAsync(int bookId)
    {
        var book = _bookReader.Find(bookId);
        return Task.FromResult(book);
    }
}
```

The `PublicService` class defines a few methods that use the `IBookReader` abstraction to query books. `PublicService` plays the consumer role and doesn't know about any concrete class. Even if we wanted to, the implementation is not accessible from this project. We succeeded; we inverted the dependency. Yes, as easy as that.

> **Note**
>
> Having a public field such as `_bookReader` breaks encapsulation, so don't do that in your projects. I just wanted to keep the focus of the example on the DIP. We see how to take advantage of the DIP using good practices later, including leveraging dependency injection.

Without any concrete implementation, an interface does nothing, so the other part of the DIP is to configure the consumer by defining what the implementations that back those abstractions are. To help us out, let's create a private class named `Composer` inside `Program` to centralize this step of the DIP.

That is, once again, not something you usually want to do in a real project, but until we cover dependency injection, we have to rely on a more manual approach, so let's take a look at that light version, focusing on `PublicService`:

```
private static class Composer
{
    private readonly static BookStore BookStore = new
    BookStore();
    // ...
    public static PublicService CreatePublicService()
    {
        return new PublicService
        {
            _bookReader = BookStore
        };
    }
}
```

The `CreatePublicService()` method is responsible for building the `PublicService` instance. In it, we assign an instance of the concrete class, `BookStore`, to the `public IBookReader _bookReader;` field, leaving `PublicService` unaware of its `_bookReader` implementation.

> **Have you noticed any DIP violations in the PublicService class?**
>
> Yes indeed, `PublicService` is concrete, and `Program` uses it directly. This is a violation of the DIP. If you want to try out dependency inversion, you could fix this violation in a project; coding is always the best way to learn!

This little sample shows how to invert dependency, making sure of the following:

- The code always depends on abstraction (interfaces).
- The projects also depend on abstractions (depending on `DIP.Data` instead of `DIP.Data.InMemory`).

Conclusion

The conclusion of this principle is strongly tied to what is coming next (see the next section). Nevertheless, the idea is to depend on abstractions (interfaces or abstract classes). Try to stick to interfaces as much as possible. They are more flexible than abstract classes.

Depending upon concretions creates tight coupling between classes, which leads to a system that can be harder to maintain. The cohesion between your dependencies plays an essential role in whether the coupling will help or hurt you in the long run. More on that later.

What's next?

The words dependency injection came out a few times, and you may be curious about it, so let's take a peek at what that is. Dependency injection, or **Inversion of Control (IoC)**, is a mechanism (a concept) that is a first-class citizen of ASP.NET Core. It allows you to map abstractions to implementations, and, when you need a new type, the whole object tree gets created automatically for you by following your configuration. Once you get used to it, you cannot move back; but beware of the challenges as you may need to "unlearn" a part of what you know to embrace this new technique.

Enough talking. Let's get through those last sections before getting too excited about dependency injection. We will start that journey in *Chapter 7, Deep Dive into Dependency Injection*.

Other important principles

I found two other principles to talk about briefly before going further:

- Separation of concerns
- Don't repeat yourself (DRY)

Of course, after reading the SOLID principles, you may find these more basic, but they are still complementary to what we just learned.

> **Note**
> There are many other principles, some that you may already know, some that you will most likely learn about later, but at some point, I have to choose the subjects or face writing an encyclopedia-sized book.

Separation of concerns

The idea is to separate your software into logical blocks, where each block is a concern; this can go from factoring a program into modules to applying the SRP to some subsystems. That can be applied to any programming paradigm. How to encapsulate a specific concern depends on the paradigm and the concern's level. The higher the level, the broader the solution; the lower the level, the more granular it becomes.

For example, the following applies:

- By using **aspect-oriented programming (AOP)**, we could see security or logging as cross-cutting concerns, encapsulating the code in an aspect.

- By using **object-oriented programming (OOP)**, we could also see security or logging as a cross-cutting concern, encapsulating shared logic in an ASP.NET filter.

- By using OOP again, we could see the rendering of a web page and the handling of an HTTP request as two concerns, leading to the MVC pattern; the view "renders" the page, while the controller handles the HTTP request.

- By using any paradigm, we could see adding extension points as a concern, leading to a plugin-based design.

- Using any paradigm again, we could see a component, responsible for copying an object into another, as a concern. In contrast, another component's responsibility could be to orchestrate those copies efficiently by following some rules, such as limiting the amount of copy that can happen in parallel, queuing the overflowing operations, and more.

As you may have noticed with those examples, a concern can be a significant matter or a tiny detail; nonetheless, it is imperative to consider concerns when dividing your software into pieces to create cohesive units. A good separation of concerns should help you create modular designs and help you face design dilemmas more effectively.

Don't repeat yourself (DRY)

OK, this principle's name is self-explanatory, and, as we already saw with the SRP and the OCP, we can, and should, extend and encapsulate logic into smaller units, aiming at reusability and lower maintenance costs.

The DRY principle explains it more or less the other way around by stating the following:

> *"When you have duplicated logic in your system, encapsulate it and reuse that new encapsulation in multiple places instead."*

The goal is to avoid making multiple changes when a specification changes. Why? To avoid forgetting to make one, or to avoid creating inconsistencies and bugs in the program.

It is very important to regroup duplicated logic by concern, not only by the look of multiple blocks of code. Let's look at those two methods from the `Program` class of a previous sample:

```
private static async Task PublicAppAsync()
{
    var publicService = Composer.CreatePublicService();
    var books = await publicService.FindAllAsync();
    foreach (var book in books)
    {
        presenter.Display(book);
    }
}

private static async Task AdminAppAsync()
{
    var adminService = Composer.CreateAdminService();
    var books = await adminService.FindAllAsync();
    foreach (var book in books)
    {
        presenter.Display(book);
    }
}
```

The code is very similar, but trying to extract a single method out of those would be a mistake. Why? Because the public program and the admin program can have different reasons to change (adding filters in the admin panel, but not in the public section, for example).

However, we could create a display method in the presenter class that handles a collection of books, replacing the `foreach` loop with a `presenter.Display(books)` call. We could then move those two methods out of `Program` without much impact. In the future, that would allow us to support multiple implementations, one for the admins and one for the public users for added flexibility.

> **Tip**
>
> I have told you this already, but here we go again. When you don't know how to name a class or a method, you may have isolated an invalid or an incomplete concern. This is a good indicator that you should go back to the drawing board.

Summary

In this chapter, we covered many architectural principles. We began by exploring the five SOLID principles and their importance in modern software engineering to then jump to the DRY and separation of concerns principles, which add some more guidance to the mix. By following those principles, you should be able to build better, more maintainable software. As we also covered, principles are only principles, not laws. You must always be careful not to abuse them so they remain helpful instead of harmful. The context is always important; internal tools and critical business apps require different levels of tinkering. Try not to over-engineer everything.

With all of those principles in our toolbox, we are now ready to jump into design patterns and get our designing level one step further! In the next few chapters, we explore how to implement some of the most frequently used GoF patterns and how those are applied at another level with dependency injection. Dependency injection is going to help follow the SOLID principles in our day-to-day designs, but before that, in the next two chapters, we explore ASP.NET Core MVC.

Questions

Let's take a look at a few practice questions:

1. How many principles are represented by the SOLID acronym?

2. Is it true that when following the SOLID principles, the idea is to create bigger components that can each manage more elements of a program by creating God-sized classes?

3. By following the DRY principle, you want to remove all code duplication from everywhere, irrespective of the source, and encapsulate that code into a reusable component. Is this affirmation correct?

4. Is it true that the ISP tells us that creating multiple smaller interfaces is better than creating one large one?

5. What principle tells us that creating multiple smaller classes that handle a single responsibility is better than one class handling multiple responsibilities?

Section 2: Designing for ASP.NET Core

This section introduces ASP.NET Core 5 **Model View Controller** (**MVC**) and its web API counterpart. We explore Razor Pages, MVC, and HTTP-based RESTful services. Then we explore a number of more advanced techniques used to push the MVC pattern a bit further, such as view models and data transfer objects.

Afterward, we dig into some classic design patterns to warm us up. Finally, we take those patterns to the next level using dependency injection, which is at the core of modern ASP.NET applications. All of those subjects lay out the fundamental knowledge that we will build upon until the end of the book and, most likely, for the rest of your career as an ASP.NET developer.

Finally, we dig into some ASP.NET-specific patterns, such as the options pattern and the .NET logging abstractions.

This section comprises the following chapters:

4

The MVC Pattern using Razor

The Model View Controller (MVC) pattern is probably one of the most extensively adapted architectural patterns for displaying web user interfaces. Why? Because it matches the concept behind HTTP and the web almost to perfection, especially for a typical server-rendered web application. For page-oriented applications, Razor Pages can also be a contestant to this claim.

From the old ASP.NET MVC to ASP.NET Core, the MVC framework is cleaner, leaner, faster, and more flexible than ever before. Moreover, dependency injection is now built-in at the heart of ASP.NET, which helps leverage its power. We will be covering dependency injection in greater depth in *Chapter 7, Deep Dive into Dependency Injection*.

MVC is an opt-in feature now, like pretty much everything else. You can opt-in MVC, Razor Pages, or web APIs and configure them with only a few statements. The ASP.NET pipeline is based on a series of middleware that can be leveraged to handle cross-cutting concerns, such as authentication and routing.

This chapter is essential for any developer desiring to create ASP.NET Core 5 MVC applications. Those technologies and the patterns learned in this chapter are used throughout the book. We are building web APIs more than Razor, but the MVC framework remains the backbone of both.

In this chapter, we will cover the following topics:

- The Model View Controller design pattern
- MVC using Razor
- The View Model design pattern

The Model View Controller design pattern

When using ASP.NET Core 5 MVC, there are two types of applications that developers can build.

- The first use is to display a web user interface, using a classic client-server application model where the page is composed on the server. The result is then sent back to the client. To build this type of application, you can take advantage of Razor, which allows developers to mix C# and HTML to build rich user interfaces elegantly. From my perspective, Razor is the technology that made me embrace MVC in the first place when ASP.NET MVC 3 came out in 2011.

- The second use of MVC is to build web APIs. In a web API, the presentation (or the view) becomes a data contract instead of a user interface. The contract is defined by the expected input and output, like any API. The most significant difference is that a web API is called over the wire and acts as a remote API. Essentially, inputs and outputs are serialized data structures, usually JSON or XML, mixed with HTTP verbs such as GET and POST. More on that in *Chapter 5, The MVC Pattern for Web APIs*.

One of the many nice facets of ASP.NET Core 5 MVC is that you can mix both techniques in the same application without any additional effort. For example, you could build a complete website and a full fledged web API in the same project.

MVC using Razor

Let's explore the first type of application, the classic server-rendered web user interface. In this kind of application using MVC, you divide the application into three distinct parts, where each has a single responsibility:

- **Model**: The model represents a data structure, a representation of the domain that we are trying to model.
- **View**: The view's responsibility is to present a model to a user, in our case, as a web user interface, so mainly HTML, CSS, and JavaScript.

- **Controller**: The controller is the key component of MVC. It plays the coordinator role between a request from a user to its response. The code of a controller should remain minimal and should not include complex logic or manipulation. The controller's primary responsibility is to handle a request and dispatch a response. The controller is an HTTP bridge.

If we put all of that back together, the controller is the entry point of every request, the view composes the response (UI), and both share the model. The model is fetched or manipulated by the controller, and then sent to the view for rendering. The user then sees the requested resource in their browser.

The following diagram illustrates the MVC concept:

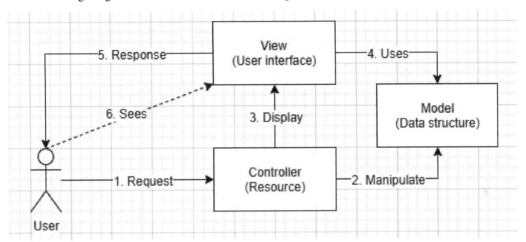

Figure 4.1 – MVC Workflow

We can interpret Figure 4.1 as the following:

1. The user requests an HTTP resource (routed to an action of a controller).

2. The controller reads or updates the model to be used by the view.

3. The controller then dispatches the model to the view for rendering.

4. The view uses the model to render the HTML page.

5. That rendered page is sent to the user over HTTP.

6. The user's browser displays the page, like any other web page; it is only HTML after all.

Next, we are looking into ASP.NET Core MVC itself, how the directories are organized by default, what controllers are, and how routing works. Then, we will dig into some code before improving on those default features using **view models**.

Directory structure

The default ASP.NET Core MVC directory structure is very explicit. There is a `Controllers` directory, a `Models` directory, and a `Views` directory. By convention, we create controllers in the `Controllers` directory, models in the `Models` directory, and views in the `Views` directory.

That said, the `Views` directory is a little different. To keep your project organized, each controller has its own subdirectory under `Views`. For example, the views for `HomeController` are found in the `Views/Home` directory.

The `Views/Shared` directory is a particular case. The views in that subdirectory are accessible by all other views and controllers alike; they are shared views. We usually create global views, such as layouts, menus, and other similar elements, in that directory.

Structure of a controller

The easiest way to create a controller is to create a class inheriting from `Microsoft.AspNetCore.Mvc.Controller`. By convention, the class's name is suffixed by `Controller`, and the class is created in the `Controllers` directory. This is not mandatory.

That base class adds all of the utility methods that you should need in order to return the appropriate view, like the `View()` method.

Once you have a controller class, you need to add actions. Actions are public methods that represent the operations that a user can perform.

More precisely, the following defines a controller:

- A controller exposes one or more actions.
- An action can take zero or more input parameters.
- An action can return zero or one output value.
- The action is what handles the actual request.
- We can group cohesive actions under the same controller, thus creating a unit.

For example, the following represents the `HomeController` class containing a single `Index` action:

```
public class HomeController : Controller
{
    public IActionResult Index() => View();
}
```

The `HomeController.Index` action is called by default when sending a `GET /` request to the server. In that case, it returns the `Home/Index.cshtml` view, without further processing or any model manipulation. Let's now explore why.

Default routing

To know which controller should handle a specific HTTP request, ASP.NET Core 5 has a routing mechanism that allows developers to define one or more routes. A route is a URI template that maps to C# code. Those definitions are created in the `Configure()` method of the `Startup` class. By default, MVC defines the following pattern: `"{controller=Home}/{action=Index}/{id?}"`.

The first fragment is about controllers, where the following applies:

- `{controller}` maps the request to a `{controller}Controller` class. For example, `Home` would map to the `HomeController` class.
- `{controller=Home}` means that the `HomeController` class is the default controller, which is used if no `{controller}` is supplied.

The second fragment is about actions:

- `{action}` maps the request to a controller method (the action).
- Like its controller counterpart, `{action=Index}` means that the `Index` method is the default action. For example, if we had a `ProductsController` class in our application, making a `GET` request to `https://somedomain.tld/Products` would make MVC invoke the `ProductsController.Index()` method. As a side note, **TLD** means **top-level domain**, such as `.com`, `.net`, and `.org`.

> **Note**
>
> In a **CRUD** controller (**Create, Read, Update, Delete**), `Index` is where you usually define your list.

The last fragment is about an optional `id` parameter:

- `{id}` means that any value following the action name maps to the parameter named `id` of that action method.
- The `?` in `{id?}` means the parameter is optional.

Let's take a look at some examples to wrap up our study of the default routing template:

- Calling `/Some/Action` would map to `SomeController.Action()`
- Calling `/Some` would map to `SomeController.Index()`
- Calling `/` would map to `HomeController.Index()`
- Calling `/Some/Action/123` would map to `SomeController.Action(123)`

> **Endpoint routing**
>
> From ASP.NET Core 2.2 onward, the team introduced a new routing system, named endpoint routing. If you are interested in advanced routing or in extending the current routing system, that would be an excellent starting point.

Project: MVC

Let's explore some code created using VS Code and the .NET CLI. The project aims at visiting certain MVC concepts.

> **Reminder**
>
> To generate a new MVC project, you can execute the `dotnet new mvc` command or the `dotnet new web` command, depending on how much boilerplate code you want in your project. In this case, I used `dotnet new web` and added the files myself to create a leaner project, but both are viable options.

The `HomeController` class defines the following actions. This should give you an overview of what we can do with ASP.NET Core 5 MVC:

- `Index`
- `ActionWithoutResult`
- `ActionWithoutResultV2Async`
- `DownloadTheImageAsync`

- `ActionWithSomeInput`

- `ActionWithSomeInputAndAModel`

Index

The `Index()` method is the default action and, in this case, the home page. It returns a view that contains some HTML. The view uses other actions to generate URLs. The view is defined in the `Views/Home/Index.cshtml` file.

The C# code to load the view is as simple as the following:

```
public IActionResult Index() => View();
```

In the preceding code snippet, the `Controller.View()` method tells ASP.NET Core to render the default view associated with the current action. By default, it loads `Views/[controller]/[action].cshtml`, where `[controller]` is the name of the controller without the `Controller` suffix, and `[action]` is the name of the action method.

The view itself looks like this:

```
@{
    ViewData["Title"] = "Home Page";
    var imageUri = Url.Action("ActionWithoutResultV2");
}
<p>Use the left menu to navigate through the examples.</p>

<h2>The result of ActionWithoutResultV2</h2>
<figure>
    <img src="@imageUri" alt="ASP.NET Core logo" />
    <figcaption>
        The result of <em>ActionWithoutResultV2</em> displayed
using the following HTML markup:
        <code>&lt;img src="@imageUri" alt="ASP.NET Core logo"
/></code>.
    </figcaption>
</figure>

<p>You can download the image by clicking <a href="@Url.
Action("DownloadTheImage")">here</a>.</p>
```

We will talk about the download and image links later, but besides that, the view only contains basic HTML written using Razor.

Expression-bodied function members (C# 6)

In the previous example, we used an expression-bodied function member, which is a C# 6 feature. It allows a single statement method to be written without curly braces by using the arrow operator.

Before C# 6, `public IActionResult Index() => View();` would have been written like this:

```
public IActionResult Index()
{
    return View();
}
```

The arrow operator can also be applied to read-only properties, as follows:

```
public int SomeProp => 123;
```

Instead of the previous, more explicit, method of rendering:

```
public int SomeProp
{
    get
    {
        return 123;
    }
}
```

ActionWithoutResult

The `ActionWithoutResult()` method does nothing. But if you navigate to `/Home/ActionWithoutResult` using a browser, it displays a blank page with an HTTP status code of `200 OK`, which means the action was executed successfully.

This is not very UI-centric applications, but it is a case supported by ASP.NET Core 5:

```
public void ActionWithoutResult()
{
    var youCanSetABreakpointHere = "";
}
```

There is no view associated with this action. Next, we add some usefulness to this type of action.

ActionWithoutResultV2Async

As a more complex example, we could use this type of action to write to the HTTP response stream manually. We could load a file from disk, make some modifications in memory, and write that updated version to the output stream without saving it back to disk. For example, we could be updating an image that is dynamically rendered or pre-filling a PDF form before sending it to the user.

Here is an example:

```
public async Task ActionWithoutResultV2Async()
{
    var filePath = Path.Combine(
        Directory.GetCurrentDirectory(),
        "wwwroot/images/netcore-logo.png"
    );
    var bytes = System.IO.File.ReadAllBytes(filePath);
    //
    // Do some processing here
    //
    Response.ContentLength = bytes.Length;
    Response.ContentType = "image/png";
    await Response.Body.WriteAsync(bytes, 0, bytes.Length);
}
```

The preceding code loads an image and then manually sends it to the client using HTTP; no MVC magic is involved. Then we can load that image using the following markup in a Razor page or view:

```
<img src="@Url.Action("ActionWithoutResultV2")" />
```

There are two important details here that are easy to miss:

1. From .NET Core 3.0 onward, we cannot do `Response.Body.Write(...)`; we must use `Response.Body.WriteAsync(...)` instead (hence the asynchronous method).

2. We must remove the `Async` suffix when calling the `Url.Action(...)` helper.

By using an action without a result, we could force the downloading of the image or do many other interesting things. I recommend studying HTTP if you are not already familiar with it. It should help you understand what can be done and how. Sometimes, you don't need the full power of MVC, and some use cases can be trivialized by using the lower-level APIs, such as the `HttpResponse` class available through the `ControllerBase.Response` property.

Routing (endpoint to delegate)

When you need that kind of action, you can also define your endpoint manually by mapping a URI to a delegate without the need to create a controller. You don't even need MVC.

A downside of this technique is that you need to do the model binding and everything else by hand as your delegate is not run inside the MVC pipeline, so no MVC magic.

The following example defines two GET endpoint; one with a route parameter and one without:

```
public class Startup
{
    public void ConfigureServices(IServiceCollection services)
    { }
    public void Configure(IApplicationBuilder app)
    {
        app.UseRouting();
        app.UseEndpoints(endpoints =>
        {
            endpoints.MapGet("/", async context =>
            {
                await context.Response.WriteAsync("Hello World!");
            });
            endpoints.MapGet("/echo/{content}", async context =>
            {
                var text = context.Request.Path.Value.Replace("/echo/", "");
                await context.Response.WriteAsync(text);
            });
        });
```

```
        }
}
```

This is a great feature worth studying, for small applications, demos, microservices, and more. I suggest creating a similar app to play with it if you are interested.

DownloadTheImageAsync

As a follow-up example, to download the image previously rendered by the `ActionWithoutResultV2Async` action, you only need to add a `Content-Disposition` header (that's HTTP, not MVC/.NET). The new method looks like this:

```
public async Task DownloadTheImageAsync()
{
    var filePath = Path.Combine(
        Directory.GetCurrentDirectory(),
        "wwwroot/images/netcore-logo.png"
    );
    var bytes = System.IO.File.ReadAllBytes(filePath);
    //
    // Do some processing here
    //
    Response.ContentLength = bytes.Length;
    Response.ContentType = "image/png";
    Response.Headers.Add("Content-Disposition", "attachment;
filename=\"netcore.png\"");
    await Response.Body.WriteAsync(bytes, 0, bytes.Length);
}
```

Now, if you call that action from a page, the browser prompts you to download the file instead of displaying it.

Here is an example from the home page:

```
<p>You can download the image by clicking <a href="@Url.
Action("DownloadTheImage")">here</a>.</p>
```

As stated in the previous example, this uses basic elements of HTTP.

ActionWithSomeInput

The `ActionWithSomeInput` method has an `id` parameter and renders a simple view, with that number displayed on the page. The code of the action appears as follows:

```
public IActionResult ActionWithSomeInput(int id)
{
    var model = id;
    return View(model);
}
```

The code of the view is as follows:

```
@model int
@{
    ViewData["title"] = "Action with some input";
}
<h2>This action has an input</h2>
<p>The input was: @Model</p>
```

When following the link from the menu (`/Home/ActionWithSomeInput/123`), we can see the MVC pattern in action:

1. MVC is routing the call to `HomeController`, requesting the `ActionWithSomeInput` action, and binding the value `123` to the `id` parameter.

2. In `ActionWithSomeInput`, the `id` parameter is assigned to the `model` variable.

    This step serves only to be explicit and demonstrates that we are passing a model to the view. We could have passed the `id` parameter directly to the `View` method. For example, we could have simplified the action as follows: `public IActionResult ActionWithSomeInput(int id) => View(id);`.

3. Then, the `model` variable is dispatched to the `ActionWithSomeInput` view for rendering, returning the result to the user.

4. Then, MVC renders the view, `ActionWithSomeInput.cshtml`, by means of the following:

    a) It implicitly uses the default layout (`Shared/_Layout.cshtml`) set in `ViewStart.cshtml`.

b) It uses the inputted `model`, typed using the `@model int` directive at the top of the view.

c) It renders the value of the model in the page using the `@Model` property; notice the different casing of both **m** and **M** (see below).

@Model and @model

`Model` is a property from `Microsoft.AspNetCore.Mvc.Razor.RazorPage<TModel>` of type TModel. Each view in ASP.NET Core MVC inherits from `RazorPage`, which is where all of those "magic properties" come from. `@model` is a Razor directive allowing us to strongly type a view (in other words, the TModel type parameter). I do recommend strongly typing all of your views unless there is no way to do so, or if it's not using a model (such as `Home/Index`). In the background, your Razor files are compiled into C# classes, which explains how the `@model` directive becomes the value of the TModel generic parameter.

ActionWithSomeInputAndAModel

As the last action method, `ActionWithSomeInputAndAModel` takes an integer parameter, named `id`, as input, but instead of sending it directly to the view, it sends a `SomeModel` instance. This is a better simulation of a real-life application, where objects are used to share and persist information, such as using a unique identifier (an `id` parameter) to load a record from the database, and then sending that data to the view for rendering (in this case, there is no database):

```
public IActionResult ActionWithSomeInputAndAModel(int id)
{
    var model = new SomeModel
    {
        SelectedId = id,
        Title = "This title was set in HomeController!"
    };
    return View(model);
}
```

When calling this action, the flow is the same as the previous one. The only exception is that the model is an object instead of an integer. The streamlined flow is as follows:

1.   The HTTP request is routed to the controller's action.

2.   The controller manipulates the model (in this case, creates it).

3. The controller dispatches the model to the view.

4. The view engine renders the page.

5. The page is sent back to the client that requested it.

Here is the view displaying the `Title` and the `SelectedId` properties of the model:

```
@model MVC.Models.SomeModel
@{
    ViewData["title"] = Model.Title;
}
<h2>This action has an input and uses a model</h2>
<p>The input was: @Model.SelectedId</p>
```

From the preceding code, we can see that we are using the `Model` property to access the anonymous object that we passed to the `View` method in our action.

Conclusion

We could talk about MVC for the remainder of the book, but we would be missing the point. This chapter and the next aim at covering as many possibilities as possible to help you understand the MVC pattern and ASP.NET Core, but nothing too in-depth, just an overview.

We covered different types of actions and the basic routing mechanism, which should be enough to continue. We use ASP.NET Core 5 throughout the book, so don't worry, we will cover many other aspects, in different contexts. Next, we improve the MVC pattern a bit.

View Model design pattern

The **View Model** pattern is used when building server-rendered web applications using Razor and can be applied to other technologies. Typically, you access data from a data source and then render a view based on that data. That is where the view model comes into play. Instead of sending the raw data directly to the view, you copy the required data to another class that carries only the required information to render that view, nothing more.

Using this technique, you can even compose a complex view model based on multiple data models, add filtering, sorting, and much more, without altering your data or domain models. Those features are presentation-centric and, as such, the view model responsibility is to meet the view's requirements in terms of presentation of the information, which is in line with the *Single Responsibility Principle,* which we explored in *Chapter 3, Architectural Principles.*

We could even see the last example, `ActionWithSomeInputAndAModel`, as a crude implementation of the View Model pattern. You get an `int` as input and **output a model for the view**, a **view model**.

Goal

The goal of the View Model pattern is to **create a model, specific to a view**, decoupling the other parts of the software from the view. As a rule of thumb, you want each view to be strongly typed with its own view model class to make sure that views are not coupled with each other, thereby causing possible maintenance issues in the long run.

View models allow developers to gather data in a particular format and send it to the view in another format that's better suited for the rendering of that specific view. That improves the application's testability, which in turn should increase the overall code quality and stability.

Design

Here is a revised MVC workflow that supports view models:

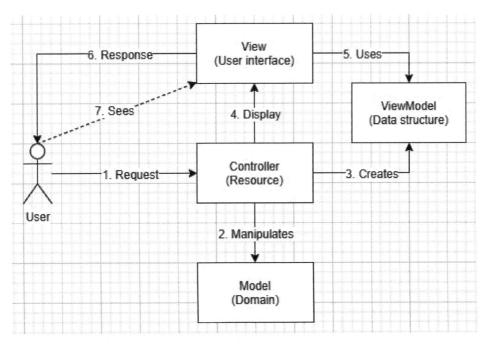

Figure 4.2 – MVC workflow with view models

We can interpret Figure 4.2 as the following:

1. The user requests an HTTP resource (routed to an action of a controller).

2. The controller reads or updates the model.

3. The controller creates the view model (or uses a view model created elsewhere).

4. The controller dispatches that data structure to the view for rendering.

5. The view uses the view model to render the HTML page.

6. That rendered page is sent to the user over HTTP.

7. The browser displays the page like any other web page.

Have you noticed that the model is now decoupled from the view?

Project: View models (a list of students)

Context: We have to build a list of students. Each list item must display a student's name and the number of classes that student is registered in.

Our graphic designers came up with the following Bootstrap 3 list with badges:

Figure 4.3 – Students list with their number of classes

To keep things simple and to create our prototype, we load in-memory data through the `StudentService` class.

It is important to remember that the view model must only contain the required information to display the view. The view model classes, located in `StudentListViewModels.cs`, looks like the following:

```
public class StudentListViewModel
{
    public IEnumerable<StudentListItemViewModel> Students {
get; set; }
}
public class StudentListItemViewModel
```

```
{
    public int Id { get; set; }
    public string Name { get; set; }
    public int ClassCount { get; set; }
}
```

That is one of the scenarios where keeping more than one class in the same file makes sense, hence the plural filename. That said, if you can't stand having multiple classes in a single file, feel free to split them up in your project.

> **Note**
>
> In a larger application, we could create subdirectories or use namespaces to keep our view model classes name unique and organized, for example, `/Models/Students/ListViewModels.cs`.
>
> Another alternative is to create view models in a `/ViewModels/` directory instead of using the default `/Models/` one.
>
> We could also create the view model classes as nested classes under their controller. For example, a `StudentsController` class could have a nested `ListViewModel` class, callable like this: `StudentsController.ListViewModel`.
>
> These are all valid options. Once again, do as you prefer and what suits your project best.

The `StudentController` class is the key element and has an `Index` action that handles `GET` requests. For each request, it fetches the students, creates the view model, and then dispatches it to the view. Here is the controller code:

```
public class StudentsController : Controller
{
    private readonly StudentService _studentService = new
StudentService();

    public async Task<IActionResult> Index()
    {
        // Get data from the datastore
        var students = await _studentService.ReadAllAsync();

        // Create the View Model, based on the data
```

```
        var viewModel = new StudentListViewModel
        {
            Students = students.Select(student => new
StudentListItemViewModel
            {
                Id = student.Id,
                Name = student.Name,
                ClassCount = student.Classes.Count()
            })
        };

        // Return the View
        return View(viewModel);
    }
}
```

The view renders the students as a Bootstrap `list-group`, using a badge to display the `ClassCount` property, as defined by our initial specifications.

```
@model StudentListViewModel
@{
    ViewData["Title"] = "Students";}
<h2>Students list</h2>
<ul class="list-group">
    @foreach (var item in Model.Students)
    {
        <li class="list-group-item">
            <span class="badge">@Html.DisplayFor(modelItem
=> item.ClassCount)</span>
            @Html.DisplayFor(modelItem => item.Name)
        </li>
    }
</ul>
```

With the preceding few lines of code and the View Model pattern, we decoupled the `Student` model from the view by using an intermediate class, `StudentListViewModel`, which is composed of a list of `StudentListItemViewModel`. Moreover, we limited the amount of information passed to the view by replacing the `Student.Classes` property with the `StudentListItemViewModel.ClassCount` property, which only contains the required information to render the view (the number of classes a student is in).

Project: View models (a student form)

Context: Now that we have a list, some clever person at the company thought that it would be a good idea to be able to create and update students; makes sense, right?

To achieve that, we have to do the following:

1. Create a GET action named `Create`.
2. Create a POST action that handles the student creation.
3. Add a `Create` view.
4. Add a view model named `CreateStudentViewModel`.
5. Repeat steps 1 to 4 for the `Edit` view.
6. Add some navigation links to the list.

After some thinking, we figured that it would be way better to reuse the same form for both views. For simplicity's sake, our student model is minimal, but, in a real-world application, it would most likely not be the case. So, extracting that form should help us with maintenance in the long run, if both forms are the same.

> **Note**
>
> In another case, if both forms are different, I'd suggest you keep them separated to avoid breaking one when updating the other.

From a technical standpoint, this requires the following:

- A partial view shared by both views.
- A `StudentFormViewModel` class shared by both `Create` and `Edit` view models.

From here, to build our view models, we have two options:

- Inheritance
- Composition

As with everything in the software engineering world, both options have their advantages and drawbacks. Composition is the most flexible technique and is the most widely used throughout the book. When facing a dilemma, I recommend composition over inheritance. That said, inheritance can also be a valid option, which is why I decided to demo both techniques. We will first implement the `Create` view using inheritance, and then the `Edit` view using composition. Let's take a look at the differences, starting with the view model classes.

The `CreateStudentViewModel` class inherits from `StudentFormViewModel` (inheritance):

```
// StudentFormViewModels.cs
public class CreateStudentViewModel : StudentFormViewModel { }
```

The `EditStudentViewModel` class has a property of the `StudentFormViewModel` type instead (composition):

```
public class EditStudentViewModel
{
    public int Id { get; set; }
    public IEnumerable<string> Classes { get; set; }
    public StudentFormViewModel Form { get; set; }
}
```

The `StudentFormViewModel` class represents the form itself that we share between the `Create` and `Edit` views:

```
public class StudentFormViewModel
{
    public string Name { get; set; }
}
```

Next, let's have a look at the `StudentsController` GET actions:

```
public IActionResult Create()
{
    return View();
}

public async Task<IActionResult> Edit(int id)
{
    var student = await _studentService.ReadOneAsync(id);
    var viewModel = new EditStudentViewModel
    {
        Id = student.Id,
        Form = new StudentFormViewModel
        {
            Name = student.Name,
        },
        Classes = student.Classes.Select(x => x.Name)
    };
    return View(viewModel);
}
```

In the preceding code, the `Create` action returns an empty view model. The `Edit` action loads a student from the database and copy the needed information in its view model, before sending that view model to the edit view. Next, let's take a look at the views, starting by the **partial view**.

A partial view is a smaller view that can be rendered as part of other views. By default, Razor passes the view's `Model` property to a partial view. In this case, since `CreateStudentViewModel` inherits from `StudentFormViewModel`, the model is directly sent to `_CreateOrEdit` as a `StudentFormViewModel` (polymorphism);

```
// Create.cshtml
@model CreateStudentViewModel
...
<partial name="_CreateOrEdit" />
...
```

We will be exploring partial views more in *Chapter 17, ASP.NET Core User Interfaces*.

Reminder

Polymorphism is one of the core concepts behind object-oriented programming. It represents the ability of an object of a given type to be considered an instance of another type. For example, all subclasses of `ClassA` (say `ClassB` and `ClassC`) can be used as `ClassA` and themselves. So, `ClassB` is a `ClassB` and a `ClassA`.

For the `Edit` view, since `EditStudentViewModel` does not inherit from `StudentFormViewModel` but has a property of that type named `Form` instead, we need to specify that as a result of using the `for` attribute, as follows:

```
// Edit.cshtml
@model EditStudentViewModel
...
<partial name="_CreateOrEdit" for="Form" />
...
```

The `for` attribute lets us specify the model to pass to the partial view; in our case, the `EditStudentViewModel.Form` property.

Next, is the content of the partial view:

```
// _CreateOrEdit.cshtml
@model StudentFormViewModel

<div class="form-group">
    <label asp-for="Name" class="control-label"></label>
    <input asp-for="Name" class="form-control" />
    <span asp-validation-for="Name" class="text-
    danger"></span>
</div>
```

As you can see in the preceding code, regardless of the option chosen, it does not change the partial view itself, just the consumers (the `Create` and `Edit` views and the structure of the view models in our case). The consumers must adapt themselves to the model defined by `_CreateOrEdit` partial view. If there is a mismatch, an error is thrown at runtime. This means that you have the flexibility to use either or both techniques in your application. Choose what best fits your needs.

In this precise use case, it is important to note that both the `Create` and `Edit` pages are tightly coupled over the shared part of the form. It can be very convenient as long as both forms are identical. For most data-oriented user interfaces using CRUD operations, I like to reuse forms like this as it helps save time. For simple view models, I would go for inheritance since we don't have to write the `for` attribute in that case. For more complex or modular view models containing many properties that need a partial view, I would start by exploring composition to make sure all partial views use a `for` attribute (linearity). The goal here was to demo the possibilities so you can use a technique or the other in a different scenario.

Composition versus inheritance

For that matter, I'd say that inheritance is more natural at first, but it can be harder to maintain in the long term. Composition is the most flexible of the two techniques. While composition leads to a more reusable and flexible design, it also creates complexity, especially when abstractions come into play. Composition helps follow the SOLID principles.

When using inheritance, you must make sure that the **sub-class is-a parent-class**. Do not inherit an unrelated class to reuse some elements of it or some implementations details. We talk more about composition in subsequent chapters.

Conclusion

If you are still uncertain or perplexed about this pattern, we use view models and other similar concepts throughout the book. That said, when you choose a pattern over another, it is essential to review the requirements of that specific project or feature as it dictates whether your choice is rational.

For example, if the following applies to your project:

- It is a simple data-driven user interface, tightly coupled with a database.
- It has no logic.
- It is not going to evolve.

In that case, the use of view models may only add development time to your project, while you could have Visual Studio almost scaffold it all for you instead. Nothing stops you from using a view model or two when you need it, such as when creating a dashboard or some more complex views.

For more complex projects, I recommend using view models by default. If you are still uncertain or perplexed about this pattern, we are exploring multiple ways to build applications as a whole later in the book, which should help you.

Summary

In this chapter, we explored one part of ASP.NET Core 5 MVC, which allows us to create rich web user interfaces with Razor and C#.

We saw how to decouple the model from the presentation, using view models. View models are classes specially crafted around a view or a partial view. For example, rather than passing a data model to a view, and letting the view do some calculations, you instead do the calculation on the server side and pass just the results to the view. This way, the view only has one responsibility: displaying the user interface, the page.

Finally, we elaborated on the fact that it is imperative to reduce the tight coupling of our components in our systems, which follow the SOLID principles.

In the next few chapters, we will explore the web API counterpart to the MVC and View Models patterns. We will also look at our first **Gang of Four** (**GoF**) design patterns and deep dive into ASP.NET Core 5 dependency injection. All of that will push us further down the path of designing better applications.

Questions

Let's take a look at a few practice questions:

1. What is the role of the **controller** in the MVC pattern?
2. What Razor directive indicates the type of **model** that a view accepts?
3. With how many views should a **view model** be associated?
4. Can a **view model** add flexibility to a system?
5. Can a **view model** add robustness to a system?

Further reading

Routing in ASP.NET Core: `https://net5.link/YHVJ`

5
The MVC Pattern for Web APIs

As we saw in the previous chapter, the Model View Controller pattern is probably one of the most extensively adapted architectural patterns for displaying web user interfaces because it matches the concept behind HTTP and the web almost to perfection.

In this chapter, we cover the web API version of ASP.NET Core, which is a crucial part of most modern technology stacks. Moreover, we use those technologies and the patterns learned in this chapter throughout the book. Avoiding user interfaces makes code easier to follow. Web APIs are used in projects of all types and sizes, from microservices to mobile apps.

In this chapter, we will cover the following topics:

- An overview of REST
- Anatomy of a web API
- A few C# language features
- The Data Transfer Object (DTO) design pattern
- API contracts

An overview of REST

REST, or **Representational State Transfer**, is a way to create internet-based services, known as web services or web APIs, that commonly use HTTP as their transport protocol. It allows the well-known HTTP specifications to be reused instead of recreating new ways of exchanging data. For example, returning an HTTP status code 200 OK indicates success, while 400 Bad Request indicates failure.

In a nutshell, we can state the following:

- Each HTTP endpoint is a resource.

- Each resource can be secured independently.

- Calling the same resource twice should result in the same operation executed twice.

  For example, executing two POST /entities should result in two new entities, while fetching GET /entities/some-id should return the same entity twice.

- The service should be stateless, meaning that it does not persist information about the client between requests.

- The response from a RESTful service should be cacheable; you should be able to control that cache using HTTP standards.

There are multiple other elements that we could talk about here, but those are the fundamental ones that should allow a neophyte to get a good initial idea of what a RESTful service is.

We could write entire books devoted to web APIs, but I'm keeping the information to a minimum for this one, just enough to get started. Nevertheless, here is some broadly applicable guidance about HTTP methods and status codes used in web APIs that should kickstart you.

Request HTTP methods

The HTTP method used is a good indicator of the operation that a web API endpoint can perform. It helps to make the intent clear. Here is a list of the most frequently used methods, what they are for, and their expected success status code:

Method	Role	Success status code
GET	Read data: a list or a single entity.	200 OK
POST	Create a new entity.	201 CREATED
PUT	Replace an entity.	200 OK or 204 No Content
DELETE	Delete an entity.	200 OK or 204 No Content
PATCH	Partially update an entity.	200 OK

Response status code

HTTP status codes are the way to transmit what has happened, back to the web API's consumers. The following table explains the most common ones before exploring status codes' predefined groups:

Status Code	Role
200 OK	Tells the client the request has succeeded. It usually includes data related to an operation or an entity in the body of the response.
201 Created	Tells the client the request has succeeded, but is more specific than 200 OK by specifying that a resource was created as a result of the request. It should also include a `Location` HTTP header that links to the newly created resource and includes the new entity in the response body.
202 Accepted	Tells the client the request has been accepted for processing but that it's not processed yet. In an event-driven system (see *Chapter 16, Introduction to Microservices Architecture*), this could mean that an event has been published, the current resource has completed its job (published the event), but to know more, the client needs to contact another resource, wait for a notification, just wait, or can't know. That depends on how the system was designed.
204 No Content	Tells the client the request has succeeded but that no content is returned. When receiving that status code, a client usually does not need to update the state (page) displayed to its user.
302 Found	Tells the client to follow the specified location. This represents an HTTP redirection. For old-timers, this is what happens under the hood of the good old .NET Framework method, `System.Web.HttpResponse.Redirect()`.
400 Bad Request	Tells the client about a validation error, generally related to badly formatted input data, missing data, or something similar.
401 Unauthorized	Tells the client that it must authenticate to access the resource.
403 Forbidden	Tells the client that it does not have the required rights to access the resource (authorization).
404 Not Found	Tells the client that the resource does not exist or was not found.
409 Conflict	Tells the client that a conflict has occurred. A common scenario would be that the entity has changed between its last `GET` and its current operation (likely a `PUT` request), in other words, handling concurrency.
500 Internal Server Error	Tells the client that an unhandled error occurred on the server side, and that this prevented it from fulfilling the request.

If you take a second look at the previous table, you may notice that status codes touching similar subjects are grouped under the same "hundredth," for example:

- The 1XX status code (omitted from the preceding table) represents informational continuation results, usually handled automatically by the server, such as **100 Continue** and **101 Switching Protocols**.

- 2XX are successful results.

- 3XX are related to redirections.

- 4XX are request errors (from the client side), usually introduced by the user, such as an empty required field.

- 5XX are server-side errors that the client cannot do anything about.

If you are not familiar with REST and are interested in web APIs, I recommend reading more on that subject after completing this book or building a few projects to grasp it by yourself.

Anatomy of a web API

Now that we have explored the basics of ASP.NET MVC in *Chapter 4, The MVC Pattern using Razor*, and a way to render web pages, it is time to jump into web APIs and return data instead of a user interface. In the past few years, the number of web APIs just exploded from a few to a gazillion of them; everybody does that nowadays. In this case, I don't think that's because people are blindly following a trend, but based on good reasons that make web APIs so appealing, such as the following:

- It is an efficient way of sharing data between systems.

- It allows interoperability between technologies by dialoguing in universal languages, such as JSON or XML.

- It allows your backend to be centralized and shared with multiple frontends such as mobile, desktop, and web applications.

Those reasons make it easier to reuse backend systems and share them with multiple user interfaces or other backend systems. For example, think of any mobile app that you know; they most probably have an iOS app, an Android app, and a web app to maintain. In that case, sharing the backend is an excellent way to save time and money.

I updated the MVC diagram to represent the flow of a web API:

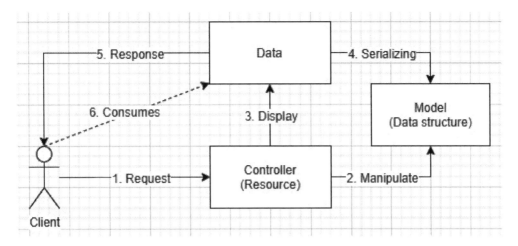

Figure 5.1 – Workflow of a web API

There are only a few differences between rendering a user interface and building a web API:

- Instead of sending HTML to the browser, the API outputs a serialized data structure.

- The client usually wants to consume the data instead of displaying it directly.

Based on this diagram, we are sending our model directly to the client. In most scenarios, we don't want to do that. Instead, we want to send only the portion of the data that we need in the format that we want. We will be covering this next with the DTO pattern, but first, let's dig into ASP.NET Core 5 web APIs.

Setting up a web API

To use the full power of ASP.NET Core 5 MVC, without loading the Razor engine and other view-related components, in the `Startup` class, the minimum requirements are as follows:

```
public class Startup
{
    public void ConfigureServices(IServiceCollection services)
    {
        services.AddControllers();
    }
    public void Configure(IApplicationBuilder app)
    {
```

```
        app.UseRouting();
        app.UseEndpoints(endpoints =>
        {
            endpoints.MapControllers();
        });
    }
}
```

The `AddControllers()` extension method adds the classes related to web API controllers, without the extra elements required to use Razor Pages or render views.

Then, we add the routing middleware and endpoint routing as we would in any MVC project. The part that interests us, however, is the `endpoints.MapControllers();` extension method. It enables the usage of attribute-based routing (see below). That's it; we don't need any more services. From there, we could add controllers and start coding.

That separation of registration is a significant improvement compared with the ASP.NET Core 2.x `AddMvc()` method. Previously, we had to register the web API, Razor Pages, and MVC with `IServiceCollection`. Now, we can cherry-pick what part of ASP.NET we want. Next, we are going to explore a way to route HTTP requests to our code using attributes.

Attribute routing

Attribute routing allows an HTTP request to be mapped to a **controller**. A controller either inherits from `ControllerBase` or is decorated with the `[ApiController]` attribute. Like MVC, the controller then implements actions.

To cover attribute routing, let's use the following controller template:

```
[Route("api/[controller]")]
[ApiController]
public class ValuesController : ControllerBase
{
    [HttpGet]
    public ActionResult<IEnumerable<string>> Get()
        => new string[] { "value1", "value2" };
    [HttpGet("{id}")]
    public ActionResult<string> Get(int id) => "value";
    // POST api/values
    [HttpPost]
```

```
    public void Post([FromBody] string value){}
    [HttpPut("{id}")]
    public void Put(int id, [FromBody] string value){}
    [HttpDelete("{id}")]
    public void Delete(int id){}
}
```

From that template, we use `RouteAttribute` and `Http[Method]Attribute` in the controller. Those attributes define what a user should query to reach a specific resource.

`RouteAttribute` allows you to define a routing pattern, similar to what we used in the previous chapter, that applies to all HTTP methods. `Http[Method]Attribute` defines a specific HTTP method and offers the possibility to set an optional route pattern. Those attributes are very helpful in crafting URIs that are concise and clear while keeping the routing close to the controller.

Based on the code, `[Route("api/[controller]")]` means that actions of this controller are reachable through `api/values` (the `Controller` suffix is ignored like with MVC). Then, the other attributes tell ASP.NET to map specific requests to specific methods. For example, `[HttpGet]` tells ASP.NET that `GET /api/values` should map to the `Get()` method. The `[HttpGet("{id}")]` attribute tells the routing engine that `GET /api/values/1` requests should be routed to the `Get(int id)` method instead. Both are mapping the `GET` method, but the `id` parameter helps differentiate them; it is the discriminator. The other attributes are doing the same, but aiming at a different HTTP method.

The `FromBody` attribute tells the model binder to look into the HTTP request body for that value. Other attributes tell the model binder what direction to look in to fetch the decorated value. Here is the list:

- `FromBody`, to look into the body and choose a formatter based on `Content-Type`.
- `FromForm`, to look into the form collection (posted form values).
- `FromHeader`, to look into the HTTP headers.
- `FromQuery`, to look at the query string.
- `FromRoute`, to look into the MVC route data.
- `FromServices`, to inject a service from the dependency injection container.

If we look back at `ValuesController`, it defines the following endpoints:

URL	Action/Method
GET api/values	ActionResult<IEnumerable<string>> Get()
GET api/values/1	ActionResult<string> Get(int id)
POST api/values	void Post([FromBody] string value)
PUT api/values/1	void Put(int id, [FromBody] string value)
DELETE api/values/1	void Delete(int id)

When designing a web API, the URI leading to your endpoints should be clear and concise, making it easier for your consumer to discover and learn your API. The rules are similar to crafting software in a sense: you want to group your resources by concern, often hierarchically, creating a cohesive URI space that is easy to browse and use. Clients must be able to understand the logic behind the endpoints easily. Think about your endpoints as a user of the web API. I would even extend that suggestion to any API, always think about the consumer of your code to create the best possible API.

Next, we are going to explore different ways to return values from our endpoint, in response to an HTTP request.

Returning values

There are multiple ways to return data to the client when using ASP.NET Core 5. Here we look at two different return types:

- `ActionResult<TValue>`
- `IActionResult`

Then, we explore how to use the same techniques to return values asynchronously.

ActionResult<TValue>

When an action specifies a return type of `ActionResult<TValue>`, you use the methods provided by the `ControllerBase` class, such as `Ok()`, `NotFound()`, and `BadRequest()`, to return a serialized object.

The following code reflects this:

```
[HttpGet("ActionResultMyResult/{input}")]
public ActionResult<MyResult> GetActionResultMyResult(int
input)
{
    return Ok(new MyResult
    {
        Input = input,
        Value = nameof(GetActionResultMyResult)
    });
}
```

The output of `https://localhost:5010/ActionResultMyResult/1` is as follows:

```
{
    "input": 1,
    "value": "GetActionResultMyResult"
}
```

You can also return the `TValue` directly, without calling the `Ok()` method, like this:

```
[HttpGet("GetMyResult/{input}")]
public ActionResult<MyResult> GetMyResult(int input)
{
    return new MyResult
    {
        Input = input,
        Value = nameof(GetMyResult)
    };
}
```

The "magic" is programmed using class conversion operators (see the *C# features* section). Navigating to `https://localhost:5010/GetMyResult/1` should output the following result:

```
{
    "input": 1,
    "value": "GetMyResult"
}
```

IActionResult

You can also use a more general return type—the `IActionResult` interface. Doing so gives you the opportunity of using the methods defined on the `ControllerBase` class, such as `Ok()`, `NotFound()`, and `BadRequest()`, as well. However, you cannot return an object directly.

The following code reflects the usage of the `Ok()` method:

```
[HttpGet("ActionResultMyResult/{input}")]
public IActionResult GetIActionResult(int input)
{
    return Ok(new MyResult
    {
        Input = input,
        Value = "GetActionResultMyResult"
    });
}
```

The output of `https://localhost:5010/GetIActionResult/1` is as follows:

```
{
    "input": 1,
    "value": "GetIActionResult"
}
```

Next, we explore how to leverage the `async/await` C# feature when returning values from our endpoints.

Async return values

To keep it simple, all examples that do not require asynchronous processing returns the values directly. In some future examples, we will use asynchronous return values. Whenever you have asynchronous tasks to execute, it is imperative to use asynchronous controller actions. To do that, it is as simple as returning `Task<T>` or `ValueTask<T>`, where `T` implements the `IActionResult` interface or another possible return type that we previously explored. Here's an example:

```
public async Task<IActionResult> GetAsync()
{
    var result = await SomeAsynMethod();
    return Ok(result);
}
```

The `async/await` pattern in .NET will improve the performance of your application. In a nutshell, when the task is waiting for a resource to respond, it will process other tasks. In conclusion, you will be able to serve more requests with the same hardware.

Another subtlety is `CancellationToken`. I think the official documentation nailed it pretty well, so I'll quote it here:

> *"A CancellationToken enables cooperative cancellation between threads, thread pool work items, or Task objects."*

In short, cancel the request, and cancel all running tasks. With ASP.NET, you can simply inject a `CancellationToken` into any action. Here is an example:

```
public async Task<IActionResult> GetAsync(CancellationToken
cancellationToken)
{
    var result = await SomeAsynMethod(cancellationToken);
    return Ok(result);
}
```

In that code, we inject the token, and then pass it to the method, which can also pass it to its underlying asynchronous operations, and so on. Whenever possible, use `CancellationToken`.

Next, we explore a few C# features before getting into the **Data Transfer Object** pattern to isolate the API's model from the domain model. We will dig deeper into models, data, and domains in *Chapter 12, Understanding Layering*.

C# features

This short section digs deeper into the class conversion operators briefly discussed in the previous section. Then we explore local functions, allowing us to create functions inside methods. These are general features that we can use everywhere, not just when building web APIs.

Class conversion operators (C#)

Class conversion operators are user-defined functions crafted to implicitly or explicitly convert one type to another. Many built-in types offer such conversions, such as converting an int to a long without any cast or method call:

```
int var1 = 5;
long var2 = var1; // This is possible due to a class conversion
operator
```

Next is an example of custom conversion. We convert a string to an instance of the SomeGenericClass<string> class without a cast:

```
using System;
using Xunit;


namespace ConversionOperator
{
    public class SomeGenericClass<T>
    {
        public T Value { get; set; }

        public static implicit operator
        SomeGenericClass<T>(T value)
        {
            return new SomeGenericClass<T>
            {
                Value = value
            };
        }
    }
}
```

SomeGenericClass<T> defines a generic property named Value that can be set to
any type. The highlighted code block is the conversion operator, allowing conversion
from the type T to SomeGenericClass<T> without a cast. Let's look at the result next:

```
public class Tests
{
    [Fact]
    public void Value_should_be_set_implicitly()
    {
        var value = "Test";
        SomeGenericClass<string> result = value;
        Assert.Equal("Test", result.Value);
    }
```

That first test method uses the conversion operator that we just examined to convert
a string to an instance of the SomeGenericClass<string> class. It works with
methods and even generics, as the next test method will show you:

```
    [Fact]
    public void Value_should_be_set_implicitly_using_local_
function()
    {
        var result1 = GetValue("Test");
        Assert.Equal("Test", result1.Value);

        var result2 = GetValue(123);
        Assert.Equal(123, result2.Value);

        static SomeGenericClass<T> GetValue<T>(T value)
        {
            return value;
        }
    }
}
```

The preceding code implicitly converts a `string` into a `SomeGenericClass<string>` object and then an `int` into a `SomeGenericClass<int>` object. That's how action results are converted, exactly like we did in the highlighted line. We returned the value of type `T` as an instance of the `SomeGenericClass<T>` class directly.

This is not the most important topic of the book, but if you were curious about how .NET was able to do that implicit conversion, this is how. Now you know that you can implement custom conversion operators in your classes when you want that kind of behavior.

Local functions (C# 7) and a static local function (C# 8)

In the previous example, we used a static local function, new to C# 8, to demonstrate the class conversion operator.

Local functions are definable inside methods, constructors, property accessors, event accessors, anonymous methods, lambda expressions, finalizers, and other local functions. Those functions are private to their containing members. They are very useful for making the code more explicit and self-explanatory without polluting the class itself, keeping them in the consuming member's scope. Local functions can access the declaring member's variables and parameters, like this:

```
[Fact]
public void With_no_parameter_accessing_outer_scope()
{
    var x = 1;
    var y = 2;
    var z = Add();
    Assert.Equal(3, z);

    x = 2;
    y = 3;
    var n = Add();
    Assert.Equal(5, n);

    int Add()
    {
        return x + y;
    }
}
```

That is not a robust function, and the code is not that elegant either, but it shows how a local function can access its parent scope's members. The following code block shows a mix:

```
[Fact]
public void With_one_parameter_accessing_outer_scope()
{
    var x = 1;
    var z = Add(2);
    Assert.Equal(3, z);

    x = 2;
    var n = Add(3);
    Assert.Equal(5, n);

    int Add(int y)
    {
        return x + y;
    }
}
```

That block shows how to pass an argument and how the local function can still use its outer scope's variables to alter its result. Now, if we want an independent function, decoupled from its outer scope, we could code the following instead:

```
[Fact]
public void With_two_parameters_not_accessing_outer_scope()
{
    var a = Add(1, 2);
    Assert.Equal(3, a);

    var b = Add(2, 3);
    Assert.Equal(5, b);

    int Add(int x, int y)
    {
        return x + y;
    }
}
```

That code is clearer and more explicit than our other alternatives. But it still allows someone to alter it later and to use the outer scope (nothing tells the intent of limiting access to the outer scope), like this:

```csharp
[Fact]
public void With_two_parameters_accessing_outer_scope()
{
    var z = 5;
    var a = Add(1, 2);
    Assert.Equal(8, a);

    var b = Add(2, 3);
    Assert.Equal(10, b);

    int Add(int x, int y)
    {
        return x + y + z;
    }
}
```

To clarify that intent, **static local functions** come to the rescue. They remove the option to access the enclosing scope variables, and clearly state that with the `static` keyword. The following is the static equivalent of a previous function:

```csharp
[Fact]
public void With_two_parameters()
{
    var a = Add(1, 2);
    Assert.Equal(3, a);

    var b = Add(2, 3);
    Assert.Equal(5, b);

    static int Add(int x, int y)
    {
        return x + y;
    }
}
```

Then, with that clear definition, the updated version could become the following instead, keeping the local function independent:

```csharp
[Fact]
public void With_three_parameters()
{
    var c = 5;
    var a = Add(1, 2, c);
    Assert.Equal(8, a);

    var b = Add(2, 3, c);
    Assert.Equal(10, b);

    static int Add(int x, int y, int z)
    {
        return x + y + z;
    }
}
```

Nothing can stop someone from removing the `static` modifier, maybe a good code review, but at least no one can say that the intent was not clear enough.

Using the enclosing scope can be useful sometimes, but I prefer to avoid that whenever possible, for the same reason that I do my best to avoid global stuff: the code can become messier, faster.

To recap, we can create a local function by declaring it inside another supported member without specifying any access modifier (`public`, `private`, and so on). That function can access its declaring scope, expose parameters, and do almost everything that a method can do, including being `async` and `unsafe`. Then comes C# 8, which adds the option to define a local function as `static`, blocking the access to its outer scope and clearly stating the intent of an independent, standalone, private local function.

Now that we have had a sneak peek of those C# features, it is time to go back to web APIs and explore **Data Transfer Objects**.

The Data Transfer Object design pattern

The **Data Transfer Object (DTO)** pattern is the equivalent of the View Model pattern, but for web APIs. Instead of targeting a view, we are targeting the consumers of a web API endpoint.

Goal

The goal is to limit and control the inputs and outputs of an endpoint to the data that we need, decoupling the API's contract from the application's inner workings. DTOs should empower us to define our APIs without thinking about the underlying data structures, leaving us the choice to craft our web services the way we want. More precisely, we can craft them the way we want the consumers to interact with them. So no matter the underlying system, we can use DTOs to design endpoints that are easy to consume and maintain. Another possible outcome would be to save bandwidth by limiting the amount of information that the API transits.

Design

Let's start by analyzing a schema, which you may find similar to the one we saw when visiting view models:

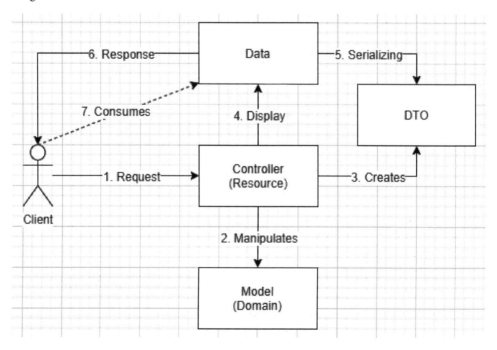

Figure 5.2 – MVC workflow with a DTO

The same few differences between view models and DTOs can be applied here, following the same idea: decoupling the domain from the view. These design patterns are the same, but one is targeting a view and the other the input and output of a web service.

Project – DTO

Context: In a new application, our UX experts figured that displaying statistics about the contracts of our clients on a new dashboard would be a fantastic idea, and that would save lots of time for the managers. In addition to that, when a user clicks on a client, our UX experts decided it would be best to display the client's full details, in the case where the manager needs to dig deeper into that client's data.

The system is composed of multiple user interfaces querying a single web API. However, we are only focusing on the backend part of the system.

Following a roundtable on designing the new features, here are the requirements for the two new endpoints:

The first endpoint should return a list of clients comprising the following information:

```
[
    {
        "id": 0,
        "name": "...",
        "totalNumberOfContracts": 0,
        "numberOfOpenContracts": 0
    }
]
```

The second endpoint should return the specified client with its full list of contracts. We need to provide the information in the following format:

```
{
    "id": 0,
    "name": "...",
    "contracts": [
        {
            "id": 0,
            "name": "...",
            "description": "...",
            "workTotal": 0,
```

```
            "workDone": 0,
            "workState": "Completed",
            "primaryContactFirstname": "...",
            "primaryContactLastname": "...",
            "primaryContactEmail": "..."
        }
    ]
}
```

Our data structure looks like this:

```
public class Client
{
    public int Id { get; set; }
    public string Name { get; set; }
    public List<Contract> Contracts { get; set; }
}


public class Contract
{
    public int Id { get; set; }
    public string Name { get; set; }
    public string Description { get; set; }
    public ContractWork Work { get; set; }
    public ContactInformation PrimaryContact { get; set; }
}


public class ContractWork
{
    public int Total { get; set; }
    public int Done { get; set; }

    public WorkState State =>
        Done == 0 ? WorkState.New :
        Done == Total ? WorkState.Completed :
        WorkState.InProgress;
}
```

```
public enum WorkState
{
    New,
    InProgress,
    Completed
}

public class ContactInformation
{
    public string Firstname { get; set; }
    public string Lastname { get; set; }
    public string Email { get; set; }
}
```

As a good developer, we started by analyzing the feature. A problem quickly arises: the data that we have and the data that we need to provide to the UI are not the same.

If we were to be using our data structure directly, the user interfaces would have to make multiple HTTP requests to build the dashboard. That would push the logic to the UI and possibly even duplicate it. That could become tedious to maintain, especially if we add other user interfaces.

Solution: We need to create two specialized resources in our web API that run the computation and return only the required data.

> **Note**
> To keep it simple and abstract away the data access logic from the controller, we moved that code to the `ClientRepository` class, which provides static data to the controller, omitted here.

For the first endpoint, let's create a new class named `ClientSummaryDto` that holds our two statistics and our client info:

```
public class ClientSummaryDto
{
    [JsonPropertyName("id")]
    public int Id { get; set; }
    [JsonPropertyName("name")]
    public string Name { get; set; }
```

```
[JsonPropertyName("totalNumberOfContracts")]
public int TotalNumberOfContracts { get; set; }
[JsonPropertyName("numberOfOpenContracts")]
public int NumberOfOpenContracts { get; set; }
}
```

The properties are decorated by `JsonPropertyNameAttribute` to define the serialized property name explicitly. That is one of the advantages of the DTO pattern. Since the DTOs are unrelated to our other objects, we can manipulate them without any impact on the source of the data, lowering the chance of unforeseen consequences, such as updating a DTO and breaking the database.

For example, adding `JsonPropertyNameAttribute` to `ClientSummaryDto` has no impact on the `Client` class.

The action that returns the data, representing our first endpoint, goes as follows:

```
[HttpGet]
public ActionResult<IEnumerable<ClientSummaryDto>> Get()
{
    var clients = _clientRepository.ReadAll();
    var dto = clients.Select(client => new ClientSummaryDto
    {
        Id = client.Id,
        Name = client.Name,
        TotalNumberOfContracts = client.Contracts.Count,
        NumberOfOpenContracts = client.Contracts.Count(x =>
x.Work.State != WorkState.Completed)
    }).ToArray();
    return dto;
}
```

What is happening is this:

1. We read the data from the `ClientRepository` instance (could be from a database).

2. We transform it into an array of DTO objects (copying the data into new objects).

3. We return that DTO to the client.

If we run the application and navigate to GET /api/clients, we should see the following output:

```
[
    {
        "id": 1,
        "name": "Jonny Boy Inc.",
        "totalNumberOfContracts": 2,
        "numberOfOpenContracts": 1
    },
    {
        "id": 2,
        "name": "Some mega-corporation",
        "totalNumberOfContracts": 1,
        "numberOfOpenContracts": 1
    }
]
```

Now that the first endpoint is working, let's attack the second one. Based on our requirements, we need to create two classes for this one:

```
public class ClientDetailsDto
{
    [JsonPropertyName("id")]
    public int Id { get; set; }

    [JsonPropertyName("name")]
    public string Name { get; set; }

    [JsonPropertyName("contracts")]
    public IEnumerable<ContractDetailsDto> Contracts { get;
set; }
}

public class ContractDetailsDto
{
    [JsonPropertyName("id")]
    public int Id { get; set; }
```

```csharp
    [JsonPropertyName("name")]
    public string Name { get; set; }

    [JsonPropertyName("description")]
    public string Description { get; set; }

    [JsonPropertyName("workTotal")]
    public int WorkTotal { get; set; }

    [JsonPropertyName("workDone")]
    public int WorkDone { get; set; }

    [JsonPropertyName("workState")]
    [JsonConverter(typeof(JsonStringEnumConverter))]
    public WorkState WorkState { get; set; }

    [JsonPropertyName("primaryContactFirstname")]
    public string PrimaryContactFirstname { get; set; }

    [JsonPropertyName("primaryContactLastname")]
    public string PrimaryContactLastname { get; set; }

    [JsonPropertyName("primaryContactEmail")]
    public string PrimaryContactEmail { get; set; }
}
```

Once again, we decorated the properties with attributes to control the output, with no impact on our data model classes.

We used the [JsonConverter(typeof(JsonStringEnumConverter))] attribute attribute on the ContractDetailsDto.WorkState property to tell the serializer that the WorkState enumeration should be serialized as a string instead of a numeric index.

> **Note**
>
> In the past, ASP.NET Core used JSON.NET as the underlying JSON
> serializer. Since .NET Core 3.0, they have added the `System.Text.`
> `Json` namespace, which contains a brand new serializer. The new serializer
> is faster but has fewer features. If you need JSON.NET features, or for
> compatibility reasons, you can use it by referencing the `Microsoft.`
> `AspNetCore.Mvc.NewtonsoftJson` NuGet package. Then, add
> a call to the `AddNewtonsoftJson()` extension method on your
> `IMvcBuilder` object, like `services.AddControllers().`
> `AddNewtonsoftJson();`.

Now that we have a data structure to represent our DTO, let's take a look at the
controller's code:

```csharp
// GET api/clients/1
[HttpGet("{id}")]
public IActionResult Get(int id)
{
    var client = _clientRepository.ReadOne(id);
    if (client == default(Client))
    {
        return NotFound();
    }
    var dto = new ClientDetailsDto
    {
        Id = client.Id,
        Name = client.Name,
        Contracts = client.Contracts.Select(contract => new
ContractDetailsDto
        {
            Id = contract.Id,
            Name = contract.Name,
            Description = contract.Description,

            // Flattening PrimaryContact
            PrimaryContactEmail = contract.PrimaryContact.
Email,
            PrimaryContactFirstname = contract.PrimaryContact.
Firstname,
            PrimaryContactLastname = contract.PrimaryContact.
```

```
Lastname,

            // Flattening Work
            WorkDone = contract.Work.Done,
            WorkState = contract.Work.State,
            WorkTotal = contract.Work.Total
        })
    };
    return Ok(dto);
}
```

As you may have noticed, this action returns an `IActionResult` instead of an
`ActionResult<ClientDetailsDto>`; that's to show you the possibilities
that we saw earlier.

That action flattens the details of a `Client` into a `ClientDetailsDto` and returns `404
Not Found` if the `Client` does not exist.

If we run the application and navigate to `GET /api/clients/2`, we should have the
following output:

```
{
    "id": 2,
    "name": "Some mega-corporation",
    "contracts": [
        {
            "id": 3,
            "name": "Huge contract",
            "description": "This is a huge contract of Some
mega-corporation.",
            "workTotal": 15000,
            "workDone": 0,
            "workState": "New",
            "primaryContactFirstname": "Kory",
            "primaryContactLastname": "O'Neill",
            "primaryContactEmail": "kory.oneill@megacorp.com"
        }
    ]
}
```

And voilà! Our little application is working as expected, and without much effort. We took some data, converted it into a different format, computed some statistics, flattened some objects, and serialized that as JSON so consumers could start using those two endpoints. All of that was made without any alteration to our initial model, but by creating DTOs instead.

> **Note**
>
> In a more significant project, I would recommend moving as much logic as possible out of the controller because we don't want to break the single responsibility principle. However, flattening the model into a DTO could arguably be considered the responsibility of the controller. We could also use AutoMapper to do that. More on that in *Chapter 13, Getting Started with Object Mappers*.
>
> Think of a controller as a bridge between HTTP and your application logic, or if you prefer, a very thin layer allowing users to access your software over HTTP.

Now that we have explored DTOs, let's dig deeper and discuss API contracts, which define our web APIs.

API contracts

An API contract is the definition of a web API. Like any standard API, a consumer should know how to call an endpoint and what to expect from it in return. Each endpoint should have a signature, like a method, and should enforce that signature.

Using DTOs as input and output makes them part of that contract, adding even more value to them, locking in place the contract instead of using a more volatile model, shared across multiple parts of the system. From this point forward, a DTO is more than a simple "object used to transfer data." It becomes an integral part of the contract, and the only reason for a DTO to change is directly linked to that contract.

Now that we have an idea of an API contract, let's see how to share those contracts that define our APIs. For teamwork, communication is the key, and the same goes for system collaboration. So, consumers of an API should have access to the contracts to consume the exposed resources more efficiently.

To do that, we could do the following:

- Open any text editor, such as MS Word or Notepad, and start writing out a document describing our web APIs; this is probably the most tedious and least flexible way of doing it.

- Use an existing standard, such as the OpenAPI Specification (formerly Swagger).

- Use any other tools that fit our requirements.

> **Tip**
>
> I like to use Postman to build web API's documentation, describing the contracts. Postman also allows tests to be written, which are organized into collections and folders, and can be shared with other people or publicly. Tools are not exclusive, and using multiple tools can lead to even greater productivity gain. I'd recommend that you explore existing and new tools whenever you can.

Some persons go even further when defining API contracts, but once again, it depends on each project, your team, teams, or the company you are working for. For now, let's stay minimalist and define an API contract as the API surface: its input and output.

Analyzing the DTO sample

From a developer perspective, a contract is a model associated with a URI and an HTTP method. For example, if we dissect `ClientsController` from the previous code sample, we would end up with the two following endpoints:

1. Read all clients.
2. Read one client.

"Read all clients" uses the GET method and listens to the `api/clients` URI. It has no input parameter, and it returns a collection of `ClientSummaryDto`.

"Read one client" also uses the GET method, but listens to the `api/clients/{id}` URI. The discriminator between the two GET actions is the `id` parameter. When successful, the action returns an instance of `ClientDetailsDto`.

These are the contracts defining our API in a textual format. That is not the most technical way of sharing this information, but it should help understand the idea. Nonetheless, when you cannot explain an idea using a spoken language, it may indicate that your analysis or understanding is incomplete.

Project – OpenAPI

Based on the previous code sample and our quick analysis, let's see how easy it is to generate an OpenAPI Specification document. Multiple tools allow automatic generation of OpenAPI specifications. Two of the most common ones are Swashbuckle and NSwag. We will use the latter in this sample because of the minimal amount of code needed to get started.

> **Tip**
>
> I'm in no way telling you that NSwag is better than Swashbuckle, I instead recommend you take a look at both and make up your own mind.
>
> The .NET 5 template now includes Swashbuckle plumbing by default. So as a bonus, you won't have to do anything to have that one ready to go.

Based on a copy of the DTO sample, to create an OpenAPI document using NSwag, we need to do the following:

1. Install the `NSwag.AspNetCore` NuGet package by running `dotnet add package NSwag.AspNetCore` or by using the VS package manager.

2. Add the dependencies to the container by calling the `services.AddSwaggerDocument();` extension method.

3. Configure the middleware that generates the OpenAPI document by calling the `app.UseOpenApi();` extension method.

4. Optionally configure the middleware that generates a user interface over the OpenAPI document by calling the `app.UseSwaggerUi3();` extension method.

With only those few lines of code, when running the project and navigating to
/swagger, we should access the following UI:

Figure 5.3 – Swagger UI generated using NSwag

Then, by navigating to /swagger/v1/swagger.json, we can consult the generated OpenAPI document. To be brief, I won't copy the whole JSON document here. Let's explore only the relevant part instead, starting with our DTO's descriptor:

```json
"ClientSummaryDto": {
  "type": "object",
  "required": ["id", "totalNumberOfContracts",
"numberOfOpenContracts"],
  "properties": {
    "id": {
      "type": "integer",
      "format": "int32"
    },
    "name": {
      "type": "string"
    },
    "totalNumberOfContracts": {
      "type": "integer",
      "format": "int32"
    },
    "numberOfOpenContracts": {
      "type": "integer",
      "format": "int32"
    }
  }
}
```

That's a clear representation of our C# class:

```csharp
public class ClientSummaryDto
{
    [JsonPropertyName("id")]
    public int Id { get; set; }
    [JsonPropertyName("name")]
    public string Name { get; set; }
    [JsonPropertyName("totalNumberOfContracts")]
    public int TotalNumberOfContracts { get; set; }
    [JsonPropertyName("numberOfOpenContracts")]
```

```
        public int NumberOfOpenContracts { get; set; }
}
```

Then, here is the "read all clients" endpoint, which returns an array of
ClientSummaryDto:

```
"/api/Clients": {
    "get": {
        "tags": ["Clients"],
        "operationId": "Clients_GetAll",
        "produces": ["text/plain", "application/json", "text/
json"],
        "responses": {
            "200": {
                "x-nullable": false,
                "description": "",
                "schema": {
                    "type": "array",
                    "items": {
                        "$ref": "#/definitions/ClientSummaryDto"
                    }
                }
            }
        }
    }
}
```

All of that was generated for us in a few lines of code. There are multiple extension points,
and there are many ways to extend those definitions, but the OpenAPI Specification is
beyond the scope of this book.

One last thing to note is that since we used `IActionResult` in the "read one client" endpoint, the OpenAPI middleware was not able to understand what was returned by that action automatically. The responses are limited to the following descriptor, which is very unclear:

```
"responses": {
  "200": {
    "x-nullable": true,
    "description": "",
    "schema": {
      "type": "file"
    }
  }
}
```

ASP.NET Core 5 provides a mechanism that generators such as NSwag can exploit to mitigate this problem (namely, `ApiExplorer`). For example, by adding two `ProducesResponseType` attributes to the action, the OpenAPI generator now knows what to generate. Here is the decorated method:

```
[HttpGet("{id}")]
[ProducesResponseType(StatusCodes.Status200OK, Type =
typeof(ClientDetailsDto))]
[ProducesResponseType(StatusCodes.Status404NotFound)]
public IActionResult Get(int id)
// ...
```

The OpenAPI Specification is now clearer. Here is the updated `responses` object for that endpoint:

```
"responses": {
  "200": {
    "x-nullable": false,
    "description": "",
    "schema": {
      "$ref": "#/definitions/ClientDetailsDto"
    }
  },
  "404": {
```

```
    "x-nullable": false,
    "description": "",
    "schema": {
      "$ref": "#/definitions/ProblemDetails"
    }
  }
}
```

The missing objects have also been created under the `definitions` node, describing the `ClientDetailsDto` class. A new `404` response is also explicitly defined there, returning the default `ProblemDetails` object.

Keep in mind that most of the elements are customizable. ASP.NET Core 5 also supports API conventions that describe APIs using conventions, instead of decorating every action one by one. That could save you a lot of time if you are building CRUD APIs or can follow a predefined set of conventions. You can also decorate a controller with a `ProducesResponseType` attribute, stating that all actions can return that response. We won't dig any further into the OpenAPI subject, but knowing this should help you get started whenever the need to have an OpenAPI document arises. Feel free to explore other tools as well. I picked NSwag for its simplicity but normally use Swagger. Perhaps another tool would suit your needs better.

Project – API contracts

Context: We are building multiple .NET applications, and we want to share our contract classes (DTOs) between projects so that we don't have to copy/paste them in every project. We know that we are going to end up having multiple clients communicating with a single backend web API.

To achieve our goal, we must move the contract classes into an external assembly. The best target for class libraries is .NET Standard to use our library with .NET 5, older .NET Core, and even .NET Framework projects.

For this scenario, we created the following projects:

- `My.Api`, which references `My.Api.Contracts` and exposes the same actions as the *Data Transfer Object* code sample.
- `My.Api.Contracts`, which contains the DTOs.
- `My.Client`, which references `My.Api.Contracts` and queries `My.Api` using an instance of `HttpClient`.

> **Note**
>
> I find the name [name of the api project].Contracts
> for these types of assembly to be explicit, but once again, that is a personal
> preference. You could also opt for [name of the api project].
> DTOs or [name of the api project].DTO instead, or any other
> name that you prefer. When naming something, the important thing is to make
> sure that the name is clear even without much knowledge of the project.

The dependency graph looks like this:

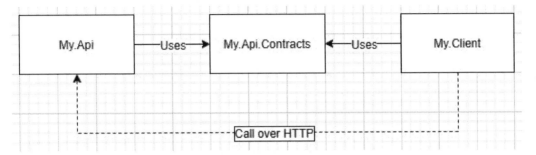

Figure 5.4 – Dependencies between assemblies; sharing the contracts

Since all classes representing the data contracts are in the shared My.Api.Contracts
library, My.Client can directly serialize them when querying My.Api. On the other
hand, My.Api can deserialize the same classes, making this design great for reusing
DTOs between projects.

There is not much code to show here since it is the same as the last example, but split into
multiple assemblies. You can always take a look and run the full sample to explore the
design: https://net5.link/HYCY.

The following screenshot shows the new solution structure and the dependencies
between projects:

Figure 5.5 – Visual Studio Solution Explorer exposing dependencies between projects

However, before moving on, I'll paste the `My.Client.Program` class here, which is the only new code to visualize:

```
namespace My.Client
{
    public class Program
    {
        private static readonly HttpClient http = new
HttpClient();

        static async Task Main(string[] args)
        {
            var uri = "https://localhost:5002/api/clients";

            // Read all summaries
            WriteTitle("All clients summaries");
            var clients = await FetchAndWriteFormattedJson
<ClientSummaryDto[]>(uri);

            // Read all details
            foreach (var summary in clients)
            {
                WriteTitle($"Details of {summary.Name} (id:
{summary.Id})");
                await FetchAndWriteFormattedJson
<ClientDetailsDto>($"{uri}/{summary.Id}");
            }

            Console.ReadLine();
        }

        private static async Task<TContract>
FetchAndWriteFormattedJson<TContract>(string uri)
        {
            var response = await http.GetStringAsync(uri);
var deserializedObject = JsonSerializer.Deserialize<TContract>
(response);
            var formattedJson = JsonSerializer.Serialize
```

```
(deserializedObject, new JsonSerializerOptions { WriteIndented
= true });
            Console.WriteLine(formattedJson);
            return deserializedObject;
    }

        private static void WriteTitle(string title)
        {
            var initialColor = Console.ForegroundColor;
            Console.ForegroundColor = ConsoleColor.Yellow;
            Console.WriteLine();
            Console.WriteLine(title);
            Console.ForegroundColor = initialColor;
        }
    }
}
```

That code reads all clients and writes that output to the console. Then it queries the details of each client one by one and outputs those details into the console.

This is the result:

```
All clients summaries
[
  {
    "id": 1,
    "name": "Jonny Boy Inc.",
    "totalNumberOfContracts": 2,
    "numberOfOpenContracts": 1
  },
  {
    "id": 2,
    "name": "Some mega-corporation",
    "totalNumberOfContracts": 1,
    "numberOfOpenContracts": 1
  }
]

Details of Jonny Boy Inc. (id: 1)
{
  "id": 1,
  "name": "Jonny Boy Inc.",
  "contracts": [
    {
      "id": 1,
      "name": "First contract",
      "description": "This is the first contract of Jonny Boy Inc.",
      "workTotal": 100,
      "workDone": 100,
      "workState": "Completed",
      "primaryContactFirstname": "John",
      "primaryContactLastname": "Doe",
      "primaryContactEmail": "john.doe@jonnyboy.com"
    },
    {
      "id": 2,
      "name": "Some other contract",
      "description": "This is another contract of Jonny Boy Inc.",
      "workTotal": 100,
      "workDone": 25,
      "workState": "InProgress",
      "primaryContactFirstname": "Jane",
      "primaryContactLastname": "Doe",
      "primaryContactEmail": "jane.doe@jonnyboy.com"
    }
  ]
}

Details of Some mega-corporation (id: 2)
{
  "id": 2,
  "name": "Some mega-corporation",
  "contracts": [
    {
      "id": 3,
      "name": "Huge contract",
      "description": "This is a huge contract of Some mega-corporation.",
      "workTotal": 15000,
      "workDone": 0,
      "workState": "New",
      "primaryContactFirstname": "Kory",
      "primaryContactLastname": "O\u0027Neill",
      "primaryContactEmail": "kory.oneill@megacorp.com"
    }
  ]
}
```

Figure 5.6 – All clients displayed in the console as JSON

Without sharing the DTOs, we would have needed to duplicate that information and have twice the number of DTOs to maintain.

As a little warning, this is not a magic solution to fix all of your problems. Sharing means coupling, which means that you could break one part of your application by updating the contracts for another. One benefit of having duplicated DTOs is the fact that before changing a contract, you must think about it more seriously due to the amount of work that would be required. You would need to manually update multiple projects instead of hitting *F2* in Visual Studio to rename a property or by adding or removing a property and assuming that everything else still works. On top of that, by updating each project manually, it forces you to analyze the impact of the changes, which could lead to avoiding bugs. A reliable test suite should help with these kinds of changes.

Nonetheless, this is a great way to share DTOs between projects. As with everything, don't just blindly pick this solution every time, but weigh the pros and cons upfront first.

Idea – Creating a typed client library

An extension to the previous code sample could be to create another project that plays the role of a typed HTTP client. The project would then be inserted between `My.Client` and `My.Api.Contract`. By following the same naming style, we could name it `My.Api.Client`. It would reference `My.Api.Contract` and expose more defined methods, such as `http.Clients.ReadAllAsync()` and `http.Clients.ReadOneAsync(id)`, for example:

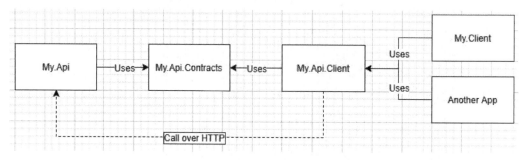

Figure 5.7 – Multiple projects using the API Client to communicate with the API

This would allow `My.Api.Client` to be reused in multiple applications, even distributing an SDK for `My.Api`.

If you are looking to practice, this could be a good project to play around with: creating a typed library that queries the web API over HTTP.

In this case, we only have a single controller, but let's assume that we have more, say the following two controllers:

- Clients
- Contracts

Our typed client interface could look like this:

```
public interface IMyApiClient
{
    IClientsClient Clients { get; }
    IContractsClient Contracts { get; }
}
public interface IClientsClient
{
    Task<IEnumerable<ClientSummaryDto>> ReadAllAsync();
    Task<ClientDetailsDto> ReadOneAsync(int clientId);
    // ...
}
public interface IContractsClient
{
    // ...
}
```

If you are not too sure, don't worry. We are talking more about interfaces later and are introducing techniques such as dependency injection and the strategy pattern, which should help you design such a typed client.

One last observation

I don't know whether you noticed that in those last designs, by sharing DTOs, we've been able to share our API contracts without exposing our domain model to other applications. Think about it; if we were not using DTOs, we would have exposed our internal classes directly. This could lead to friction when that model evolves because multiple applications directly depend on these internal classes. Now, with DTOs shielding our system, we can share a model but keep the internal data model hidden from the outside world, thereby making it easier to maintain our API in the long run.

As stated before, the DTOs are shared, but as long as we don't change them, we can make changes to the way the data is modeled without any impact on the external consumers.

Summary

In this chapter, we explored how to leverage web APIs and create web services that expose REST endpoints to share data over HTTP. We also saw how to decouple the model from the "presentation" using DTOs.

DTOs are the equivalent of view models, but for web services. They are classes specially crafted around a specific resource: an HTTP endpoint. Instead of returning raw data to the client, a DTO can encapsulate the result of computations, limit the number of exposed properties, aggregate results, and flatten data structures to carefully craft the API contract representing the input and output of its endpoint.

Then we dug a little further along that path by defining that DTOs are part of the API contracts. A contract is the definition of our web APIs, so its consumers know how to communicate with it. We also looked at sharing DTOs between .NET projects.

In the end, we established that it is imperative to decouple the components from our systems, which follows up on the previous chapters, where we explored architectural principles, automated testing, and more.

In the next two chapters, we explore our first **Gang of Four** (**GoF**) design patterns and take a deep dive into ASP.NET Core **dependency injection** (**DI**) systems. All of this will help us to continue on the path we started: **to design better software**.

Questions

Let's look at a few practice questions:

1. In a REST API, what is the most common status code sent after creating an entity?
2. What attribute tells ASP.NET to bind the data of the request body to a parameter?
3. If you want to read data from the server, what HTTP method would you use?
4. Can DTOs add flexibility and robustness to a system?
5. Are DTOs part of an API contract?

Further reading

Here is a link to build on what we have learned in the chapter:

- OpenAPI Specification: `https://net5.link/M4Uz`

6

Understanding the Strategy, Abstract Factory, and Singleton Design Patterns

This chapter explores object creation using a few classic, simple, and yet powerful design patterns from the GoF. These patterns allow developers to encapsulate behaviors, centralize object creation, add flexibility to their design, or control object lifetime. Moreover, they will most likely be used in every software you build directly or indirectly in the future.

> **GoF**
>
> Erich Gamma, Richard Helm, Ralph Johnson, and John Vlissides are the
> authors of *Design Patterns: Elements of Reusable Object-Oriented Software*
> (1994), also known as the **GoF** (**GoF**). In that book, they introduce
> 23 design patterns, some of which we will look at in this book.

Why are they that important? Because they are the building blocks of robust object
composition and they help to create flexibility and reliability. Moreover, in *Chapter 7,
Deep Dive into Dependency Injection*, we will leverage Dependency Injection to make
those patterns even more powerful!

But first things first. The following topics will be covered in this chapter:

- The Strategy design pattern

- A brief look at a few C# features

- The Abstract Factory design pattern

- The Singleton design pattern

The Strategy design pattern

The Strategy pattern is a behavioral design pattern that allows us to change object
behaviors at runtime. We can also use this pattern to compose complex object trees and
rely on it to follow the **Open/Closed Principle (OCP)** without much effort. As a follow
up on that last point, the Strategy pattern plays a significant role in the *composition over
inheritance* way of thinking. In this chapter, we focus on the behavioral part of the Strategy
pattern. In the next chapter, we cover how to use the Strategy pattern to compose systems
dynamically.

Goal

The Strategy pattern's goal is to extract an algorithm (strategy) away from the host class
needing it (context). That allows the consumer to decide on the strategy (algorithm) to use
at runtime.

For example, we could design a system that fetches data from two different types of databases. Then we could apply the same logic over that data and use the same user interface to display it. To achieve this, using the Strategy pattern, we could create two strategies, one named `FetchDataFromSql` and the other `FetchDataFromCosmosDb`. Then we could plug the strategy that we need at runtime in the `context` class. That way, when the consumer calls the `context`, the `context` does not need to know from where the data comes from, how it is fetched, or what strategy is in use; it only gets what it needs to work, delegating the fetching responsibility to an abstracted strategy.

Design

Before any further explanation, let's take a look at the following class diagram:

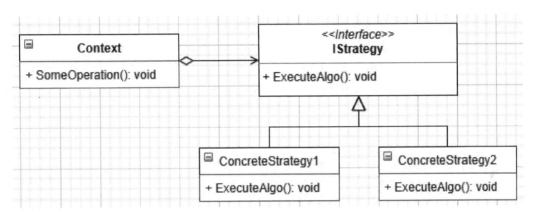

Figure 6.1 – Strategy pattern class diagram

The building blocks of the Strategy pattern go as follows:

- `Context` is a class that delegates one or more operations to an `IStrategy` implementation.

- `IStrategy` is an interface defining the strategies.

- `ConcreteStrategy1` and `ConcreteStrategy2` represent one or more different concrete implementations of the `IStrategy` interface.

In the following diagram, we explore what happens at runtime. The *actor* represents any code consuming the `Context` object.

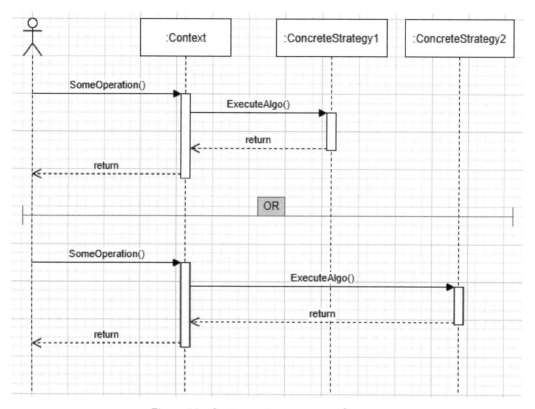

Figure 6.2 – Strategy pattern sequence diagram

When the consumer calls the `Context.SomeOperation()` method, it does not know which implementation is executed, which is an essential part of this pattern. `Context` should not be aware of the strategy being used either. It should execute it through the interface without any knowledge of the implementation past that point. That is the strength of the Strategy pattern: it abstracts the implementation away from both the `Context` and the consumer.

> **Note**
>
> We could even generalize that last sentence and extend it to the use of any interface. Using an interface removes the ties between the consumer and the implementation by relying on the abstraction instead.

Project: Strategy

Context: We want to sort a collection using different strategies. Initially, we want to support sorting the elements of a list in ascending or descending order.

To achieve this, we need to implement the following building blocks:

- The **Context** is the `SortableCollection` class.

- The **Strategy** is the `ISortStrategy` interface.

- The concrete strategies are:

  a) `SortAscendingStrategy`

  b) `SortDescendingStrategy`

The consumer is a small program that allows the user to choose a strategy, sort the collection, and display the items. Let's start with the `ISortStrategy` interface:

```
public interface ISortStrategy
{
    IOrderedEnumerable<string> Sort(IEnumerable<string> input);
}
```

That interface contains only one method that expects a collection of strings as input, and that returns an ordered collection of strings. Now let's inspect the two implementations:

```
public class SortAscendingStrategy : ISortStrategy
{
    public IOrderedEnumerable<string> Sort(IEnumerable<string> input)
        => input.OrderBy(x => x);
}
public class SortDescendingStrategy : ISortStrategy
{
    public IOrderedEnumerable<string> Sort(IEnumerable<string> input)
        => input.OrderByDescending(x => x);
}
```

Both implementations are super simple as well, using LINQ to sort the input and return the result directly. Both implementations use expression-bodied methods, which we talked about in *Chapter 4, The MVC Pattern using Razor*.

> **Tip**
> When using expression-bodied methods, please ensure that you do not make the method harder to read for your colleagues.

The next building block to inspect is the `SortableCollection` class. It is not a collection in itself (it does not implement `IEnumerable` or other collection interfaces), but it is composed of items and can sort them using an `ISortStrategy`, like this:

```
public sealed class SortableCollection
{
    public ISortStrategy SortStrategy { get; set; }
    public IEnumerable<string> Items { get; private set; }

    public SortableCollection(IEnumerable<string> items)
    {
        Items = items;
    }

    public void Sort()
    {
        if (SortStrategy == null)
        {
            throw new NullReferenceException("Sort strategy not found.");
        }
        Items = SortStrategy.Sort(Items);
    }
}
```

This class is the most complex one so far, so let's take a more in-depth look:

- The SortStrategy property holds a reference to an ISortStrategy implementation (that can be null).

- The Items property holds a reference to the collection of strings contained in the SortableCollection class.

- We set the initial IEnumerable<string> when creating an instance of SortableCollection, through its constructor.

- The Sort method uses the current SortStrategy to sort the Items. When there is no strategy set, it throws a NullReferenceException.

With that code, we can see the Strategy pattern in action. The SortStrategy property represents the current algorithm, respecting an ISortStrategy contract, which is updatable at runtime. The SortableCollection.Sort() method delegates the work to that ISortStrategy implementation (the concrete strategy). Therefore, changing the value of the SortStrategy property leads to a change of behavior of the Sort() method, making this pattern very powerful yet simple.

Let's experiment with this by looking at MyConsumerApp, a console application that uses the previous code:

```csharp
public class Program
{
    private static readonly SortableCollection _data = new
SortableCollection(new[] { "Lorem", "ipsum", "dolor", "sit",
"amet." });
```

The _data instance represents the **context**, our sortable collection of items. Next, an empty Main method:

```csharp
    public static void Main(string[] args) { /*...*/ }
```

To keep it focused on the pattern, I took away the console logic, which is irrelevant for now.

```csharp
    private static string SetSortAsc()
    {
        _data.SortStrategy = new SortAscendingStrategy();
        return "The sort strategy is now Ascending!";
    }
```

The preceding method sets the **strategy** to a new instance of
SortAscendingStrategy.

```
private static string SetSortDesc()
{
    _data.SortStrategy = new SortDescendingStrategy();
    return "The sort strategy is now Descending!";
}
```

The preceding method sets the **strategy** to a new instance of
SortDescendingStrategy.

```
private static string SortData()
{
    try
    {
        _data.Sort();
        return "Data sorted!";
    }
    catch (NullReferenceException ex)
    {
        return ex.Message;
    }
}
```

The SortData method calls the Sort() method, which delegates the call to an optional
ISortStrategy implementation.

```
private static string PrintCollection()
{
    var sb = new StringBuilder();
    foreach (var item in _data.Items)
    {
        sb.AppendLine(item);
    }
    return sb.ToString();
}
```

This last method displays the collection in the console to visually validate the correctness of the code.

When we run the program, the following menu appears:

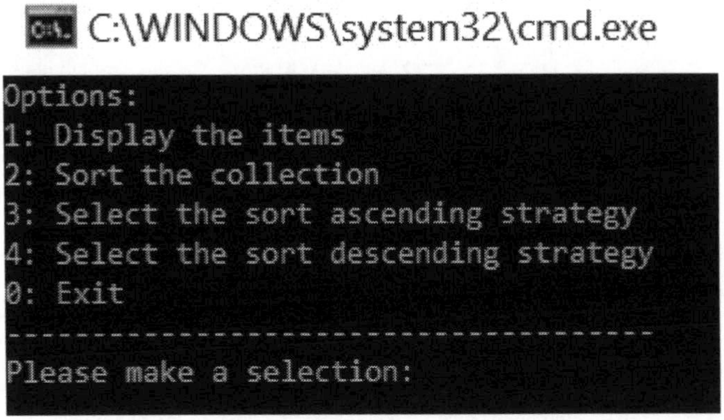

Figure 6.3 – Output showing the Options menu

When a user selects an option, the program calls the appropriate method, as described earlier.

When executing the program, if you display the items (1), they appear in their initial order. If you assign a strategy (3 or 4), sort the collection (2), then display the list again, the order will have changed and would now be different based on the selected algorithm.

Let's analyze the sequence of events when you select the following options:

1. Select the sort ascending strategy (**3**).

2. Sort the collection (**2**).

    Next, is a sequence diagram that represents this:

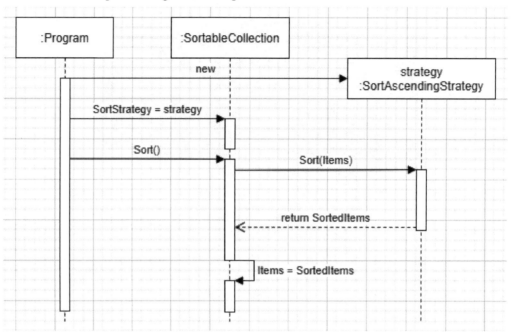

Figure 6.4 – Sequence diagram sorting the items using the "sort ascending" strategy (options 3 then 2)

The preceding diagram shows the Program creating a strategy and assigning it to SortableCollection. Then, when the Program calls the Sort() method, the SortableCollection instance delegates the sorting computation to the underlying algorithm implemented by the SortAscendingStrategy class, a.k.a. the **strategy**.

From the pattern standpoint, the SortableCollection class, a.k.a. the **context**, is responsible for keeping a hold on the current **strategy** and to use it.

Conclusion

The Strategy design pattern is very effective at delegating responsibilities to other objects. It also allows having a rich interface (context) with behaviors that can change during the program's execution.

The strategy does not have to be exposed directly; it can also be private to the class, hiding its presence to the outside world (the consumers); we talk more about this in the next chapter. Meanwhile, the Strategy pattern is excellent at helping us follow the **SOLID** principles:

- **S**: It helps to extract responsibilities to external classes and use them, interchangeably, later.

- **O**: It allows extending classes without updating its code by changing the current strategy at runtime.

- **L**: It does not rely on inheritance. Moreover, it plays a large role in the *composition over inheritance principle*, helping us avoid inheritance altogether and, at the same time, the LSP.

- **I**: By creating smaller strategies based on lean and focused interfaces, the Strategy pattern is an excellent enabler for respecting the ISP.

- **D**: The creation of dependencies is moved from the class using the strategy (the context) to the class's consumer. That makes the context depends on abstraction instead of implementation, inverting the flow of control.

Before getting into the Abstract Factory pattern, we will look at a few C# features to help write cleaner code.

A brief look at a few C# features

Let's get back to the `Main` method of the Strategy pattern code sample. There, I used a few newer C# features. I omitted the implementation there because it was not relevant to the pattern itself, but here is that missing code, to analyze it:

```csharp
public static void Main(string[] args)
{
    string input = default;
    do
    {
        Console.Clear();
        Console.WriteLine("Options:");
        Console.WriteLine("1: Display the items");
        Console.WriteLine("2: Sort the collection");
        Console.WriteLine("3: Select the sort ascending
strategy");
        Console.WriteLine("4: Select the sort descending
strategy");
```

```
        Console.WriteLine("0: Exit");
        Console.
WriteLine("------------------------------------------");
        Console.WriteLine("Please make a selection: ");
        input = Console.ReadLine();


        Console.Clear();
        var output = input switch
        {
            "1" => PrintCollection(),
            "2" => SortData(),
            "3" => SetSortAsc(),
            "4" => SetSortDesc(),
            "0" => "Exiting",
            _   => "Invalid input!"
        };
        Console.WriteLine(output);
        Console.WriteLine("Press **enter** to continue.");
        Console.ReadLine();
    } while (input != "0");
}
```

Default literal expressions (C# 7.1)

This first C# feature to explore was introduced in C# 7.1 and is called **default literal expressions**. It allows us to reduce the amount of code required to use **default value expressions**.

Previously, we'd need to write this:

```
string input = default(string);
```

Or this:

```
var input = default(string);
```

Now, we can write this:

```
string input = default;
```

It can be very useful for optional parameters, like this:

```
public void SomeMethod(string input1, string input2 = default)
{
    // ...
}
```

In that code block, we can pass one or two arguments to the method. When we omit the `input2` parameter, it is instantiated to `default(string)`. The default value of a `string` is `null`.

Switch expressions (C# 8)

The second C# feature to explore was introduced in C# 8 and is named **switch expressions**. Previously, we'd need to write this:

```
string output = default;
switch (input)
{
    case "1":
        output = PrintCollection();
        break;
    case "2":
        output = SortData();
        break;
    case "3":
        output = SetSortAsc();
        break;
    case "4":
        output = SetSortDesc();
        break;
    case "0":
        output = "Exiting";
        break;
    default:
        output = "Invalid input!";
        break;
}
```

Now, we can write this:

```
var output = input switch
{
    "1" => PrintCollection(),
    "2" => SortData(),
    "3" => SetSortAsc(),
    "4" => SetSortDesc(),
    "0" => "Exiting",
    _   => "Invalid input!"
};
```

That makes the code shorter and simpler. Once you get used to it, I find this new way even easier to read. You can think about a switch expression as if the switch returns a value.

Discards (C# 7)

The **discards** are the last C# feature that we'll explore here. It was introduced in C# 7. In this case, it became the default case of the switch (see the highlighted line):

```
var output = input switch
{
    "1" => PrintCollection(),
    "2" => SortData(),
    "3" => SetSortAsc(),
    "4" => SetSortDesc(),
    "0" => "Exiting",
    _   => "Invalid input!"
};
```

The discards (_) are also useable in other scenarios. It is a special variable that cannot be used, a placeholder, like a variable that does not exist. By using discards, you don't allocate memory for that variable, which help optimize your application.

It can also be useful when deconstructing a tuple where you only use some of its members. It is also very convenient when calling a method with an `out` parameter that you don't want to use, for example:

```
if (bool.TryParse("true", out _))
{
    /* ... */
}
```

In that last code block, we only want to do something if the input is a Boolean, but we do not use the Boolean value itself, which is a great scenario for a discard variable.

I'll skip tuples for now as we discuss them in the next chapter.

The Abstract Factory design pattern

The Abstract Factory design pattern is a creational design pattern from the GoF. We use creational patterns to create other objects, and factories are a very popular way of doing that.

Goal

The Abstract Factory pattern is used to abstract the creation of a family of objects. It usually implies the creation of multiple object types within that family. A family is a group of related or dependent objects (classes).

Let's think about creating vehicles. There are multiple types of vehicles, and for each type, there are multiple models. We can use the Abstract Factory pattern to make our life easier for this type of scenario.

> **Note**
>
> There is also the *Factory Method* pattern, which focuses on creating a single type of object instead of a family. We only cover Abstract Factory here, but we use other types of factories later in the book.

Design

With Abstract Factory, the consumer asks for an abstract object and gets one. The factory is an abstraction, and the resulting objects are also abstractions, decoupling the object creation from the consumers. That also allows us to add or remove families of objects without impacting the consumers.

If we think about vehicles, we could have the ability to make low- and high-grade versions of each type of vehicle. Let's take a look at a class diagram representing this:

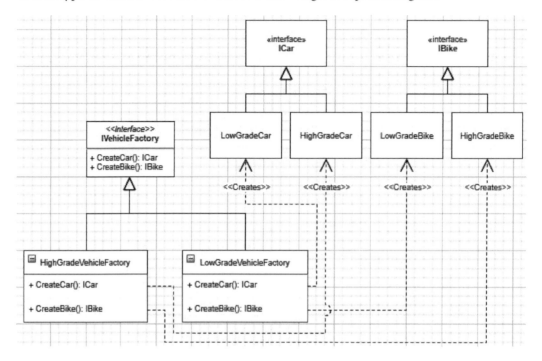

Figure 6.5 – Abstract Factory class diagram

In the diagram, we have the following:

- `IVehicleFactory` is an abstract factory, defining two methods: one that creates cars of type `ICar` and another that creates bikes of type `IBike`.

- `HighGradeVehicleFactory` is an implementation of the abstract factory that handles high-grade vehicle creation. This concrete factory returns instances of type `HighGradeCar` or `HighGradeBike`.

- `LowGradeVehicleFactory` is an implementation of our abstract factory that handles low-grade vehicle creation. This concrete factory returns instances of type `LowGradeCar` or `LowGradeBike`.

- `LowGradeCar` and `HighGradeCar` are two implementations of `ICar`.

- `LowGradeBike` and `HighGradeBike` are two implementations of `IBike`.

Based on that diagram, a consumer uses the `IVehicleFactory` interface and should not be aware of the concrete factory used underneath, abstracting away the vehicle creation process.

Project: AbstractVehicleFactory

Context: We need to support the creation of multiple types of vehicles. We also need to be able to add new types as they become available without impacting the system. To begin with, we only support high-grade and low-grade vehicles. Moreover, the program only supports the creation of cars and bikes.

For the sake of our demo, the vehicles are just empty classes and interfaces:

```
public interface ICar { }
public interface IBike { }
public class LowGradeCar : ICar { }
public class LowGradeBike : IBike { }
public class HighGradeCar : ICar { }
public class HighGradeBike : IBike { }
```

Let's now look at the part that we want to study – the factories:

```
public interface IVehicleFactory
{
    ICar CreateCar();
    IBike CreateBike();
}
public class LowGradeVehicleFactory : IVehicleFactory
{
    public IBike CreateBike() => new LowGradeBike();
    public ICar CreateCar() => new LowGradeCar();
}
public class HighGradeVehicleFactory : IVehicleFactory
{
    public IBike CreateBike() => new HighGradeBike();
    public ICar CreateCar() => new HighGradeCar();
}
```

The factories are simple implementations that describe the pattern well:

- `LowGradeVehicleFactory` creates low-grade vehicles.
- `HighGradeVehicleFactory` creates high-grade vehicles.

The consumer is an xUnit test project. Unit tests are often your first consumers, especially if you are doing TDD.

The `AbstractFactoryBaseTestData` class encapsulates some of our test data classes' utilities and is not relevant to our pattern study. Nevertheless, it can be useful to have all of the code on hand, and it is a very small class; so let's start there:

```
public abstract class AbstractFactoryBaseTestData :
IEnumerable<object[]>
{
    private readonly TheoryData<IVehicleFactory, Type> _data =
new TheoryData<IVehicleFactory, Type>();

    protected void AddTestData<TConcreteFactory,
TExpectedVehicle>()
        where TConcreteFactory : IVehicleFactory, new()
    {
        _data.Add(new TConcreteFactory(),
typeof(TExpectedVehicle));
    }

    public IEnumerator<object[]> GetEnumerator() => _data.
GetEnumerator();
    IEnumerator IEnumerable.GetEnumerator() => GetEnumerator();
}
```

That class is an `IEnumerable<object[]>` with a private collection of `TheoryData<T1, T2>`, and an `AddTestData<TConcreteFactory, TExpectedVehicle>()` method that is used by other classes, to feed our theories.

Let's take a look at the concrete test class and its theories:

```
public class AbstractFactoryTest
{
    [Theory]
    [ClassData(typeof(AbstractFactoryTestCars))]
    public void Should_create_a_Car_of_the_specified_
type(IVehicleFactory vehicleFactory, Type expectedCarType)
    {
        // Act
        ICar result = vehicleFactory.CreateCar();
```

```csharp
        // Assert
        Assert.IsType(expectedCarType, result);
    }


    [Theory]
    [ClassData(typeof(AbstractFactoryTestBikes))]
    public void Should_create_a_Bike_of_the_specified_
type(IVehicleFactory vehicleFactory, Type expectedBikeType)
    {
        // Act
        IBike result = vehicleFactory.CreateBike();

        // Assert
        Assert.IsType(expectedBikeType, result);
    }
}
```

In the preceding code, we have two theories that each use the data contained in a class, defined by the [ClassData(...)] attribute (see highlighted code). That data is used by the test runner to populate the value of the test method's parameters. So the test runner executes a test once per set of data. In this case, each method runs twice (the test data is covered next).

The execution of each test method goes as follows:

1. We use the Abstract Factory IVehicleFactory vehicleFactory to create an ICar or an IBike instance.

2. We test that instance against the expected concrete type to ensure it is the right type; that type is specified by Type expectedCarType or Type expectedBikeType, depending on the test method.

> **Note**
>
> I used ICar and IBike to type the variables instead of var, to make the type of the result variable clearer. In another context, I would have used var instead.

Now to the `Theory` data:

```
public class AbstractFactoryTestCars :
AbstractFactoryBaseTestData
{
    public AbstractFactoryTestCars()
    {
        AddTestData<LowGradeVehicleFactory, LowGradeCar>();
        AddTestData<HighGradeVehicleFactory, HighGradeCar>();
    }
}

public class AbstractFactoryTestBikes :
AbstractFactoryBaseTestData
{
    public AbstractFactoryTestBikes()
    {
        AddTestData<LowGradeVehicleFactory, LowGradeBike>();
        AddTestData<HighGradeVehicleFactory, HighGradeBike>();
    }
}
```

With the implementation details abstracted, the code is straightforward. If we take a closer look at the `AbstractFactoryTestCars` class, it creates two sets of test data:

- A `LowGradeVehicleFactory` that should create a `LowGradeCar` instance.
- A `HighGradeVehicleFactory` that should create a `HighGradeCar` instance.

The same goes for the `AbstractFactoryTestBikes` data:

- A `LowGradeVehicleFactory` that should create a `LowGradeBike` instance.
- A `HighGradeVehicleFactory` that should create a `HighGradeBike` instance.

We now have four tests. Two bike tests (`Vehicles.AbstractFactoryTest.Should_create_a_Bike_of_the_specified_type`) executed with the following arguments:

```
(vehicleFactory: HighGradeVehicleFactory { }, expectedBikeType:
typeof(Vehicles.Models.HighGradeBike))
```
```
(vehicleFactory: LowGradeVehicleFactory { }, expectedBikeType:
typeof(Vehicles.Models.LowGradeBike))
```

And two car tests (`Vehicles.AbstractFactoryTest.Should_create_a_Car_of_the_specified_type`) executed with the following arguments:

```
(vehicleFactory: HighGradeVehicleFactory { }, expectedCarType:
typeof(Vehicles.Models.HighGradeCar))
```
```
(vehicleFactory: LowGradeVehicleFactory { }, expectedCarType:
typeof(Vehicles.Models.LowGradeCar))
```

If we review the tests' execution, both test methods are unaware of types. They use the abstract factory (`IVehicleFactory`) and test the `result` against the expected type.

In a real program, we would use the `ICar` or the `IBike` instances to execute some logic, compute statistics, or do anything relevant to that program. Maybe that could be a racing game or a rich person's garage management system, who knows!

The important part of this project is the abstraction of the object creation process. The consumer code was not aware of the implementations.

Project: MiddleEndVehicleFactory

To prove our design's flexibility, based on the Abstract Factory pattern, let's add a new concrete factory named `MiddleEndVehicleFactory`. That factory should return a `MiddleEndCar` or a `MiddleEndBike` instance. Once again, the car and bike are just empty classes (of course, in your programs they will do something):

```
public class MiddleGradeCar : ICar { }
public class MiddleGradeBike : IBike { }
```

The new `MiddleEndVehicleFactory` looks pretty much the same as the other two:

```
public class MiddleEndVehicleFactory : IVehicleFactory
{
    public IBike CreateBike() => new MiddleGradeBike();
    public ICar CreateCar() => new MiddleGradeCar();
}
```

As for the test class, we don't need to update the test methods (the consumers); we only need to update the setup to add new test data (see the lines in bold):

```
public class AbstractFactoryTestCars :
AbstractFactoryBaseTestData
{
    public AbstractFactoryTestCars()
    {
        AddTestData<LowGradeVehicleFactory, LowGradeCar>();
        AddTestData<HighGradeVehicleFactory, HighGradeCar>();
        AddTestData<MiddleEndVehicleFactory, MiddleGradeCar>();
    }
}

public class AbstractFactoryTestBikes :
AbstractFactoryBaseTestData
{
    public AbstractFactoryTestBikes()
    {
        AddTestData<LowGradeVehicleFactory, LowGradeBike>();
        AddTestData<HighGradeVehicleFactory, HighGradeBike>();
        AddTestData<MiddleEndVehicleFactory,
MiddleGradeBike>();
    }
}
```

If we run the tests, we now have six passing tests (two theories with three test cases each). So, without updating the consumer (the `AbstractFactoryTest` class), we were able to add a new family of vehicles, the middle-end cars and bikes; kudos to the Abstract Factory pattern for that wonderfulness!

Conclusion

The Abstract Factory is an excellent pattern to abstract away the creation of object families, isolating each family and its concrete implementation, leaving the consumers unaware (decoupled) of the family being created at runtime.

We talk more about factories in the next chapter; meanwhile, let's see how the Abstract Factory pattern can help us follow the **SOLID** principles:

- **S**: Each concrete factory has the sole responsibility of creating a family of objects. You could combine Abstract Factory with other creational patterns such as the **Prototype** and **Builder** patterns for more complex creational needs.

- **O**: The consumer is open to extension but closed for modification; as we did in the "expansion" sample, we can add new families without modifying the code that uses it.

- **L**: We are aiming at composition, so there's no need for any inheritance, implicitly discarding the need for the LSP. If you use abstract classes in your design, you'll need to keep an eye open for compatibility issues that could arise when creating new abstract factories.

- **I**: By extracting an abstraction that creates other objects, it makes that interface very focused on one task, which is in line with the ISP, creating flexibility at a minimal cost.

- **D**: By depending only on interfaces, the consumer is not aware of the concrete types that it is using.

The Singleton design pattern

The Singleton design pattern allows creating and reusing a single instance of a class. We could use a static class to achieve almost the same goal, but not everything is doable using static classes. For example, implementing an interface or passing the instance as an argument cannot be done with a static class; you cannot pass static classes around, you can only use them directly.

In my opinion, the Singleton pattern in C# is an anti-pattern. Unless I cannot rely on Dependency Injection, I don't see how this pattern could serve a purpose. That said, it is a classic, so let's start by studying it, then move to a better alternative in the next chapter.

Here are a few reasons why we are covering this pattern:

- It translates into a singleton scope in the next chapter.

- Without knowing about it, you cannot locate it, nor try to remove it – or avoid its usage.

- It is a simple pattern to explore, and it leads to other patterns, such as the **Ambient Context** pattern.

Goal

The Singleton pattern limits the number of instances of a class to one. Then, the idea is to reuse the same instance subsequently. A singleton encapsulates both the object logic itself and its creational logic. For example, the Singleton pattern could lower the cost of instantiating an object with a large memory footprint since it's instantiated only once.

Can you think of a SOLID principle that gets broken right there?

Design

This design pattern is straightforward and is limited to a single class. Let's start with a class diagram:

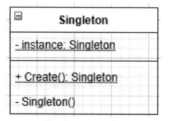

Figure 6.6 – Singleton pattern class diagram

The `Singleton` class is composed of the following:

- A private static field that holds its unique instance.

- A public static `Create()` method that creates or returns the unique instance.

- A private constructor, so external code cannot instantiate it without passing by the `Create` method.

> **Note**
>
> You can name the `Create()` method anything or even get rid of it, as we'll see in the next example. We could name it `GetInstance()`, or it could be a static property named `Instance` or bear any other relevant name.

Now, in code, it can be translated to the following:

```
public class MySingleton
{
    private static MySingleton _instance;
    private MySingleton() { }
    public static MySingleton Create()
    {
        if(_instance == default(MySingleton))
        {
            _instance = new MySingleton();
        }
        return _instance;
    }
}
```

We can see in the following unit test that `MySingleton.Create()` always returns the same instance:

```
public class MySingletonTest
{
    [Fact]
    public void Create_should_always_return_the_same_instance()
    {
        var first = MySingleton.Create();
        var second = MySingleton.Create();
        Assert.Same(first, second);
    }
}
```

And voilà! We have a working Singleton pattern, which is extremely simple – probably the most simple design pattern that I can think of.

Here is what is happening under the hood:

1. The first time that a consumer calls `MySingleton.Create()`, it creates the first instance of `MySingleton`. Since the only constructor is `private`, it can only be created from the inside. You cannot instantiate `MySingleton` (using `new MySingleton()`) from the outside of the class because there is no public constructor.

2. That first instance is then persisted to the `_instance` field for future use.

3. When a consumer calls `MySingleton.Create()` a second time, it returns the `_instance` field, reusing the previous (and only) instance of the class.

If you want your singleton to be thread-safe, you may want to `lock` the instance creation, like this:

```
public class MySingletonWithLock
{
    private readonly static object _myLock = new object();

    private static MySingletonWithLock _instance;
    private MySingletonWithLock() { }

    public static MySingletonWithLock Create()
    {
        lock (_myLock)
        {
            if (_instance == default(MySingletonWithLock))
            {
                _instance = new MySingletonWithLock();
            }
        }
        return _instance;
    }
}
```

An alternate (better) way

Previously, we used the "long way" of implementing the Singleton pattern and had to implement a thread-safe mechanism. Now that classic is behind us. We can shorten that to get rid of the `Create()` method, like this:

```
public class MySimpleSingleton
{
    public static MySimpleSingleton Instance { get; } = new
MySimpleSingleton();
    private MySimpleSingleton() { }
}
```

This way, you can use the **singleton** instance directly through its `Instance` property, like this:

```
MySimpleSingleton.Instance.SomeOperation();
```

We can prove the correctness of that claim by executing the following test method:

```
[Fact]
public void Create_should_always_return_the_same_instance()
{
    var first = MySimpleSingleton.Instance;
    var second = MySimpleSingleton.Instance;
    Assert.Same(first, second);
}
```

By doing this, our **singleton** becomes thread-safe as the property initializer creates the **singleton** instance instead of nesting it inside an `if` statement. It is usually best to delegate responsibilities to the language or the framework whenever possible.

Beware of the Arrow operator

It may be tempting to use the arrow operator `=>` to initialize the `Instance` property like this: `public static MySimpleSingleton Instance => new MySimpleSingleton();`, but doing so would return a new instance every time. This would defeat the purpose of what we want to achieve. On the other hand, the property initializer is run only once.

The use of a static constructor would also be a valid, thread-safe alternative, once again delegating the job to the language.

Code smell: Ambient Context

That last implementation of the **Singleton** pattern led us to the **Ambient Context** pattern. We could even call the Ambient Context an anti-pattern, but let's just state that it is a consequential code smell.

I don't like ambient contexts for multiple reasons. First, I do my best to stay away from anything global. Globals can be very convenient at first because they are easy to use. They are always there and accessible whenever needed: easy. However, they can bring many drawbacks in terms of flexibility and testability.

When using an ambient context, the following occurs:

- The system will most likely become **less flexible**. A global object is harder to replace and cannot easily be swapped for another object. And the implementation cannot be different based on its consumer.

- Global objects are harder to mock, which can lead to a system that is **harder to test**.

- The system can become **more brittle**; for example, if some part of your system messes up your global object, that may have unexpected consequences on other parts of your system, and you may have a hard time finding out the root cause of those errors.

- Another thing that does not help is the lack of isolation since consumers are usually directly coupled with the ambient context. Not being able to isolate components from those global objects can be a hassle, as stated in the previous points.

> **Fun fact**
>
> Many years ago, before the JavaScript frameworks era, I ended up fixing a bug in a system where some function was overriding the value of `undefined` due to a subtle error. This is an excellent example of how global variables could impact your whole system and make it more brittle. The same is true for the Ambient Context and Singleton patterns in C#; globals can be dangerous and annoying.
>
> Rest assured that, nowadays, browsers won't let developers update the value of `undefined`, but back then, it was possible.

Now that we've talked about globals, an **ambient context** is a global instance, usually available through a static property. The Ambient Context pattern is not purely evil, but it is a **code smell** that smells bad. There are a few examples in .NET Framework, such as `System.Threading.Thread.CurrentPrincipal` and `System.Threading.Thread.CurrentThread`. In this last case, `CurrentThread` is scoped instead of being purely global like `CurrentPrincipal`. An ambient context does not have to be a singleton, but that is what they are most of the time. Creating a scoped ambient context is harder and is out of the scope of this book.

Is the Ambient Context pattern good or bad? I'd go with both! It is useful primarily because of its convenience and ease of use while it is usually global. Most of the time, it could and should be designed differently to reduce the drawbacks that globals bring.

There are many ways of implementing an ambient context; it can be more complicated than a simple singleton, and it can aim at another, more dynamic scope than a single global instance. However, to keep it brief and straightforward, we are focusing only on the singleton version of the ambient context, like this:

```csharp
public class MyAmbientContext
{
    public static MyAmbientContext Current { get; } = new
MyAmbientContext();

    private MyAmbientContext() { }

    public void WriteSomething(string something)
    {
        Console.WriteLine($"This is your something:
{something}");
    }
}
```

That code is an exact copy of the `MySimpleSingleton` class, with a few subtle changes:

- `Instance` is named `Current`.
- The `WriteSomething` method is new but has nothing to do with the Ambient Context pattern itself; it is just to make the class do something.

If we take a look at the test method that follows, we can see that we use the ambient context by calling MyAmbientContext.Current, just like we did with the last singleton implementation:

```
[Fact]
public void Should_echo_the_inputted_text_to_the_console()
{
    // Arrange (make the console write to a StringBuilder
    // instead of the actual console)
    var expectedText = "This is your something: Hello World!" +
Environment.NewLine;
    var sb = new StringBuilder();
    using (var writer = new StringWriter(sb))
    {
        Console.SetOut(writer);

        // Act
        MyAmbientContext.Current.WriteSomething("Hello
World!");
    }

    // Assert
    var actualText = sb.ToString();
    Assert.Equal(expectedText, actualText);
}
```

The property could include a public setter (public static MyAmbientContext Current { get; set; }), and it could support more complex mechanics. As always, it is up to you and your specifications to build the right classes exposing the right behaviors.

To conclude this interlude: try to avoid ambient contexts and use instantiable classes instead. We'll see how to replace a singleton with a single instance of a class using Dependency Injection in the next chapter. That gives us a more flexible alternative to the Singleton pattern.

Conclusion

The Singleton pattern allows the creation of a single instance of a class for the whole lifetime of the program. It leverages a `private static` field and a `private` constructor to achieves its goal, exposing the instantiation through a `public static` method or property. We can use a field initializer, the `Create` method itself, a static constructor, or any other valid C# options to encapsulate the initialization logic.

Now let's see how the Singleton pattern can help us (not) follow the SOLID principles:

- **S**: The singleton violates this principle because it has two clear responsibilities:

  a) It has the responsibility for which it has been created (not illustrated here), like any other class.

  b) It has the responsibility of creating and managing itself (lifetime management).

- **O**: The Singleton pattern also violates this principle. It enforces a single static instance, locked in place by itself, which limits extensibility. The class must be modified to be updated, impossible to extend without changing the code.

- **L**: There is no inheritance directly involved, which is the only good point.

- **I**: There is no interface involved, which is a violation of this principle.

- **D**: The singleton class has a rock-solid hold on itself. It also suggests using its static property (or method) directly without using an abstraction, breaking the DIP with a sledgehammer.

As you can see, the Singleton pattern does violate all the SOLID principles but the LSP and should be used with caution. Having only a single instance of a class and always using that same instance is a legitimate concept. However, we'll see how to properly do this in the next chapter, leading me to the following advice: do not use the Singleton pattern, and if you see it used somewhere, try refactoring it out. Another good idea is to avoid the use of `static` members as much as possible as they create global elements that can make your system less flexible and more brittle. There are occasions where `static` members are worth using, but try keeping their number as low as possible. Ask yourself if that `static` member or class could be replaced with something else before coding one.

Some may argue that the Singleton design pattern is a legitimate way of doing things. However, in ASP.NET Core 5, I cannot agree with them: we have a powerful mechanism to do it differently, called Dependency Injection. When using other technologies, maybe, but not with .NET.

Summary

In this chapter, we explored our first GoF design patterns. These patterns expose some of the essential basis of software engineering, not necessarily the patterns themselves, but the concepts behind them:

- The Strategy pattern is a behavioral pattern that we use to compose most of our future classes. It allows swapping behavior at runtime by composing an object with smaller pieces and coding against interfaces, following the SOLID principles.

- The Abstract Factory pattern brings the idea of abstracting away object creation, leading to a better separation of concerns. More specifically, it aims to abstract the creation of object families and follow the SOLID principles.

- Even if we defined it as an anti-pattern, the Singleton pattern brings the application-level objects to the table. It allows creating a single instance of an object that lives for the whole lifetime of a program. The pattern itself violates most SOLID principles.

We also peeked at the Ambient Context code smell, which is used to create an omnipresent entity accessible from everywhere. It is often implemented as a singleton and is a global object usually defined using the `static` modifier.

In the next chapter, we'll finally jump into Dependency Injection to see how it helps us compose complex yet maintainable systems. We'll also revisit the Strategy, the Factory, and the Singleton patterns to see how to use them in a Dependency Injection oriented context and how powerful they really are.

Questions

Let's take a look at a few practice questions:

1. Why is the Strategy pattern a behavioral pattern?

2. How could we define the goal of the creational patterns?

3. If I write the code `public MyType MyProp => new MyType();`, and I call the property twice (`var v1 = MyProp; var v2 = MyProp;`), are `v1` and `v2` the same instance or two different instances?

4. Is it true that the Abstract Factory pattern allows us to add new families of elements without modifying the existing consuming code?

5. Why is the Singleton pattern an anti-pattern?

7

Deep Dive into Dependency Injection

In this chapter, we'll explore the ASP.NET Core 5 Dependency Injection system and how to leverage it efficiently, its limits, and its capabilities. We'll also cover how to compose objects using Dependency Injection, the meaning of Inversion of Control, and how to use the built-in Dependency Injection container. We'll cover the concepts behind Dependency Injection too. And we'll also revisit our first three GoF design patterns using Dependency Injection. This chapter is crucial to your journey into modern application design.

The following topics will be covered in this chapter:

- What is Dependency Injection?
- Revisiting the Strategy pattern
- Revisiting the Singleton pattern
- Understanding the Service Locator pattern
- Revisiting the Factory pattern

What is Dependency Injection?

Dependency Injection (**DI**) is a way to apply the **Inversion of Control** (**IoC**) principle. We could see IoC as a broader version of the Dependency Inversion principle (the D in SOLID).

The idea behind DI is to move the creation of dependencies from the objects themselves to the entry point of the program (the composition root). That way, we can delegate the management of dependencies to an IoC container (also known as a DI container), which does the heavy lifting.

For example, object A should not know about object B that it is using. A should instead use an interface I implemented by B, and B should be resolved and injected at runtime.

Let's decompose this:

- Object A should depend on interface I instead of concretion B.

- Instance B, injected into A, should be resolved at runtime by the IoC container.

- A should not be aware of the existence of B.

- A should not control the lifetime of B.

To go all out LEGO®, we could see IoC as drawing a plan to build a castle: you draw it, make or buy the blocks, then you press the start button, and the blocks assemble themselves following your plan. By following that logic, you could create a new 4x4 block with a unicorn painted on its side, update your plan, then press the restart button to rebuild the castle with that new block inserted into it, replacing an old one without affecting the structural integrity of the castle. By respecting the 4x4 block contract, everything should be updatable without impacting the rest of the castle.

By following that idea, if we needed to manage every single LEGO® block one by one, it would become incredibly complex very fast! Therefore, managing all dependencies by hand in a project would be super tedious and error-prone, even in the smallest program. To help us solve this issue, IoC containers come into play.

> **Note**
>
> A DI container or IoC container is the same thing – they're just different words that people use. I use both interchangeably in real life, but I'll do my best to stick with IoC container in this book.
>
> I chose the term "IoC container" because it seems more accurate than "DI container." IoC is the concept (the principle), while DI is a way of inverting the flow of control (applying IoC). For example, you apply the IoC principle (inverting the flow) by injecting dependencies at runtime (doing DI) using a container.

The role of an IoC container is to manage objects for you. You configure them, then when you ask for some abstraction, the associated implementation is resolved by the container. Moreover, the lifetime of dependencies is also managed by the container, leaving your classes to do only one thing: the job you designed them for, without thinking about their dependencies, their implementation, or their lifetime!

The bottom line is that an IoC container is a DI framework that does the auto-wiring for you. We could see Dependency Injection as follows:

1. The *consumer* of a dependency states its needs about one or more dependencies.

2. The IoC container injects that dependency (implementation) upon creating the *consumer*, fulfilling its needs at runtime.

Next, we'll explore different DI areas: where to configure the container, available options, and a common object-oriented technique that is now a code smell.

The composition root

One of the first concepts behind DI is the composition root. The composition root is where you tell the container about your dependencies: where you compose your dependency trees. The composition root should be as close to the starting point of the program as possible.

In ASP.NET Core 5, it is in `Program.cs`, `Startup.cs`, or both.

> **Note**
> As a LEGO® analogy, the composition root could be the paper sheet on which you draw your plan.

The starting point of an ASP.NET Core 5 application is the `Program` class. From there, you can use the `ConfigureServices` extension method available on the `IHostBuilder` interface to configure your services, like this:

```
public class Program
{
    public static void Main(string[] args)
    {
        CreateHostBuilder(args).Build().Run();
    }
    public static IHostBuilder CreateHostBuilder(string[] args)
=>
```

```
        Host.CreateDefaultBuilder(args)
            .ConfigureServices(services =>
            {
                // This could be the composition root
            })
            .ConfigureWebHostDefaults(webBuilder =>
            {
                webBuilder.UseStartup<Startup>();
            });
}
```

Using the `IHostBuilder` to configure services is very useful in some scenarios, including configuring test hosts or small microservices.

However, you usually want to build the host and run the program in the `Program` class, while delegating the composition of ASP.NET Core 5 to the `Startup` class, which is the second closest location to the entry point. That class is usually generated for you when you create a new project. That said, both locations are valid composition roots:

```
public class Startup
{
    public void ConfigureServices(IServiceCollection services)
    {
        // This could be the composition root
    }
    // ...
}
```

The `Startup` class is the composition root of most applications, and it is where you will most likely configure the DI container and the ASP.NET Core 5 pipeline. You can also use both, like so:

```
Host.CreateDefaultBuilder(args)
    .ConfigureServices(services =>
    {
        services.AddSingleton<Dependency1>();
    })
    .ConfigureWebHostDefaults(webBuilder =>
    {
```

```
        webBuilder.UseStartup<Startup>();
    });
//...
public void ConfigureServices(IServiceCollection services)
{
    services.AddSingleton<Dependency2>();
    services.AddSingleton<Dependency3>();
}
```

> **Note**
>
> In the `Startup` class, you can create specific methods for each environment
> (`Development`, `Staging`, `Production`) to compose applications
> effectively. You can even create multiple startup classes. See the official
> documentation for more information about this powerful feature.

It is imperative to remember that your program's composition should be done in the
composition root. That removes the need for all of those pesky new keywords spread
around your codebase and all the responsibilities that come with them. It centralizes the
application's composition into that location (that is, creating the plan to assemble the
LEGO® blocks).

Extending IServiceCollection

As we just saw, you should register dependencies in the composition root, but you can
still organize your registration code. For example, you could split your application's
composition into multiple methods or classes, then call them from your composition root.
You could also use an auto-discovery mechanism to automate the registration of some
services; we'll use packages that do that in subsequent chapters.

> **Note**
>
> The critical part remains centralizing the program composition.

As an example, most features of ASP.NET Core 5 and other popular libraries provide one
or more `Add[Feature name]()` extension methods to manage the registration of their
dependencies, allowing you to register a "bundle of dependencies" with one method call.
That's very useful to organize program composition into smaller, more cohesive units,
such as by feature.

> **Side note**
>
> A feature has the right size as long as it stays cohesive. If your feature becomes too big, does too many things, or starts to share dependencies with other features, it may be the time for a redesign before losing control over it. That's usually a good indicator of undesired coupling.

By using extension methods, it is reasonably easy to achieve. As a rule of thumb, you should do the following:

1. Create a static class named `[subject]Extensions`.

2. As per the Microsoft recommendation, create that class in the `Microsoft.Extensions.DependencyInjection` namespace (the same as `IServiceCollection`).

3. From there, create your `IServiceCollection` extension methods. Unless you need to return something else, make sure to return the extended `IServiceCollection`; this allows chaining method calls.

For example, if my feature were named `Demo Feature`, I'd write the following extension method:

```csharp
using CompositionRoot.DemoFeature;

namespace Microsoft.Extensions.DependencyInjection
{
    public static class DemoFeatureExtensions
    {
        public static IServiceCollection AddDemoFeature(this IServiceCollection services)
        {
            return services
                .AddSingleton<MyFeature>()
                .AddSingleton<IMyFeatureDependency, MyFeatureDependency>()
                ;
        }
    }
}
```

Then, to use it, we could enter the following in the composition root:

```
public void ConfigureServices(IServiceCollection services)
{
    services.AddDemoFeature();
}
```

If you are not familiar with extension methods, they come in handy to extend existing code (what we just did). For example, you could build a sophisticated library and a set of easy-to-use extension methods that allow consumers to learn and use your library easily while keeping advanced options and customization opportunities to a maximum; think ASP.NET Core 5 MVC or `System.Linq`.

Object lifetime

I've talked about this a few times already: no more new; that time is over! From now on, the DI container should do most of the jobs related to instantiating and managing objects for us.

However, before trying this out, we need to cover one last thing: object lifetime. When you create instances manually, using the new keyword, you create a hold on that object; you know when you create them, and you know when you destroy them. That leaves no chance to control these objects from the outside, enhance them, intercept them, or swap them for another implementation. This is known as the **Control Freak** anti-pattern or code smell, explained in the *Code smell: Control Freak* section.

When using DI, you need to forget about controlling objects and start to think about using dependencies – more explicitly, using their interfaces. In ASP.NET Core 5, there are three possible lifetimes to choose from:

Lifetime	Description	Code sample

Transient	The container creates a new object every time you ask for one.	`services.`
		`AddTransient<ISomeService,`
		`SomeService>();`

Scoped	The container creates an object per HTTP request and passes that object around to all other objects that want to use it.	`services.`
		`AddScoped<ISomeService,`
		`SomeService>();`

Singleton	The container creates a single instance of that dependency and always passes that unique object around.	`services.`
		`AddSingleton<ISomeService,`
		`SomeService>();`

From now on, we'll manage most of our objects using one of those three scopes. Here are some questions to help you choose:

- Do I need a single instance of my dependency? Yes? Use the **singleton** lifetime.
- Do I need a single instance of my dependency shared over an HTTP request? Yes? Use the **scoped** lifetime.
- Do I need a new instance of my dependency every time? Yes? Use the **transient** lifetime.

If you need a more complex lifetime, you may need to swap the built-in container to a third-party one (see the *Using external IoC container* section) or create your dependency tree manually in the composition root.

> **Note**
>
> A more general approach to object lifetime would be to design your components to be **singletons**. If you can't, then go for **scoped**. If **scoped** is also impossible, go for **transient**. This way, you maximize instances reuse, lower the overhead of creating objects, lower the memory cost of keeping those objects in memory, and lower the amount of garbage collection needed to remove unused instances.
>
> For example, long-lived objects are inspected only once in a while by the garbage collector, while short-lived ones are often scanned and disposed of.

There are multiple variants of the three preceding examples, but the lifetimes remain. We use the built-in container throughout the book with many of its registration methods, so you should grow familiar with it by the end. The system offers good discoverability, so you could explore the possibilities using IntelliSense or by reading the documentation.

Code smell: Control Freak

We've already stated that using the new keyword is a **code smell** or even an **anti-pattern**. But do not ban the new keyword just yet. Instead, every time you use it, ask yourself whether the object you instanciated using the new keyword is a dependency that could be managed by the container and injected instead. To help out with that, I borrowed two terms from Mark Seemann's book *Dependency Injection in .NET*; the name Control Freak also comes from that book. He describes the following two categories of dependencies:

- Stable dependencies
- Volatile dependencies

Stable dependencies are dependencies that should not break your application when a new version of it is released. They should use deterministic algorithms (input X should always produce output Y; a.k.a. respecting the LSP), and you should not expect to change them with something else in the future. I'd say that most data structures could fall into this category: DTOs, ViewModels, List<T>, and so on. You can still instantiate objects using the new keyword when they fall into this category; it is acceptable since they are not likely to break anything nor to change. But be careful because foreseeing whether a dependency is likely to change or not is very hard, even impossible, as we can't know for sure what the future has to offer. For example, elements that are part of .NET 5 could be considered stable dependencies.

Volatile dependencies are dependencies that can change, behaviors that could be swapped, or elements you may want to extend. Basically, most of the classes you create for your programs such as data access and business logic classes. These are the dependencies that you should not instanciate using the new keyword anymore. The primary way to break the tight coupling between implementations is to rely on interfaces instead.

To conclude this interlude: don't be a control freak anymore, those days are behind you!

> **Tip**
> When in doubt, inject the dependency instead of using the new keyword.

Next, we'll briefly explore an ASP.NET Core extension point before revisiting three design patterns, but this time, by exploiting Dependency Injection.

Using external IoC containers

ASP.NET Core 5 provides an extensible built-in IoC container out of the box. It is not the most powerful IoC container because it lacks some advanced features, but it can do the job for most applications. Rest assured, if it does not, you can change it for another. You might want to do that if you are used to another IoC container and want to stick to it or need missing advanced features.

As of today, Microsoft recommends using the built-in container first. If you don't know ahead of time all of the DI features that you will need, I'd go with the following strategy:

1. Use the built-in container.

2. When something cannot be done with it, look at your design and see if you can redesign your feature to work with the built-in container. This could help simplify your design, and at the same time, help maintain your software in the long run.

3. If it is impossible to achieve your goal, then swap it for another IoC container.

Assuming the container supports it, it is super simple to swap. You need to update the `ConfigureServices` method of the `Startup` class to return an `IServiceProvider` (instead of `void`), like this:

```
public IServiceProvider ConfigureServices(IServiceCollection services)
{
    // Build and return the custom IServiceProvider here
}
```

Then, inside the method, you can build the service provider, compose your application, then return it. As I sense that you don't feel like implementing your own IoC container just yet (or even ever), don't worry, multiple types of third-party integration already exist. Here is a non-exhaustive list:

- Autofac
- DryIoc
- Grace
- LightInject
- Lamar
- Stashbox
- Unity

Some libraries extend the default container and add functionalities to it, which is an option that we explore in *Chapter 9, Structural Patterns*.

Next, we'll revisit the Strategy pattern, which will become the primary tool to compose our applications and add flexibility to our systems.

Revisiting the Strategy pattern

In this section, we'll leverage the Strategy pattern to compose complex object trees and use DI to dynamically create those instances without using the new keyword, moving away from being control freaks and toward writing DI-ready code.

The Strategy pattern is a behavioral design pattern that we can use to compose object trees at runtime, allowing extra flexibility and control over objects' behavior. Composing our objects using the Strategy pattern should make our classes easier to test and maintain, as well as putting us on a SOLID path.

From now on, we want to compose objects and lower the amount of inheritance to a minimum. We call that principle **composition over inheritance**. The goal is to inject dependencies (composition) into the current class instead of depending on base class features (inheritance). Moreover, that allows behaviors to be extracted in external classes (SRP/ISP), then reused in one or more other classes (composition) through their interface (DIP).

The following list covers the most popular ways of injecting dependencies into objects:

- Constructor injection
- Property injection
- Method injection

We can also ask the container directly to resolve a dependency, which is known as the Service Locator (anti-)pattern. We'll explore the Service Locator pattern later in this chapter.

Let's look at some theory and then jump into the code to see DI in action.

Constructor injection

Constructor injection consists of injecting dependencies into the constructor, as parameters. This is the most popular and preferred technique by far. Constructor injection is useful to inject **required dependencies**; you can add null checks to ensure that, also known as the **Guard Clause** (see the *Adding a guard clause to HomeController* section).

Property injection

The built-in IoC container does not support **property injection** out of the box. The concept is to inject **optional dependencies** into properties. Most of the time, you want to avoid doing this, so it is not bad that ASP.NET Core left this one out of the built-in container. You can usually remove the property injection requirements by reworking your design a bit, leading to a better design. If you cannot avoid using property injection, you must use a third-party container.

Nevertheless, from a high-level view, the container would do something like this:

1. Create a new instance of the class and inject all required dependencies into the constructor.

2. Find extension points by scanning properties (this could be attributes, contextual bindings, or something else).

3. For each extension point, inject (set) a dependency, leaving unconfigured properties untouched, hence its definition of an optional dependency.

There are a couple of exceptions to the previous statement about the lack of support:

- Razor components (Blazor) support property injection through the use of the `[Inject]` attribute.

- Razor contains the `@inject` directive, which generates a property to hold a dependency (ASP.NET Core manages to inject it).

We can't call that property injection per se because they are not optional but required, and the `@inject` directive is more about generating code than doing DI. They are more about an internal workaround than "real" property injection. That said, that is as close as .NET 5 can get to property injection.

> **Tip**
> I recommend aiming at constructor injection instead. Not having property injection should not cause you any problems.

Method injection

ASP.NET Core supports **method injection** only at a few locations, such as in a controller's actions (methods), in the `Startup` class, and in middlewares' `Invoke` or `InvokeAsync` methods. You are not able to liberally use method injection in your classes without some work on your part.

Method injection is also used to inject **optional dependencies** into classes. We can also validate those at runtime using null checks or any other required logic.

> **Tip**
> **I recommend aiming for constructor injection whenever you can.** Only rely on method injection when it is the only way or if it adds something. For example, in a controller, injecting a transient service in the only action that needs it instead of the constructor could save a lot of useless object instantiation and, by doing so, increase performance (less instantiation and less garbage collection).

Project: Strategy

In the Strategy project, we use the Strategy pattern and constructor injection to add (compose) a `IHomeService` dependency to the `HomeController` class.

The goal is to inject a dependency of type `IHomeService` into the `HomeController` class. Then send a view model to the view to renders the page.

The service goes like this:

```
namespace Strategy.Services
{
    public interface IHomeService
    {
        IEnumerable<string> GetHomePageData();
    }

    public class HomeService : IHomeService
    {
        public IEnumerable<string> GetHomePageData()
        {
            yield return "Lorem";
            yield return "ipsum";
            yield return "dolor";
            yield return "sit";
            yield return "amet";
        }
```

```
        }
}
```

The IHomeService interface is the dependency that we want the HomeController class to have. The HomeService class is the implementation that we want to inject when instanciating the HomeController, inverting the flow of dependency.

To do that, we inject IHomeService into the controller using constructor injection. Textually, we do the following:

1. Create a private IHomeService field into the HomeController class.

2. Create a HomeController constructor with a parameter of type IHomeService.

3. Assign the argument to the field.

In code, it looks like this:

```
using Strategy.Services;
namespace Strategy.Controllers
{
    public class HomeController : Controller
    {
        private readonly IHomeService _homeService;
        public HomeController(IHomeService homeService)
        {
            _homeService = homeService;
        }
        // ...
    }
}
```

The use of private readonly fields is beneficial for two reasons:

- They are private, so you do not expose your dependencies outside of the class (encapsulation).

- They are readonly, so you can only set the value once. In the case of constructor injection, this ensures that the injected dependency, referenced by the private field, cannot be changed by other parts of the class.

If we run the application now, we get the following error:

```
InvalidOperationException: Unable to resolve service for type
 'Strategy.Services.IHomeService' while attempting to activate
 'Strategy.Controllers.HomeController'.
```

This error tells us that we forgot about something essential: to tell the container about the dependency.

To do that, we need to map the injection of `IHomeService` to an instance of `HomeService`. Due to our class's nature, we are safe to use the singleton lifetime (one single instance). Using the provided extension methods, in the composition root, we only need to add the following line:

```
public void ConfigureServices(IServiceCollection services)
{
    services.AddSingleton<IHomeService, HomeService>();
    //...
}
```

Now, if we rerun the app, the home page should load. That tells ASP.NET to inject a `HomeService` instance when a class depends on the `IHomeService` interface.

We just completed our first implementation of constructor injection using ASP.NET Core 5 – it's as easy as that.

To recap constructor injection, we need to do the following:

1. Create a dependency and its interface.

2. Inject that dependency into another class through its constructor.

3. Create a binding that tells the container how to handle the dependency.

> **Note**
> We can also inject classes directly, but until you feel that you've mastered the SOLID principles, I'd recommend sticking with injecting interfaces.

Adding the View Model

Now that we've injected the service that contains the data to display in the `HomeController` class, we need to display it. To achieve that, we decided to use the View Model pattern. The view model's goal is to create a view-centric model, then use it to render that view.

Here is what we need to do:

1.   Create a View Model class (`HomePageViewModel`).

2.   Update the `Home/Index` view to use the view model and display the information that it contains.

3.   Create and send an instance of `HomePageViewModel` to the view from the controller.

The `HomePageViewModel` class is exposing the `SomeData` property publicly and expects that data to be injected when instantiated; the code looks like this:

```
namespace Strategy.Models
{
    public class HomePageViewModel
    {
        public IEnumerable<string> SomeData { get; }
        public HomePageViewModel(IEnumerable<string> someData)
        {
            SomeData = someData;
        }
    }
}
```

That's another example of constructor injection.

Then, after a few updates, the `Views/Home/Index.cshtml` view looks like this:

```
@model HomePageViewModel
@{
    ViewData["Title"] = "Home Page";
}


<div class="text-center">
    <h1 class="display-4">Welcome</h1>
    <p>Here are your data:</p>
    <ul class="list-group">
    @foreach (var item in Model.SomeData)
    {
        <li class="list-group-item">@item</li>
```

```
        }
    </ul>
</div>
```

Now we need to pass an instance of `HomePageViewModel` to the view. We are doing that in the `Index` action, like this:

```
public IActionResult Index()
{
    var data = _homeService.GetHomePageData();
    var viewModel = new HomePageViewModel(data);
    return View(viewModel);
}
```

In that code, we used the `_homeService` field to retrieve the data through the `IHomeService` interface. It is important to note that at this point, the controller is not aware of the implementation; it depends only on the contract (the interface). Then we create the `HomePageViewModel` class using that data. Finally, we dispatch the instance of `HomePageViewModel` to the view for rendering.

> **Note**
>
> As you may have noticed, I used the new keyword here. In this case, I find that instantiating a view model inside the controller's action is acceptable. However, we could have used method injection or any other technique to help with object creation, such as a factory.

Adding a guard clause to HomeController

We've already stated that constructor injection is reliable and is used to inject the required dependencies. However, one thing bothers me from the last code sample: nothing guarantees us that `homeService` is not null.

We could check for nulls in the `Index` method, like this:

```
public IActionResult Index()
{
    var data = _homeService?.GetHomePageData();
    var viewModel = new HomePageViewModel(data);
    return View(viewModel);
}
```

But as the controller grows, we may end up writing null checks for that one dependency many times, in multiple locations. Then we should do the same null check in the view. Otherwise, we would loop a `null` value, which is not good.

To avoid that duplication of logic, and the number of possible errors that could come with it at the same time, we can add a **guard clause**.

A guard clause does as its name implies: it guards against invalid values. Most of the time, it *guards against null*. When you pass a `null` dependency into an object, the guard clause testing that parameter should throw an `ArgumentNullException`.

By using a `throw` expression, from C# 7, we can simply write this:

```
public HomeController(IHomeService homeService)
{
    _homeService = homeService ?? throw new
ArgumentNullException(nameof(homeService));
}
```

That throws an `ArgumentNullException` when `homeService` is `null`; otherwise, it assigns the `homeService` parameter value to the `_homeService` field.

> **Important note**
>
> A built-in container will automatically throw an exception if it can fulfill all dependencies during the instantiation of a class (such as `HomeController`). That said, it does not mean that all third-party containers act the same. Moreover, that does not protect you from passing `null` to a manually instantiated instance (even if we should use DI, it does not mean it won't happen). As a matter of preference, I like to add them no matter what, but they are not required.

Throw expressions (C# 7)

This feature allows us to use the `throw` statement as an expression, giving us the possibility to throw exceptions on the right side of the null-coalescing operator.

The good old way of writing the guard clause, before throw expressions, was as follows:

```
public HomeController(IHomeService homeService)
{
    if (homeService == null)
    {
        throw new ArgumentNullException (nameof(homeService));
    }
    _homeService = homeService;
}
```

First, we check for null, and if homeService is null, we throw an
ArgumentNullException; otherwise, we assign the value to the field.

Now, with throw expressions, we can write the previous code instead, outlined here again:

```
public HomeController(IHomeService homeService)
{
    _homeService = homeService ?? throw new
ArgumentNullException(nameof(homeService));
}
```

The ?? operator is a binary operator. In the result = left ?? right block, the ??
operator express that if the left value is null, use the right value instead. If the left
value is not null, use the left value.

In the past, we could not throw an exception from the right side (it was a statement),
but now we can (it is an expression).

In other cases, if you are not already familiar with that null-coalescing operator, we could
use ?? like this as well:

```
public string ValueOrDefault(string value, string defaultValue)
{
    return value ?? defaultValue;
}
```

That method returns defaultValue when value is null; otherwise, it returns
value – very convenient.

Adding a guard clause to HomePageViewModel

Let's now add a guard clause to our `HomePageViewModel` class as well:

```
public HomePageViewModel(IEnumerable<string> someData)
{
    SomeData = someData ?? throw new
ArgumentNullException(nameof(someData));
}
```

And voilà! We now have everything that we need to render the home page. More importantly, we achieved that without directly coupling the `HomeController` class with `HomeService`. Instead, we depend only on the `IHomeService` interface, a contract. By centralizing composition into the composition root, we could change the resulting home page by swapping the `IHomeService` implementation in the `Startup` class without impacting the controller or the view.

I invite you to create another class that implements `IHomeService` and change the mapping in the `Startup` class from `HomeService` to your new class and see how easy it is to change the home page's list. To go even further, you could connect your implementation to a database, an Azure Table, Redis, a JSON file, or any other data source that you can think of.

Next, we'll revisit a design pattern that is now an anti-pattern, while exploring the singleton lifetime replacing it.

Revisiting the Singleton pattern

The Singleton pattern is obsolete, goes against the SOLID principles, and we replace it with a lifetime, as we've already seen. This section explores that lifetime and recreates the good old application state, which turns out to be nothing more than a singleton scoped dictionary.

We'll explore two examples here; one about the application state, in case you wondered where that feature disappeared to. Then, the Wishlist project also uses the singleton lifetime to provide an application-level feature. There are a few unit tests as well to play with the testability and to allow safe refactoring.

The application state

If you programmed ASP.NET using .NET Framework, or the "good" old classic ASP with VBScript, you might remember the application state. If you don't, the application state was a key/value dictionary that allowed you to store data globally in your application, shared between all sessions and requests. That is one of the things that ASP always had and other languages, such as PHP, did not (or does not easily allow).

For example, I remember designing a generic reusable typed shopping cart system with classic ASP/VBScript. VBScript was not a strongly typed language and had limited object-oriented capabilities. The shopping cart fields and types were defined at the application level (once per application), then each user had their own "instance" containing the products in their "private shopping cart" (created once per session).

In ASP.NET Core 5, there is no more `Application` dictionary. To achieve the same goal, you could use a static class or static members, which is not the best approach; remember that global objects (`static`) make your application harder to test and less flexible. We could also use the Singleton pattern or create an ambient context, which would allow us to create an application-level instance of an object. We could maybe even mix that with a factory to create end user shopping carts, but we won't; these are not the best solution either.

Another way could be to use one of the ASP.NET Core 5 caching mechanisms, memory cache or distributed cache, but it is a stretch.

We could also save everything in a database to persist the shopping cart between visits, but that is not related to the application state and requires a user account, so we will not do that either.

We could save the shopping cart on the client side using cookies, local storage, or any other modern mechanism to save data on the user's computer. However, we'd get even further from the application state than using a database.

For most cases requiring an application state-like feature, the best approach would be to create a standard class and an interface, then register the binding with a singleton lifetime in the container. Finally, you inject it into the component that needs it, using constructor injection. Doing so allows the mocking of dependencies and changing the implementations without touching the code but the composition root.

> **Note**
> Sometimes, the best solution is not the technically complex one or design pattern-oriented; the best solution is often the simplest. Less code means less maintenance and fewer tests, resulting in a simpler application.

Project: Application state

Let's implement a small program that simulates the application state. The API is a single interface with two implementations. The program also exposes part of the API over HTTP, allowing users to get or set a value associated with the specified key. We use the singleton lifetime to make sure the data is shared between all requests.

The interface looks like the following:

```csharp
public interface IApplicationState
{
    TItem Get<TItem>(string key);
    bool Has<TItem>(string key);
    void Set<TItem>(string key, TItem value);
}
```

We can get the value associated with a key, associate a value with a key (set), and validate whether a key exists.

The `Startup` class contains the code responsible for handling HTTP requests. It is not using MVC, but raw request management. All of that code is not interesting to us, but I invite you to run it if you want to experiment with it. The two implementations can be swapped by commenting or uncommenting the first line of the `Startup.cs` file, which is `#define USE_MEMORY_CACHE`, which changes the way code is compiled in the `ConfigureServices` method:

```csharp
    public void ConfigureServices(IServiceCollection services)
    {
#if USE_MEMORY_CACHE
        services.AddMemoryCache();
        services.AddSingleton<IApplicationState,
ApplicationMemoryCache>();
#else
        services.AddSingleton<IApplicationState,
ApplicationDictionary>();
#endif
    }
```

The first implementation uses the memory cache system. First, I felt that it would be educational to show that to you. Second, we are hiding the cache system behind our implementation, which is also educational. Finally, we needed two implementations, and using the cache system was a pretty straightforward implementation.

Here is the `ApplicationMemoryCache` class:

```csharp
public class ApplicationMemoryCache : IApplicationState
{
    private readonly IMemoryCache _memoryCache;

    public ApplicationMemoryCache(IMemoryCache memoryCache)
    {
        _memoryCache = memoryCache ?? throw new
ArgumentNullException(nameof(memoryCache));
    }

    public TItem Get<TItem>(string key)
    {
        return _memoryCache.Get<TItem>(key);
    }

    public bool Has<TItem>(string key)
    {
        return _memoryCache.TryGetValue<TItem>(key, out _);
    }

    public void Set<TItem>(string key, TItem value)
    {
        _memoryCache.Set(key, value);
    }
}
```

> **Note**
>
> The `ApplicationMemoryCache` class is a thin layer over
> `IMemoryCache`, hiding the implementation details. That type of class is
> called a façade. We talk more about the Façade design pattern in *Chapter 9,
> Structural Patterns.*

The second implementation is using a `Dictionary<string, object>` to store the application state data. The `ApplicationDictionary` class is almost as simple as `ApplicationMemoryCache`:

```
public class ApplicationDictionary : IApplicationState
{
    private readonly Dictionary<string, object> _memoryCache =
new Dictionary<string, object>();

    public TItem Get<TItem>(string key)
    {
        if (!Has<TItem>(key))
        {
            return default;
        }
        return (TItem)_memoryCache[key];
    }

    public bool Has<TItem>(string key)
    {
        return _memoryCache.ContainsKey(key) &&
_memoryCache[key] is TItem;
    }

    public void Set<TItem>(string key, TItem value)
    {
        _memoryCache[key] = value;
    }
}
```

We can now use any of the two implementations without impacting the rest of the program. That demonstrates the strength of DI when it comes to dependency management. Moreover, we control the lifetime of the dependencies from the composition root.

If we were to use the `IApplicationState` interface into another class, say
`SomeConsumer`, its usage could look similar to the following:

```
namespace ApplicationState
{
    public class SomeConsumer
    {
        private readonly IApplicationState
_myApplicationWideService;

        public SomeConsumer(IApplicationState
myApplicationWideService)
        {
            _myApplicationWideService =
myApplicationWideService ?? throw new
ArgumentNullException(nameof(myApplicationWideService));
        }

        public void Execute()
        {
            if (_myApplicationWideService.Has<string>("some-
key"))
            {
                var someValue = _myApplicationWideService.Get
<string>("some-key");
                // Do something with someValue
            }
            // Do something else like:
            _myApplicationWideService.Set("some-key", "some-
value");
            // More logic here
        }
    }
}
```

In that code, `SomeConsumer` depends only on the `IApplicationState` interface,
not on `IMemoryCache` nor `Dictionary<string, object>`. Using DI allows us
to hide the implementation by inverting the control of dependencies. It also breaks direct
coupling between concretions, programming against interfaces (DIP).

Here is a diagram illustrating our application state system, making it visually easier to notice how it breaks coupling:

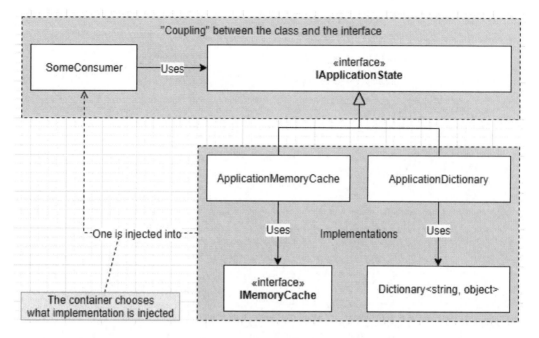

Figure 7.1 – DI-oriented diagram representing the application state system

From this sample, let's remember that the singleton lifetime allows us to reuse objects between requests and share them application-wide. Moreover, hiding implementation details behind interfaces can improve the flexibility of our design.

Default literal expressions (C# 7.1)

In the last sample, we used the `default` operator in a way new to C# 7.1. The `default` operator allows us to initialize a variable to its default value, which is often `null`. In the past, we needed to pass an argument to the default operator, like this: `int someVariable = default(int);`, which would be the equivalent of `int someVariable = 0;`, as 0 is the default value of `int`.

From C# 7.1 onward, we can use default literal expressions instead, which allow us to do the following:

- Initialize a variable to its default value.

- Set the default value of an optional method parameter.

- Provide a default argument value to a method call.

- Return a default value in a `return` statement or an expression-bodied member (the arrow `=>` operator introduced in C# 6 and 7).

Here is an example covering those use cases:

```
public class DefaultLiteralExpression<T>
{
    public void Main()
    {
        // Initialize a variable to its default value
        T myVariable = default;

        var defaultResult1 = SomeMethod();

        // Provide a default argument value to a method call
        var defaultResult2 = SomeOtherMethod(myVariable,
default);
    }

    // Set the default value of an optional method parameter
    public object SomeMethod(T input = default)
    {
        // Return a default value in a return statement
        return default;
    }

    // Return a default value in an expression-bodied member
    public object SomeOtherMethod(T input, int i) => default;
}
```

We used the generic T type parameter in the examples, but that could be any type. The default literal expressions become handy with complex generic types such as Func<T>, Func<T1, T2>, or tuples.

We won't go into more details about tuples since we talk about them after the next code sample, but here is a good example of how simple it is to return a tuple and default its three components using a default literal expression:

```
public (object, string, bool) MethodThatReturnATuple()
{
    return default;
}
```

Project: Wishlist

Let's get into another sample to illustrate the use of the singleton lifetime and Dependency Injection. Seeing DI in action should help with understanding it, then leveraging it to create SOLID software.

Context: The application is a site-wide wish list, where users can add items. Items should expire every 30 seconds. When a user adds an existing item, the system should increment the count and reset the item's expiration time. That way, popular items stay on the list longer, making it to the top. The system should sort the items by count (highest first) when displayed.

> **Note**
>
> 30 seconds is very fast, but I'm sure that you don't want to wait for days before an item expires when running the app.

The program is a tiny web API that exposes two endpoints:

- Add an item to the wish list (POST)
- Read the wish list (GET)

The wishlist should be in the singleton scope, so all users share the same instance. To keep it simple, the wishlist only stores the names of items.

Our wishlist interface looks like this:

```
public interface IWishList
{
    Task<WishListItem> AddOrRefreshAsync(string itemName);
    Task<IEnumerable<WishListItem>> AllAsync();
}
```

```
public class WishListItem
{
    public int Count { get; set; }
    public DateTimeOffset Expiration { get; set; }
    public string Name { get; set; }
}
```

Our two operations are there, and by making them async (returning a `Task<T>`), we could implement another version that relies on a remote system, such as a database, instead of an in-memory store.

> **Note**
>
> Trying to foresee the future is not usually a good idea, but designing APIs to be awaitable is generally a safe bet. Other than this, I'd recommend you stick to your specifications and use cases. When you try to solve problems that do not exist yet, you usually end up coding a lot of useless stuff, leading to additional unneeded maintenance and testing time.

The `WishListItem` class is part of the `IWishList` contract; it is the model.

The last piece of plumbing is `WishListController`, which handles the HTTP requests:

```
[Route("/")]
public class WishListController : ControllerBase
{
    private readonly IWishList _wishList;

    public WishListController(IWishList wishList)
    {
        _wishList = wishList ?? throw new
ArgumentNullException(nameof(wishList));
    }

    [HttpGet]
    public async Task<IActionResult> GetAsync()
    {
        var items = await _wishList.AllAsync();
        return Ok(items);
    }
}
```

```csharp
    [HttpPost]
    public async Task<IActionResult>
PostAsync([FromBody,Required]CreateItem newItem)
    {
        if (!ModelState.IsValid)
        {
            return BadRequest(ModelState);
        }
        var item = await _wishList.AddOrRefreshAsync(newItem.
Name);
        return Created("/", item);
    }


    public class CreateItem
    {
        [Required]
        public string Name { get; set; }
    }
}
```

The controller primarily delegates the logic to the injected IWishList implementation. It also validates the POST model, defined as a nested class, to keep it simple.

To help us implement the InMemoryWishList class, we started by writing some tests to back our specifications up. Since static members are hard to configure in tests (remember globals?), we borrowed a concept from the ASP.NET Core memory cache and created an ISystemClock interface that abstracts away the static call to DateTimeOffset. UtcNow. This way, we can program the value of UtcNow in our tests to create expired items.

The unit tests file was quite long, so here is the outline:

```csharp
namespace Wishlist
{
    public class InMemoryWishListTest
    {
        // ...
        public class AddOrRefreshAsync : InMemoryWishListTest
        {
```

```
        [Fact]
        public async Task Should_create_new_item() { /* ...
*/ }
        [Fact]
        public async Task Should_increment_Count_of_an_
existing_item() { /* ... */ }
        [Fact]
        public async Task Should_set_the_new_Expiration_
date_of_an_existing_item() { /* ... */ }
        [Fact]
        public async Task Should_set_the_Count
_of_expired_items_to_1() { /* ... */ }
        [Fact]
        public async Task Should_remove_expired_items() {
/* ... */ }
    }
    public class AllAsync : InMemoryWishListTest
    {
        [Fact]
        public async Task Should_return_items_ordered_by_
Count_Descending() { /* ... */ }
        [Fact]
        public async Task Should_not_return_expired_items()
{ /* ... */ }
    }
    // ...
    }
}
```

Let's analyze that code (see the source code on GitHub: `https://net5.link/code`).
We mocked the `ISystemClock` interface and programmed it to obtain the desired
results, based on each test case. We also programmed some helper methods to make
the tests easier to read. Those helpers use tuples to return multiple values; see the *Tuples*
(C# 7+) section for more information about tuples.

Now that we have those failing tests, we can start implementing `InMemoryWishList`. Here is the outline of the implementation that makes all tests pass:

```
public class InMemoryWishList : IWishList
{
    private readonly InMemoryWishListOptions _options;
    private readonly Dictionary<string, InternalItem> _items;

    public InMemoryWishList(InMemoryWishListOptions options)
    {
        _options = options ?? throw new
ArgumentNullException(nameof(options));
        _items = new Dictionary<string, InternalItem>();
    }
    public Task<WishListItem> AddOrRefreshAsync(string
itemName)
    {
        // ...
    }
    public Task<IEnumerable<WishListItem>> AllAsync()
    {
        // ...
    }
    private class InternalItem
    {
        public int Count { get; set; }
        public DateTimeOffset Expiration { get; set; }
    }
}
```

> **Note**
>
> Please consult the full code in GitHub for the two omitted methods as they are quite long: `https://net5.link/code`.

The `InMemoryWishList` uses a `Dictionary<string, InternalItem>` internally to store the items. The `AllAsync` method filters out expired items while the `AddOrRefreshAsync` method removes expired items. The implementation is not thread-safe, and multiple simultaneous `AddOrRefreshAsync` calls could yield false results.

The code is not necessarily the most elegant of all code, so we could use our tests to refactor it.

Exercise

I invite you to refactor the two methods of the `InMemoryWishList` class; you have tests to help you out. I took a few minutes to refactor it myself and saved it as `InMemoryWishListRefactored`. You can also uncomment the first line of `InMemoryWishListTest.cs` to test that class instead of the main one. My refactoring is just a way to make the code cleaner; I left it there to give you ideas. It is not the only way, nor the best way to write that class (the "best way" being subjective). It is not thread-safe either.

Back to Dependency Injection, the line that makes the wishlist shared between users is in the composition root. Yes, only the highlighted line makes all the difference between creating multiple instances and a single shared instance:

```
public void ConfigureServices(IServiceCollection services)
{
    services
        .ConfigureOptions<InMemoryWishListOptions>()
        .AddTransient<IValidateOptions
<InMemoryWishListOptions>, InMemoryWishListOptions>()
        .AddSingleton(serviceProvider => serviceProvider.
GetRequiredService<IOptions <InMemoryWishListOptions>>().Value)
        ;

    services.AddSingleton<IWishList, InMemoryWishList>();
    services.AddControllers();
}
```

By setting the lifetime to singleton, you can open multiple browsers and share the wishlist. To POST to the API, I recommend using Postman or any other tool you like that is more suited than a browser. From a console, you can use `curl` or `Invoke-WebRequest` depending on your OS. There are instructions in the GitHub repository and a link to a Postman collection that contains the HTTP requests to test the Wishlist API.

That's it! All of that code to demo what a single line can do, and we have a working program, as tiny as it is.

We cover the Options pattern in more depth in the next chapter if you were wondering where `IConfigureOptions`, `IValidateOptions`, and `IOptions` came from.

Next, we'll explore tuples, in case you are not familiar with that C# feature.

Tuples (C# 7+)

A tuple is a type that allows returning multiple values from a method or stores multiple values in a variable without declaring a type and without using the `dynamic` type. Since C# 7, the tuples support has greatly improved.

> **Note**
>
> Using `dynamic` objects is okay in some cases, but beware that it could reduce performance and increase the number of runtime exceptions thrown due to the lack of type. Compile-time errors can be fixed right away, without the need to wait for them to arise during runtime, or worse, be reported by a user. Moreover, `dynamic` objects bring limited tooling support, making it harder to discover what an object can do, and it is more error-prone (there is no type to get auto-completion from).

The C# language adds syntactic sugar regarding tuples that makes the code clearer and easier to read. Microsoft calls that **lightweight syntax**.

If you've used the `Tuple` type before, you know that `Tuple` members are accessed through `Item1`, `Item2`, and `ItemN` fields. This newer syntax allows us to eliminate those fields from our codebase and replace them with user-defined names. If you've never heard of tuples, we'll explore them right away.

Let's jump right into a few samples, coded as xUnit tests. The first shows how we can create an unnamed tuple and access its fields using `Item1`, `Item2`, and `ItemN`, which we talked about earlier:

```
[Fact]
public void Unnamed()
{
    var unnamed = ("some", "value", 322);
    Assert.Equal("some", unnamed.Item1);
    Assert.Equal("value", unnamed.Item2);
```

```
        Assert.Equal(322, unnamed.Item3);
}
```

Then, we can create a named tuple – very useful when you don't like those 1, 2, 3 fields:

```
[Fact]
public void Named()
{
        var named = (name: "Foo", age: 23);
        Assert.Equal("Foo", named.name);
        Assert.Equal(23, named.age);
}
```

Since the compiler does most of that naming, and even if IntelliSense is not showing it to you, we can still access those 1, 2, 3 fields:

```
[Fact]
public void Named_equals_Unnamed()
{
        var named = (name: "Foo", age: 23);
        Assert.Equal(named.name, named.Item1);
        Assert.Equal(named.age, named.Item2);
}
```

Moreover, we can create a named tuple using variables where names follow "magically":

```
[Fact]
public void ProjectionInitializers()
{
        var name = "Foo";
        var age = 23;
        var projected = (name, age);
        Assert.Equal("Foo", projected.name);
        Assert.Equal(23, projected.age);
}
```

Since the values are stored in those 1, 2, 3 fields, and the programmer-friendly names are compiler-generated, equality is based on field order, not field name. Partly due to that, comparing whether two tuples are equal is pretty straightforward:

```
[Fact]
public void TuplesEquality()
{
    var named1 = (name: "Foo", age: 23);
    var named2 = (name: "Foo", age: 23);
    var namedDifferently = (Whatever: "Foo", bar: 23);
    var unnamed1 = ("Foo", 23);
    var unnamed2 = ("Foo", 23);

    Assert.Equal(named1, unnamed1);
    Assert.Equal(named1, named2);
    Assert.Equal(unnamed1, unnamed2);
    Assert.Equal(named1, namedDifferently);
}
```

If you don't like to access the tuple's members using the . notation, we can also deconstruct them into variables:

```
[Fact]
public void Deconstruction()
{
    var tuple = (name: "Foo", age: 23);
    var (name, age) = tuple;
    Assert.Equal("Foo", name);
    Assert.Equal(23, age);
}
```

Methods can also return tuples, and can be used the same way that we saw in previous examples:

```
[Fact]
public void MethodReturnValue()
{
    var tuple1 = CreateTuple1();
    var tuple2 = CreateTuple2();
```

```
        Assert.Equal(tuple1, tuple2);

    static (string name, int age) CreateTuple1()
    {
        return (name: "Foo", age: 23);
    }

    static (string name, int age) CreateTuple2()
        => (name: "Foo", age: 23);
}
```

The methods are inline, but the same applies to normal methods as well.

To conclude this interlude on tuples, I suggest avoiding them on public APIs that are exported (a shared library, for example). However, they can come in handy internally to code helpers without creating a class that holds only data and is used once or a few times.

I think that tuples are a great addition to .NET, but I prefer fully-defined types on public APIs for many reasons. The first reason is encapsulation; tuple's members are fields, which breaks encapsulation. Then, accurately naming classes that are part of an API (contract/interface) is essential.

> **Tip**
> When you can't find an exhaustive name for a type, the chances are that some business requirements are blurry, what is under development is not exactly what is needed, or the domain language is not clear. Sometimes, your imagination is simply failing you though, but this one is okay – it happens.

Next, we'll explore the Service Locator anti-pattern/code smell.

Understanding the Service Locator pattern

Service Locator is an anti-pattern that reverts the IoC principle to its **Control Freak** roots. The only difference is the use of the IoC container to build the dependency tree instead of the new keyword.

There is some use of this pattern in ASP.NET, and some may argue that there are some reasons for one to use the Service Locator pattern, but it should happen very rarely or never. For that reason, in this book, let's call Service Locator a **code smell** instead of an **anti-pattern**.

The Service Locator pattern is used internally by the DI container to find dependencies, which is the correct way of using it. In your applications, you want to avoid injecting an `IServiceProvider` to get the dependencies you need from it, which revert to the classic flow of control.

My strong recommendation is *don't use Service Locator* unless you know what you are doing and have no other option.

A good use of Service Locator could be to migrate a legacy system that is too big to rewrite. So you could build the new code using DI and update the legacy code using the Service Locator pattern, allowing both systems to live together or migrate one into the other, depending on your goal.

Project: ServiceLocator

The best way to avoid something is to know about it, so let's see how to implement the Service Locator pattern using the `IServiceProvider` to find a dependency:

```csharp
public class MyController : ControllerBase
{
    private readonly IServiceProvider _serviceProvider;
    public MyController(IServiceProvider serviceProvider)
    {
        _serviceProvider = serviceProvider ?? throw new
ArgumentNullException(nameof(serviceProvider));
    }

    [Route("/")]
    public IActionResult Get()
    {
        var myService = _serviceProvider.
GetService<IMyService>();
        myService.Execute();
        return Ok("Success!");
    }
}
```

In the code sample, instead of injecting `IMyService` into the constructor, we are injecting `IServiceProvider`. Then, we use it to find `IMyService` in the `Get()` method. Doing so moves the responsibility of creating the object from the container to the class (`MyController`, in this case). `MyController` should not be aware of the `IServiceProvider` and should let the container do its job without interference.

What could go wrong? Let's implement `IDisposable` from `IMyService`, and let's add a `using` statement in the `Get()` method. That shows what kind of problem could arise from controlling a dependency's life outside of the container.

`MyServiceImplementation` looks like this, simulating the use of some external, disposable dependencies:

```
public class MyServiceImplementation : IMyService
{
    public bool IsDisposed { get; private set; }
    public void Dispose() => IsDisposed = true;

    public void Execute()
    {
        if (IsDisposed)
        {
            throw new NullReferenceException("Some dependencies
has been disposed.");
        }
    }
}
```

Then, by updating `MyController` to dispose of `IMyService`, we created some instability:

```
[Route("/")]
public IActionResult Get()
{
    using (var myService = _serviceProvider.
GetService<IMyService>())
    {
        myService.Execute();
        return Ok("Success!");
```

```
        }
    }
```

If we run the application and navigate to /, everything works as expected. If we reload the page, we get an error, thrown by `Execute()`, because we called `Dispose()` in the previous call. `MyController` should not control its injected dependencies, which is the point that I am trying to emphasize here: leave the container to control the lifetime of dependencies rather than trying to be a control freak. Using the Service Locator pattern opens pathways toward those wrong behaviors, which will most likely cause more harm than good in the long run.

Moreover, even though the ASP.NET Core 5 container does not natively support this, we lose the ability to inject dependencies contextually when using Service Locator because the consumer controls its dependencies. What do I mean by contextually? One could inject instance A into a class, but instance B into another class.

Project: ServiceLocatorFixed

To fix our controller, we need to navigate away from Service Locator and inject our dependencies instead. In the sample, we tackle the following:

- Method injection
- Constructor injection

Implementing method injection

Let's start by using *method injection* to demonstrate its use:

```
public class MethodInjectionController : ControllerBase
{
    [Route("/method-injection")]
    public IActionResult GetUsingMethodInjection([FromServices]
IMyService myService)
    {
        if (myService == null) { throw new
ArgumentNullException(nameof(myService)); }
        myService.Execute();
        return Ok("Success!");
    }
}
```

Let's analyze the code:

- The `FromServicesAttribute` class tells the model binder about method injection. We can inject zero or more services in any action by decorating its parameters with `[FromServices]`.

- We added a guard clause to protect us from `null`s.

- Finally, we kept the original code.

> **Note**
> Method injection like this would be of good use for a controller with multiple actions but that uses `IMyService` in only one of them.

Implementing constructor injection

Let's continue by implementing the same solution using constructor injection. Our new controller looks like this:

```
public class ConstructorInjectionController : ControllerBase
{
    private readonly IMyService _myService;
    public ConstructorInjectionController(IMyService myService)
    {
        _myService = myService ?? throw new
ArgumentNullException(nameof(myService));
    }

    [Route("/constructor-injection")]
    public IActionResult GetUsingConstructorInjection()
    {
        _myService.Execute();
        return Ok("Success!");
    }
}
```

When using constructor injection, we enforce that `IMyService` is not null, upon class instantiation. Since it is a class member, it is less tempting to call its `Dispose()` method in an action, leaving that responsibility to the container (as it should be).

Both techniques are an acceptable replacement for the Service Locator anti-pattern. Let's analyze the code:

- We implemented the strategy pattern.
- We used constructor injection.
- We added a guard clause.
- We simplified the action back to what it should do, to a bare minimum, the original code.

Conclusion

Most of the time, by following the Service Locator anti-pattern, we only hide that we are taking control of objects, instead of decoupling our components. The last example demonstrated a problem when disposing of an object, which could happen using constructor injection. However, when thinking about it, it is more tempting to dispose of an object that we created than one that is injected.

Moreover, the service locator takes control away from the container and moves it into the consumer, going against the OCP. One should be able to update the consumer by updating the composition root's bindings. In this case, we could change the binding, and it would work. In a more advanced case, when requiring contextual injection, we would have a hard time binding two implementations to the same interface, one for each context; it could even be impossible.

This anti-pattern also complicates testing; when unit testing your class, you need to mock a container that returns a mocked service, instead of mocking only the service.

One place where I can see its usage justified is in the composition root, as bindings are defined there, and sometimes, especially using the built-in container, we can't avoid it. Another place would be a library that adds functionalities to the container. Other than that, try to stay away!

> **Beware**
> Moving the service locator elsewhere does not make it disappear; it only moves it around, like any dependency.

Revisiting the Factory pattern

In the Strategy pattern example, we implemented a solution that instantiated a `HomePageViewModel` using the `new` keyword. While doing that is acceptable, we could use method injection instead, mixed with the use of a factory. The Factory patterns are handy tools when the time comes to construct objects. Let's take a look at a few rewrites using factories to explore some possibilities.

Factory mixed with method injection

Our first option would be to inject the view model directly into our method instead of injecting `IHomeService`. To achieve this, let's rewrite the `HomeController` class like this:

```csharp
public class HomeController : Controller
{
    public IActionResult Index([FromServices]HomePageViewModel viewModel)
    {
        return View(viewModel);
    }
    // Omitted Privacy() and Error()
}
```

The `FromServicesAttribute` class tells the ASP.NET Core pipeline to inject an instance of `HomePageViewModel` directly into the method.

Now that we've coded the consumer, we need to tell the container how to feed us that view model. To do so, we use a factory instead of a static binding, like this:

```csharp
public void ConfigureServices(IServiceCollection services)
{
    services.AddSingleton<IHomeService, HomeService>();
    services.AddTransient(serviceProvider => {
        var homeService = serviceProvider.GetService<IHomeService>();
        var data = homeService.GetHomePageData();
        return new HomePageViewModel(data);
    });
}
```

In the preceding code, we used another overload of the `AddTransient()` extension method and passed a `Func<IServiceProvider, TService>` `implementationFactory` as an argument. The highlighted code represents our factory. That factory is implemented as a service locator using the `IServiceProvider` instance to create the `IHomeService` dependency that we use to instantiate the `HomePageViewModel`.

We are using the `new` keyword here, but is this wrong? The composition root is where elements should be created (or configured), so instantiating objects there is okay, as it is to use the Service Locator pattern. However, you should aim to avoid it whenever possible. It is harder to avoid when using the default container versus a full-featured third-party one, but we can avoid it in many cases.

We could also create a factory class to keep our composition root clean (see the *HomeViewModelFactory* code sample). While that is true, we would only move the code around, adding complexity to our program. That is the reason why creating view models inside your controller's actions is acceptable to reduce unneeded complexity.

Moreover, in most cases, creating view models inside actions should not negatively impact the program's maintainability since a view model is bound to a single view, controlled by a single action, leading to a one-on-one relationship.

Lastly, it is way cheaper to implement. It is also way easier to understand than roaming around the code to find what binding does what.

The biggest downsize is testability; it is easier to inject the data we want from a test case than dealing with hardcoded object creation.

The use of a factory can be considered for multiple scenarios, so we cover that in the following example, killing two birds with one stone. So far, we've seen the following:

- We can create a factory in the composition root that manages the creation of dependencies (a `Func<IServiceProvider, TService>`).

- An example of method injection.

- That sometimes, the `new` keyword should be used instead of trying to implement more complex code that would, in the end, only move the problem around, leading to false decoupling with added complexity.

HomeViewModelFactory

For more complex scenarios, or to clean the `Startup` class, we could create a class to handle the factory logic. We could also create a class and an interface to directly use the factory inside our other classes. This approach comes in handy to create your dependencies only when you need them; this is also known as lazy loading. Lazy loading means to create the object only when needed, deferring the overhead of doing so at the time of use (or during its first use).

> **Note**
>
> There is an existing `Lazy<T>` class to help with lazy loading, but that is not the point of this code sample. The idea is the same though: we create the object only when first needed.

Unless you need to reuse that creation logic in multiple places, creating a factory class may not be worth it. Nevertheless, this is a very handy pattern worth remembering. Here is how to implement a factory that returns an instance of `PrivacyViewModel`:

```
public interface IHomeViewModelFactory
{
    PrivacyViewModel CreatePrivacyViewModel();
}


public class HomeViewModelFactory : IHomeViewModelFactory
{
    public PrivacyViewModel CreatePrivacyViewModel() => new
PrivacyViewModel
    {
        Title = "Privacy Policy (from
        IHomeViewModelFactory)",
        Content = new HtmlString("<p>Use this page to detail
your site's privacy policy.</p>")
    };
}
```

The preceding code encapsulates the creation of `PrivacyViewModel` instances into `HomeViewModelFactory`. The code is very basic, it creates an instance of the `PrivacyViewModel` class and fills its propeties with hardcoded values.

Now to use that new factory, we need to update the controller. To do so, we use constructor injection to inject `IHomeViewModelFactory` into `HomeController`, then use it from the `Privacy()` action method, like this:

```
private readonly IHomeViewModelFactory _homeViewModelFactory;
public HomeController(IHomeViewModelFactory
homeViewModelFactory)
{
    _homeViewModelFactory = homeViewModelFactory ?? throw new
ArgumentNullException(nameof(homeViewModelFactory));
}
// ...
public IActionResult Privacy()
{
    var viewModel = _homeViewModelFactory.
CreatePrivacyViewModel();
    return View(viewModel);
}
```

The preceding code is clear, simple, and easy to test.

By using this technique, we are not limited to one method. We can write multiple methods, that each encapsulate its own creational logic, in the same factory. We could also pass additional objects to the `Create[object to create]()` method, like this:

```
public HomePageViewModel
CreateHomePageViewModel(IEnumerable<string> someData)
{
    return new HomePageViewModel(someData);
}
```

The possibilities are almost endless when you think about it, so now that you've seen a few in action, you may find other uses for a factory when you need to inject some classes with complex instantiation logic into other objects.

You can also inject dependencies into your factory and use them for that complex instantiation logic.

Just keep in mind that *moving code around your codebase does not make that code, logic, dependencies, or coupling disappear.*

As a rule of thumb, creating view models in controller actions is acceptable. Classes that contain logic are the ones we want to inject and break tight coupling with.

Summary

This chapter covered the basics of **Dependency Injection** and how to leverage it to follow the **Dependency Inversion Principle** helped by the **Inversion of Control** principle.

We then revisited the **Strategy** design pattern, and we saw how to use it to create a flexible, DI-ready system. We also revisited the **Singleton** pattern, seeing that we can inject the same instance, system-wide, by using the singleton lifetime when configuring dependencies in the container. We finally saw how to leverage factories to handle complex object creation logic.

We also talked about moving code around, the illusion of improvement, and the cost of engineering. We saw that the new keyword could help reduce complexity when the construction logic is simple enough and that it could save time and money.

On the other hand, we also explored a few techniques to handle object creation complexity to create maintainable and testable programs, such as factories, and get away from the **Control Freak** code smell.

In between those important subjects, we also visited the **guard clause** to guard our injected dependencies against null. This way, we can demand some required services using constructor injection and use them from the class methods without testing for null every time.

We explored how the **Service Locator** (anti-)pattern can be harmful and how it can be leveraged from the composition root to dynamically create complex objects. We also discussed why to keep its usage frequency as close to never as possible.

Understanding these patterns and code smells is very important to keep your systems maintainable as your programs grow in size.

Additionally, we explored a few newer elements of the C# language, such as tuples, default literal expressions, and throw expressions.

For programs that require complex DI logic, conditional injection, multiple-scopes, auto-implemented factories, and other advanced features, we saw that it is possible to use third-party containers instead of the built-in one.

In subsequent sections, we will explore tools that add functionality to the default container, reducing the need to swap it for another. If you are building multiple smaller projects (microservices) instead of a big one (a monolith), that may save you from requiring those extra features, but nothing is free, and everything has a cost; more on this in *Chapter 16, Introduction to Microservices Architecture*.

In the next chapter, we explore options and logging patterns. These ASP.NET Core patterns aim to ease our lives when managing such common problems.

Questions

Let's take a look at a few practice questions:

1. What are the three Dependency Injection lifetimes that we can assign to objects in ASP.NET Core?

2. What is the composition root for?

3. Is it true that we should avoid the `new` keyword when instantiating volatile dependencies?

4. What is the pattern that we revisited in this chapter that helps compose objects to eliminate inheritance?

5. Is the Service Locator pattern a design pattern, a code smell, or an anti-pattern?

Further reading

Here are some links to build upon what we learned in the chapter:

- Startup environment-specific composition root: `https://net5.link/GdjP`

- If you need more options, such as contextual injection, you can check out an open source library that I built. It adds support for new scenarios: `https://net5.link/S3aT`

8
Options and Logging Patterns

In this chapter, we will cover .NET-specific patterns, such as the Options pattern, and logging. We will explore these abstractions while keeping it to a level where we use them, not master every aspect of them. Once you've read this chapter, you should know how to leverage the .NET 5 options and settings infrastructure, as well as how to write application logs. We will also briefly explore how to customize those systems.

The following topics will be covered in this chapter:

- An overview of the Options pattern
- Getting familiar with .NET logging abstractions

Let's get started!

An overview of the Options pattern

In ASP.NET 5, we can use predefined mechanisms to enhance the usage of application settings. These allow us to divide our configuration into multiple smaller objects, configure them during multiple stages of the startup flow, validate them, and even watch for runtime changes with minimal effort.

The Options pattern's goal is to use settings at runtime, allowing changes to the application to happen without changes being made to the code. The settings could be as simple as a `string`, a `bool`, a database connection string, or a complex object that holds an entire subsystem's configuration.

This section explores different tools offered by ASP.NET Core to manage, inject, and load configurations and options into our programs. We will tackle different scenarios, from common ones to more advanced ones.

Getting started

The **Options pattern** in ASP.NET Core 5 allows us to load settings from multiple sources seamlessly. We can customize these sources when creating `IHostBuilder`, or even use the default ones that are set by calling `Host.CreateDefaultBuilder(args)`. The default sources, in order, are as follows:

1. `appsettings.json`.
2. `appsettings.{Environment}.json`.
3. User secrets; these are only loaded when the environment is `Development`.
4. Environment variables.
5. Command-line arguments.

The order is also very important as the last to be loaded overrides any previous values. For example, you can set a value in `appsettings.json` and override it in `appsettings.Staging.json` by redefining the value in that file, user secrets, or an environment variable or by passing it as a command-line argument when you run your application.

There are four main ways to use settings: `IOptionsMonitor<TOptions>`, `IOptionsFactory<TOptions>`, `IOptionsSnapshot<TOptions>`, and `IOptions<TOptions>`. In all these cases, we can inject that dependency into a class to use the available settings. `TOptions` is the type that represents the settings that we want to access.

As mentioned in the following three notes, the framework often returns an empty instance of your options class if you don't configure it. We will learn how to configure options properly in the next subsection, but keep in mind that using property initializers inside your options class can also be a great way to ensure certain defaults are used. Don't use initializers for default values that change based on the environment (dev, staging, or production) or for secrets such as connection strings and passwords. You can also use constants to centralize those defaults somewhere in your codebase (making them easier to maintain). Nevertheless, proper configuration and validation is always preferred, but both combined can add a safety net.

Based on the `MyListOption` class, because the default value of an `int` is 0, the default number of items to display per page would be 0, leading to an empty list. However, we can configure this using a property initializer, as shown in the example below:

```
public class MyListOption
{
    public int ItemsPerPage { get; set; } = 20;
}
```

The default number of items to display per page is now 20.

> **Note**
>
> In the source code for *Chapter 8, Options and Logging Patterns*, I've included a few tests in the `CommonScenarios.Tests` project that assert the lifetime of the different options interfaces. I haven't included this code here for brevity, but it describes the different options' behaviors via unit tests. See `https://net5.link/T8Ro` for more information.

Next, we explore the different interfaces provided by .NET 5.

IOptionsMonitor<TOptions>

This interface is the most versatile of them all. It allows us to receive notifications about reloading the configuration. It also supports caching and can have multiple configurations, each associated with a name (named configuration). The injected `IOptionsMonitor<TOptions>` instance is always the same (**singleton lifetime**). It also supports default settings (without a name) through its `Value` property.

> **Note**
>
> You receive an empty `TOptions` instance (`new TOptions()`) if you only configured named options or configured no instance at all.

IOptionsFactory<TOptions>

This interface is a factory, as we saw in *Chapter 6, Understanding the Strategy, Abstract Factory, and Singleton Design Patterns* and *Chapter 7, Deep Dive Into Dependency Injection*. We use factories to create instances; this one is no different. Unless it's absolutely necessary, I'd suggest sticking with `IOptionsMonitor<TOptions>` or `IOptionsSnapshot<TOptions>` instead.

One use of this factory could be to create multiple instances of settings while injecting only one dependency, but that sounds more like a design flaw than a solution to me. Nevertheless, this could be useful in some rare situations. Why a flaw? You revert to controlling your dependencies instead of doing IoC.

How it works is simple: a new factory is created every time you ask for one (**transient lifetime**), and each factory creates a new options instance every time you call its `Create(name)` method (**transient lifetime**).

> **Note**
>
> You receive an empty `TOptions` instance (`new TOptions()`) if you only configured the named options or configured no instance at all when calling `factory.Create(Options.DefaultName)`.
>
> `Options.DefaultName` is the name that's given to non-named options; this is usually handled for you by the framework.

IOptionsSnapshot<TOptions>

This interface is useful when you need a snapshot of the settings, and is created once per request (**scoped lifetime**). We can use it to get named options as well, such as `IOptionsMonitor<TOptions>`. We can access the default options with the `CurrentValue` property.

> **Note**
>
> You receive an empty `TOptions` instance (`new TOptions()`) if you only configured the named options or configured no instance at all.

IOptions<TOptions>

This interface is the first that was added to ASP.NET Core. It does not support advanced scenarios such as what snapshots and monitors do. Whenever you request an `IOptions<TOptions>`, you get the same instance (**singleton lifetime**).

> **Note**
>
> `IOptions<TOptions>` does not support named options, so you can only access the default options.

Project – CommonScenarios

This first example covers multiple basic use cases, such as injecting options, using named options, and storing options values in settings.

Common usage

In this first use case, we will learn how to use `IOptions<TOptions>`. We will also define the common ground for multiple other scenarios. Let's go over what we will do, step by step:

1. Create an interface for our services, named `IMyNameService`.

2. Create options classes.

3. Code some unit tests against that interface. We will reuse these tests for each implementation.

4. Code our first implementation.

5. Run our tests against it.

Our interface is very simple and looks like this:

```
public interface IMyNameService
{
    string GetName(bool someCondition);
}
```

It contains a single `GetName` method that takes `someCondition` as a parameter and returns a string, from which we can expect its content to be a name.

Next, we create two options classes: one for this scenario and one for the others. The class that we will use in the other scenarios is as follows:

```
public class MyOptions
{
    public string Name { get; set; }
}
```

The class that we will use in this scenario is as follows:

```
public class MyDoubleNameOptions
{
    public string FirstName { get; set; }
```

```
    public string SecondName { get; set; }
}
```

> **Note**
>
> I have shown both classes here to save space later, so that I don't have to copy the same tests again while only making a small change. Moreover, they are small and straightforward classes.

Now, as practitioners of TDD, let's see the unit tests that act as our initial code consumers. Our simple specifications are that when `someCondition` is `true`, `GetName` returns the value of `Option1Name`, but when `someCondition` is `false`, `GetName` returns the value of `Option2Name`.

> **Note**
>
> `Option1Name` and `Option2Name` are two constants containing irrelevant values (but different ones so that we can compare their output).

Let's begin with our unit test:

```
public abstract class MyNameServiceTest<TMyNameService>
    where TMyNameService : class, IMyNameService
{
    protected readonly IMyNameService _sut;

    public const string Option1Name = "Options 1";
    public const string Option2Name = "Options 2";

    public MyNameServiceTest()
    {
        var services = new ServiceCollection();
        services.AddTransient<IMyNameService,
TMyNameService>();
        services.Configure<MyOptions>("Options1", myOptions =>
        {
            myOptions.Name = Option1Name;
        });
        services.Configure<MyOptions>("Options2", myOptions =>
        {
```

```
            myOptions.Name = Option2Name;
    });
    services.Configure<MyDoubleNameOptions>(options =>
    {
        options.FirstName = Option1Name;
        options.SecondName = Option2Name;
    });
    _sut = services.BuildServiceProvider()
        .GetRequiredService<IMyNameService>();
}
```

Let's analyze the first part of our test class:

- Our test class is abstract and generic, making it the base class of all
  IMyNameService tests.

- We created our subject under test by using the generic TMyNameService type
  as our implementation.

- We configured two named MyOptions and one MyDoubleNameOptions. These
  are injected into the service's implementations; more on that later. In this case, we
  have configured the options' properties manually. In programs, we usually move
  those values to configuration files or other providers, such as appsettings.json;
  more on that later.

> **Note**
>
> The name of each option is passed as an argument to the services.
> Configure<MyOptions>("name", ...) method.

Then, we need to create the two test cases we discussed earlier:

```
[Fact]
public void GetName_should_return_Name_from_options1_when_
someCondition_is_true()
{
    var result = _sut.GetName(true);
    Assert.Equal(Option1Name, result);
}


[Fact]
```

```
    public void GetName_should_return_Name_from_options2_when_
someCondition_is_false()
    {
        var result = _sut.GetName(false);
        Assert.Equal(Option2Name, result);
    }
}
```

Now, let's create our implementation, named
MyNameServiceUsingDoubleNameOptions. It uses the
IOptions<MyDoubleNameOptions> interface, which make it the simplest
implementation we can use:

```
public class MyNameServiceUsingDoubleNameOptions :
IMyNameService
{
    private readonly MyDoubleNameOptions _options;

    public MyNameServiceUsingDoubleNameOptions
(IOptions<MyDoubleNameOptions> options)
    {
        _options = options.Value;
    }

    public string GetName(bool someCondition)
    {
        return someCondition ? _options.FirstName : _options.
SecondName;
    }
}
```

This is a fairly simple implementation; we inject IOptions<MyDoubleNameOptions>
into the constructor and use the tertiary operator to return the first or
second name from the options. Now that we have our reusable tests and the
MyNameServiceUsingDoubleNameOptions class, we can add the concrete test
class, which runs the actual tests against our implementation:

```
public class MyNameServiceUsingDoubleNameOptionsTest :
MyNameServiceTest<MyNameServiceUsingDoubleNameOptions> { }
```

Yes, that's it; all of the plumbing has been done in the base test. If we run our tests, everything should be green!

Named options

Using the options pattern, we can register multiple instances of the same type and access them by name.

> **Note**
>
> Doing this breaks the inversion of control, dependency inversion, and open/closed principles by giving back the dependencies' creation control to the consuming class instead of moving that responsibility out of it, up to the composition root.
>
> Since the .NET teams deemed it appropriate to implement named options, we are going to cover it here. We could use this pattern to build a dynamic application without compromising any principles by dynamically accessing the name of the options to create, instead of hardcoding magic string inside constructors. This could use a database or some other settings, for example.
>
> The feature is not wrong in itself, but problems could arise based on its usage.

For this example, we are going to create three different implementations: one using `IOptionsFactory<MyOptions>`, one using `IOptionsMonitor<MyOptions>`, and one using `IOptionsSnapshot<MyOptions>`. All three use the test suite we created in the previous sample. Let's take a look at the code:

```
public class MyNameServiceUsingNamedOptionsFactory :
IMyNameService
{
    private readonly MyOptions _options1;
    private readonly MyOptions _options2;

    public MyNameServiceUsingNamedOptionsFactory
(IOptionsFactory<MyOptions> myOptions)
    {
        _options1 = myOptions.Create("Options1");
        _options2 = myOptions.Create("Options2");
    }

    public string GetName(bool someCondition)
```

```
    {
        return someCondition ? _options1.Name : _options2.Name;
    }
}

public class MyNameServiceUsingNamedOptionsMonitor :
IMyNameService
{
    private readonly MyOptions _options1;
    private readonly MyOptions _options2;

    public MyNameServiceUsingNamedOptionsMonitor
(IOptionsMonitor<MyOptions> myOptions)
    {
        _options1 = myOptions.Get("Options1");
        _options2 = myOptions.Get("Options2");
    }

    public string GetName(bool someCondition)
    {
        return someCondition ? _options1.Name : _options2.Name;
    }
}

public class MyNameServiceUsingNamedOptionsSnapshot :
IMyNameService
{
    private readonly MyOptions _options1;
    private readonly MyOptions _options2;

    public MyNameServiceUsingNamedOptionsSnapshot
(IOptionsSnapshot<MyOptions> myOptions)
    {
        _options1 = myOptions.Get("Options1");
        _options2 = myOptions.Get("Options2");
    }
```

```
public string GetName(bool someCondition)
{
    return someCondition ? _options1.Name : _options2.Name;
}
}
```

These three classes are very similar, except for their constructors; each is expecting a different dependency.

> **Note**
>
> My note about magic strings may make more sense now; each class requests a specific set of options using a hardcoded name; that is, a *magic string*. Doing so limits our ability to change the injected options in any single class from the composition root. To make a change, we need to open the class, change the magic strings, save the class, and then recompile. Moreover, strings are not automatically refactored using the tooling, leading to inconsistencies and runtime errors. So, all in all, magic strings are harder to maintain and should be avoided as much as possible.

Next, we need to, create the following three simple classes:

```
public class MyNameServiceUsingNamedOptionsFactoryTest :
MyNameServiceTest<MyNameServiceUsingNamedOptionsFactory> {}

public class MyNameServiceUsingNamedOptionsMonitorTest :
MyNameServiceTest<MyNameServiceUsingNamedOptionsMonitor> {}

public class MyNameServiceUsingNamedOptionsSnapshotTest :
MyNameServiceTest<MyNameServiceUsingNamedOptionsSnapshot> {}
```

Running these tests proves that our three new classes respect our use cases. With that, we have created multiple classes that use named options.

Using settings

Now that we've explored how to manually create options, let's explore how to make that happen in an ASP.NET Core 5 application using `appsettings.json` instead.

The appsettings.json file allows you to define any setting, structured as you want, in the JSON syntax. It is a great improvement from the key/value settings that we had in the web.config file before ASP.NET Core. You can now define complex object hierarchies, which allow for better organization. You also don't need to program complex plumbing code, like you had to do to create custom web.config sections.

Here are our JSON settings:

```
{
  "options1": {
    "name": "Options 1"
  },
  "options2": {
    "name": "Options 2"
  },
  "myDoubleNameOptions": {
    "firstName": "Options 1",
    "secondName": "Options 2"
  }
}
```

The data structures here are the same as our previously defined classes; that is, MyOptions and MyDoubleNameOptions. That's because we are about to load (deserialize) those settings into our classes using the provided options utilities.

In the Startup.ConfigureServices method, we can add the following:

```
services.Configure<MyOptions>(
    "Options1",
    _configuration.GetSection("options1")
);
services.Configure<MyOptions>(
    "Options2",
    _configuration.GetSection("options2")
);
services.Configure<MyDoubleNameOptions>(
    _configuration.GetSection("myDoubleNameOptions")
);
```

We are using two different extension methods here instead of configuring the options manually, as we did previously. The `_configuration` field is of the `IConfiguration` type, which allows us to access to the entire configuration. Calling `_configuration.GetSection("...")` gives us another `IConfiguration` object – more precisely, an `IConfigurationSection` object – where the keys match our settings.

> **Note**
>
> If you need to access a subsection, you can use the `:` sign. For example, with a configuration that looks like `{ "object1": { "object2": {} } }`, you could `GetSection("object1:object2")` to get the nested configuration object directly.

After that, we need to register our services. In this case, we need to use the following code:

```
services.AddTransient<MyNameServiceUsingDoubleNameOptions>();
services.AddTransient<MyNameServiceUsingNamedOptionsFactory>();
services.AddTransient<MyNameServiceUsingNamedOptionsMonitor>();
services.
AddTransient<MyNameServiceUsingNamedOptionsSnapshot>();
```

Then, we can inject any of those dependencies anywhere we want to; for this example, I've decided to go for a simple endpoint using the `MapGet` extension method:

```
endpoints.MapGet("/{serviceName}/{someCondition?}", async
context =>
{
    var serviceName = (string)context.Request.
RouteValues["serviceName"];
    if (bool.TryParse((string)context.Request
.RouteValues["someCondition"], out var someCondition))
    {
        var myNameService = GetMyNameService(serviceName);
        var name = myNameService.GetName(someCondition);

        context.Response.ContentType = "application/json";
        await context.Response.WriteAsync("{");
        await context.Response.WriteAsync("\"name\":");
        await context.Response.WriteAsync($"\"{name}\"");
        await context.Response.WriteAsync("}");
    }
```

```
    IMyNameService GetMyNameService(string serviceName) =>
serviceName
    switch
    {
        "factory" => context.RequestServices
            .GetRequiredService<MyNameServiceUsingNamed
OptionsFactory>(),
        "monitor" => context.RequestServices
            .GetRequiredService<MyNameServiceUsingNamed
OptionsMonitor>(),
        "snapshot" => context.RequestServices
            .GetRequiredService<MyNameServiceUsingNamed
OptionsSnapshot>(),
        "options" => context.RequestServices
            .GetRequiredService<MyNameServiceUsingDoubleName
Options>(),
        _ => throw new NotSupportedException($"The service
named '{serviceName}' is not supported."),
    };
});
```

> **Note**
>
> I also added an endpoint that responds with a list of links when a user calls GET /. I omitted the code as it is not relevant to the example, but it is convenient when running it. If you have a plugin in your browser that formats the JSON string for you, the links should be clickable. I use *JSON Viewer*, an open source project, in both Chrome and Edge on Chromium for this.

That's it! We've loaded options from JSON to our objects using a few lines of code. Feel free to run the code, add breakpoints, and explore how the app behaves.

Project – OptionsConfiguration

Now that we have covered some simple scenarios, let's attack some more advanced possibilities, such as creating types that will help configure, initialize, and validate our options.

Configuring options

We can create types that implement `IConfigureOptions<TOptions>`, then register these implementations as services to dynamically configure our options.

> **Note**
>
> We can implement `IConfigureNamedOptions<TOptions>` for named options as well.

First, let's lay out the groundwork for our little program:

1. The first building block is the options class that we want to configure:

```
public class ConfigureMeOptions
{
    public string Title { get; set; }
    public IEnumerable<string> Lines { get; set; }
}
```

2. Now, let's define our application settings (`appsettings.json`):

```
{
    "configureMe": {
        "title": "Configure Me!",
        "lines": [
            "This comes from appsettings!"
        ]
    }
}
```

3. Next, let's make an endpoint that accesses the settings, serializes the result to a JSON string, and then writes it to the response stream:

```
endpoints.MapGet("/configure-me", async context =>
{
    var options = context.RequestServices
        .GetRequiredService<IOptionsMonitor<ConfigureMe
Options>>();
    var json = JsonSerializer.Serialize(options);
```

```
context.Response.ContentType = "application/json";
await context.Response.WriteAsync(json);
});
```

This endpoint displays the latest options, even if we change the content of appsettings.json without changing the code or restarting the server.

4. Before we can run the program, we need to tell ASP.NET about those settings:

```
services.Configure<ConfigureMeOptions>(_configuration.
GetSection("configureMe"));
```

5. Now, when running the program and navigating to /configure-me, we should see the following:

```
{
    "CurrentValue": {
        "Title": "Configure Me!",
        "Lines": [
            "This comes from appsettings!"
        ]
    }
}
```

CurrentValue is the property name and can be accessed from IOptionsMonitor<TOptions>. Besides that, the rest of the code looks very familiar to the value we configured in the appsettings.json file. The only exception is the casing; we did not configure the serializer, so it used our property's casing (**Pascal case** or **upper camel case**).

6. To take care of this, we can pass an instance of JsonSerializerOptions to the Serialize method, like this:

```
var json = JsonSerializer.Serialize(
    options,
    new JsonSerializerOptions {
        PropertyNamingPolicy = JsonNamingPolicy.CamelCase
    }
);
```

> **Note**
> **Camel case** (also known as **lower camel case**) is a broadly accepted standard for JSON and JavaScript.

IConfigureOptions<TOptions>

Now, let's configure our options in another class. That type will add a line to our options dynamically.

To achieve this, we can create a class that implements the IConfigureOptions<TOptions> interface, like this:

```
public class Configure1ConfigureMeOptions :
IConfigureOptions<ConfigureMeOptions>
{
    public void Configure(ConfigureMeOptions options)
    {
        options.Lines = options.Lines.Append("Added line 1!");
    }
}
```

Now, we must register it with the service collection:

```
services.AddSingleton<IConfigureOptions<ConfigureMeOptions>,
Configure1ConfigureMeOptions>();
```

From there, navigating to /configure-me should output the following:

```
{
  "currentValue": {
    "title": "Configure Me!",
    "lines": [
      "This comes from appsettings!",
      "Added line 1!"
    ]
  }
}
```

And voilà – we have a neat result that took almost no effort. This can lead to so many possibilities! Implementing the `IConfigureOptions<TOptions>` is the best way to configure default values of an options class.

Multiple IConfigureOptions<TOptions>

You probably found the previous example fun, but we're just getting started! We can register many `IConfigureOptions<TOptions>` for the same `TOptions`, and this is as easy as registering a new binding. For our purposes, let's create another class that adds another line to the array since this allows us to follow what is happening in the background:

```
public class Configure2ConfigureMeOptions :
IConfigureOptions<ConfigureMeOptions>
{
    public void Configure(ConfigureMeOptions options)
    {
        options.Lines = options.Lines.Append("Added line 2!");
    }
}
```

Now, we can register it:

```
services.AddSingleton<IConfigureOptions<ConfigureMeOptions>,
Configure2ConfigureMeOptions>();
```

The new output should be as follows:

```
{
  "currentValue": {
    "title": "Configure Me!",
    "lines": [
      "This comes from appsettings!",
      "Added line 1!",
      "Added line 2!"
    ]
  }
}
```

It is important to note that the dependencies that have been registered with
IServiceCollection are ordered, so by swapping the registration of
Configure1ConfigureMeOptions and Configure2ConfigureMeOptions,
we would end up with the following output instead:

```
{
   "currentValue": {
      "title": "Configure Me!",
      "lines": [
         "This comes from appsettings!",
         "Added line 2!",
         "Added line 1!"
      ]
   }
}
```

Great, right?

More configurations

There are other ways to configure options; for instance:

- We can call the Configure extension methods multiple times.

- ConfigureAll allows us to run configuration on all the options of any given
  TOptions. This is primarily used to configure named options, but unnamed
  options are just named options associated with the default name, so in our example,
  this works as well.

- PostConfigure and PostConfigureAll are the equivalents of Configure
  and ConfigureAll, respectively, but they run at the end of the initialization
  process.

By adding the following to the composition root,

```
services.Configure<ConfigureMeOptions>(options =>
{
    options.Lines = options.Lines.Append("Another Configure
call");
});
services.PostConfigure<ConfigureMeOptions>(options =>
{
```

```
        options.Lines = options.Lines.Append("What about
PostConfigure?");
    });
    services.PostConfigureAll<ConfigureMeOptions>(options =>
    {
        options.Lines = options.Lines.Append("Did you forgot about
PostConfigureAll?");
    });
    services.ConfigureAll<ConfigureMeOptions>(options =>
    {
        options.Lines = options.Lines.Append("Or ConfigureAll?");
    });
```

we should end up with the following output:

```
{
  "currentValue": {
    "title": "Configure Me!",
    "lines": [
      "This comes from appsettings!",
      "Added line 1!",
      "Added line 2!",
      "Another Configure call",
      "Or ConfigureAll?",
      "What about PostConfigure?",
      "Did you forgot about PostConfigureAll?"
    ]
  }
}
```

The registration order matters here because, under the hood, the framework is creating instances that implement IConfigureOptions<ConfigureMeOptions> and registers them with the service collection.

The post-configuration is a bit of a rule-breaker as they run after the configure methods, but the order between them also matters. If options configuration is still unclear, please play around with this example. I find experimentation to be one of the best ways to learn and improve.

Project – OptionsValidation

Another feature is to run validation code when a TOptions object is created. This code is guaranteed to run the first time an option is created and does not account for subsequent options modifications. If the lifetime is transient, the validation runs every time you get an options object. If its lifetime is scoped, it runs once per scope (most likely per HTTP request). If its lifetime is singleton, it runs once per application.

To validate our options, we can create validation types that implement the IValidateOptions<TOptions> interface or use data annotations such as [Required].

Data annotations

Let's start by using System.ComponentModel.DataAnnotations types to decorate our options with validation attributes. To demonstrate this, let's look at two small tests:

```csharp
using System.ComponentModel.DataAnnotations;
using Microsoft.Extensions.DependencyInjection;
using Microsoft.Extensions.Options;
using Xunit;

namespace OptionsValidation
{
    public class ValidateOptionsWithDataAnnotations
    {
        [Fact]
        public void Should_pass_validation()
        {
            var services = new ServiceCollection();
            services.AddOptions<Options>()
                .Configure(o => o.MyImportantProperty = "Some important value")
                .ValidateDataAnnotations();
            var serviceProvider = services.BuildServiceProvider();
            var options = serviceProvider.GetService<IOptionsMonitor<Options>>();
            Assert.Equal("Some important value", options.CurrentValue.MyImportantProperty);
        }
```

```
        [Fact]
        public void Should_fail_validation()
        {
            var services = new ServiceCollection();
            services.AddOptions<Options>()
                .ValidateDataAnnotations();
            var serviceProvider = services.
BuildServiceProvider();
            var options = serviceProvider.GetService
<IOptionsMonitor<Options>>();
            var error = Assert.
Throws<OptionsValidationException>(() => options.CurrentValue);
            Assert.Collection(error.Failures,
                f => Assert.Equal("DataAnnotation validation
failed for members: 'MyImportantProperty' with the error: 'The
MyImportantProperty field is required.'.", f)
            );
        }


        private class Options
        {
            [Required]
            public string MyImportantProperty { get; set; }
        }
    }
}
```

From these tests, we can see that setting MyImportantProperty allows us to use
our options object, while not setting it throws an OptionsValidationException,
alerting us of the error.

> **Note**
>
> At the time of writing, eager validation is not possible (failing at startup) but is
> under consideration.
>
> Due to this, validation is run during the first usage of the options'
> value, not when injecting the options. For example, in the case of
> IOptionsMonitor<TOptions>, validation runs when the
> CurrentValue property is being retrieved.

To tell .NET to validate data annotations on options, we must call the
ValidateDataAnnotations extension method, which is available from the
Microsoft.Extensions.Options.DataAnnotations assembly, like this:

```
services.AddOptions<Options>().ValidateDataAnnotations();
```

That's it – .NET does the job for us from there.

Validation types

To implement validation types for options (options validators), we can create a class that
implements one or more IValidateOptions<TOptions> interfaces. One type can
validate multiple options, and multiple types can validate the same options, so the possible
combinations should be covering all possible use cases.

Using a custom class is not harder than using data annotations. However, it allows us to
remove the validation concerns away from the options class itself and code more complex
validation logic. You should pick the way that makes the more sense for your project.

Here is how to do this via code:

```
using Microsoft.Extensions.DependencyInjection;
using Microsoft.Extensions.Options;
using Xunit;

namespace OptionsValidation
{
    public class ValidateOptionsWithTypes
    {
        [Fact]
        public void Should_pass_validation()
        {
            var services = new ServiceCollection();
            services.AddSingleton<IValidateOptions<Options>,
OptionsValidator>();
            services.AddOptions<Options>()
                .Configure(o => o.MyImportantProperty = "Some
important value");

            var serviceProvider = services.
BuildServiceProvider();
```

```
                    var options = serviceProvider.GetService
<IOptionsMonitor<Options>>();
            Assert.Equal("Some important value", options.
CurrentValue.MyImportantProperty);
        }


        [Fact]
        public void Should_fail_validation()
        {
            var services = new ServiceCollection();
            services.AddSingleton<IValidateOptions<Options>,
OptionsValidator>();
            services.AddOptions<Options>();
            var serviceProvider = services.
BuildServiceProvider();
            var options = serviceProvider.GetService
<IOptionsMonitor<Options>>();
            var error = Assert.
Throws<OptionsValidationException>(() => options.CurrentValue);
            Assert.Collection(error.Failures,
                f => Assert.Equal("'MyImportantProperty' is
required.", f)
            );
        }


        private class Options
        {
            public string MyImportantProperty { get; set; }
        }


        private class OptionsValidator :
IValidateOptions<Options>
        {
            public ValidateOptionsResult Validate(string name,
Options options)
            {
                if (string.IsNullOrEmpty(options.
MyImportantProperty))
```

```
                {
                    return ValidateOptionsResult.Fail
("'MyImportantProperty' is required.");
                }
                return ValidateOptionsResult.Success;
            }
        }
    }
}
```

As you can see, this is the same options we used in the previous example, without the data annotation, and both test cases are very similar as well. The difference is that instead of using the [Required] attribute, we created the OptionsValidator class, which contains the validation logic.

OptionsValidator implements IValidateOptions<Options>, which only contains the ValidateOptionsResult Validate(string name, Options options) method. This method allows named and default options to be validated. The name argument represents the options' name. In our case, we implemented the required logic for all options. The ValidateOptionsResult class exposes a few members to help us out, such as the Success and Skip fields, as well as two Fail() methods.

ValidateOptionsResult.Success indicates success. ValidateOptionsResult.Skip indicates that the validator did not validate the options, most likely because it only validates certain named options but not the given one. For failure, we can either fail with a single message or a collection of messages by calling ValidateOptionsResult.Fail(message) or ValidateOptionsResult. Fail(messages).

The next step is to make the validator available in the IoC container. In our case, we could do this using a simple services.AddSingleton<IValidateOptions<Options>, OptionsValidator>() call, but we could also scan one or more assemblies to register all our validators "automagically."

Then, as with the data annotations, when we first use the options, the validation is executed against that instance.

Injecting options directly

My only negative point about the .NET Options pattern is that we need to tie our code to the framework's interfaces, meaning that we need to inject IOptionsMonitor<Options> instead of Options. I'd prefer to inject Options directly, controlling its lifetime from the composition root, instead of letting the class itself control its dependencies. I'm a little *anti-control-freak*, I know.

It just so happens that we can circumvent this easily with a little trick. Here, we need to do two things:

1. Set up the Options pattern, as shown previously in this chapter.

2. Create a dependency binding that tells the container how to inject the options class that we want directly.

The following code does the same thing as our previous examples and uses scopes to demonstrates scoping:

```
using Microsoft.Extensions.DependencyInjection;
using Microsoft.Extensions.Options;
using Xunit;

namespace OptionsValidation
{
    public class ByPassingInterfaces
    {
        [Fact]
        public void Should_support_any_scope()
        {
            var services = new ServiceCollection();
            services.AddOptions<Options>()
                .Configure(o => o.MyImportantProperty = "Some important value");
```

Here, we are registering the Options class, then configuring the default value of MyImportantProperty.

```
            services.AddScoped(serviceProvider =>
                serviceProvider.GetService <IOptionsSnapshot<Options>>().
                Value);
```

In the preceding code block, we registered the `Options` class using a factory method. That way, we can inject the `Options` class directly (with a scoped lifetime). We control the creation and the lifetime from that delegate (highlighted code).

And voilà, we can now inject `Options` directly into our system without the need to tie our classes with any .NET-specific options interface. Next, we test that out:

```
var serviceProvider = services.
BuildServiceProvider();

using var scope1 = serviceProvider.CreateScope();
var options1 = scope1.ServiceProvider.
GetService<Options>();
var options2 = scope1.ServiceProvider.
GetService<Options>();
Assert.Same(options1, options2);
```

The preceding code asserts that the two instances acquired from the same scope are the same.

```
using var scope2 = serviceProvider.CreateScope();
var options3 = scope2.ServiceProvider.
GetService<Options>();
Assert.NotSame(options2, options3);
}
```

The preceding code asserts that the options from two different scopes are not the same.

```
private class Options
{
    public string MyImportantProperty { get; set; }
}
}
}
```

Finally, we have our `Options` class, which allowed us to write those tests. There's nothing special here.

This can also be a good workaround for an existing system that could benefit from the Options pattern without us having to update its code, assuming the system is *DI-ready*. We can also use this trick to compile an assembly that does not depend on `Microsoft.Extensions.Options`.

Conclusion

The Options pattern is a great way to inject options so that we can configure our apps. We saw that we can choose between different options:

- `IOptionsMonitor<TOptions>` or `IOptions<TOptions>` for singleton
- `IOptionsSnapshot<TOptions>` for scoped
- `IOptionsFactory<TOptions>` for transient

We also covered multiple ways to configure and validate our options classes. All in all, these .NET options provide us with very flexible ways to inject options into our systems, and I strongly recommend that you start using them today, if you haven't been using them already. This can help you test your systems, and it also makes it easier to manage the changes of your applications.

Getting familiar with .NET logging abstractions

Another improvement of .NET Core over .NET Framework is its logging abstractions. Instead of relying on third-party libraries, the new, uniform system offers clean interfaces that are backed by a flexible and robust mechanism that helps implement logging into your application. It also supports third-party libraries that are streamlined through that abstraction. Before we look at the implementation in more detail, let's talk about logging.

About logging

Logging is the practice of writing messages into a log and cataloging information for later use. That information can be used to debug errors, trace operations, analyze usage, or any other reason that creative people can come up with. Logging is a cross-cutting concern, meaning it applies to every piece of your application. We will talk about layers in *Chapter 12, Understanding Layering*, but until then, let's just say that a cross-cutting concern affects all layers and cannot be centralized in just one.

A log is made up of log entries. We can view each log entry as an event that happened during the execution of the program. Those events are then written to the log. This log can be a file, a remote system, simply `stdout`, or a combination of multiple destinations.

When creating a log entry, we must also think about the *level* of that log entry. In a way, this level represents the *type of message* or the *level of importance* that we want to log. It can also be used to filter those logs. `Trace`, `Error`, and `Debug` are examples of log entry levels. Those levels are defined in the `Microsoft.Extensions.Logging.LogLevel` enum.

Another important aspect of a log entry is how it is structured. You can log a single string. Everyone on your team could log single strings in their own way. But what happens when someone searches for information? Chaos ensues! There's the stress of not being able to find what that person is looking for, and the displeasure of the log's structure, as experienced by that same person. One way to fix this is by using structured logging. It is simple yet complex; you need to create a structure that every log entry follows. That structure could be more or less complex. It could be serialized into JSON. The important part is that the log entries are structured. We won't get into this subject here, but if you have to decide on a logging strategy, I recommend digging into structured logging first. If you are part of a team, then chances are someone else already did. If that's not the case, you can always bring it up. Continuous improvement is a key aspect of life.

We could write a whole book on logging, best logging practices, structured logging, and distributed logging, but the aim of this chapter is learning how to use .NET logging abstractions.

Writing logs

First, the logging system is provider-based, meaning that you must register one or more `ILoggerProvider` if you want your log entries to go somewhere. By default, when calling `Host.CreateDefaultBuilder(args)`, it registers the *Console*, *Debug*, *EventSource*, and *EventLog* (Windows-only) providers, but this list can be modified. You can add and remove providers if you need to. `CreateDefaultBuilder` also registers the required dependencies for using logging in the application.

Before we look at the code, let's learn how to create log entries, which is the objective behind logging. To create an entry, we can use one of the following interfaces: `ILogger`, `ILogger<T>`, or `ILoggerFactory`. Let's take a look at them in more detail:

- `ILogger` is the base abstraction.

- `ILogger<T>` uses T to automatically creates the logging *category*.

- `ILoggerFactory` allows us to create an `ILogger` with a custom category name. We won't explore this one here.

The following is the more commonly used pattern, which consists of injecting an
`ILogger<T>` interface and storing it in an `ILogger` field before using it, like this:

```
public class Service : IService
{
    private readonly ILogger _logger;
    public Service(ILogger<Service> logger)
    {
        _logger = logger ?? throw new
ArgumentNullException(nameof(logger));
    }

    public void Execute()
    {
        _logger.LogInformation("Service.Execute()");
    }
}
```

In the preceding code, we have the private `ILogger` `_logger` field in the `Service`
class. We inject an `ILogger<Service>` `logger` that we store in that field, then use
that member in the `Execute` method to write an information-level message to the log.

To test this out, I loaded a small library that I created, which provides additional logging
providers for testing purposes:

```
namespace Logging
{
    public class BaseAbstractions
    {
        [Fact]
        public void Should_log_the_Service_Execute_line()
        {
            // Arrange
            var lines = new List<string>();
            var args = new string[0];
            var host = Host.CreateDefaultBuilder(args)
                .ConfigureLogging(loggingBuilder =>
                {
                    loggingBuilder.ClearProviders();
```

```
                    loggingBuilder.AddAssertableLogger(lines);
            })
            .ConfigureServices(services =>
            {
                services.AddSingleton<IService, Service>();
            })
            .Build();
        var service = host.Services.
GetRequiredService<IService>();
```

In the `Arrange` phase of the test, we create some variables, configure `IHost`, and get an instance of `IService` that we want to test (the code for this is after the test case).

In the highlighted code, we removed all providers using the `ClearProviders` method, and then we used the `AddAssertableLogger` extension method from the library that we loaded to add a new provider. We could have just added a new provider if we wanted to, but I wanted to show you how to remove existing providers so that we can start from a clean slate. That's something you might need someday.

> **Note**
>
> The library that I loaded is available on NuGet and is named `ForEvolve.`
> `Testing.Logging`, but this is irrelevant to understanding logging
> abstractions.

Usually, `IHost` is built in the `Program` class and can be customized there. It is also there that you can load a third-party library of your choice. Now that we covered that, let's continue with the test case:

```
        // Act
        service.Execute();


        // Assert
        Assert.Collection(lines,
            line => Assert.Equal("Service.Execute()", line)
        );
    }
```

In the `Act` phase, we call the `Execute` method of our service. This method is supposed to log a line (see the following code). Then, we assert that line was written in the `lines` list (that's what `AssertableLogger` does; that is, it writes to a `List<string>`). Next, we have the other building blocks:

```
public interface IService
{
    void Execute();
}
public class Service : IService
{
    private readonly ILogger _logger;
    public Service(ILogger<Service> logger)
    {
        _logger = logger ?? throw new
ArgumentNullException(nameof(logger));
    }

    public void Execute()
    {
        _logger.LogInformation("Service.Execute()");
    }
}
}
```

The `Service` class is a simple consumer of an `ILogger<Service>` and uses that `ILogger`. You can do the same for any class that you want to add logging support to. Change `Service` by the name of that class.

To wrap this up, this test case allowed us to implement the most commonly used logging pattern in ASP.NET Core 5 and add a custom provider to make sure that we logged the correct information. Since all log entries are not created equal, we will look at **log levels** next.

Log levels

We used the `LogInformation` method to log an information message, but there are other levels as well, shown in the following table:

Level	Method	Description	Production
Trace	LogTrace	This is used to capture detailed information about the program, instrument execution speed, and debugging. You can also log sensitive information when using traces.	Disabled
Debug	LogDebug	This is used to log debugging and development information.	Disabled unless troubleshooting
Information	LogInformation	This is used to track the flow of the application. Normal events that occur in the system are often information-level events, such as the system started, the system stopped, and a user has signed in.	Enabled
Warning	LogWarning	This is used to log abnormal behavior in the application flow that does not cause the program to stop, but that may need to be investigated; for example, handled exceptions, failed network calls, and accessing resources that do not exist.	Enabled
Error	LogError	This is used to log errors in the application flow that do not cause the application to stop. Errors must usually be investigated. Examples include the failure of the current operation and an exception that cannot be handled.	Enabled
Critical	LogCritical	This is used to log errors that require immediate attention and represent a catastrophic state. The program is most likely about to stop, and the integrity of the application might be compromised; for example, a hard drive is full, the server is out of memory, or the database is in a deadlocked state.	Enabled with some alerts that could be configured to trigger automatically

Optimization

In a project that I lead, we benchmarked multiple ways to log simple and complex messages using ASP.NET Core because we wanted to build clear guidelines. We could not come up with a fair conclusion when the messages were logged (too much variance), but we observed a constant when they were not. Based on that conclusion, I recommend logging the `Trace` and `Debug` messages using the following construct instead of interpolation, `string.Format`, or other means. Here is the fastest way to not write log entries:

```
_logger.LogTrace("Some: {variable}", variable);
// Or
_logger.LogTrace("Some: {0}", variable);
```

When the log level is disabled, such as `Trace` in production, you only pay the price of a method call because no processing is done on your log entries. On the other hand, if we use interpolation, the processing is done, so that one argument is passed to the `Log[Level]` method, leading to a higher cost in processing power for each log entry.

Logging providers

To give you an idea of the possible built-in logging providers, here is a list from the official documentation (see *Further reading* section at the end of this chapter):

- Console
- Debug
- EventSource
- EventLog (Windows only)
- ApplicationInsights

The following is a list of third-party logging providers, also from the official documentation:

- elmah.io
- Gelf
- JSNLog
- KissLog.net
- Log4Net
- Loggr

- NLog
- Sentry
- Serilog
- Stackdriver

Now, if you need any of those or if your favorite logging library is part of the preceding list, you know that you can use it. If it is not, maybe it supports ASP.NET Core 5 but was not part of the documentation when I consulted it.

Configuring logging

As with most of ASP.NET Core 5, we can configure logging. The default host that is created when calling `Host.CreateDefaultBuilder(args)` does a lot for us. As we saw earlier, it registers many configuration providers, and it also loads the `Logging` section of the configuration. That section is present, by default, in the `appsettings.json` file. Like all configurations, it is cumulative, so we can redefine part of it in another. If you don't use the default builder, you have to configure logging yourself; please beware of the additional work involved.

I don't want to spend too many pages on this, but it is good to know that you can customize the minimum level of what you are logging. You can also use transformation files (such as `appsettings.Development.json`) to customize those levels per environment. For example, you can define your defaults in `appsettings.json`, then update a few for development purposes in `appsettings.Development.json`, change production settings in `appsettings.Production.json`, then the staging settings in `appsettings.Staging.json`, and add some testing settings in `appsettings.Testing.json`.

Before we move on, let's take a peek at the default settings:

```
{
    "Logging": {
        "LogLevel": {
            "Default": "Information",
            "Microsoft": "Warning",
            "Microsoft.Hosting.Lifetime": "Information"
        }
    }
}
```

We can define default levels (using `Logging:LogLevel:Default`) and a custom level for each category (such as `Logging:LogLevel:Microsoft`). Then, we can filter what we want to log using configuration or code, by provider. In the configuration, we can change the default level of the console provider to `Trace`, like this:

```json
{
  "Logging": {
    "LogLevel": {
      "Default": "Information",
      "Microsoft": "Warning",
      "Microsoft.Hosting.Lifetime": "Information"
    },
    "Console": {
      "LogLevel": {
        "Default": "Trace"
      }
    }
  }
}
```

We kept the same default values but added the `Logging:Console` section (see highlighted code) with a default `LogLevel`. We could have defined more settings here, but that's outside the scope of this book.

Then, we can use one of the `AddFilter` extension methods, as shown in the following experimental test code:

```csharp
[Fact]
public void Should_filter_logs_by_provider()
{
    // Arrange
    var lines = new List<string>();
    var args = new string[0];
    var host = Host.CreateDefaultBuilder(args)
        .ConfigureLogging(loggingBuilder =>
        {
            loggingBuilder.ClearProviders();
            loggingBuilder.AddConsole();
            loggingBuilder.AddAssertableLogger(lines);
```

```
                loggingBuilder.AddxUnitTestOutput(_output);

                loggingBuilder.
AddFilter<XunitTestOutputLoggerProvider>(
                    level => level >= LogLevel.Warning
                );
            })
        .ConfigureServices(services =>
        {
                services.AddSingleton<IService, Service>();
        })
        .Build();
    var service = host.Services.GetRequiredService<IService>();

    // Act
    service.Execute();

    // Assert
    Assert.Collection(lines,
        line => Assert.Equal("[info] Service.Execute()", line),
        line => Assert.Equal("[warning] Service.Execute()",
line)
    );
}

public class Service : IService
{
    //...
    public void Execute()
    {
        _logger.LogInformation("[info] Service.Execute()");
        _logger.LogWarning("[warning] Service.Execute()");
    }
}
```

Here, we added three providers: the console and two test providers – one that logs to a list and another that logs to the xUnit output. Then, we told the system to filter out everything that is not at least a `Warning` from `XunitTestOutputLoggerProvider` (see highlighted code); other providers are unaffected.

You now have two options:

- Code
- Configuration

All of that should be enough to get you started.

Conclusion

Logging is essential, and ASP.NET Core gives us various ways to log independently of third-party libraries while allowing us to use our favorite logging framework. We can customize the way the logs are written and categorized. We can use zero or more logging providers. We can also create custom logging providers. Finally, we can use configurations or code to filter logs and much more.

What you must remember is the most useful pattern for logging:

1. Inject an `ILogger<T>`, where `T` is the type of the class into which the logger is injected. `T` becomes the category.

2. Save a reference of that logger into a `private readonly ILogger` field.

3. Use that logger in your methods to log messages using the appropriate log level.

Summary

.NET Core added many features, such as configuration and logging, that are now part of .NET 5. The new APIs are better and provide a lot of value compared to the old .NET Framework ones. Most of the boilerplate code is gone, and almost everything is on an opt-in basis.

Options allow us to load and compose configurations from multiple sources while using those easily in our systems through simple C# objects. It removes the hassle of the previous configuration from `web.config` and makes it easy to use. No more complex boilerplate code is needed to create custom `web.config` sections; just add a JSON object to `appsettings.json`, tell the system what section to load, what the type should be, and voilà – you have your strongly-typed options! The same simplicity applies to consuming settings: inject the desired interface or the class itself and use it. With that, you are up and running; no more static `ConfigurationManager` or other structures that are hard to test.

Logging is also a great addition; it allows us to standardize the logging mechanism, making our systems easier to maintain in the long run. For example, if you want to use a new third-party library or even a custom-made one, you can just load the provider into your `Program`, and the entire system will adapt and start using it without any further changes. That's what well-designed abstractions are supposed to bring to a system.

This chapter closes the second section of this book that had ASP.NET Core 5 at its center. In the next three chapters, we will explore design patterns to design flexible and robust components.

Questions

Let's take a look at a few practice questions:

1. What is the lifetime of `IOptionsMonitor<TOptions>`?
2. What is the lifetime of `IOptionsSnapshot<TOptions>`?
3. What is the lifetime of `IOptionsFactory<TOptions>`?
4. Can we write log entries to the console and a file at the same time?
5. Is it true that we should log the trace- and debug-level log entries in a production environment?

Further reading

Here are some links to build upon what we learned in the chapter:

- [Official docs] *Logging in .NET Core and ASP.NET Core*: `https://net5.link/MUVG`

- [Official docs] *Options pattern in ASP.NET Core*: `https://net5.link/RTGc`

Section 3: Designing at Component Scale

This section focuses on component design, where we study how an individual piece of software can be crafted to achieve a specific goal. We do that by exploring a few structural GoF patterns to help design SOLID data structures and components. They also help simplify the complexity of our code by encapsulating our logic in smaller units.

We continue with two behavioral patterns that help manage shared logic or simplify the efforts needed to manage complex logic. We end the section by exploring how to transmit structured information between components regarding operations' errors and successes.

This section comprises the following chapters:

- *Chapter 9, Structural Patterns*
- *Chapter 10, Behavioral Patterns*
- *Chapter 11, Understanding the Operation Result Design Pattern*

9
Structural Patterns

In this chapter, we'll explore four design patterns from the well-known Gang of Four (GoF). These are structural patterns that are used to create complex, flexible, and fine-grained classes.

The following topics will be covered in this chapter:

- Implementing the Decorator design pattern
- Implementing the Composite design pattern
- Implementing the Adapter design pattern
- Implementing the Façade design pattern

Let's get started!

Implementing the Decorator design pattern

The Decorator pattern allows us to extend objects at runtime while keeping responsibilities separated. It is a simple but powerful pattern. In this section, we'll explore how to implement this pattern in the traditional way, as well as how to leverage an open source tool named Scrutor to help us create powerful DI-ready decorators using .NET 5.

Goal

The decorator's goal is to extend an existing object, at runtime, without changing its code. Moreover, the decorated object should not be aware that it is being decorated, leaving it as a great candidate for long-lived or complex systems that need to evolve. This pattern fits systems of all sizes.

I often use this pattern to add flexibility and create adaptability to a program for next to no cost. In addition, small classes are easier to test, so the Decorator pattern adds ease of testability into the mix, making it worth mastering.

The Decorator pattern makes it easier to encapsulate a single responsibility into multiple classes, instead of packing multiple responsibilities inside a single class.

Design

A **decorator** class must both implement and use the interface that's being implemented by the **decorated** class. Let's see this step by step, starting with a non-decorated class design:

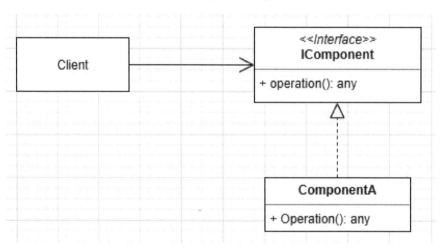

Figure 9.1 – A class diagram representing the ComponentA class
implementing the IComponent interface

In the preceding diagram, we have the following components:

- A client that calls the Operation() method of IComponent.

- ComponentA, which implements the IComponent interface.

This translates into the following sequence diagram:

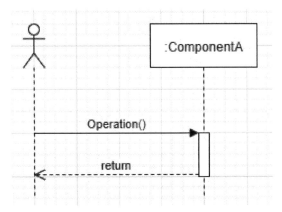

Figure 9.2 – A sequence diagram showing a consumer calling the
Operation method of the ComponentA class

Now, say that we want to add some new behavior to `ComponentA`, but only in some cases. In other cases, we want to keep the initial behavior. To do so, we could choose the Decorator pattern and implement it as follows:

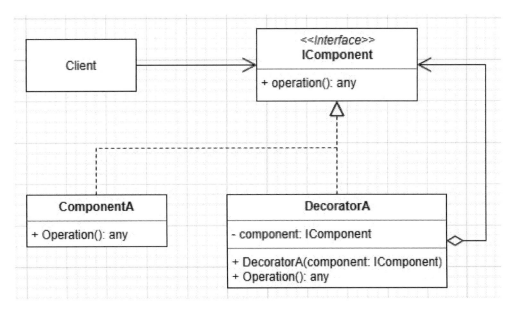

Figure 9.3 – Decorator class diagram

Instead of modifying the ComponentA class, we created DecoratorA, which implements IComponent as well. This way, Client can use an instance of DecoratorA instead of ComponentA and have access to the new behavior, without impacting the other consumers of ComponentA. Then, to avoid rewriting the whole component, an implementation of IComponent is injected when creating a new DecoratorA instance (constructor injection). This new instance is stored in the component field and used by the Operation() method (implicit use of the **Strategy** pattern).

We can translate the updated sequence like so:

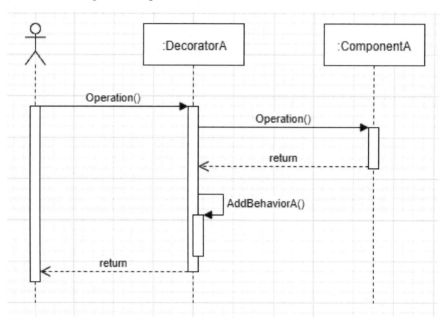

Figure 9.4 – Decorator sequence diagram

In the preceding diagram, instead of calling ComponentA directly, Client calls DecoratorA, which in turn calls ComponentA. Finally, DecoratorA does some postprocessing by calling its private method; that is, AddBehaviorA().

The way you implement the changes in behavior or its internal state is irrelevant to the pattern, which is why I excluded the `AddBehaviorA()` method from the class diagram. However, I added it to the next one to clarify the idea since we added a second decorator into the mix, hoping it makes it easier to follow.

To show you how powerful the Decorator pattern is before we jump into the code, know this: we can chain decorators! Since our decorator depends on the interface (not the implementation), we could inject another decorator, say `DecoratorB`, inside `DecoratorA` (or vice versa). We could then create an infinite chain of rules that decorate one another, leading to a very powerful yet simple design.

Let's take a look at the following class diagram, which represents our chaining example:

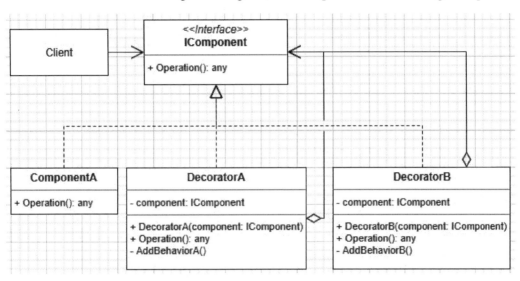

Figure 9.5 – Decorator class diagram, including two decorators

Here, we created the `DecoratorB` class, which looks very similar to `DecoratorA` but has a private `AddBehaviorB()` method instead of `AddBehaviorA()`. Let's take a look at the sequence diagram for this:

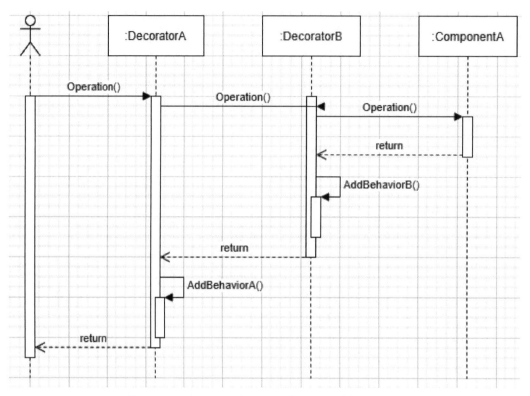

Figure 9.6 – Sequence diagram of two nested decorators

With this, we are beginning to see the power of decorators. In the preceding diagram, we can assess that `ComponentA`'s behaviors have been changed twice without `Client` knowing about it. All those classes are unaware of the next `IComponent` in the chain. They don't even know that they are being decorated. They only play their role in the plan – that's all.

It is also important to note that the Decorator's power resides in its dependency on the interface, not on a concretion, making it reusable. Based on that fact, we could swap `DecoratorA` and `DecoratorB` to invert the order the new behaviors are applied, without touching the code itself.

Project: Adding behaviors

To help visualize the Decorator pattern, let's implement the previous example, which adds some arbitrary behaviors. Each `Operation()` method returns a string that is then outputted to the response stream. It is not fancy, but it shows how this works.

First, let's take a look at the `Client` class, the `IComponent` interface, and the `ComponentA` class. `Client` uses the `IComponent` interface, and outputs the result:

```csharp
public class Client
{
    private readonly IComponent _component;
    public Client(IComponent component)
    {
        _component = component ?? throw new
ArgumentNullException(nameof(component));
    }
    public Task ExecuteAsync(HttpContext context)
    {
        var result = _component.Operation();
        return context.Response.WriteAsync($"Operation:
{result}");
    }
}

public interface IComponent
{
    string Operation();
}

public class ComponentA : IComponent
{
    public string Operation()
    {
        return "Hello from ComponentA";
    }
}
```

The IComponent interface only states that an implementation should have an Operation() method that returns a string. The Client class takes an IComponent dependency upon creation and uses it in its ExecuteAsync() method later. ExecuteAsync() simply writes the result of Operation() to the response stream.

Now that we have our Client class, let's take a look at the composition root:

```
public class Startup
{
    public void ConfigureServices(IServiceCollection services)
    {
        services
            .AddSingleton<Client>()
            .AddSingleton<IComponent, ComponentA>()
        ;
    }
    public void Configure(IApplicationBuilder app,
IHostingEnvironment env, Client client)
    {
        app.Run(async (context) => await client.
ExecuteAsync(context));
    }
}
```

In the ConfigureServices() method, we tell the container that Client has a singleton lifetime. Then, we register ComponentA as the implementation of IComponent, also with a singleton lifetime. In the Configure() method, we inject a Client instance and call its ExecuteAsync() method when an HTTP request occurs – any request.

At this point, running the application (from any URL) will result in the following output:

```
Operation: Hello from ComponentA
```

This happened because the system injected an implementation of the IComponent interface of type ComponentA into the Client constructor, so the client outputs Operation:, followed by the result of ComponentA, which is Hello from ComponentA, leading to the final result.

Decorator A

Here, we want to modify the response without touching `ComponentA`. To do so, let's create a decorator named `DecoratorA` that wraps the `Operation()` result into a `<DecoratorA>` tag:

```
public class DecoratorA : IComponent
{
    private readonly IComponent _component;
    public DecoratorA(IComponent component)
    {
        _component = component ?? throw new
ArgumentNullException(nameof(component));
    }
    public string Operation()
    {
        var result = _component.Operation();
        return $"<DecoratorA>{result}</DecoratorA>";
    }
}
```

`DecoratorA` depends on an implementation of `IComponent`. It uses that `IComponent` in the `Operation()` method and wraps its result in an HTML-like (XML) tag.

Now that we have a decorator, to change the program, we need to tell the IoC container to send an instance of `DecoratorA` instead of `ComponentA` when injecting an `IComponent` interface.

`DecoratorA` should decorate `ComponentA`; or more precisely, `ComponentA` should be injected into `DecoratorA`.

To achieve this, we could do the following:

```
public void ConfigureServices(IServiceCollection services)
{
    services
        .AddSingleton<Client>()
        .AddSingleton<IComponent>(serviceProvider => new
DecoratorA(new ComponentA()));
}
```

Here, we are telling ASP.NET Core to inject an instance of `DecoratorA` that decorates an instance of `ComponentA` when injecting an `IComponent` interface. When we run the application, we should see the following result in the browser:

```
Operation: <DecoratorA>Hello from ComponentA</DecoratorA>
```

> **Note**
>
> You may have noticed a few new keywords there, but even though it is not very elegant, we can manually create new instances in the composition root without jeopardizing our application's health. We'll learn how to get rid of some of them later.

Decorator B

Now that we have a decorator, it is time to create a second decorator to demonstrate the power of chaining decorators.

Context: At some point, we need to wrap that content once again, but we don't want to modify any existing classes. To achieve this, we concluded that creating a second decorator would be perfect, so we created the following `DecoratorB` class:

```csharp
public class DecoratorB : IComponent
{
    private readonly IComponent _component;
    public DecoratorB(IComponent component)
    {
        _component = component ?? throw new
ArgumentNullException(nameof(component));
    }
    public string Operation()
    {
        var result = _component.Operation();
        return $"<DecoratorB>{result}</DecoratorB>";
    }
}
```

It is very similar to `DecoratorA`, but the HTML-like tag is `DecoratorB` instead. The important and similar part here is that we always depend on the `IComponent` abstraction, never on any concrete class. This is what gives us the flexibility of decorating any `IComponent`, and this is what enables us to chain decorators.

To complete this example, we need to update our composition root to the following:

```
public void ConfigureServices(IServiceCollection services)
{
    services
        .AddSingleton<Client>()
        .AddSingleton<IComponent>(serviceProvider => new
DecoratorB(new DecoratorA(new ComponentA())));
}
```

Now, we can decorate `DecoratorA` with `DecoratorB`, which, in turn, decorates `ComponentA`. Upon running the application, we should see the following output:

```
Operation: <DecoratorB><DecoratorA>Hello from ComponentA</
DecoratorA></DecoratorB>
```

And voilà! These decorators allowed us to modify the behavior of `ComponentA` without having an impact on the code. However, our composition root is beginning to get messy as we are instantiating multiple dependencies inside each other. This could make our application harder to maintain and the code is becoming harder to read. That would be even worse if the decorators were depending on other classes as well.

As we mentioned previously, you can use decorators to change the behavior or state of an object; be creative. For example, you could create a class that queries remote resources, say over HTTP, then decorate that class with a small component that manages a memory cache of the results, limiting the round trip to the remote server. You could then create another decorator that monitors the time needed to query those resources and then log that somewhere. This could be a nice exercise to code if you are looking to practice.

Project: Decorator using Scrutor

The objective is to simplify the composition of the system we have created. To achieve this, we will use **Scrutor**, an open source library that allows us to do just that, among other things.

The first thing we need to do is load the NuGet package using Visual Studio or the CLI. When using the CLI, run the following command:

```
dotnet add package Scrutor
```

Once Scrutor has been installed, you can use the `Decorate<TService, TDecorator>()` extension method on `IServiceCollection` to add decorators; it is a fantastic little tool.

By using Scrutor, we can update the following messy line:

```
.AddSingleton<IComponent>(serviceProvider => new DecoratorB(new
DecoratorA(new ComponentA())))
```

And convert it into these three more elegant lines:

```
services
    .AddSingleton<Client>()
    .AddSingleton<IComponent, ComponentA>()
    .Decorate<IComponent, DecoratorA>()
    .Decorate<IComponent, DecoratorB>()
    ;
```

OK; what happened here?

We registered ComponentA as the implementation of IComponent, with a singleton lifetime.

Then, by using Scrutor, we told the IoC container to override that first binding and to decorate the already registered IComponent (ComponentA) with an instance of DecoratorA instead. Then, we overrode the second binding by telling the IoC container to return an instance of DecoratorB that decorates the last known binding of IComponent instead (DecoratorA).

The result is the same as what we did previously but is now written in a more elegant and flexible matter. The IoC container injects the equivalent of the following instance with a singleton lifetime:

```
var instance = new DecoratorB(new DecoratorA(new
ComponentA()));
```

> **Note**
>
> Why am I saying that it is more elegant and flexible? This is a simple example, but if we start adding other dependencies to those classes, it could quickly end up as a complex code block that could turn into a maintenance nightmare, become very hard to read, and have manually managed lifetimes. Of course, if the system is simple, you can always instantiate the decorators manually without loading an external library. Using methods to encapsulate the initialization of some part of the system is also an option.

Whenever possible, keep your code simple. Using Scrutor is one way to achieve this. Code simplicity helps in the long run as it is easier to read and follow, even for someone else reading it. Always think about that someone else that may maintain your code.

To validate that both programs behave the same, with or without Scrutor, the following integration test runs for both projects and ensures their correctness, see `StartupTest.cs` (https://net5.link/QzwS):

```
[Fact]
public async Task Should_return_a_double_decorated_string()
{
    // Arrange
    var client = _webApplicationFactory.CreateClient();

    // Act
    var response = await client.GetAsync("/");

    // Assert
    response.EnsureSuccessStatusCode();
    var body = await response.Content.ReadAsStringAsync();
    Assert.Equal(
        "Operation: <DecoratorB><DecoratorA>Hello from
ComponentA</DecoratorA></DecoratorB>",
        body
    );
}
```

The preceding test sends an HTTP request to one of the applications running in memory and compares the server response to the expected value. Since both projects should have the same output, that test is reused in both `DecoratorPlainStartupTest` and `DecoratorScrutorStartupTest`.

> **Scrutor**
>
> You can also do assembly scanning using Scrutor (https://net5.link/xvfS), which allows you to perform automatic dependency registration. This is outside the scope of this chapter, but it is worth looking into. Scrutor allows you to use the built-in IoC container for more complex scenarios, postponing the need to replace it with a third-party one.

Conclusion

The Decorator pattern is one of the simplest but most powerful design patterns out there. It augments existing classes without modifying them. Moreover, if you don't need to decorate all instances of X by Y, you can encapsulate small blocks of logic, then create complex and granular object trees to fit different needs; this can even be modified at runtime.

The Decorator pattern helps us stay in line with the **SOLID** principles, as follows:

- **S**: The Decorator pattern suggests creating small classes to add behaviors to other classes, which segregates responsibilities.

- **O**: Decorators add behaviors to other classes without modifying them, which is almost literally the definition of the OCP.

- **L**: N/A.

- **I**: By following the ISP, it should be easy to create decorators for your specific needs. If your interfaces are too complex, packing in too many responsibilities, using decorators could be harder. Having a hard time creating a decorator is a good indicator that something is wrong with the design. A well-segregated interface should be easy to decorate.

- **D**: Using abstractions is the key to the Decorator's power.

Implementing the Composite design pattern

The Composite design pattern is another structural GoF pattern that helps us manage complex object structures.

Goal

The goal behind the Composite pattern is to create a hierarchical data structure where you don't need to differentiate groups of elements from a single element. You could think of it as a way of building a graph or a tree with self-managing nodes.

Design

The design is straightforward; we have *components* and *composites*. Both implement a common interface that defines the shared operations. The *components* are the single nodes, while the *composites* are collections of *components*. Let's take a look at a diagram:

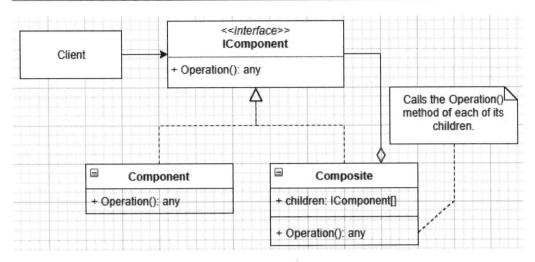

Figure 9.7 – Composite class diagram

In the preceding diagram, `Client` depends on an `IComponent` interface. By doing so, it is unaware of the implementation it is using; it could be a `Component` or a `Composite`. Then, we have two implementations:

- `Component` represents a single element; a leaf.

- `Composite` represents a collection of `IComponent`. The `Composite` object uses its children to manage the hierarchy's complexity by delegating part of the process to them.

Those three pieces, when put together, create the Composite design pattern. Considering that it is possible to add `Composite` and `Component` as children of other `Composite` objects, it is possible to create complex, non-linear, and self-managed data structures with next to no effort.

> **Note**
>
> You are not limited to one implementation of `Component` and one implementation of `Composite`; you can create as many implementations of `IComponent` as you need to, based on your use case. Then, you can mix and match them so your data structure fits your needs. We'll explore how to display complex composites in *Chapter 17, ASP.NET Core User Interfaces*.

Project: BookStore

Let's revisit the bookstore that we built in *Chapter 3, Architectural Principles*.

Context: The store is going so well that our little program is not enough anymore. Our fictional company now owns multiple stores, so they need to divide those stores into sections, and they need to manage book sets and single books. After a few minutes of gathering information, we realize that they can have sets of sets, subsections, and possibly sub-stores, so we need a flexible design.

Let's use the Composite pattern to solve this problem. The user interface that we are aiming to build looks like this:

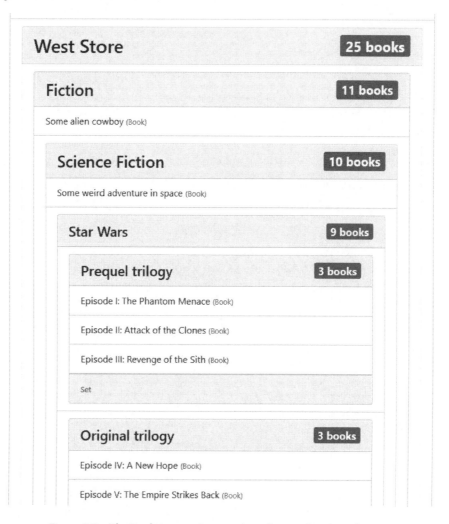

Figure 9.8 – The Bookstore project user interface rendered in a browser

First, let's look at the `IComponent` interface, which is the primary building block of the Composite pattern:

```
public interface IComponent
{
    void Add(IComponent bookComponent);
    void Remove(IComponent bookComponent);
    string Display();
    int Count();
    string Type { get; }
}
```

This interface defines the following:

- The `Add()` and `Remove()` sub-components.
- `Display()` the current component.
- `Count()` the number of books available from the current component.
- Know the `Type` of the component (displayed in the card's footer).

From there, we need components. First, let's focus on the `BookComposite` class, which abstracts away most of the composite logic:

```
public abstract class BookComposite : IComponent
{
    protected readonly List<IComponent> children;
    public BookComposite(string name)
    {
        Name = name ?? throw new
ArgumentNullException(nameof(name));
        children = new List<IComponent>();
    }
    public string Name { get; }
    public virtual string Type => GetType().Name;
    protected abstract string HeadingTagName { get; }

    public virtual void Add(IComponent bookComponent)
    {
        children.Add(bookComponent);
```

```
    }
    public virtual int Count()
    {
        return children.Sum(child => child.Count());
    }
    public virtual string Display()
    {
        var sb = new StringBuilder();
        sb.Append("<section class=\"card\">");
        AppendHeader(sb);
        AppendBody(sb);
        AppendFooter(sb);
        sb.Append("</section>");
        return sb.ToString();
    }
    private void AppendHeader(StringBuilder sb)
    {
        sb.Append($"<{HeadingTagName} class=\"card-header\">");
        sb.Append(Name);
        sb.Append($"<span class=\"badge badge-secondary float-right\">{Count()} books</span>");
        sb.Append($"</{HeadingTagName}>");
    }
    private void AppendBody(StringBuilder sb)
    {
        sb.Append($"<ul class=\"list-group list-group-flush\">");
        children.ForEach(child =>
        {
            sb.Append($"<li class=\"list-group-item\">");
            sb.Append(child.Display());
            sb.Append("</li>");
        });
        sb.Append("</ul>");
    }
    private void AppendFooter(StringBuilder sb)
    {
```

```
        sb.Append("<div class=\"card-footer text-muted\">");
        sb.Append($"<small class=\"text-muted text-
right\">{Type}</small>");
        sb.Append("</div>");
    }

    public virtual void Remove(IComponent bookComponent)
    {
        children.Remove(bookComponent);
    }
}
```

> **Note**
>
> In this case, to focus on the Composite pattern, `IComponent`'s implementations handle how its data is presented. However, most of the time, I would not recommend doing so. Why? Because we are giving too many responsibilities to those classes since we are tightly coupling them with the HTML language. It makes the components harder to reuse. Think SRP. We will revisit these concepts in subsequent chapters and fix this problem.

The `BookComposite` class implements the following shared features:

- Children management.
- Setting the `Name` property of the composite object.
- Automatically finding the `Type` name of its derived class.
- Counting the number of children (and, implicitly, the children's children).
- Displaying the composite and its children. The `protected abstract string HeadingTagName { get; }` property is used to set a different heading tag per sub-class.

> **Note**
>
> Using the LINQ `Sum()` extension method in the `children.Sum(child => child.Count());` expression allowed us to replace a more complex `for` loop and an accumulator variable.

Now, let's take a look at a more complex composite example. By creating multiple classes, we can pinpoint what responsibilities we have. In a real scenario, we may need to handle more than a name and a count. Moreover, it shows how flexible the Composite pattern is.

Here is the full hierarchy that represents our bookstore:

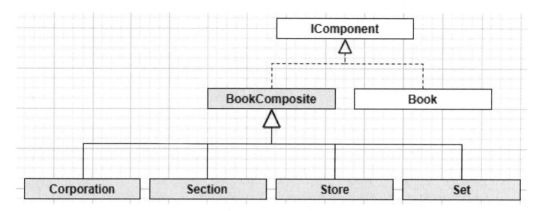

Figure 9.9 – Inheritance hierarchy of the Bookstore project

Under `BookComposite`, we have the following:

- `Corporation`, which represents the corporation that owns multiple stores. However, it is not limited to owning stores; a corporation could own other corporations and stores, or any other `IComponent` for that matter.

- `Store`, which represents a bookstore.

- `Section`, which is a section of a bookstore, or a category of books.

- `Set`, which is a book set, such as a trilogy.

All of these can be composed of any `IComponent`, making this an ultra-flexible data structure – maybe even too flexible in this case. Before we move on, let's take a look at the code for these `BookComposite` subclasses:

```
public class Corporation : BookComposite
{
    public Corporation(string name) : base(name) { }
    protected override string HeadingTagName => "h1";
}
public class Store : BookComposite
{
    public Store(string name) : base(name) { }
```

```
        protected override string HeadingTagName => "h2";
}
public class Section : BookComposite
{
    public Section(string name) : base(name) { }
    protected override string HeadingTagName => "h3";
}
public class Set : BookComposite
{
    public Set(string name, params IComponent[] books)
        : base(name)
    {
        foreach (var book in books)
            Add(book);
    }
    protected override string HeadingTagName => "h4";
}
```

As you can see, the code is straightforward; the subclasses inherit from `BookComposite`, which does most of the work, leaving them to specify only the value of the `HeadingTagName` property. `Set` is different and allows us to inject other `IComponent` objects in its constructor. This is going to be convenient later when we assemble the tree (hint: a book set contains multiple books).

The last part of our Composite pattern's implementation is the `Book` class:

```
public class Book : IComponent
{
    public Book(string title)
    {
        Title = title ?? throw new
ArgumentNullException(nameof(title));
    }
    public string Title { get; set; }
    public string Type => "Book";

    public int Count() => 1;
    public string Display() => $"{Title} <small class=\"text-
```

```
muted\">({Type})</small>";


    public void Add(IComponent bookComponent) => throw new
NotSupportedException();
    public void Remove(IComponent bookComponent) => throw new
NotSupportedException();


}
```

The Book class is a little different as it is not a collection of other objects, but a single node. Let's look at the differences:

- It has a Title property, instead of Name. How to name a component is not defined in the IComponent interface, so we can do what we want; in this case, a book has a title, not a name.

- It returns "Book" as the value of its Type property.

- It tells the callers that both the Add() and Remove() operations are not supported by throwing an exception.

- Its Count() method always returns 1 because it is a single book; this is the leaf.

- The Display() method is also way simpler because it only needs to handle itself; there are no children.

Before we jump into the program, let's look at the last part that was added to help encapsulate the data structure's creation. This is not part of the Composite pattern, but now that we know what a factory is, we can use one to encapsulate the creation logic of our data structure. The factory interface looks like the following:

```
public interface ICorporationFactory
{
    Corporation Create();
}
```

The default concrete implementation of ICorporationFactory is DefaultCorporationFactory, and it creates the following structure (visual representation; see https://net5.link/2Vqw for the full-size image):

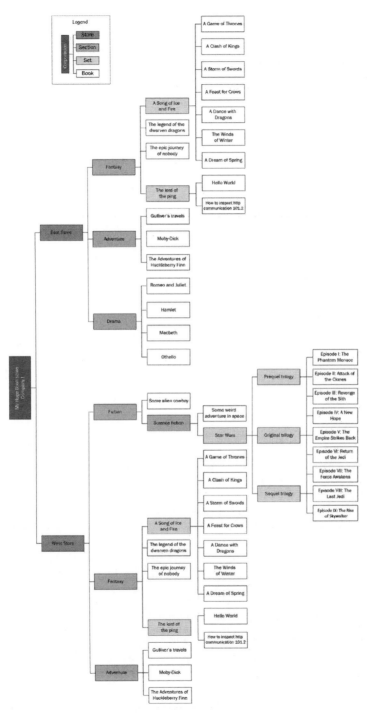

Figure 9.10 – A partial representation of the data that the DefaultCorporationFactory class creates

If we take a close look, we can see that the structure is non-linear. There are sections, subsections, sets, and subsets. We could even add books directly to the store if we want. This whole structure is defined using our composite model in `DefaultCorporationFactory`.

To keep it simple, let's focus on the West Store's Fiction section:

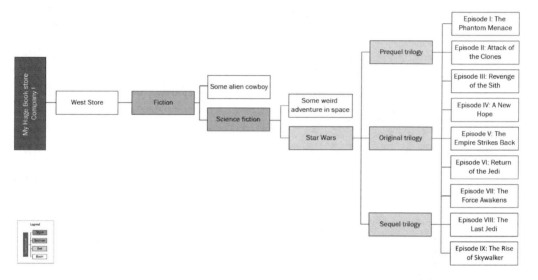

Figure 9.11 – The Fiction section of the West Store data

In the West Store, we have a section that contains a fabricated book and a subsection named Science fiction. In Science fiction, there is another fabricated book and a set of books named Star Wars. Three subsets represent the three trilogies under the Star Wars set, which reveal the flexibility of the design.

Let's take a look at the code that builds that section in isolation. Feel free to consult the full source code for the complete example (`https://net5.link/DD8e`). Here is the code:

```
public class DefaultCorporationFactory : ICorporationFactory
{
    public Corporation Create()
    {
        var corporation = new Corporation("My Huge Book Store Company!");
        corporation.Add(CreateEastStore());
        corporation.Add(CreateWestStore());
        return corporation;
    }
```

```
private IComponent CreateWestStore()
{
    var store = new Store("West Store");
    store.Add(CreateFictionSection());
    store.Add(CreateFantasySection());
    store.Add(CreateAdventureSection());
    return store;
}

private IComponent CreateFictionSection()
{
    var section = new Section("Fiction");
    section.Add(new Book("Some alien cowboy"));
    section.Add(CreateScienceFictionSection());
    return section;
}

private IComponent CreateScienceFictionSection()
{
    var section = new Section("Science Fiction");
    section.Add(new Book("Some weird adventure in space"));
    section.Add(new Set(
        "Star Wars",
        new Set(
            "Prequel trilogy",
            new Book("Episode I: The Phantom Menace"),
            new Book("Episode II: Attack of the Clones"),
            new Book("Episode III: Revenge of the Sith")
        ),
        new Set(
            "Original trilogy",
            new Book("Episode IV: A New Hope"),
            new Book("Episode V: The Empire Strikes Back"),
            new Book("Episode VI: Return of the Jedi")
        ),
        new Set(
```

```
            "Sequel trilogy",
            new Book("Episode VII: The Force Awakens"),
            new Book("Episode VIII: The Last Jedi"),
            new Book("Episode IX: The Rise of Skywalker")
        )
    ));
    return section;
}
// ...
}
```

I find the preceding code very exhaustive, making the creation of this part of the data structure clear. Now that we've read part of the code of the factory, let's head back to the Composite pattern and learn how to display it. In short, we only need to call the `Display()` method of the root node of our composite model, like this:

```
public class Startup
{
    public void ConfigureServices(IServiceCollection services)
    {
        services.AddSingleton<ICorporationFactory,
        DefaultCorporationFactory>();
    }

    public void Configure(IApplicationBuilder
app, IHostingEnvironment env, ICorporationFactory
corporationFactory)
    {
        if (env.IsDevelopment())
        {
            app.UseDeveloperExceptionPage();
        }

        app.Run(async (context) =>
        {
            var compositeDataStructure = corporationFactory.
Create();
            var output = compositeDataStructure.Display();
```

```
            context.Response.Headers.Add("Content-Type", "text/
html; charset=utf-8");
            await context.Response.WriteAsync("[removed for
brevity]");
            await context.Response.WriteAsync(output);
            await context.Response.WriteAsync("[removed for
brevity]");
        });
    }
}
```

Let's take a look at what's happening in the preceding code:

- In ConfigureServices(), we're telling the IoC container to bind the DefaultCorporationFactory class to the ICorporationFactory interface.

- In Configure(), we're injecting an implementation of ICorporationFactory in order to build the data structure.

- In app.Run(), which is executed for every request, we display the data structure. This is the part that represents the consumer of our Composite pattern implementation.

Now, let's analyze the content of app.Run() in more detail:

1. We use the injected ICorporationFactory corporationFactory parameter to create the data structure.

2. We call the Display() method to generate the output; the highlighted line. This is where the composite magic happens.

3. Finally, we write that output to the response stream by calling await context.Response.WriteAsync(output);.

The Composite pattern allowed us to render a complex data structure in a small method call. Since each component handles itself in an autonomous fashion, the burden of handling this complexity is taken away from the consumer.

In another scenario, we could have used the data instead of blindly displaying it; we could have also implemented a way of browsing that data or any other use cases that may come to mind. In this code example, I added a bit of complexity on purpose so that we could experiment with the Composite pattern in a more complex scenario while keeping extraneous details away from the code as much as possible.

I encourage you to play around with the existing data structure so that you understand the pattern. You could also try adding a `Movie` class to manage movies; a bookstore must diversify its activities. You could also differentiate movies from books so that customers are not confused. The bookstores could have physical and digital books as well.

If, after all of that, you are still looking for more, try building a new application from scratch and using the Composite pattern to create, manage, and display a multi-level menu.

Conclusion

The Composite pattern is very effective at building, managing, and maintaining complex non-linear data structures. Its power is primarily in its self-management capabilities. Each node, component, or composite is responsible for its own logic, leaving little to no work for the composite's consumers.

Using the Composite pattern helps us follow the **SOLID** principles in the following ways:

- **S**: It helps divide multiple elements of a complex data structure into small classes, in order to split responsibilities.

- **O**: By allowing us to "mix and match" different implementation of `IComponent`, the Composite pattern allows us to extend the data structure without impacting the other existing classes. For example, you could create a new class that implements `IComponent` and start using it right away, with no need to modify any other component classes.

- **L**: N/A.

- **I**: The Composite pattern may violate the ISP when single items implement operations that only impact the collections.

- **D**: All of the Composite pattern actors depend solely on `IComponent`.

Implementing the Adapter design pattern

The Adapter pattern is another structural GoF pattern that helps adapt the API of one class to the API of another interface.

Goal

The adapter's goal is to plug in a component that does not respect the expected contract and adapt it so that it does. The adapter comes in handy when you cannot change the adaptee's code or if you do not want to change it.

Design

Think of the adapter as a power outlet's universal adapter; you can connect a North American device to a European outlet by connecting it to the adapter and then connecting it to the power outlet. The Adapter design pattern does exactly that, but for APIs.

Let's start by looking at the following diagram:

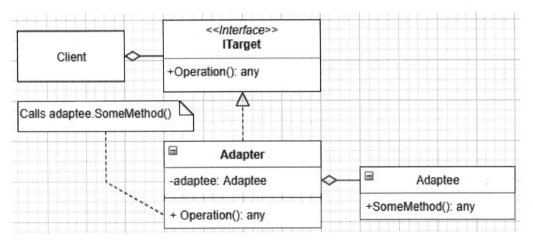

Figure 9.12 – Adapter class diagram

In the preceding diagram, we have the following actors:

- `ITarget`, which is the interface that holds the contract that we want (or have) to use.

- `Adaptee`, which is the concrete component that we want to use that does not conform to `ITarget`.

- `Adapter`, which adapts the `Adaptee` class to the `ITarget` interface.

There is a second way of implementing the Adapter pattern that implies inheritance. If you can go for composition, go for it, but if you need access to `protected` methods or other internal states of `Adaptee`, you can go for inheritance instead, like this:

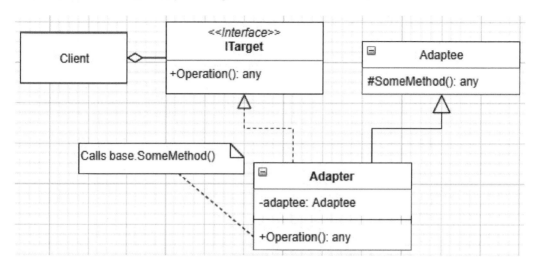

Figure 9.13 – Adapter class diagram inheriting the Adaptee

The actors are the same, but instead of composing `Adapter` with `Adaptee`, `Adapter` inherits from `Adaptee`. This makes `Adapter` become both an `Adaptee` and an `ITarget`.

Project: Greeter

Context: We've programmed a highly sophisticated greeting system that we want to reuse in a new program. However, its interface does not match the new design, and we cannot modify it because other systems use that greeting system.

To fix this problem, we decided to apply the Adapter pattern. Here is the code of the external greeter (`ExternalGreeter`), and the new interface (`IGreeter`) used in the new system. This code must not directly modify the `ExternalGreeter` class to prevent any breaking changes from occurring in other systems:

```
public interface IGreeter
{
    string Greeting();
}
public class ExternalGreeter
{
```

```
    public string GreetByName(string name)
    {
        return $"Adaptee says: hi {name}!";
    }
}
```

Next is how the external greeter is adapted to meet the latest requirements:

```
public class ExternalGreeterAdapter : IGreeter
{
    private readonly ExternalGreeter _adaptee;
    public ExternalGreeterAdapter(ExternalGreeter adaptee)
    {
        _adaptee = adaptee ?? throw new
ArgumentNullException(nameof(adaptee));
    }
    public string Greeting()
    {
        return _adaptee.GreetByName("System");
    }
}
```

In the preceding code, the actors are as follows:

- `IGreeter`, which represents `ITarget`. This is the interface that we want to use.

- `ExternalGreeter`, which represents `Adaptee`. This is the external component that already contains all the logic that's been programmed and tested. This could be located in an external assembly, maybe even loaded using NuGet.

- `ExternalGreeterAdapter`, which represents `Adapter`. This is where the adapter's job is done: `ExternalGreeterAdapter.Greeting()` calls `ExternalGreeter.GreetByName("System")`, which implements the greeting logic.

Now, we can call the `IGreeter.Greeting()` method and get the result of the `ExternalGreeter.GreetByName("System")` call. With this in place, we can reuse the existing logic. We can test any `IGreeter` consumers by mocking the `IGreeter` interface, without caring about the `ExternalGreeterAdapter` class.

I have to admit that the "complex logic" in this case is pretty simple, but we are here for the Adapter pattern, not for imaginary business logic. Now, let's take a look at the consumer:

```
public class Startup
{
    public void ConfigureServices(IServiceCollection services)
    {
        services.AddSingleton<ExternalGreeter>();
        services.AddSingleton<IGreeter,
ExternalGreeterAdapter>();
    }
    public void Configure(IApplicationBuilder app,
IHostingEnvironment env, IGreeter greeter)
    {
        app.Run(async (context) =>
        {
            var greeting = greeter.Greeting();
            await context.Response.WriteAsync(greeting);
        });
    }
}
```

In the preceding code, we composed our application by specifying that the same instance of `ExternalGreeterAdapter` should be provided every time we ask for an `IGreeter` interface. We also told the container to provide a single instance of `ExternalGreeter` whenever it's requested (in this case, it's injected into `ExternalGreeterAdapter`).

Then, the consumer (**Client** in the diagrams) is the `app.Run()` delegate (see the highlighted code). `IGreeter` is injected as a parameter of the `Configure` method. Then, it calls the `Greeting` method on that injected instance. Finally, it outputs the greeting to the response stream.

The following diagram represents what's happening in this system:

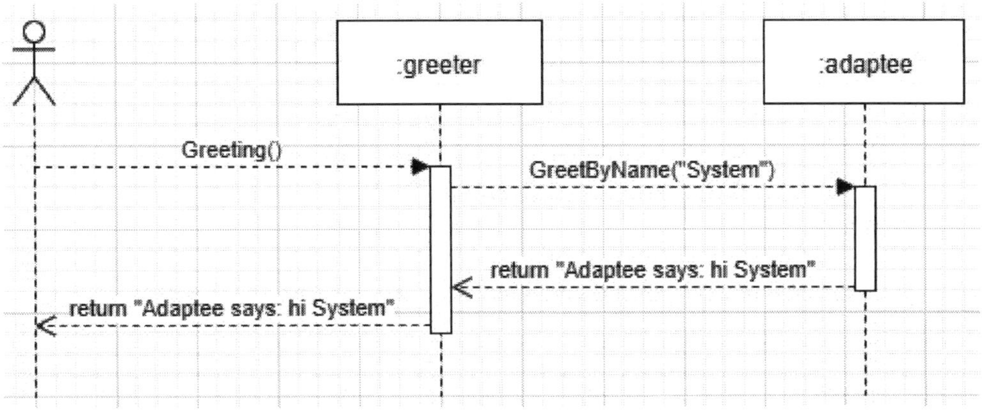

Figure 9.14 – Greeter system sequence diagram

And voilà! We've adapted the `ExternalGreeterAdapter` class to the `IGreeter` interface with little effort.

Conclusion

The Adapter pattern is another simple pattern that offers flexibility. With it, we can use older or non-conforming components without rewriting them. Of course, depending on the `ITarget` and `Adaptee` interfaces, you may need to put more or less effort into writing the code of the `Adapter` class.

Now, let's learn how the Adapter pattern can help us follow the **SOLID** principles:

- **S**: The Adapter pattern has only one responsibility: make an interface work with another interface.

- **O**: The Adapter pattern allows us to modify the Adaptee's interface, without the need to modify its code.

- **L**: Inheritance is not much of a concern when it comes to the Adapter pattern, so once again, this principle does not apply. If `Adapter` inherits from `Adaptee`, the goal is to change its interface, not its behavior, which should conform to the LSP.

- **I**: Since we could see the `Adapter` class as a means to an end where `ITarget` is *the end*, the Adapter pattern is directly depending on the design of `ITarget` and has no direct impact on it (good or bad). Your only concern for this principle is to design `ITarget` well enough so that it follows the ISP, which is not part of the pattern, but the reason to use the pattern.

- **D**: The Adapter pattern introduces only an implementation of the `ITarget` interface. Even if the adapter depends on a concrete class, its goal is to break the direct dependency on that external component by adapting it to the `ITarget` interface.

Implementing the Façade design pattern

The Façade pattern is another structural GoF pattern, similar to the Adapter pattern. It creates a wall (a facade) between one or more subsystems. The big difference between the adapter and the façade is that instead of adapting an interface to another, the façade simplifies the use of a subsystem, typically by using multiple classes of that subsystem.

> **Note**
>
> The same idea can be applied to shielding one or more programs, but in this case, the façade is called a gateway – more on that in *Chapter 16, Introduction to Microservices Architecture.*

The Façade pattern is an extremely useful pattern that can be adapted to multiple situations.

Goal

The goal of the Façade pattern is to simplify the use of one or more subsystems by providing an interface that is easier to use than the subsystems themselves, shielding the consumers from that complexity.

Design

We could create multiple diagrams representing a multitude of subsystems, but let's keep things simple here. Remember that you can replace the single subsystem shown in the following diagram with as many subsystems as you need to adapt:

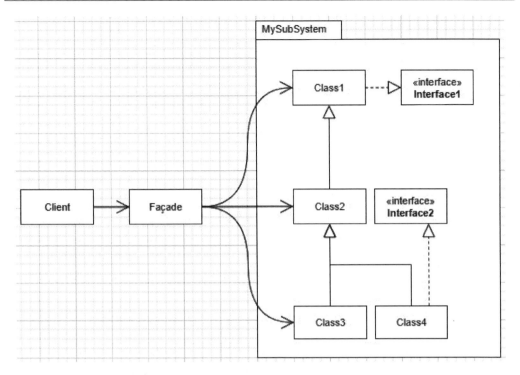

Figure 9.15 – A class diagram representing a Façade object that hides a complex subsystem

As we can see, Façade plays the intermediary between Client and the subsystem, simplifying its usage. Let's see this in action as a sequence diagram:

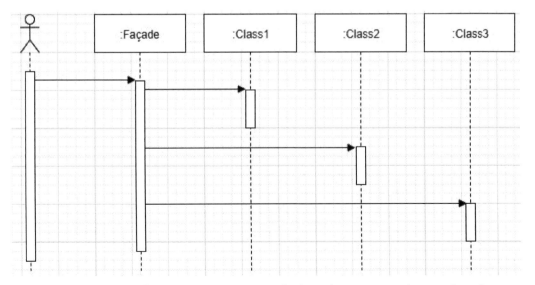

Figure 9.16 – A sequence diagram representing a Façade object that interacts with a complex subsystem

In the preceding diagram, `Client` calls `Façade` once, while `Façade` places multiple calls against different classes.

There are multiple ways of implementing a façade:

- **Opaque façades**: In this form, the `Façade` class is inside the subsystem. All other classes of the subsystem have an `internal` visibility modifier. This way, only the classes inside the subsystem can interact with the other internal classes, forcing the consumers to use the `Façade` class.

- **Transparent façades**: In this form, the classes can have a `public` modifier, allowing the consumers to use them directly or to use the `Façade` class. This way, we can create the `Façade` class inside or outside the subsystem.

- **Static façades**: In this form, the `Façade` class is `static`. We can implement a **static façade** as **opaque** or **transparent**. I do not recommend this approach because global (`static`) elements tend to limit flexibility and testability.

Project: The façades

In this example, we will play with three C# projects:

- An empty ASP.NET Core 5 application that is using routing to expose four HTTP endpoints. Two endpoints aim at the `OpaqueFacadeSubSystem`, while the other two endpoints aim at the `TransparentFacadeSubSystem`. This is our `Client`, our consumer.

- The `OpaqueFacadeSubSystem` class library implements an **opaque façade**.

- The `TransparentFacadeSubSystem` class library implements a **transparent façade**.

Let's start with the class libraries.

> **Note**
>
> To follow the SOLID principles, adding some interfaces representing the elements of the subsystem seemed appropriate. In subsequent chapters, we will explore how to organize our abstractions to be more reusable, but for now, both abstractions and implementations are in the same assembly.

Opaque façade

In this assembly, only the façade is public; all the other classes are internal, which means they are hidden from the external world. In most cases, this is not ideal; hiding everything makes the subsystem less flexible and harder to extend.

However, in some scenarios, you may want to control access to your internal APIs. This may be because they are not mature enough and you don't want any third party to depend on them, or for any other reasons you may deem appropriate for your specific use case.

Let's start by taking a look at the following subsystem code:

```
// An added interface for flexibility
public interface IOpaqueFacade
{
    string ExecuteOperationA();
    string ExecuteOperationB();
}


// A hidden component
internal class ComponentA
{
    public string OperationA() => "Component A, Operation A";
    public string OperationB() => "Component A, Operation B";
}


// A hidden component
internal class ComponentB
{
    public string OperationC() => "Component B, Operation C";
    public string OperationD() => "Component B, Operation D";
}


// A hidden component
internal class ComponentC
{
    public string OperationE() => "Component C, Operation E";
    public string OperationF() => "Component C, Operation F";
}
```

```csharp
// The opaque façade using the other hidden components
public class OpaqueFacade : IOpaqueFacade
{
    private readonly ComponentA _componentA;
    private readonly ComponentB _componentB;
    private readonly ComponentC _componentC;

    // Using constructor injection
    internal OpaqueFacade(ComponentA componentA, ComponentB
componentB, ComponentC componentC)
    {
        _componentA = componentA ?? throw new
ArgumentNullException(nameof(componentA));
        _componentB = componentB ?? throw new
ArgumentNullException(nameof(componentB));
        _componentC = componentC ?? throw new
ArgumentNullException(nameof(componentC));
    }

    public string ExecuteOperationA()
    {
        return new StringBuilder()
            .AppendLine(_componentA.OperationA())
            .AppendLine(_componentA.OperationB())
            .AppendLine(_componentB.OperationD())
            .AppendLine(_componentC.OperationE())
            .ToString();
    }

    public string ExecuteOperationB()
    {
        return new StringBuilder()
            .AppendLine(_componentB.OperationC())
            .AppendLine(_componentB.OperationD())
            .AppendLine(_componentC.OperationF())
            .ToString();
```

```
        }
    }
```

As you can see, the `OpaqueFacade` class is coupled with `ComponentA`, `ComponentB`, and `ComponentC` directly. There was no point in extracting any `internal` interfaces since the subsystem is not extensible anyway. We could have done this to offer some kind of internal flexibility, but in this case, there was no advantage in doing so.

Besides this coupling, `ComponentA`, `ComponentB`, and `ComponentC` define two methods each, which returns a string describing their source. With that code in place, we can observe what is happening and how the final result was composed.

`OpaqueFacade` also exposes two methods, but each composes a different message by using the underlying subsystem's components. This is a classic use of a façade; the façade queries other objects in a more or less complicated way and then does something with the results, taking away the caller's burden of knowing the subsystem.

Moreover, to register the `OpaqueFacadeSubSystem` façade against the IoC container, we needed some "magic" to overcome the `internal` visibility modifiers. To solve this problem, I added the following extension method that registers the dependencies, as we explored in *Chapter 7, Deep Dive into Dependency Injection*. The extension method is accessible by the consumer application:

```
public static class StartupExtensions
{
    public static IServiceCollection
AddOpaqueFacadeSubSystem(this IServiceCollection services)
    {
        services.AddSingleton<IOpaqueFacade>(serviceProvider
            => new OpaqueFacade(new ComponentA(), new
ComponentB(), new ComponentC()));
        return services;
    }
}
```

Next, to the transparent façade implementation.

Transparent façade

The transparent façade is the most flexible type of façade, extremely suitable for a system that leverages dependency injection. The implementation is very similar to the opaque façade, but the `public` visibility modifier changes how consumers can access the class library elements. For this system, it was worth adding interfaces to allow the consumers of the subsystem to extend it when needed.

First, let's take a look at the abstractions:

```
namespace TransparentFacadeSubSystem.Abstractions
{
    public interface ITransparentFacade
    {
        string ExecuteOperationA();
        string ExecuteOperationB();
    }
    public interface IComponentA
    {
        string OperationA();
        string OperationB();
    }
    public interface IComponentB
    {
        string OperationC();
        string OperationD();
    }
    public interface IComponentC
    {
        string OperationE();
        string OperationF();
    }
}
```

The API of this subsystem is the same as the opaque façade. The only difference is how we can use the subsystem and extend it (from a consumer standpoint). The implementations are mostly the same as well, but the classes implement the interfaces and are `public`; the elements in bold represent the changes that have been made:

```
namespace TransparentFacadeSubSystem
{
    public class ComponentA : IComponentA
    {
        public string OperationA() => "Component A, Operation A";
        public string OperationB() => "Component A, Operation B";
    }
    public class ComponentB : IComponentB
    {
        public string OperationC() => "Component B, Operation C";
        public string OperationD() => "Component B, Operation D";
    }
    public class ComponentC : IComponentC
    {
        public string OperationE() => "Component C, Operation E";
        public string OperationF() => "Component C, Operation F";
    }


    public class TransparentFacade : ITransparentFacade
    {
        private readonly IComponentA _componentA;
        private readonly IComponentB _componentB;
        private readonly IComponentC _componentC;

        public TransparentFacade(IComponentA componentA,
IComponentB componentB, IComponentC componentC)
        {
```

```
            _componentA = componentA ?? throw new
ArgumentNullException(nameof(componentA));
            _componentB = componentB ?? throw new
ArgumentNullException(nameof(componentB));
            _componentC = componentC ?? throw new
ArgumentNullException(nameof(componentC));
        }

        public string ExecuteOperationA()
        {
            return new StringBuilder()
                .AppendLine(_componentA.OperationA())
                .AppendLine(_componentA.OperationB())
                .AppendLine(_componentB.OperationD())
                .AppendLine(_componentC.OperationE())
                .ToString();
        }

        public string ExecuteOperationB()
        {
            return new StringBuilder()
                .AppendLine(_componentB.OperationC())
                .AppendLine(_componentB.OperationD())
                .AppendLine(_componentC.OperationF())
                .ToString();
        }
    }
}
```

Before going further, note that the following extension method was also created to simplify the use of the subsystem. However, everything that's defined there can be overridden (which was not the case for the opaque façade):

```
public static class StartupExtensions
{

    public static IServiceCollection
AddTransparentFacadeSubSystem(this IServiceCollection services)
    {
```

```
            services.AddSingleton<ITransparentFacade,
TransparentFacade>();
            services.AddSingleton<IComponentA, ComponentA>();
            services.AddSingleton<IComponentB, ComponentB>();
            services.AddSingleton<IComponentC, ComponentC>();
            return services;
    }
}
```

As you can see, all the new elements are gone and have been replaced by simple dependency registration (singleton lifetimes, in this case). These little differences give you the tools to reimplement any part of the subsystem if you want to; see the following subsection for an example.

Besides those differences, the transparent façade plays the same role as the opaque façade, outputting the same result.

The program

Now, let's analyze the client, a tiny ASP.NET Core 5 application that forwards HTTP requests to the façades.

The first step is to register the dependencies in the composition root, like this:

```
public void ConfigureServices(IServiceCollection services)
{
    services
        .AddRouting()
        .AddOpaqueFacadeSubSystem()
        .AddTransparentFacadeSubSystem()
        ;
}
```

> **Note**
>
> With these extension methods, the application root is so clean that it is hard to know that we registered two subsystems against the IoC container. This is a good way of keeping your code organized and clean, especially when you're building class libraries.

Now that everything has been registered, the second thing we need to do is route those HTTP requests to the façades. Let's take a look at the code first:

```
public void Configure(IApplicationBuilder app, IOpaqueFacade
opaqueFacade, ITransparentFacade transparentFacade)
{
    app.UseRouter(routeBuilder =>
    {
        routeBuilder.MapGet("/opaque/a", async context =>
        {
            var result = opaqueFacade.ExecuteOperationA();
            await context.Response.WriteAsync(result);
        });
        routeBuilder.MapGet("/opaque/b", async context =>
        {
            var result = opaqueFacade.ExecuteOperationB();
            await context.Response.WriteAsync(result);
        });
        routeBuilder.MapGet("/transparent/a", async context =>
        {
            var result = transparentFacade.ExecuteOperationA();
            await context.Response.WriteAsync(result);
        });
        routeBuilder.MapGet("/transparent/b", async context =>
        {
            var result = transparentFacade.ExecuteOperationB();
            await context.Response.WriteAsync(result);
        });
    });
}
```

In the preceding block (see highlighted code), the following is happening:

1. The dependencies are injected into the Configure() method.

2. Using the router, we define four routes, with each route dispatching the request to one of the façade's methods.

If you run the program and navigate to `https://localhost:9004/transparent/a`, the page should display the following:

```
Component A, Operation A
Component A, Operation B
Design Pattern
Component C, Operation E
```

Figure 9.17 – The result of executing the ExecuteOperationA method of the ITransparentFacade instance

What happened is located inside the delegates. It uses the injected `ITransparentFacade` service and calls its `ExecuteOperationA()` method, then outputs the `result` variable to the response stream.

Now, let's define how `ITransparentFacade` is composed:

- `ITransparentFacade` is an instance of `TransparentFacade`.
- We inject `IComponentA`, `IComponentB`, and `IComponentC` in the `TransparentFacade` class.
- These dependencies are instances of `ComponentA`, `ComponentB`, and `ComponentC`, respectively.

Visually, the following flow happens:

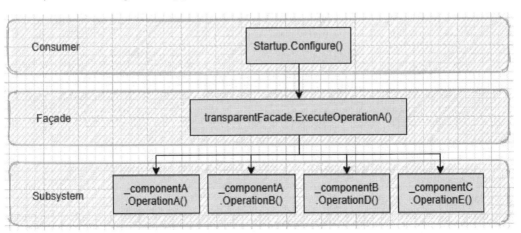

Figure 9.18 – A representation of the call hierarchy that occurs when the consumer executes the ExecuteOperationA method

In the preceding diagram, we can see the shielding that's done by the façade and how it has made the consumer's life easier. Here, there's one call instead of four.

> **Note**
>
> One of the hardest parts of using dependency injection is its abstractness. If you are not sure how all those parts are assembled, add a breakpoint into Visual Studio (let's say, on the `var result = transparentFacade.ExecuteOperationA()` line) and run the application in debug mode. From there, **Step Into** each method call. That should help you figure out what is happening. Using the debugger to find the concrete types and their states can help find details about a system or diagnose bugs.

To use **Step Into**, you can use the following button or hit *F11*:

Figure 9.19 – The Visual Studio Step Into (F11) button

Next, we update the result without changing the component's code.

Flexibility in action

Now, let's see the added flexibility of the transparent façade in action.

Context: We want to change the behavior of the `TransparentFacade` class. At the moment, the result of the endpoint `transparent/b` looks like this:

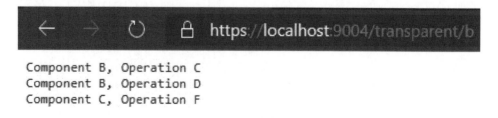

```
Component B, Operation C
Component B, Operation D
Component C, Operation F
```

Figure 9.20 – The result of executing the ExecuteOperationB
method of the ITransparentFacade instance

We want to change it to the following:

```
Flexibility
Design Pattern
Component C, Operation F
```

Figure 9.21 – The expected result once the change has been made

We also want to achieve this result without modifying `ComponentB`. To do this, we executed the following steps:

1. Create the following class:

```
public class UpdatedComponentB : IComponentB
{
    public string OperationC() => "Flexibility";
    public string OperationD() => "Design Pattern";
}
```

2. Tell the IoC container about it, like this:

```
services
    .AddRouting()
    .AddOpaqueFacadeSubSystem()
    .AddTransparentFacadeSubSystem()
    .AddSingleton<IComponentB, UpdatedComponentB>()
    ;
```

3. From there, if you run the program, you should see the desired result!

> **Note**
>
> Adding a dependency for a second time makes that dependency resolved by the container, thus overriding the first one. However, both registrations remain present in the services collection; for example, calling `GetServices<IComponentB>()` on `IServiceProvider` would return two dependencies. Do not confuse the `GetServices()` and `GetService()` methods (plural vs singular); one returns a collection while the other returns a single instance. That single instance is always the last that has been registered.

That's it! We updated the system without modifying it. This is what dependency injection can do for you when you're designing a program around it.

Alternative façade patterns

One alternative would be to create *a hybrid between a transparent façade and an opaque façade* by exposing the abstractions using the `public` visibility modifier (all of the interfaces) while keeping the implementations hidden under an `internal` visibility modifier. This hybrid design offers the right balance between **control and flexibility**.

Another alternative would be to create *a façade outside of the subsystem*. In the previous examples, we created the façades inside the class libraries, but this is not mandatory; the façade is just a class that creates an accessible wall between your system and one or more subsystems. It should be located wherever you see fit. Creating external façades like this would be especially useful when you do not control the source code of the subsystem(s), such as if you only have access to the binaries. This could also be used to create project-specific façades over the same subsystem, giving you extra flexibility without cluttering your subsystems with multiple façades, shifting the maintenance cost from the subsystems to the client applications that use them.

This one is more of a note than an alternative: you do not need to create an assembly per subsystem. I did it because it helped me explain different concepts to you in the examples, but you could create multiple subsystems in the same assembly. You could even create a single assembly that includes all your subsystems, façades, and the client code (all in a single project).

Conclusion

The Façade pattern is handy for simplifying consumers' lives as it allows you to hide subsystems' implementation details behind a wall. There are multiple flavors to it; the two most prominent ones are:

- The **transparent façade**, which flexibility by exposing at least part of the subsystem(s).
- The **opaque façade**, which control access by hiding most of the subsystem(s).

Now, let's see how the **transparent façade** pattern can help us follow the **SOLID** principles:

- **S**: A well-designed **transparent façade** serves this exact purpose by providing a cohesive set of functionalities to its clients by hiding overly complex subsystems or internal implementation details.

- **O**: A well-designed **transparent façade** and its underlying subsystem's components can be extended without direct modification, as we saw in the *Flexibility in action* section.

- **L**: N/A.

- **I**: By exposing a façade that uses different smaller objects implementing small interfaces, we could say that the segregation is done at both the façade and the component levels.

- **D**: The Façade pattern does not specify anything about interfaces, so it is up to the developers to enforce this principle by using other patterns, principles, and best practices.

Finally, let's see how the **opaque façade** pattern can help us follow the **SOLID** principles:

- **S**: A well-designed **opaque façade** serves this exact purpose by providing a cohesive set of functionalities to its clients by hiding overly complex subsystems or internal implementation details.

- **O**: By hiding the subsystem, the **opaque façade** limits our ability to extend it. However, we could implement a **hybrid façade** to help with that.

- **L**: N/A.

- **I**: The **opaque façade** does not help nor diminish our ability to apply the ISP.

- **D**: The Façade pattern does not specify anything about interfaces, so it is up to the developers to enforce this principle by using other patterns, principles, and best practices.

Summary

In this chapter, we covered multiple fundamental GoF structural design patterns. They help us extend our systems from the outside, without modifying the actual classes, leading to a higher degree of cohesion by composing our object graph dynamically.

We started with the Decorator pattern, which extends other objects, at runtime, by using them internally. Decorators can also be chained, allowing even greater flexibility (decorating other decorators). We also used an open source tool named Scrutor to simplify the decorator's use with the built-in ASP.NET Core 5 dependency injection system.

Then, we covered the Composite pattern, which allows us to create complex and flexible data structures. To make the life of its consumer easier, the composite delegates the navigation responsibility to each component.

After that, we covered the Adapter pattern, which allows us to adapt an object to another interface. This pattern is very helpful when we need to adapt the components of external systems that we have no control over.

Finally, we dug into the Façade pattern, which is similar to the Adapter pattern, but at the subsystem level. It allows us to create a wall in front of one or more subsystems, simplifying its usage. It could also be used to hide a subsystem from its consumers.

In the next chapter, we will explore two GoF behavioral design patterns: the Template Method and the Chain of Responsibility design pattern.

Questions

Here are a few revision questions:

1. Can we decorate a decorator with another decorator?
2. Name one of the advantages of the Composite pattern.
3. Can we use the Adapter pattern to migrate an old API to a new system in order to adapt its APIs before rewriting it?
4. Why should we use a façade?
5. What is the difference between the Adapter the Façade patterns?

Further reading

- To learn more about Scrutor, please visit `https://net5.link/xvfS`.

10
Behavioral Patterns

In this chapter, we explore two new design patterns from the well-known **Gang of Four** (**GoF**). Those are behavioral patterns, which means that they help simplify the management of system behavior.

The following topics will be covered in this chapter:

- Implementing the Template Method pattern
- Implementing the Chain of Responsibility pattern
- How to mix both

Implementing the Template Method pattern

The Template Method is a GoF behavioral pattern using inheritance to share code between the base class and its subclasses. It is a very powerful, yet simple, design pattern.

Goal

The goal of the Template Method pattern is to encapsulate the outline of an algorithm in a base class while leaving some parts of that algorithm open for modification by the subclasses.

Design

As mentioned earlier, the design is simple but extensible. First, we need to define a base class that contains the `TemplateMethod()`, and then defines one or more sub-operations that need to be implemented by its subclasses (`abstract`), or that can be overridden (`virtual`). Using UML, it looks like this:

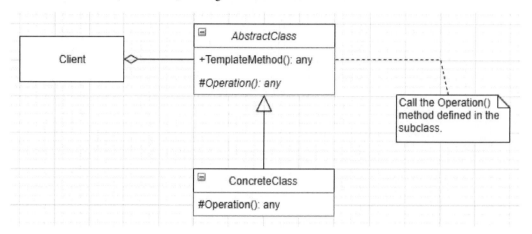

Figure 10.1 – Class diagram representing the Template Method pattern

How does this work?

- `AbstractClass` implements the shared code: the algorithm.
- `ConcreteClass` implements its specific part of the algorithm.
- `Client` calls the `TemplateMethod()`, which calls the subclass implementation of one or more specific algorithm elements.

> **Note**
>
> We could also extract an interface from `AbstractClass` to allow for even more flexibility, but that's beyond the scope of the Template Method pattern.

Let's now get into some code to see the Template Method pattern in action.

Project – Building a search machine

Let's start with a simple, classic example to demonstrate how the Template Method works.

Context: We want to use a different search algorithm depending on the collection to be searched. When the collection is sorted, we want to use a binary search, but when it is not, we want to use a linear search.

Let's start by breaking down the full code listing by class (actors):

```
namespace TemplateMethod
{
    public class Startup
    {
        public void ConfigureServices(IServiceCollection
services)
        {
            services.AddSingleton<SearchMachine>(x => new
LinearSearchMachine(1, 10, 5, 2, 123, 333, 4));
            services.AddSingleton<SearchMachine>(x => new
BinarySearchMachine(1, 2, 3, 4, 5, 6, 7, 8, 9, 10));
        }

        public void Configure(IApplicationBuilder app,
IHostingEnvironment env, IEnumerable<SearchMachine>
searchMachines)
        {
            app.Run(async (context) =>
            {
                context.Response.ContentType = "text/html";
                var elementsToFind = new int[] { 1, 10, 11 };
                await context.WriteLineAsync("<pre>");
                foreach (var searchMachine in searchMachines)
                {
                    var heading = $"Current search machine is
{searchMachine.GetType().Name}";
                    await context.WriteLineAsync("".
PadRight(heading.Length, '='));
                    await context.WriteLineAsync(heading);
                    foreach (var value in elementsToFind)
                    {
                        var index = searchMachine.IndexOf
(value);
                        var wasFound = index.HasValue;
                        if (wasFound)
                        {
```

```
                                    await context.WriteLineAsync($"The
element '{value}' was found at index {index.Value}.");
                            }
                            else
                            {
                                    await context.WriteLineAsync ($"The
element '{value}' was not found.");
                            }
                        }
                    }
                    await context.WriteLineAsync("</pre>");
                });
            }
        }
    internal static class HttpContextExtensions
    {
        public static async Task WriteLineAsync(this
HttpContext context, string text)
        {
            await context.Response.WriteAsync(text);
            await context.Response.WriteAsync (Environment.
NewLine);
        }
    }
}
```

The Startup class is the consumer, the Client. The HttpContextExtensions class is a helper that has nothing to do with the template method. In the Startup class, we configure two SearchMachine services (the AbstractClass). One as an instance of the LinearSearchMachine class and the other as an instance of the BinarySearchMachine class. Both instances are initialized with a different collection of numbers.

We then inject all registered SearchMachine services into the Configure method (highlighted code). We then register a delegate to handle HTTP requests. That handler iterates all SearchMachine instances and tries to find all elements of the elementsToFind array, before outputting the results.

Next is the `AbstractClass`, the `SearchMachine` class itself:

```csharp
public abstract class SearchMachine
{
    protected int[] Values { get; }

    protected SearchMachine(params int[] values)
    {
        Values = values ?? throw new
 ArgumentNullException(nameof(values));
    }

    public int? IndexOf(int value)
    {
        var result = Find(value);
        if (result < 0) { return null; }
        return result;
    }
    public abstract int Find(int value);
}
```

The `SearchMachine` class represents the `AbstractClass`. It exposes the `IndexOf()` template method, which uses the required hook represented by the abstract `Find()` method (see highlighted code). The hook is required because each subclass must implement that method, thereby making that method a required extension point (or hook).

Next, we explore our first implementation of the `ConcreteClass`, the `LinearSearchMachine` class:

```csharp
public class LinearSearchMachine : SearchMachine
{
    public LinearSearchMachine(params int[] values)
        : base(values) { }

    public override int Find(int value)
    {
        var index = 0;
        foreach (var item in Values)
```

```
            {
                if (item == value) { return index; }
                index++;
            }
            return -1;
        }
    }
```

The `LinearSearchMachine` class is a `ConcreteClass`, representing the linear search implementation used by `SearchMachine`. It's part of the algorithm implemented by the `Find` method.

Finally, we move on to the `BinarySearchMachine` class:

```
    public class BinarySearchMachine : SearchMachine
    {
        public BinarySearchMachine(params int[] values)
            : base(values) { }

        public override int Find(int value)
        {
            return Array.BinarySearch(Values, value);
        }
    }
}
```

The `BinarySearchMachine` class is a `ConcreteClass`, representing the binary search implementation of `SearchMachine`. As you may have noticed, we skipped the binary search algorithm's implementation by delegating it to the `Array.BinarySearch` built-in method. Thanks to the .NET team!

Important

For a binary search algorithm to work, the collection must be sorted.

Now that we have defined the actors and explored the code, let's see what is happening in client:

1. client uses the registered SearchMachine instances and searches for a set of values (1, 10, and 11).

2. Once that is done, client displays to the user whether the numbers were found.

In this case, the template method returns null when a value is not found, while the implementing classes return a negative number with their Find method.

By running the program, we get the following output:

```
==============================================
Current search machine is LinearSearchMachine
The element '1' was found at index 0.
The element '10' was found at index 1.
The element '11' was not found.
==============================================
Current search machine is BinarySearchMachine
The element '1' was found at index 0.
The element '10' was found at index 9.
The element '11' was not found.
```

And voilà! We have covered the template method, as easy as that. We could add one or more virtual methods in the base class that would become optional extension points, implemented, or not, by the subclasses for added flexibility. That would allow a more complex and more versatile scenario to be supported.

Conclusion

The Template Method is a powerful and easy-to-implement design pattern that allows subclasses to reuse the algorithm's skeleton while implementing (abstract) or overriding (virtual) some of its subparts.

Now, let's see how the Template Method pattern can help us follow the **SOLID** principles:

- **S**: The Template Method pushes algorithm-specific portions of the code to subclasses while keeping the core algorithm in the base class. By doing that, it follows the **single responsibility principle** (**SRP**), distributing responsibilities.

- **O**: By opening extension hooks, it opens the template for extensions (allowing subclasses to extend it) and closes it from modifications (no need to modify the base class since the subclasses can extend it).

- **L**: Since the subclasses are the implementations, there are no base behaviors to make sure they work the same in subclasses, so following the **Liskov substitution principle** (**LSP**) should not be a problem when implementing a Template Method. That said, this principle is tricky, so it could be possible to create a subclass (or a subclass of a subclass) that breaks the LSP, thereby altering the program logic. Just keep an eye open for this principle when using the Template Method pattern.

- **I**: As long as the base class implements the smallest cohesive surface possible, using the Template Method pattern should not negatively impact the program.

- **D**: The Template Method is based on an abstraction, so as long as consumers depend on that abstraction, it should help to get in line with the **dependency inversion principle** (**DIP**).

We will now move to the Chain of Responsibility design pattern and how we can mix both to improve our project.

Implementing the Chain of Responsibility pattern

The Chain of Responsibility is a GoF behavioral pattern to chain classes to handle complex scenarios efficiently, with limited effort. Once again, the goal is to take a complex problem and break it into multiple smaller units.

Goal

The goal behind the Chain of Responsibility pattern is to chain multiple handlers that each solves a limited number of problems. If a handler cannot solve the specific problem, it passes the resolution to the chain's next handler. There could be a default handler executing some logic at the end of the chain, such as throwing an exception (for example, `OperationNotHandledException`), or a handler that makes sure of the opposite (in other words, that nothing happens, especially no exception).

Design

The most basic chain of responsibility starts by defining an interface that handles a request (`IHandler`). Then we add classes that handle one or more scenarios (`Handler1` and `Handler2`):

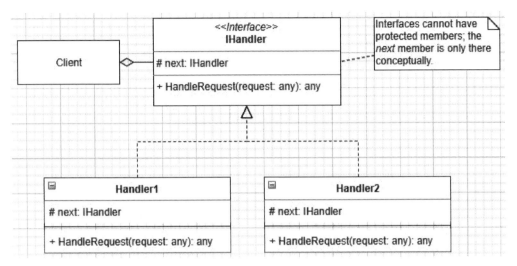

Figure 10.2 – Class diagram representing the Chain of Responsibility pattern

> **Tip**
>
> When creating the chain of responsibility, you can order the handlers so that the most requested handlers are closer to the beginning of the chain and the least requested handlers are closer to the end. This helps limit the amount of "chain links" that are visited for each request before reaching the right handler.

A big difference between the Chain of Responsibility and many other patterns is that no central dispatcher knows the handlers; all handlers are independent. The consumer receives a handler and tells it to handle the request, so no more complexity. Each handler is also simple, handling the request or not, and then passing it, or not, to the next handler in the chain. Enough theory. Let's look at some code.

Project – Message interpreter

Context: We need to create the receiving end of a messaging application where each message is unique, making it impossible to create a single algorithm to handle them all.

After analyzing the problem, we decided to build a chain of responsibility where each handler can manage a single message. The pattern seems more than perfect!

> **Background**
>
> This project is based on something that I built a few years ago. Physical (IoT) devices were sending bytes (messages) due to limited bandwidth. Then, in a web application, we had to associate those bytes with real values. Each message had the same header, but with a different body. The headers were handled in a base handler (template method), and each individual handler in the chain was managing a different message type. For the current example, we keep it simpler than parsing bytes, but the concept is the same.

For our demo application, the messages are as simple as this:

```
public class Message
{
    public string Name { get; set; }
    public string Payload { get; set; }
}
```

The Name property is used as a discriminator to differentiate messages, and each handler's responsibility is to do something with the Payload property. We won't do anything with the payload as it is irrelevant to the pattern itself, but conceptually, that's what should happen.

The handlers are also very simple:

```
public interface IMessageHandler
{
    void Handle(Message message);
}
```

The only thing a handler can do is to handle a message. Our initial application can handle the following messages:

- The AlarmTriggeredHandler class handles AlarmTriggered messages.
- The AlarmPausedHandler class handles AlarmPaused messages.
- The AlarmStoppedHandler class handles AlarmStopped messages.

The three handlers are very similar and share quite a bit of logic, but we are fixing that later. In the meantime, we have the following:

```
public class AlarmTriggeredHandler : IMessageHandler
{
    private readonly IMessageHandler _next;
    public AlarmTriggeredHandler(IMessageHandler next = null)
    {
        _next = next;
    }

    public void Handle(Message message)
    {
        if (message.Name == "AlarmTriggered")
        {
            // Do something cleaver with the Payload
        }
        else if (_next != null)
        {
            _next.Handle(message);
        }
    }
}

public class AlarmPausedHandler : IMessageHandler
{
    private readonly IMessageHandler _next;
    public AlarmPausedHandler(IMessageHandler next = null)
    {
        _next = next;
    }

    public void Handle(Message message)
    {
        if (message.Name == "AlarmPaused")
        {
            // Do something cleaver with the Payload
```

```
            }
        else if (_next != null)
        {
            _next.Handle(message);
        }
    }
}

public class AlarmStoppedHandler : IMessageHandler
{
    private readonly IMessageHandler _next;
    public AlarmStoppedHandler(IMessageHandler next = null)
    {
        _next = next;
    }

    public void Handle(Message message)
    {
        if (message.Name == "AlarmStopped")
        {
            // Do something cleaver with the Payload
        }
        else if (_next != null)
        {
            _next.Handle(message);
        }
    }
}
```

Each handler does two things:

1. It allows an optional "next handler" to be injected into its constructor (highlighted in the code).

2. It handles only the request that it knows about, delegating the others to the next handler in the chain.

In this case, if the next handler is null, nothing happens. In a real scenario, you may want to know that a handler is missing or that the message was invalid. Let's add a fourth handler that notifies us of invalid requests:

```
public class DefaultHandler : IMessageHandler
{
    public void Handle(Message message)
    {
        throw new NotSupportedException($"Messages named
'{message.Name}' are not supported.");
    }
}
```

That new default handler throws an exception that notifies the consumer of the chain of responsibility about the error.

> **Note**
>
> We can create custom exceptions to make it easier to differentiate between system errors and application errors. But sometimes, throwing a system exception is good enough. For example, here are a few exceptions that are often thrown *as is*: NotSupportedException, NotImplementedException, and ArgumentNullException.

Let's use Startup as the client and use the HTTP request to build the message. Usually, the GET method is used to read data, while other methods such as POST, PUT, and PATCH are used to create, replace, or update data. For testing purposes, it is easier to send arbitrary data to our chain of responsibility by using GET (don't do that in your apps), so we are cheating on this one:

```
public class Startup
{
    public void ConfigureServices(IServiceCollection services)
    {
        // Create the chain of responsibility,
        // ordered by the most called handler (or the one
        // that must be executed the faster)
        // to the less called handler (or the one that can
        // take more time to be executed),
        // followed by the DefaultHandler.
```

```
        services.AddSingleton<IMessageHandler>(new
AlarmTriggeredHandler(new AlarmPausedHandler(new
AlarmStoppedHandler(new DefaultHandler())))));
    }


    public void Configure(IApplicationBuilder app,
IHostingEnvironment env, IMessageHandler messageHandler)
    {
        app.Run(async (context) =>
        {
            var message = new Message
            {
                Name = context.Request.Query["name"],
                Payload = context.Request.Query["payload"]
            };
            try
            {
                // Send the message into the chain of
responsibility
                messageHandler.Handle(message);
                await context.Response.WriteAsync($"Message
'{message.Name}' handled successfully.");
            }
            catch (NotSupportedException ex)
            {
                await context.Response.WriteAsync (ex.Message);
            }
        });
    }
}
```

In `Startup`, we manually create the chain of responsibility in the `ConfigureServices` method by registering the following instance as a singleton of `IMessageHandler`:

```
new AlarmTriggeredHandler(
    new AlarmPausedHandler(
        new AlarmStoppedHandler(
            new DefaultHandler())))
```

In that code each handlers are injected in the previous constructor manually (created with the new keyword).

Then, in the Configure method, we inject the IMessageHandler messageHandler instance and, for every request, we do the following:

1. Create a Message based on the query string.

2. Pass that message to the first handler of the chain of responsibility (injected into the Configure method): messageHandler.Handle(message);.

3. Write an error message when a NotSupportedException has been thrown, or a success message otherwise.

If we run the application, we should obtain the following message:

```
URL: https://localhost:10001/
Messages named '' are not supported.
```

By specifying a valid name such as AlarmTriggered, we should get the following result:

```
URL: https://localhost:10001/?name=AlarmTriggered
Message 'AlarmTriggered' handled successfully.
```

By specifying an invalid name such as SomeUnhandledMessageName, we should get the following result:

```
URL: https://localhost:10001/?name=SomeUnhandledMessageName
Messages named 'SomeUnhandledMessageName' are not supported.
```

And voilà. We have built a simple chain of responsibility that handles messages. Next, let's use both the Template Method and the Chain of Responsibility patterns to encapsulate our handlers' duplicated logic.

Project – Improved message interpreter

Now that we know both the Chain of Responsibility and the Template Method patterns, it is time to *DRY* out our handlers by extracting the shared logic into an abstract base class, using the Template Method pattern, and providing extension points to the subclasses.

DRY

We cover the **D**on't **R**epeat **Y**ourself principle in *Chapter 3, Architectural Principles*.

OK, so what has been duplicated?

- The `next` handler injection code has been duplicated, and, as an important part of the pattern, could be encapsulated into the base class.

- The logic testing whether the current handler can handle the message has been duplicated.

The new base class looks like this:

```csharp
public abstract class MessageHandlerBase : IMessageHandler
{
    private readonly IMessageHandler _next;
    public MessageHandlerBase(IMessageHandler next = null)
    {
        _next = next;
    }

    public void Handle(Message message)
    {
        if (CanHandle(message))
        {
            Process(message);
        }
        else if (HasNext())
        {
            _next.Handle(message);
        }
    }

    private bool HasNext()
    {
        return _next != null;
    }

    protected virtual bool CanHandle(Message message)
    {
        return message.Name == HandledMessageName;
    }
    protected abstract string HandledMessageName { get; }
```

```
    protected abstract void Process(Message message);
}
```

Based on those few changes, what is the template method, and what are the extension points (hooks)?

The MessageHandlerBase class adds the Handle template method. That template method's algorithm is easier to read than it was before. Then, MessageHandlerBase exposes the following extension points:

- CanHandleMessage(Message message) tests whether the HandledMessageName is equal to message.Name. This could be overridden if a handler required more complex comparison logic.

- HandledMessageName must be implemented by all subclasses, driving the default logic of CanHandleMessage.

- Process(Message message) must be implemented by all subclasses, allowing them to run logics against the message.

Let's now take a look at the three simplified alarm handlers:

```
public class AlarmTriggeredHandler : MessageHandlerBase
{
    protected override string HandledMessageName =>
"AlarmTriggered";
    public AlarmTriggeredHandler(IMessageHandler next = null) :
base(next) { }
    protected override void Process(Message message)
    {
        // Do something clever with the Payload
    }
}


public class AlarmPausedHandler : MessageHandlerBase
{
    protected override string HandledMessageName =>
"AlarmPaused";
    public AlarmPausedHandler(IMessageHandler next = null) :
base(next) { }
    protected override void Process(Message message)
    {
```

```
            // Do something clever with the Payload
    }
}


public class AlarmStoppedHandler : MessageHandlerBase
{
    protected override string HandledMessageName =>
"AlarmStopped";
    public AlarmStoppedHandler(IMessageHandler next = null) :
base(next) { }
    protected override void Process(Message message)
    {
        // Do something clever with the Payload
    }
}
```

As we can see from the updated alarm handlers, they are now limited to a single responsibility: processing the messages they can handle. In contrast, `MessageHandlerBase` now handles the chain of responsibility's plumbing.

By mixing those two patterns, we created a complex messaging system that divides responsibilities into handlers. There is one handler per message, and the chain logic is pushed into a base class. The beauty of such a system is that we don't have to think about all messages at once; we can focus on just one message at a time. When dealing with a new type of message, we can concentrate on that precise message and implement its handler and forget about the *N* other types. The consumers can also be super dumb, sending the request into the pipe without knowing about the chain of responsibility, and like magic, the right handler shall prevail!

Project – A final, finer-grained design

In the last example, we were using `HandledMessageName` and `CanHandleMessage` to decide whether a handler could handle a request. There is one problem with that code: if a subclass decides to override `CanHandleMessage`, and then decides that it no longer requires `HandledMessageName`, we would end up having a lingering, unused property in our system.

> **Note**
> There are worse situations, but we are talking component design here, so why not push that system a little further toward a better design.

One solution for fixing this is to create a finer-grained class hierarchy as follows:

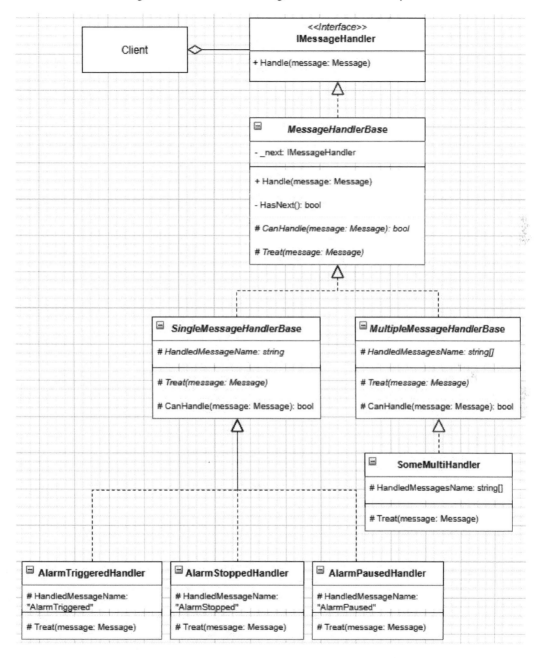

Figure 10.3 – Class diagram representing the design of the finer-grained project
that implements the Chain of Responsibility and Template Method patterns

That looks more complicated than it is, really. Before digging into what it actually does, let's take a look at the refactored code:

```
namespace FinalChainOfResponsibility
{
    public interface IMessageHandler
    {
        void Handle(Message message);
    }

    public abstract class MessageHandlerBase : IMessageHandler
    {
        private readonly IMessageHandler _next;
        public MessageHandlerBase(IMessageHandler next = null)
        {
            _next = next;
        }


        public void Handle(Message message)
        {
            if (CanHandle(message))
            {
                Process(message);
            }
            else if (HasNext())
            {
                _next.Handle(message);
            }
        }
        private bool HasNext()
        {
            return _next != null;
        }
        protected abstract bool CanHandle(Message message);
        protected abstract void Process(Message message);
    }
```

```csharp
    public abstract class SingleMessageHandlerBase :
MessageHandlerBase
    {
        public SingleMessageHandlerBase(IMessageHandler next =
null)
            : base(next) { }

        protected override bool CanHandle(Message message)
        {
            return message.Name == HandledMessageName;
        }
        protected abstract string HandledMessageName { get; }
    }

    public abstract class MultipleMessageHandlerBase :
MessageHandlerBase
    {
        public MultipleMessageHandlerBase(IMessageHandler next
= null)
            : base(next) { }

        protected override bool CanHandle(Message message)
        {
            return HandledMessagesName.Contains (message.Name);
        }
        protected abstract string[] HandledMessagesName { get;
}
    }
}
```

The omitted `AlarmPausedHandler`, `AlarmStoppedHandler`, and
`AlarmTriggeredHandler` classes now inherit from `SingleMessageHandlerBase`
instead of `MessageHandlerBase`, but nothing else has changed. `DefaultHandler`
has not changed either. For demonstration purposes, I added `SomeMultiHandler`,
which simulates a message handler that can handle `"Foo"`, `"Bar"`, and `"Baz"` messages.
That one looks like the following:

```
namespace FinalChainOfResponsibility
{
    public class SomeMultiHandler : MultipleMessageHandlerBase
    {
        public SomeMultiHandler(IMessageHandler next = null)
            : base(next) { }

        protected override string[] HandledMessagesName
            => new string[] { "Foo", "Bar", "Baz" };

        protected override void Process(Message message)
        {
            // Do something cleaver with the Payload
        }
    }
}
```

Now that we have seen the code and the UML representation of the class hierarchy, let's
analyze the actors of the new structure:

- `MessageHandlerBase` manages the chain of responsibility by handling the next
  handler logic and by exposing two hooks (Template Method pattern) for subclasses
  to extend:

  a) `bool CanHandle(Message message)`

  b) `void Process(Message message)`

- `SingleMessageHandlerBase` inherits from `MessageHandlerBase`
  and implements (override) the `bool CanHandle(Message message)`
  method. It implements the logic related to it and adds the `abstract string
  HandledMessageName { get; }` property that subclasses must define
  (override) for the `CanHandle` method to work (a required extension point).

- The subclasses of `SingleMessageHandlerBase` implement the `HandledMessageName` property that returns the message name that they can handle and implements the handling logic by overriding the `void Process(Message message)` method.

- `MultipleMessageHandlerBase` does the same as `SingleMessageHandlerBase`, but it uses a string array instead of a single string, supporting multiple handler names.

This may sound complicated, but what we did was to allow extensibility without the need to keep any unnecessary code in the process, leaving each class with a single responsibility:

- `MessageHandlerBase` handles _next.

- `SingleMessageHandlerBase` handles the `CanHandle` method of handlers, supporting just a single message.

- `MultipleMessageHandlerBase` handles the `CanHandle` method of handlers supporting multiple messages.

- Other classes must implement their version of `void Process(Message message)`.

And voilà! This is another example demonstrating the strength of the Template Method and the Chain of Responsibility patterns put together. That last example also emphasizes the importance of the SRP by allowing for greater flexibility while keeping the code reliable and maintainable.

Another strength of that design is the interface at the top. Anything that does not fit the class hierarchy can be implemented directly from the interface instead of trying to adapt logic from inappropriate structures—tricking code into doing your bidding often leads to half-baked solutions that become hard to maintain.

Conclusion

The Chain of Responsibility is another great GoF pattern. It allows dividing a large problem into smaller cohesive units, each doing its one job: handling its specific request. Mixed with the Template Method pattern, it can become even simpler to handle the chain, moving each part closer toward single responsibilities.

Now, let's see how the Chain of Responsibility pattern can help us follow the **SOLID** principles:

- **S**: The Chain of Responsibility aims toward this exact principle, making it a perfect SRP advocate: single units of logic!

- **O**: The Chain of Responsibility allows the addition, removal, and moving of handlers around without touching the code by only changing the composition of the chain.

- **L**: N/A.

- **I**: By creating a small interface with multiple handlers (implementations), the Chain of Responsibility should help with the ISP. The handler interface is not limited to a single method; it can expose multiple methods as long as they aim toward the same responsibility. Cohesion is key.

- **D**: By using the handler interface, no element of the chain, nor consumers, depend on a specific handler; they only depend on the interface.

Summary

In this chapter, we covered two GoF behavioral patterns. Those patterns can help us create a flexible, yet easy-to-maintain, system. As its name states, behavioral patterns aim at encapsulating application behaviors into cohesive software pieces.

First, we looked at the Template Method, which allowed us to encapsulate an algorithm's core inside a base class. It then allows its subclasses to "fill in the gaps" and extend that algorithm at predefined locations. These locations can be required (`abstract`) or optional (`virtual`).

Then, we explored the Chain of Responsibility pattern that opens the possibility of chaining multiple small handlers into a chain of processing, inputting the message to be processed at the beginning of the chain, and waiting for one or more handlers to execute the actual logic related to that message against it. That is an important nuance: you don't have to stop the chain's execution at the first handler. In some cases, the chain of responsibility could become more like a pipeline than a clear association of one message to one handler.

Lastly, using the Template Method pattern to encapsulate the chain of responsibility's chaining logic led us to a simpler implementation without any sacrifice.

In the next chapter, we are going to dig into the operation result design pattern to discover efficient ways of managing return values.

Questions

Let's take a look at a few practice questions:

1. Is it true that we can only add one `abstract` method when implementing the Template Method design pattern?

2. Can we use the strategy pattern in conjunction with the Template Method pattern?

3. Is it true that there is a limit of 32 handlers in a Chain of Responsibility?

4. In a Chain of Responsibility, can multiple handlers process the same message?

5. In what way can the Template Method help implement the Chain of Responsibility pattern?

11
Understanding the Operation Result Design Pattern

In this chapter, we explore the Operation Result pattern starting from simple to more complex cases. An operation result aims at communicating the success or the failure of an operation to its caller. It also allows that operation to return both a value and one or more messages to the caller.

Imagine any system in which you want to display user-friendly error messages, achieve some small speed gain, or even handle failure easily and explicitly. The **Operation Result** design pattern can help you achieve these goals. One way to use it is as the result of a remote operation, such as after querying a remote web service.

The following topics will be covered in this chapter:

- The Operation Result design pattern basics
- The Operation Result design pattern returning a value
- The Operation Result design pattern returning error messages
- The Operation Result design pattern returning messages with severity levels
- Using sub-classes and static factory methods for better isolation of successes and failures

Goal

The role of the **Operation Result** pattern is to give an operation (a method) the possibility to return a complex result (an object), which allows the consumer to:

- [Mandatory] Access the success indicator of the operation (that is, whether the operation succeeded or not).

- [Optional] Access the result of the operation, in case there is one (the return value of the method).

- [Optional] Access the cause of the failure, in case the operation was not successful (error messages).

- [Optional] Access other information that documents the operation's result. This could be as simple as a list of messages or as complex as multiple properties.

This can go even further, such as returning the severity of a failure or adding any other relevant information for the specific use case. The success indicator could be binary (`true` or `false`), or there could be more than two states, such as success, partial success, and failure. Your imagination (and your needs) is your limit!

> **Tip**
>
> Focus on your needs first, then use your imagination to reach the best possible solution. Software engineering is not only about applying techniques that others told you to. It's an art! The only difference is that you are crafting software instead of painting or woodworking. And that most people won't see any of that art (code).

Design

It is easy to rely on throwing exceptions when an operation fails. However, the Operation Result pattern is an alternative way of communicating success or failure between components when you don't want to, or can't, use exceptions.

To be used effectively, a method must return an object containing one or more elements presented in the *Goal* section. As a rule of thumb, a method returning an operation result should not throw an exception. This way, consumers don't have to handle anything else other than the operation result itself. For special cases, you could allow exceptions to be thrown, but at that point, it would be a judgment call based on clear specifications or facing a real problem.

Instead of walking you through all of the possible UML diagrams, let's jump into the code and explore multiple smaller examples after taking a look at the basic sequence diagram that describes the simplest form of this pattern, applicable to all examples:

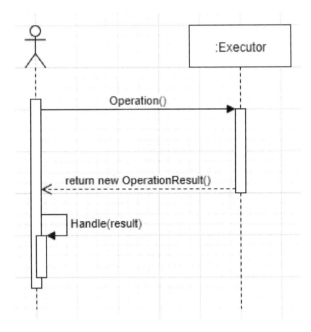

Figure 11.1 – Sequence diagram of the Operation Result design pattern

As we can see from the diagram, an operation returns a result (an object), and then the caller can handle that result. What can be included in that result object is covered in the following examples.

Project – Implementing different Operation Result patterns

In this project, a consumer routes the HTTP requests to the right handler. We are visiting each of those handlers one by one, which will help us implement simple to more complex operation results. This should show you the many alternative ways to implement the Operation Result pattern to help you understand it, make it your own, and implement it as required in your projects.

The consumer

The consumer in all examples is the `Startup` class. The following code routes the request toward a handler:

```
app.UseRouter(builder =>
{
    builder.MapGet("/simplest-form", SimplestFormHandler);
    builder.MapGet("/single-error", SingleErrorHandler);
    builder.MapGet("/single-error-with-value",
SingleErrorWithValueHandler);
    builder.MapGet("/multiple-errors-with-value",
MultipleErrorsWithValueHandler);
    builder.MapGet("/multiple-errors-with-value-and-severity",
MultipleErrorsWithValueAndSeverityHandler);
    builder.MapGet("/static-factory-methods",
StaticFactoryMethodHandler);
});
```

Next, we cover each handler one by one.

Its simplest form

The following diagram represents the simplest form of the Operation Result pattern:

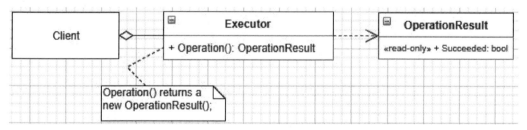

Figure 11.2 – Class diagram of the Operation Result design pattern

We can translate that class diagram into the following blocks of code:

```
namespace OperationResult
{
    public class Startup
    {
        // ...
```

```csharp
        private async Task SimplestFormHandler(HttpRequest
request, HttpResponse response, RouteData data)
        {
            // Create an instance of the class that contains
the operation
            var executor = new SimplestForm.Executor();

            // Execute the operation and handle its result
            var result = executor.Operation();
            if (result.Succeeded)
            {
                // Handle the success
                await response.WriteAsync("Operation
succeeded");
            }
            else
            {
                // Handle the failure
                await response.WriteAsync("Operation failed");
            }
        }
    }
}
```

The preceding code handles the /simplest-form HTTP request. It is the consumer of the operation.

```csharp
namespace OperationResult.SimplestForm
{
    public class Executor
    {
        public OperationResult Operation()
        {
            // Randomize the success indicator
            // This should be real logic
            var randomNumber = new Random().Next(100);
            var success = randomNumber % 2 == 0;
```

```
                    // Return the operation result
                    return new OperationResult(success);
            }
    }
    public class OperationResult
    {
        public OperationResult(bool succeeded)
        {
            Succeeded = succeeded;
        }

        public bool Succeeded { get; }
    }
}
```

The `Executor` class implements the operation to execute with the `Operation` method. That method returns an instance of the `OperationResult` class. The implementation is based on a random number. Sometimes it succeeds, and sometimes it fails. You would usually code some application logic in that method instead.

The `OperationResult` class represents the result of the operation. In this case, it is a simple read-only boolean value stored in the `Succeeded` property.

In this form, the difference between the `Operation()` method returning a `bool` and an instance of `OperationResult` is thin, but it exists nonetheless. By returning an `OperationResult` object, you can extend the return value over time, adding to it, which you cannot do with a `bool` without updating all consumers.

A single error message

Now that we know whether the operation succeeded or not, we want to know what went wrong. To do that, we can add an `ErrorMessage` property to the `OperationResult` class. By doing that, we no longer need to set whether the operation succeeded or not; we could compute that using the `ErrorMessage` property instead.

The logic behind this improvement is as follows:

- When there is no error message, the operation succeeded.
- When there is an error message, the operation failed.

The `OperationResult` implementing this logic looks like the following:

```
namespace OperationResult.SingleError
{
    public class OperationResult
    {
        public OperationResult() { }
        public OperationResult(string errorMessage)
        {
            ErrorMessage = errorMessage ?? throw new
ArgumentNullException(nameof(errorMessage));
        }
        public bool Succeeded => string.
IsNullOrWhiteSpace(ErrorMessage);
        public string ErrorMessage { get; }
    }
}
```

In the preceding code, we have the following:

- Two constructors:

    a) The parameterless constructor that handles successes.

    b) The constructor that takes an error message as a parameter that handles errors.

- The `Succeeded` property that checks for an `ErrorMessage`.

- The `ErrorMessage` property that contains an optional error message.

The executor of that operation looks similar but uses the new constructors, setting an error message instead of directly setting the success indicator:

```
namespace OperationResult.SingleError
{
    public class Executor
    {
        public OperationResult Operation()
        {
            // Randomize the success indicator
            // This should be real logic
            var randomNumber = new Random().Next(100);
```

```
            var success = randomNumber % 2 == 0;


            // Return the operation result
            return success
                ? new OperationResult()
                : new OperationResult($"Something went wrong
with the number '{randomNumber}'.");
        }
    }
}
```

The consuming code does the same as in the previous sample but writes the error message
in the response output instead of a generic failure string:

```
namespace OperationResult
{
    public class Startup
    {
        // ...
        private async Task SingleErrorHandler(HttpRequest
request, HttpResponse response, RouteData data)
        {
            // Create an instance of the class that contains
the operation
            var executor = new SingleError.Executor();

            // Execute the operation and handle its result
            var result = executor.Operation();
            if (result.Succeeded)
            {
                // Handle the success
                await response.WriteAsync("Operation
succeeded");
            }
            else
            {
```

```
                // Handle the failure
                await response.WriteAsync (result.
ErrorMessage);
            }
        }
    }
}
```

When looking at that example, we can begin to comprehend the Operation Result pattern's usefulness. It gets us further away from the simple success indicator that looked like an overcomplicated boolean. And this is not the end of our exploration because many more forms can be designed and used in more complex scenarios.

Adding a return value

Now that we have a reason for failure, we may want the operation to return a value. To achieve this, let's start from the last example and add a Value property to the OperationResult class as follows (we cover **init-only properties** in *Chapter 17, ASP.NET Core User Interfaces*):

```
namespace OperationResult.SingleErrorWithValue
{
    public class OperationResult
    {
        // ...
        public int? Value { get; init; }
    }
}
```

The operation is also very similar, but we are setting the Value using the object initializer:

```
namespace OperationResult.SingleErrorWithValue
{
    public class Executor
    {
        public OperationResult Operation()
        {
            // Randomize the success indicator
            // This should be real logic
```

```
            var randomNumber = new Random().Next(100);
            var success = randomNumber % 2 == 0;meet


            // Return the operation result
            return success
                ? new OperationResult { Value =
                randomNumber }
                : new OperationResult($"Something went wrong
with the number '{randomNumber}'.")
                {
                    Value = randomNumber
                };
        }
    }
}
```

With that in place, the consumer can use the `Value` as follows:

```
namespace OperationResult
{
    public class Startup
    {
        // ...
        private async Task SingleErrorWithValueHandler
(HttpRequest request, HttpResponse response, RouteData data)
        {
            // Create an instance of the class that contains
the operation
            var executor = new SingleErrorWithValue.Executor();


            // Execute the operation and handle its result
            var result = executor.Operation();
            if (result.Succeeded)
            {
                // Handle the success
                await response.WriteAsync($"Operation succeeded
with a value of '{result.Value} '.");
            }
```

```
            else
            {
                // Handle the failure
                await response.WriteAsync (result.
ErrorMessage);
            }
        }
    }
}
```

As we can see from this sample, we can display a relevant error message when the operation fails and use a return value when it succeeds (or even when it fails in this case), and all of that without throwing an exception. With this, the power of the Operation Result pattern starts to emerge. We are not done yet, so let's jump into the next evolution.

Multiple error messages

Now we are at the point where we can transfer a `Value` and an `ErrorMessage` to the operation consumers, but what about transferring multiple errors, such as validation errors? To achieve this, we can convert our `ErrorMessage` property into an `IEnumerable<string>` and add methods to manage messages:

```
namespace OperationResult.MultipleErrorsWithValue
{
    public class OperationResult
    {
        private readonly List<string> _errors;
        public OperationResult(params string[] errors)
        {
            _errors = new List<string>(errors ?? Enumerable.
Empty<string>());
        }

        public bool Succeeded => !HasErrors();
        public int? Value { get; set; }

        public IEnumerable<string> Errors => new
ReadOnlyCollection<string>(_errors);
        public bool HasErrors()
```

```
        {
                return Errors?.Count() > 0;
        }


        public void AddError(string message)
        {
                _errors.Add(message);
        }
    }
}
```

Let's take a look at the new pieces in the preceding code before continuing:

- The errors are now stored in List<string> _errors and returned to
  the consumers through a ReadOnlyCollection<string> instance
  that is hidden under an IEnumerable<string> interface. The
  ReadOnlyCollection<string> instance denies the ability to change the
  collection from the outside, assuming the consumer is clever enough to cast
  IEnumerable<string> to List<string>, for example.

- The Succeeded property was updated to account for a collection instead of
  a single message and follows the same logic.

- The HasErrors method was added for convenience.

- The AddError method allows adding errors after the instance creation, which
  could happen in more complex scenarios, such as multi-step operations where parts
  could fail without the operation itself failing.

> **Note**
>
> For additional control over the result, the AddError method should be
> hidden from the outside of the operation. That way, a consumer could not add
> errors to the result after the completion of the operation. Of course, the level of
> control that is required depends on each specific scenario. A way to code this
> would be to return an interface that does not contain the method, instead of
> the concrete type that does.

Now that the operation result is updated, the operation itself can stay the same, but
we could add more than one error to the result. The consumer must handle that slight
difference and support multiple errors.

Let's take a look at that code:

```
namespace OperationResult
{
    public class Startup
    {
        private async Task
MultipleErrorsWithValueHandler(HttpRequest request,
HttpResponse response, RouteData data)
        {
            // Create an instance of the class that contains
the operation
            var executor = new MultipleErrorsWithValue.
Executor();

            // Execute the operation and handle its result
            var result = executor.Operation();
            if (result.Succeeded)
            {
                // Handle the success
                await response.WriteAsync($"Operation succeeded
with a value of '{result.Value}'.");
            }
            else
            {
                // Handle the failure
                var json = JsonSerializer.Serialize (result.
Errors);
                response.Headers["ContentType"] = "application/
json";
                await response.WriteAsync(json);
            }
        }
    }
}
```

The code serializes the IEnumerable<string> Errors property to JSON before outputting it to the client to help visualize the collection.

> **Tip**
>
> Returning a `plain/text` string when the operation succeeds and an
> `application/json` array when it fails is usually not a good idea. I suggest
> not doing something similar to this in a real application. Either return JSON
> or plain text. Try not to mix content types in a single endpoint. In most cases,
> mixing content types will only create avoidable complexity. We could say that
> reading `content-type` and the status code headers would be enough to
> know what has been returned by the server, and that's the purpose of those
> headers in the HTTP specifications. But, even if that is true, it is way easier for
> your fellow developers to always be able to expect the same content type when
> consuming your APIs.
>
> When designing systems' contracts, consistency and uniformity are usually
> better than incoherency, ambiguity, and variance.

Our Operation Result pattern implementation is getting better and better but still lacks
a few features. One of those features is the possibility of propagating messages that are
not errors, such as information messages and warnings, which we will implement next.

Adding message severity

Now that our operation result structure is materializing, let's update our last iteration
to support message severity.

First, we need a severity indicator. An enum is a good candidate for this kind of work,
but it could be something else. Let's name it `OperationResultSeverity`.

Then we need a message class to encapsulate both the message and the severity level; let's
name that class `OperationResultMessage`. The new code looks like this:

```
namespace OperationResult.WithSeverity
{
    public class OperationResultMessage
    {
        public OperationResultMessage(string message,
OperationResultSeverity severity)
        {
            Message = message ?? throw new
ArgumentNullException(nameof(message));
            Severity = severity;
        }
```

```
        public string Message { get; }
        public OperationResultSeverity Severity { get; }
    }

    public enum OperationResultSeverity
    {
        Information = 0,
        Warning = 1,
        Error = 2
    }
}
```

As you can see, we have a simple data structure to replace our `string` messages.

Then we need to update the `OperationResult` class to use that new `OperationResultMessage` class. We need to ensure that the operation result indicates a success only when there is no `OperationResultSeverity.Error`, allowing it to transmit the `OperationResultSeverity.Information` and `OperationResultSeverity.Warnings` messages:

```
namespace OperationResult.WithSeverity
{
    public class OperationResult
    {
        private readonly List<OperationResultMessage>
_messages;
        public OperationResult(params OperationResultMessage[]
errors)
        {
            _messages = new List<OperationResultMessage>
(errors ?? Enumerable.Empty <OperationResultMessage>());
        }

        public bool Succeeded => !HasErrors();
        public int? Value { get; init; }

        public IEnumerable<OperationResultMessage> Messages
            => new ReadOnlyCollection
<OperationResultMessage>(_messages);
```

```csharp
        public bool HasErrors()
        {
            return FindErrors().Count() > 0;
        }

        public void AddMessage(OperationResultMessage message)
        {
            _messages.Add(message);
        }

        private IEnumerable<OperationResultMessage> FindErrors()
            => _messages.Where(x => x.Severity ==
OperationResultSeverity.Error);
    }
}
```

The highlighted lines represent the new logic setting the success state only when no error is present in the _messages list.

With that in place, the Executor class also needs to be revamped.

So let's look at that new version of the Executor class:

```csharp
namespace OperationResult.WithSeverity
{
    public class Executor
    {
        public OperationResult Operation()
        {
            // Randomize the success indicator
            // This should be real logic
            var randomNumber = new Random().Next(100);
            var success = randomNumber % 2 == 0;

            // Some information message
            var information = new OperationResultMessage(
                "This should be very informative!",
```

```
                OperationResultSeverity.Information
            );


            // Return the operation result
            if (success)
            {
                var warning = new OperationResultMessage(
                    "Something went wrong, but we will try
again later automatically until it works!",
                    OperationResultSeverity.Warning
                );
                return new OperationResult(information,
warning) { Value = randomNumber };
            }
            else
            {
                var error = new OperationResultMessage(
                    $"Something went wrong with the number
'{randomNumber}'.",
                    OperationResultSeverity.Error
                );
                return new OperationResult(information, error)
{ Value = randomNumber };
            }
        }
    }
}
```

As you may have noticed, we removed the tertiary operator to make the code easier to read.

> **Tip**
> You should always aim to write code that is easy to read. It is OK to use the
> language features, but nesting statements over statements on a single line has its
> limits and can quickly become a mess.

In that last code block, both successes and failures return two messages:

- When it is successful, the messages are an information message and a warning.

- When it is unsuccessful, the messages are an information message and an error.

From the consumer standpoint (see the following code), we now only serialize the result to the output to clearly show the outcome. Here is the `/multiple-errors-with-value-and-severity` endpoint delegate that consumes this new operation:

```csharp
namespace OperationResult
{
    public class Startup
    {
        // ...
        private async Task
MultipleErrorsWithValueAndSeverityHandler(HttpRequest request,
HttpResponse response, RouteData data)
        {
            // Create an instance of the class that contains
the operation
            var executor = new WithSeverity.Executor();

            // Execute the operation and handle its result
            var result = executor.Operation();
            if (result.Succeeded)
            {
                // Handle the success
            }
            else
            {
                // Handle the failure
            }
            var json = JsonSerializer.Serialize(result);
            response.Headers["ContentType"] = "application/
json";
            await response.WriteAsync(json);
        }
```

```
        }
}
```

As you can see, it is still as easy to use, but now with more flexibility added to it. We could do something with the different types of messages, such as displaying them to the user, retrying the operation, and more.

For now, if you run the application and call that endpoint, successful calls should return a JSON string that looks like the following:

```
{
    "Succeeded": true,
    "Value": 86,
    "Messages": [
        {
            "Message": "This should be very informative!",
            "Severity": 0
        },
        {
            "Message": "Something went wrong, but we will try
again later automatically until it works!",
            "Severity": 1
        }
    ]
}
```

Failures should return a JSON string that looks like this:

```
{
    "Succeeded": false,
    "Value": 87,
    "Messages": [
        {
            "Message": "This should be very informative!",
            "Severity": 0
        },
        {
            "Message": "Something went wrong with the
            number '87'.",
```

```
            "Severity": 2
        }
    ]
}
```

One more idea to improve this design would be to add a `Status` property that returns a complex success result based on each message's severity level. To do that, we could create another `enum`:

```
public enum OperationStatus{ Success, Failure, PartialSuccess}
```

Then we could access that through a new property named `Status`, on the `OperationResult` class. With this, a consumer could handle partial successes without digging into the messages themselves. I will leave you to play with this one on your own.

Now that we've expanded our simple example into this, what happens if we want the `Value` to be optional? To do that, we could create multiple operation result classes that each hold more or less information (properties); let's try that next.

Sub-classes and factories

In this iteration, we keep all of the properties, but we change how we instantiate the `OperationResult` objects.

A **static factory method** is nothing more than a static method with the responsibility to create objects. As you are about to see, it can become handy for ease of use. As always, I cannot stress this enough: be careful when designing something static, or it could haunt you later.

Let's start with some already-visited code:

```
namespace OperationResult.StaticFactoryMethod
{
    public class OperationResultMessage
    {
        public OperationResultMessage(string message,
OperationResultSeverity severity)
        {
            Message = message ?? throw new
ArgumentNullException(nameof(message));
            Severity = severity;
        }
```

```
        public string Message { get; }
        public OperationResultSeverity Severity { get; }
    }

    public enum OperationResultSeverity
    {
        Information = 0,
        Warning = 1,
        Error = 2
    }
}
```

The preceding code is the same as we used before. In the following block of code, the severity is not considered when computing the operation's success or failure result. Instead, we create an abstract OperationResult class with two sub-classes:

- SuccessfulOperationResult, which represents successful operations.
- FailedOperationResult, which represents failed operations.

Then the next step is to force the use of the specifically designed class by creating two static factory methods:

- public static OperationResult Success(), which returns a SuccessfulOperationResult.
- public static OperationResult Failure(params OperationResultMessage[] errors), which returns a FailedOperationResult.

Doing this moves the responsibility of deciding whether the operation is a success or not from the OperationResult class itself to the Operation method.

The following code block shows the new OperationResult implementation (the static factory is highlighted):

```
namespace OperationResult.StaticFactoryMethod
{
    public abstract class OperationResult
    {
        private OperationResult() { }
```

```csharp
        public abstract bool Succeeded { get; }
        public virtual int? Value { get; init; }
        public abstract IEnumerable<OperationResultMessage>
Messages { get; }


        public static OperationResult Success(int? value =
null)
        {
            return new SuccessfulOperationResult { Value =
value };
        }


        public static OperationResult Failure(params
OperationResultMessage[] errors)
        {
            return new FailedOperationResult(errors);
        }


        public sealed class SuccessfulOperationResult :
OperationResult
        {
            public override bool Succeeded => true;
            public override IEnumerable
<OperationResultMessage> Messages
                => Enumerable.Empty <OperationResultMessage>();
        }


        public sealed class FailedOperationResult :
OperationResult
        {
            private readonly List<OperationResultMessage>
_messages;
            public FailedOperationResult(params
OperationResultMessage[] errors)
            {
                _messages = new
List<OperationResultMessage>(errors ?? Enumerable.
Empty<OperationResultMessage>());
```

```
                    }

            public override bool Succeeded => false;

            public override IEnumerable
<OperationResultMessage> Messages
                => new ReadOnlyCollection
<OperationResultMessage>(_messages);
        }
    }
}
```

After analyzing the code, there are two closely related particularities:

- The `OperationResult` class has a private constructor.
- Both the `SuccessfulOperationResult` and `FailedOperationResult` classes are nested inside `OperationResult` and inherit from it.

Nested classes are the only way to inherit from the `OperationResult` class because, as a member of the class, nested classes have access to its private members, including the constructor. Otherwise, it is impossible to inherit from `OperationResult`.

Since the beginning of the book, I have repeated **flexibility** many times; but you don't always want flexibility. Sometimes you want control over what you expose and what you allow consumers to do.

In this specific case, we could have used a protected constructor instead, or we could have implemented a fancier way of instancing successes and failures instances. However, I decided to use this opportunity to show you how to lock an implementation in place, making it impossible to extend by inheritance from the outside. We could have built mechanisms in our classes to allow controlled extensibility, but for this one, let's keep it locked in tight!

From there, the only missing pieces are the operation itself and the client that consumes that operation. Let's take a look at the operation first:

```
namespace OperationResult.StaticFactoryMethod
{
    public class Executor
    {
        public OperationResult Operation()
        {
```

```
// Randomize the success indicator
// This should be real logic
var randomNumber = new Random().Next(100);
var success = randomNumber % 2 == 0;


// Return the operation result
if (success)
{
    return OperationResult.Success(randomNumber);
}
else
{
    var error = new OperationResultMessage(
        $"Something went wrong with the number
'{randomNumber}'.",
        OperationResultSeverity.Error
    );
    return OperationResult.Failure(error);
    }
  }
 }
}
```

The two highlighted lines in the preceding code block show the elegance of this new improvement. I find this code very easy to read, which was the objective. We now have two methods that clearly define our intentions when using them: Success or Failure.

The consumer uses the same code that we saw before in other examples, so I'll omit it here.

Advantages and disadvantages

Here are a few advantages and disadvantages that come with the Operation Result design pattern.

Advantages

It is more explicit than throwing an Exception since the operation result type is specified explicitly as the method's return type. That makes it more evident than knowing what type of exceptions the operation and its dependencies can throw.

Another advantage is the execution speed; returning an object is faster than throwing an exception. Not that much faster, but faster nonetheless.

Disadvantages

Using operation results is more complex than throwing exceptions because we must *manually propagate it up the call stack* (a.k.a. returned by the callee and handled by the caller). This is especially true if the operation result must go up multiple levels, which could be an indicator not to use the pattern.

It is easy to expose members that are not used in all scenarios, creating an API surface that is bigger than needed, where some parts are used only in some cases. But, between this and spending countless hours designing the perfect system, sometimes exposing an `int?` `Value { get; }` property can be a more than viable option. From there, you have lots of options to reduce that surface to a minimum. Use your imagination and your designing skills to overcome those challenges!

Summary

In this chapter, we visited multiple forms of the Operation Result pattern, from an augmented boolean to a complex data structure containing messages, values, and success indicators. We also explored static factories and private constructors to control external access. Furthermore, after all of that exploring, we can conclude that there are almost endless possibilities around the Operation Result pattern. Each specific use case should dictate how to make it happen. From here, I am confident that you have enough information about the pattern to explore the many more possibilities by yourself, and I highly encourage you to.

At this point, we would usually explore how the **Operation Result** pattern can help us follow the SOLID principles. However, it depends too much on the implementation, so here are a few points instead:

- The `OperationResult` class encapsulates the result, extracting that responsibility from the other system's components (SRP).

- We violated the ISP with the `Value` property in multiple examples. This was minor and could have been done differently, which could lead to a more complex design.

- We could compare an **operation result** to a **view model** or a **DTO**, but returned by an operation (method). From there, we could add an abstraction or stick with returning a concrete class, which we could see as a violation of the DIP.

- When the advantages surpass the minor and limited impacts of those two violations, I don't mind letting them slide (principles are ideals, rules, not laws).

This chapter concludes the *Designing at Component Scale* section and leads to the *Designing at Application Scale* section, in which we'll explore higher-level design patterns.

Questions

Let's take a look at a few practice questions:

1. Is returning an operation result when doing an asynchronous call, such as an HTTP request, a good idea?

2. What is the name of the pattern that we implemented using static methods?

3. Is it faster to return an operation result than throwing an exception?

Further reading

Here are some links to build on what we learned in this chapter:

- An article on my blog about exceptions (title: *A beginner guide to exceptions | The basics*): `https://net5.link/PpEm`

- An article on my blog about Operation Result (title*: Operation result | Design Pattern*): `https://net5.link/4o2q`

- I have a generic open source implementation of the Operation Result pattern, allowing you to use it by adding a NuGet package to your project: `https://net5.link/FeGZ`

Section 4: Designing at Application Scale

In this section, we enter the realm of application design. Instead of focusing on a smaller part of an application, we look at how we want to design the application itself. We start by looking into layering, which exposes the bases of application design, where we focus on the three most common layers used in layered applications before moving toward the evolution of layering. We explore two ways of modeling the domain model. We then explore a way to encapsulate and lower the burden of layering and model copy before moving on to newer architectural styles, such as vertical slice and microservices.

Each of these chapters could make a book by themselves, so we explore them at a higher level, helping you make more informed decisions when the time to choose an architectural style will arrive. This section is a starting point to further reading, while still filled with useful content, patterns, tips, and technologies to use straight away in your everyday projects.

The goal is to cover as many application-level patterns as possible. The reason is that knowing a little about many techniques helps choose the right method for the job at hand instead of picking the same one every time. Getting better at something is easier when you know where to start, but impossible if you don't know what options are available.

This section comprises the following chapters:

- *Chapter 12, Understanding Layering*
- *Chapter 13, Getting Started with Object Mappers*
- *Chapter 14, Mediator and CQRS Design Patterns*
- *Chapter 15, Getting Started with Vertical Slice Architecture*
- *Chapter 16, Introduction to Microservices Architecture*

12
Understanding Layering

In this chapter, we'll explore the inherent concepts behind layering. Layering is a popular way of organizing computer systems by encapsulating major concerns into layers. Those concerns are related to a "computer vocation" such as "data access" instead of a "business concern" such as "inventory." It is essential to understand the concepts behind layering as other concepts were born from them.

We'll start this chapter by exploring the initial ideas behind layering. Then, we'll explore alternatives that can help us solve different problems. We will use both an **anemic model** and a **rich model** and expose pros and cons of both in action. Finally, we will quickly explore **Clean Architecture**, which is what I call the evolution of layering.

The following topics will be covered in this chapter:

- Introduction to layering
- Responsibilities of the common layers
- Abstract data layer
- Shared rich model
- Clean Architecture

Let's get started!

Introduction to layering

Now that we've explored a few design patterns and played with ASP.NET Core 5 a little, it is time to jump into layering. In most computer systems, there are layers. Why? Because it is an efficient way to partition and organize units of logic together. We could conceptually represent layers as horizontal chunks of software, each encapsulating a concern.

Let's start by examining a classic three-layer application design:

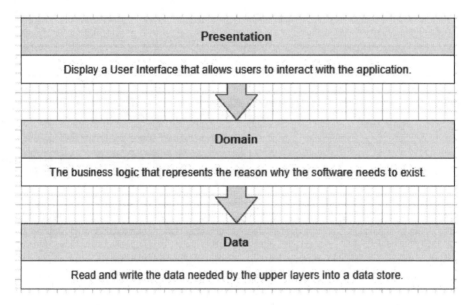

Figure 12.1 – A classic three layer application design

The **presentation layer** represents any user interface that a user can interact with to reach the **domain**. In our case, it could be an ASP.NET Core 5 web application. However, anything from WPF to WinForms to Android could be a valid non-web presentation layer alternative.

The **domain layer** represents the core logic driven by the business rules; this is the solution to the problem that the application should be solving. The domain layer is also called the **business logic layer** (**BLL**).

The **data layer** represents the bridge between the data and the application. The data could be stored in a SQL Server database, hosted elsewhere, a NoSQL database hosted in the cloud, a mix of all of those, or anything else that fits the business needs. The data layer is also called the **data access layer (DAL)** and the **persistance layer**.

Let's jump to an example. Given that a user has been authenticated and authorized, here is what happens when they want to create a book in a bookstore application that's been built using those three layers:

1. The user requests the page by sending a GET request to the server.

2. The server handles that GET request (**presentation layer**) and then returns the page to the user.

3. The user fills out the form and sends a POST request back to the server.

4. The server handles the POST request (**presentation layer**) and then sends it to the **domain layer** for processing.

5. The **domain layer** executes the *create a book routine* and then tells the **data layer** to persist the data.

6. The server then returns the appropriate response to the user, most likely a page containing a list of books and a message telling them that the operation was successful.

Following a classic layering architecture, a layer can only talk to the next layer in the stack. **Presentation** talks to **domain**, which talks to **data**, and so on. The important part is that **each layer must be independent and isolated to limit tight coupling**.

Moreover, each layer should own its **model**. For example, the **view models** should not be sent to the **domain**; only **domain objects** should be used there. The opposite is also true: since the **domain** returns its own objects to the **presentation layer**, the **presentation layer** should not leak them to the **views**, but organize the required information into **view models** instead.

Here is a visual example:

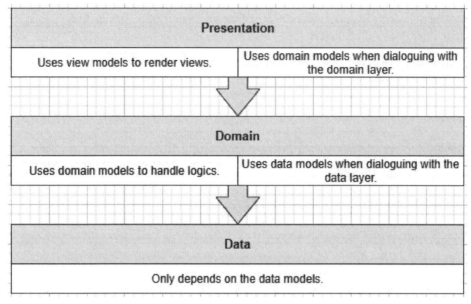

Figure 12.2 – Diagram representing how the layers interact with one another

Let's examine the advantages and disadvantages of layering, starting with the advantages:

- Knowing the purpose of a layer makes it easy to understand what its elements are doing for the application. For example, it is easy to guess that the components of the **data layer** read or write some data somewhere.

- It creates a cohesive unit built around a single concern. For example, our **data layer** should not render any user interface; it should stick to accessing data.

- It allows us to decouple the layer from the rest of the system (the other layers). You can isolate and work with a layer without any knowledge of the others. For example, suppose you are tasked with optimizing a query in a data access layer. In that case, you don't need to know about the user interface that eventually displays that data to a user. You only need to focus on that element, optimize it, test it in isolation, and then ship the layer or redeploy the application.

- Like any other isolated unit, it should be possible to reuse a layer. For example, we could reuse our **data access layer** in another application that needs to query the same database for a different purpose (a different **domain layer**).

> **Tip**
>
> Some layers are theoretically easier to reuse than others, and reusability could add more or less value, depending on the software you are building. I have never seen a layer being integrally reused in practice, and I've rarely heard or read about people that did – each time rather ends in a not-so-reusable-after-all situation.
>
> Based on my experience, I would strongly suggest not over-aiming at reusability when it is not a precise specification that adds value to your application. By limiting your overengineering endeavors, you and your employers could save a lot of time and money. We must not forget that our job is to deliver value.
>
> As a rule of thumb, do what needs to be done, not more, but do it well.

Ok, now, let's look at the drawbacks:

- By splitting your software horizontally (into layers), each feature crosses all of the layers. This often leads to cascading changes between layers. For example, if we decide to add a field to our bookstore database, we would need to update the database, the code that accesses it (**data layer**), the business logic (**domain layer**), and the user interface (**presentation layer**). With volatile specs or low-budget projects, this can become painful! Newcomers could also have a harder time implementing a full-stack feature that crosses all layers.

- Since a layer directly depends on the layer under it, using dependency injection is impossible without introducing an **abstraction layer** or referencing lower layers from the **presentation layer**. For example, if the **domain layer** depends on the **data layer**, changing the data layer would require a rewrite and thus, rewriting all of that coupling from the **domain** to the **data**. *Don't worry about this just yet; it is a fairly easy challenge to overcome.*

- Since each layer owns its entities, the more layers you add, the more copies there are of the entities, leading to performance loss. For example, the **presentation layer** takes a **view model** and copies it to a **domain object**. Then, the **domain layer** copies it to a **data object**. Finally, the **data layer** translates it into SQL to persist it into a **database** (SQL Server, for example). The opposite is also true when reading from the database.

We'll explore ways to combat some of those drawbacks later. Until then, I'd like to point out that even if three is probably the most popular number of layers, we can create as many as we need; we are not limited to three layers.

I strongly recommend that you don't do what we just explored. It is an old, more basic way of doing layering. We will be looking at multiple improvements we can make to this layering system during this chapter, so keep reading before jumping to a conclusion. I decided to explore layering from the beginning in case you have to work with that kind of application. Furthermore, studying its chronological evolution, fixing some flaws, and adding options should help you understand the concepts instead of just knowing a single way of doing things. Understanding the patterns is the key to software architecture, not just learning to apply them.

Splitting the layers

Now that we've talked about layers and saw them as big horizontal slices of responsibilities, we can organize our applications more granularly by splitting those big slices vertically, creating multiple smaller layers. This can help us organize applications by features or by bounding context. It could also allow us to compose multiple different user interfaces using the same building blocks, which would be easier than reusing colossal-size layers.

Here is a conceptual representation of this idea:

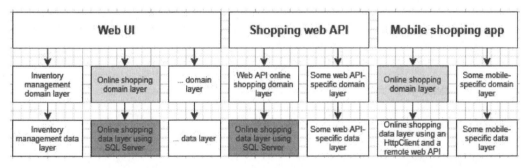

Figure 12.3 – Organizing multiple applications using smaller partially shared layers

We can split an application into multiple features (vertically) and divide each into layers (horizontally). Based on the previous diagram, we named those features as follows:

- Inventory management
- Online shopping
- Others

So, we can bring in the online shopping domain and data layers to our Shopping web API without bringing everything else with it. Moreover, we can bring the online shopping domain layer to the mobile app and swap its data layer for another that talks to the web API.

We could also use our web API as a plain and simple data access application with different logic attached to it, while keeping the shopping data layer underneath.

We could end up with the following recomposed applications (this is just one possible outcome):

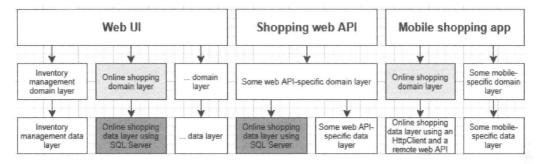

Figure 12.4 – Organizing multiple applications using smaller partially shared layers

These are just examples of what we can conceptually do with layers. However, the most important thing to remember is not how the diagrams are laid out, but the specifications of the applications that you are building. Only those specs and a good analysis can help you create the best possible design for that exact problem. Here, I used a hypothetical shopping example, but it could have been anything.

By splitting huge horizontal slices vertically, each piece becomes easier to reuse and share. This improvement can yield interesting results, especially if you have multiple frontend apps or plan to migrate away from a monolith in the future.

Layers versus tiers versus assemblies

So far in this chapter, we have been talking about layers without talking about making them into code. Before we jump into that subject, I'd like to talk about **tiers**. You may have seen the term **3-tier architecture** somewhere before or read people talking about **tiers** and **layers**, and possibly even interchanging them in the same context as synonyms. However, they are not the same. Let's take a look:

- **Tiers** are **physical**; each **tier** can be deployed on its own machine. For example, you could have a database server, a server hosting your web API that contains the business logic (the **domain**), and another server that serves an Angular application (**presentation**); these are three tiers (three distinct machines), and each **tier** can scale independently.

- **Layers** are **logical**; each **layer** is only the logical organization of code, with concerns organized and divided in a layered way. For example, you may create one or more projects in Visual Studio and organize your code into three layers. Then, you deploy your application, and all of these layers are deployed together on the same server. This would be one tier and three layers.

Now that we've talked about **tiers**, let's take a look at a **layer** versus an **assembly**. You do not have to split your layers into different assemblies; you can have your three layers residing in the same assembly. It can be easier to create undesirable coupling when all of the code is in the same project, but with some rigor, some rules, and some conventions, it is a viable option. That being said, moving each layer to an assembly does not necessarily make the application better; the code inside each of those layers (or assemblies) can become mixed up as well and coupled with other parts of the system.

So, what is an assembly?

Assemblies are commonly compiled into `.dll` or `.exe` files; you can compile and consume them directly. You can also deploy them as NuGet packages and consume them from `nuget.org` or a custom NuGet repository of your choosing. But there is no one-to-one relationship between a layer and an assembly or a tier and an assembly; assemblies are only a consumable unit of compiled code: a library or a program.

Don't get me wrong here; you can create an assembly per layer. There is nothing wrong with doing that, but doing so does not mean that the layers are not tightly coupled. A layer is simply a logical unit of organization.

To be or not to be a purist?

In your day-to-day work, you may not always need the rigidity of a **domain layer** creating a wall in front of your data. Maybe you just don't have the time or the money, or it's just not worth doing it.

Taking the data and presenting it can often work well enough, especially for simple data-driven applications that are only a user interface over a database, like many internal tools.

The answer to the *"To be or not to be a purist"* question is, based on my experience: it depends!

OK; you are probably not liking my answer right now, but I'll do my best not to let you down, and I will be more specific. It depends on the following:

- The project; for example:

    a) **Domain-heavy or logic-intensive projects** should benefit from the domain layer, helping you centralize those bits for an augmented level of reusability and maintainability.

    b) **Data management projects** tend to have less logic in them. They can often be built without the complexity of adding a domain layer as the **domain** is often only a tunnel from the **presentation** to the **data**. These systems can often be simplified into two layers: **data** and **presentation**.

- Your team; for example, a highly skilled team may tend to use advanced concepts and patterns more efficiently, and the learning curve for newcomers should be easier due to the number of seasoned engineers that can support them on the team. This does not mean that less skilled teams should aim lower; on the contrary, it may just be harder or take longer to start. Analyze each project individually and find the best patterns to drive them accordingly.

- Your boss; if the company you work for puts pressure on you and your team to deliver complex applications in record time and nobody tells your boss that it is impossible, you may need to cut corners a lot and enjoy many maintenance headaches with crashing systems, painful deployments, and more. That being said, if it is inevitable, for these types of projects, I'd go with a very simple design that does not aim at reusability – aim at low to average testability and code stuff that just works. I also suggest you to continue reading and try **Vertical Slice Architecture**.

- Your budget; once again, this often depends on the people selling the application and the features. I often saw promises that were impossible to keep but were delivered anyway with a lot of effort, extra hours, and corner cutting. The thing to keep in mind when going down that path is that at some point, there is no return from the amount of accumulated **technical debt**, and it will just get worse.

- The audience; the people who use the software can make a big difference to how you build it: ask them. For example, if you are building a tool for your fellow developers, you can probably cut many corners that you would not for other, less technically skilled, users. On the other hand, if you're aiming your application at multiple clients (web, mobile, and so on), isolating your application's components and focusing on reusability could be a winning design.

- The expected quality; depending on if you are building a prototype or a high-quality piece of software, you should not tackle the problem in the same way. It is acceptable for a prototype to have no test and not follow best practices, but I'd recommend the opposite for a production-quality application.

- Any other things that life throws at you; yes, life is unpredictable, and no one can cover every possible scenario in a book, so just keep the following in mind when building your next piece of software:

    a) Do not over-engineer your applications.

    b) Only implement features that you need to, not more, as per the **YAGNI principle** (*You aren't gonna need it*).

I hope that you find this enumeration good enough and that it will be helpful at some point in your career. For now, let's learn more about layers and how to share a model between layers.

Sharing the model

Another alternative to copying models from one layer to another is to share a model between multiple layers, generally as an assembly. Visually, it looks like this:

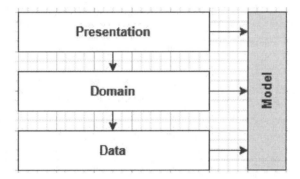

Figure 12.5 – Sharing a model between all three layers

As we discussed previously, there are pros and cons to everything. Doing this can help save some time initially and will most likely become a pain point later as the project advances and becomes bigger and more complex.

Suppose you feel that sharing a model is worth it for your application. In that case, you could also use **view models** or **DTOs** at the presentation level to control and keep the input and output of your application decoupled from your domain/data model. This can be represented as follows:

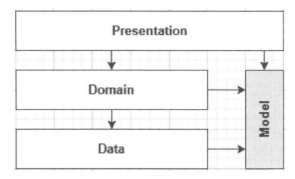

Figure 12.6 – Sharing a model between the domain and data layers

By doing that, you may save some time initially by sharing your model between your domain and data layers. The good thing is that by hiding that shared model under the presentation layer, you will most likely dodge many problems in the long run, making this a good compromise between quality and development time. Moreover, since your presentation layer shields your application from the outside world, you can rework or rewrite your other layers without impacting your consumers.

View models and **DTOs** are key elements to successful programs and developers' sanity; they should save you many headaches for long-running projects. We will revisit and explore the concepts of controlling the input and output later in this section, with **CQRS**, where inputs become **commands** and **queries**. Meanwhile, let's explore the reality of small- to medium-sized enterprises (SMEs).

The reality of small- to medium-sized enterprises

Data-driven programs are the type of software that I often saw in enterprises. Every company needs internal tools, and many needed them yesterday. The reason is simple; every company is unique. Because it's unique, due to its business model, its leadership, or its employees, it also needs unique tools to help with its day-to-day operations. Often, those small tools are simple user interfaces over a database, controlling access to that data. In these cases, you don't need over-engineered solutions, as long as everyone is informed that the tool is not going to evolve beyond what it is: a small tool.

In real life, this one is tough to explain to non-programmers and managers. This is because they tend to see complex use cases as being easy to implement and simple use cases as being hard to implement. It's normal; they don't know, and we all don't know something. A big part of our job is to educate people. Advising decision makers about the differences in a small tool's quality or a large business application's quality should help. By educating and working with the stakeholders, they become aware of the situation and decide with you, leading to higher project quality that meets everyone's expectations. This can also reduce the "it's not my fault syndrome" from both sides.

I found that immersing clients (decision makers) in the decision process and having them follow the development cycle helps them understand the reality behind the programs, and also helps both sides stay happy and grow more satisfied. Management not getting what they want is no better than if you are super stressed over unreachable deadlines.

That being said, our educational part does not end with decision makers. Teaching new tools and techniques to our peers is also a major way to improve your team, peers, and yourself. Explaining concepts is not always as easy as it sounds.

Nevertheless, data-driven programs may be hard to avoid, especially if you are working for SMEs, so try to get the best out of it. Another tip is to remember that someday, someone is going to do the maintenance of those small tools. Think of that person as being you and think about how you'd like to have some guidelines or documentation to help you out. I'm not saying to over-document projects either, as documentation often gets out of sync with the code and becomes more of a problem than a solution. However, a simple README.md file at the root of the project explaining how to build the program, run the program, and some general guidelines could be very beneficial. Always think about documentation like you were the one reading it. Most people don't like to read hours upon hours of documentation to understand something simple, so keep it simple.

When building a *façade over a database*, you want to keep it simple. Also, you should make it clear that it should not evolve past that role. One way to build this would be to use Entity Framework Core as your data layer and scaffold an MVC application as your presentation layer, shielding your database. If you need access control, you can use the built-in authentication and authorization providers with attributes, go role-based, policy-based, or any other way that makes sense for your tool and allows you to control access to the data the way you need to.

Keeping it simple should help you build more tools in less time, making everyone happy. Most likely, improving your non-tech colleagues' productivity, which should lead to more profit for the company, could lead to prosperity, which should mean more work for you; it should be a win-win situation.

From a layering standpoint, using my previous example, you will end up having two layers sharing the data model:

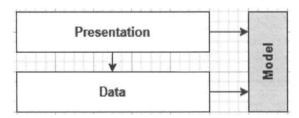

Figure 12.7 – A façade-like presentation layer over a database application's design

Nothing stops you from creating a **view model** here and there for more complex views, but the key is to keep the logic's complexity to a minimum. Otherwise, you may discover the hard way that sometimes, rewriting a program from scratch takes less time than trying to fix it. Moreover, nothing stops you from using other presentation tools and components that are available to you; we will explore this option later in this book.

Using this data-driven architecture as a temporary application while the main application is in development is also a good solution. It takes a fraction of the time to build, and the users have access to it right away. You can even get some feedback from it, which allows you to fix any mistakes before you implement them in the real (future) application.

Now, let's get into some code. We have many layers and techniques to explore before we can complete this chapter on layering.

Responsibilities of the common layers

In this section, we will explore each of the most commonly used layers in more depth. We will not dig too deep into each one as there are countless resources online and other books covering these. However, I still want to overview each since hopefully, this will help you understand the essential ideas behind layering.

I've built a small project that explores the basic ideas behind layering, and I've ensured it is easy to follow. The project allows for the following:

- Listing products.
- Adding and removing stocks (inventory).

We will iterate on this project throughout this chapter and in the next two. Moreover, since we are exploring two types of domain model, the solution comprises the following projects (layers):

- A shared data layer at the bottom.
- An anemic domain layer and a presentation layer that depends on that domain layer.
- A rich domain layer and a presentation layer that depends on that domain layer.

The following is the visual representation of those layers:

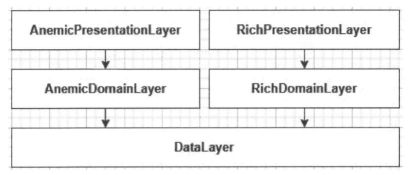

Figure 12.8 – Representation of the project's (layers) relationships

Both presentation layers use the same HTTP port, so you can't start them simultaneously. I intentionally did that to allow the Postman tests to be run on both apps without parameterization. Please have a look at the source code's README.md file for more information about the Postman tests (https://net5.link/code).

> **Note**
>
> Both presentation layers are identical, but one uses the rich domain layer while the other uses the anemic one. I could have only created one, used interfaces as a trick to share both domain layers, or even preprocessor directives, but that would have led to a more confusing codebase.
>
> Since the data layer is independent of the domain and presentation layers, it was possible to reuse it in both domain layers, which is the point of layering.

Presentation

The **presentation layer** is probably the easiest layer to understand because it is the only one that we can see: the user interface. However, the presentation layer can also be the data contracts in case of a REST, OData, GraphQL, or other type of web service. The presentation layer is what the user uses to access your program.

As another example, a CLI program can be a presentation layer. You write commands in a terminal, and the CLI dispatches those commands to its **domain layer**, which executes the required business logic.

Let's start with the first iteration of our example. In it, we have two controllers and three HTTP endpoints:

- `GET https://localhost:12001/products` lists all products.
- `POST https://localhost:12001/products/{productId}/add-stocks` adds products to the inventory.
- `POST https://localhost:12001/products/{productId}/remove-stocks` removes products from the inventory.

> **Note**
>
> The only lines that are different between the two presentation projects are a `using` statement and the root namespace. One project is `using AnemicDomainLayer;`, while the other is `using RichDomainLayer;` (omitted in the code block). The root namespace is either `AnemicPresentationLayer` or `RichPresentationLayer`, respectively.

Let's explore the `StocksController` class, which interests us more than the `ProductsController`:

```csharp
namespace RichPresentationLayer.Controllers
{
    [ApiController]
    [Route("products/{productId}/")]
    public class StocksController : ControllerBase
    {
        private readonly IStockService _stockService;
        public StocksController(IStockService stockService)
        {
            _stockService = stockService ?? throw new
ArgumentNullException(nameof(stockService));
        }
```

The preceding code injects an `IStockService` into `StocksController`, then we use it in the following two code blocks to execute business logic, such as adding or removing stocks from the inventory:

```
[HttpPost("add-stocks")]
public ActionResult<StockLevel> Add(int productId,
[FromBody]AddStocksCommand command)
{
    var quantityInStock = _stockService.
AddStock(productId, command.Amount);
    var stockLevel = new StockLevel(quantityInStock);
    return Ok(stockLevel);
}
```

The preceding code uses the `IStockService` interface to add inventory, based on the value of the `AddStocksCommand` DTO. It then returns the updated stock value using the `StockLevel` DTO. Both DTOs are described at the end of the listing, after the `remove-stock` action:

```
[HttpPost("remove-stocks")]
public ActionResult<StockLevel> Remove(int productId,
[FromBody]RemoveStocksCommand command)
{
    try
    {
        var quantityInStock = _stockService.
RemoveStock(productId, command.Amount);
        var stockLevel = new
StockLevel(quantityInStock);
        return Ok(stockLevel);
    }
    catch (NotEnoughStockException ex)
    {
        return Conflict(new
        {
            ex.Message,
            ex.AmountToRemove,
            ex.QuantityInStock
        });
```

```
        }
    }
```

Besides using the `RemoveStocksCommand` DTO and copying the updated quantity in stock into a `StockLevel` instance, the `Remove` method contains a small piece of logic. It changes the HTTP status code from `200` to `409` when a `NotEnoughStockException` is thrown. We explored that HTTP status code in *Chapter 5, The MVC Pattern for Web APIs*. In a nutshell, it allows the consumer to know about the nature of the error.

Mapping an `Exception` to an HTTP status code can be part of the controller's responsibility. However, filters and middlewares can handle that kind of logic if you want to centralize it and avoid managing exceptions in each controller (see the *Further reading* section for more information):

```csharp
public class AddStocksCommand
{
    public int Amount { get; set; }
}

public class RemoveStocksCommand
{
    public int Amount { get; set; }
}

public class StockLevel
{
    public StockLevel(int quantityInStock)
    {
        QuantityInStock = quantityInStock;
    }

    public int QuantityInStock { get; set; }
}
```

Finally, there are two input DTOs and an output DTO. The inputs are `AddStocksCommand` and `RemoveStocksCommand`, and they represent the data that we `POST` to the controller (see the Postman collection for more information about the requests). The output is the `StockLevel` class, which represents an item's current stock level. This is returned once we update the quantity of a product.

In the preceding controller code, we can see the role of the presentation layer in action. It gathers information from the HTTP request and formats that information in the way the domain expects it. After the domain completes its work, it then converts the result back to HTTP.

I can't stress this enough: controllers should remain thin because they are **simple translators between HTTP and the domain layer**. Here is a visual representation of this:

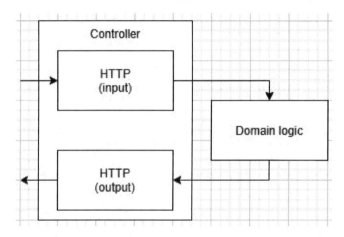

Figure 12.9 – The flow of an HTTP request through a controller

The controller's responsibility is to map HTTP requests to the domain and then map the domain's output back to HTTP.

Now, let's take a look at the **domain layer** to see where these calls are going.

Domain

The **domain layer** is where the software's value resides; it is also where most of the complexity lies. The **domain layer** is the home of your business logic rules.

Unfortunately, it is easier to sell a **user interface** than a **domain layer**. This makes sense since this is how the users connect to the domain; that's what they see. However, as a developer, it is important to remember that the **domain** is responsible for solving the problems and automating the solutions. The **presentation layer** is only there to link users' actions to the **domain**.

There are two big points of view about how to build that layer:

- Using a rich model.

- Using an anemic model.

No matter which one you choose, the domain layer is usually built around a domain model. **Domain-driven design (DDD)** can be used to build that model and the program around it. A well-crafted model should help simplify the maintenance of the program. Doing DDD is not mandatory, and you can achieve the required level of correctness without it.

Another dilemma is whether to **persist the domain model directly into the database or use an intermediate data model**. We will talk about that in more detail in the *Data* section, but we are using a separate data model for now (incremental steps).

To go back to the **domain layer**, we can use a pattern that we've seen emerge over the years that gets more and more adoption, shielding the **domain model** using a **service layer**, splitting the **domain layer** into two distinct pieces.

Service layer

The **service layer** shields the domain model and encapsulates domain logic. The service layer is usually designed to be highly reusable, orchestrating the complex interactions with the model or external resources such as databases. Multiple components can then use the service layer while having limited knowledge of the model:

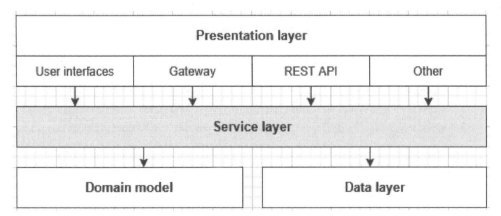

Figure: 12.10 – Service layer relationships with other layers

Based on the preceding diagram, the **presentation layer** talks to the **service layer**, which manages the **domain model** and implements the business logic.

The **service layer** contains services, which are classes that interact with other **domain objects**, such as the **domain model** and the **data layer**.

We can divide services into two categories: **domain services** and **application services**.

Domain services are those services we are talking about here. They contain domain logic and allow consumers to read or write data. They access and mutate the domain model.

Application services are services that are not related to the domain, such as `[I]EmailService`, a class/interface that sends emails. These could live in the domain layer or not, depending on their use. Since they are not tied to the domain (no domain logic), it can be wise to extract them into a library so that you can share them between the domain and other layers or with other applications (why rewrite an email service for every project, right?).

As with other layers, your service layer could expose its own model, shielding its consumers from domain model (internal) changes. In other words, the service layer should only exposes its contracts and interfaces (keyword: shield). **A service layer is a form of façade.**

There are many ways to interpret this layer, and I'll try to illustrate as many as possible in a condensed manner (from simpler to more complex ones). Let's get started:

1. The classes and interfaces of the service layer could be part of the domain layer's assembly, created in a *Services* directory, for example.

    This is less reusable, but it paves the way to sharing services in the future without managing multiple projects at first. It needs rigor not to depend on what you should not.

2. The service layer could be an assembly containing interfaces and implementation.

    This is a great compromise between reusability and maintenance time. Chances are you will never need two implementations (see the next point) because the services are tied to the logic, which makes the domain. You could even hide the implementation, as we did with the **opaque façade** in *Chapter 9, Structural Patterns*.

3. The service layer could be divided into two assemblies – one containing abstractions (referenced by consumers) and one containing implementations.

    For most projects, this is just plain overkill and useless, but I'll leave that choice to you; maybe you are building a project that requires such level of abstraction.

4.   The service layer could be an actual web service tier (such as a web API).

5.   A web service tier using a service layer assembly.

This is a combination of points *2* and *4*. A service layer as an assembly that can be used as-is with a web API on top of it exposing some or all of its features to external systems.

By convention, people usually suffix a service class with `Service`, such as `ProductService` and `InventoryService`; the same goes for interfaces (`IProductService` and `IInventoryService`).

No matter which technique you choose, keep in mind that the service layer contains the domain logic and shields the domain model from direct access.

Before we get lost in the details, let's take a look at the two primary ways to think about the **domain model**. The following code represent the services interface that each domain layer project exposes. Those interfaces represent the link between the presentation and the domain, encapsulating more or less responsibilities, depending on the domain model type. There are two different interfaces with the same signature, one per project:

```
public interface IProductService
{
    IEnumerable<Product> All();
}
```

`IProductService` only exposes one method that returns all `Product` instances of the system.

```
public interface IStockService
{
    int AddStock(int productId, int amount);
    int RemoveStock(int productId, int amount);
}
```

`IStockService` exposes two methods: one that adds stocks and one that removes stocks from the inventory. Both return the updated stock level.

Let's explore the **rich domain model** first and see how those services are implemented.

Rich domain model

A rich domain model is more object-oriented, in the "purest" sense of the term, and encapsulates the domain logic as part of the model, inside methods. For example, the following class is the rich version of the `Product` class:

```
namespace RichDomainLayer
{
    public class Product
    {
        public Product(string name, int quantityInStock)
        {
            Name = name ?? throw new
ArgumentNullException(nameof(name));
            QuantityInStock = quantityInStock;
        }
        public Product(int id, string name, int
quantityInStock)
            : this(name, quantityInStock)
        {
            Id = id;
        }
```

The preceding two constructors force the consumers to provide the required data when creating the `Product` instance. This gives us an additional layer of control over what can go in.

```
        public int Id { get; private set; }
        public string Name { get; private set; }
        public int QuantityInStock { get; private set; }
```

To force the consumers to use the following methods, all the setters have been set to `private` so that they can't be altered from the outside.

```
        public void AddStock(int amount)
        {
            QuantityInStock += amount;
        }
        public void RemoveStock(int amount)
        {
```

```
                if (amount > QuantityInStock)
                {
                    throw new
NotEnoughStockException(QuantityInStock, amount);
                }
                QuantityInStock -= amount;
            }
        }
    }
```

Finally, we have the AddStock and RemoveStock methods. They encapsulate the logic related to our product. They manage the process of adding and removing stock for that product. Of course, in this case, we only increment and decrement a property's value, but the concept would be the same in a more complex model.

The **service layer** that shields that model is represented by the following code:

```
namespace RichDomainLayer
{
    public class StockService : IStockService
    {
        private readonly ProductContext _db;
        public StockService(ProductContext db)
        {
            _db = db ?? throw new
ArgumentNullException(nameof(db));
        }
        public int AddStock(int productId, int amount)
        {
            var data = _db.Products.Find(productId);
            var product = new Product(
                id: data.Id,
                name: data.Name,
                quantityInStock: data.QuantityInStock
            );
            product.AddStock(amount);
            data.QuantityInStock = product.QuantityInStock;
            _db.SaveChanges();
```

```
            return product.QuantityInStock;
    }
    public int RemoveStock(int productId, int amount)
    {
        var data = _db.Products.Find(productId);
        var product = new Product(
            id: data.Id,
            name: data.Name,
            quantityInStock: data.QuantityInStock
        );
        product.RemoveStock(amount);
        data.QuantityInStock = product.QuantityInStock;
        _db.SaveChanges();
        return product.QuantityInStock;
    }
  }
}
```

In the preceding service code, there is a mapping between our data objects and our business objects. We then call that reconstructed domain model to add or remove some stocks before saving that updated entity back to the database and returning the updated quantity to the consumer (we will simplify this later).

The rich model's flow usually goes as follows:

1. Reconstruct the model (load it from the database and map it to objects).

2. Use the logic embedded in the model.

3. Optionally, save the changes back to the database (save and map objects to the database).

Now, let's take a look at the advantages and disadvantages.

Advantages and disadvantages

The biggest advantage of this approach is that all the logic is built into the model. It is very domain-centric since operations are programmed on model entities as methods. Moreover, it reaches the basic ideas behind object-oriented design, where behaviors should be part of the objects, making them a virtual representations of their real-life counterparts.

The biggest drawback is the accumulation of responsibilities by a single class. Even if the object-oriented design tells us to put logic into the objects, this does not mean that it is always a good idea. If flexibility is important for your system, hardcoding logic into the domain model may hinder your ability to make business rules evolve without changing the code itself (it can still be done). If the domain is built to be robust and fixed, then a rich model might be a good choice for your project.

A relative drawback of this approach is that injecting dependencies into the domain model may be harder to do than in other objects, such as into services, possibly cutting up on flexibility once again or increasing the complexity of creating the model.

If you are building a stateful application where the domain model can live in memory longer than the time of an HTTP request, a rich domain model could be of use to you. There are also other patterns, such as **Model-View-ViewModel** (**MVVM**) and **Model-View-Update** (**MVU**) to help you with that. We'll tackle MVU in *Chapter 18, A Brief Look into Blazor*.

If you believe that your application would benefit from keeping the data and the logic together, then a rich domain model is most likely a good idea for your project.

If your program is built around your domain models, persisting those classes directly to your database could be a better idea than having yet another model. If you are using an object-relational mapper (ORM) such as Entity Framework Core, you can even configure how the model is persisted. Using a document database such as CosmosDB, Firebase, MongoDB, Azure Blob Storage, or any other document database could make it very easy to store complex models as a single document instead of a collection of tables (this applies to anemic models too).

As you may have noticed, there is a lot of "if" in this section because I don't think there is an absolute answer to whether a rich model is better or not. It is more of a question of whether it is better for your specific case than overall. You also need to take your personal preferences into account.

Experience is most likely your best ally here, so I'd recommend coding, coding, and coding more applications to acquire that experience.

Anemic domain model

An anemic domain model does not contain methods but is composed of dumb data structures, containing mostly just getters and setters. The same product we had previously would look like this:

```
namespace AnemicDomainLayer
{
    public class Product
    {
        public int Id { get; set; }
        public string Name { get; set; }
        public int QuantityInStock { get; set; }
    }
}
```

As you can see, there is no more method in the class, only the three properties with public setters. We moved that logic to the service layer. The model is now a simple data structure. Here is the updated `StockService` class:

```
namespace AnemicDomainLayer
{
    public class StockService : IStockService
    {
        private readonly ProductContext _db;
        public StockService(ProductContext db)
        {
            _db = db ?? throw new
ArgumentNullException(nameof(db));
        }
        public int AddStock(int productId, int amount)
        {
            var product = _db.Products.Find(productId);
            product.QuantityInStock += amount;
            _db.SaveChanges();

            return product.QuantityInStock;
        }
        public int RemoveStock(int productId, int amount)
```

```
        {
            var product = _db.Products.Find(productId);
            if (amount > product.QuantityInStock)
            {
                throw new NotEnoughStockException(product.
QuantityInStock, amount);
            }
            product.QuantityInStock -= amount;
            _db.SaveChanges();

            return product.QuantityInStock;
        }
    }
}
```

We have almost the same code as we did previously, but with the logic handled in the service instead. The anemic model flow usually goes as follows:

1. Reconstruct the model (load it from the database and map it to objects).

2. Handle the logic while using the model as a simple data structure.

3. Optionally, save the changes back to the database (save and map objects to the database).

Now, let's look at the advantages and disadvantages.

Advantages and disadvantages

With the anemic model, separating the operations from the data can help us add flexibility to a system. However, it can be harder to enforce the state of the model at any given time since external actors (services) are modifying the model instead of the model managing itself.

Encapsulating logic into smaller units makes it easier to manage each of them. It is easier to inject those dependencies into the service classes than injecting them into the entities themselves. Having more smaller units of code can make a system more dreading for a newcomer as it can be more complex to understand, since it has more moving parts. On the other hand, if the system is built around well-defined abstractions, it can be easier to test each unit in isolation.

However, the tests can be quite different. In the case of our rich model, we can test the rules in isolation (see `RichDomainLayer.Tests/ProductTest.cs`) and the persistence in another test (see `RichDomainLayer.Tests/StockServiceTest.cs`); see `https://net5.link/FP7q`. We call this **persistence ignorance**. It allows us to test business rules in isolation. Here is the `Product` model unit test file showing that concept into action:

```
namespace RichDomainLayer
{
    public class ProductTest
    {
        public class AddStock : ProductTest
        {
            [Fact]
            public void Should_add_the_specified_amount_to_
QuantityInStock()
            {
                // Arrange
                var sut = new Product("Product 1",
quantityInStock: 0);
                // Act
                sut.AddStock(2);
                // Assert
                Assert.Equal(2, sut.QuantityInStock);
            }
        }
// ...
    }
}
```

The preceding code shows the `Product.AddStock` method test, which is only testing the business logic rules. Next, we have some integration tests covering the `StockService` class:

```
namespace RichDomainLayer
{
    public class StockServiceTest
    {
        private readonly DbContextOptionsBuilder _builder=...;
```

```csharp
public class AddStock : StockServiceTest
{
    [Fact]
    public void Should_add_the_specified_amount_to_
QuantityInStock()
    {
        // Arrange
        using var arrangeContext = new ProductContext(
_builder.Options);
        using var actContext = new ProductContext(
_builder.Options);
        using var assertContext = new ProductContext(
_builder.Options);

        arrangeContext.Products.Add(new() { Name =
"Product 1", QuantityInStock = 1 });
        arrangeContext.SaveChanges();

        var sut = new StockService(actContext);

        // Act
        var quantityInStock = sut.AddStock(productId:
1, amount: 2);

        // Assert
        Assert.Equal(3, quantityInStock);
        var actual = assertContext.Products.Find(1);
        Assert.Equal(3, actual.QuantityInStock);
    }
}
// ...
    }
}
```

The code above shows a test of persistence, making sure StockService persists the entity in the database after executing the AddStock operation.

With our anemic model, we need to test both the rules and the persistence in the same test, transforming the unit test into an integration test (see `AnemicDomainLayer.Tests/StockServiceTest.cs`):

```csharp
namespace AnemicDomainLayer
{
    public class StockServiceTest
    {
        private readonly DbContextOptionsBuilder _builder =
...;
        public class AddStock : StockServiceTest
        {
            [Fact]
            public void Should_add_the_specified_amount_to_
QuantityInStock()
            {
                // Arrange
                using var arrangeContext = new ProductContext(_
builder.Options);
                using var actContext = new ProductContext(_
builder.Options);
                using var assertContext = new ProductContext(_
builder.Options);

                arrangeContext.Products.Add(new() { Name =
"Product 1", QuantityInStock = 1 });
                arrangeContext.SaveChanges();

                var sut = new StockService(actContext);

                // Act
                var quantityInStock = sut.AddStock(1, 9);

                // Assert
                Assert.Equal(10, quantityInStock);
                var actual = assertContext.Products.Find(1);
                Assert.Equal(10, actual.QuantityInStock);
            }
```

```
              }
// ...
          }
    }
```

The preceding code is almost identical to the rich model integration test. It tests both the logic and persistence at the same time. We can simplify the anemic model integration tests using different techniques. We will cover some of them later in this chapter and subsequent chapters. Nonetheless, all of this is a matter of choice; having three integration tests covering your needs can be better than three unit tests and two integration tests that achieve the same. Often, **less is more**. Remember that you are not paid by the line of code written but to deliver results. For complex business rules, I would strongly advise encapsulating the rules on their own. This allows you to write many unit tests that cover every scenario without the need for a database.

All in all, if the same rigorous domain analysis process is followed, an anemic model should be as complex as a rich domain model. The biggest difference should be where the methods are located; that is, in what classes.

For stateless systems, such as RESTful APIs, an anemic model is a good option. Since you have to recreate the state of the model for every request, this can offer you a way to recreate a smaller portion of the model, in smaller classes, optimized for each use case independently. Stateless systems tend to require a more procedural type of thinking than a pure object-oriented one, leaving the anemic models to be excellent candidates for that.

> **Note**
>
> I personally love anemic models behind a service layer, but some people would not agree with me. As always, I recommend choosing what you think is best for the system that you are building instead of doing something based on what someone else said about another system.
>
> Another good tip is to let the refactoring flow *top-down* to the right location. For example, if you feel that a method is bound to an entity, nothing stops you from moving that piece of logic into that entity instead of a service class. If a service is more fitting, then move the logic to a service class. This approach is instrumental to the Vertical Slice architecture, which we will cover in *Chapter 15, Getting Started with Vertical Slice Architecture*.

Now, let's look at the data layer.

Data

The **data layer** is where the persistence code goes. In most programs, we need some kind of persistence to store our application data, which is often a database. Several patterns come to mind when talking about the data layer, including the **Unit of Work** and the **Repository patterns**, which are very common patterns. We will cover these two patterns briefly at the end of this subsection.

We can persist our **domain model** as-is or create a **data model** that is more suited to be stored. For example, a many-to-many relationship is not a thing in the object-oriented world, while it is from a relational database standpoint. You can view a **data model** like a **view model** or a **DTO**, but for data. The **data model** is the way the data is stored in your data store; that is, how you modeled your data. In a classic layering project, you have no choice but to have a data model. However, you may find better solutions as we continue to explore additional options.

I used **Entity Framework Core (EF Core)** as the **object-relational mapper (ORM)** for this project. An **ORM** is a piece of software that translates objects into a database language such as SQL automatically. In the case of **EF Core**, it allows us to choose between multiple providers, from SQL to Cosmos DB, passing by in-memory. The great thing about EF Core is that it already implements the **Unit of Work** and the **Repository** patterns for us, among other things. In our case, we are using the in-memory provider to cut down setup time. In the case of a SQL Server database, we could use migrations to maintain our database schema based on our **data model**.

> **Note**
> If you've used EF6 before and dread Entity Framework, know that they learned from their mistakes and that EF Core is lighter, faster, and easier to test.
> Feel free to give it a second shot. It is far from perfect, but it works well for a multitude of scenarios. If you want full control over your SQL code, look for Dapper (not to be confused with Dapr).

The data layer of this project is very thin, so let's take a look at it in its entirety here first:

```
namespace DataLayer
{
    public class Product
    {
        public int Id { get; set; }
        public string Name { get; set; }
        public int QuantityInStock { get; set; }
```

```
    }


    public class ProductContext : DbContext
    {
        public ProductContext(DbContextOptions options)
            : base(options) { }

        public DbSet<Product> Products { get; set; }
    }
}
```

In the preceding code, the `Product` class is the **data model**, while the `ProductContext` class is a **unit of work**. `DbSet<Product>` is a `Product` **repository**. The service layers that we previously explored are using the `ProductContext` and the `Product` class already.

I don't want to go into too much detail about these patterns, but they are important enough that they deserve an overview. I wrote a multi-part article series about the Repository pattern (see *Further reading* section). When using EF Core, you don't have to deal with that level of detail, which can be a good thing.

Meanwhile, let's at least study their goals so that you know what they are for and if the time arises that you need to write such components, you know where to look.

Repository pattern

The goal of the Repository pattern is to allow consumers to query the database in an object-oriented way. Usually, this implies memory caching of objects and the possibility to filter the data dynamically. EF Core represents this concept with a `DbSet<T>` and provides dynamic filtering using LINQ and the `IQueryable<T>` interface.

People also use the term **repository** to represent the **Table Data Gateway pattern**, which is another pattern that models a class that gives us access to a single table in a database and provides access to operations such as creating, updating, deleting, and fetching entities from that database table. Both patterns are from the *Patterns of Enterprise Application Architecture*.

For example, we can use `DbSet<Product>` to add new products to the database, like this:

```
db.Products.Add(new Product
{
    Id = 1,
    Name = "Banana",
    QuantityInStock = 50
});
```

For the querying part, we use it to find a single product, like this:

```
var product = _db.Products.Find(productId);
```

However, we could use LINQ instead:

```
_db.Products.Single(x => x.Id == productId);
```

These are the kind of querying capabilities that a **repository** should provide and that EF Core supports seamlessly, translating LINQ into the configured provider expectations like SQL.

The `ProductService.All()` method (from `AnemicDomainLayer`) fetches all the products and it projects that data to domain objects using LINQ:

```
public IEnumerable<Product> All()
{
    return _db.Products.Select(p => new Product
    {
        Id = p.Id,
        Name = p.Name,
        QuantityInStock = p.QuantityInStock
    });
}
```

We can also filter further using LINQ here; for example, by querying all the products that are out of stock:

```
var outOfStockProducts = _db.Products
    .Where(p => p.QuantityInStock == 0);
```

We could also allow a margin for error, like so:

```
var mostLikelyOutOfStockProducts = _db.Products
    .Where(p => p.QuantityInStock < 3);
```

With that, we've explored how EF Core implements the Repository pattern and how to use it. It would require considerable work to implement custom repositories that are on par with EF Core features.

That's enough for the **Repository pattern**. Now, let's jump into an overview of the **Unit of Work pattern** before going back to layering.

Unit of Work pattern

A **unit of work** keeps track of the object representation of a transaction. In other words, it manages a registry of what object should be created, updated, and deleted. It allows us to combine multiple changes in a single transaction (one database call), which offers multiple advantages over calling the database every time we make a change. Here are two:

- First, it can speed up data access; calling a database is slow, so limiting the number of calls and connections can improve performance.

- Second, running a transaction instead of individual operations allows us to roll back all operations if one fails or commit the transaction as a whole if everything succeeds.

In EF Core, this pattern is implemented by the DbContext class and its underlying types, such as the DatabaseFacade and ChangeTracker classes.

In our small application, we did not take advantage of transactions, but the concept remains the same. Let's look at the anemic StockService for an example of what happens inside the unit of work:

```
var product = _db.Products.Find(productId);
product.QuantityInStock += amount;
_db.SaveChanges();
```

The preceding code does the following:

1. Queries the database for a single entity.

2. Changes the value of the QuantityInStock property.

3. Persists the changes back into the database.

In reality, what happened is closer to the following:

1. We ask EF Core for a single entity through the `ProductContext` (a **unit of work**), which exposes the `DbSet<Product>` property (the product **repository**). Under the hood, EF Core does the following:\

    a) Queried the database.

    b) Cached the entity.

    c) Begun tracking changes for that entity.

    d) Returned it to us.

2. We changed the value of the `QuantityInStock` property; EF Core detects the change and marks the object as dirty.

3. We tell the **unit of work** to persist the changes that it tracked, saving the dirty product back to the database.

In a more complex scenario, we could have written the following code:

```
_db.Products.Add(newProduct);
_db.Products.Remove(productToDelete);
product.Name = "New product name";
_db.SaveChanges();
```

Here, the `SaveChanges()` method triggers saving the three operations instead of sending them one by one. You can control database transactions using the `Database` property of a `DbContext` (see *Further reading* section for more information).

Now that we've explored the **unit of work**, we could implement one by ourselves. Would that add value to our application? Probably not. If you want to build a custom **unit of work** or a wrapper over EF Core, there are plenty of existing resources to guide you. Unless you want to experiment or need a custom **unit of work** and **repository** (which is possible), I recommend staying away from doing that. Remember: **do only what needs to be done for your program to be correct**.

> **Tip**
>
> Don't get me wrong when I say *do only what needs to be done*; wild engineering endeavors and experimentations are a great way to explore, and I encourage you to do so. However, I recommend doing so in parallel so that you can innovate, learn, and possibly even migrate that knowledge to your application later instead of wasting time and breaking things. If you are using Git, a good way of doing this would be to create an experimental branch. You can then delete it when your experimentation does not work but merge the branch if it yields positive results.

Now, let's go back to layering and continue our journey of using layers in a robust, flexible, and efficient way.

Abstract data layer

In this section, we will be implementing an abstract data layer to explore **repository interfaces**. This type of abstraction can be very useful and is another step closer to the **Clean Architecture**.

Let's start with the problem: the **domain layer** is where the logic lies, and the **UI** is the link between the user and the **domain**, exposing the features built into that **domain**. On the other hand, the **data layer** should be an implementation detail that the **domain** blindly uses. The **data layer** contains the code that knows where the data is stored, which should be irrelevant to the **domain**, but the **domain** indirectly depends on it.

The solution is to **break the tight coupling** between the **domain** and the **data** persistence implementations by creating an additional layer that is abstract, as shown in the following diagram:

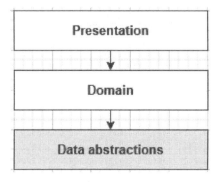

Figure 12.11 – Replacing the data (persistence) layer with a data abstraction layer

New rule: **only interfaces and model classes go into the data abstractions layer**. This new layer now defines our data access API and does nothing but expose a set of interfaces – a contract.

Then, **we can create one or more data implementations** based on that layer. In our case, we are implementing an EF Core version of our **data abstractions layer**. The link between the abstractions and the implementations is done with dependency injection bindings, which are defined in the **composition root**.

The new dependency tree looks like this:

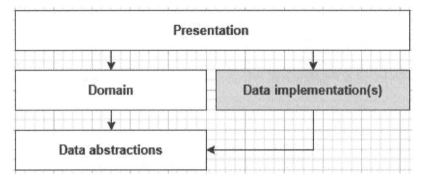

Figure 12.12 – The relationships between layers

The **presentation layer** references a **data implementations layer** for the sole reason of creating the DI bindings. We need those bindings to inject the correct implementation when creating **domain** classes. Besides that, **the presentation layer must not use the data layer's abstractions and implementations**.

For example, our program could inject an instance of the EFCore.ProductRepository class when a consumer asks for an object that implements the IProductRepository interface.

Here is part of the `ProductService` class that uses `IProductRepository`:

```
public class ProductService : IProductService
{
    private readonly IProductRepository _repository;
    public ProductService(IProductRepository repository)
    {
        _repository = repository ?? throw new
ArgumentNullException(nameof(repository));
    }
    // ...
}
```

`ProductService` only depends on the `IProductRepository` abstraction and does not care about what implementation is injected.

Abstract layers are about organizing the code rather than writing new code. Figure 12.13 shows the dependencies between projects illustrated by *the relationships between layers* diagram (figure 12.12). Textually, the dependencies are as follow:

- `DataLayer` depends on nothing and contains abstractions and the data model.

- `DataLayer.EFCore` depends on `DataLayer` and implements its abstractions using EF Core, which are abstracted away from the concrete consumers of `DomainLayer`.

- `DomainLayer` depends only on the `DataLayer` abstractions.

- `PresentationLayer` depends only on `DomainLayer` but loads `DataLayer. EFCore` for dependency injection purposes.

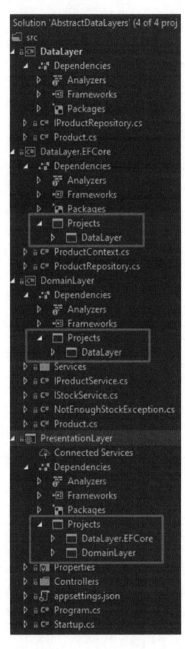

Figure 12.13 – The Solution Explorer window highlighting the dependencies between projects (layers)

With that updated architecture, we are inverting the flow of dependency on `DataLayer` while following the **Dependency Inversion Principle**. We also cut out the dependency on EF Core, allowing us to implement a new `DataLayer` and swap one for another without it impacting our code. As I mentioned previously, I can foresee that swapping layers will not happen anytime soon for most of us. Nonetheless, this is an important part of the evolution of layering. Moreover, this technique can be applied to any layer (or project), not just the data layer, so it is very important to understand how to invert the dependency flow. This can also be applied to a single project; we don't need four projects to depend only on abstractions – we could copy all of that code into a single project, and the dependency flow would be the same.

Even if splitting projects into multiple assemblies is not mandatory, it can be done for another reason, such as for sharing code between multiple projects. Obviously, having one big project is not always ideal and can have drawbacks. What I'm saying here is that as long as you depend on the right abstractions, your system can be loosely coupled, testable, and invert the dependency flow. For example, don't use data interfaces in the presentation layer and don't use domain services in the data layer.

I kept the code of the abstract data layer project out of this book since it is almost the same as the previous example, and comparing project structures should be easier to do with a computer and the full source code than using a book. See `https://net5.link/Xzgf` for the `AbstractDataLayers` project source code. That being said, here is a list of changes to help you find them:

- We added the `DataLayer.EFCore` project.
- The dependencies between projects changed, as seen previously.
- The domain layer only contains an anemic model and one set of services.

Next, let's explore how to share and persist a rich domain model. This will lead us to the Clean Architecture.

Shared rich model

In this section, we will look at a layering solution with a shared model. Then, we will piece the notions that have been provided in this chapter together into a Clean Architecture. We saw a similar diagram at the beginning of this chapter, and that's what we are building here: a shared model between the **domain** and **data layers**. In the previous project, the **data abstraction layer** owned the **data model**, and the **domain layer** owned the **domain model**.

In this architectural alternative, we are sharing the model between the two layers; that is, we are using a **rich product model**. Here is a visual representation of that:

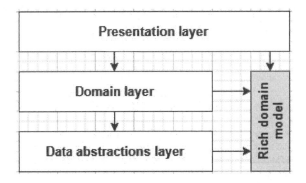

Figure 12.14 – Diagram representing a shared rich model

The objective is to directly persist the **domain model** and skip the copy from the **domain layer** to the **data layer**.

We can do this for **anemic models** too, but it is well-suited for **rich models**. With a **rich domain model**, you delegate the job of reconstructing the model to the ORM; then, you can immediately start calling methods on that rich domain model.

Not much has changed from the previous project, especially with *the transitive dependencies restoration* introduced by .NET Core. The **data abstraction layer** now contains only the data access abstractions, such as the repositories, and it references the new `SharedModels` project.

Conceptually, it cleans up a few things:

- The data abstraction layer's only responsibility is to contain data access abstractions.

- With a rich model, the domain layer's only responsibility is to implement the domain services and domain logic that is not part of the rich model.

- In the case of an anemic model, the domain layer's responsibility would be to encapsulate all of the domain logic.

- The `SharedModels` project contains the entities themselves; whether they are anemic or rich does not matter.

Using a shared rich model leads to very lean services compared to the first project. Here is the rewrite of the `StockService` class:

```
namespace DomainLayer.Services
{
    public class StockService : IStockService
    {
        private readonly IProductRepository _repository;
        public StockService(IProductRepository repository)
        {
            _repository = repository ?? throw new
ArgumentNullException(nameof(repository));
        }
```

Here, we are injecting an implementation of the `IProductRepository` interface that we use in the next two methods.

```
        public int AddStock(int productId, int amount)
        {
            var product = _repository.FindById(productId);
            product.AddStock(amount);
            _repository.Update(product);
            return product.QuantityInStock;
        }
```

The fun starts in the preceding code, which does the following:

1. The repository recreates the product (model) that contains the logic.

2. We use that model to call the `AddStock` method.

3. We tell the repository to update the product.

4. We return the updated product's `QuantityInStock` to the consumer of the service.

```
        public int RemoveStock(int productId, int amount)
        {
            var product = _repository.FindById(productId);
            product.RemoveStock(amount);
            _repository.Update(product);
            return product.QuantityInStock;
```

```
            }
        }
    }
```

The same logic as the `AddStock` method was applied to `RemoveStock`, but we called the `Product.RemoveStock` method instead.

Pushing logic into the model is not always possible or desirable, which is why we are exploring multiple types of domain models and ways to share them. To make a good design, it is often about options and making the right decision about what option to use for each scenario.

Next, the `ProductService` becomes a façade in front of the repository:

```
namespace DomainLayer.Services
{
    public class ProductService : IProductService
    {
        private readonly IProductRepository _repository;
        public ProductService(IProductRepository repository)
        {
            _repository = repository ?? throw new
ArgumentNullException(nameof(repository));
        }

        public IEnumerable<Product> All()
        {
            return _repository.All();
        }
    }
}
```

The rest of the code is the same, but the classes were moved around a bit. Feel free to explore the source code (`https://net5.link/izwK`) and compare it with the other projects. The best way to learn is to practice, so play with the samples, add features, update the current features, remove stuff, or even build your own project. Understanding these concepts should help you apply them to different scenarios, sometimes creating unexpected but efficient constructs.

Now, let's look at another evolution of layering: Clean Architecture.

Clean Architecture

Now that we've covered many layering approaches, it is time to combine them into Clean Architecture, also known as Hexagonal Architecture, Onion Architecture, Ports and Adapters, and more. Clean Architecture is an evolution of the layers, yet very similar to what we just built. Instead of presentation, domain, and data (or persistence), Clean Architecture suggests **UI**, **Core**, and **Infrastructure**.

As we saw previously, we can design a layer so that it contains abstractions or implementations. Then, when implementations depend only on abstractions, that inverts the flow of dependency. Clean Architecture emphasizes on such layers, but with its own set of guidance about how to organize them.

We also explored the theoretical concept of breaking layers into smaller ones (or multiple projects), thus creating "fractured layers" that are easier to port and reuse. Clean Architecture leverages that concept at the infrastructure layer level.

There are probably as many points of view and variants of this that there are names for it, so I'll try to be as general as possible while keeping the essence. By doing this, if you are interested in this type of architecture, you'll be able to pick a resource and dig deeper into it, following the style that you prefer.

Let's take a look at a diagram that resembles what we can find online:

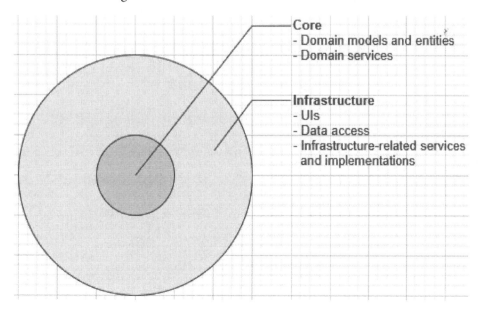

Figure 12.15 – A diagram representing the most basic Clean Architecture layout

From a layering diagram-like standpoint, the preceding diagram could look like this:

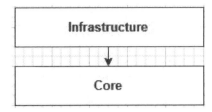

Figure 12.16 – A two-layer view of the previous Clean Architecture diagram

From here, depending on what method you choose, you can split those layers into multiple other sublayers. One thing that everyone agrees upon (I think) is that the **Core** layer can be divided into **Entities** and **Use Cases,** like this:

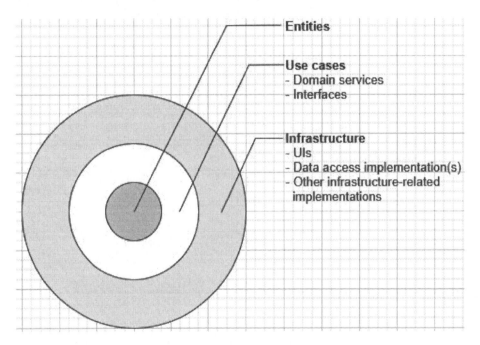

Figure 12.17 – Widespread Clean Architecture layout diagram

Since people in the tech industry are creative, there are many names for many things, but the concepts remain the same. From a layering diagram-like standpoint, that diagram could look like this:

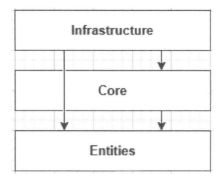

Figure 12.18 – A layer-like view of the previous Clean Architecture diagram

The infrastructure layer is conceptual and can represent multiple projects, such as an infrastructure assembly that contains EF Core implementations and a website project that represents the web UI. We could also add more projects to the infrastructure layer.

The dependency rule of Clean Architecture states that dependencies can only point inward, from the outer layers to the inner layers. This means that abstractions lie inside it and concretions lie outside it. Based on my layer-like diagram, inside translates to downward. That means a layer can use any of its direct or transitive dependencies, which means that infrastructure can use core and entities.

Clean Architecture follows all of the principles that we've been talking about since the beginning of this book, such as decoupling our implementations using abstractions, dependency inversion, and separation of concerns. These implementations are glued over abstractions using dependency injection (this is not mandatory, but it should help).

I've always found those circle diagrams a bit confusing, so here is my take on an updated, more linear diagram:

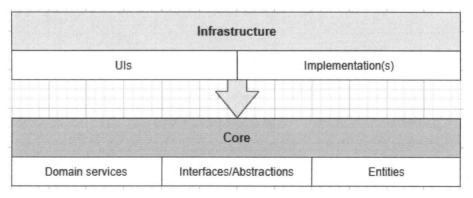

Figure 12.19 – A two-layer view of the Clean Architecture's common elements

Now, let's revisit our layered application using Clean Architecture, starting with the **core layer**. The core project contains the domain model, the use cases, and the interfaces needed to fulfill those use cases.

No external resource should be accessed here: no database calls, no disk access, and no HTTP requests. This layer contains the interfaces that expose such interaction, but the implementations must live in the **infrastructure layer**.

Starting with the entities, we have a `Product` class, which is the same as what we used in our previous implementations:

```
namespace Core.Entities
{
    public class Product
    {
        public int Id { get; set; }
        public string Name { get; set; }
        public int QuantityInStock { get; set; }
    }
}
```

Then, we have a repository interface that exposes the way we store and retrieve those products:

```
namespace Core.Interfaces
{
    public interface IProductRepository
    {
        Ienumerable<Product> All();
        Product FindById(int productId);
        void Update(Product product);
        void Insert(Product product);
        void DeleteById(int productId);
    }
}
```

Then, besides `NotEnoughStockException`, we have two use cases: `AddStocks` and `RemoveStocks`. Each use case encapsulates its own logic. We could have ported the service instead, but this use case approach is neat and gets us closer to Vertical Slice Architecture (see *Chapter 15, Getting Started with Vertical Slice Architecture*, for more information). Let's start with the more complex one; that is, `RemoveStocks`:

```
namespace Core.UseCases
{
    public class RemoveStocks
    {
        private readonly IproductRepository _productRepository;
        public RemoveStocks(IproductRepository
productRepository)
        {
            _productRepository = productRepository ?? throw new
ArgumentNullException(nameof(productRepository));
        }

        public int Handle(int productId, int amount)
        {
            var product = _productRepository
.FindById(productId);
            if (amount > product.QuantityInStock)
            {
                throw new NotEnoughStockException (product.
QuantityInStock, amount);
            }
            product.QuantityInStock -= amount;
            _productRepository.Update(product);
            return product.QuantityInStock;
        }
    }
}
```

Once again, the preceding code is very similar to the previous samples. We are injecting `IProductRepository`, then migrating the other sample's logic in the `Handle` method while using `IProductRepository` to access data. The `Handle` method takes a `productId` and an `amount` as input and returns the updated quantity. This is simple – the class has one responsibility and all of the logic is there; that's all we need.

The `AddStock` use case is built by following the same pattern. As a reference, here is its `Handle` method:

```
public int Handle(int productId, int amount)
{
    var product = _productRepository.FindById(productId);
    product.QuantityInStock += amount;
    _productRepository.Update(product);
    return product.QuantityInStock;
}
```

Now that we have those business rules in place, let's look at how we can consume them from `StocksController`. Both use cases are encapsulated in their individual classes, so we can use method injection and inject the use case directly into the action method (this is not mandatory, nor part of Clean Architecture; it is just a possibility that feels natural):

```
[HttpPost("remove-stocks")]
public ActionResult<StockLevel> Remove(
    int productId,
    [FromBody] RemoveStocksCommand command,
    [FromServices] RemoveStocks useCase
)
{
    try
    {
        var quantityInStock = useCase.Handle(productId,
command.Amount);
        var stockLevel = new StockLevel(quantityInStock);
        return Ok(stockLevel);
    }
    catch (NotEnoughStockException ex)
    {
        return Conflict(new
        {
            ex.Message,
            ex.AmountToRemove,
            ex.QuantityInStock
```

```
        });
    }
}
```

This is the same code that we had previously, but instead of _stockService. RemoveStock, we call useCase.Handle. The same applies to the AddStocks use case, as follows:

```
[HttpPost("add-stocks")]
public ActionResult<StockLevel> Add(
    int productId,
    [FromBody] AddStocksCommand command,
    [FromServices] AddStocks useCase
)
{
    var quantityInStock = useCase.Handle(productId, command.
Amount);
    var stockLevel = new StockLevel(quantityInStock);
    return Ok(stockLevel);
}
```

In the composition root, we must replace the bindings of IProductService and IStockService with the following:

```
services.AddScoped<AddStocks>();
services.AddScoped<RemoveStocks>();
```

As you may have noticed, we have no interface for those use cases. Since they are concrete business rules that we consume as-is from the infrastructure layer, interfaces are not needed. There is nothing to abstract away.

Now, let's take a look at the infrastructure. As we saw previously, we can have a data model or not, but since the entities are located in a more inward layer, any project from the infrastructure layer can use them directly. Moreover, we often don't need a different data model, so persisting entities directly saves some mapping along the way and removes useless complexity.

We can continue on the same path that we initiated in the *Shared Rich Model* project, which has a design that is close to Clean Architecture.

Knowing that we persist domain entities directly, our `ProductRepository` implementation is simple. There's no mapping and it looks like this:

```
namespace Infrastructure.Data.Repositories
{
    public class ProductRepository : IProductRepository
    {
        private readonly ProductContext _db;
        public ProductRepository(ProductContext db)
        {
            _db = db ?? throw new
ArgumentNullException(nameof(db));
        }
        public IEnumerable<Product> All()
        {
            return _db.Products;
        }
        public void DeleteById(int productId)
        {
            var product = _db.Products.Find(productId);
            _db.Products.Remove(product);
            _db.SaveChanges();
        }
        public Product FindById(int productId)
        {
            var product = _db.Products.Find(productId);
            return product;
        }
        public void Insert(Product product)
        {
            _db.Products.Add(product);
            _db.SaveChanges();
        }
        public void Update(Product product)
        {
            _db.Entry(product).State = EntityState.Modified;
            _db.SaveChanges();
```

```
        }
    }
}
```

The preceding code is very clean; it takes entities in and persists them. Since the entities are the heart of the system, there is no need for more copies or a data model.

> **Tip**
>
> Suppose you need to save the data using a different structure than the domain model. The data-specific classes should live in the project that's implementing the persistence, which resides in the infrastructure layer. This means that no other layer should be aware of it, which does not create tight coupling between other layers and the database while becoming the solution to your persistence problem.

That's it for the stocks part of the system; we have the same use cases as we had previously, following the same web API contract but using Clean Architecture.

For the "get all products" use case, I decided to inject `IProductRepository` directly into the controller. Since the UI (**infrastructure layer**) can depend on the **core layer**, we could technically do that because the layer's flow points inward.

> **Note**
>
> There are many code examples on the web that suggest this approach. My take is that as long as the feature is data-driven, very close to the database, and has no business logic, it is acceptable; programming empty shells and adding complexity is rarely helpful. However, as soon as business logic is involved, create a service, a use case, or any other domain entity that you deem necessary for that scenario. Don't pack business logic into your controllers.

Next is `ProductsController`, which consumes that "use case":

```
namespace Web.Controllers
{
    [ApiController]
    [Route("[controller]")]
    public class ProductsController : ControllerBase
    {
        // ...
        [HttpGet]
```

```
public ActionResult<IEnumerable<ProductDetails>> Get()
{
    var products = _productRepository
        .All()
        .Select(p => new ProductDetails(
            id: p.Id,
            name: p.Name,
            quantityInStock: p.QuantityInStock
        ));
    return Ok(products);
}
public class ProductDetails
{
    // omitted for brevity
}
}
}
```

Here, we have limited logic that copies the domain model to a DTO and returns a 200 OK to the consumer. In this example, the controller follows its role and plays the bridge between HTTP and the business logic.

Nevertheless, you should analyze your needs and specs; each project is different, so maybe loading repositories from your controllers is good enough for one scenario while not good at all for another.

To wrap this up, Clean Architecture is a proven pattern for building applications. It is fundamentally an evolution of layering. There are many variants out there that can help you manage use cases, entities, and infrastructure; however, we will not cover those here. If you think this is a great fit for you, your team, your project, or your organization, feel free to dig deeper and adopt this pattern. In subsequent chapters, we will explore some patterns, such as CQRS, Publish-Subscribe, and domain events that can be used with Clean Architecture to add more flexibility and robustness, which is particularly useful as your system grows in size or complexity.

Summary

Layering is one of the most used architectural techniques when it comes to designing applications. An application is often split into three different layers, each managing a single responsibility. The three most popular layers are **presentation**, **domain**, and **data**. You are not limited to three layers, and you can split each one into smaller layers (or smaller pieces inside the same conceptual layer). This allows you to create composable, manageable, and maintainable applications. Moreover, you can create abstraction layers to invert the flow of dependency and separate interfaces from implementations, as we saw with the *Abstract Data Layer* project. You can persist the domain entities directly or create an independent model for the data layer. You can also use an anemic model (no logic or method) or a rich model (packed with entity-related logic).

From there, out of layering was born Clean Architecture, which provides guidance about how you can organize your application into concentric layers, often dividing the application into use cases.

Let's see how this approach can help us move toward the **SOLID** principles, at app-scale:

- **S**: Layering leads us toward splitting responsibilities horizontally, with each layer oriented around a single macro-concern. So, the goal of layering is responsibility segregation.

- **O**: N/A.

- **L**: N/A.

- **I**: Splitting layers based on features (or cohesive groups of features) is a way of segregating a system into smaller blocks (interfaces).

- **D**: Abstraction layers lead directly to the dependency flow's inversion, while classic layering leads to the opposite direction.

In the next chapter, we will learn how to centralize the logic of copying objects (models) using the object mapper pattern and use an open source tool to help us skip the implementation (this is also known as productive laziness).

Questions

Let's take a look at a few practice questions:

1. Is it true that, when creating a layered application, we must have presentation, domain, and data layers?

2. Is a rich domain model better than an anemic domain model?

3. Does EF Core implements the Repository and Unit of Work patterns?

4. Do we need to use an ORM in the data layer?

5. Can a layer, in Clean Architecture, access any inward layers?

Further reading

Here are a few links that can help you build on what we learned in this chapter:

- **ExceptionMapper** is an ASP.NET Core middleware that reacts to `Exception`. You can map certain exception types to HTTP status codes and more. It is one of the open source projects that I created in 2020: `https://net5.link/i8jb`.

- **Dapper** is a simple yet powerful ORM for .NET, made by the people of Stack Overflow. If you like writing SQL, but don't like mapping data to objects, this ORM might be for you: `https://net5.link/pTYs`.

- An article that I wrote in 2017, talking about the Repository pattern; that is, *Design Patterns: ASP.NET Core Web API, services, and repositories | Part 5: Repositories, the ClanRepository, and integration testing*: `https://net5.link/D53Z`.

- *Entity Framework Core – Using Transactions*: `https://net5.link/gxwD`.

13
Getting Started with Object Mappers

In this chapter, we'll explore object mapping. As we saw in the previous chapter, working with layers often leads to copying models from one layer to another. Object mappers solve that problem. We will first take a look at manually implementing an object mapper. Then, we'll improve our design. Finally, I will introduce you to an open source tool that helps us generate business value instead of writing mapping code.

The following topics will be covered in this chapter:

- Overview of object mapping
- Implementing an object mapper, and exploring a few alternatives
- Using the **Service Locator** pattern to create a service in front of our mappers
- Using **AutoMapper** to map an object to another, replacing our homebrewed code

Overview of object mapping

What is object mapping? In a nutshell, it is the action of copying the value of an object's properties into the properties of another object. But sometimes, properties' names do not match; an object hierarchy may need to be flattened, and more. As we saw in the previous chapter, each layer can own its own model, which can be a good thing, but that comes at the price of copying objects from one layer to another. We can also share models between layers, but we will need some sort of mapping at some point. Even if it's just to map your models to DTOs or view models, it is almost inevitable, unless you are building a tiny application, but even then, you may want or need DTOs and view models.

> **Note**
> Remember that DTOs define your API's contract. Having independent contract classes should help you maintain a system, making you choose when to modify them. If you skip that part, each time you change your model, it automatically updates your endpoints' contracts, possibly breaking some clients. Moreover, if you input your model directly, a malicious user could try to bind the value of properties that he should not, leading to potential security issues.

In the previous projects, we instantiated the objects manually where the conversion happened, duplicating the mapping logic, and adding additional responsibilities to the class doing the mapping. To fix that issue, we are going to extract the mapping logic into other components.

Goal

The object mapper's goal is to copy the value of an object's properties into the properties of another object. It encapsulates the mapping logic away from where the mapping takes place. The mapper is also responsible for transforming the values from the original format to the destination format if both objects do not follow the same structure. We could want to flatten the object hierarchy, for example.

Design

We could design this in many ways, but we could represent the basic design with the following:

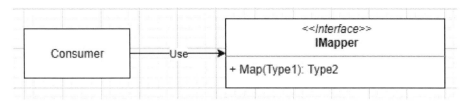

Figure 13.1 – Basic design of the object mapper

From the diagram, the **Consumer** uses the IMapper interface to map an object of Type1 to an object of Type2. That's not very reusable, but it illustrates the concept. By using the power of generics, we can upgrade that simple design to this more reusable version:

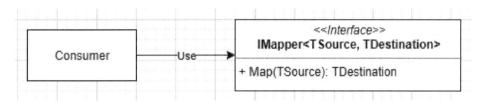

Figure 13.2 – Updating the design of the object pattern

We can now implement the IMapper<TSource, TDestination> interface, and create one class per mapping rule or one class that implements multiple mapping rules. For example, we could implement the mapping of Type1 to Type2 and Type2 to Type1 in the same class.

We could also use the following design and create an IMapper interface with a single method that handles all of the application's mapping:

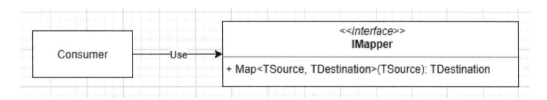

Figure 13.3 – Object mapping using a single IMapper as the entry point

The biggest advantage of that last design is the ease of use. We always inject a single IMapper instead of one IMapper<TSource, TDestination> per type of mapping, which should reduce the number of dependencies and the complexity of consuming such a mapper. The biggest downside could be the complexity of the implementation, but we can take that out of the equation, as we are about to discover.

You could implement object mapping using any way that your imagination allows, but the critical part to remember is that the mapper has the responsibility of mapping an object to another. A mapper should not do crazy stuff such as loading data from a database and whatnot. It should copy the values of one object into another; that's it.

Let's jump into some code to explore the designs in more depth with each project.

Project: Mapper

This project is an updated version of the Clean Architecture code from the last chapter, which contains both a **data model** and a **domain model**. I used that version to showcase the mapping of both data to domain and domain to DTO. If you don't need a data model, don't create one, especially using Clean Architecture. Nonetheless, the goal is to demonstrate the design's versatility and encapsulate the mapping of entities into mapper classes to extract that logic from the repositories and the controllers.

First, we need an interface that resides in the `Core` project so the other projects can implement the mapping that they need. Let's adopt the second design that we saw:

```csharp
namespace Core.Interfaces
{
    public interface IMapper<TSource, TDestination>
    {
        TDestination Map(TSource entity);
    }
}
```

With that interface, we can start by creating the data mappers. Since we are mapping `Data.Models.Product` to a `Core.Entities.Product` and vice versa, I opted for a single class to implement both mappings:

```csharp
namespace Infrastructure.Data.Mappers
{
    public class ProductMapper : IMapper<Data.Models.Product,
Core.Entities.Product>, IMapper<Core.Entities.Product, Data.
Models.Product>
    {
        public Core.Entities.Product Map(Data.Models.Product
entity)
        {
            return new Core.Entities.Product
```

```
            {
                Id = entity.Id,
                Name = entity.Name,
                QuantityInStock = entity.QuantityInStock
            };
        }

        public Data.Models.Product Map(Core.Entities.Product
entity)
        {
            return new Data.Models.Product
            {
                Id = entity.Id,
                Name = entity.Name,
                QuantityInStock = entity.QuantityInStock
            };
        }
    }
}
```

These are simple methods that copy the value of an object's properties into the other. Nonetheless, now that we have done that, we are ready to update the `ProductRepository` class to use the new mapper:

```
namespace Infrastructure.Data.Repositories
{
    public class ProductRepository : IProductRepository
    {
        private readonly ProductContext _db;
        private readonly IMapper<Data.Models.Product, Core.
Entities.Product> _dataToEntityMapper;
        private readonly IMapper<Core.Entities.Product, Data.
Models.Product> _entityToDataMapper;
        public ProductRepository(ProductContext db,
IMapper<Data.Models.Product, Core.Entities.Product>
productMapper, IMapper<Core.Entities.Product, Data.Models.
Product> entityToDataMapper)
        {
            _db = db ?? throw new
```

```
ArgumentNullException(nameof(db));
        _dataToEntityMapper = productMapper ?? throw new
ArgumentNullException (nameof(productMapper));
        _entityToDataMapper = entityToDataMapper ?? throw
new ArgumentNullException (nameof(entityToDataMapper));
    }
```

In the preceding code, we've injected the two mappers that we need. Even if we created a single class that implements both interfaces, the consumer (`ProductRepository`) does not know that. Next are the methods that use the mappers:

```
public IEnumerable<Core.Entities.Product> All()
{
    return _db.Products.Select(p =>
_dataToEntityMapper.Map(p));
}


public void DeleteById(int productId)
{
    var product = _db.Products.Find(productId);
    _db.Products.Remove(product);
    _db.SaveChanges();
}


public Core.Entities.Product FindById(int productId)
{
    var product = _db.Products.Find(productId);
    return _dataToEntityMapper.Map(product);
}


public void Insert(Core.Entities.Product product)
{
    var data = _entityToDataMapper.Map(product);
    _db.Products.Add(data);
    _db.SaveChanges();
}


public void Update(Core.Entities.Product product)
```

```
        {
            var data = _db.Products.Find(product.Id);
            data.Name = product.Name;
            data.QuantityInStock = product.QuantityInStock;
            _db.SaveChanges();
        }
    }
}
```

Then, the `ProductRepository` class uses the mappers to replace its copy logic (the preceding highlighted lines). That simplifies the repository, moving the mapping responsibility into mapper objects instead—one more step towards the Single Responsibility Principle (SRP – the "S" in SOLID).

The same principle was then applied to the web application, creating `ProductMapper` and `StockMapper`, and updating the controllers to use them. I omitted the code for brevity, but it is basically the same. Please look at the code on GitHub (`https://net5.link/rZdN`).

The only missing piece is in the composition root, where we bind the mapper implementations with the `IMapper<TSource, TDestination>` interface. The data bindings look like this:

```
services.AddSingleton<IMapper<Infrastructure.Data.Models.
Product, Core.Entities.Product>, Infrastructure.Data.Mappers.
ProductMapper>();
```

```
services.AddSingleton<IMapper<Core.Entities.Product,
Infrastructure.Data.Models.Product>, Infrastructure.Data.
Mappers.ProductMapper>();
```

Since `ProductMapper` implements both interfaces, we bind both to that class. That is one of the beauties of abstractions; `ProductRepository` asks for two mappers but receives the same instance of `ProductMapper` twice, without even knowing it.

> **Note**
>
> Yes, I did that on purpose. That proves that we can compose an application as we want it to be, without impacting the **consumers**. That is done by depending on abstractions instead of concretions, as per the dependency inversion principle. Moreover, the division into small interfaces, as per the Interface Segregation Principle (ISP – the "I" in SOLID), makes that kind of scenario possible. Finally, all of those pieces are put back together using the power of **Dependency Injection (DI)**.
>
> I hope you are starting to see what I have in mind, as we are putting more and more pieces together.

Code smell: Too many dependencies

Using that kind of mapping could become tedious in the long run, and we would rapidly see scenarios such as injecting three or more mappers into a single controller. That controller would most likely have other dependencies already, leading to four or more dependencies.

That should raise the following flag:

- Does that class do too much and have too many responsibilities?

In that case, not really, but our fine-grained interface would be polluting our controllers with tons of dependencies on mappers, which is not ideal and makes our code harder to read.

If you are curious, here is how I came up with the number three:

- Mapping from `Entity` to `DTO` (`GetOne`, `GetAll`, `Insert`, `Update`, and maybe `Delete`)
- Mapping from `DTO` to `Entity` (`Insert`)
- Mapping from `DTO` to `Entity` (`Update`)

As a rule of thumb, you want to limit the number of dependencies to three or less. Over that number, ask yourself if there is a problem with that class; does it have too many responsibilities? Having more than four dependencies is not inherently bad; it is just an indicator that you should reconsider some part of the design. If nothing is wrong, keep it at 4 or 5 or 10; it does not matter.

If you don't like to have that many dependencies, you could extract service aggregates that encapsulate two or more of those dependencies and inject that aggregate instead. Beware that moving your dependencies around does not fix anything; it just moves the problem elsewhere if there was a problem in the first place. Using aggregates could increase the readability of the code though.

Instead of blindly moving dependencies around, analyze the problem to see if you could create classes with actual logic that could do something useful to reduce the number of dependencies.

Pattern – Aggregate Services

Even if aggregate services is not a magic problem-solving pattern, it is a viable alternative to injecting tons of dependency into another class. Its goal is to aggregate many dependencies in another class to reduce the number of injected services in other classes, grouping dependencies together. The way to manage aggregates would be to group those by concerns or responsibility. Putting a bunch of exposed services in another service just for the sake of it is rarely the way to go; aim for cohesion.

> **Note**
>
> Creating one or more central aggregation services that expose other services can be a great way to implement service (interface) discovery in a project. I'm not telling you to put everything into an aggregate firsthand. However, if the discovery of services is a concern in your project or you and your team find it hard, that is a possibility worth investigating.

Here is an example of a hypothetical mapping aggregate to reduce the dependency of our imaginary CRUD controller:

```
public interface IProductMappers
{
    IMapper<Product, ProductDetails> EntityToDto { get; }
    IMapper<InsertProduct, Product> InsertDtoToEntity { get; }
    IMapper<UpdateProduct, Product> UpdateDtoToEntity { get; }
}


public class ProductMappers : IProductMappers
{
    public ProductMappers(IMapper<Product, ProductDetails>
entityToDto, IMapper<InsertProduct, Product> insertDtoToEntity,
```

```
IMapper<UpdateProduct, Product> updateDtoToEntity)
    {
        EntityToDto = entityToDto ?? throw new
ArgumentNullException(nameof(entityToDto));
        InsertDtoToEntity = insertDtoToEntity ?? throw new
ArgumentNullException(nameof(insertDtoToEntity));
        UpdateDtoToEntity = updateDtoToEntity ?? throw new
ArgumentNullException(nameof(updateDtoToEntity));
    }

    public IMapper<Product, ProductDetails> EntityToDto { get;
}
    public IMapper<InsertProduct, Product> InsertDtoToEntity {
get; }
    public IMapper<UpdateProduct, Product> UpdateDtoToEntity {
get; }
}


public class ProductsController : ControllerBase
{
    private readonly IProductMappers _mapper;
    // …

    public ProductDetails Method()
    {
        var product = default(Product);
        var dto = _mapper.EntityToDto.Map(product);
        return dto;
    }
}
```

From that example, the IProductMappers aggregate could make sense as it regroups all mappers used in the ProductsController class. It has the single responsibility of mapping ProductsController-related domain objects to DTOs and vice versa. You can create aggregates with anything, not just mappers. That's a fairly common pattern in DI-heavy applications.

> **Note**
>
> As long as an aggregate service is not likely to change and implements no logic, we could omit the interface and directly inject the concrete type. Since we are focusing heavily on the SOLID principles here, I decided to include the interface (which is not a bad thing in itself). One advantage of not having an interface is that using the concrete type could reduce the complexity of mocking the aggregate in unit tests. And as long as you don't try to put logic in there, I see no drawback.

Pattern – Mapping Façade

Instead of what we did in the previous case, we could create a mapping façade instead of an aggregate. The code consuming the façade is more elegant. The responsibility of the façade is the same as the aggregate, but it implements the interfaces instead of exposing properties.

Here is an example:

```
public interface IProductMapperService : IMapper<Product,
ProductDetails>, IMapper<InsertProduct, Product>,
IMapper<UpdateProduct, Product>
{
}
```

```
public class ProductMapperService : IProductMapperService
{
    private readonly IMapper<Product, ProductDetails>
_entityToDto;
    private readonly IMapper<InsertProduct, Product>
_insertDtoToEntity;
    private readonly IMapper<UpdateProduct, Product>
_updateDtoToEntity;
    // ...
    public ProductDetails Map(Product entity)
    {
        return _entityToDto.Map(entity);
    }

    public Product Map(InsertProduct dto)
    {
```

```
            return _insertDtoToEntity.Map(dto);
    }


    public Product Map(UpdateProduct dto)
    {
            return _updateDtoToEntity.Map(dto);
    }
}


public class ProductsController : ControllerBase
{
    private readonly IProductMapperService _mapper;
    // ...
    public ProductDetails Method()
    {
        var product = default(Product);
        var dto = _mapper.Map(product);
        return dto;
    }
}
```

From the `ProductsController` standpoint, I always find it way cleaner to write
`_mapper.Map(...)` instead of `_mapper.SomeMapper.Map(...)`. The controller does
not want to know what mapper is doing what mapping; the only thing it wants is to map
what needs mapping.

Now that we've covered a few mapping options and explored the *too many dependencies*
code smell, it is time to continue our journey into object mapping, with a "mapping façade
on steroids."

Project – Mapping service

The goal is to simplify the implementation of the mapper façade with a universal interface.

We are going to use our third diagram to achieve that goal. Here's a reminder:

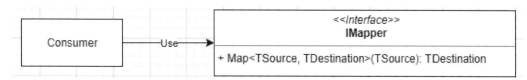

Figure 13.4 – Object mapping using a single IMapper interface

Instead of naming the interface `IMapper`, I found `IMappingService` to be more suitable because it is not mapping anything; it is a dispatcher, sending the mapping request to the right mapper. Let's take a look:

```
namespace Core.Interfaces
{
    public interface IMappingService
    {
        TDestination Map<TSource, TDestination>(TSource
entity);
    }
}
```

That interface is self-explanatory; it maps any `TSource` to any `TDestination`.

On the implementation side, we are leveraging the **Service Locator** pattern, so I called the implementation `ServiceLocatorMappingService`:

```
namespace Web.Services
{
    public class ServiceLocatorMappingService : IMappingService
    {
        private readonly IServiceProvider _serviceProvider;
        public ServiceLocatorMappingService(IServiceProvider
serviceProvider)
        {
            _serviceProvider = serviceProvider ?? throw new
ArgumentNullException(nameof(serviceProvider));
        }

        public TDestination Map<TSource, TDestination>(TSource
entity)
        {
            var mapper = _serviceProvider.
GetService<IMapper<TSource, TDestination>>();
```

```
            if (mapper == null)
            {
                throw new MapperNotFoundException
(typeof(TSource), typeof(TDestination));
            }
            return mapper.Map(entity);
        }
    }
}
```

The logic is simple:

- Find the appropriate `IMapper<TSource, TDestination>` service, then map the entity with it.

- If you don't find any, throw a `MapperNotFoundException`.

The key to that design is to register the mappers with the IoC container instead of with the service itself. Then we use the mappers without knowing every single one of them, like in the previous example. The `ServiceLocatorMappingService` class doesn't know any mappers; it just dynamically asks for one whenever needed.

> **Tip**
>
> I do not like the **Service Locator** pattern much in the application's code. The Service Locator is a code smell, and sometimes even worse, an anti-pattern. However, sometimes it can come in handy, as in this case. We are not trying to cheat dependency injection here; on the contrary, we leverage its power. Moreover, that service location needs to be done somewhere. Usually, I prefer to let the framework do it for me, but in this case, we explicitly did it, which was fine.
>
> The use of a service locator is wrong when acquiring dependencies in a way that removes the possibility of controlling the program's composition from the composition root. That would break the IoC principle.
>
> In this case, we load mappers dynamically from the IoC container, which does, however, limit the container's ability to control what to inject a little, but it is acceptable enough for this type of implementation.

Now, we can inject that service everywhere that we need mapping, then use it directly. We already registered the mappers, so we just need to bind the `IMappingService` to its `ServiceLocatorMappingService` implementation and update the consumers.

If we look at this new version of the `ProductRepository`, we now have the following:

```
namespace Infrastructure.Data.Repositories
{
    public class ProductRepository : IProductRepository
    {
        private readonly ProductContext _db;
        private readonly IMappingService _mappingService;
        public ProductRepository(ProductContext db,
IMappingService mappingService)
        {
            _db = db ?? throw new
ArgumentNullException(nameof(db));
            _mappingService = mappingService ?? throw new
ArgumentNullException(nameof(mappingService));
        }
```

Here, unlike the last sample, we inject a single service instead of one per mapper:

```
        public IEnumerable<Product> All()
        {
            return _db.Products.Select(p => _mappingService.
Map<Models.Product, Product>(p));
        }
        // ...
        public Product FindById(int productId)
        {
            var product = _db.Products.Find(productId);
            return _mappingService.Map<Models.Product,
Product>(product);
        }
        public void Insert(Product product)
        {
            var data = _mappingService.Map<Product, Models.
Product>(product);
            _db.Products.Add(data);
            _db.SaveChanges();
        }
        //...
```

```
        }
    }
```

That's very similar to the previous sample, but we replaced the mappers with the new service (the highlighted lines). The last piece is the DI binding:

```
services.AddSingleton<IMappingService,
    ServiceLocatorMappingService>();
```

And that's it; we now have a universal mapping service that delegates the mapping to any mapper that we register with the IoC container.

> **Note**
>
> I used the singleton lifetime because `ServiceLocatorMappingService` has no state; it can be reused every time without any impact on the mapping logic.

The nicest part is that this is not the apogee of object mapping just yet. We have one tool to explore, named AutoMapper.

Project – AutoMapper

We just covered different ways to implement object mapping, but here we will leverage an open source tool named AutoMapper, which does it for us instead of us implementing our own.

Why bother learning all of that if there is a tool that already does it? There are a few reasons to do so:

- It is important to understand the concepts; you don't always need a full-fledged tool like AutoMapper.

- It gives us the chance to cover multiple patterns that we applied to the mappers that can also be applied elsewhere to any components with different responsibilities. So, all in all, you should have learned multiple new techniques during this object mapping progression.

- Lastly, we dug deeper into applying the SOLID principles to write better programs.

This project is also a copy of the Clean Architecture sample. The biggest difference between this project and the others is that we don't need to define any interface because AutoMapper exposes an `IMapper` interface with all of the methods we need and more.

To install AutoMapper, you can load the `AutoMapper` NuGet package using the CLI (`dotnet add package AutoMapper`), Visual Studio's NuGet Package Manager, or by updating your `.csproj` manually.

The best way to define our mappers is by using AutoMapper's profile mechanism. A profile is a simple class that inherits from `AutoMapper.Profile` and that contains maps from one object to another. We can use a similar grouping to earlier, but without implementing interfaces.

Finally, instead of manually registering our profiles, we can scan one or more assemblies to load all of the profiles into AutoMapper by using the `AutoMapper.Extensions.Microsoft.DependencyInjection` package.

There is more to AutoMapper than this, but it has enough resources online, including the official documentation, to help you dig deeper into the tool.

In the *Infrastructure* project, we need to map `Data.Models.Product` to `Entities.Product` and vice versa. We can do that in a profile that we are naming `ProductProfile`:

```
namespace Infrastructure.Data.Mappers
{
    public class ProductProfile : Profile
    {
        public ProductProfile()
        {
            CreateMap<Data.Models.Product, Core.Entities.
Product>().ReverseMap();
        }
    }
}
```

A profile in AutoMapper is nothing but a class where you create maps in the constructor. The `Profile` class adds the required methods for you to do that, such as the `CreateMap` method. What does that do?

`CreateMap<Data.Models.Product, Core.Entities.Product>()` tells AutoMapper to register a mapper that maps `Data.Models.Product` to `Core.Entities.Product`. Then the `ReverseMap()` method tells AutoMapper to reverse that map, so from `Core.Entities.Product` to `Data.Models.Product`. That's all that we need for now because AutoMapper maps properties using conventions, and both of our classes have the same set of properties with the same names.

From the *Web* project perspective, we needed some mappers too, which I divided into the two following profiles:

```
namespace Web.Mappers
{
    public class StocksProfile : Profile
    {
        public StocksProfile()
        {
            CreateMap<Product, StocksController.StockLevel>();
        }
    }
    public class ProductProfile : Profile
    {
        public ProductProfile()
        {
            CreateMap<Product, ProductsController.
ProductDetails>();
        }
    }
}
```

We could have merged them into just one, but I decided not to because I felt one profile per controller made sense, especially as the application grows.

Here is an example that illustrates multiple maps in a single profile:

```
namespace Web.Mappers
{
    public class ProductProfile : Profile
    {
        public ProductProfile()
        {
            CreateMap<Product, ProductsController.
ProductDetails>();
            CreateMap<Product, StocksController.StockLevel>();
        }
    }
}
```

To scan for profiles from the composition root, we can use one of the `AddAutoMapper` extension methods to do that (from the `AutoMapper.Extensions.Microsoft.DependencyInjection` package):

```
services.AddAutoMapper(
    GetType().Assembly,
    typeof(Infrastructure.Data. Mappers.ProductProfile).
Assembly
);
```

That method accepts a `params Assembly[] assemblies` argument, which means that we can pass an array or multiple `Assembly` instances to it.

The first `Assembly` is the *Web* assembly, acquired from the `Startup` class by calling `GetType().Assembly` (that code is in the `Startup.ConfigureServices` method). From there, AutoMapper should find the `StocksProfile` and the `ProductProfile` classes.

The second `Assembly` is the *Infrastructure* assembly, acquired using the `Data.Mappers.ProductProfile` class. It is important to note that any type from that assembly would have given us a reference on the `Infrastructure` assembly; there's no need to find a class inheriting from `Profile`. From there, AutoMapper should find the `Data.Mappers.ProductProfile` class.

The beauty of scanning for types like this is that once you register AutoMapper with the IoC container, you can add profiles in any of the registered assemblies, and they get loaded automatically; there's no need to do anything else afterward but to write useful code. Scanning assemblies also encourages composition by convention, making it easier to maintain in the long run. The downside of assembly scanning is that it can be hard to debug when something does not get registered. It can also be hard to find what *registration module* is doing something wrong.

Now that we've created the profiles and registered them with the IoC container, it is time to use AutoMapper. Let's take a look at the `ProductRepository` class:

```
namespace Infrastructure.Data.Repositories
{
    public class ProductRepository : IProductRepository
    {
        private readonly ProductContext _db;
        private readonly IMapper _mapper;
```

```
        public ProductRepository(ProductContext db, IMapper
mapper)
        {
            _db = db ?? throw new
ArgumentNullException(nameof(db));
            _mapper = mapper ?? throw new
ArgumentNullException(nameof(mapper));
        }
```

In the preceding code, we've injected AutoMapper's IMapper interface.

```
        public IEnumerable<Product> All()
        {
#if USE_PROJECT_TO
            // Transposed to a Select() possibly optimal in
some cases; previously known as "Queryable Extensions".
            return _mapper.ProjectTo<Product>(_db.Products);
#else
            // Manual Mapping (query the whole object, then map
it; could lead to "over-querying" the database)
            return _db.Products.Select(p => _mapper.
Map<Product>(p));
#endif
        }
```

The All method (preceding code block) exposes two ways of mapping collections that I describe later. Next, are the two other updated methods:

```
        // ...
        public Product FindById(int productId)
        {
            var product = _db.Products.Find(productId);
            return _mapper.Map<Product>(product);
        }
        public void Insert(Product product)
        {
            var data = _mapper.Map<Models.Product>(product);
            _db.Products.Add(data);
            _db.SaveChanges();
        }
```

```
            // ...
        }
}
```

As you can see, it is very similar to the other options; we inject an `IMapper`, then use it to map the entities. The only method that has a bit more code is the `All()` method. The reason is that I added two ways to map the collection.

The first way implies the `ProjectTo<TDestination>()` method that uses the `IQueryable` interface to limit the number of queried fields. In our case, that changes nothing because we need the whole entity. Using that method is recommended with EF.

The `All()` method should have been as simple as the following:

```
public IEnumerable<Product> All()
{
    return _mapper.ProjectTo<Product>(_db.Products);
}
```

The second method uses the `Map` method directly, as we did with our implementations, and is used in the projection like this:

```
public IEnumerable<Product> All()
{
    return _db.Products.Select(p => _mapper.Map<Product>(p));
}
```

All of the other cases are very straightforward and use the `Map` method of AutoMapper. The two controllers are doing the same, like this:

```
namespace Web.Controllers
{
    [ApiController]
    [Route("[controller]")]
    public class ProductsController : ControllerBase
    {
        private readonly IProductRepository _productRepository;
        private readonly IMapper _mapper;

        public ProductsController(IProductRepository
productRepository, IMapper mapper)
```

```
        {
            _productRepository = productRepository ?? throw new
ArgumentNullException (nameof(productRepository));
            _mapper = mapper ?? throw new
ArgumentNullException(nameof(mapper));
        }
        [HttpGet]
        public ActionResult<IEnumerable<ProductDetails>> Get()
        {
            var products = _productRepository
                .All()
                .Select(p => _mapper.Map<ProductDetails>(p));
            return Ok(products);
        }
        // ...
    }
```

Here is the `StocksController` using `AutoMapper` to maps domain entities to DTOs (highlighted lines):

```
    [ApiController]
    [Route("products/{productId}/")]
    public class StocksController : ControllerBase
    {
        private readonly IMapper _mapper;
        public StocksController(IMapper mapper)
        {
            _mapper = mapper ?? throw new
ArgumentNullException(nameof(mapper));
        }

        [HttpPost("add-stocks")]
        public ActionResult<StockLevel> Add(
            int productId,
            [FromBody] AddStocksCommand command,
            [FromServices] AddStocks useCase
        )
        {
```

```
            var product = useCase.Handle(productId, command.
Amount);
            var stockLevel = _mapper.Map<StockLevel>(product);
            return Ok(stockLevel);
        }


    [HttpPost("remove-stocks")]
    public ActionResult<StockLevel> Remove(
        int productId,
        [FromBody] RemoveStocksCommand command,
        [FromServices] RemoveStocks useCase
    )
    {
        try
        {
            var product = useCase.Handle(productId,
command.Amount);
            var stockLevel = _mapper.
Map<StockLevel>(product);
            return Ok(stockLevel);
        }
        catch (NotEnoughStockException ex)
        {
            return Conflict(new
            {
                ex.Message,
                ex.AmountToRemove,
                ex.QuantityInStock
            });
        }
    }
    // ...
    }
}
```

The last detail that I'd like to add is that we can assert whether our mapper configurations are valid when the application starts. That will not point to missing mappers, but it validates that the registered ones are configured correctly. From the `Startup` class, you can write the following code:

```
public void Configure(IApplicationBuilder app,
IWebHostEnvironment env, IMapper mapper)
{
    // ...
    mapper.ConfigurationProvider.AssertConfigurationIsValid();
    // ...
}
```

And this closes the AutoMapper project. At this point, you should begin to be familiar with object mapping.

I'd recommend that you evaluate whether AutoMapper is the right tool for the job whenever a project needs object mapping. If it is not, you can always load another tool or implement your own mapping logic.

> **Final note**
> AutoMapper is convention-based and does a lot on its own without any configuration from us, the developers. It is also configuration based, caching the conversions to improve performance. We can also create **type converters, value resolvers, value converters,** and more. AutoMapper keeps us away from writing that boring mapping code, and I have yet to find a better tool.

Summary

Object mapping is an avoidable reality in most cases. However, as we saw in this chapter, there are several ways of implementing object mapping, taking that responsibility away from the other components of our applications. One of those ways is AutoMapper, an open source tool that does that for us, offering us many options to configure the mapping of our objects.

Now let's see how object mapping can help us follow the **SOLID** principles:

- **S**: It helps extract the mapping responsibility away from the other classes, encapsulating mapping logic into mapper objects or AutoMapper profiles.

- **O**: By injecting mappers, we can change the mapping logic without changing the code of their consumers.

- **L**: N/A.

- **I**: We saw different ways of dividing mappers into smaller interfaces. AutoMapper is no different; it exposes the `IMapper` interface and uses other interfaces and implementations under the hood.

- **D**: All of our code depends only on interfaces, moving the implementation's binding to the composition root.

Now that we are done with object mapping, in the next chapter, we'll explore the **Mediator** and **CQRS** patterns. Then we will combine our knowledge to learn about a new style of application-level architecture named **Vertical Slice Architecture**.

Questions

Let's take a look at a few practice questions:

1. Is it true that injecting an **Aggregation Service** instead of multiple services makes our system better?

2. Is it true that using mappers helps us extract responsibilities from consumers to mapper classes?

3. Is it true that you should always use AutoMapper?

4. When using AutoMapper, should you encapsulate your mapping code into profiles?

5. How many dependencies should start to raise a flag telling you that you are injecting too many dependencies into a single class?

Further reading

Here are some links to build upon what we learned in the chapter:

- If you want more object mapping, I wrote an article about that in 2017, titled *Design Patterns: ASP.NET Core Web API, Services, and Repositories | Part 9: the NinjaMappingService and the Façade Pattern*: `https://net5.link/hxYf`

- AutoMapper official website: `https://net5.link/5AUZ`

- *AutoMapper Usage Guidelines* is an excellent do/don't list to help you do the right thing with AutoMapper, written by the library's author: `https://net5.link/tTKg`

14

Mediator and CQRS Design Patterns

In this chapter, we explore the building blocks that we will use in the next chapter about **Vertical Slice Architecture**. We begin with a quick overview of Vertical Slice Architecture to give you an idea of the end goal to understand where we are heading. Then we explore the **Mediator** design pattern, which plays the role of the middleman between the components of our application. That leads us to the **Command Query Responsibility Segregation (CQRS)** pattern, which describes how to organize our logic. Finally, to piece all of that together, we explore MediatR, an open source implementation of the Mediator design pattern.

The following topics will be covered in this chapter:

- A high-level overview of Vertical Slice Architecture
- Implementing the Mediator pattern
- Implementing the CQRS pattern
- Using MediatR as a mediator

Let's begin with the end goal.

A high-level overview of Vertical Slice Architecture

Before starting, let's look at the end goal of this chapter and the next. This way, it should be easier to follow the progress toward that goal throughout the chapter.

As we just covered in the chapter on layering, a layer groups classes together based on shared responsibility. So, classes that contain data access code are part of the data access layer (or infrastructure). In diagrams, layers are often represented by horizontal slices, like this:

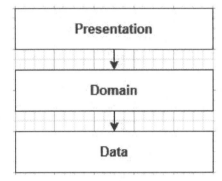

Figure 14.1 – Diagram representing layers as horizontal slices

The name "vertical slice" comes from that; a vertical slice represents the part of each layer that creates a specific feature. So, instead of dividing the application into layers, we are dividing it by feature. A feature manages its data access code, its domain logic, and possibly even its presentation code. By doing this, we are decoupling the features from one another but keeping each feature's components close together. When we add, update, or remove a feature using layering, we make changes to one or more layers. Unfortunately, "one or more layers" too often translates to "all layers." With vertical slices, all features are kept in isolation, allowing us to design them independently.

From a layering perspective, it's like flipping your way of thinking about software to a 90° angle:

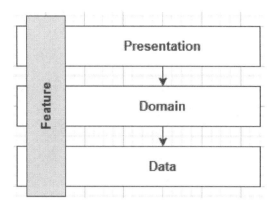

Figure 14.2 – Diagram representing a vertical slice crossing all layers

Vertical Slice Architecture does not dictate the use of **CQRS**, the **Mediator** pattern, or **MediatR**, but these tools and patterns flow very well together, as we see in the next chapter.

Our goal is to encapsulate features together, use CQRS to divide the application into requests (commands and queries), and use MediatR as the mediator of that CQRS pipeline, decoupling the pieces from one another.

You now know the plan – we will explore Vertical Slice Architecture later; meanwhile, let's start with the Mediator design pattern.

Implementing the Mediator pattern

The **Mediator** pattern is another GoF design pattern that controls how objects interact with one another (making it a behavioral pattern).

Goal

The mediator's role is to manage the communication between objects (colleagues). Those colleagues should not communicate together directly but use the mediator instead. The mediator helps break tight coupling between these colleagues.

To keep it short, **a mediator is a middleman that relays messages between colleagues**.

Design

Let's start with some UML diagrams. From a very high level, the Mediator pattern is composed of a mediator and colleagues:

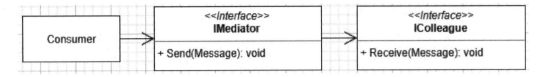

Figure 14.3 – Class diagram representing the Mediator pattern

When an object in the system wants to send a message to one or more colleagues, it uses the mediator. Here is an example of how it works:

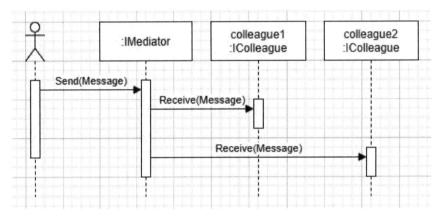

Figure 14.4 – Sequence diagram of a mediator relaying messages to colleagues

That is also good for colleagues; to talk to each other, a colleague must use the mediator as well. We could update the diagram as follows:

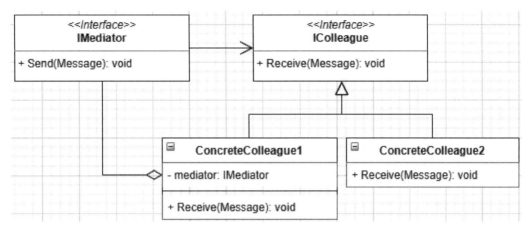

Figure 14.5 – Class diagram representing the Mediator pattern including colleagues' collaboration

In that diagram, `ConcreteColleague1` is a colleague but also the consumer of the mediator. For example, that colleague could send a message to another colleague using the mediator, like this:

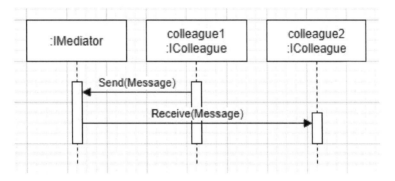

Figure 14.6 – Sequence diagram representing colleague1 communicating
with colleague2 through the mediator

From the mediator standpoint, its implementation will most likely contain a collection of colleagues to communicate with, like this:

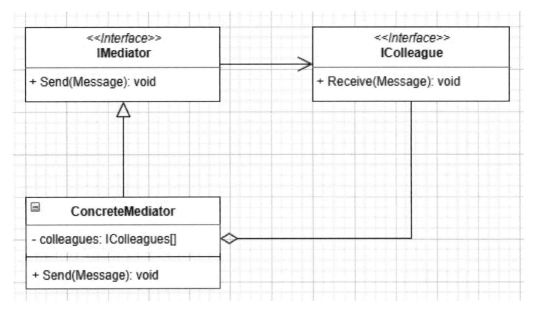

Figure 14.7 – Class diagram representing a simple hypothetical concrete mediator implementation

All of those UML diagrams are useful, but enough of that; it is now time to look at some code.

Project – Mediator (IMediator)

The Mediator project represents a simplified chat system using the Mediator pattern. Let's start with the interfaces:

```
namespace Mediator
{
    public interface IMediator
    {
        void Send(Message message);
    }

    public interface IColleague
    {
        string Name { get; }
        void ReceiveMessage(Message message);
```

```
        }


    public class Message
    {
        public Message(IColleague from, string content)
        {
            Sender = from ?? throw new
ArgumentNullException(nameof(from));
            Content = content ?? throw new
ArgumentNullException(nameof(content));
        }


        public IColleague Sender { get; }
        public string Content { get; }
    }
}
```

The system is composed of the following:

- `IMediator`, which sends messages.

- `IColleague`, which receives messages and has a `Name` property (to output something).

- The `Message` class, which represents a message sent by an `IColleague` implementation.

Now to the implementation of the `IMediator` interface. `ConcreteMediator` broadcasts the messages to all `IColleague` instances without discrimination:

```
public class ConcreteMediator : IMediator
{
    private readonly List<IColleague> _colleagues;
    public ConcreteMediator(params IColleague[] colleagues)
    {
        if (colleagues == null) { throw new
ArgumentNullException(nameof(colleagues)); }
        _colleagues = new List<IColleague>(colleagues);
    }
```

```
    public void Send(Message message)
    {
        foreach (var colleague in _colleagues)
        {
            colleague.ReceiveMessage(message);
        }
    }
}
```

That mediator is simple; it forwards all the messages that it receives to every colleagues that it knows. The last part of the pattern is ConcreteColleague, which delegates the messages to an IMessageWriter<TMessage> interface:

```
public class ConcreteColleague : IColleague
{
    private readonly IMessageWriter<Message> _messageWriter;
    public ConcreteColleague(string name,
IMessageWriter<Message> messageWriter)
    {
        Name = name ?? throw new
ArgumentNullException(nameof(name));
        _messageWriter = messageWriter ?? throw new
ArgumentNullException(nameof(messageWriter));
    }

    public string Name { get; }

    public void ReceiveMessage(Message message)
    {
        _messageWriter.Write(message);
    }
}
```

That class could hardly be simpler: it takes a name and an
IMessageWriter<TMessage> implementation when created, then it stores
a reference for future use.

The `IMessageWriter<TMessage>` interface serves as a presenter to control how the messages are displayed and has nothing to do with the Mediator pattern. Nevertheless, it is an excellent way to manage how a `ConcreteColleague` object handles messages. Here is the code:

```
namespace Mediator
{
    public interface IMessageWriter<TMessage>
    {
        void Write(TMessage message);
    }
}
```

Let's use that chat system now. The consumer of the system is the following integration test:

```
public class MediatorTest
{
    [Fact]
    public void Send_a_message_to_all_colleagues()
    {
        // Arrange
        var (millerWriter, miller) =
CreateConcreteColleague("Miller");
        var (orazioWriter, orazio) =
CreateConcreteColleague("Orazio");
        var (fletcherWriter, fletcher) =
CreateConcreteColleague("Fletcher");
```

The test starts by defining three colleagues with their own `TestMessageWriter` implementation (names were randomly generated).

```
        var mediator = new ConcreteMediator(miller, orazio,
fletcher);
        var expectedOutput = @"[Miller]: Hey everyone!
[Orazio]: What's up Miller?
[Fletcher]: Hey Miller!
";
```

In the second part of the preceding `Arrange` block, we create the subject under test (`mediator`) and register the three colleagues. At the end of that `Arrange` block, we also define the expected output of our test. It is important to note that we control the output from the `TestMessageWriter` implementation (defined at the end of the `MediatorTest` class).

```
// Act
mediator.Send(new Message(
    from: miller,
    content: "Hey everyone!"
));
mediator.Send(new Message(
    from: orazio,
    content: "What's up Miller?"
));
mediator.Send(new Message(
    from: fletcher,
    content: "Hey Miller!"
));
```

In the preceding `Act` block, we send three messages through `mediator`, in the expected order.

```
// Assert
    Assert.Equal(expectedOutput, millerWriter.Output.
ToString());
    Assert.Equal(expectedOutput, orazioWriter.Output.
ToString());
    Assert.Equal(expectedOutput, fletcherWriter.Output.
ToString());
    }
```

In the `Assert` block, we ensure that all colleagues received all of the messages.

```
    private (TestMessageWriter, ConcreteColleague)
CreateConcreteColleague(string name)
    {
        var messageWriter = new TestMessageWriter();
        var concreateColleague = new ConcreteColleague(name,
messageWriter);

        return (messageWriter, concreateColleague);
    }
```

The `CreateConcreteColleague` method is a helper method that encapsulates the creation of the colleagues, enabling us to write the one-liner declaration used in the `Arrange` section of the test.

```
    private class TestMessageWriter : IMessageWriter<Message>
    {
        public StringBuilder Output { get; } = new
StringBuilder();

        public void Write(Message message)
        {
            Output.AppendLine($"[{message.Sender.Name}]:
{message.Content}");
        }
    }
}
```

Finally, the `TestMessageWriter` class writes the messages into `StringBuilder`, making it easy to assert the output. If we were to build a GUI for that, we could write an implementation of `IMessageWriter<Message>` that writes to that GUI; in the case of a web UI, it could be using **SignalR**, for example.

To summarize the sample, the consumer (the unit test) sent messages to the colleagues through the mediator. Those messages were written in the `StringBuilder` instance of each `TestMessageWriter`. Finally, we asserted that all colleagues received the expected messages. That illustrates the Mediator design pattern's basic idea.

In theory, colleagues should communicate through the mediator, so the Mediator pattern would not be complete without that. Let's implement a chatroom to tackle that concept.

Project – Mediator (IChatRoom)

In the last code sample, the classes were named after the Mediator pattern actors, as shown in the diagram of Figure 14.7. While this example is very similar, it uses domain-specific names instead and implements a few more methods to manage the system. Let's start with the abstractions:

```
namespace Mediator
{
    public interface IChatRoom
    {
        void Join(IParticipant participant);
        void Send(ChatMessage message);
    }
```

The IChatRoom interface is the mediator and it defines two methods instead of one:

- Join, which allows IParticipant to join IChatRoom.
- Send, which sends a message to the others.

```
    public interface IParticipant
    {
        string Name { get; }
        void Send(string message);
        void ReceiveMessage(ChatMessage message);
        void ChatRoomJoined(IChatRoom chatRoom);
    }
```

The IParticipant interface also has a few more methods:

- Send, to send messages.
- ReceiveMessage, to receive messages from the other IParticipant objects.
- ChatRoomJoined, to confirm that the IParticipant object has successfully joined a chatroom.

```
    public class ChatMessage
    {
        public ChatMessage(IParticipant from, string content)
        {
            Sender = from ?? throw new
```

```
ArgumentNullException(nameof(from));
        Content = content ?? throw new
ArgumentNullException(nameof(content));
        }


    public IParticipant Sender { get; }
    public string Content { get; }
    }
}
```

ChatMessage is the same as the previous Message class, but it references
IParticipant instead of IColleague.

Let's now look at the IParticipant implementation:

```
public class User : IParticipant
{
    private IChatRoom _chatRoom;
    private readonly IMessageWriter<ChatMessage>
_messageWriter;

    public User(IMessageWriter<ChatMessage> messageWriter,
string name)
    {
        _messageWriter = messageWriter ?? throw new
ArgumentNullException(nameof(messageWriter));
        Name = name ?? throw new
ArgumentNullException(nameof(name));
    }

    public string Name { get; }

    public void ChatRoomJoined(IChatRoom chatRoom)
    {
        _chatRoom = chatRoom;
    }

    public void ReceiveMessage(ChatMessage message)
    {
```

```
        _messageWriter.Write(message);
    }

    public void Send(string message)
    {
        _chatRoom.Send(new ChatMessage(this, message));
    }
}
```

The `User` class represents our default `IParticipant`. A `User` instance can chat in only one `IChatRoom`; that is set when calling the `ChatRoomJoined` method. When it receives a message, it delegates it to its `IMessageWriter<ChatMessage>`. Finally, a `User` instance can send a message by delegating it to the mediator (`IChatRoom`).

We could create a `Moderator`, `Administrator`, `SystemAlerts`, or any other `IParticipant` implementations as we see fit, but not in this sample. I will leave that to you to experiment with the Mediator pattern.

Now to the `IChatRoom` implementation:

```
public class ChatRoom : IChatRoom
{
    private readonly List<IParticipant> _participants = new
List<IParticipant>();

    public void Join(IParticipant participant)
    {
        _participants.Add(participant);
        participant.ChatRoomJoined(this);
        Send(new ChatMessage(participant, "Has joined the
channel"));
    }

    public void Send(ChatMessage message)
    {
        _participants.ForEach(participant => participant.
ReceiveMessage(message));
    }
}
```

ChatRoom is even slimmer than User; it allows IParticipant to join in and sends ChatMessage to all registered participants. When joining a ChatRoom, it keeps a reference on that IParticipant, tells that IParticipant that it has successfully joined, then sends a ChatMessage to all participants announcing the newcomer.

That's it; we have a classic Mediator implementation. Before moving to the next section, let's take a look at the Consumer instance of IChatRoom, which is another integration test:

```
public class ChatRoomTest
{
    [Fact]
    public void ChatRoom_participants_should_send_and_receive_
messages()
    {
        // Arrange
        var (kingChat, king) = CreateTestUser("King");
        var (kelleyChat, kelley) = CreateTestUser("Kelley");
        var (daveenChat, daveen) = CreateTestUser("Daveen");
        var (rutterChat, _) = CreateTestUser("Rutter");

        var chatroom = new ChatRoom();
```

We created four users with their respective TestMessageWriter instances in the Arrange section, as we did before (names were also randomly generated).

```
        // Act
        chatroom.Join(king);
        chatroom.Join(kelley);
        king.Send("Hey!");
        kelley.Send("What's up King?");
        chatroom.Join(daveen);
        king.Send("Everything is great, I joined the
CrazyChatRoom!");
        daveen.Send("Hey King!");
        king.Send("Hey Daveen");
```

In the `Act` block, our test users join the `chatroom` instance and send messages into it.

```
// Assert
Assert.Empty(rutterChat.Output.ToString());
```

Since Rutter did not join the chatroom, we expect no message.

```
Assert.Equal(@"[King]: Has joined the channel
[Kelley]: Has joined the channel
[King]: Hey!
[Kelley]: What's up King?
[Daveen]: Has joined the channel
[King]: Everything is great, I joined the CrazyChatRoom!
[Daveen]: Hey King!
[King]: Hey Daveen
", kingChat.Output.ToString());
```

Since King is the first to join the channel, he is expected to have received all messages.

```
Assert.Equal(@"[Kelley]: Has joined the channel
[King]: Hey!
[Kelley]: What's up King?
[Daveen]: Has joined the channel
[King]: Everything is great, I joined the CrazyChatRoom!
[Daveen]: Hey King!
[King]: Hey Daveen
", kelleyChat.Output.ToString());
```

Kelley was the second user to join the chatroom, so the output contains almost all messages.

```
Assert.Equal(@"[Daveen]: Has joined the channel
[King]: Everything is great, I joined the CrazyChatRoom!
[Daveen]: Hey King!
[King]: Hey Daveen
", daveenChat.Output.ToString());
    }
```

Daveen joined after King and Kelley exchanged a few words, so the conversation is expected to start later.

```
    private (TestMessageWriter, User) CreateTestUser(string
name)
    {
        var writer = new TestMessageWriter();
        var user = new User(writer, name);
        return (writer, user);
    }
```

The `CreateTestUser` method helps simplify the `Arrange` section of the test case, similar to before.

```
    private class TestMessageWriter :
IMessageWriter<ChatMessage>
    {
        public StringBuilder Output { get; } = new
StringBuilder();

        public void Write(ChatMessage message)
        {
            Output.AppendLine($"[{message.Sender.Name}]:
{message.Content}");
        }
    }
}
```

The `TestMessageWriter` implementation is the same as the previous example, accumulating messages in a `StringBuilder` instance.

To summarize the test case, we had four users; three of them joined the same chatroom at a different time and chatted a little. The output is different for everyone since the time you join now matters.

Conclusion

As we explored in the two preceding projects, a **mediator** allows us to decouple the components of our system. **The mediator is the middleman between colleagues**, and it served us well in the small chatroom samples.

Now let's see how the Mediator pattern can help us follow the **SOLID** principles:

- **S**: The Mediator extracts the communication responsibility from colleagues.

- **O**: With a mediator relaying the messages, we can create new colleagues and change the existing colleagues' behaviors without impacting the others. If we need a new colleague; we can just register it with the mediator, and voilà! On the other hand, if we need new mediation behavior, we can always implement a new mediator and keep the existing colleagues' implementation.

- **L**: N/A.

- **I**: The system is divided into multiple small interfaces (`IMediator` and `IColleague`).

- **D**: All actors of the Mediator pattern solely depend on other interfaces.

Next, we explore CQRS, which will allow us to clearly separate commands and queries, leading to a more maintainable application.

Implementing the CQRS pattern

CQRS stands for **Command Query Responsibility Segregation**. We can apply CQRS in two ways:

- Dividing requests into commands and queries.

- Applying the CQRS concept to a higher level, leading to a distributed system.

In this chapter, we stick with the first one, but we will tackle the second definition in *Chapter 16, Introduction to Microservices Architecture.*

Goal

The goal is to divide all requests into two categories: commands and queries.

A command mutates the state of an application. For example, creating, updating, and deleting an entity are commands. Commands do not return a value.

On the other hand, a query reads the state of the application but never changes it. For example, reading an order, reading your order history, and retrieving your user profile are all queries.

By performing this division, we create a clear separation of concerns between mutator and accessor requests.

Design

There is no definite design for this, but for us, the flow of a command should look like the following:

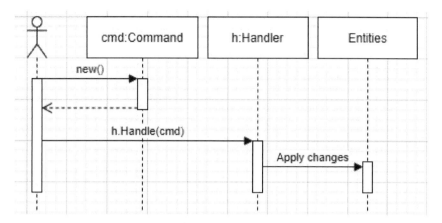

Figure 14.8 – Sequence diagram representing the abstract flow of a command

The consumer creates a command object and sends it to a command handler, which then applies mutation to the application. In this case, I called it `Entities`, but it could have sent a SQL `UPDATE` command to a database or a web API call over HTTP; the implementation details do not matter.

The concept is the same for a query, but it returns a value instead. Very importantly, the query must not change the state of the application but query for data instead, like this:

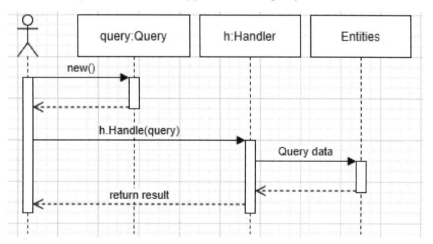

Figure 14.9 – Sequence diagram representing the abstract flow of a query

Like the command, the consumer creates a query object and sends it to a handler, which then executes some logic to retrieve and return the requested data. You can replace `Entities` with anything that your handler needs to query the data.

Enough talk – let's look at a CQRS project.

Project: CQRS

Context: We need to build an improved version of our chat system. The old system was working so well that we now need to scale it up. The mediator was of help to us, so we kept that part, and we picked CQRS to help us with this new, improved design. A participant was limited to a single chatroom in the past, but now a participant should be able to chat in multiple rooms at the same time.

The new system is composed of three commands and two queries:

- A participant must be able to join a chatroom.

- A participant must be able to leave a chatroom.

- A participant must be able to send a message into a chatroom.

- A participant must be able to obtain the list of participants that joined a chatroom.

- A participant must be able to retrieve the existing messages from a chatroom.

The first three are commands, and the last two are queries. The system is backed by a mediator that makes heavy use of C# generics as follows:

```
public interface IMediator
{
    TReturn Send<TQuery, TReturn>(TQuery query)
        where TQuery: IQuery<TReturn>;
    void Send<TCommand>(TCommand command)
        where TCommand : ICommand;

    void Register<TCommand>(ICommandHandler<TCommand>
commandHandler)
        where TCommand : ICommand;
    void Register<TQuery, TReturn>(IQueryHandler<TQuery,
TReturn> commandHandler)
        where TQuery : IQuery<TReturn>;
}
```

```
public interface ICommand { }
public interface ICommandHandler<TCommand>
    where TCommand : ICommand
{
    void Handle(TCommand command);
}


public interface IQuery<TReturn> { }
public interface IQueryHandler<TQuery, TReturn>
    where TQuery : IQuery<TReturn>
{
    TReturn Handle(TQuery query);
}
```

If you are not familiar with generics, this might look daunting, but that code is way simpler than it looks. First, we have two empty interfaces: `ICommand` and `IQuery<TReturn>`. We could omit them, but they help identify the commands and the queries; they help describe our intent.

Then we have two interfaces that handle commands or queries. Let's start with the interface to implement for each type of command that we want to handle:

```
public interface ICommandHandler<TCommand>
    where TCommand : ICommand
{
    void Handle(TCommand command);
}
```

That interface defines a `Handle` method that takes the command as a parameter. The generic parameter `TCommand` represents the type of command handled by the class implementing the interface. The query handler interface is the same, but it specifies a return value as well:

```
public interface IQueryHandler<TQuery, TReturn>
    where TQuery : IQuery<TReturn>
{
    TReturn Handle(TQuery query);
}
```

The mediator abstraction allows registering command and query handlers using the generic interfaces that we just explored. It also supports sending commands and queries. Then we have `ChatMessage`, which is similar to the last two samples (with an added creation date):

```
public class ChatMessage
{
    public ChatMessage(IParticipant sender, string message)
    {
        Sender = sender ?? throw new
ArgumentNullException(nameof(sender));
        Message = message ?? throw new
ArgumentNullException(nameof(message));
        Date = DateTime.UtcNow;
    }

    public DateTime Date { get; }
    public IParticipant Sender { get; }
    public string Message { get; }
}
```

That's followed by the updated `IParticipant` interface:

```
public interface IParticipant
{
    string Name { get; }
    void Join(IChatRoom chatRoom);
    void Leave(IChatRoom chatRoom);
    void SendMessageTo(IChatRoom chatRoom, string message);
    void NewMessageReceivedFrom(IChatRoom chatRoom, ChatMessage
message);
    IEnumerable<IParticipant> ListParticipantsOf(IChatRoom
chatRoom);
    IEnumerable<ChatMessage> ListMessagesOf(IChatRoom
chatRoom);
}
```

All methods of the `IParticipant` interface accept an `IChatRoom` parameter to support multiple chatrooms. Next, the updated `IChatRoom` interface:

```
public interface IChatRoom
{
    string Name { get; }

    void Add(IParticipant participant);
    void Remove(IParticipant participant);
    IEnumerable<IParticipant> ListParticipants();

    void Add(ChatMessage message);
    IEnumerable<ChatMessage> ListMessages();
}
```

Before going into commands and the chat itself, let's take a peek at the `Mediator` class:

```
public class Mediator : IMediator
{
    private readonly HandlerDictionary _handlers = new
    HandlerDictionary();

    public void Register<TCommand>(ICommandHandler<TCommand>
commandHandler)
        where TCommand : ICommand
    {
        _handlers.AddHandler(commandHandler);
    }

    public void Register<TQuery, TReturn>
(IQueryHandler<TQuery, TReturn> commandHandler)
        where TQuery : IQuery<TReturn>
    {
        _handlers.AddHandler(commandHandler);
    }

    public TReturn Send<TQuery, TReturn>(TQuery query)
        where TQuery : IQuery<TReturn>
```

```
    {
        var handler = _handlers.Find<TQuery, TReturn>();
        return handler.Handle(query);
    }

    public void Send<TCommand>(TCommand command)
        where TCommand : ICommand
    {
        var handlers = _handlers.FindAll<TCommand>();
        foreach (var handler in handlers)
        {
            handler.Handle(command);
        }
    }
}
```

The `Mediator` class supports registering commands and queries as well as sending a query to a handler or sending a command to zero or more handlers.

> **Note**
>
> I omitted the implementation of `HandlerDictionary` because it does not add anything, and it is just an implementation detail. It is available on GitHub (`https://net5.link/CWCe`).

Now to the commands. To keep it clean, I've grouped the commands and the handlers together, but you could use another way to classify yours:

```
public class JoinChatRoom
{
    public class Command : ICommand
    {
        public Command(IChatRoom chatRoom, IParticipant requester)
        {
            ChatRoom = chatRoom ?? throw new
ArgumentNullException(nameof(chatRoom));
            Requester = requester ?? throw new
ArgumentNullException(nameof(requester));
```

```
        }

        public IChatRoom ChatRoom { get; }
        public IParticipant Requester { get; }
    }

    public class Handler : ICommandHandler<Command>
    {
        public void Handle(Command command)
        {
            command.ChatRoom.Add(command.Requester);
        }
    }
}
```

The JoinChatRoom.Command class represents the command itself, a data structure that carries the command data. The JoinChatRoom.Handler class handles that type of command. When executed, it adds the specified IParticipant to the specified IChatRoom, from the ChatRoom and Requester properties. Next command:

```
public class LeaveChatRoom
{
    public class Command : ICommand
    {
        public Command(IChatRoom chatRoom, IParticipant requester)
        {
            ChatRoom = chatRoom ?? throw new
ArgumentNullException(nameof(chatRoom));
            Requester = requester ?? throw new
ArgumentNullException(nameof(requester));
        }

        public IChatRoom ChatRoom { get; }
        public IParticipant Requester { get; }
    }
    public class Handler : ICommandHandler<Command>
    {
```

```
        public void Handle(Command command)
        {
            command.ChatRoom.Remove(command.Requester);
        }
    }
}
```

That code represents the exact opposite of the `JoinChatRoom` command, the `LeaveChatRoom` handler removes an `IParticipant` from the specified `IChatRoom`. To the next command:

```
public class SendChatMessage
{
    public class Command : ICommand
    {
        public Command(IChatRoom chatRoom, ChatMessage message)
        {
            ChatRoom = chatRoom ?? throw new
ArgumentNullException(nameof(chatRoom));
            Message = message ?? throw new
ArgumentNullException(nameof(message));
        }

        public IChatRoom ChatRoom { get; }
        public ChatMessage Message { get; }
    }

    public class Handler : ICommandHandler<Command>
    {
        public void Handle(Command command)
        {
            command.ChatRoom.Add(command.Message);
            foreach (var participant in command.ChatRoom.
ListParticipants())
            {
                participant.NewMessageReceivedFrom(command.
ChatRoom, command.Message);
            }
```

```
        }
    }
}
```

The `SendChatMessage` command, on the other hand, handles two things:

- It adds the specified `Message` to `IChatRoom` (which is now only a data structure that keeps track of users and past messages).

- It also sends the specified `Message` to all `IParticipant` that joined that `IChatRoom`.

We are starting to see many smaller pieces interacting with each other to create a more developed system. But we are not done; let's look at the two queries, then the chat implementation:

```
public class ListParticipants
{
    public class Query : IQuery<IEnumerable<IParticipant>>
    {
        public Query(IChatRoom chatRoom, IParticipant
requester)
        {
            Requester = requester ?? throw new
ArgumentNullException(nameof(requester));
            ChatRoom = chatRoom ?? throw new
ArgumentNullException(nameof(chatRoom));
        }

        public IParticipant Requester { get; }
        public IChatRoom ChatRoom { get; }
    }

    public class Handler : IQueryHandler<Query,
IEnumerable<IParticipant>>
    {
        public IEnumerable<IParticipant> Handle(Query query)
        {
            return query.ChatRoom.ListParticipants();
        }
```

```
        }
    }
```

The `ListParticipants` query's handler uses the specified `IChatRoom` and returns its participants. Now, to the last query:

```
public class ListMessages
{
    public class Query : IQuery<IEnumerable<ChatMessage>>
    {
        public Query(IChatRoom chatRoom, IParticipant
requester)
        {
            Requester = requester ?? throw new
ArgumentNullException(nameof(requester));
            ChatRoom = chatRoom ?? throw new
ArgumentNullException(nameof(chatRoom));
        }

        public IParticipant Requester { get; }
        public IChatRoom ChatRoom { get; }
    }

    public class Handler : IQueryHandler<Query,
IEnumerable<ChatMessage>>
    {
        public IEnumerable<ChatMessage> Handle(Query query)
        {
            return query.ChatRoom.ListMessages();
        }
    }
}
```

The `ListMessages` query's handler uses the specified `IChatRoom` instance and returns its messages.

> **Note**
>
> All of the commands and queries reference `IParticipant` so we could enforce rules such as "`IParticipant` must join a channel before sending messages," for example. I decided to omit these details to keep the code simple, but feel free to add those features if you want to.

Next, let's take a look at the `ChatRoom` class, which is a simple data structure that holds the state of a chatroom:

```csharp
public class ChatRoom : IChatRoom
{
    private readonly List<IParticipant> _participants = new
List<IParticipant>();
    private readonly List<ChatMessage> _chatMessages = new
List<ChatMessage>();

    public ChatRoom(string name)
    {
        Name = name ?? throw new
ArgumentNullException(nameof(name));
    }

    public string Name { get; }

    public void Add(IParticipant participant)
    {
        _participants.Add(participant);
    }

    public void Add(ChatMessage message)
    {
        _chatMessages.Add(message);
    }

    public IEnumerable<ChatMessage> ListMessages()
    {
        return _chatMessages.AsReadOnly();
    }
```

```
    public IEnumerable<IParticipant> ListParticipants()
    {
        return _participants.AsReadOnly();
    }

    public void Remove(IParticipant participant)
    {
        _participants.Remove(participant);
    }
}
```

If we take a second look at the ChatRoom class, it has a Name property, and it contains a list of IParticipant instances and a list of ChatMessage instances. Both ListMessages() and ListParticipants() return the list AsReadOnly() so a clever programmer cannot mutate the state of ChatRoom from the outside. That's it, the new ChatRoom class is a façade over its underlying dependencies.

Finally, the Participant class is probably the most exciting part of this system because it is the one that makes heavy use of our **Mediator** and **CQRS** implementations:

```
public class Participant : IParticipant
{
    private readonly IMediator _mediator;
    private readonly IMessageWriter _messageWriter;

    public Participant(IMediator mediator, string name,
IMessageWriter messageWriter)
    {
        _mediator = mediator ?? throw new
ArgumentNullException(nameof(mediator));
        Name = name ?? throw new
ArgumentNullException(nameof(name));
        _messageWriter = messageWriter ?? throw new
ArgumentNullException(nameof(messageWriter));
    }

    public string Name { get; }
```

```
    public void Join(IChatRoom chatRoom)
    {
        _mediator.Send(new JoinChatRoom.Command(chatRoom,
this));
    }

    public void Leave(IChatRoom chatRoom)
    {
        _mediator.Send(new LeaveChatRoom.Command(chatRoom,
this));
    }

    public IEnumerable<ChatMessage> ListMessagesOf(IChatRoom
chatRoom)
    {
        return _mediator.Send<ListMessages.Query,
IEnumerable<ChatMessage>>(new ListMessages.Query(chatRoom,
this));
    }

    public IEnumerable<IParticipant>
ListParticipantsOf(IChatRoom chatRoom)
    {
        return _mediator.Send<ListParticipants.Query,
IEnumerable<IParticipant>>(new ListParticipants.Query(chatRoom,
this));
    }

    public void NewMessageReceivedFrom(IChatRoom chatRoom,
ChatMessage message)
    {
        _messageWriter.Write(chatRoom, message);
    }

    public void SendMessageTo(IChatRoom chatRoom, string
message)
    {
        _mediator.Send(new SendChatMessage.Command (chatRoom,
```

```
            new ChatMessage(this, message)));
        }
    }
```

Every method of the `Participant` class, apart from `NewMessageReceivedFrom`, sends a command or a query through `IMediator`, breaking the tight coupling between `Participant` and the system's operations (that is, the commands and queries). If we think about it, the `Participant` class is also a simple façade over its underlying dependencies, delegating most of the work to the mediator.

Now, let's take a look at how it works when everything's put together. I've grouped several test cases together; here is the shared setup code:

```
public class ChatRoomTest
{
    private readonly IMediator _mediator = new Mediator();
    private readonly TestMessageWriter _reagenMessageWriter =
new TestMessageWriter();
    private readonly TestMessageWriter _garnerMessageWriter =
new TestMessageWriter();
    private readonly TestMessageWriter _corneliaMessageWriter =
new TestMessageWriter();

    private readonly IChatRoom _room1 = new ChatRoom("Room 1");
    private readonly IChatRoom _room2 = new ChatRoom("Room 2");

    private readonly IParticipant _reagen;
    private readonly IParticipant _garner;
    private readonly IParticipant _cornelia;

    public ChatRoomTest()
    {
        _mediator.Register(new JoinChatRoom.Handler());
        _mediator.Register(new LeaveChatRoom.Handler());
        _mediator.Register(new SendChatMessage.Handler());
        _mediator.Register(new ListParticipants.Handler());
        _mediator.Register(new ListMessages.Handler());

        _reagen = new Participant(_mediator, "Reagen",
```

```
_reagenMessageWriter);
        _garner = new Participant(_mediator, "Garner",
_garnerMessageWriter);
        _cornelia = new Participant(_mediator, "Cornelia",
_corneliaMessageWriter);
    }

    // ...
}
```

Our test program is composed of the following:

- One `IMediator`, which enables all colleagues to interact with each other.
- Two `IChatRoom` instances.
- Three `IParticipant` instances and their `TestMessageWriter`.

In the constructor, all handlers are registered with the `Mediator` instance, so it knows how to handle commands and queries. The names of the participants are randomly generated. Here is the first test case:

```
[Fact]
public void A_participant_should_be_able_to_list_the_
participants_that_joined_a_chatroom()
{
    _reagen.Join(_room1);
    _reagen.Join(_room2);
    _garner.Join(_room1);
    _cornelia.Join(_room2);

    var room1Participants = _reagen.ListParticipantsOf(_room1);
    Assert.Collection(room1Participants,
        p => Assert.Same(_reagen, p),
        p => Assert.Same(_garner, p)
    );
}
```

In that test case, Reagen and Garner join Room 1, and Reagen and Cornelia join Room 2. Then Reagen requests the list of participants from Room 1, which outputs Reagen and Garner. The code is easy to understand and use. Under the hood, it uses commands and queries through a mediator, which breaks tight coupling between the colleagues. Here is a sequence diagram representing what is happening when a participant joins a chatroom:

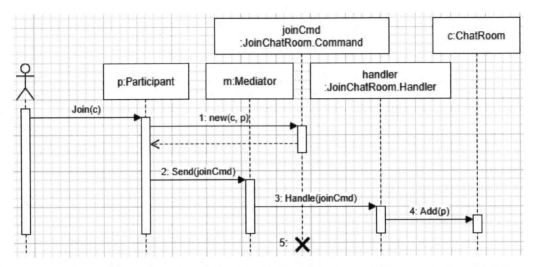

Figure 14.10 – Sequence diagram representing the flow of a participant (p) joining a chatroom (c)

1. The participant (p) creates a `JoinChatRoom` command (`joinCmd`).

2. p sends `joinCmd` through the mediator (m).

3. m finds and dispatches `joinCmd` to its handler (`handler`).

4. `handler` executes the logic (adds p to the chatroom).

5. `joinCmd` ceases to exist afterward; commands are ephemeral.

That means `Participant` never interacts directly with `ChatRoom`, or other participants.

Then a similar workflow happens when a participant requests the list of participants of a chatroom:

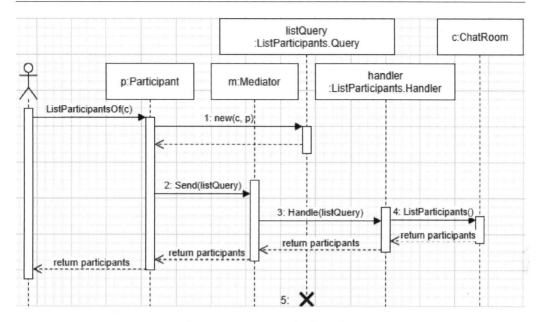

Figure 14.11 – Sequence diagram representing the flow of a participant (p) requesting the list of participants of a chatroom (c)

1. Participant (p) creates a ListParticipants query (listQuery).

2. p sends listQuery through the mediator (m).

3. m finds and dispatches the query to its handler (handler).

4. handler executes the logic (lists the participants of the chatroom).

5. listQuery ceases to exist afterward; queries are also ephemeral.

Once again, Participant does not interact directly with ChatRoom.

Here is another test case where Participant sends a message to a chatroom and another Participant receives it:

```
[Fact]
public void A_participant_should_receive_new_messages()
{
    _reagen.Join(_room1);
    _garner.Join(_room1);
    _garner.Join(_room2);
    _reagen.SendMessageTo(_room1, "Hello!");

    Assert.Collection(_garnerMessageWriter.Output,
```

```
        line =>
        {
            Assert.Equal(_room1, line.chatRoom);
            Assert.Equal(_reagen, line.message.Sender);
            Assert.Equal("Hello!", line.message.Message);
        }
    );
}
```

In that test case, Reagen joins Room 1 while Garner joins Rooms 1 and 2. Then Reagen sends a message to Room 1, and we verify that Garner received it once. The SendMessageTo workflow is very similar to the other one that we saw, but with a more complex command handler:

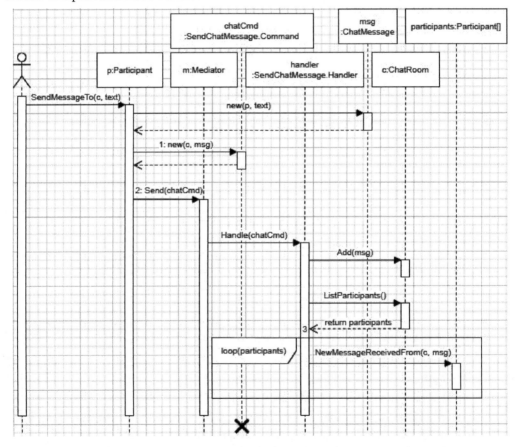

Figure 14.12 – Sequence diagram representing the flow of a participant (p) sending a message (msg) to a chatroom (c)

From that diagram, we can observe that the logic was pushed to the `ChatMessage.Handler` class. All of the other actors work together with limited knowledge of each other (see even no knowledge of each other).

That demonstrates how CQRS works with a mediator:

1. Create a command (or a query).

2. Send that command through the mediator.

3. Have one or more handlers execute the logic for that command.

You can explore the other test cases to familiarize yourself with the program and the concepts.

> **Note**
>
> You can debug the tests in Visual Studio; use breakpoints combined with *Step Into (F11)* and *Step Over (F10)* to explore the sample.

I also created a `ChatModerator` instance that sends a message in a "moderator chatroom" when a message contains a word from the `badWords` collection. That test case executes multiple handlers for each `SendChatMessage.Command`. I'll leave you to explore these other test cases yourself.

Code smell – marker interfaces

We used the empty `ICommand` and `IQuery<TReturn>` interfaces in the code samples to make the code more explicit and self-descriptive. Empty interfaces are a sign that something may be wrong: a code smell. We call those **marker interfaces**.

In our case, they help identify commands and queries but are empty and add nothing. We could discard them without any impact on our system. On the other hand, we are not performing any kind of magic tricks or violating any principles, so it seems OK to have them; they help define the intent.

Here are two examples of marker interfaces.

Metadata

Markers can be used to define metadata. A class "implements" the empty interface, and some consumer does something with it later. It could be an assembly scanning for specific types, a choice of strategy, or something else.

Instead of creating marker interfaces to add metadata, try to use custom attributes. The idea behind attributes is to add metadata to classes or members. On the other hand, interfaces exist to create a contract, and they should define at least one member; empty contracts are like a blank sheet.

In a real-world scenario, you may want to consider the cost of one versus the other. Markers are very cheap to implement but can violate the SOLID principles. Attributes could be as cheap to implement if the mechanism is already implemented or supported by the framework but could cost a lot more than a marker interface to implement if you need to program everything by hand. You must always evaluate money, time, and skills as crucial factors when making a decision.

Dependency identifier

If you need markers to inject some specific dependency in a particular class, you are most likely cheating the **inversion of control**. You should find a way to achieve the same goal using dependency injection instead, such as by contextually injecting your dependencies.

Let's start with the following interface:

```
public interface IStrategy
{
    string Execute();
}
```

In our program, we have two implementations and two markers, one for each implementation:

```
public interface IStrategyA : IStrategy { }
public interface IStrategyB : IStrategy { }

public class StrategyA : IStrategyA
{
    public string Execute() => "StrategyA";
}

public class StrategyB : IStrategyB
{
    public string Execute() => "StrategyB";
}
```

The code is barebone, but all the building blocks are there:

- `StrategyA` implements `IStrategyA`, which inherits from `IStrategy`.
- `StrategyB` implements `IStrategyB`, which inherits from `IStrategy`.
- Both `IStrategyA` and `IStrategyB` are empty marker interfaces.

Now, the consumer needs to use both strategies, so instead of controlling dependencies from the composition root, the consumer requests the markers:

```csharp
public class Consumer
{
    public IStrategyA StrategyA { get; }
    public IStrategyB StrategyB { get; }

    public Consumer(IStrategyA strategyA, IStrategyB strategyB)
    {
        StrategyA = strategyA ?? throw new
ArgumentNullException(nameof(strategyA));
        StrategyB = strategyB ?? throw new
ArgumentNullException(nameof(strategyB));
    }
}
```

In this case, the `Consumer` class exposes the strategies through properties to assert its composition later but in a non-demo scenario, it would most likely use them directly instead. Let's test that out by building a dependency tree, simulating the composition root, and then asserting the value of the consumer properties:

```csharp
[Fact]
public void ConsumerTest()
{
    // Arrange
    var serviceProvider = new ServiceCollection()
        .AddSingleton<IStrategyA, StrategyA>()
        .AddSingleton<IStrategyB, StrategyB>()
        .AddSingleton<Consumer>()
        .BuildServiceProvider();
    // Act
    var consumer = serviceProvider.GetService<Consumer>();
```

```
    // Assert
    Assert.IsType<StrategyA>(consumer.StrategyA);
    Assert.IsType<StrategyB>(consumer.StrategyB);
}
```

Both properties are of the expected type, but that is not the problem. Consumer controls what dependencies to use and when to use them by injecting markers A and B instead of two IStrategy instances. Due to that, we cannot control the dependency tree from the composition root. For example, we cannot change IStrategyA to IStrategyB and IStrategyB to IStrategyA, nor inject two IStrategyB instances or two IStrategyA instances, or even create an IStrategyC instance to replace IStrategyA or IStrategyB.

How do we fix this? Let's start by deleting our markers and by injecting two IStrategy instances instead. After doing that, we end up with the following object structure:

```
public class StrategyA : IStrategy
{
    public string Execute() => "StrategyA";
}
public class StrategyB : IStrategy
{
    public string Execute() => "StrategyB";
}
public class Consumer
{
    public IStrategy StrategyA { get; }
    public IStrategy StrategyB { get; }

    public Consumer(IStrategy strategyA, IStrategy strategyB)
    {
        StrategyA = strategyA ?? throw new
ArgumentNullException(nameof(strategyA));
        StrategyB = strategyB ?? throw new
ArgumentNullException(nameof(strategyB));
    }
}
```

With the new implementation, the `Consumer` class no longer controls the narrative, and the composition responsibility falls back to the composition root. Unfortunately, there is no way to do contextual injections using the default dependency injection container, and I don't want to get into a third-party framework for this. But all is not lost yet; we can use a factory to help ASP.NET build the `Consumer` instance, like this:

```
// Arrange
var serviceProvider = new ServiceCollection()
    .AddSingleton<StrategyA>()
    .AddSingleton<StrategyB>()
    .AddSingleton(serviceProvider =>
    {
        var strategyA = serviceProvider.GetService<StrategyA>();
        var strategyB = serviceProvider.GetService<StrategyB>();
        return new Consumer(strategyA, strategyB);
    })
    .BuildServiceProvider();

// Act
var consumer = serviceProvider.GetService<Consumer>();

// Assert
Assert.IsType<StrategyA>(consumer.StrategyA);
Assert.IsType<StrategyB>(consumer.StrategyB);
```

From that point forward, we control the composition of the program, and we can swap A by B or do anything else that we want to, as long as the implementation respects the `IStrategy` contract.

To conclude, using markers instead of doing contextual injection breaks the inversion of control principle, making the consumer control its dependencies. That's very close to using the `new` keyword to instantiate objects. Inverting back the dependency control is easy to do, even using the default container. If you need to inject dependencies contextually, I started an open source project in 2020 that does that. See *Further reading* section.

Conclusion

CQRS suggests dividing the operations of a program into **commands** and **queries**. A command mutates data, and a query returns data. We can apply the **Mediator** pattern as a way to send those commands and queries, which break the tight coupling between the pieces of that software.

You may find the codebase more intimidating when using CQRS this way due to the multiple classes. However, keep in mind that each of those classes does less (having a single responsibility), making them easier to test than a more sizable class that has many responsibilities.

Now let's see how CQRS can help us follow the **SOLID** principles:

- **S**: Dividing an application into commands, queries, and handlers takes us toward encapsulating single responsibilities into different classes.

- **O**: CQRS helps extend the software without modifying the existing code, such as by adding handlers and creating new commands.

- **L**: N/A.

- **I**: CQRS makes is easier to create multiple small interfaces with a clear distinction between commands, queries, and their respective handlers.

- **D**: N/A.

Now that we have explored CQRS and the Mediator pattern, it is time to get lazy and look at a tool that will save us some hassle.

Using MediatR as a mediator

In this section, we are exploring MediatR, an open source mediator implementation. What is MediatR? Let's start with its maker's description from its GitHub repository, which brands it as this:

"Simple, unambitious mediator implementation in .NET"

MediatR is a simple but very powerful tool for in-process communication through messaging. It supports a request/response flow through commands, queries, notifications, and events, synchronously and asynchronously. That resumes what the README says.

You can install the NuGet package using the .NET CLI: `dotnet add package MediatR`.

Now that I have quickly introduced the tool, we are going to explore the migration of our Clean Architecture sample but use MediatR to dispatch the `StocksController` requests to the core use cases. Let's jump into the code to see how it works.

Project – Clean Architecture with MediatR

Context: We want to break some more of the coupling in the Clean Architecture project that we built in *Chapter 12, Understanding Layering* by leveraging the **Mediator** pattern and **CQRS**-inspired approach.

The `CleanArchitectureWithoutDataModel` solution was already solid, but MediatR will pave the way to even more good things later. There is another major change that was introduced in this updated sample: everything is now async, from the controller to the repository. That is reflected by minor code changes here and there, thanks to the C# 5.0 `async`/`await` programming model.

> **Note**
>
> I would recommend going async whenever you can, which should be nearly always, unless something is blocking you from doing so. This is especially true for code that accesses external resources. Doing this should give you performance gain with next to no effort.
>
> When running an async task, that task does not block the thread that it runs in. Moreover, in the case of long-running operations, that thread can do other work while waiting (between the HTTP request and the response, for example). Having an async web application should increase the number of simultaneous requests that it can handle, without any complicated work on your side. So, why not?
>
> I chose not to have the previous samples as async to keep them more focused on what we were studying and keep some noise away. Now that we know all of that, it is time to take it up a notch, revisiting the same notion and looking at a new tool, and all of that in an async app.

Here is the updated `IProductRepository`:

```
namespace Core.Interfaces
{
    public interface IProductRepository
    {
        Task<IEnumerable<Product>> AllAsync(CancellationToken
cancellationToken);
        Task<Product> FindByIdAsync(int productId,
```

```
CancellationToken cancellationToken);
        Task UpdateAsync(Product product, CancellationToken
cancellationToken);
        Task InsertAsync(Product product, CancellationToken
cancellationToken);
        Task DeleteByIdAsync(int productId, CancellationToken
cancellationToken);
    }
}
```

Next is the implementation, which is very similar because Entity Framework Core exposes both synchronous and asynchronous operations:

```
namespace Infrastructure.Data.Repositories
{
    public class ProductRepository : IProductRepository
    {
        private readonly ProductContext _db;
        public ProductRepository(ProductContext db)
        {
            _db = db ?? throw new
ArgumentNullException(nameof(db));
        }
        public async Task<IEnumerable<Product>>
AllAsync(CancellationToken cancellationToken)
        {
            var products = await _db.Products.
ToArrayAsync(cancellationToken);
            return products;
        }
        public async Task DeleteByIdAsync(int productId,
CancellationToken cancellationToken)
        {
            var product = await _db.Products.
FindAsync(productId, cancellationToken);
            _db.Products.Remove(product);
            await _db.SaveChangesAsync(cancellationToken);
        }
        public async Task<Product> FindByIdAsync(int productId,
```

```
CancellationToken cancellationToken)
        {
            var product = await _db.Products.
FindAsync(productId, cancellationToken);
            return product;
        }
        public async Task InsertAsync(Product product,
CancellationToken cancellationToken)
        {
            _db.Products.Add(product);
            await _db.SaveChangesAsync(cancellationToken);
        }
        public async Task UpdateAsync(Product product,
CancellationToken cancellationToken)
        {
            _db.Entry(product).State = EntityState.Modified;
            await _db.SaveChangesAsync(cancellationToken);
        }
    }
}
```

In the preceding code, we are persisting the domain entities directly to the database using Entity Framework Core. We have explored many ways of organizing the layers, but in many cases, this one makes the most sense in terms of simplicity and efficiency.

Back to MediatR: first, we installed the `MediatR.Extensions.Microsoft.DependencyInjection` NuGet package in the web project. That package adds a helper method to scan one or more assemblies for MediatR handlers, preprocessors, and postprocessors. It adds those to the IoC container with a transient lifetime.

With that package in hand, in `Startup`, we can do this:

```
services.AddMediatR(typeof(NotEnoughStockException).Assembly);
```

Note that the `NotEnoughStockException` class is part of the core project. We can also specify more than one assembly here; as of version 8.0.0 of MediatR, there are five overloads to that method.

MediatR exposes two types of messages, request/response and notifications. The first model executes a single handler while the second allows multiple handlers to handle each message. The request/response model is perfect for both commands and queries, while notifications are more suited as an event-based model applying the Publish-Subscribe pattern. We will cover the Publish-Subscribe pattern in *Chapter 16, Introduction to Microservices Architecture*.

Now that everything is "magically" registered, we can start by updating the use cases. Both use cases were expecting `int productId` and `int amount` as parameters and were returning an `int`. Let's have a look at the updated `AddStocks` code first:

```
namespace Core.UseCases
{
    public class AddStocks
    {
        public class Command : IRequest<int>
        {
            public int ProductId { get; set; }
            public int Amount { get; set; }
        }

        public class Handler : IRequestHandler<Command, int>
        {
            private readonly IProductRepository
_productRepository;
            public Handler(IProductRepository
productRepository)
            {
                _productRepository = productRepository ?? throw
new ArgumentNullException (nameof(productRepository));
            }

            public async Task<int> Handle(Command request,
CancellationToken cancellationToken)
            {
                var product = await _productRepository.
FindByIdAsync(request.ProductId, cancellationToken);
                product.QuantityInStock += request.Amount;
                await _productRepository. UpdateAsync(product,
```

```
cancellationToken);
                    return product.QuantityInStock;
        }
    }
  }
}
```

Let's jump right to the `RemoveStocks` use case, which is very similar:

```
namespace Core.UseCases
{
    public class RemoveStocks
    {
        public class Command : IRequest<int>
        {
            public int ProductId { get; set; }
            public int Amount { get; set; }
        }

        public class Handler : IRequestHandler<Command, int>
        {
            private readonly IProductRepository
_productRepository;
            public Handler(IProductRepository
productRepository)
            {
                _productRepository = productRepository ?? throw
new ArgumentNullException (nameof(productRepository));
            }

            public async Task<int> Handle(Command request,
CancellationToken cancellationToken)
            {
                var product = await _productRepository.
FindByIdAsync(request.ProductId, cancellationToken);
                if (request.Amount > product.QuantityInStock)
```

```
        {
            throw new NotEnoughStockException (product.
QuantityInStock, request.Amount);
        }
        product.QuantityInStock -= request.Amount;
        await _productRepository. UpdateAsync(product,
cancellationToken);
        return product.QuantityInStock;
      }
    }
  }
}
```

As you may have noticed in the code, I chose the same pattern to build the commands that I did with the CQRS sample, so we have a class per use case that contains two nested classes: Command and Handler. I find this structure to make very clean code. Unfortunately, I noticed that the tooling sometimes does not like that.

By using the request/response model, the command (or query) becomes a request and must implement the IRequest<TResponse> interface. The handlers must implement the IRequestHandler<TRequest, TResponse> interface. We can also implement the IRequest and IRequestHandler<TRequest> interfaces instead, for a command that returns nothing (void).

> **Note**
>
> There are more options that are part of MediatR, and the documentation is complete enough for you to dig deeper by yourself. Not that I don't want to, but I have to limit the subjects that I talk about or risk rewriting the internet in an encyclopedia.

Let's analyze the anatomy of the AddStocks use case. Here is the old code as a reference:

```
public class AddStocks
{
    private readonly IProductRepository _productRepository;
    public AddStocks(IProductRepository productRepository)
    {
        _productRepository = productRepository ?? throw new
ArgumentNullException(nameof(productRepository));
    }
```

```
    public int Handle(int productId, int amount)
    {
        var product = _productRepository.FindById(productId);
        product.QuantityInStock += amount;
        _productRepository.Update(product);
        return product.QuantityInStock;
    }
}
```

The first difference is that we moved the loose parameters (int productId and int amount) into the Command class, which encapsulates the whole request:

```
public class Command : IRequest<int>
{
    public int ProductId { get; set; }
    public int Amount { get; set; }
}
```

Then the Command class specifies the handler's expected return value by implementing the IRequest<TResponse> interface, where TResponse is a int. That gives us a typed response when sending the request through MediatR. This is not "pure CQRS" because the command handler returns an integer representing the updated QuantityInStock. We could call that optimization, as executing one command and one query would be overkill for this scenario (possibly leading to two database calls). Moreover, we are exploring MediatR using a CQRS-like approach, which is more than fine for in-process communication.

Then the Handler class is almost identical to the AddStocks class from the CleanArchitectureWithoutDataModel solution, but it calls the asynchronous methods of the repository and passes an instance of CancellationToken to them.

```
public class Handler : IRequestHandler<Command, int>
{
    // ...
    public async Task<int> Handle(Command request,
CancellationToken cancellationToken)
    {
        var product = await _productRepository.
FindByIdAsync(request.ProductId, cancellationToken);
        product.QuantityInStock += request.Amount;
```

```
        await _productRepository.UpdateAsync(product,
cancellationToken);
        return product.QuantityInStock;
    }
}
```

> **Note**
>
> CancellationToken can be used if the asynchronous operation is
> canceled. In the sample, we pass that token to Entity Framework Core. In
> another case, we could also implement our own cancellation logic. That's out
> of the current sample's scope, but it is worth knowing. I highly suggest that you
> pass that token around every time you can.

The RemoveStocks use case follows the same pattern, so I am omitting to talk about
it to not be repetitive. Instead, let's look at the consumption of those use cases in
StocksController:

```
namespace Web.Controllers
{
    [ApiController]
    [Route("products/{productId}/")]
    public class StocksController : ControllerBase
    {
        private readonly IMediator _mediator;
        public StocksController(IMediator mediator)
        {
            _mediator = mediator ?? throw new
ArgumentNullException(nameof(mediator));
        }
```

Here we inject IMediator in the constructor since we use it in all methods. Previously,
we were injecting a different use case per action, that we replaced by the command
objects. We also let ASP.NET inject a CancellationToken, that we pass to MediatR:

```
        [HttpPost("add-stocks")]
        public async Task<ActionResult<StockLevel>> AddAsync(
            int productId,
            [FromBody] AddStocks.Command command,
CancellationToken cancellationToken
        )
```

```
        {
            command.ProductId = productId;
            var quantityInStock = await _mediator.Send(command,
cancellationToken);
            var stockLevel = new
            StockLevel(quantityInStock);
            return Ok(stockLevel);
        }
```

Here, we let the model binder load the data from the HTTP request into objects, and we `Send` the command through `_mediator`. Then we map the result into the `StockLevel` DTO before returning its value and an HTTP status code of `200 OK`. After the note, we look at the remove stock action.

> **Note**
>
> The default model binder cannot load data from multiple sources. Because of that, we must inject `productId` and assign its value to the `command.ProductId` property manually. Even if both values could be taken from the body, the resource identifier of that endpoint would become less exhaustive (no `productId` in the URI).

```
        [HttpPost("remove-stocks")]
        public async Task<ActionResult<StockLevel>>
RemoveAsync(
            int productId,
            [FromBody] RemoveStocks.Command command,
CancellationToken cancellationToken
        )
        {
            try
            {
                command.ProductId = productId;
                var quantityInStock = await _mediator.
Send(command, cancellationToken);
                var stockLevel = new
StockLevel(quantityInStock);
                return Ok(stockLevel);
            }
            catch (NotEnoughStockException ex)
```

```
        {
            return Conflict(new
            {
                ex.Message,
                ex.AmountToRemove,
                ex.QuantityInStock
            });
        }
    }
```

The preceding method does the same but sends `RemoveStocks.Command` instead. If `NotEnoughStockException` is thrown, it returns `Conflict`. Exceptions could be handled by ASP.NET Core middlewares, MVC filters, or extending the MediatR pipeline.

```
    public class StockLevel
    {
        public StockLevel(int quantityInStock)
        {
            QuantityInStock = quantityInStock;
        }

        public int QuantityInStock { get; }
    }
}
```

Finally, we have the `StockLevel` DTO, that has not changed.

> **Note about DTOs**
>
> Now, with C# 9 records, we could convert our DTOs to record classes. For example, the `StockLevel` class would look like this: `public record StockLevel(int QuantityInStock);`.
>
> We talk about records in *Chapter 17, ASP.NET Core User Interfaces*.

All in all, it is almost the same code as before, but we use MediatR instead and all the code is now asynchronous. Here is the previous implementation of the Add method to compare with:

```
[HttpPost("add-stocks")]
public ActionResult<StockLevel> Add(
    int productId,
    [FromBody] AddStocksCommand command,
    [FromServices] AddStocks useCase
)
{
    var quantityInStock = useCase.Handle(productId, command.
Amount);
    var stockLevel = new StockLevel(quantityInStock);
    return Ok(stockLevel);
}
```

Conclusion

With MediatR, we packed the power of a CQRS-inspired pipeline with the Mediator pattern into a Clean Architecture application. We were able to break the coupling between the controller and the use case handler. A simple DTO such as a command object makes controllers unaware of the handlers, leaving MediatR to be the middleman between the commands and their handlers. Due to that, the handlers could change along the way without any impact on the controller. Moreover, we could configure more interaction between the command and the handler with IRequestPreProcessor, IRequestPostProcessor, and IRequestExceptionHandler. As expected, we now control even more elements from the composition root.

MediatR help us follow the SOLID principles the same the same as the Mediator and CQRS patterns combined. The only drawback (if it is one) is that the use cases now also control the API's input contracts. The command objects are now the input DTOs. If this is something that you must avoid in a project, you can input a DTO in the action method instead, create the command object, then send it to MediatR.

Summary

In this chapter, we looked at the Mediator pattern. That pattern allows us to cut the ties between collaborators, mediating the communication between them. Then we attacked the CQRS pattern, which advises the division of software behaviors into commands and queries. Those two patterns are tools that cut tight coupling between components.

Then we updated a Clean Architecture project to use MediatR, an open source generic Mediator implementation that is CQRS-oriented. There are many more possible uses than what we explored, but that's still a great start. This concludes another chapter where we explored techniques to break tight coupling and divide systems into smaller parts.

All of those building blocks lead us to the next chapter, where we will be piecing all of those patterns and tools together to explore the Vertical Slice Architecture.

Questions

Let's take a look at a few practice questions:

1. Can we use a mediator inside a colleague to call another colleague?
2. In CQRS, can a command return a value?
3. How much does MediatR cost?
4. Imagine a design has a marker interface to add metadata to some classes. Do you think you should review that design?

Further reading

Here are a few links to build on what we have learned in the chapter:

- MediatR: `https://net5.link/ZQap`
- To get rid of setting `ProductId` manually in the *Clean Architecture with MediatR* project, you can use the open source project `HybridModelBinding` or read the official documentation about custom model binding and implement your own:

  a) Custom Model Binding in ASP.NET Core: `https://net5.link/65pb`

  b) `HybridModelBinding` (open source project on GitHub): `https://net5.link/EyKK`
- `ForEvolve.DependencyInjection` is an open source project of mine that adds support for contextual dependency injection and more: `https://net5.link/myW8`

15
Getting Started with Vertical Slice Architecture

In this chapter, we'll explore Vertical Slice Architecture, which moves all elements of a feature back together. It is almost the opposite of layering, but not totally. Vertical Slice Architecture also gives us a clean separation between requests, leading to an implicit **Command Query Responsibility Segregation (CQRS)** design. We piece all of that together using MediatR, which we explored in the previous chapter.

The following topics will be covered in this chapter:

- Vertical Slice Architecture
- A small project using Vertical Slice Architecture
- Continuing your journey: A few tips and tricks

Vertical Slice Architecture

As was said at the beginning of the previous chapter, instead of separating an application horizontally, a vertical slice groups all horizontal concerns together to encapsulate a feature. Here is a diagram that illustrates that:

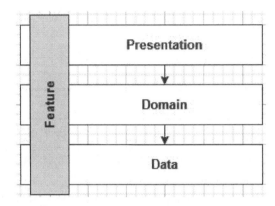

Figure 15.1 – Diagram representing a vertical slice crossing all layers

Jimmy Bogard, who is the pioneer of this type of architecture and who promotes it frequently, says the following:

> *[The goal is to] minimize coupling between slices and maximize coupling within a slice.*

What does that mean? Let's split that sentence into two distinct points:

- "minimize coupling between slices" (improved maintainability, loose coupling)
- "maximize coupling within a slice" (cohesion)

We could see the former as: instead of spreading code around multiple layers, with potentially superfluous abstractions along the way, let's regroup that code together. That helps keep the tight coupling inside a vertical slice to create a cohesive unit of code that serves a single purpose: handling the feature's logic.

We could see the latter as: one vertical slice should not depend on another. With that in mind, when you modify a vertical slice, you don't have to worry about the impact on the other slices because the coupling is minimal.

Then we could wrap that to create software around the business problem that you are trying to solve instead of around the developer's concerns, which your client has no interest in (such as data access).

What are the advantages and disadvantages?

On the upside, we have the following:

- We reduce coupling between features, making it easier to work on such a project. We only need to think about a single vertical slice, not *N* layers, improving **maintainability** by centralizing the code around a shared concern.

- We can choose how each vertical slice interacts with the external resources they require without thinking about the other slices. That adds **flexibility** since one slice can use T-SQL while another uses EF Core.

- We can start small with a few lines of code (described as **Transaction Scripts** in *Patterns of Enterprise Application Architecture* by Martin Fowler) without extravagant design or over-engineering. Then we can refactor our way to a better design when the need arises, and patterns start to emerge, leading to a **faster time to market**.

- Each vertical slice should contain precisely the right amount of code needed for it to be correct – not more, not less. That leads to a **more robust** codebase (less code means less extraneous code).

- It is easier for newcomers to find their way around an existing system since each feature is independent, with its code grouped, leading to a **faster onboarding time**.

- All that you already know still applies.

> **Tip**
>
> From my experience, features tend to start small and grow over time. While using a software, the users often find out what they really need, updating the workflow they thought they initially required, which leads to changes in the software. There are many projects that I wish were built using Vertical Slice Architecture instead of layering.

Now some downsides:

- It may take time to wrap your head around it if you're used to layering, leading to an adaptation period to learn a new way to think about your software.

- It is a "newer" type of architecture, and people don't like change.

> **Note**
>
> Another thing that I learned the hard way is to embrace change. I don't think that I've seen one project end as it was supposed to. Everyone figures out the missing pieces of the business processes while using the software. That leads to the following advice: release as fast as you can and have your customer use the software as soon as possible. That advice can be easier to achieve with Vertical Slice Architecture because you are building value for your customers instead of more or less useful abstractions and layers.
>
> At the beginning of my career, I was frustrated when specifications changed, and I thought that better planning would have fixed that. Sometimes better planning would have helped, but sometimes, the client just did not know and had to try the application to figure it out. My advice here is don't be frustrated when the specs change, even if that means rewriting a part of the software that took you days or more to code in the first place; that will happen all the time. Learn to accept that instead, and find ways to reduce the number of times it happens by helping your clients figure out their needs.

The following points are downsides that can become upsides:

- If you are used to working in silos, it may be harder to assign tasks by concerns (such as the data guys doing the data stuff). But in the end, it should be an advantage; everyone in your team (or teams) should work more closely together, leading to more learning and collaboration and possibly a new cross-functional team(s) (which definitely is an excellent thing).

- Refactoring: You need refactoring skills. Over time, most systems need some refactoring. That can be caused by changes in the requirements, or due to technical debt. No matter the reason, if you don't, you may very well end up with a **Big Ball of Mud**. Writing isolated code at first then refactoring to patterns is a crucial part of Vertical Slice Architecture. That's one of the best ways to keep cohesion high inside a slice and coupling as low as possible between slices.

> **Note**
>
> A way to start refactoring that business logic would be to push the logic into the **domain model**, creating a **rich domain model**. You can also use other design patterns and techniques to fine-tune the code and make it more maintainable, such as by creating services or even layers. A layer does not have to cross all vertical slices; it can cross only a subset of them. Compared to other application-level patterns, such as layering, there are fewer Vertical Slice Architecture rules, leading to more choices on your end. *You can use all design patterns, principles, and best practices inside a vertical slice without exporting those choices to other vertical slices.*

How do you organize a project into Vertical Slice Architecture? Unfortunately, there is no definitive answer to that; it's like everything when designing software: it depends. We will explore one way in the next project, but you can organize your project as you see fit. Then we will dig deeper into refactoring and organization. Before that, let's have a quick look at the **Big Ball of Mud** anti-pattern.

Anti-pattern: Big Ball of Mud

Big Ball of Mud describes a system that ended up badly, or that was never designed. Sometimes a system starts great but evolves into a Big Ball of Mud due to pressure, volatile requirements, impossible deadlines, bad practices, or any other reasons. Big Ball of Mud is often referred to as **spaghetti code**, which means pretty much the same thing.

That's it for this anti-pattern; it is simply an unmaintainable codebase or a very hard to maintain codebase. Next, we will get into that Vertical Slice Architecture project.

Project: Vertical Slice Architecture

Context: We are getting tired of layering, and we got asked to rebuild our small demo shop using Vertical Slice Architecture.

Here is an updated diagram that shows how the project is conceptually organized:

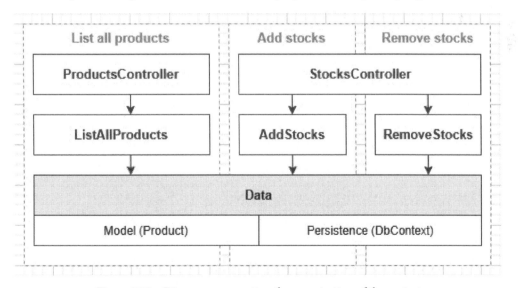

Figure 15.2 – Diagram representing the organization of the project

Each vertical box is a use case (or slice), while each horizontal arrow is a crosscutting concern or some shared components. This is a small project, so the data access code (`DbContext`) and the `Product` model are shared between all use cases. That sharing has nothing to do with Vertical Slice Architecture, but as a tiny project, it is hard to split it up more. I'll go into more detail at the end of the section.

Here are the actors:

- `ProductsController` is the web API entry point to manage products.
- `StocksController` is the web API entry point to manage inventory (add or remove stocks).
- `AddStocks`, `RemoveStocks`, and `ListAllProducts` are the same use cases that we are copying around in our project.
- The **persistence** "layer" consists of an EF Core `DbContext` that persists the `Product` model.

We could add other crosscutting concerns on top of our vertical slices, such as authorization, error management, and logging, to name a few. We will explore only validation in this sample.

Next, let's take a look at how the project is organized.

Project organization

Here is how we organized the project:

- The `Data` directory contains EF Core-related classes.
- The `Features` directory contains the features. Each subfolder contains its underlying use cases (vertical slices).
- Each use case is self-contained and exposes the following classes:

  a) `Command` represents the MediatR request.

  b) `Result` is the return value of that request.

  c) `MapperProfile` instructs AutoMapper how to map the objects that are use case-related.

  d) `Validator` contains the validation rules to validate the `Command` objects.

  e) `Handler` contains the use case logic: how to handle the request.

- The `Models` directory contains the domain model.

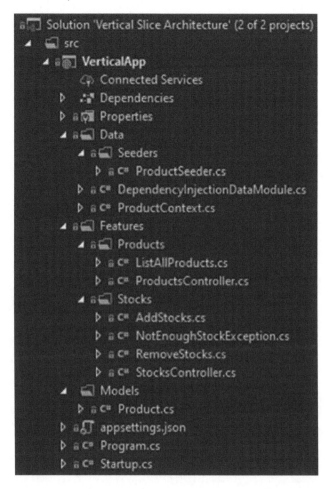

Figure 15.3 – Solution Explorer view of the file organization

We have a `MapperProfile` class for each use case in this project, but we could share one per feature instead, moving the `MapperProfile` class to the same level as the controller.

In this project, we add request validation. To achieve that, we are using **FluentValidation**. You could also use `System.ComponentModel.DataAnnotations` or any other validation system that you want to. What is great about FluentValidation is that it is easy to keep the validation within our vertical slice but outside of the class to be validated (compared to `DataAnnotations`, for example). Moreover, it is easy to test and extend.

Like other tools, FluentValidation can scan assemblies for validators with the following line (highlighted):

```
var currentAssembly = GetType().Assembly;
services.AddAutoMapper(currentAssembly);
services.AddMediatR(currentAssembly);
services.AddDependencyInjectionModules(currentAssembly);
services
    .AddControllers()
    .AddFluentValidation(config => config.
RegisterValidatorsFromAssembly(currentAssembly));
```

The validators themselves are part of each vertical slice. Let's take a look at those features next.

Exploring a feature

In this subsection, we'll explore the RemoveStocks feature. We had the same logic in previous samples but organized differently (which is pretty much the difference between one architectural style and another). Let's look at the code, which I describe after each block:

```
namespace VerticalApp.Features.Stocks
{
    public class RemoveStocks
    {
```

The RemoveStocks class contains multiple nested classes to help organize our feature and save us some headache about naming collision.

```
        public class Command : IRequest<Result>
        {
            public int ProductId { get; set; }
            public int Amount { get; set; }
        }
```

The Command class is the **input of the use case**: the request. The request contains everything needed to execute the operation (that is, to remove stocks from the inventory). The IRequest<TResult> interface tells MediatR that the Command class is a request and should be routed to its handler. The Result class (which follows here) is the return value of that handler:

```csharp
public class Result
{
    public int QuantityInStock { get; set; }
}
```

The Result class represents the **output of the use case**. That's what the handler will return.

```csharp
public class MapperProfile : Profile
{
    public MapperProfile()
    {
        CreateMap<Product, Result>();
    }
}
```

The mapper profile is optional, but it allows encapsulating AutoMapper *maps* that are related to the use case. In the preceding code, we registered the map from a Product instance to a Result instance.

```csharp
public class Validator : AbstractValidator<Command>
{
    public Validator()
    {
        RuleFor(x => x.Amount).GreaterThan(0);
    }
}
```

The validator is optional but allows validating the input (`Command`)
before it hits the handler. To make this work, we need to implement an
`IPipelineBehavior<TRequest, TResponse>` interface that is added to the
MediatR pipeline (after we are done with the `RemoveStock` feature). Next is the
`Handler` class, which implements the use case logic:

```csharp
public class Handler : IRequestHandler<Command, Result>
{
    private readonly ProductContext _db;
    private readonly IMapper _mapper;

    public Handler(ProductContext db, IMapper mapper)
    {
        _db = db ?? throw new
ArgumentNullException(nameof(db));
        _mapper = mapper ?? throw new
ArgumentNullException(nameof(mapper));
    }

    public async Task<Result> Handle(Command request,
CancellationToken cancellationToken)
    {
        var product = await _db.Products.
FindAsync(request.ProductId);
        if (request.Amount > product.QuantityInStock)
        {
            throw new NotEnoughStockException(product.
QuantityInStock, request.Amount);
        }
        product.QuantityInStock -= request.Amount;
        await _db.SaveChangesAsync();

        var result = _mapper.Map<Result>(product);
        return result;
    }
}
}
```

The `Handler` class inherits from `IRequestHandler<Command, Result>`, which links it to the `Command` class. It implements the same logic as the previous implementations, beginning in *Chapter 12, Understanding Layering.*

To summarize, the `RemoveStocks` class contains all the required sub-classes for that specific use case. As a reminder, now that we read the code, the pieces of each use case are the following:

- `Command` is the input DTO.
- `Result` is the output DTO.
- `MapperProfile` is the AutoMapper profile that maps DTOs to domain models (and vice versa).
- `Validator` validates the `Command` DTO (the input).
- `Handler` encapsulates the use case logic.

Let's now look at the `StocksController` class, which translates the HTTP requests to the MediatR pipeline:

```
namespace VerticalApp.Features.Stocks
{

    [ApiController]
    [Route("products/{productId}/")]
    public class StocksController : ControllerBase
    {
        private readonly IMediator _mediator;
        public StocksController(IMediator mediator)
        {
            _mediator = mediator ?? throw new
ArgumentNullException(nameof(mediator));
        }
```

We inject an `IMediator` implementation in the controller since we are using it in all of the actions that follow.

```
[HttpPost("add-stocks")]
public async Task<ActionResult<AddStocks.Result>>
AddAsync(
    int productId,
    [FromBody] AddStocks.Command command
)
{
    command.ProductId = productId;
    var result = await _mediator.Send(command);
    return Ok(result);
}
```

In the preceding code, we read the content of an `AddStocks.Command` instance from the body, then we set `ProductId` for the reasons discussed in *Chapter 12, Understanding Layering*, to finally send the `command` object into the MediatR pipeline. From there, MediatR routes the request to the handler that we explored a few pages ago, before returning the result of that operation with an HTTP `200 OK` status code.

```
[HttpPost("remove-stocks")]
public async Task<ActionResult<RemoveStocks.Result>>
RemoveAsync(
    int productId,
    [FromBody] RemoveStocks.Command command
)
{
    try
    {
        command.ProductId = productId;
        var result = await _mediator.Send(command);
        return Ok(result);
    }
    catch (NotEnoughStockException ex)
    {
        return Conflict(new
        {
```

```
                    ex.Message,
                    ex.AmountToRemove,
                    ex.QuantityInStock
            });
        }
    }
}
}
```

The `remove-stocks` action has the same logic as the `add-stocks` one, with the added `try/catch` block (like the previous implementations of this code).

One of the differences between the preceding code and previous implementations is that we moved the DTOs to the vertical slice itself (highlighted lines). Each vertical slice defines the input, the logic, and the output of that feature, as follows:

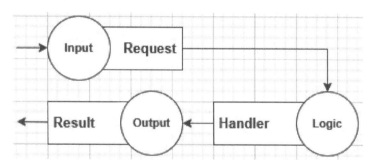

Figure 15.4 – Diagram representing the three primary pieces of a vertical slice

When we add input validation, we have the following:

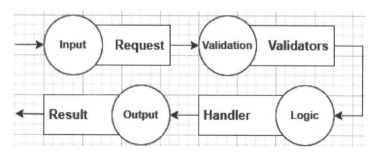

Figure 15.5 – Diagram representing the three primary pieces of a vertical slice, with added validation

All in all, the code of the controller is thin, creating a tiny layer between HTTP and our domain, mapping the HTTP requests to the MediatR pipeline, and the responses back to HTTP. We still have the extra line for the `productId` and that `try/catch` block, but we could get rid of these using custom model binders (see the end of the chapter for some additional resources).

With that in place, it is now straightforward to add new features to the project. Visually, we end up with the following vertical slices (bold), possible expansions (normal), and shared classes (italics):

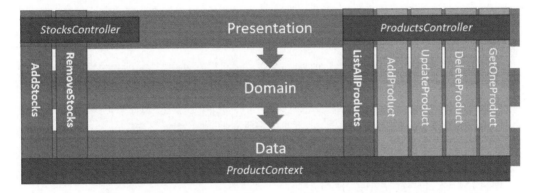

Figure 15.6 – Diagram representing the project and possible extensions related to product management

Next, we add the missing parts to use those `IValidator` implementations.

Request validation

We now have most of the code to run our little project. However, we still have no validation in our MediatR pipeline, only validators. Fortunately, MediatR has an `IPipelineBehavior<in TRequest, TResponse>` interface that allows us to extend the request pipeline. It works like an MVC filter. Speaking of which, we also need a filter to control the HTTP response when a validation error occurs. That will allow us to encapsulate validation logic in two small classes. Those two classes will intercept and handle all validation exceptions thrown by any feature.

Let's start with a high-level view:

1. The HTTP request passes through the ASP.NET MVC pipeline up to the controller.
2. The controller sends a command that passes through the MediatR pipeline:

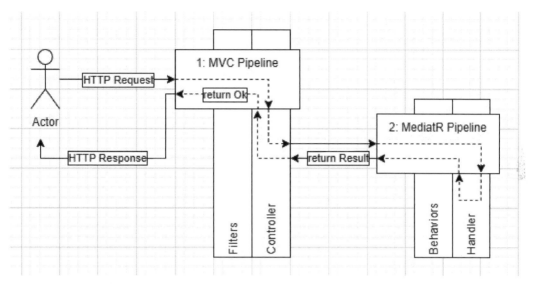

Figure 15.7 – High-level flow of a successful HTTP request

What we want to do is the following:

1. Add an `IExceptionFilter` that catches `ValidationException` (from FluentValidation) in the MVC pipeline (in the **Filters** section of the diagram).
2. Add a MediatR `IPipelineBehavior` that validates requests and throws a `ValidationException` when the request validation fails (in the **Behaviors** section of the diagram).

After adding those two pieces, our request flow will become something like this:

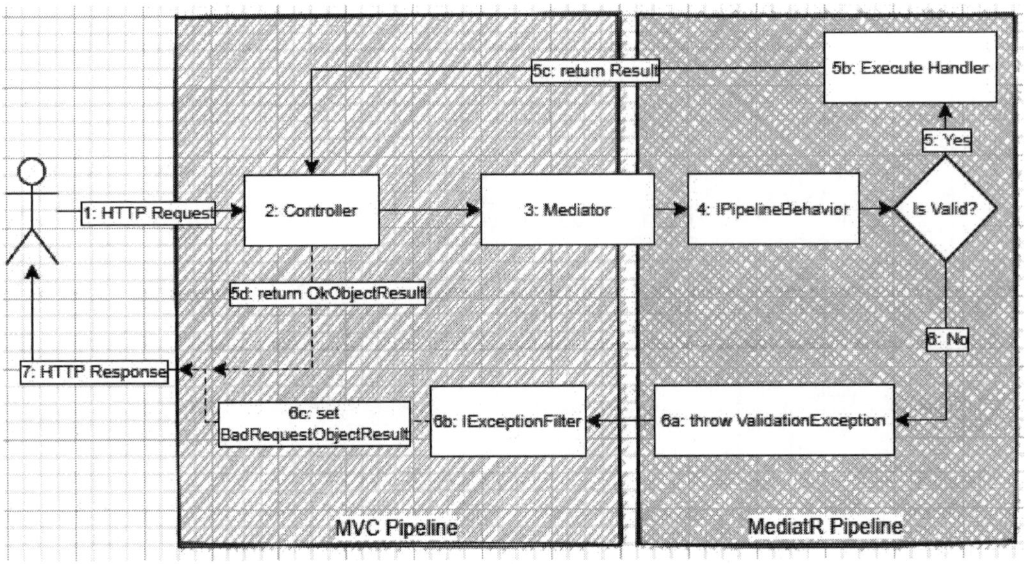

Figure 15.8 – Request flow including request validation details

1. The user sends an HTTP request.

2. The controller sends a command through the mediator.

3. The mediator runs the request through its pipeline.

4. The `IPipelineBehavior` implementation validates the request.

5. If the request is valid, the following occurs:

   a) The request continues through the MediatR pipeline until it reaches the handler.

   b) The `Handler` is executed.

   c) The `Handler` returns a `Result` instance.

   d) The controller transfers that `Result` object into an `OkObjectResult` object.

6. If the validation of the request fails, the following occurs:

   a) The `IPipelineBehavior` implementation throws a `ValidationException`.

   b) The `IActionFilter` implementation catches and handles the exception.

   c) The filter sets the action result to a `BadRequestObjectResult`.

7. MVC transforms the resulting `IActionResult` into a `200 OK` (success) or a `400 BadRequest` (validation failure) response and serializes the resulting object into the response body.

Now that we understand the theoretical aspects of the changes, let's start by coding the `IPipelineBehavior` implementation. I named it `ThrowFluentValidationExceptionBehavior` because it throws a `ValidationException` (from FluentValidation), and it is a MediatR behavior:

```
namespace VerticalApp
{

    public class
ThrowFluentValidationExceptionBehavior<TRequest, TResponse> :
IPipelineBehavior<TRequest, TResponse>
        where TRequest : IBaseRequest
```

We start by implementing the `IPipelineBehavior<TRequest, TResponse>` interface. Our class forwards both generic parameters to the `IPipelineBehavior` interface to serve all types of requests, as long as the request implements `IBaseRequest`. The `IRequest<out TResponse>` interface that the `Command` class implements inherits from `IBaseRequest`.

```
    {
        private readonly IEnumerable<IValidator<TRequest>> _
validators;
        public ThrowFluentValidationExceptionBehavior
(IEnumerable<IValidator<TRequest>> validators)
        {
            _validators = validators ?? throw new
ArgumentNullException(nameof(validators));
        }
```

Here is part of the magic; by injecting a list of `IValidator<TRequest>`, our behavior will have access to the validators of the current request (any type of request).

```
        public Task<TResponse> Handle(TRequest
request, CancellationToken cancellationToken,
RequestHandlerDelegate<TResponse> next)
        {
            var failures = _validators
                .Select(v => v.Validate(request))
```

```
                    .SelectMany(r => r.Errors);
            if (failures.Any())
            {
                    throw new ValidationException(failures);
            }
            return next();
        }
    }
}
```

Finally, in the `Handle` method, we run all validators (see the highlighted code) and project the errors into the `failures` variable. If there are any failures, it throws a `ValidationException` that contains all the failures. If the validation succeeds, it returns the next element of the pipeline. This concept is similar to the **Chain of Responsibility** pattern, which we explored in *Chapter 10, Behavioral Patterns*.

Next, to make it work, we must register it in the composition root. Since we don't want to register it for every feature in our project, we are going to register it as an **open generic type** like this (in the `Startup` class):

```
services.AddSingleton(
    typeof(IPipelineBehavior<,>),
    typeof(ThrowFluentValidationExceptionBehavior<,>)
);
```

This code means: "add and instance of `ThrowFluentValidationExceptionBehavior` in the pipeline for all requests." So our behavior runs every time, no matter the type of the request.

If we run the code, we get the following error, which is not elegant:

```
1   FluentValidation.ValidationException: Validation failed:
2    -- Amount: 'Amount' must be greater than '0'.
3      at VerticalApp.ThrowFluentValidationExceptionBehavior`2.
       Core\C14\Vertical Slice Architecture\src\VerticalApp\Thr
4      at MediatR.Internal.RequestHandlerWrapperImpl`2.<>c__Disp
5      at MediatR.Pipeline.RequestExceptionProcessorBehavior`2.H
6      at MediatR.Pipeline.RequestExceptionProcessorBehavior`2.H
7      at MediatR.Pipeline.RequestExceptionActionProcessorBehavi
```

Figure 15.9 – The result of the ThrowFluentValidationExceptionBehavior without the MVC filter

To manage the way MVC outputs those exceptions, we can create
and add an `IExceptionFilter` to its pipeline. I decided to call it
`FluentValidationExceptionFilter` because it is an exception filter
that handles exeptions of type `FluentValidation.ValidationException`.
That class looks like the following:

```
namespace VerticalApp
{
    public class FluentValidationExceptionFilter :
IExceptionFilter
    {
        public void OnException(ExceptionContext context)
        {
            if (context.Exception is ValidationException ex)
            {
                context.Result = new BadRequestObjectResult(new
                {
                    ex.Message,
                    ex.Errors,
                });
                context.ExceptionHandled = true;
            }
        }
    }
}
```

The preceding code validates whether the value of the `Exception` property (the
current exception) is a `ValidationException`. If it is, it sets the `Result` property's
value to an instance of `BadRequestObjectResult`. It creates an anonymous
object with two properties directly taken from the `ValidationException` object:
`Message` and `Errors`. `Message` is the error message, and `Errors` is a collection of
`ValidationFailure` objects.

Afterward, it sets the `ExceptionHandled` property to true, so MVC knows the
exception was handled and stops caring about it, like it never happened. Those few lines
of code are the equivalent of returning a `BadRequest(new {...})` from a controller
action, but applied globally, for all controllers' actions.

One last step: we must register it with the MVC pipeline so it gets used. In the `Startup` class, we replace the empty `services.AddControllers()` method call with the following:

```
services.AddControllers(options => options
        .Filters.Add<FluentValidationExceptionFilter>())
```

That adds our new filter to the MVC pipeline. From now on, whenever an unhandled exception occurs, our filter will be executed.

Now, if we run a request that should not pass validation (such as *add 0 new stock*), we get the following result:

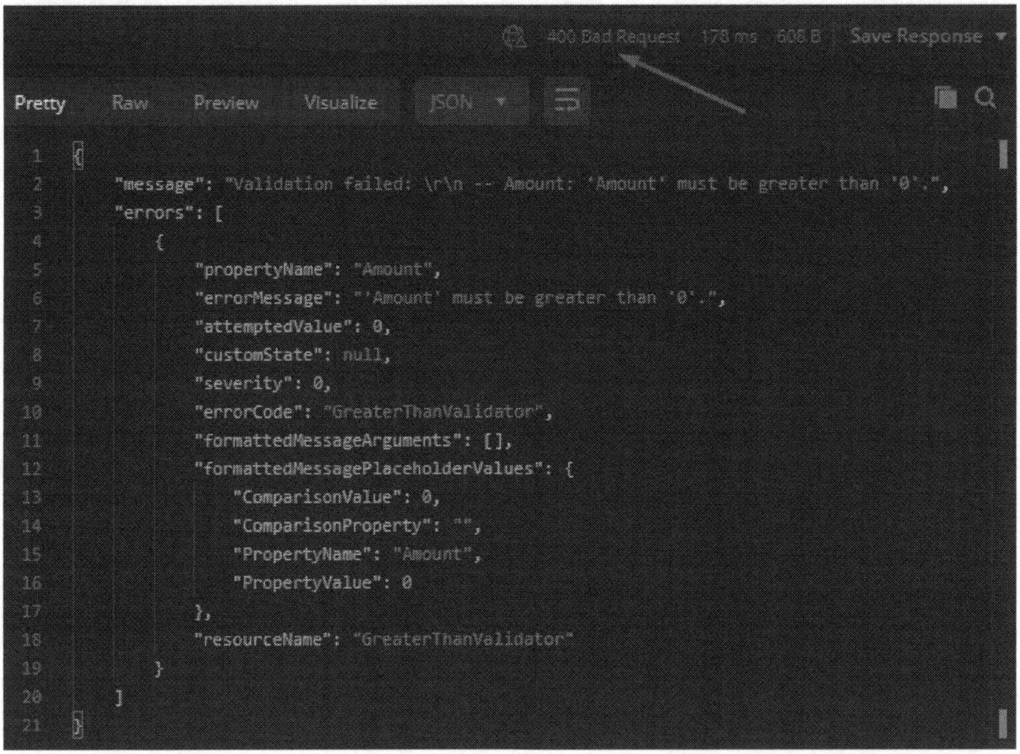

Figure 15.10 – The result of the ThrowFluentValidationExceptionBehavior handled by the FluentValidationExceptionFilter

That is more elegant and can be handled by clients more easily. You can also customize the exception you throw in your implementation of the `IPipelineBehavior` interface and the object you serialize in your implementation of the `IExceptionFilter`. You can also leverage custom implementation of the `IExceptionFilter` interface in non-MediatR-based projects since it is MVC. There are other types of filters too. Filters are really good at handling cross-cutting concerns in MVC.

Next, we'll explore a bit of testing. I won't test the whole application, but I'll get into a few advantages of testing Vertical Slice Architecture versus other architecture types.

Testing

For this project, I wrote one integration test per use case outcome, which lowers the number of unit tests required while increasing the level of confidence in the system at the same time. Why? Because we are testing the features themselves instead of many abstracted parts independently. We could also add as many unit tests as we want. I'm not telling you to stop writing unit tests; on the contrary, I think this approach helps you to write fewer but better feature-oriented tests, diminishing the need for mock-heavy unit tests.

Let's take a look at the *Stocks* use cases tests:

```
namespace VerticalApp.Features.Stocks
{
    public class StocksTest : BaseIntegrationTest
    {
        public StocksTest()
            : base(databaseName: "StocksTest") { }
```

The `BaseIntegrationTest` class encapsulates the boilerplate code of the dependency injection and database seeding logic. I'm going to omit it for brevity reasons, but you can consult the full source code in the GitHub repository (`https://net5.link/DfSf`).

```
        protected async override Task SeedAsync(ProductContext db)
        {
            await db.Products.AddAsync(new Product
            {
                Id = 4,
                Name = "Ghost Pepper",
                QuantityInStock = 10
```

```
        });
        await db.Products.AddAsync(new Product
        {
            Id = 5,
            Name = "Carolina Reaper",
            QuantityInStock = 10
        });
        await db.SaveChangesAsync();
    }
```

In the SeedAsync method, we insert two products in the in-memory test database.

```
        public class AddStocksTest : StocksTest{...}
        public class RemoveStocksTest : StocksTest
        {
            private const int _productId = 5;

            [Fact]
            public async Task Should_decrement_
QuantityInStock_by_the_specified_amount()
            {
                // Arrange
                var serviceProvider = _services.
BuildServiceProvider();
                using var scope = serviceProvider.
CreateScope();
                var mediator = scope.ServiceProvider.
GetRequiredService<IMediator>();

                // Act
                var result = await mediator.Send(new
RemoveStocks.Command
                {
                    ProductId = _productId,
                    Amount = 10
                });

                // Assert
```

```
                    using var assertScope = serviceProvider.
CreateScope();

                    var db = assertScope.ServiceProvider.
GetRequiredService<ProductContext>();

                    var peppers = await db.Products.FindAsync(
_productId);

                    Assert.Equal(0, peppers.QuantityInStock);

                }


            [Fact]
            public async Task Should_throw_a_
NotEnoughStockException_when_the_resulting_QuantityInStock_
would_be_less_than_zero()
                {
                    // Arrange
                    using var scope = _services.
BuildServiceProvider().CreateScope();

                    var mediator = scope.ServiceProvider.
GetRequiredService<IMediator>();


                    // Act & Assert
                    await Assert.
ThrowsAsync<NotEnoughStockException>(() => mediator.Send(new
RemoveStocks.Command
                    {
                        ProductId = _productId,
                        Amount = 11
                    }));

                }

            }

        }

}
```

The `RemoveStocksTest` class contains two test cases:

- Should decrement `QuantityInStock` by the specified amount.
- Should throw a `NotEnoughStockException` when the resulting `QuantityInStock` would be less than zero.

In the **Arrange** phase, the test methods get services from the IoC container, creating a `ServiceProvider` instance, then creating a scope that simulates the scope of an HTTP request. From that scope, both test cases get an instance of `IMediator`.

Then, in the **Act** phase, both tests send the command to `IMediator`, just like the controller does, testing the whole pipeline in the process.

In the **Assert** phase, the first test creates a new scope to make sure it receives a new instance of the `ProductContext` class and that the query does not return some uncommitted EF Core entities. Then it validates whether the saved data is correct. The second test case validates that `Handler` has thrown a `NotEnoughStockException`.

That's it; with that little amount of code, we tested the three primary logic path of our two stocks use cases. We could also test the whole web API by sending an HTTP request to the controller instead. On the other hand, we could unit test the controller by mocking the `IMediator` interface. Your testing strategy depends on your needs, but testing from the `IMediator` will work for any type of application that uses MediatR, which is why I opted for that strategy here.

Next, we'll look at a few tricks and processes to get started with a bigger application. These are ways that I found work for me, and that may well suit you too. Take what works for you and leave the rest; we are all different and work differently.

Continuing your journey

The previous project was tiny. It had a shared model that served as the data layer because that model was composed of only a single class. When you are building a bigger application, you will most likely have more than a class, so I'll try to give you a good starting point to tackle bigger apps. The idea is to create slices that are as small as possible, limit interactions with other slices as much as possible, then refactor that code into better code. We cannot remove coupling, so we need to organize it instead.

Here is a workflow that we could call "start small and refactor":

1. Write the contracts that cover your feature (input and output).

2. Write one or more integration tests that cover your feature, using those contracts; the `Query` or `Command` class (`IRequest`) as input and the `Result` class as output.

3. Implement your `Handler`, `Validator`, `MapperProfile`, and any other bit that needs to be coded. At this point, the code could be a giant `Handler`; it does not matter.

4. Once your integration tests pass, refactor that code by breaking down your giant `Handler.Handle` method (if needed).

5. Make sure your tests still pass.

During *step 2*, you may also want to test the validation rules as unit tests. It is way easier and faster to test multiple combinations and scenarios from unit tests, and you don't need to access a database for that. The same also applies to any other part of your system that is not tied to an external resource.

During *step 4*, you may find duplicated logic between features. If that's the case, it is time to encapsulate that logic elsewhere, in a shared place. That could be to create a method in the model, create a service class, or any other pattern and technique that you know that might solve your logic duplication problem. Working from isolated features and extracting shared logic will help you design the application. You want to push that shared logic outside of a handler, not the other way around (well once you have that shared logic, you can use it wherever needed). Here, I want to emphasize *shared logic*, which means a business rule. When a business rule changes, all consumers of that business rule must also change their behavior. Avoid sharing *similar code* but do share business rules.

What is very important when designing software is to focus on the functional needs, not the technical ones. Your clients and users don't care about the technical stuff; they want results, new features, bug fixes, and improvements. Simultaneously, beware of the technical debt and don't skip that refactoring step, or your project may end up in trouble. That advice also applies to all types of architecture.

Another piece of advice is to keep all of the code that makes a vertical slice as close as possible. You don't have to keep all classes of a use case in a single file, but I feel that helps. You can also create a folder hierarchy where the deeper levels share the previous levels. For example, I recently implemented a workflow in an MVC application related to shipments. The creation process was in multiple steps. So I ended up with a hierarchy that looked like the following (directories are bold):

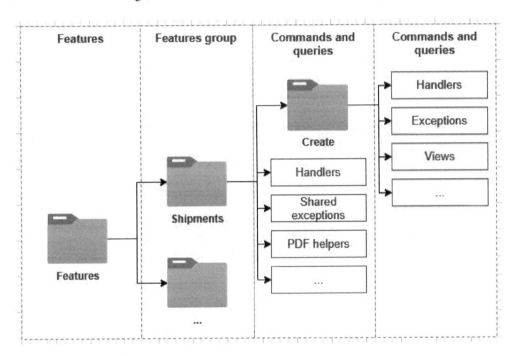

Figure 15.11 – The organizational hierarchy of directories and elements

Initially, I just coded all the handlers one by one, then I saw patterns emerge, so I took that shared logic and encapsulated it into shared classes. Then I started to reuse some exceptions at upper levels, so I moved those up from the Features/Shipments/ Create folder/namespace to the Features/Shipments folder/namespace. I also extracted a service class to manage shared logic between multiple use cases and more (I'll skip all the details as they are irrelevant). In the end, I have only the code that I need, no duplicated logic, and the collaborators (classes, interfaces) are close to each other. I registered only three interfaces with the IoC container, and two of them are related to PDF generation. The coupling between features is minimal, while parts of the system work in synergy (cohesion). Moreover, there is very little to no coupling with other parts of the system. If we compare that result to another type of architecture such as layering, I would most likely have needed more abstractions such as repositories, services, and whatnot; the end result with Vertical Slice Architecture is simpler.

The key point here is to code your handlers independently, organize them the best you can, keep an eye open for shared logic and emerging patterns, extract and encapsulate that logic, and try to limit interactions between use cases and slices.

Now, what is a slice? Personally, I see slices as composites. Each Features/Shipments/Create/[*]Handler is a slice. When put together, they compose the Features/Shipments/Create slice (a bigger slice). Then, all slices from Features/Shipments become another big slice, leading to something like this:

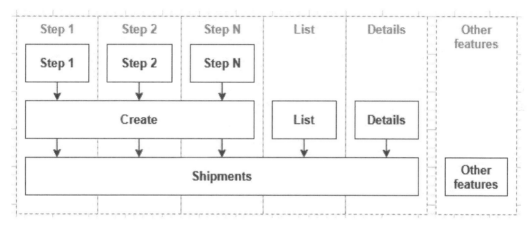

Figure 15.12 – A diagram displaying a top-down coupling structure where smaller parts (top) depend on bigger parts (middle) of complex features (bottom) based on their cohesion with one another (vertically)

There is strong coupling inside of **Step 1**, with limited coupling between the other steps; they share some creation code as part of the **Create** slice. **Create**, **List**, and **Details** also share some code, but in a limited way; they are all part of the **Shipments** slice and access or manipulate the same entity: one or more shipments. Finally, the **Shipments** slice shares no code (or very little) with **Other Features**.

OK, this was my definition of a slice and how I see them; maybe other people have other points of view on that, which is fine. I find that by following the pattern that I just described, I end up with limited coupling and maximum cohesion.

Summary

In this chapter, we overviewed Vertical Slice Architecture, which flips layers by 90°. Vertical Slice Architecture is about writing minimal code to generate maximum value by getting superfluous abstractions and rules out of the equation by relying on the developers' skills and judgment instead.

Refactoring is a critical factor in a Vertical Slice Architecture project; success or failure will most likely depend on it. All patterns, including layers, can be used in conjunction with Vertical Slice Architecture. It has lots of advantages over layering with little to no disadvantages. Teams who work in silos (horizontal teams) may need to rethink that before switching to Vertical Slice Architecture and create multi-functional teams instead (vertical teams).

With Vertical Slice Architecture, we replaced the low-value abstraction with commands and queries (CQRS-inspired). Those are then routed to their respective `Handler` using the Mediator pattern (helped by MediatR). That allows encapsulating the business logic and decoupling it from its callers (the controllers in the sample). Those commands and queries ensure that each bit of domain logic is centralized in a single location.

We can encapsulate crosscutting concerns using a classic MVC filter, an ASP.NET middleware, or a MediatR `IPipelineBehavior`, depending on where we want that concern handled. We can also implement a composite solution using many of those options, as we did in the code sample to handle validation.

We can significantly reduce the number of mocks required for our tests by testing each vertical slice with integration tests. That could also lower the number of unit tests significantly, testing features instead of mocked units of code. Our focus should be on producing features, not on the details behind querying the infrastructure or the code itself (OK, that's important too).

> **Note**
>
> It is important to note that you can still write as many unit tests as you need; nothing from Vertical Slice Architecture stops you from doing that. That's one of the advantages: use all that you know in the slice you are working on, without the need to export it globally to other slices.

All in all, we explored a modern way to design an application that aligns well with Agile development, and that helps generate value for your customers.

Now let's see how Vertical Slice Architecture can help us follow the **SOLID** principles:

- **S**: Each vertical slice (feature) becomes a cohesive unit that changes as a whole, leading to the segregation of responsibilities per feature. Based on a CQRS-inspired approach, each feature splits the application's complexity into commands and queries, leading to multiple small pieces. Each piece handles a part of the process. For example, we can define an input, a validator, a mapper profile, a handler, a result, an HTTP bridge (controller), and as many more pieces as we need to craft the slice.

- **O**: We can enhance the system globally by extending the ASP.NET, MVC, or MediatR pipelines. The features themselves can be designed as one see fit, having a limited direct impact on the OCP.

- **L**: N/A.

- **I**: By organizing features by units of domain-centric use cases, we end up with many client-specific components instead of general-purpose elements, like layers.

- **D**: All of the pieces of a slice depend only on interfaces and are tied together using dependency injection. Furthermore, by cutting the less useful abstractions out of the system, we simplify it, making it more maintainable and more concise. By having so many pieces of a feature living close to each other, the system becomes easier to maintain with improved discoverability.

In the next chapter, we will explore another architectural style and talk about microservices.

Questions

Let's take a look at a few practice questions:

1. What design patterns can we use in a vertical slice?

2. Is it true that when using Vertical Slice Architecture, you must pick a single ORM and stick with it, such as a data layer?

3. What will likely happen if you don't refactor your code and pay the technical debt in the long run?

4. Can we handle crosscutting concerns using behaviors and MVC filters in other types of applications or are they enabled by Vertical Slice Architecture?

5. What does cohesion mean?

6. What does tight coupling mean?

Further reading

Here are a few links to build upon what we learned in the chapter:

- For UI implementations, you can look at how Jimmy Bogard upgraded ContosoUniversity:

  a) ContosoUniversity on ASP.NET Core with .NET Core `https://net5.link/UXnr`

  b) ContosoUniversity on ASP.NET Core 3.1 on .NET Core and Razor Pages `https://net5.link/6Lbo`

- FluentValidation `https://net5.link/xXgp`

- ExceptionMapper is an open source project of mine, which is an ASP.NET Core middleware that reacts to **Exception**. You can map certain exception types to HTTP **status codes**, automatically serialize them as JSON `ProblemDetails`, and so on: `https://net5.link/dtRi`

- AutoMapper `https://net5.link/5AUZ`

- MediatR `https://net5.link/ZQap`

- To avoid setting `ProductId` manually in the Vertical Slice project, you can use the open source **HybridModelBinding** project, or read the official documentation about custom model binding and implement your own:

  a) Custom Model Binding in ASP.NET Core `https://net5.link/65pb`

  b) HybridModelBinding `https://net5.link/EyKK`

16

Introduction to Microservices Architecture

This chapter is the last chapter that talks about application design. It covers some of the essential microservices architecture concepts. This chapter is designed to get you started with those principles and give you a good idea of the microservices architecture.

The goal of this chapter is to give you an overview of the concepts surrounding microservices, which should help you make informed decisions about whether you should go for a microservices architecture or not. Monolithic architecture patterns, such as Vertical Slice and Clean Architecture, are still good to know, as you can apply those to individual microservices. Don't worry – all of the knowledge you have acquired since the beginning of this book is not forfeit and is still worthwhile.

The following topics will be covered in this chapter:

- What are microservices?
- Getting started with message queues
- An overview of events
- Implementing the Publish-Subscribe pattern

- Introducing Gateway patterns
- Revisiting the CQRS pattern
- An overview of containers

Let's get started!

What are microservices?

Besides being a buzzword, microservices represent an application that is divided into multiple smaller applications. Each application, or microservice, interacts with the others to create a scalable system.

Here are a few principles to keep in mind when building microservices:

- Each microservice should be a cohesive unit of business.
- Each microservice should own its data.
- Each microservice should be independent of the others.

Furthermore, everything we have studied so far – that is, the other principles of designing software – apply to microservices but on another scale. For example, you don't want tight coupling between microservices (solved by microservices independence), but the coupling is inevitable (as with any code). There are numerous ways to solve this problem, such as the Publish-Subscribe pattern.

There are no hard rules about how to design microservices, how to divide them, how big they should be, and what to put where. That being said, I'll lay down a few foundations to help you get started and orient your journey into microservices.

Cohesive unit of business

A microservice should have a single business responsibility. Always design the system with the domain in mind, which should help you divide the application into multiple pieces. If you know **Domain-Driven Design (DDD)**, a microservice will most likely represent a **Bounded Context**, which in turn is what I call a *cohesive unit of business*.

Even if a **microservice** has *micro* in its name, it is more important to group logical operations under it than to aim at a micro-size. Don't get me wrong here; if your unit is tiny, that's even better. However, suppose you split a unit of business into multiple smaller parts instead of keeping it together (breaking cohesion).

In that case, you are likely to introduce useless chattiness within your system (coupling between microservices). This could lead to performance degradation and to a system that is harder to debug, test, maintain, monitor, and deploy.

Try to apply the SRP to your microservices: a microservice should have only one reason to change unless you have a good reason to do otherwise.

Own its data

Each microservice is the source of truth of its chunk of business (bounded context; its data). It should own that data, and it should not share that data with other microservices directly at the database level. A microservice should share its data through itself (a web API/HTTP, for example) or another mechanism (integration events, for example).

For instance, in a relational database, a table should never be accessed from two different microservices. If a second microservice needs some of the same data, it can create its own cache, duplicate the data, or query the owner of that data, but not access the database directly; **never**.

This data-ownership concept is probably the most critical part of the microservices architecture and leads to microservices independence. Failing at this will most likely lead to a tremendous amount of problems.

Independence

At this point, we have microservices that are cohesive units of business that own their data. This defines **independence**.

What this independence offers to the system is the ability to scale while having minimum to no impact on the other microservices. Each microservice can also scale independently, without the need for the whole system to be scaled. Additionally, when the business requirements are growing, each part of that domain can grow independently.

Furthermore, you could update one microservice without impacting the others or even have a microservice go offline without the whole system stopping.

Of course, microservices have to interact with one another, but the way they do should define how well your system runs. A little like the Vertical Slice architecture, you are not limited to using one set of architectural patterns; you can make specific decisions for each microservice independently. For example, you could choose a different way for how two microservices communicate with each other versus two others. You could even use different programming languages for each microservice.

> **Tip**
>
> I recommend sticking to one or a few programming languages for smaller businesses and organizations as you most likely have fewer developers, and each has more to do. Based on my experience, you want to ensure business continuity when people leave and make sure you can replace them and not sink the ship due to some obscure technologies used here and there (or too many technologies).

Now that we've defined the basics, let's jump into the different ways microservices can communicate. We will first explore ways to mediate communication between microservices. We will then learn ways to shield and hide the complexity of the microservices cluster. After that, we will dig in more detail into the CQRS pattern and provide a conceptual serverless example. Finally, we will conclude by providing an overview of containers, which allow us to deploy a whole microservices cluster, or part of it, more efficiently.

Getting started with message queues

A **message queue** is nothing more than a queue that we leverage to send ordered messages. A queue works on a **First In, First Out** (**FIFO**) basis. If our application runs in a single process, we could use one or more `Queue<T>` to send messages between our components or a `ConcurrentQueue<T>` to send messages between threads. Moreover, queues can be managed by an independent program to send messages in a distributed fashion (between applications or microservices).

A distributed message queue can add more or less features to the mix, which is especially true for cloud programs that have to handle failures at more levels than a single server does. One of those features is the **dead letter queue**, which stores messages that failed some criteria in another queue. For example, if the target queue is full, a message could be sent to the **dead letter queue** instead.

Many messaging queue protocols exist; some are proprietary, while others are open source. Some messaging queues are cloud-based and used *as a service*, such as Azure Service Bus and Amazon Simple Queue Service. Others are open source and can be deployed to the cloud or on-premises, such as Apache ActiveMQ.

If you need to process messages in order and want each message to be delivered to a single recipient at a time, a **message queue** seems like the right choice. Otherwise, the **Publish-Subscribe** pattern could be a better fit for you.

Here is a basic example that illustrates what we just discussed:

Figure 16.1 – A publisher that enqueues a message with a subscriber that dequeues it

For a more concrete example, let's say that we want our user registration process to be distributed. When a user registers, we want to do the following:

1. Send an email confirmation.

2. Process their picture and save one or more thumbnails.

3. Send an onboarding message to their in-app mailbox.

To sequentially achieve this, one operation after the other, we could do the following:

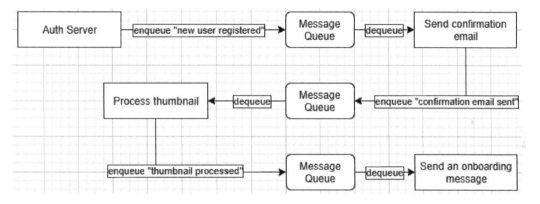

Figure 16.2 – A process flow that sequentially executes three operations that happen after a user creates an account

In this case, if the process crashes during the *Process Thumbnail* operation, the user would not receive the *Onboarding Message*. Another drawback would be that to insert a new operation between *Process Thumbnail* and *Send an onboarding message*, we would have to modify both the *Process Thumbnail* and *Send an onboarding message* operations (tight coupling).

If the order does not matter, we could queue all the messages from the *Auth Server* instead, right after the user's creation, like this:

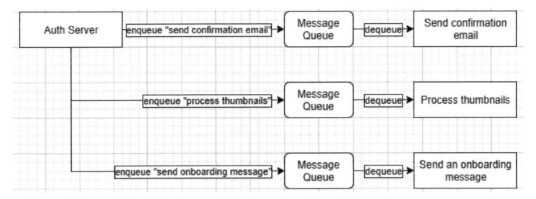

Figure 16.3 – The Auth Server is queuing the operations sequentially while different processes execute them in parallel

This process is better, but the *Auth Server* is now controlling what should be happening once a new user has been created. In the previous workflow, the *Auth Server* was queuing an event that told the system that a new user was registered. However, now, it has to be aware of the post-processing workflow to queue each operation sequentially. Doing this is not wrong in itself and is easier to follow when you dig into the code, but it creates tighter coupling between the services where the *Auth Server* is aware of the external processes. By the SRP, I don't see how an authentication/authorization server should be responsible for anything other than authentication, authorization, and managing that data.

If we continue from there and want to add a new operation between two existing steps, we would only have to modify the *Auth Server*, which is less error-prone than the preceding workflow.

If we want the best of both worlds, we could use the **Publish-Subscribe** pattern instead, which we will cover next. We will revisit this example there.

Conclusion

If you need messages to be delivered sequentially, in the order they were queued, a queue might well be the right tool to use. The example that we explored was "doomed to failure" from the beginning, but it allowed us to explore the thinking process behind designing the system. Sometimes, the first idea is not the best and can be improved by exploring new ways of doing things or learning new skills. Being open-minded to the ideas of others can also lead to better solutions.

Now, let's see how message queues can help us follow the **SOLID** principles at app-scale:

- **S**: Helps centralize and divide responsibilities between applications or components without them directly knowing each other, breaking tight coupling.
- **O**: Allows us to change the message producer's or subscriber's behaviors without the other knowing about it.
- **L**: N/A.
- **I**: Each message and handler can be as small as needed, while in the bigger scheme of things, the microservices interact with each other to solve the bigger problem.
- **D**: By not knowing the other dependencies (that is, breaking tight coupling between microservices), microservices depend on messages (abstractions) instead of concretions (other microservices' APIs).

One drawback is the delay between enqueuing a message and processing a message. We will talk about delay and latency in more detail in subsequent sections.

An overview of events

We talked about messages in the previous section. Now, we are about to see those messages become events. So, let's dig into this before we learn about the Pub-Sub pattern.

An event is a message that represents something that happened in the past.

We can use events to divide a complex system into smaller pieces or have multiple systems talk to each other without creating tight couplings. Those systems could be subsystems or external applications, such as microservices.

We can regroup events into two broad categories:

- Domain events
- Integration events

Let's look at each in detail.

Domain events

A domain event is a term based on DDD that represents an event in the domain. This event could then trigger other pieces of logic to be executed subsequently. It allows a complex process to be divided into multiple smaller processes. These events can be executed sequentially or could be "fired and forgot." Domain events work well with the Clean Architecture and can be used to simplify complex domains. We can use MediatR to publish domain events.

Integration events

Integration events are events, just like domain events, but are used to propagate messages to an external system, most likely out of process. For example, that could be one or more other microservices, such as when sending a `new user registered` event message.

We use a message broker (see the following section) to publish integration events. We can also use a message queue to publish these events sequentially.

Now, let's see what the Publish-Subscribe pattern is all about.

Implementing the Publish-Subscribe pattern

The **Publish-Subscribe** pattern (Pub-Sub) is very similar to what we did using **MediatR** and what we explored in the *Getting started with message queues* section. However, instead of sending one message to one handler (or enqueuing a message), we publish (send) a message (or event) to zero or more subscribers (handlers). Moreover, the publisher is not aware of the subscribers; it only sends messages out, hoping for the best (also known as **fire and forget**).

We can use **publish-subscribe** in-process or in a distributed system through a **message broker**. The message broker is responsible for delivering the messages to the subscribers. That is the way to go for microservices and other types of distributed systems since they are not running in a single process.

This pattern has many advantages over other ways of communication. For example, we could recreate the state of a database by replaying the events (messages) that happened in the system, leading to the **event sourcing** pattern. More on that later.

The design depends on the technology that's used to deliver the messages and the configuration of that system. For example, you could use **MQTT** to deliver messages to **Internet of Things (IoT)** devices and configure them to retain the last message that was sent on each topic. That way, when a device connects to a topic, it receives the last message. You could also configure a **Kafka** broker that keeps a long history of messages and asks for all of them when a new system connects to it. All of that depends on your needs and requirements.

MQTT and Apache Kafka

If you were wondering what MQTT was, here is a quote from their website `https://net5.link/mqtt`:

"MQTT is an OASIS standard messaging protocol for the Internet of Things (IoT). It is designed as an extremely lightweight publish/subscribe messaging transport [...]"

Here is a quote from Apache Kafka's website `https://net5.link/kafka`:

"Apache Kafka is an open-source distributed event streaming platform [...]"

We cannot cover every single scenario of every single system that follows every single protocol. Therefore, I'll highlight some shared concepts behind the Pub-Sub design pattern so that you know how to get started. Then, you can dig into the specific technology that you want (or need) to use.

To receive messages, subscribers must subscribe to topics (or the equivalent of a topic):

Figure 16.4 – A subscriber subscribes to a pub-sub topic

The second part of the Pub-Sub pattern is to publish messages, like this:

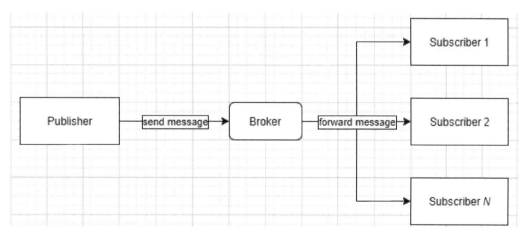

Figure 16.5 – A publisher is sending a message to the message broker. The broker then forwards that message to *N* subscribers, where *N* can be zero or more

There are many abstracted details here that depend on the broker and the protocol. However, the following are the two primary concepts behind the Publish-Subscribe pattern:

- Publishers publish messages to topics.
- Subscribers subscribe to topics to receive messages.

> **Note**
>
> For example, one crucial implementation detail that is not illustrated here is security. Security is mandatory in most systems, and not every subsystem or device should have access to all topics.

Publishers and subscribers could be any part of any system. For example, many Microsoft Azure services are publishers (for example, Blob storage). You can then have other Azure services (for example, Azure Functions) subscribe to those events to react to them.

You can also use the **Publish-Subscribe** pattern inside your applications – there's no need to use cloud resources for that; this can even be done inside the same process.

The most significant advantage of the Publish-Subscribe pattern is its ability to break tight coupling between systems. One system can publish events, while others consume these events without the systems knowing about each other.

That loose coupling leads to scalability, where each system can scale independently and where messages can be processed in parallel using the amount of resources it requires to do so. It is easier to add new processes to a workflow as well since the systems are unaware of the others. To add a new process that reacts to an event, you only have to create a new microservice, deploy it, then start to listen to one or more events and process them.

On the downside, the message broker can become the single point of failure of an application and must be configured appropriately. It is also essential to consider the best message delivery policies for each type of message. An example of a policy could be to ensure the delivery of crucial messages while delaying less time-sensitive messages and dropping unimportant messages during load surges.

If we revisit our previous example using **publish-subscribe**, we end up with the following simplified workflow:

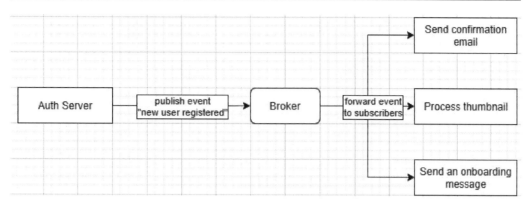

Figure 16.6 – The Auth Server is publishing an event representing the creation of a new user. The broker then forwards that message to the three subscribers that are then executing their tasks in parallel

Based on this workflow, we decoupled the Auth Server from the post-registration process. The Auth Server is not aware of the workflow, and the individual services are unaware of each other. Moreover, if we want to add a new task, we only have to create or update a microservice, then subscribe it to the right topic (in this case, the "new user registered" topic).

The current system does not support synchronization and does not handle process failures or retries, but it is a good start since we are combining the pros of the message queue examples and leaving the cons behind.

Message brokers

A message broker is a program that allows us to send (**publish**) and receive (**subscribe**) messages. It plays the mediator role at scale, allowing multiple applications to talk to each other without knowing each other (**loosely coupled**). The message broker is usually the central piece of any event-based distributed system that's implementing the publish-subscribe pattern.

An application (**publisher**) usually publishes messages to topics, while other applications (**subscribers**) receive messages from those topics. The notion of **topics** may differ from one protocol or system to another, but all systems that I know have some kind of topic-like concept to route messages to the right place. For example, you can publish to the `Devices` topic using Kafka, but to `devices/abc-123/do-something` using MQTT.

The message broker is responsible for forwarding the messages to the registered recipients. The lifetime of those messages can vary by broker or even per individual message.

There are multiple message brokers out there using different protocols. Some brokers are cloud-based, such as Azure Event Grid. Other brokers are lightweight and more suited for IoT, such as Eclipse Mosquitto/MQTT. In contrast to MQTT, others are more robust and allow for high-velocity streaming of data, such as Apache Kafka.

What message broker to use should be based on the requirements of the software that you are building. Moreover, you are not limited to one broker. Nothing stops you from picking a message broker that handles the dialogs between your microservices and uses another to handle the dialogs between your system and external IoT devices. If you are building a system in Azure, want to go serverless, or prefer paying for SaaS components that scale without investing maintenance time, you can leverage Azure services such as Event Grid, Service Bus, and Queue Storage.

The event sourcing pattern

Now that we explored the Publish-Subscribe pattern, learned what an event is, and talked about event brokers, it is time to explore **how to replay the state of an application**. To achieve this, we can follow the **event sourcing pattern**.

The idea behind event sourcing is to **store a chronological list of events** instead of a single entity, where that collection of events becomes the source of truth. That way, every single operation is saved in the right order, helping with concurrency. Moreover, we could replay all of these events to generate an object's actual state in a new application, allowing us to deploy new microservices more easily.

Instead of just storing the data, if the system propagates it using an event broker, other systems can cache some of the data as one or more **materialized views**.

> **Materialized views**
>
> A materialized view is a model that's created and stored to serve a specific purpose. The data can come from one or more sources, leading to improved performance when querying that data. For example, the application returns the materialized view instead of querying multiple other systems to acquire the data. You can view the materialized view as a cached entity that a microservice stores in its own database.

One of the drawbacks of event sourcing is data consistency. There is an unavoidable delay between the time a service adds an event to the store and the time all the other systems update their materialized views. This leads to **eventual consistency**.

> **Eventual consistency**
>
> Eventual consistency means that the data will be consistent at some point in the future, but not outright. The delay can be from a few milliseconds to a lot longer, but the goal is usually to keep that delay as small as possible.

Another drawback is the complexity of creating such a system compared to a single application that queries a single database. Like the microservices architecture, event sourcing is not just rainbows and unicorns. It comes at a price: **operational complexity**.

> **Operational complexity**
>
> In a microservices architecture, each piece is smaller, but gluing them together has a cost. For example, the infrastructure to support microservices is more complex than a monolith (one app and one database). The same goes for event sourcing; all applications must subscribe to one or more events, cache data (materialized view), publish events, and more. This operational complexity represents the shift of complexity from the application code to the operational infrastructure. In other words, it requires more work to deploy and maintain multiple microservices and databases, as well as to fight the possible instability of network communication between those external systems than it does for a single application containing all of the code. Monoliths are simple: they work, or they don't; they rarely partially work.

A crucial aspect of event sourcing is appending new events to the store and never changing existing events (append-only). In a nutshell, microservices communicating using the Pub-Sub pattern publish events, subscribe to topics, and generate materialized views to serve their clients.

Example

Let's explore an example of what could happen if we mix what we just studied together. **Context**: We need to build a software that manages IoT devices. We begin by creating two microservices:

- One that handles IoT devices twin's data (that is, a digital representation of the device) that we name `DeviceTwin`.

- One that manages the networking-related information of IoT devices (that is, how to reach a device) that we name `Networking`.

As a visual reference, the final system could look as follows:

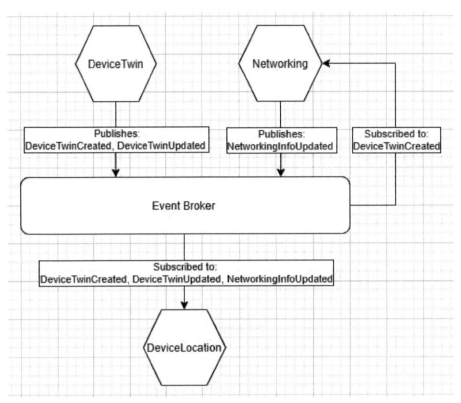

Figure 16.7 – Three microservices communicating using the Publish-Subscribe pattern

Here are the user interactions and the published events:

1. A user creates a twin in the system named *Device 1*. `DeviceTwin` saves the data and publishes the `DeviceTwinCreated` event with the following payload:

```
{
    "id": "some id",
    "name": "Device 1",
    "other": "properties go here..."
}
```

In parallel, the `Networking` microservice needs to know when a device is created, so it is subscribed to the `DeviceTwinCreated` event. When a new device is created, it creates default networking information for that device in its database; the default is `unknown`. This way, the `Networking` microservice knows what devices exist or not:

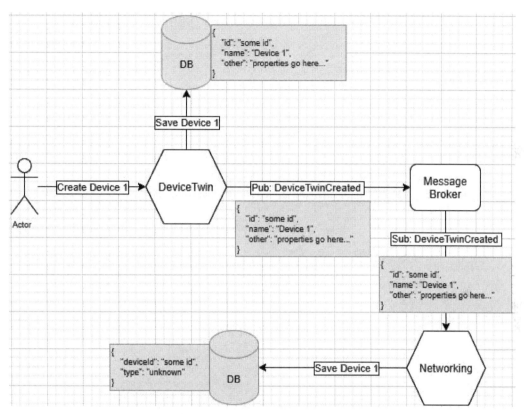

Figure 16.8 – A workflow representing the creation of a device twin and its default networking information

2. A user then updates the networking information of that device and sets it to `MQTT`. `Networking` saves the data and publishes the `NetworkingInfoUpdated` event with the following payload:

```
{
    "deviceId": "some id",
    "type": "MQTT",
    "other": "networking properties..."
}
```

This is demonstrated by the following diagram:

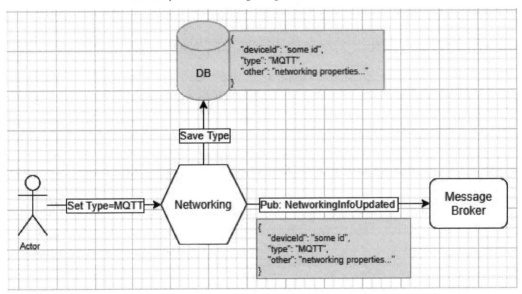

Figure 16.9 – A workflow representing updating the networking type of a device

3. A user changes the display name of the device to `Kitchen Thermostat`, which is more relevant. `DeviceTwin` saves the data and publishes the `DeviceTwinUpdated` event with the following payload. The payload uses **JSON patch** to publish only the differences instead of the whole object (see the *Further reading* section for more information):

```
{
    "id": "some id",
    "patches": [
        { "op": "replace", "path": "/name", "value":
"Kitchen Thermostat" },
```

```
    ]
  }
```

This is demonstrated by the following diagram:

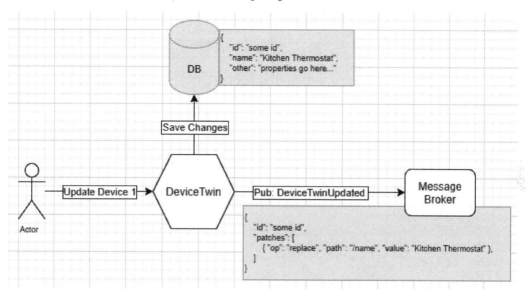

Figure 16.10 – A workflow representing a user updating the name of the device to Kitchen Thermostat

Let's say that a team designed and completed a new microservice that organizes the devices at physical locations. This allows users to visualize the location of their devices on a map, such as the map of their house.

The team named that microservice `DeviceLocation`. `DeviceLocation` subscribes to all three events to manage its materialized view, like this:

- When receiving a `DeviceTwinCreated` event, it saves its unique identifier and its display name.

- When receiving a `NetworkingInfoUpdated` event, it saves the communication type (HTTP, MQTT, and so on).

- When receiving a `DeviceTwinUpdated` event, it updates the display name of the device.

When the service is deployed for the first time, it is set to replay all events from the beginning (**event sourcing**); here is what happens:

1. `DeviceLocation` receives the `DeviceTwinCreated` event and creates the following model for that object:

```
{
    "device": {
        "id": "some id",
        "name": "Device 1"
    },
    "networking": {},
    "location": {...}
}
```

This is demonstrated by the following diagram:

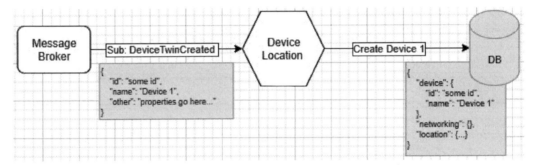

Figure 16.11 – The DeviceLocation microservice replaying the DeviceTwinCreated event to create its materialized view of the device twin

2. `DeviceLocation` receives the `NetworkingInfoUpdated` event, which updates the networking type to `MQTT`, leading to the following:

```
{
    "device": {
        "id": "some id",
        "name": "Device 1"
    },
    "networking": {
        "type": "MQTT"
    },
```

```
    "location": {...}
}
```

This is demonstrated by the following diagram:

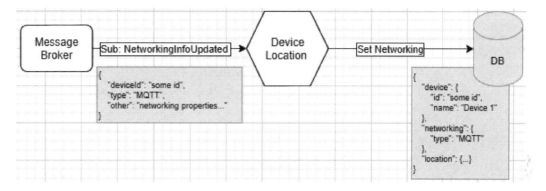

Figure 16.12 – The DeviceLocation microservice replaying the NetworkingInfoUpdated event to update its materialized view of the device twin

3. `DeviceLocation` receives the `DeviceTwinUpdated` event, updating the device's name. The final model looks like this:

```
{
    "device": {
        "id": "some id",
        "name": "Kitchen Thermostat"
    },
    "networking": {
        "type": "MQTT"
    },
    "location": {...}
}
```

This is demonstrated by the following diagram:

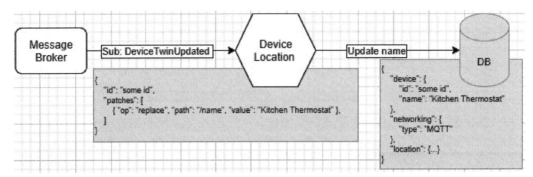

Figure 16.13 – The DeviceLocation microservice replaying the DeviceTwinUpdated event to update its materialized view of the device twin

From there, the `DeviceLocation` microservice is initialized and ready. A user could set the kitchen thermostat's location on the map or continue to play with the other parts of the system. When a user queries the `DeviceLocation` microservice for information about `Kitchen Thermostat`, it displays the **materialized view**, which contains all the required information without sending external requests.

With that in mind, we could spawn new instances of `DeviceLocation` or other microservices, and they could generate their materialized views from past events – all of that with very limited to no knowledge of other microservices. In this type of architecture, a microservice can only know about events, not the other microservices. How a microservice handles events should be relevant only to that microservice, never to the others. The same applies to both publishers and subscribers.

This example illustrates the event sourcing pattern, integration events, the materialized view, the use of a message broker, and the Publish-Subscribe pattern.

In contrast, using direct communication (HTTP, gRPC, and so on) would look like this:

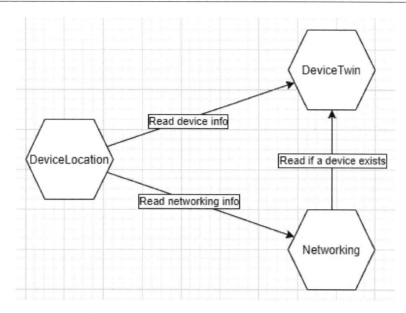

Figure 16.14 – Three microservices communicating directly with one another

If we compare both approaches, by looking at the first diagram (*Figure 16.7*), we can see that the message broker plays the role of a **mediator** and breaks the direct coupling between the microservices. By looking at the preceding diagram (*Figure 16.14*), we can see the tight coupling between the microservices, where DeviceLocation would need to call DeviceTwin and Networking directly to build the equivalent of its materialized view. Furthermore, DeviceLocation translates one call into three, since Networking also has to talk to DeviceTwin.

Suppose eventual consistency is not an option, or the Publish-Subscribe pattern cannot be applied or could be too hard to apply to your scenario. In this case, microservices can directly call each other. They can achieve this using HTTP, RPC, or any other means that best suits that particular system's needs.

I won't be covering this topic in this book, but one thing to be careful of when calling microservices directly is the indirect call chain that could bubble up fast. You don't want your microservices to create a super deep call chain, or your system will most likely become very slow, very fast. Here is an abstract example of what could happen to illustrate what I mean. A diagram is often better than words:

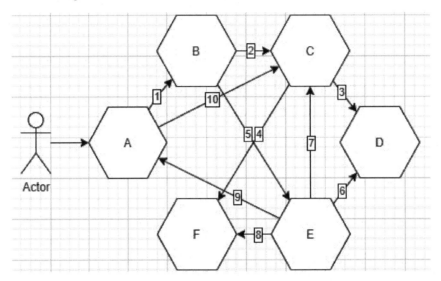

Figure 16.15 – A user calling microservice A, which then triggers a chain reaction of subsequent calls, leading to disastrous performance

In terms of the preceding diagram, let's think about failures. If microservice C goes offline, the whole request ends with an error. Of course, we could put retry policies in place to create a more robust and more stable system, but that would also mean a longer delay between the initial call and the response. This would be better than a system crash, but still far from optimal.

Conclusion

The Publish-Subscribe pattern uses events to decouple parts of an application. In a microservices architecture, we can use a message broker and integration events to allow microservices to talk to each other. Then, we can leverage the event sourcing pattern to persist those events, allowing a new microservice to populate its database by replaying past events.

Such patterns can be very powerful together but can also take time to implement. Cloud providers also offer similar services. Those can be faster to get started with than building your own infrastructure. If building servers is your thing, you can use open source software to "economically" build your stack.

Now, let's see how the Publish-Subscribe pattern can help us follow the **SOLID** principles at app-scale:

- **S**: Helps centralize and divide responsibilities between applications or components without them directly knowing each other, breaking tight coupling.
- **O**: Allows us to change how publishers and subscribers behave without directly impacting the other microservices (breaking tight coupling between them).
- **L**: N/A.
- **I**: Each event (abstraction/contract) can be as small as needed.
- **D**: The microservices depend on events (abstractions) instead of concretions (the other microservices), breaking tight coupling between them.

As you may have noticed, these are very similar to the message queue; the only difference is the way messages are read:

- One at a time with queues.
- Up to multiple at the same time with the Pub-Sub pattern.

> **Observer design pattern**
>
> I voluntarily kept the Observer pattern out of this book since we rarely need it in .NET. C# offers multicast events, which are well versed in replacing the Observer pattern (in most cases). If you don't know the Observer pattern, don't worry – chances are, you will never need it anyway. Nevertheless, if you already know the Observer pattern, here are the differences between it and the Pub-Sub pattern.
>
> In the Observer pattern, the subject keeps a list of its observers, creating direct knowledge of their existence. Concrete observers also often know about the subject, which leads to even more knowledge of other entities, leading to more coupling.
>
> In the Pub-Sub pattern, the publisher is not aware of the subscribers; it is only aware of the message broker. The subscribers are not aware of the publishers either, only of the message broker. The publishers and subscribers are linked only through the data contract of the messages they are either publishing or receiving.
>
> We could view the Pub-Sub pattern as the distributed evolution of the Observer pattern or more precisely, like adding a mediator to the Observer pattern.

Next, we'll explore some patterns that directly call other microservices by visiting a new kind of **Façade**: the **Gateway**.

Introducing Gateway patterns

When building a microservices-oriented system, the number of services grows with the number of features; the bigger the system, the more microservices you will have. When you think about a user interface that has to interact with such a system, this can become tedious, complex, and inefficient (dev-wise and speed-wise). Gateways can help us achieve the following:

- Hide complexity by routing requests to the appropriate services.
- Hide complexity by aggregating responses, translating one external request into many internal ones.
- Hide complexity by exposing only the subset of features that a client needs.
- Translate an external request into another protocol that's used internally.

A gateway can also centralize different processes, such as logging and caching requests, authenticating and authorizing users and clients, enforcing request rate limits, and other similar policies.

You can see gateways as façades, but instead of being a class in a program, it is a program of its own, shielding other programs. There are multiple variants of the Gateway pattern, and we will explore many of them.

Regardless of the type of gateway you need, you can code it yourself or leverage existing tools to speed up the development process.

> **Tip**
> Beware that there is a strong chance that your homemade gateway version 1.0 has more flaws than a proven solution. This tip is not only applicable to gateways but to most complex systems. That being said, sometimes, there is no proven solution that does exactly what we want, and we have to code it ourselves, which is where the real fun begins!

An open source project that could help you out is Ocelot (`https://net5.link/Uwiy`). It is an application gateway written in .NET Core that supports many things that we expect from a gateway. You can route requests using configuration or write custom code to create advanced routing rules. Since it is open source, you can contribute to it, fork it, and explore the source code if you need to.

A gateway is a **reverse proxy** that fetches the information that's been requested by a client. That information can come from one or more resources, possibly located on one or more servers. Microsoft is working on a reverse proxy named YARP, which is also open source (`https://net5.link/YARP`). At the time of writing, it is in preview, but I suggest that you take a look as they seem to build it for Microsoft's internal teams, so it will most likely evolve and be maintained over time.

Now, let's explore a few types of gateway.

Gateway Routing pattern

We can use this pattern to hide the complexity of our system by having the gateway route requests to the appropriate services.

For example, let's say that we have two microservices: one that holds our device data and another that manages device locations. We want to show the latest known location of a specific device (`id=102`) and display its name and model.

To achieve that, a user requests the web page, and then the web page calls two services (see the following diagram). The `DeviceTwin` microservice is accessible from `service1.domain.com`, and the location microservice is accessible from `service2.domain.com`. From there, the web application has to keep track of what services use what domain name. The UI has to handle more complexity as we add more microservices. Moreover, if, at some point, we decide to change `service1` to `device-twins` and `service2` to `location`, we'd need to update the web application as well. If there is only a UI, it is still not so bad, but if you have multiple user interfaces, that means each of them has to handle that complexity.

Furthermore, if we want to hide the microservices inside a private network, it would be impossible unless all the user interfaces are also part of that private network:

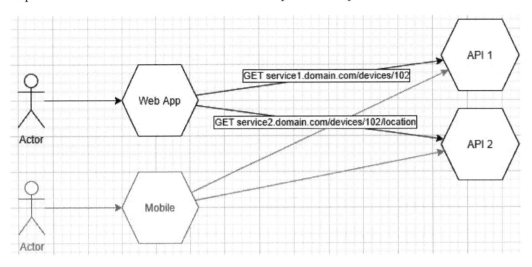

Figure 16.16 – A web application and a mobile app that are calling two microservices directly

To fix some of these issues, we can implement a gateway that does the routing for us. That way, instead of knowing what services are accessible through what DNS, the UI only has to know the gateway:

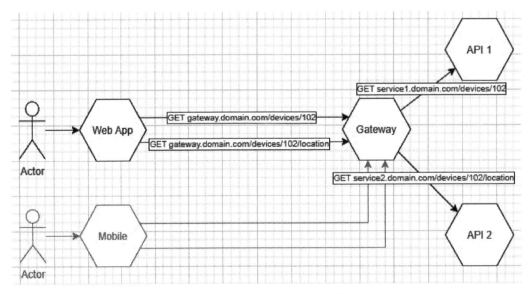

Figure 16.17 – A web application and a mobile app that are calling two microservices through a gateway application

Of course, this brings some possible issues to the table as your gateway could become a single point of failure. You could consider using a load balancer to ensure that you have strong enough availability and fast enough performance. Since all requests pass through the gateway, you may need to scale it up at some point.

You should also make sure that your gateway supports failure by implementing different resiliency patterns, such as **Retry** and **Circuit Breaker**. The chances that an error occurs on the other side of the gateway increases with the number of microservices you deploy and the number of requests that are sent to those microservices.

You can also use a routing gateway to reroute the URI to create easier to use URI patterns. You can also reroute ports; add, update, or remove HTTP headers; and more. Let's explore the same example but using different URIs. Let's assume the following:

Microservice	URI
API 1 (get a device)	internal.domain.com:8001/{id}
API 2 (get a device location)	internal.domain.com:8002/{id}

UI developers would have a harder time remembering what port is leading to what microservice and what is doing what (and who could blame them?). Moreover, we could not transfer the requests as we did earlier (only routing the domain). We could use the gateway as a way to create memorable URI patterns for developers to consume, like these:

Gateway URI	Microservice URI
gateway.domain.com/devices/{id}	internal.domain.com:8001/{id}
gateway.domain.com/devices/{id}/location	internal.domain.com:8002/{id}

As you can see, we took the ports out of the equation to create usable, meaningful, and easy-to-remember URIs.

However, we are still making two requests to the gateway to display one piece of information (the location of a device and its name/model), which leads us to our next Gateway pattern.

Gateway Aggregation pattern

Another role that we can give to a gateway is one that allows it to aggregate requests to hide complexity from our systems' consumers.

Continuing with our previous example, we have two UI applications that contain a feature to show a device's location on a map before identifying it using its name/model. To achieve this, they must call the device twin endpoint to obtain the device's name and model, as well as the location endpoint to get its last known location. So, two requests to display a small box, times two UIs, means four requests to maintain for a simple feature. If we extrapolate, we could end up managing a near-endless number of HTTP requests for a handful of features.

Here is a diagram showing our feature in its current state:

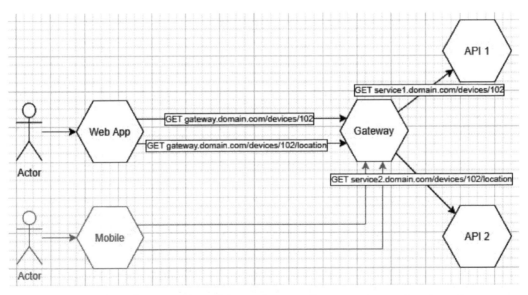

Figure 16.18 – A web application and a mobile app that are calling two microservices through a gateway application

To remedy this problem, we can apply the Gateway Aggregation pattern to simplify our UIs and offload the responsibility of managing those details to the gateway.

By applying the Gateway Aggregation pattern, we end up with the following simplified flow:

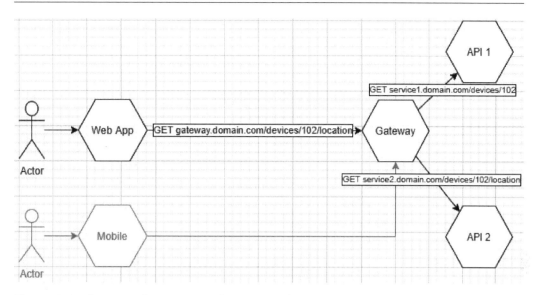

Figure 16.19 – A gateway that aggregates the response of two requests to serve a single request from both a web application and a mobile app

Next, let's explore the steps that occurred, in order. Here, we can see that the Web App makes a single request, while the gateway makes two calls. In the following diagram, the requests are sent in series, but we could have sent them in parallel to speed things up:

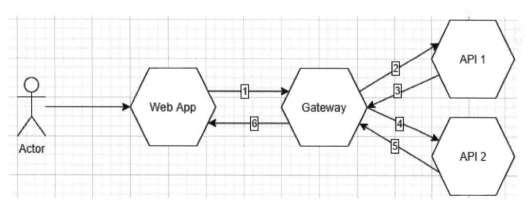

Figure 16.20 – The order in which the requests take place

Like the routing gateway, an aggregation gateway can become the bottleneck of your application and a single point of failure, so beware of that.

Another important point to note is the latency between the gateway and the internal APIs. If the latency is too high, your clients are going to wait for every response. So, deploying the gateway close to the microservices that it is interacting with could become crucial for your system's performance.

The gateway can implement caching to improve performance so that sub-requests are only sent once in a while.

Backends for Frontends pattern

The Backends for Frontends pattern is yet another variation of the Gateway pattern. With Backends for Frontends, instead of building a general-purpose gateway, you build a gateway per user interface (or for an application that interacts with your system), lowering complexity. Moreover, it allows for fine-grained control of what endpoints are exposed. It removes the chances of app B being broken when changes are being made to app A. Many optimizations can come out of this pattern, such as sending only the data that's required for each call instead of sending data that only a few applications are using, saving some bandwidth along the way.

Let's say that our Web App needs to display more data about a device. To achieve that, we would need to change the endpoint and send that extra information to the mobile app as well. However, the mobile app doesn't need that information since it doesn't have room on its screen to display it. Here is an updated diagram that replaces the single gateway with two gateways, one per frontend.

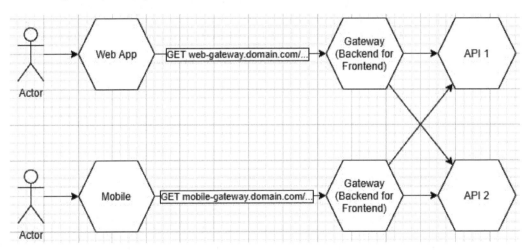

Figure 16.21 – Two backends for frontends gateways; one for the Web App and one for the Mobile App

By doing this, we can now develop specific features for each frontend without impacting the other. Each gateway is now shielding its particular frontend from the rest of the system and the other frontend.

Once again, the Backends for Frontends pattern is a gateway. And like other variations of the Gateway pattern, it can become the bottleneck of its frontend and its single point of failure. The good news is that the outage of one backend for frontend gateway limits the impact to a single frontend, shielding the other frontends from that downtime.

Mixing and matching gateways

Now that we've explored three variations of the Gateway pattern, it is important to note that we can mix and match them, either at the codebase level or as multiple microservices.

For example, a gateway can be built for a single client (backend for frontend), perform simple routing, and aggregate results.

We can also mix them as different applications, for example, by putting multiple backend for frontend gateways in front of a more generic gateway to simplify the development and maintenance of those backends for frontends.

Beware that each hop has a cost. The more pieces you add between your clients and your microservices, the more time it will take for those clients to receive the response (latency). Of course, you can put mechanisms in place to lower that overhead, such as caching or non-HTTP protocols such as gRPC, but you still must consider it. That goes for everything, not just gateways.

Here is an example illustrating this:

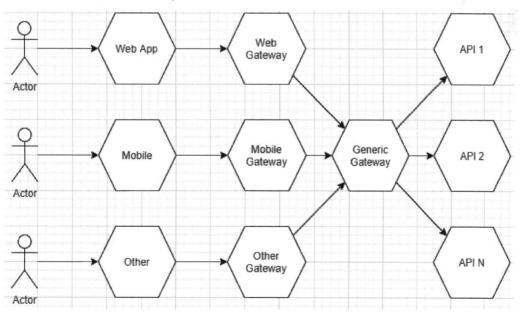

Figure 16.22 – A mix of the Gateway patterns

As you've possibly guessed, the Generic Gateway is the single point of failure of all applications, while at the same time, each backend for frontend gateway is a point of failure for its specific client.

> **Service mesh**
>
> A service mesh is an alternative to help microservices communicate with one another. It is a layer, outside of the application, that proxies communications between services. Those proxies are injected on top of each service and are referred to as **sidecars**. The service mesh can also help with distributed tracing, instrumentation, and system resiliency. If your system needs service-to-service communication, a service mesh would be an excellent place to look.

Conclusion

A gateway is a façade or reverse proxy that shields or simplifies access to one or more other services. In this section, we explored the following:

- **Routing**: This forwards a request from point A to point B.
- **Aggregation**: This combines the result of multiple sub-requests into a single response.
- **Backends for Frontends**: This is used in a one-to-one relationship with a frontend.

We can use microservices patterns like any other and mix and match them. Just consider the advantages, but also the drawbacks, that they bring to the table. If you can live with them, well, you've got your solution.

Gateways often end up being the single point of failure, so that is a point to consider. Moreover, we must also consider the delay that's added by calling a service that calls another service since that slows down the response time.

All in all, a gateway is a great tool to simplify consuming microservices. They also allow hiding the microservices topology behind them, possibly even isolated in a private network. They can also handle cross-cutting concerns such as security.

Now, let's see how gateways can help us follow the **SOLID** principles at app-scale:

- **S**: A gateway can handle routing, aggregation, and other logic that would otherwise be implemented in different components or applications.

- **O**: I see many ways to attack this one, but here are two takes on this:

  a) Externally, a gateway could reroute its sub-requests to new URIs without its consumers knowing about it, as long as its contract does not change.

  b) Internally, a gateway could load its rules from configurations, allowing it to change without updating its code.

- **L**: We could see the previous point (b) as *not changing the correctness of the application.*

- **I**: Since a backend for frontend gateway serves a single frontend system. That means one contract (interface) per frontend systems, leading to multiple smaller interfaces instead of one big general-purpose gateway.

- **D**: We could see a gateway as an abstraction, hiding the real microservices (implementations).

Now, let's revisit CQRS on a distributed scale.

Revisiting the CQRS pattern

Command Query Responsibility Segregation (**CQRS**), explored in *Chapter 14, Mediator and CQRS Design Patterns*, applies the **Command Query Separation** (**CQS**) principle. Compared to what we saw in *Chapter 14, Mediator and CQRS Design Patterns*, we can push CQRS further using microservices or serverless computing. Instead of simply creating a clear separation between commands and queries, we can divide them even more by using multiple microservices and data sources.

CQS is a principle stating that a method should either return data or mutate data, but not both. On the other hand, **CQRS** suggests using one model to read the data and one model to mutate the data.

Serverless computing is a cloud execution model where the cloud provider manages the servers and allocates the resources on-demand, based on usage. Serverless resources fall into the platform as a service (PaaS) offering.

Let's use IoT again as an example; we were querying the last known location of a device in the previous examples, but what about the device updating that location? This can mean pushing many updates every minute. To solve this issue, we are going to use CQRS. We will focus on two operations:

- Updating the device location.

- Reading the last known location of a device.

Simply put, we have a `Read Location` microservice, a `Write Location` microservice, and two databases. Remember that each microservice should own its data. That way, a user can access the last known device location through the read microservice (query model), while a device can punctually send its current position to the write microservice (command model). By doing that, we split the load from reading and writing the data as both occur at different frequencies:

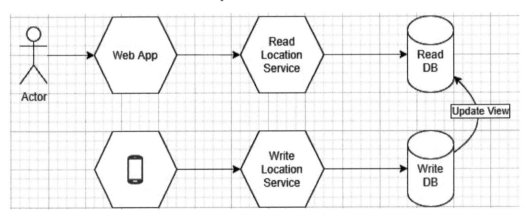

Figure 16.23 – Microservices that apply CQRS to divide the reads and writes of a device's location

This is a simplified version, but basically, the reads are queries, while the writes are commands. The way we update the Read DB once a new value is added to the Write DB depends on the systems that we are using/building. One essential thing in this type of architecture is that, per the CQRS pattern, a command should not return a value, enabling a "fire and forget" scenario. With that rule in place, consumers don't have to wait for the command to complete before doing something else.

One way to do this would be to leverage an existing cloud infrastructure, such as Azure Functions and Table Storage. Let's revisit this example using those components:

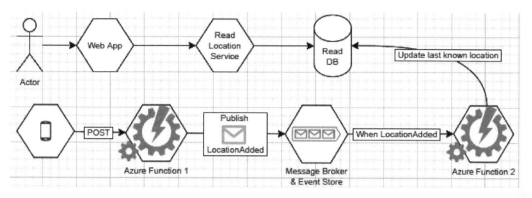

Figure 16.24 – Using Azure services to manage a CQRS implementation

The previous diagram illustrates the following:

1. The device sends its location every *T* times by posting it to Azure Function 1.

2. Azure Function 1 then publishes the `LocationAdded` event to the event broker, which is also an event store (the Write DB).

3. All subscribers to the `LocationAdded` event can now handle the event appropriately; in this case, Azure Function 2.

4. Azure Function 2 updates the last known location of the device in the Read DB.

5. Any subsequent queries should result in getting the new location.

This is a good example of **eventual consistency**. Any call to read the last known location between *steps 1* and *4* is getting the old value (the system is processing the new value).

In the preceding example, the message broker is also the event store, but we could store events elsewhere, such as in an Azure Storage Table or in a time-series database in this case. Moreover, I abstracted this component for multiple reasons, including the fact that there are multiple ways to publish events in Azure, and there are multiple ways of using third-party components (open source and proprietary).

> **Time-series databases**
>
> Time-series databases are optimized for temporally querying and storing data, where you always append new records without updating old ones. This kind of NoSQL database can be useful for temporal-intensive usage.

Once again, we used the Publish-Subscribe pattern to get another scenario going. Assuming that events are persisted forever, the previous example could also support event sourcing. Furthermore, new services could subscribe to the `LocationAdded` event without impacting the code that has already been deployed. For example, we could create a SignalR microservice that pushes the updates to its clients. It is not CQRS-related, but it flows well with everything that we've explored so far, so here is an updated diagram:

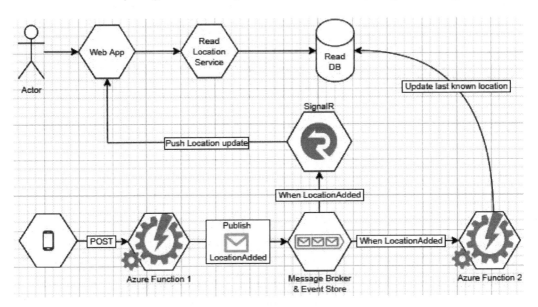

Figure 16.25 – Adding a SignalR service as a new subscriber without impacting the other part of the system

The SignalR microservice could be custom code or an Azure SignalR Service (backed by another Azure Function); it doesn't matter. The idea is to illustrate that it is easier to drop new services into the mix with a pub-sub model, rather than doing so with a monolith or a more traditional way of providing communication between microservices.

As you can see, a microservices system adds more and more small pieces that indirectly interconnect with each other over one or more message broker. Maintaining, diagnosing, and debugging such systems is harder than with a single application; that's the **operational complexity** we talked about earlier. However, containers can help out with deploying and maintaining such systems, which is our next subject.

Starting in ASP.NET Core 3.0, the ASP.NET team invested much effort into **distributed tracing**. Distributed tracing is necessary to find failures and bottlenecks related to an event that flows from one program to another (such as microservices). If something bugs out, it is important to trace what the user did to isolate the error, reproduce it, and then fix it. The more independent pieces there are, the harder it can become to make that trace possible. This is outside the scope of this book, but now you know one more ASP.NET Core 5 feature.

Conclusion

CQRS helps clearly divide queries and commands and helps encapsulate and isolate each block of logic independently. When we mix that concept with serverless computing or microservices architecture, it allows us to scale reads and writes independently. We can also use different databases, empowering us with the tools that we need for the data rate required by each part of that system (for example, frequent writes and occasional reads).

Now, let's see how CQRS can help us follow the **SOLID** principles at app-scale:

- **S**: Dividing an application into smaller reads and writes applications (or functions) leans toward encapsulating single responsibilities into different programs.

- **O**: CQRS, mixed with serverless computing or microservices, helps extend the software without the need for us to modify the existing code by adding, removing, or replacing applications.

- **L**: N/A.

- **I**: With a clear distinction between commands and queries, it should be easier to create multiple small interfaces (or programs) instead of a bigger one.

- **D**: N/A.

Next, we'll explore containers, which help us develop and deploy microservices.

An overview of containers

Containers are an evolution of virtualization. With containers, we virtualize applications instead of machines. To share resources, we can leverage virtual or physical machines. A container contains everything that is required for the containerized app to run, including an OS.

Containers can help us set up environments, ensure the correctness of applications when moving them between environments (local, staging, and production), and more. By packaging everything into a single container image, our application becomes more portable than ever before; no more "it was working on my machine." Another perk of containers is the possibility to configure the networking and relationships between containers. Moreover, containers are lightweight, allowing us to create a new one in a matter of seconds, leading to on-demand provisioning of resources that can scale up with traffic spikes, then scale back down when the demand decreases.

Containers can be very abstract and seem very complicated at first glance. However, nowadays, the tools have matured and improved, making it easier than ever to understand and debug containers, but it can still be a steep learning curve. The upside is that once you grasp it, it is hard to go back to non-containerized applications.

In this section, we will explore the following topics related to containers:

- Docker, which is a container engine.

- Docker Compose, which allows us to compose complex Docker applications.

- Orchestration, which is the concept of managing complex containerized applications. We will explore two orchestrators in this section.

- Finally, we will talk about scaling, which is a key point of using containers and microservices, where each microservice can scale independently.

Let's get started with Docker.

Docker

Docker is by far the most popular container engine out there. Getting started is now easy, while mastering it is another story. You can use Docker on Linux or Windows and even on Linux on Windows using WSL or WSL2. The Getting Started page (see Further reading) describes how to install Docker and what Docker Hub is.

The following is what we are about to discuss:

- Docker Desktop
- Docker Hub
- Docker images
- Docker containers
- `Dockerfile`
- `.dockerignore`

Docker Desktop is the runtime that allows you to run containers locally (you must install it first). It also comes bundled with the `docker` and `docker-compose` CLIs.

Docker Hub is a web-based repository where you can publish, share, and download **Docker images**.

A **Docker image** is the plan to build a **Docker container**. It's similar to a ghost image, for those who are familiar with Norton Ghost, or a Virtual Machine image.

A **Docker container** is a running **Docker image**; basically, the running application. You can run multiple instances (containers) of an image.

A `Dockerfile` is a text file that describes the building process of a **Docker image**.

A `.dockerignore` file works similarly to a `.gitignore` file and allows you to exclude certain files from being copied to the image by the `ADD` and `COPY` instructions.

Docker Compose is a utility that allows you to build a complex topology that could include multiple Docker images, public and private networks, volumes, and more. **Docker Compose** uses YAML files as configuration (the default is `docker-compose.yml`) and is run using the `docker-compose` CLI.

Regarding these concepts, both Visual Studio and Visual Studio Code have very useful tools that help with Docker. Moreover, the newer Docker Desktop user interface is very handy and includes a dashboard and settings. 2020 was a great year for Docker tooling.

Here is the basic idea:

1. Install Docker and other prerequisites (you only need to do this once).
2. Create a `Dockerfile` per application.
3. Create a `docker-compose.yml` file to manage multiple applications as a whole (optional).
4. Deploy your images to an image repository (locally, Docker Hub, or any cloud provider).
5. Run your images as containers (using Docker, container as a service, Kubernetes, or something else).

To create a Dockerfile, from Visual Studio, do the following:

1. Right-click the project that you want to dockerize.
2. In the contextual menu, select **Add > Docker Support**.
3. Choose Linux or Windows.

The generated Dockerfile of a web project named WebApp running on Ubuntu-18.04 (WSL2), looks as follows:

```
FROM mcr.microsoft.com/dotnet/aspnet:5.0-buster-slim AS base
WORKDIR /app
EXPOSE 80
EXPOSE 443


FROM mcr.microsoft.com/dotnet/sdk:5.0-buster-slim AS build
WORKDIR /src
COPY ["WebApp/WebApp.csproj", "WebApp/"]
RUN dotnet restore "WebApp/WebApp.csproj"
COPY . .
WORKDIR "/src/WebApp"
RUN dotnet build "WebApp.csproj" -c Release -o /app/build


FROM build AS publish
RUN dotnet publish "WebApp.csproj" -c Release -o /app/publish


FROM base AS final
WORKDIR /app
COPY --from=publish /app/publish .
ENTRYPOINT ["dotnet", "WebApp.dll"]
```

Microsoft's engineers, working on Docker tools, leveraged a Docker feature named **multistage build** to generate optimized layers, making sure the final image is as small as possible while still having access to the .NET SDK during the build process (see highlighted lines and spot the **base**, **build**, **publish**, and **final** stages).

> **Visual Studio tip**
>
> When using Visual Studio tools to run and debug Docker containers, Visual Studio only uses the first stage, so if you have logic that must run during startup or any other dependencies such as fonts that need to be installed in the micro-Linux distro, you have to put that logic into the base layer.

An essential part of the Dockerfile is the FROM [base image] AS [alias] instruction. FROM loads an existing Docker image as its base image. It's similar to inheriting from a class; we inherit from the whole base image. Then, we can add more content to that image, creating a new image of our own. Furthermore, each FROM defines a new stage of a multi-stage build.

> **.NET SDK versus runtime images**
>
> In the preceding Dockerfile, the first stage contains the .NET runtime (mcr. microsoft.com/dotnet/aspnet:5.0-buster-slim), while the second contains the SDK (mcr.microsoft.com/dotnet/sdk:5.0-buster-slim). This opens up the possibility of building the application inside Docker using the SDK and publishing the app inside an image (stage) that only contains the runtime. The runtime is much lighter than the full SDK. The smaller the resulting image, the faster it will be to download and start a new container from it.

The WORKDIR instruction specifies the execution context's directory from which other instructions are executed, such as RUN, COPY, and ENTRYPOINT. COPY does what you think it does; it copies files from your machine to the image.

RUN executes the specified command inside the container's OS. It could be a simple dotnet build command, a more complex one, or a series of commands that download and install the .NET SDK, for example.

EXPOSE tells Docker what ports the application is listening to. These ports must also be opened using the -p (one port) or -P (all exposed ports) flags. Don't forget that your application must listen to the ports that you expose; otherwise, nothing will happen when you query your container. We can also open and map ports inside the docker-compose.yml file.

ENTRYPOINT represents the executable that runs when you start a container. In this case, it is dotnet WebApp.dll, which runs the web application by using the .NET CLI.

> **More Information**
>
> For more information about the way Microsoft builds Dockerfiles, take a look at https://net5.link/L2PD.
>
> For more information about the Dockerfiles syntax, take a look at https://net5.link/j1Kv.

Docker comes with a CLI, which could take a whole book to describe, but here are a few useful commands. I think these snippets will help you get started with Docker.

`docker build` allows you to create an image. The `--rm` flag removes intermediate containers, the `-f` flag points to the Dockerfile, and the `-t` flag allows you to specify a tag (which is useful for identifying and running the image). Here is an example (the `.` at the end is important and represents the current directory):

```
docker build --rm -f "WebApp/Dockerfile" -t webapp:latest .
```

`docker run` allows you to start a container based on an image. If you don't want the shell to be attached, you can run a container in the background (detached mode) using the `-d` flag. The `--rm` flag removes the container when it exits, which is very useful when developing. Here is an example:

```
docker run --rm -d -p 443:8443/tcp -p 80:8080/tcp webapp:latest
```

Specifying `tcp` is optional and is the default value when mapping ports. It can also be replaced by another value, such as `udp`. The `--name` flag can be handy for accessing the container later, by name; for example:

```
docker run --rm -d -p 8080:80 --name MyWebApp webapp:latest
```

`docker image ls` lists all Docker images, while `docker ps` lists all running images (containers). `docker stop` stops a running container, while `docker rm` removes a stopped container. For example, we could start, stop, and then remove a container using the following commands:

```
docker run -d -p 8080:80 --name MyWebApp webapp:latest
docker stop MyWebApp
docker rm MyWebApp
```

For an unnamed container, we'd need to use its ID (run `docker ps` to find the ID of a running container). We can stop and remove a container by ID like so:

```
docker stop 0d5bffe4071f
docker rm 0d5bffe4071f
```

You can label your containers with both the `docker` CLI and `docker-compose`. You can then use those labels for many useful things, such as filtering. We can use the `-l` option when executing `docker build` to label a container. We can also use the `--filter "label=[label to filter here]"` option when executing a `docker ps` command to filter running containers that share a label; for example:

```
docker run -d -p 8080:80 --name MyWebApp -l webapp
webapp:latest
docker ps --filter "label=webapp"
```

Here, we cover two more options of the `docker ps` command. The first is the `-a` flag, which can come in handy for listing stopped containers (such as when they crash or did not start properly). The second is the `-q` flag, which only output IDs (which can be useful for chaining commands). For example, if you want to stop all containers that are labeled webapp, you could run the following command (in both bash and PowerShell):

```
docker stop $(docker ps --filter "label=webapp" -a -q)
```

That's enough Docker CLI commands for now; let's take a peek at `docker-compose`.

Docker Compose

Docker Compose allows you to create a complex system and link multiple applications together by creating one or more YAML files. Both Visual Studio and Visual Studio Code offer tools that can help you create and edit `docker-compose` files, which can be very useful when you're just starting out. Visual Studio creates two complementary files: the default `docker-compose.yml` file and one for local overrides called `docker-compose.override.yml`. You can use any number of files that you want when using the `docker-compose` CLI so that you can define overrides for *staging*, *production*, and whatnot. Here is a slightly modified version of that `docker-compose.yml` file:

```
version: '3.4'
services:
    webapp:
        image: ${DOCKER_REGISTRY-}webapp
        build:
            context: .
            dockerfile: WebApp/Dockerfile
        container_name: MyWebApp
        ports:
```

```
            - '8080:80'
    labels:
            - webapp
```

This file does the same as the previous command that we executed to run the container; it maps the ports, adds the `webapp` label, names the container `MyWebApp`, and uses `WebApp/Dockerfile`.

To build the images, we can use the `docker-compose build` command. The `--no-cache` flag is convenient in making sure that we are rebuilding the images; caches can sometimes be a pain. The `--force-rm` flag acts like the `docker build --rm` flag and removes intermediate containers. The following command builds the images using the `docker-compose.yml` file combined with the `compose.override.yml` file (if one exists):

```
docker-compose build --no-cache --force-rm
```

To specify certain files and the order in which they are applied, we can use the `-f` option, like this:

```
docker-compose -f docker-compose.yml build --no-cache
--force-rm
```

It is important to note that `-f` options must be located **before** `build`, not after, like the other options. It is also possible to specify multiple files, like this:

```
docker-compose -f docker-compose.yml -f another-docker-compose-
file.yml build --no-cache --force-rm
```

To run (start) the system, we can use `docker-compose up`. Like the `build` command, we can specify one or more files, using the `-f` option before the up command. You can also use the `-d` flag to run containers in detached mode and the `--build` flag to build the images before you start them. Here is an example:

```
docker-compose -f docker-compose.yml up --build -d
```

Finally, to take down the system, we can use the `docker-compose down` command, which also supports the `-f` option, like this:

```
docker-compose -f docker-compose.yml down
```

Now that we've explored all of those commands, let's add a SQL Server instance to the `docker-compose.yml` file and make our WebApp depend on it. Achieving this is as easy as adding a service to the `docker-compose.yml` file and, optionally, specifying that our WebApp `depends_on` it:

```yaml
version: '3.4'
services:
  webapp:
    image: webapp:latest
    build:
      context: .
      dockerfile: WebApp/Dockerfile
    container_name: MyWebApp
    ports:
      - '8080:80'
    labels:
      - webapp
    depends_on:
      - sql-server

  sql-server:
    image: 'mcr.microsoft.com/mssql/server'
    ports:
      - '1433:1433'
    environment:
      SA_PASSWORD: Some_Super_Strong_Password_123
      ACCEPT_EULA: 'Y'
    labels:
      - db
```

The WebApp could use the following connection string:

```
Server=sql-server;Database=[database name
here];User=sa;Password=Some_Super_Strong_Password_123;
```

The server name in the connection string (**highlighted**) matches the service name (**highlighted**) from the `docker-compose.yml` file. This is because `Docker Compose` automatically creates a DNS entry based on the service name. These DNS are accessible from the other containers.

Now that we've created a connection string, we don't want the password in the
`docker-compose.yml` file so that we don't accidentally commit that value into
Git. We could do this in many ways, such as by passing environment variables to the
`docker/docker-compose` commands, but we are going to create a `.env` file instead.

> **Tip**
>
> When using Git, add your `.env` file to your `.gitignore` file so that you
> don't commit it to your repository. Moreover, don't forget to document the
> values that should go there somewhere, without the secret values, so that
> your colleagues can create and update their personal `.env` file. For example,
> you could create a `.env.template` file that contains the keys but not the
> sensitive values, and check that file into Git.

At the same level of the `docker-compose.yml` file, if we add a `.env` file, we can reuse
the environment variables that we define in there, like this:

.env:

```
# Don't commit this file in Git
SQL_SERVER_SA_PASSWORD=Some_Super_Strong_Password_123
SQL_SERVER_CONNECTION_STRING=Server=sql-server;Database=webapp;
User=sa;Password=Some_Super_Strong_Password_123;
```

docker-compose.yml:

```
version: '3.4'
services:
    webapp:
        image: webapp:latest
        build:
            context: .
            dockerfile: WebApp/Dockerfile
        container_name: MyWebApp
        ports:
            - '8080:80'
        environment:
            - ConnectionString=${SQL_SERVER_CONNECTION_STRING}
        labels:
            - webapp
```

```
        depends_on:
            - sql-server

    sql-server:
        image: 'mcr.microsoft.com/mssql/server'
        ports:
            - '1433:1433'
        environment:
            SA_PASSWORD: ${SQL_SERVER_SA_PASSWORD}
            ACCEPT_EULA: 'Y'
        labels:
            - db
```

With these two files, when we run `docker-compose up`, two containers start up:
a SQL Server and an ASP.NET Core 5 web application that connects to that SQL Server.
Moreover, we opened and mapped port `1433` to itself, allowing us to connect to that
container using SQL Management Studio or the tool of your choosing.

> **Tip**
>
> Port `1433` is the default SQL Server port. Don't leave port `1433` open in
> production. The fewer attack vectors that you leave open, the harder it will be
> for intruders to hack your system.

From a .NET 5 perspective (inside the web application), we have access to the
connection string like we have access to any other setting (`_configuration` is of the
`IConfiguration` injected into the `Startup` class):

```
var connectionString = _configuration.
GetValue<string>("ConnectionString");
```

And we could load an Entity Framework Core context from there as well, like this:

```
services.AddDbContext<MyDbContext>(options => options.
UseSqlServer(connectionString))
```

Now that we've explored Docker in more detail, let's take a look at a tool that we can use
to manage a production environment.

Orchestration

Once we have a containerized microservices application, we need to deploy it. The challenges pass from the number of features in a single application to the number of applications to deploy, maintain, and orchestrate.

Each cloud provider has its own offering, which can be serverless, such as **Azure Container Instances** (**ACI**) and **Azure Kubernetes Service** (**AKS**). You can also maintain your own **virtual machines** (**VM**) in the cloud or on-premises.

Kubernetes is the most popular container orchestrator out there. It allows you to deploy, manage, and scale containers. Kubernetes can help you manage multiple VMs, add load balancing, monitor your containers, auto-scale based on demands, and more.

> K8s
>
> **Kubernetes** is also called **K8s**, short for "K", 8 other letters, and then "s". K8s is pronounced *K-eights*.

A tool that can help you get started with K8s, when using Docker Compose, is **Kompose** (`https://net5.link/NKqu`). It is an open source project that converts docker-compose YAML files into K8s YAML files. This process can also be automated in a **continuous integration** (**CI**) pipeline by running the following command:

```
kompose convert -f docker-compose.yaml
```

There are so many tools to help with orchestrating and deploying containers but we can't cover them all here. That is also why I've kept this section as lean as possible; I don't want to overwhelm you with information about tools that may become irrelevant or that you may never use. Instead, I think it is important to lay out some foundations to help you get started. Let's start with Project Tye, before we explore K8s jargon.

Project Tye

Project Tye (`https://net5.link/tye`) is an open source project started by Microsoft employees David Fowler, Glenn von Breadmeister, Justin Kotalik, and Ryan Nowak. The .NET Foundation now sponsors the project. Here is their README description:

> *"Tye is a developer tool that makes developing, testing, and deploying microservices and distributed applications easier. Project Tye includes a local orchestrator to make developing microservices easier and the ability to deploy microservices to Kubernetes with minimal configuration."*

If you did not watch Build 2020, many praised the tool, so I figured that I would include a short introduction in this book so that you know it exists.

In a nutshell, Tye is another YAML-based tool that allows you to compose multiple programs for a distributed application (that was my initial thought). Now, I see Tye as a tool used to simplify distributed .NET application development, the initial cost of setup, and its deployment.

Among its features, Tye offers the following:

- A dashboard that shows your application and services.
- Allows you to load Docker images.
- A proxy server that allows you to easily configure an **ingress**, which does the job of a **routing gateway**.
- Enables **distributed tracing**.
- Enables **service discovery**.
- Allows you to connect to **log aggregation systems**, such as **Elastic Stack** and **Seq**.
- Allows you to deploy to Kubernetes.
- Allows you to deploy to cloud providers, such as AKS.
- And more!

I only played slightly with Tye, but it sounds very promising. For example, I started an existing solution by only executing the `dotnet tye` command without any additional configuration (`tye` is a global tool installed via NuGet). That solution contains about 15 docker-compose files, 15 Dockerfiles, and most of the containers started. I looked at Tye from afar since its inception, but it's on my to-try-more list. The chances are that by the time you read this, Project Tye will have matured even more, so I thought it would be a great idea to tell you about it. It is under active development.

Next, let's look at Kubernetes!

Kubernetes

In this section we will discuss a few concepts related to Kubernetes so that you know, as the bare minimum, what is going on if you start reading more about K8s. A **cluster** is a group of nodes. A **node** is a machine (physical or virtual) that contains pods. Containers run inside **pods**. Pods are volatile; to quote the official documentation:

> *"[Pods] are born and when they die, they are not resurrected."*

Services come to the rescue by identifying a set of pods that serve a resource – say, the *DeviceLocation microservice*. Services are the conceptual identifiers of the applications running inside Kubernetes, so external clients don't have to know about the pods getting spawned and destroyed all the time. **Ingress** exposes services outside the cluster. **Volumes** are directories where you store files. They outlive containers but die with their associated pod. **Persistent Volumes (PVs)** are dedicated resources used to store files in the cluster. PVs can be provisioned on a **Network File System (NFS)**, iSCSI, or cloud storage system. Beware that the lifetimes of the files saved inside a container are tied to the life of that container.

> **Tip**
>
> A container can be destroyed at any time, so don't store important files inside a container; otherwise, you will lose them. Each container has its own filesystem, so files are not shared between them, even if two containers come from the same image. Use volumes or PVs instead, depending on your needs.

I understand this sub-section contains many concepts and, at the same time, not that much information. However, I think this high-level overview of Kubernetes is sufficient to save you hours of reading and deciphering information from diverse sources. You can always come back to this chapter later.

Scaling

Everyone is talking about scaling; all the cloud providers are selling auto-scaling and near-unlimited scaling capabilities, but what does that mean, microservices-wise?

Let's go back to our IoT example. Let's say that there are so many devices sending real-time information about their location that the server needs more power to run the *Location microservice*. What we can do here is put more power into the server (CPU and RAM), which is called **vertical scaling**. Then, at some point, when a single server is not enough, we can add more servers, which is called **horizontal scaling**. However, more servers means multiple instances of the application running on all of those servers. Using containers and an orchestrator such as Kubernetes makes it possible to create containers when the demand gets high enough, then remove them when it goes back to normal. Moreover, we can run a minimum number of instances so that if one crashes, there is always one or more others running to serve the requests while the one that crashed gets restarted (more precisely, it gets removed while a new one starts).

When multiple instances of the same application are running simultaneously, the requests need to be routed to the right node (server). For that to be possible, all nodes hosting that app must have a common entry point. None of the consumers can be in charge of reaching the instance they want or it would create chaos (and be unmanageable). To fix that, we can use a load balancer to balance the load between the different applications running on different servers.

A load balancer is a sort of routing gateway; it takes a request and routes it to the right server while managing the load between servers. We will not go into the implementation details of all of this, but here is a contextual diagram that represents this:

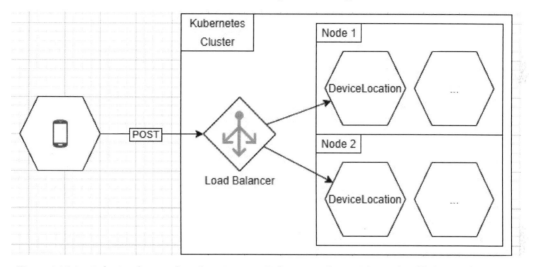

Figure 16.26 – A device that sends its location to a Kubernetes cluster. Then, a load balancer dispatches the request to the right instance of the DeviceLocation microservice

That is a little simplified, but it shows the idea behind load balancing:

1. A request enters the cluster and reaches the load balancer.

2. The load balancer dispatches the request to the appropriate instance of the *DeviceLocation microservice.*

Some load balancers can also serve the same server to the same client after subsequent calls, allowing stateful applications to be more dependable.

Conclusion

Containers are very helpful for creating portable applications. Docker Compose and orchestration programs come in handy to compose and deploy complex applications. All of this leads to scaling individual parts of the system more easily than ever before.

Now, let's see how containers can help us follow the **SOLID** principles at app-scale:

- **S**: They help us orchestrate, test, and deploy smaller microservices with one responsibility.
- **O**: They help us change the system's behaviors by adding and removing containers without stopping the application.
- **L**: N/A.
- **I**: They help us orchestrate, test, and deploy smaller microservices (a smaller app exposes a smaller public contract/interface).
- **D**: N/A.

Summary

The microservices architecture is something different from everything else that we've covered in this book and how we build monoliths. Instead of one big application, we split it into multiple smaller ones that we call microservices. Microservices must be decoupled from one another; otherwise, we face the possible problems associated with tightly coupling classes, times infinity.

We can leverage the Publish-Subscribe design pattern to decouple microservices while keeping them connected through events. Message brokers are software that dispatch those messages. We can use event sourcing to recreate the state of the application at any point in time, including when spawning new containers. We can use application gateways to shield clients from the microservices cluster's complexity and expose only a subset of services publicly.

We also took a look at how we can build upon the CQRS design pattern to decouple reads and writes of the same entities, allowing us to scale queries and commands independently. We also looked at using serverless resources to create that kind of system.

We then overviewed concepts about containers, Docker, Kubernetes, and scaling. Since we could write multiple books on these, we only glanced at what microservices can do.

On the other hand, microservices come at a cost and are not intended to replace all that exists. Building a monolith is still a good idea for many projects. Starting with a monolith and migrating it to microservices when scaling is another solution. This allows us to develop the application faster (monolith). It is also easier to add new features to a monolith than it can be to add them to a microservice application. Most of the time, mistakes cost less in a monolith than in a microservices application. You can also plan your future migration toward microservices, which leads to the best of both worlds while keeping operational complexity low. For example, you could leverage the Publish-Subscribe pattern through MediatR notifications in your monolith and migrate the events dispatching responsibility to a message broker later when migrating your system to a microservices architecture (if the need ever arises).

I don't want you to discard the microservices architecture, but I just want to make sure that you weigh up the pros and cons of such a system before blindly jumping in. The skill level of your team and their ability to learn new technologies may also impact the cost of jumping into the microservices boat.

DevOps (development [Dev] and IT operations [Ops]) and **DevSecOps** (adding security to the DevOps mix), which we do not cover in the book, are essential when building microservices. They bring deployment automation, automated quality checks, auto-composition, and more. Without that your project will be very hard to deploy and maintain.

Microservices are great when you need scaling, want to go serverless, or split responsibilities between multiple teams, but keep the operational costs in mind.

This chapter concludes the application-scale section of this book. Next, we'll explore user interfaces options provided by ASP.NET Core 5, including Blazor and the MVU pattern.

Questions

Let's take a look at a few practice questions:

1. What is the most significant difference between a **message queue** and a **pub-sub** model?

2. What is **event sourcing**?

3. Can an **application gateway** be both a **routing gateway** and an **aggregation gateway**?

4. Is it true that real CQRS requires the use of a serverless cloud infrastructure?

5. Do you need to use containers when you're building microservices applications?

Further reading

Here are a few links that will help you build on what you learned in this chapter:

- *Docker Getting Started*: https://net5.link/1zfM
- *Learn Kubernetes Basics*: https://kubernetes.io/docs/tutorials/kubernetes-basics/
- Event Sourcing pattern by Martin Fowler: https://net5.link/oY5H
- Event Sourcing pattern by Microsoft: https://net5.link/ofG2
- Publisher-Subscriber pattern by Microsoft: https://net5.link/amcZ
- Event-driven architecture by Microsoft: https://net5.link/rnck
- Microservices architecture and patterns on microservices.io: https://net5.link/41vP
- Microservices architecture and patterns by Martin Fowler: https://net5.link/Mw97
- Microservices architecture and patterns by Microsoft: https://net5.link/s2Uq
- JSON Patch: https://net5.link/PsqU
- RFC 6902 (JSON Patch): https://net5.link/bGGn
- JSON Patch in ASP.NET Core web API: https://net5.link/u6dw

Section 5: Designing the Client Side

In this section, we explore the options given by ASP.NET Core 5 to build user interfaces, the client-side aspect of our programs. We dig into the possibilities provided by ASP.NET Razor Pages and multiple ways to divide our UIs into smaller, easier-to-reuse components. Most content applies to both Razor Pages and MVC. We also learn many new powerful C# 9 features that are game-changers in the way we write .NET code. Finally, we cover a type-oriented way to build complex UIs.

Afterward, we move on to Blazor, which enables us to build full stack .NET programs. We quickly explore Blazor Server and dig into Blazor WebAssembly, a .NET SPA framework. We take a look at different ways to create Razor components and we explore the Model-View-Update (MVU) pattern. We complete the section with a medley of Blazor features that I cannot cover in more detail in the book, but I will give you an outline and many pointers to help you start your Blazor journey.

This section comprises the following chapters:

- *Chapter 17, ASP.NET Core User Interfaces*
- *Chapter 18, A Brief Look into Blazor*

17
ASP.NET Core User Interfaces

In this chapter, we'll explore different ways to create user interfaces using ASP.NET Core 5 and its extensive offerings. We have MVC, Razor Pages, and Blazor (*Chapter 18, A Brief Look into Blazor*) as macro-models. Then we have partial views, view components, Tag Helpers, display templates, editor templates, and Razor components to micro-manage our UIs. Furthermore, the .NET 5 ecosystem includes other non-web technologies to build UIs, such as WinForm, WPF, UWP, and Xamarin.

The goal of this chapter is not to cover every aspect of all of those elements and technologies but to lay out a plan explaining their roles and ways to use them.

The following topics will be covered in this chapter:

- Getting familiar with Razor Pages
- Organizing the user interface
- C# 9 features
- Display and Editor Templates

Getting familiar with Razor Pages

As its name implies, Razor Pages is a server-side way of rendering web content, organized by pages. That applies very well to the web, as people visit pages, not controllers. Razor Pages shares many components with MVC under the hood.

If you want to know if using MVC or Razor Pages is the best for your project, ask yourself if organizing your project into pages would be more suitable for your scenario. If yes, go Razor Pages; otherwise, pick something else, such as MVC or a SPA. We can also use both Razor Pages and MVC in the same application, so there is no need to choose only one.

Using Razor Pages is very similar to MVC. In the `Startup.ConfigureServices` method, instead of `services.AddControllersWithViews();` or `services.AddControllers();`, we can call the `services.AddRazorPages();` extension method.

The same applies to the `Startup.Configure` method where we must map Razor Pages routes using the `endpoints.MapRazorPages();` method.

The use of the other middlewares is the same. Here is an example of `Startup`:

```
public class Startup
{
    public void ConfigureServices(IServiceCollection services)
    {
        services.AddRazorPages();
    }
    public void Configure(IApplicationBuilder app,
IWebHostEnvironment env)
    {
        if (env.IsDevelopment())
        {
            app.UseDeveloperExceptionPage();
        }
        else
        {
            app.UseExceptionHandler("/Error");
            app.UseHsts();
        }
        app.UseHttpsRedirection();
        app.UseStaticFiles();
```

```
        app.UseRouting()
        app.UseAuthorization();
        app.UseEndpoints(endpoints =>
        {
            endpoints.MapRazorPages();
        });
    }
}
```

With the two highlighted lines, ASP.NET handles the routing and the model binding for us, as with MVC.

We can use the `webapp` project template to create a Razor Pages project:

```
dotnet new webapp
```

Design

Each page can handle one or more GET or POST methods. The idea is that each page is self-sufficient (SRP). To get started, a page consists of two parts: a view and a model. The model must inherit from `PageModel`. The view must use the `@model` directive to link to its page model, and the `@page` directive tells ASP.NET that it is a Razor page, not just an MVC view.

Here is a visual representation of that relationship:

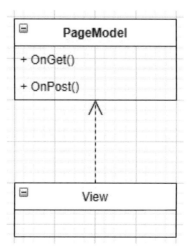

Figure 17.1 – Diagram representing a Razor page

Here is an example that I scaffolded using Visual Studio. The @page and @model directives are highlighted in the following snippet:

Pages\Employees\Create.cshtml

```
@page
@model PageController.Pages.Employees.CreateModel
@{
    ViewData["Title"] = "Create";
}
<h1>Create</h1>
<h4>Employee</h4>
<hr />
<div class="row">
    <div class="col-md-4">
        <form method="post">
            <div asp-validation-summary="ModelOnly"
class="text-danger"></div>
            <div class="form-group">
                <label asp-for="Employee.FirstName"
class="control-label"></label>
                <input asp-for="Employee.FirstName"
class="form-control" />
                <span asp-validation-for="Employee.FirstName"
class="text-danger"></span>
            </div>
            <div class="form-group">
                <label asp-for="Employee.LastName"
class="control-label"></label>
                <input asp-for="Employee.LastName" class="form-
control" />
                <span asp-validation-for="Employee.LastName"
class="text-danger"></span>
            </div>
            <div class="form-group">
                <input type="submit" value="Create" class="btn
btn-primary" />
            </div>
```

```
        </form>
    </div>
</div>
<div>
    <a asp-page="Index">Back to List</a>
</div>
@section Scripts {
    @{await Html.RenderPartialAsync ("_
ValidationScriptsPartial");}
}
```

Next is the PageModel, which we discuss here:

Pages\Employees\Create.cshtml.cs

```
namespace PageController.Pages.Employees
{
    public class CreateModel : PageModel
    {
        private readonly EmployeeDbContext _context;
        public CreateModel(EmployeeDbContext context)
        {
            _context = context;
        }

        public IActionResult OnGet()
        {
            return Page();
        }

        [BindProperty]
        public Employee Employee { get; set; }

        public async Task<IActionResult> OnPostAsync()
        {
            if (!ModelState.IsValid)
            {
```

```
        return Page();
    }

    _context.Employees.Add(Employee);
    await _context.SaveChangesAsync();

    return RedirectToPage("./Index");
  }
 }
}
```

From that code, we can see both parts: the view and the model. In the `PageModel` code, the `[BindProperty]` attribute is what tells ASP.NET to bind the form post to the `Employee` property. That's the equivalent of an MVC action that looks like this:

```
[HttpPost]
public Task<IActionResult> MyAction([FromForm] Employee
employee) {…}
```

Visually, a user requesting a page would look like this:

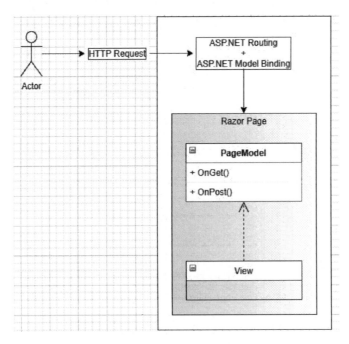

Figure 17.2 – User requesting a page

By default, pages live under the `Pages` directory instead of the `Views` directory. The layout mechanism of MVC is also available with Razor Pages. The default layout is in the `Pages/Shared/_Layout.cshtml` file; the `Pages/_ViewStart.cshtml` and `Pages/_ViewImports.cshtml` files play the same role as their MVC equivalent, but for Razor Pages.

Routing

In MVC, we can control the routing by creating global route patterns or with attributes. In Razor Pages, we can also control those routes. By default, the routing system automatically creates routes based on the filesystem, making it faster for us to get started. To use automatic routing, we just have to include the `@page` directive at the top of the page, and ASP.NET Core does the magic for us.

The routing system used by Razor Pages is simple yet powerful. The default pattern is the page's location without the `Pages` folder and the `.cshtml` extension with the `Index.cshtml` pages being optional (like the `Index` View of MVC). Instead of endless explanations, let's look at some examples:

Razor page file location	URL/Route
/Pages/Index.cshtml	/ or /index
/Pages/Contact.cshtml	/contact
/Pages/Employees/Index.cshtml	/employees
/Pages/Employees/Details.cshtml	/employees/details

In Razor Pages, the routing system chooses the page to be displayed, based on the URL.

We can also replace those defaults with custom routes. The way to replace the default route of a page is by providing a route template after the `@page` directive, such as `@page "/some-route"`. That page now handles the `/some-route` URL instead of the default one. The template supports the same as MVC routes, including parameters and constraints.

Covering every aspect of Razor Pages is out of the scope of the current book, but I encourage you to dig deeper into that way of building websites and web applications. It is enjoyable, powerful, and sometimes simpler than MVC.

However, if you need other HTTP methods than `GET` and `POST`, Razor Pages might not be for you.

Conclusion

Razor Pages is a good alternative when you want to organize your website or web application by pages instead of controllers. Many features from MVC are supported, such as validation (`ModelState` and `ValidationSummary`), the routing system, model binding, Tag Helpers, and more.

Now let's see how Razor Pages can help us follow the **SOLID** principles:

- **S**: Each `PageModel` is responsible for a single page, an essential point of Razor Pages.

- **O**: N/A.

- **L**: N/A.

- **I**: N/A.

- **D**: N/A.

> **The Single Responsibility Principle**
>
> One could see the "single responsibility" of a Razor Page as multiple responsibilities. It handles both reads and writes; the page model; HTTP requests; and could play with the HTTP response.
>
> Just keep in mind that the goal of a Razor Page is to manage a page. That's a single responsibility. A responsibility does not translate into a single operation. That said, if you think there is too much code in one of your Razor Pages, there are ways to help diminish that burden by extracting and delegating part of those responsibilities to other components, leaving the `PageModel` with fewer responsibilities and less code. For example, you could use MediatR to extract the business logic elsewhere.

We could see a Razor Page as a simplified **Page Controller** (Martin Fowler Patterns of Enterprise Application Architecture (PoEAA)). Why simplified? Because ASP.NET does most of the **Page Controller** work for us, leaving us only the **model** (domain logic) and the **view** to implement. See the *Further reading* section for more information.

Now that we know about Razor Pages and MVC, it is time to explore the options that ASP.NET Core 5 offers to us to organize our UIs.

Organizing the user interface

In this section, we will explore three options:

- **Partial views** to encapsulate reusable UI parts.

- **Tag Helpers** that enable us to write HTML-like Razor code instead of a C#-like syntax.

- **View components** that allow encapsulating logic with one or more views to create reusable components.

Keep in mind that we can use these options in both MVC and Razor Pages.

Partial views

A partial view is a part of a view created in a `cshtml` file, a Razor file. The content (markup) of the partial view is rendered at the location it was included by the `<partial>` Tag Helper or the `@Html.PartialAsync()` method. ASP.NET introduced the concept in MVC, hence the view. For Razor Pages, you could see partial views as partial pages.

We can place partial views files almost anywhere in our projects, but I'd suggest keeping them close to the views that use them. You can also keep them in the `Shared` folder. As a rule of thumb, the filename of a partial view begins with _, like `_CreateOrEditForm. cshtml`.

Partial views are good at simplifying complex views and reusing part of the UI in multiple other views. Here is an example that helps simplify the `_Layout.cshtml` file:

```
<div class="container">
    @Html.PartialAsync("_CookieConsentPartial")
    <partial name="_CookieConsentPartial" />
    <main role="main" class="pb-3">
        @RenderBody()
    </main>
</div>
```

The two highlighted lines are doing the same thing, so only one is needed. That's the two code styles to load partial views; pick the one you prefer. This example inserts the content of the `Pages/Shared/_CookieConsentPartial.cshtml` file at that location in the page. Partial views are very similar to the good old **includes** from ASP and PHP, but they don't have direct access to the caller's scope (a very good thing).

By default, the current value of the `Model` property is sent to the partial view, but it is possible to send a different model, like this:

```
@{
    var myModel = "My Model";
}
@Html.PartialAsync("_SomePartialView", myModel)
<partial name="_SomePartialView" model="myModel" />
```

In this case, `myModel` is a string, but it could also be an object of any type.

The partial view are more robust than the **includes** were with added flexibility. Let's now dig into some code.

Project: Shared form

One of the possibilities of partial views is to share presentation code. In a CRUD project, the create and edit forms are often very similar, so we can leverage partial views to simplify such duplication maintenance. This is similar to the project implemented in *Chapter 4, The MVC Pattern using Razor* but using Razor Pages instead of MVC.

The initial Razor code for this project has been scaffolded by Visual Studio, based on the `Employee` class below:

```
namespace PageController.Data.Models
{
    public class Employee
    {
        public int Id { get; set; }

        [Required]
        [StringLength(50)]
        public string FirstName { get; set; }

        [Required]
        [StringLength(50)]
        public string LastName { get; set; }
    }
}
```

Next, we explore a way to centralize the form shared by both pages to enhance our module's maintainability. First, we must extract the shared portion of `CreateModel` and `EditModel` so the form can use it. The `ICreateOrEditModel` interface contains that shared contract:

Pages/Employees/ICreateOrEditModel.cs

```
public interface ICreateOrEditModel
{
    Employee Employee { get; set; }
}
```

Then both `CreateModel` and `EditModel` must implement it:

Pages/Employees/Create.cshtml.cs

```
public class CreateModel : PageModel, ICreateOrEditModel
{
    ...
    [BindProperty]
    public Employee Employee { get; set; }
    ...
}
```

Pages/Employees/Edit.cshtml.cs

```
public class EditModel : PageModel, ICreateOrEditModel
{
    ...
    [BindProperty]
    public Employee Employee { get; set; }
    ...
}
```

Then we can isolate the shared portion of the forms and move that to the `_Form.cshtml` partial view (you can name it as you want):

Pages/Employees/_Form.cshtml

```
@model ICreateOrEditModel
<div class="form-group">
    <label asp-for="Employee.FirstName" class="control-label"></label>
    <input asp-for="Employee.FirstName" class="form-control" />
    <span asp-validation-for="Employee.FirstName" class="text-danger"></span>
</div>
<div class="form-group">
    <label asp-for="Employee.LastName" class="control-label"></label>
    <input asp-for="Employee.LastName" class="form-control" />
    <span asp-validation-for="Employee.LastName" class="text-danger"></span>
</div>
```

In the preceding code, we are using the `ICreateOrEditModel` interface as the `@model` so we have access to the `Employee` property of both the create and edit page models. Then we can include that partial view in both of our create and edit pages:

Pages/Employees/Create.cshtml

```
@page
@model PageController.Pages.Employees.CreateModel

...
<div class="row">
    <div class="col-md-4">
        <form method="post">
            <div asp-validation-summary="ModelOnly" class="text-danger"></div>
            <partial name="_Form" />
            <div class="form-group">
                <input type="submit" value="Create" class="btn btn-primary" />
```

```
            </div>
        </form>
    </div>
</div>
```

Pages/Employees/Edit.cshtml

```
@page
@model PageController.Pages.Employees.EditModel

...
<div class="row">
    <div class="col-md-4">
        <form method="post">
            <input type="hidden" asp-for="Employee.Id" />
            <div asp-validation-summary="ModelOnly"
class="text-danger"></div>
            <partial name="_Form" />
            <div class="form-group">
                <input type="submit" value="Save" class="btn
btn-primary" />
            </div>
        </form>
    </div>
</div>
```

With that in place, we have one form to maintain and two pages that do different things. In this case the form is trivial, but in the case of a more substantial entity, this could save a lot of time.

Beware that complex logic within a partial view can become more problematic than the time saved by having it. If you see the amount of conditional code grow in a partial view, I'd recommend investigating whether another technique/pattern would be better. Getting rid of the partial view or creating multiple partial views used in fewer places could also be solutions. Sometimes we think that sharing is a good idea, but it turns out it was not. When that happens, admit your failure, then fix the problem.

Conclusion

Partial views are a great way to reuse parts of a UI or to divide a complex screen into smaller, more manageable elements. Partial views are the most basic way of encapsulating chunks of UI. Use them when the display logic is limited; for more advanced use cases, we'll explore other options in the following subsections.

Now let's see how partial views can help us follow the **SOLID** principles:

- **S**: Extracting manageable parts of the UI into partial views can lead to the encapsulation of component-like views that each manage a single display responsibility.

- **O**: N/A.

- **L**: N/A.

- **I**: N/A.

- **D**: N/A.

Tag Helpers

Tag Helpers are server-side helpers allowing developers to write more HTML-like code in Razor views, reducing the amount of C#-like code mixed into the view. We used Tag Helpers in the last example, maybe without knowing it.

Let's start by having a second look at the _Form.cshtml file:

Pages/Employees/_Form.cshtml

```
@model ICreateOrEditModel
<div class="form-group">
    <label asp-for="Employee.FirstName" class="control-
label"></label>
    <input asp-for="Employee.FirstName" class="form-control" />
    <span asp-validation-for="Employee.FirstName" class="text-
danger"></span>
</div>
<div class="form-group">
    <label asp-for="Employee.LastName" class="control-label"></
label>
    <input asp-for="Employee.LastName" class="form-control" />
    <span asp-validation-for="Employee.LastName" class="text-
```

```
danger"></span>
</div>
```

In that partial view, we used built-in ASP.NET Tag Helpers to enhance the HTML `label`, `input`, and `span` tags. The `asp-*` attributes are used to set the values of certain built-in Tag Helpers' properties.

For example, the **Label Tag Helper** generates the value of the HTML `for` attribute automatically, based on its `asp-for` attribute. Moreover, it generates the text of the label based on the property name or its `[Display(Name = "Custom name")]` attribute, if the model property was decorated by one.

To get the same output using HTML helpers, the partial view would look like this:

Pages/Employees/_Form-HtmlHelpers.cshtml

```
@model ICreateOrEditModel
<div class="form-group">
    @Html.LabelFor(x => x.Employee.FirstName, new { @class =
"control-label" })
    @Html.TextBoxFor(x => x.Employee.FirstName, new { @class =
"form-control" })
    @Html.ValidationMessageFor(x => x.Employee.FirstName,
null, new { @class = "text-danger" })
</div>
<div class="form-group">
    @Html.LabelFor(x => x.Employee.LastName, new { @class =
"control-label" })
    @Html.TextBoxFor(x => x.Employee.LastName, new { @class =
"form-control" })
    @Html.ValidationMessageFor(x => x.Employee.LastName, null,
new { @class = "text-danger" })
</div>
```

In both cases, the `FirstName` form-group is rendered as the following HTML:

```
<div class="form-group">
    <label class="control-label" for="Employee_
FirstName">FirstName</label>
    <input class="form-control valid" type="text" data-
val="true" data-val-length="The field FirstName must be
```

```
a string with a maximum length of 50." data-val-length-
max="50" data-val-required="The FirstName field is required."
id="Employee_FirstName" maxlength="50" name="Employee.
FirstName" value="Bob" aria-describedby="Employee_FirstName-
error" aria-invalid="false">
```

```
    <span class="text-danger field-validation-valid" data-
valmsg-for="Employee.FirstName" data-valmsg-replace="true"></
span>
```

```
</div>
```

I find the use of Tag Helpers more elegant than the old HTML helpers (C#), but that's my
personal preference. Nevertheless, we can choose and mix both options.

Built-in Tag Helpers

There are many built-in Tag Helpers in ASP.NET Core. Some can help load different
elements depending on the environment (production or development); others help build
the `href` attribute of the `<a>` tag; and more.

Let's have a quick overview of what exists. If you want to learn more afterward, the official
documentation is getting better and better since Microsoft open sourced it. I've added
a few links in the *Further reading* section at the end of the chapter. Afterward, we will
explore how to create custom Tag Helpers.

The Anchor Tag Helper

The Anchor Tag Helper enhances the `<a>` tag to generate the `href` attribute based on
a controller action or a Razor page.

Here are a few examples for Razor Pages:

Tag	href value
`<a asp-page="/Index">...</a>`	`/`
`<a asp-page="/Employees/Index">...</a>`	`/Employees`
`<a asp-page="/Employees/Create">...</a>`	`/Employees/Create`
`<a asp-page="./Edit" asp-route-id="@item.Id">...</a>`	`/Employees/Edit/{item.Id}`

It is similar for MVC controllers:

Tag	href value
`<a asp-controller="Home"` `asp-action="Index">...</a>`	`/`
`<a asp-controller="Employees"` `asp-action="Index">...</a>`	`/Employees`
`<a asp-controller="Employees"` `asp-action="Create">...</a>`	`/Employees/Create`
`<a asp-controller="Employees" asp-action="Edit"` `asp-route-id="@item.Id">...</a>`	`/Employees/Edit/{item.Id}`

The Anchor Tag Helper is very useful in creating links that look like HTML, incredibly convenient to set the `class` attribute without an anonymous object and an escape character (if you've used HTML helpers before, you'll know what I mean).

The `asp-route-id` attribute is a little different than the others. The `asp-route-*` attributes allow specifying the value for a parameter, such as `id`. So if the GET action looks like this:

```
[HttpGet]
public IActionResult Details(int something){ ... }
```

You would need a link that specifies the `something` parameter, which could be declared like this:

```
<a asp-controller="Employees" asp-action="Details" asp-route-something="123">...</a>
```

There are many more options behind this Tag Helper that we are not covering here, but with what we did, you know that you can leverage ASP.NET to generate links based on pages and controllers.

The Link Tag Helper

The Link Tag Helper allows you to define a fallback CSS `href` in case the primary one does not load (that is, if the CDN is down). Here is an example from the Razor Pages template:

```
<link rel="stylesheet" href="https://cdnjs.cloudflare.com/ajax/
libs/twitter-bootstrap/4.1.3/css/bootstrap.min.css"
      asp-fallback-href="~/lib/bootstrap/dist/css/bootstrap.
min.css"
      asp-fallback-test-class="sr-only"
      asp-fallback-test-property="position"
      asp-fallback-test-value="absolute"
```

```
        crossorigin="anonymous"
        integrity="sha256-eSi1q2PG6J7g7ib17yAaWMcrr5GrtohYChqib
rV7PBE=" />
```

ASP.NET renders the required HTML and JavaScript to test if the CSS was loaded, based on the specified `asp-fallback-test-*` attributes. If it was not, it swaps it for the one specified in the `asp-fallback-href` attribute.

The Script Tag Helper

The Script Tag Helper allows you to define a fallback JavaScript file in case the primary one does not load (that is, if the CDN is down). Here is an example from the Razor Pages template:

```
<script src="https://cdnjs.cloudflare.com/ajax/libs/twitter-
bootstrap/4.1.3/js/bootstrap.bundle.min.js"
        asp-fallback-src="~/lib/bootstrap/dist/js/bootstrap.
bundle.min.js"
        asp-fallback-test="window.jQuery && window.jQuery.fn &&
window.jQuery.fn.modal"
        crossorigin="anonymous"
        integrity="sha256-E/V4cWE4qvAeO5MOhjtGtqDzPndRO1LBk81J/
PR7CA4=">
</script>
```

ASP.NET renders the required HTML and JavaScript to test if the script was loaded, based on the specified `asp-fallback-test` attribute. If the script did not load, the browser swaps the source for the one specified in the `asp-fallback-href` attribute. This is the equivalent of the `<link>` tag but for `<script>` tags.

The Environment Tag Helper

The Environment Tag Helper allows rendering certain parts of the UI only for specific environments. For example, you could render some debugging information only when in `Development`.

The Environment Tag Helper is also a good complement to the `<link>` and `<script>` Tag Helpers, allowing us to load local not minified scripts when developing and CDN-hosted minified files in production.

We can define what environment to target by including or excluding environments using the `include` and `exclude` attributes, respectively. The value of those attributes can be a single environment name or a comma-separated list. Here are some examples:

```
<environment include="Development">
    <div>Development Content.</div>
</environment>
```

The preceding snippet displays the `<div>` only when the environment is `Development`.

```
<environment exclude="Development">
    <div>Content not to display in Development.</div>
</environment>
```

The preceding snippet displays the `<div>` for all environments but `Development`.

```
<environment include="Staging,Production">
    <div>Staging and Production content.</div>
</environment>
```

The preceding snippet displays the `<div>` only for the `Staging` and `Production` environments.

```
<environment exclude="Staging,Production">
    <div>Content not to display in Staging nor Production.</div>
</environment>
```

The preceding snippet displays the `<div>` for all environments but `Staging` and `Production`.

The Caching Tag Helpers

ASP.NET Core also provides the following caching related Tag Helpers:

- The Cache Tag Helper
- The Distributed Cache Tag Helper
- The Image Tag Helper

The **Cache Tag Helper** allows caching part of a view for 20 minutes, by default, and leverages the ASP.NET Core cache provider mechanism. A basic example could be caching a random number like this:

```
<cache>@(new Random().Next())</cache>
```

Multiple attributes can also be set to control how the cache is invalidated and what it targets. We could want to cache the greeting to a user, for example, but if we write the following, all users would see the greeting of the first user to trigger the cache:

```
<cache>Hello @this.User.Identity.Name!</cache>
```

To fix that issue, we can set the `vary-by-user` attribute to `true`:

```
<cache vary-by-user="true">
    Hello @this.User.Identity.Name!
</cache>
```

Multiple other `vary-by-*` attributes can be used in other cases, such as `vary-by-header`, `vary-by-query`, `vary-by-route`, and `vary-by-cookie`.

To control how the cache is invalidated, we can set the `expires-on` attribute to a `DateTime` object or the `expires-after` or `expires-sliding` attributes to a `TimeSpan` object.

If that is not enough, ASP.NET Core also provides a **Distributed Cache Tag Helper** that leverages the `IDistributedCache` implementation that you register. You must configure the distributed cache provider in the `Startup` class, or the Tag Helper will use the in-memory provider. You must also specify a unique key for each element by setting the `name` attribute. The other attributes are the same as the Cache Tag Helper.

The last cache-related Tag Helper is the **Image Tag Helper**. That Tag Helper allows invalidating images when they change. To do that, ASP.NET appends a version to its enhanced `<img>` tags that get invalidated when the file changes.

Since the **Image Tag Helper** enhances the `<img>` tag, there is no new tag here. To use this functionality, you must set an `asp-append-version` attribute to `true` on an `<img>` tag that has an `src` attribute like this:

```
<img src="~/images/some-picture.jpg" asp-append-version="true">
```

While using one or more of those three Tag Helpers, it is easier than ever to cache part of your views, but caching is a subject of its own that I prefer not to dig too deeply into here.

The Form Tag Helpers

ASP.NET Core provides multiple Tag Helpers when the time comes to create forms. Since forms are the way to gather user inputs, they are quite essential. Here, we cover the **Form Tag Helper** first, which extends the `<form>` HTML tag.

Its first advantage is the automatic rendering of an `input [name="__` `RequestVerificationToken"]` element to prevent cross-site request forgery (CSRF or XSRF). **Razor Pages does the verification automatically**, but **MVC does not**. To enable XSRF/CSRF protection when using MVC, we need to decorate the action or the controller with the `[ValidateAntiForgeryToken]` attribute.

The second advantage is to help with routing. The Form Tag Helper exposes the same attributes as the Anchor Tag Helper when routing time comes, like the `asp-controller`, `asp-action`, `asp-page`, and `asp-route-*` attributes.

To submit the form, you can proceed like any normal HTML `<form>` tag: with a `button [type="submit"]` or an `input [type="submit"]`. We can also set different actions on different buttons by using the same routing attributes.

Next, let's explore the **Input Tag Helper** that we saw earlier. The key attribute of the Input Tag Helper is `asp-for`. When setting it to a property of the view's model, ASP.NET automatically generates the `name` of the `<input>` tag, its `value`, the validation information, and the `type` of that input. For example, a `bool` is rendered as `input [type=checkbox]` while a `string` is rendered as `input [type=text]`. We can decorate our view models with data annotations to control the type of input to be generated, like `[EmailAddress]`, `[Url]`, or `[DataType(DataType.*)]`.

> **Tip**
>
> When you have a property on your model representing a collection, you should use a `for` loop (not a `foreach`) to generate your form. Otherwise, in many cases, ASP.NET Core will not render the elements correctly, and you will receive a `null` value for those fields on the server after posting the form. Here is an example that works:
>
> ```
> @for (var i = 0; i < Model.Destinations.Count;
> i++)
> {
>     <input type="text" asp-for="@destinations[i].
> Name" class="control-label"></label>
>
>     <input type="text" asp-for="@destinations[i].
> Name" class="form-control" />
> }
> ```

Another advantage of Tag Helpers that enhance HTML tags is that all standard HTML attributes are usable. So when you want to create an input [type=hidden] for the Id property of the model being edited, you can set the type attribute directly and override the defaults, like this:

```
<input type="hidden" asp-for="Employee.Id" />
```

We then have the **Textarea Tag Helper** that generates a <textarea> tag like this:

```
<textarea asp-for="Employee.Description"></textarea>
```

Then comes the **Label Tag Helper** that helps render <label> tags, like this:

```
<label asp-for="Employee.Description"></label>
```

Finally, the **Select Tag Helper** helps render <select> tags using the values specified in its asp-items attribute. The items must be an IEnumerable<SelectListItem> collection. The asp-for attribute serves the same purpose as the other Tag Helpers. Here is an example of a manually generated list of items bound to the SomeProperty property of the Model:

```
@{
    var items = new[]
    {
        new SelectListItem("Make a selection", ""),
        new SelectListItem("Choice 1", "1"),
        new SelectListItem("Choice 2", "2"),
        new SelectListItem("Choice 3", "3"),
    };
}
<select asp-items="items" asp-for="SomeProperty"></select>
```

> **Tips:** enum
>
> You can use the `Html.GetEnumSelectList<TEnum>()` method to generate the list from an enum, where `TEnum` is the type of your enum. The generated `<option>` tags will have a numerical value equal to the value of the enum element and its text set to the textual representation of the enum element, like `<option value="2">SecondOption</option>`.
>
> To customize the text of each option, you can decorate your enum members with attributes, like the `[Display(Name = "Second option")]` attribute, which would render `<option value="2">Second option</option>` instead, improving readability. Here's an example:
>
> ```
> public enum MyEnum {
>     [Display(Name = "Second option")]
>     SecondOption = 2
> }
> ```

To conclude this subsection, we have two more form-related Tag Helpers to cover, the **Validation Message Tag Helper** and the **Validation Summary Tag Helper**. They exist to help validate form inputs on the client side.

The Validation Summary Tag Helper is used to display the list of error messages of the `ModelState` property (`ModelStateDictionary`). That property is accessible in most MVC and Razor Pages related base classes, such as `PageModel`, `PageBase`, `ControllerBase`, and `ActionContext` (accessible from `RazorPageBase.ViewContext` in an MVC view). The following code creates a validation summary:

```
<div asp-validation-summary="ModelOnly" class="text-danger"></div>
```

The value of the `asp-validation-summary` attribute can be `None`, `ModelOnly`, or `All`:

- `None` means that no summary will be displayed.
- `ModelOnly` means that only errors not related to the model's properties will be displayed in the validation summary (the name is counter-intuitive if you ask me).
- `All` means that all errors, including property errors, will be displayed in the validation summary.

If you are using the Validation Message Tag Helper for your properties, I'd recommend setting that value to ModelOnly, which will allow sending custom validation messages from your page or action without duplicating the model's messages on the page.

The Validation Message Tag Helpers allows us to display the error message of a single property. Usually, these are displayed close to the element they represent, but they don't have to be. Here is an example:

```html
<span asp-validation-for="Employee.FirstName" class="text-danger"></span>
```

The asp-validation-for attribute acts as the asp-for attribute but tells the element that it is for validation purposes instead of creating a form input. If the property (in this case, Employee.FirstName) is not valid, the error message is displayed; otherwise, it is not.

The class="text-danger" is a Bootstrap class that sets the text to a red color.

If we take a look again at the previous section's example, we will see that the following Razor code (first block) is rendered to the following HTML code (second block), with the Razor code highlights being translated to the HTML code highlights:

```html
<div class="form-group">
    <label asp-for="Employee.FirstName" class="control-label"></label>
    <input asp-for="Employee.FirstName" class="form-control" />
    <span asp-validation-for="Employee.FirstName" class="text-danger"></span>
</div>
```

```html
<div class="form-group">
    <label class="control-label"for="Employee_FirstName">FirstName</label>
    <input class="form-control" type="text" data-val="true" data-val-length="The field FirstName must be a string with a maximum length of 50." data-val-length-max="50" data-val-required="The FirstName field is required." id="Employee_FirstName" maxlength="50" name="Employee.FirstName" value="">
    <span class="text-danger field-validation-valid" data-valmsg-for="Employee.FirstName" data-valmsg-replace="true"></span>
</div>
```

The validation attributes (`data-val-length`, `data-val-length-max`, `data-val-required`, and `maxlength`) and the `type` attribute come from the `Employee.FirstName` property, which is defined as follows:

```
[Required]
[StringLength(50)]
public string FirstName { get; set; }
```

To conclude, the form Tag Helpers provided by ASP.NET Core are very handy at crafting readable forms, fast, and packed with functionalities.

The Partial Tag Helper

We already used the Partial Tag Helper in the previous subsection about partial views, but here are a few more use cases. The most trivial one implies to set only the `name` attribute as we did before:

```
<partial name="_Form" />
```

We can also specify a path instead of a name, like this:

```
<partial name="Employees/_PieceOfUI" />
```

That would load the `_PieceOfUI.cshtml` partial view from one of the following three files: `/Pages/Employees/_PieceOfUI.cshtml` or `/Pages/Shared/Employees/_PieceOfUI.cshtml` or `/Views/Shared/Employees/_PieceOfUI.cshtml`.

We can also pass a custom model to a partial view using the `model` attribute, like this:

Pages/Employees/PieceOfUIViewModel.cs

```
public record PieceOfUIViewModel(bool GenerateRandomNumber);
```

The `PieceOfUIViewModel` record class is a view model that we pass to the `PieceOfUI` partial view as follows. Records are a new C# 9 feature that we'll explore in the next section of this chapter. For now, think of `PieceOfUIViewModel` as a class with a read-only property named `GenerateRandomNumber`.

Pages/Employees/_PieceOfUI.cshtml

```
@model PieceOfUIViewModel
Piece of UI
```

```
@if (Model.GenerateRandomNumber) {
    <text>| </text>
    @(new Random().Next())
}
```

The preceding Razor code is the partial view that we render in the next block:

Pages/Shared/_Layout.cshtml

```
@using PageController.Pages.Employees

...

<partial name="Employees/_PieceOfUI" model="new
PieceOfUIViewModel(true)" />

...
```

In that example, we pass an instance of `PieceOfUIViewModel` to the partial view, which in turn renders a random number or not (`true` or `false`), depending on the value of the `GenerateRandomNumber` property.

The `for` attribute allows similar behavior but through the model itself. If we go back to our shared form but create a new partial view **without the need to implement any interface**, we could end up with the following code instead:

_FormFor.cshtml

```
@using PageController.Data.Models
@model Employee


<div class="form-group">
    <label asp-for="FirstName" class="control-label"></label>
    <input asp-for="FirstName" class="form-control" />
    <span asp-validation-for="FirstName" class="text-danger"></span>
</div>
<div class="form-group">
    <label asp-for="LastName" class="control-label"></label>
    <input asp-for="LastName" class="form-control" />
    <span asp-validation-for="LastName" class="text-danger"></span>
</div>
```

Next, the code used by both views:

Create.cshtml and Edit.cshtml

```
...
<partial name="_FormFor" for="Employee" />
...
```

Even if the partial view is not aware of the `Employee` property on the original `Model`, it still renders the same form because the `for` attribute preserved that context for us.

One last attribute is `view-data`, allowing us to pass a `ViewDataDictionary` instance to the partial view. I recommend sticking with fully typed objects instead of playing with dictionaries and magic strings, but if you need it one day for some obscure cases, well, you know that the attribute exists.

The Component Tag Helper

The **Component Tag Helper** is used to render **Razor Components** into an MVC or Razor Pages application. We explore Razor components in *Chapter 18, A Brief Look into Blazor,* and briefly explore this Tag Helper as well.

Creating a custom Tag Helper

Now that we've sprinted through the built-in Tag Helpers, we can also create our own quite easily. We have two options; we can extend an existing tag or create a new tag.

In this example, we are creating the `<pluralize>` tag. The objective behind it is to replace code like this:

```
<p class="card-text">
    @Model.Count
    @(Model.Count > 1 ? "Employees" : "Employee")
</p>
```

With code like this:

```
<p class="card-text">
    <pluralize count="Model.Count" singular="{0} Employee"
plural="{0} Employees" />
</p>
```

There is less context-switching with that code than with the first block as the whole block looks like HTML now.

> **Side effect**
>
> It would also be easier to localize a UI built using the `<pluralize>` Tag Helper than a UI filled with tertiary operators. As a quick change, we could inject an `IStringLocalizer<T>` into our `PluralizeTagHelper` class to localize the content of the `Singular` or `Plural` property before formatting it using `string.Format()`.
>
> Don't get me wrong here: I'm not telling you to stop writing C# into your views; I'm just pointing out another possible advantage of this versus using plain C#.

For that component, we need to create a `PluralizeTagHelper` class that we save into the `TagHelpers` directory. A Tag Helper must implement the `ITagHelper` interface but can also inherit from the `TagHelper` class. We are opting for the `TagHelper` class, which exposes a synchronous `Process` method that we can use.

> **Note**
>
> The `TagHelper` class does nothing more than adding the `Process` method to override and a default empty implementation of the `ITagHelper` interface.

The `PluralizeTagHelper` class that we are programming looks like this:

```
namespace PageController.TagHelpers
{

    [HtmlTargetElement("pluralize", TagStructure =
TagStructure.WithoutEndTag)]
```

This attribute tells Razor that we're extending the `<pluralize>` tag and that we can omit the end tag and write it like `<pluralize />` instead of `<pluralize></pluralize>`.

```
public class PluralizeTagHelper : TagHelper
{
    public int Count { get; set; }
    public string Singular { get; set; }
    public string Plural { get; set; }
```

The name of the properties directly translates to attributes in **kebab-case** format. So
`Singular` translates to `singular`, while a property named `ComplexAttributeName`
would translate to `complex-attribute-name`.

```
        public override void Process(TagHelperContext context,
    TagHelperOutput output)
        {
            var text = Count > 1 ? Plural : Singular;
            text = string.Format(text, Count);
```

The preceding code is the logic that chooses whether we display the singular or the plural
version of the text.

```
            output.TagName = null;
```

By setting the `TagName` property to `null`, we ensure that Razor does not render the
content inside a `<pluralize>` tag; we only want to generate text.

```
            output.Content.SetContent(text);
        }
    }
}
```

Finally, we set the value of what we want to output with the `SetContent` method of the
`TagHelperContent` class. The `TagHelperContent` class exposes multiple other
methods to append and set the content of the Tag Helper.

Like any other Tag Helper, we need to register it. We will register all Tag Helpers of the
project, in a few pages, in *Project: Reusable employee count*.

When loading a page that displays the Pluralize Tag Helper, we end up with the following
outputs:

```
# When count = 0
0 Employee
# When count = 1
1 Employee
# When count = 2
2 Employees
```

That's it for this one. Of course, we could create more complex Tag Helpers, but I'll leave that to you and your projects.

> **Tip**
> You can also download existing Tag Helpers from NuGet.org and publish your Tag Helpers on NuGet.org (or the third-party service of your choice) as NuGet packages.

Let's take a look at the **Tag Helper Component** next.

Creating an RSS feed TagHelperComponent

Context: We want to dynamically add a `<link>` tag into the `<head>` of every page without changing the `_Layout.cshtml` file. The expected output looks like the following:

```
<link href="/feed.xml" type="application/atom+xml"
rel="alternate" title="Chapter 17 Code Samples App">
```

We can do that by implementing an `ITagHelperComponent` interface, or we can inherit from `TagHelperComponent`. We will do the latter.

Let's first look at the `RssFeedTagHelperComponent` class and its options:

```
namespace PageController.TagHelpers
{
    public class RssFeedTagHelperComponentOptions
    {
        public string Href { get; set; } = "/feed.xml";
        public string Type { get; set; } = "application/
atom+xml";
        public string Rel { get; set; } = "alternate";
        public string Title { get; set; };
    }
```

The `RssFeedTagHelperComponentOptions` class contains some properties with default values about what to write into the `<link>` tag, for convenience.

Next, the `RssFeedTagHelperComponent` looks like this:

```
    public class RssFeedTagHelperComponent : TagHelperComponent
    {
```

```
        private readonly RssFeedTagHelperComponentOptions
_options;
        public
RssFeedTagHelperComponent(RssFeedTagHelperComponentOptions
options)
        {
            _options = options ?? throw new
ArgumentNullException(nameof(options));
        }

        public override void Process(TagHelperContext context,
TagHelperOutput output)
```

The `Process` method is where the magic happens. That can also be in the `ITagHelperComponent.ProcessAsync` method if you have asynchronous code to run.

```
        {
            if (context.TagName == "head")
```

Two sections can be extended by a Tag Helper component: the `<head>` and the `<body>`. Here, we want to append content to the `<head>`, so we are looking for that.

```
            {
                output.PostContent.AppendHtml(
                    $@"<link href=""{_options.Href}"" type=""{_
options.Type}"" rel=""{_options.Rel}"" title=""{_options.
Title}"">"
                );
            }
        }
    }
}
```

Finally, we append the `<link>` tag itself to the `<head>`, using our options object.

That code does nothing on its own; for it to run, we need to tell ASP.NET about it. To do that, we have multiple options, but as a big fan of **Dependency Injection**, that's the way that I chose here.

In the `Startup` class, we must register the `RssFeedTagHelperComponentOptions` and the `RssFeedTagHelperComponent` classes. Let's start with the options, which is a design choice and has nothing to do with the `ITagHelperComponent` itself:

```
services.
Configure<RssFeedTagHelperComponentOptions>(Configuration.
GetSection("RssFeed"));
```

```
services.AddSingleton(sp =>
sp.GetRequiredService<IOptionsMonitor
<RssFeedTagHelperComponentOptions>>().CurrentValue);
```

Here, I decided to leverage the **Options** pattern, which allows overriding our default values from any configuration source like the `appsettings.json` file. Then I needed a raw `RssFeedTagHelperComponentOptions`, so I registered it as is (see *Chapter 8, Options and Logging Pattern*, for more information about this workaround).

Now that our options are registered, we can register the `RssFeedTagHelperComponent` as an `ITagHelperComponent`. Since the component is stateless, we can register it as a singleton, like this:

```
services.AddSingleton<ITagHelperComponent,
RssFeedTagHelperComponent>();
```

That's it. When loading any page, the `<link>` tag is added to the `<head>` with the options that we defined! That's ASP.NET Core extensibility magic!

When we think about it, the options are endless; we could have components self-registering their CSS files or even minifying the `<head>` or the `<body>` or both. Here is an example of a minifier:

```
    public class MinifierTagHelperComponent :
TagHelperComponent

    {

        public override int Order => int.MaxValue;


        public async override Task
ProcessAsync(TagHelperContext context, TagHelperOutput output)

        {

            var childContent = await output.
GetChildContentAsync();

            var content = childContent.GetContent();

            var result = Minify(content);
```

```
            output.Content.SetHtmlContent(result);
    }

    private static string Minify(string input) { ... }
  }
}
```

That is most likely not the optimal way of doing minification (I did not benchmark it), but I built it because it crossed my mind, and as a quick second example to trigger your imagination. All of the code is available in Git (`https://net5.link/EcSc`).

> **More info**
>
> The `ITagHelper` interface inherits from `ITagHelperComponent`, so you can technically create a Tag Helper that adds resources to the `<head>` or `<body>` of the page by combining both methods into one class.

Conclusion

Tag Helpers are a great way to create new HTML-like tags or to expand existing ones to lower the friction from switching context between C# and HTML in Razor code. ASP.NET Core is packed with existing Tag Helpers, and you may have used some without even knowing it.

Now let's see how creating Tag Helpers can help us follow the **SOLID** principles:

- **S**: Tag Helpers can help us encapsulate tag-related logic into reusable pieces of code.
- **O**: N/A.
- **L**: N/A.
- **I**: N/A.
- **D**: N/A.

View components

Now to a new concept: **View components**. A view component is a mix between a partial view and a controller action. It is composed of two parts:

- A class that inherits from `ViewComponent` or is decorated with a `[ViewComponent]` attribute. This class contains the logic.
- One or more `cshtml` views. These are the views that knows how to render the component.

There are multiple ways to organize the files that compose a view component. Since I prefer it when the files related to a feature are close together, I like to see all of the classes live in the same directory as the view itself (let's call that vertical slice inspired), like this:

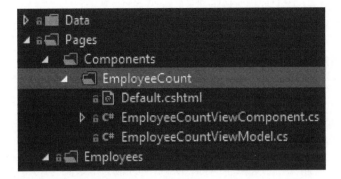

Figure 17.3: A way to organize View components keeping all files together

Project: Reusable employee count

Context: We want to create a view component in the same Razor Pages project. That component should display the number of employees that are available in the system's database. The component should always be visible.

The widget is a Bootstrap card that looks like this:

Figure 17.4: The result, rendered in a browser, of the employee count view component

I decided to inherit the view component from `ViewComponent` so I can leverage the helper methods, such as `View()`. For the `EmployeeCountViewModel`, I decided to leverage **record classes** (see *the Record classes (C# 9)* section). The view model exposes a `Count` property:

Pages/Components/EmployeeCount/EmployeeCountViewModel.cs

```
public record EmployeeCountViewModel(int Count);
```

The `EmployeeCountViewModel` class is virtually the same as a class with a `public int Count { get; }` property:

Pages/Components/EmployeeCount/Default.cshtml

```
@model PageController.Pages.Shared.Components.EmployeeCount.
EmployeeCountViewModel


<div class="card">
    <div class="card-body">
        <h5 class="card-title">Employee Count</h5>
        <p class="card-text">
            @Model.Count
            @(Model.Count > 1 ? "Employees" : "Employee")
        </p>
        <a asp-page="Employees/Index" class="card-
link">Employees list</a>
    </div>
</div>
```

As we saw in the *View Model design pattern* section of *Chapter 4, The MVC Pattern using Razor*, we inject a model, specifically crafted for this view, which is the default view of our view component, then we render the component using it. Now, to the view component:

Pages/Components/EmployeeCount/EmployeeCountViewComponent.cs

```
public class EmployeeCountViewComponent : ViewComponent
{
    private readonly EmployeeDbContext _context;
    public EmployeeCountViewComponent(EmployeeDbContext
context)
    {
        _context = context ?? throw new
ArgumentNullException(nameof(context));
    }
```

Here, we inject the `EmployeeDbContext` so we can count the employees in the `InvokeAsync` method down below:

```
public async Task<IViewComponentResult> InvokeAsync()
{
    var count = await _context.Employees.CountAsync();
    return View(new EmployeeCountViewModel(count));
}
}
```

A view component's logic must be placed inside an `InvokeAsync` method that returns a `Task<IViewComponentResult>` or an `Invoke` method that returns an `IViewComponentResult`. In our case, we access a database, so we better go `async` not to block resources while waiting for the database. Then, similar to a controller action, we use the `View<TModel>(TModel model)` method of the `ViewComponent` base class to return a `ViewViewComponentResult` that contains an `EmployeeCountViewModel` instance.

To render a view component, we can use the `Component.InvokeAsync()` extension method, like this:

```
@await Component.InvokeAsync("EmployeeCount")
```

The name of the view component must exclude the `ViewComponent` suffix.

For a more refactor-friendly method, we can also pass the type instead of its name:

```
@await Component.InvokeAsync(typeof(PageController.Pages.
Shared.Components.EmployeeCount.EmployeeCountViewComponent))
```

We can also use Tag Helpers to invoke our view components. To do so, we can register all view components as Tag Helpers by adding the following line to the `_ViewImports.cshtml` file:

```
@addTagHelper *, PageController
```

`PageController` is the name of the assembly to scan for view components (the name of the project).

Then we can use the `<vc:[view-component-name]></vc:[view-component-name]>` Tag Helper instead, like this:

```
<vc:employee-count></vc:employee-count>
```

`vc` is the default prefix that can be overridden.

We can achieve many things with view components, including passing arguments to the `InvokeAsync` method, so if you need some parameters, it is possible. Moreover, with view components and the power of dependency injection, we can create powerful UI pieces that are reusable and encapsulate complex logic, leading to a more maintainable application. We can also register components independently, no need to register them all at once.

Conclusion

View components are a mix between a partial view and a controller action, with the possibility of having a Tag Helper-like syntax. They support dependency injection for extensibility but are limited in other ways. They do not support optional parameters when using the Tag Helper syntax, only when using the `Component.InvokeAsync()` methods. The default places where we can save the views are limited but could be extended if one wants to.

In a nutshell, if you want a controller-like piece of UI that has logic or that needs to access external resources, a view component could be the right choice for you. On the other hand, if you want to create composable pieces of UI, Razor components might be a better fit (we cover those in the *Getting familiar with Razor components* section of *Chapter 18, A Brief Look into Blazor*).

Now let's see how creating view components can help us follow the **SOLID** principles:

- **S**: A view component helps us extract pieces of UI logic into independent components.
- **O**: N/A.
- **L**: N/A.
- **I**: N/A.
- **D**: N/A.

Next, we'll explore a few amazing C# features that are new to C# 9.

C# 9 features

In this section, we will visit the following new features:

- Top-level statements
- Target-typed `new` expressions
- Init-only properties
- Record classes

We will use the top-level statement to simplify some code samples, leading to one code file with less boilerplate code. Then we will dig into the `new` expressions that allow creating new instances with less typing. The init-only properties are the backbone of the record classes used in this chapter and are foundational to the MVU example presented in *Chapter 18, A Brief Look into Blazor*.

Top-level statements (C# 9)

Starting from C# 9, it is possible to write statements before declaring namespaces and other members. Those statements are compiled to an emitted `Program.Main` method.

With top-level statements, a minimal .NET "Hello World" program now looks like this:

```
using System;
Console.WriteLine("Hello world!");
```

Unfortunately, we also need a project to run, so we have to create a `.csproj` file with the following content:

```
<Project Sdk="Microsoft.NET.Sdk">
    <PropertyGroup>
        <TargetFramework>net5.0</TargetFramework>
        <OutputType>Exe</OutputType>
    </PropertyGroup>
</Project>
```

From there, we can use the .NET CLI to `dotnet run` the application.

We can also declare other members like classes and use them as we would in any console application. Classes must be declared after the top-level code.

Top-level statements are a great feature to get started with C# and write code samples by cutting out boilerplate code. I was slightly against the idea at first, but I now see many possibilities for it.

Target-typed new expressions (C# 9)

Target-typed new expressions are a new way of initializing types. Back in the day, C# 3 introduced the var keyword, which became very handy to work with generic types, LINQ return values, and more (I remember embracing that new construct with joy).

This new C# feature does the opposite of the var keyword by letting us call the constructor of a known type, like this:

```csharp
using System;
using System.Collections.Generic;

List<string> list1 = new();
List<string> list2 = new(10);
List<string> list3 = new(capacity: 10);
var obj = new MyClass(new());
AnotherClass anotherObj = new() { Name = "My Name" };

public class MyClass {
    public MyClass(AnotherClass property)
    => Property = property;
    public AnotherClass Property { get; }
}
public class AnotherClass {
    public string Name{ get; init; }
}
```

The first highlight shows the ability to create new objects when the type is known using the new() keyword and omitting the type name. The second list is created the same way, but we passed the argument 10 to its constructor. The third list uses the same approach but explicitly specifies the parameter name, as we could with any standard constructor.

The variable obj is created explicitly, but new() is used to create an instance of AnotherClass, which is inferred because the parameter type is known.

The final example demos the use of class initializers. As you may have noticed, the AnotherClass class has an init-only property, which is our next subject.

I can see the target-typed new expressions simplify many codebases. I started using them and they are one of the great addition of C# 9.0.

Init-only properties (C# 9)

Init-only properties are read-only properties that can be initialized using the class initializer. Before that, read-only properties could only be initialized in the constructor or with property initializers (such as `public int SomeProp { get; } = 2;`).

For example, let's take a class that holds the state of a counter. When using a read-only property, we would have the following class:

```
public class Counter
{
    public int Count { get; }
}
```

Without a constructor, it is impossible to initialize the Count property, so we can't initialize an instance like this:

```
var counter = new Counter { Count = 2 };
```

That's the use case that init-only properties enable. We can rewrite the Counter class to make use of that by using the `init` keyword, like this:

```
public class Counter
{
    public int Count { get; init; }
}
```

Init-only properties enable developers to create immutable properties that are settable using a class initializer. They are also a building block of the **record classes**.

Record classes (C# 9)

A record class uses init-only properties and allows making reference types (classes) **immutable**. The only way to change a record is to create a new one. Let's convert the Counter class into a record:

```
public record Counter
{
```

```
    public int Count { get; init; }
}
```

Yes, it is as simple as replacing the `class` keyword with the `record` keyword.

But that's not all:

- We can simplify record creation.
- We can also use the `with` keyword to simplify "mutating" a record (creating a mutated copy without touching the initial one).
- Records support **deconstruction**, like the **Tuple** types.
- .NET auto-implements the `Equals` and `GetHashCode` methods. Those two methods compare the value of the properties instead of the reference to the object. That means that two different instances with the same values would be equal.

All in all, that means that we end up with an immutable reference type (`class`) that behaves like a value type (`struct`) without the copy allocation cost.

Simplifying the record creation

If we don't want to use a **class initializer** when creating instances, we can simplify the code of our records to the following:

```
public record Counter(int Count);
```

That syntax reminds me of **TypeScript**, where you can define properties and fields in the constructor, and they get implemented automatically without the need to do it manually. Then, we can create a new instance like any other class:

```
var counter = new Counter(2);
Console.WriteLine($"Count: {counter.Count}");
```

Running that code would output `Count:  2` in the console. We can also add methods to the record class:

```
public record Counter(int Count)
{
    public bool CanCount() => true;
}
```

You can do everything with a record that you would do with a class, and more.

The with keyword

The `with` keyword allows us to create a copy of a record and set only the properties that we want to change, keeping the other values as they were. Let's take a look at the following code (leveraging C# 9 top-level statements):

```
using System;


var initialDate = DateTime.UtcNow.AddMinutes(-1);
var initialForecast = new Forecast(initialDate, 20, "Sunny");
var currentForecast = initialForecast with { Date = DateTime.
UtcNow };
Console.WriteLine(initialForecast);
Console.WriteLine(currentForecast);


public record Forecast(DateTime Date, int TemperatureC, string
Summary)
{
    public int TemperatureF => 32 + (int)(TemperatureC /
    0.5556);
}
```

When we execute that code, we end up with a result similar to this:

```
Forecast { Date = 9/22/2020 12:04:20 AM, TemperatureC = 20,
Summary = Sunny, TemperatureF = 67 }
Forecast { Date = 9/22/2020 12:05:20 AM, TemperatureC = 20,
Summary = Sunny, TemperatureF = 67 }
```

The power of the `with` keyword allows us to create a copy of the `initialForecast` record and only change the `Date` property's value.

The `with` keyword is a compelling addition to the language.

Deconstruction

We can **deconstruct** `record` classes automatically like a `Tuple`:

```
using System;


var current = new Forecast(DateTime.UtcNow, 20, "Sunny");
var (date, temperatureC, summary) = current;
```

```
Console.WriteLine($"date: {date}");
Console.WriteLine($"temperatureC: {temperatureC}");
Console.WriteLine($"summary: {summary}");


public record Forecast(DateTime Date, int TemperatureC, string
Summary)
{
    public int TemperatureF => 32 + (int)(TemperatureC /
0.5556);
}
```

By default, all **positional members** (defined in the constructor) are deconstructable. In that example, we cannot access the `TemperatureF` property by using deconstruction because it is not a positional member.

We can create a custom **deconstructor** by implementing one or more `Deconstruct` method that exposes `out` parameters of the properties that we want to be deconstructible, like this:

```
using System;


var current = new Forecast(DateTime.UtcNow, 20, "Sunny");
var (date, temperatureC, summary, temperatureF) = current;


Console.WriteLine($"date: {date}");
Console.WriteLine($"temperatureC: {temperatureC}");
Console.WriteLine($"summary: {summary}");
Console.WriteLine($"temperatureF: {temperatureF}");


public record Forecast(DateTime Date, int TemperatureC, string
Summary)
{
    public int TemperatureF => 32 + (int)(TemperatureC /
0.5556);


    public void Deconstruct(out DateTime date, out int
temperatureC, out string summary, out int temperatureF)
        => (date, temperatureC, summary, temperatureF) = (Date,
```

```
TemperatureC, Summary, TemperatureF);
}
```

With that updated sample, we can also access the `TemperatureF` property's value when deconstructing the record.

Equality comparison

As mentioned earlier, the default comparison between two records is made by its value and not its memory address, so two different instances with the same values are equal. The following code proves this:

```
using System;

var employee1 = new Employee("Johnny", "Mnemonic");
var employee2 = new Employee("Clark", "Kent");
var employee3 = new Employee("Johnny", "Mnemonic");

Console.WriteLine($"Does '{employee1}' equals '{employee2}'?
{employee1 == employee2}");
Console.WriteLine($"Does '{employee1}' equals '{employee3}'?
{employee1 == employee3}");
Console.WriteLine($"Does '{employee2}' equals '{employee3}'?
{employee2 == employee3}");

public record Employee(string FirstName, string LastName);
```

When running that code, the output is as follows:

```
'Employee { FirstName = Johnny, LastName = Mnemonic }' equals
'Employee { FirstName = Clark, LastName = Kent }'? False
'Employee { FirstName = Johnny, LastName = Mnemonic }' equals
'Employee { FirstName = Johnny, LastName = Mnemonic }'? True
'Employee { FirstName = Clark, LastName = Kent }' equals
'Employee { FirstName = Johnny, LastName = Mnemonic }'? False
```

In that example, even if `employee1` and `employee3` are two different objects, when we compare them using `employee1 == employee3`, the result is `true`, proving that values were compared, not instances.

You may not have noticed, but the `ToString()` method of record classes is returning a developer-friendly representation of its data. The `ToString()` method of an object is called implicitly when using string interpolation, like in the preceding code, hence the complete output.

On the other hand, if you want to know if they are the same instance, you can use the `Object.ReferenceEquals()` method like this:

```
Console.WriteLine($"Is 'employee1' the same as 'employee3'?
{Object.ReferenceEquals(employee1, employee3)}");
```

This will output the following:

```
Is 'employee1' the same as 'employee3'? False
```

Conclusion

Record classes are a great new addition that allows creating immutable types in a few keystrokes. Furthermore, they support deconstruction and implement equality comparison that compares the value of properties, not whether the instances are the same, simplifying our lives in many cases.

Init-only properties can also be beneficial for regular classes when one prefers class initializers to constructors.

> **Opinions**
>
> I think that record classes could be convenient for one-way binding UIs that follow patterns like Redux (JavaScript) and Model-View-Update (MVU). I played along those lines with C# 9.0/.NET 5 previews, leading to a very elegant MVU result, which I encapsulated in an open source library on GitHub. We'll use that library to implement the MVU pattern in the next chapter.
>
> Records could also fit well for view models and DTOs. Those are ephemeral objects that are generally not to be mutated.

Next, we'll explore display and editor templates to attach parts of UIs to types.

Display and Editor Templates

In this section, we'll look at how to use **display and editor templates** to divide our UIs into model-oriented partial views. These have been available since MVC on the .NET Framework and are not new to ASP.NET Core. Unfortunately, they are often forgotten or overlooked at the expense of brand-new things that come out.

Display templates are Razor views that override the default rendering template of a given type. Editor templates are the same, but override the editor's view of a given type.

Each type can have a display template and an editor template. They are also stored hierarchically so that each type can have globally shared templates and specific ones per area, controller, section, or page. In a complex application, this could be very handy to override an individual template for a particular section of the app.

A **display template** must be created in a `DisplayTemplates` directory, and an **editor template** must be created in an `EditorTemplates` directory. These directories can be placed at different levels. Moreover, the directory structure depends on whether you're using MVC or Razor Pages.

ASP.NET loads them in order of priority, from the more specific to the more general. That allows us to create a shared template, shared between all pages or all controllers, then override it for a specific controller or a specific page.

For MVC, the order in which they are loaded is as follows:

1. `Views/[some controller]/DisplayTemplates`
2. `Views/Shared/DisplayTemplates`

For Razor pages, the order in which they are loaded is as follows:

1. `Pages/[some directory]/DisplayTemplates`
2. `Pages/Shared/DisplayTemplates`

> **Note**
> The same logic applies to areas; MVC searches for display and editor templates like any other views.

Both display and editor templates are `.cshtml` files with a `@model` directive that points to the type they are for. For example, `Views/Shared/DisplayTemplates/SomeModel.cshtml` should have a `@model SomeModel` directive at the top. The same goes for `Views/Shared/EditorTemplates/SomeModel.cshtml`.

Let's start with display templates.

Display Templates

Let's use a CRUD UI to manage the employees that we scaffolded again for this section. See the `TransformTemplateView` project.

Context: We want to encapsulate the way employees are displayed in both `Details` and `Delete` pages. Instead of creating a partial view, we have decided to use a display template.

We don't want that template to be used elsewhere, so we create it specifically in the `Pages/Employees` directory. Let's start with that display template:

Pages/Employees/DisplayTemplates/Employee.cshtml

```
@model Data.Models.Employee
<dl class="row">
    <dt class="col-sm-2">
        @Html.DisplayNameFor(model => model.FirstName)
    </dt>
    <dd class="col-sm-10">
        @Html.DisplayFor(model => model.FirstName)
    </dd>
    <dt class="col-sm-2">
        @Html.DisplayNameFor(model => model.LastName)
    </dt>
    <dd class="col-sm-10">
        @Html.DisplayFor(model => model.LastName)
    </dd>
</dl>
```

That file is a copy of the scaffolded files that we had. To render a display template, we must call one of the `@Html.DisplayFor()` extension methods. In the details and delete views, we can replace the old code with `@Html.DisplayFor(x => x.Employee)`. From there, the rendering engine of ASP.NET Core will find the template and render it (as easy as that).

Next, we look at the two pages that consume that display template:

Pages/Employees/Details.cshtml

```
@page
@model TransformTemplateView.Pages.Employees.DetailsModel
@{
    ViewData["Title"] = "Details";
}
```

```
<h1>Details</h1>
<div>
    <h4>Employee</h4>
    <hr />
    @Html.DisplayFor(x => x.Employee)
</div>
<div>
    <a asp-page="./Edit" asp-route-id="@Model.Employee.
Id">Edit</a> |
    <a asp-page="./Index">Back to List</a>
</div>
```

Pages/Employees/Delete.cshtml

```
@page
@model TransformTemplateView.Pages.Employees.DeleteModel
@{
    ViewData["Title"] = "Delete";
}
<h1>Delete</h1>
<h3>Are you sure you want to delete this?</h3>
<div>
    <h4>Employee</h4>
    <hr />
    @Html.DisplayFor(x => x.Employee)
    <form method="post">
        <input type="hidden" asp-for="Employee.Id" />
        <input type="submit" value="Delete" class="btn btn-
danger" /> |
        <a asp-page="./Index">Back to List</a>
    </form>
</div>
```

Just like that, we centralized the display of an employee to one cshtml file, located and loaded automatically by its type, not by a string like partial views. But that's not it – display templates are more powerful than that, as we are about to see, after our overview of editor templates.

Editor Templates

The **editor templates** work in the same way as **display templates**, so let's rebuild the same thing that we did with a partial view, but with an editor template.

Reminder: We want to encapsulate the `Employee` form and reuse it in both `Create` and `Edit` views.

Once again, we don't want that template to be used elsewhere, so we create it at the same level, under `Pages/Employees`. Let's take a look at the code:

Pages/Employees/EditorTemplates/Employee.cshtml

```
@model Data.Models.Employee
<div class="form-group">
    <label asp-for="FirstName" class="control-label"></label>
    <input asp-for="FirstName" class="form-control" />
    <span asp-validation-for="FirstName" class="text-danger"></span>
</div>
<div class="form-group">
    <label asp-for="LastName" class="control-label"></label>
    <input asp-for="LastName" class="form-control" />
    <span asp-validation-for="LastName" class="text-danger"></span>
</div>
```

That's the same view as the partial view that we created in a previous sample. It is important to remember that display and editor templates are designed around a type, in this case the `Employee` class.

To tell ASP.NET Core to create an editor for a model, we can use one of the `@Html.EditorFor()` extension method overloads. In both `Create` and `Edit` views, we are replacing the form with a call to `@Html.EditorFor(m => m.Employee)`:

Pages/Employees/Create.cshtml

```
@model TransformTemplateView.Pages.Employees.CreateModel
@{
    ViewData["Title"] = "Create";
}
```

```html
<h1>Create</h1>
<h4>Employee</h4>
<hr />
<div class="row">
    <div class="col-md-4">
        <form method="post">
            <div asp-validation-summary="ModelOnly"
class="text-danger"></div>
            @Html.EditorFor(m => m.Employee)
            <div class="form-group">
                <input type="submit" value="Create" class="btn
btn-primary" />
            </div>
        </form>
    </div>
</div>
```

Pages/Employees/Edit.cshtml

```html
@page
@model TransformTemplateView.Pages.Employees.EditModel
@{
    ViewData["Title"] = "Edit";
}
<h1>Edit</h1>
<h4>Employee</h4>
<hr />
<div class="row">
    <div class="col-md-4">
        <form method="post">
            <div asp-validation-summary="ModelOnly"
class="text-danger"></div>
            <input type="hidden" asp-for="Employee.Id" />
            @Html.EditorFor(m => m.Employee)
            <div class="form-group">
                <input type="submit" value="Save" class="btn
btn-primary" />
```

```
            </div>
        </form>
    </div>
</div>
```

And like the display templates, that's the only thing that we need to do. When running the project, both create and edit pages use the same form, specifically crafted for the `Employee` class.

We are about to explore the power of display templates in the next example. Keep in mind that you can achieve the same with editor templates.

Project : Composite BookStore revisited

Context: We want to revisit how we are displaying the composite bookstore's UI that we built earlier, in *Chapter 3*, *Architectural Principles*, and *Chapter 9*, *Structural Patterns*. The goal is to get the display logic out of the classes, decoupling them from their HTML output.

What could be better than display templates to encapsulate those small blocks of UI?

Let's first inspect the steps to take:

1. Update the model classes.

2. Create the views and transfer the rendering logic there (the HTML).

Let's start by updating the model classes:

Models/*.cs

```
namespace TransformTemplateView.Models
{
    public interface IComponent
    {
        void Add(IComponent bookComponent);
        void Remove(IComponent bookComponent);
        int Count();
    }
```

First, we removed the `Display` method and the `Type` property from `IComponent`. Both are used to display the `IComponent` instance.

```csharp
    public class Book : IComponent
    {
        public Book(string title)
        {
            Title = title ?? throw new
ArgumentNullException(nameof(title));
        }
        public string Title { get; set; }
        public int Count() => 1;
        public void Add(IComponent bookComponent) => throw new
NotSupportedException();
        public void Remove(IComponent bookComponent) => throw
new NotSupportedException();
    }
```

Then we did the same for the `Book` class (both members were part of the `IComponent` interface).

```csharp
    public abstract class BookComposite : IComponent
    {
        protected readonly List<IComponent> children;
        public BookComposite(string name)
        {
            Name = name ?? throw new
ArgumentNullException(nameof(name));
            children = new List<IComponent>();
        }

        public string Name { get; }
        public virtual ReadOnlyCollection<IComponent>
Components => new ReadOnlyCollection<IComponent>(children);

        public virtual string Type => GetType().Name;
        public virtual void Add(IComponent bookComponent) =>
children.Add(bookComponent);
        public virtual int Count() => children.Sum(child =>
```

```
child.Count());
        public virtual void Remove(IComponent bookComponent) =>
children.Remove(bookComponent);
        public virtual void AddRange(IComponent[] components)
=> children.AddRange(components);
    }
```

Then, we stripped all the display code from `BookComposite` and added a property named `Components` that exposes its children to the display template.

The `Corporation`, `Section`, and `Store` classes that follow are only organizational types since we are keeping the bookstore logic to a minimum to explore patterns and features, not the business model of a fake store:

```
public class Corporation : BookComposite
{
    public Corporation(string name) : base(name) { }
}
public class Section : BookComposite
{
    public Section(string name) : base(name) { }
}
public class Store : BookComposite
{
    public Store(string name) : base(name) { }
}
```

The `Set` class is a little different. It is an organizational type, but it requires some books (see the `books` parameter of its constructor here):

```
public class Set : BookComposite
{
    public Set(string name, params IComponent[] books)
        : base(name)
    {
        AddRange(books);
    }
}
```

That code represents our first step and is conceptually very similar to what we had in the original code, without the display logic.

Now, to create the new, updated display code, we create the following three Razor files:

1. The **Razor Page** itself, displayed when a client requests it, in the `Pages/BookStore/Index.chhtml` file.

2. The **View Template** to render the books, in the `Pages/BookStore/DisplayTemplates/Book.chhtml` file.

3. The **View Template** to render all of the other `BookComposite` objects, in the `Pages/BookStore/DisplayTemplates/BookComposite.chhtml` file.

Let's look at how the files are organized, then at the code:

```
▲ ᵃ⌐ Pages
   ▲ ᵃ⌐ BookStore
      ▲ ᵃ⌐ DisplayTemplates
         ᵃ ⌐ Book.cshtml
         ᵃ ⌐ BookComposite.cshtml
      ▲ ᵃ ⌐ Index.cshtml
         ▷ ᵃ C# Index.cshtml.cs
```

Figure 17.5: Solution Explorer's view of the revised BookStore display templates and Index page

Let's start with the page model:

Pages/BookStore/Index.cshtml.cs

```csharp
using Microsoft.AspNetCore.Mvc.RazorPages;
using System;
using System.Collections.ObjectModel;
using TransformTemplateView.Models;
using TransformTemplateView.Services;


namespace TransformTemplateView.Pages.BookStore
{
    public class IndexModel : PageModel
    {
        private readonly ICorporationFactory
_corporationFactory;
```

```
        public IndexModel(ICorporationFactory
corporationFactory)
        {
            _corporationFactory = corporationFactory ?? throw
new ArgumentNullException(nameof(corporationFactory));
        }
```

First, we used **constructor injection** to gain access to the `ICorporationFactory`.

```
        public ReadOnlyCollection<IComponent> Components { get;
private set; }
```

Then we expose a collection of `IComponent` that the view needs to render the page.

```
        public void OnGet()
        {
            var corporation = _corporationFactory.Create();
            Components = new ReadOnlyCollection<IComponent>(new
IComponent[] { corporation });
        }
    }
}
```

Finally, when someone sends a `GET` request to that page, it builds the `ReadOnlyCollection<IComponent>` instance by calling the `_corporationFactory.Create()` method.

Next, the page's view:

Pages/BookStore/Index.cshtml

```
@page
@model TransformTemplateView.Pages.BookStore.IndexModel
@{
    ViewData["Title"] = "My BookStore";
}
<section class="card">
    <h1 class="card-header">@ViewData["Title"]</h1>
    <ul class="list-group list-group-flush">
        @Html.DisplayFor(x => x.Components)
```

```
    </ul>
</section>
```

That markup creates a Bootstrap 4 `.card` to hold our bookstore data. The key to that view is the `DisplayFor()` call (highlighted).

Since the `Components` property of our `PageModel` is a `ReadOnlyCollection<T>` that implements `IEnumerable<T>` that inherits from `IEnumerable`, ASP.NET Core loops and renders all elements of the `Components` collection. In our case, that's only one `Corporation` object, but it could be more.

For each of those elements, ASP.NET Core tries to find the right **display template** for that type. Since we don't have a `Corporation` template, it goes up the inheritance chain to find the `BookComposite` template and renders the element. Let's look at those templates now, starting with `BookComposite`:

Pages/BookStore/DisplayTemplates/BookComposite.cshtml

```
@model BookComposite
<li class="list-group-item">
    <section class="card">
        <h5 class="card-header">
            @Model.Name
            <span class="badge badge-secondary float-right">@Model.Count()</span>
        </h5>

        <ul class="list-group list-group-flush">
            @Html.DisplayFor(x => x.Components)
        </ul>

        <div class="card-footer text-muted">
            <small class="text-muted text-right">@Model.Type</small>
        </div>
    </section>
</li>
```

The `@model BookComposite` directive instructs the framework about the type it knows how to render.

The template renders a Bootstrap 4 `.card` inside a `.list-group-item`. Since the page renders the `Components` inside a `<ul class="list-group list-group-flush">`, those `<li>` elements will make a nice-looking UI.

The template does the same as the page and calls `@Html.DisplayFor(x => x.Components)`, which allows rendering any type that implements the `IComponent` interface.

> **Highlights**
> That's the power of the display templates right there; with them, we can craft a complex model-based recursive UI, with little effort.

In more details, what happens is the following:

1. `ReadOnlyCollection<T>` implements `IEnumerable<T>`, so ASP.NET loops and renders all its content. In our case, that's a collection containing two `Store` instances.

2. For each element, ASP.NET tries to find the right **display template** for that type. Since we don't have a `Store` template, it goes up the inheritance chain to find the `BookComposite` template and renders the elements.

3. Then, for each `Store`, it renders its children; in our case, instances of `Section` and `Set`, using the `BookComposite` template (we don't have `Set` or `Section` templates).

4. From those `Section` and `Set` objects, the `Book` objects are rendered using the `Book` template (which we are about to look at), while other non-book objects are rendered using the `BookComposite` template.

Let's start with the Razor code to render `Book` instances:

Pages/BookStore/DisplayTemplates/Book.cshtml

```
@model Book
<li class="list-group-item">
    @Model.Title
    <small class="text-muted">(Book)</small>
</li>
```

The `Book` template is a leaf of the tree and displays the details of a `Book`, nothing more (instructed by the `@model Book` directive).

If we compare that code with the initial model that we had, it is very similar. The `BookComposite` template is also very similar to what we were building in the `BookComposite.Display()` method.

The most significant difference is the level of difficulty that was required to write the presentation code. It is feasible to render a small element using a `StringBuilder`, but it can become tedious to render a complex web page. **Display templates** allowed us to write that same code very easily with IntelliSense and tooling support.

> **Important note**
> Display templates and editor templates are an excellent way to create a type-oriented UI design (model-oriented).

If we take a subset of our `BookStore`, what happens in the background is the following:

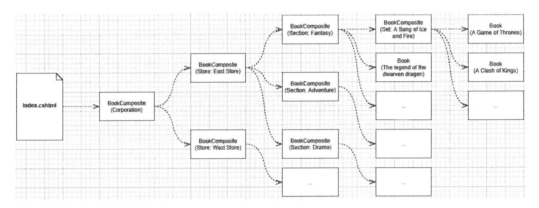

Figure 17.6: A subset of the rendering flow done by ASP.NET, based on our display templates

This completes our example. With that few lines of code, we were able to render a complex UI that supports a non-linear composite data structure. We could extend that UI, by rendering each class differently, such as including a logo for `Corporation` objects or cover images for `BookSet` objects.

Conclusion

As we explored in this chapter, we discovered many ways to render components and parts of a page, but display and editor templates are convenient ones that are often overlooked. We can render complex polymorphic UI with little effort.

Now let's see how this approach can help us follow the **SOLID** principles:

- **S**: By extracting the rendering of objects from the models, we divided both responsibilities into two different pieces.

- **O**: By managing independent, type-related pieces of the UI, we can change how a type is rendered without impacting it directly or its consumers.

- **L**: N/A.

- **I**: N/A.

- **D**: N/A.

> **Note**
>
> We could see the display and editor templates as **Transformers** from the **Transform View** pattern. We could also see **Razor** as an implementation of the **Template View** pattern. Martin Fowler introduced those patterns in his book, *Patterns of Enterprise Application Architecture* (PoEAA), in 2002. See the *Further reading* section for more information.

Summary

In this chapter, we explored **Razor Pages**, which allowed us to organize our web applications by page instead of controllers. Razor Pages leverages the same tools as **MVC**. Both technologies can also be combined and used together, allowing you to build parts of your application using Razor Pages and other parts using MVC.

Then we tackled **partial views**, which allow reusing parts of a UI and break down complex UI into smaller pieces. When we have complex logic, we can move from partial views to **view components**, a controller action-like view. We also tackled **Tag Helpers** to create reusable UI parts or extend existing HTML elements, or to just consume the built-in ones.

We explored multiple new **C# 9 features**, from top-level statements to target-typed new expressions, init-only properties, and the new record classes. We then dug deeper into record classes, which offer many possibilities as an immutable reference type.

Finally, we explored yet another way to divide UIs into smaller pieces, but this time, oriented around the model classes themselves. **Display and editor templates** give us the power to dynamically build a model-based UI for both display and modification purposes.

With all of that, we've almost dipped into everything that ASP.NET Core has to offer in terms of web UIs, but we are not done yet; we still have Blazor to explore in the next chapter to complete our full-stack journey into .NET 5.

Questions

Let's take a look at a few practice questions:

1. What is **Razor Pages** good for?

2. When using **Razor Pages**, do we have access to model binding, model validation, and routing of MVC?

3. Can we use a **partial view** to query a database?

4. Can we extend existing tags with **Tag Helpers**?

5. Can we use **view components** to query a database?

6. Does the following code compiles: `List<string> list = new();`?

7. Does the following code compiles: `public class MyDTO(int Id, string Name);`?

8. How many display templates can a class have?

9. To what do we link (or associate) a display or an editor template?

Further reading

- Here are a few links to build upon what we learned in the chapter:

- Partial views in ASP.NET Core `https://net5.link/p1oW`

- View components in ASP.NET Core `https://net5.link/DNsE`

- Tag Helpers in ASP.NET Core `https://net5.link/JaZQ`

- Page Controller (Martin Fowler PoEAA) `https://net5.link/LLQg`

- Template View (Martin Fowler PoEAA) `https://net5.link/TFM9`

- Transform View (Martin Fowler PoEAA) `https://net5.link/4Gom`

- Stator (StateR) is a simple, dependency injection-oriented, Redux-inspired, or Model-View-Update (MVU) experiment using C# 9.0 `https://net5.link/Z7Ej`

18
A Brief Look into Blazor

In this chapter, we look at Blazor. Blazor is the new kid on the block enabling full-stack .NET. Blazor is a great piece of technology. It is still relatively new, but it improved remarkably between its experimental stage, its first official release, and its current state. In about 2 years, it went from being something of a distant future to reality. Daniel Roth was most likely the most fervent believer who preached Blazor over that period. For a time, Blazor was the only thing I heard about (or maybe that was the internet spying on me).

> **Fun fact**
> Back in the day, we could use server-side JavaScript with classic ASP, making classic ASP the first full-stack technology (that I know of).

Blazor is two things:

- It is a client-side **single-page application** (**SPA**) framework compiling .NET to **WebAssembly** (**Wasm**).

- It is a client-server link over SignalR that acts as a modern `UpdatePanel` with superpowers.

> **A bit of history**
>
> If you don't know what an `UpdatePanel` is, you haven't missed much. It was an ASP.NET Web Forms control released with .NET Framework 3.5 that helped run AJAX calls "automagically."

Blazor also comes bundled with **Razor components** (why not Blazor components? I don't know). It has some experimental projects revolving around it and a growing ecosystem of libraries accessible through NuGet.

Now that I have laid out the high-level overview of Blazor, the following topics will be covered in this chapter:

- An overview of Blazor Server
- Overview of Blazor WebAssembly
- Getting familiar with Razor components
- The Model-View-Update pattern
- A medley of Blazor features

An overview of Blazor Server

Blazor Server is an ASP.NET Core web application that initially sends a page to the browser. Then, the browser updates part of the UI over a SignalR connection. The application becomes an automated AJAX client-server app on steroids. It is a mix of classic web apps and a SPA model, where the client loads the UI pieces to update from the server. So, less processing for the client and more processing for the server. There can also be a short delay (latency) since you must wait for a server response (*steps 2 to 4*); for example:

1. You click a button in the browser.
2. The action is dispatched to the server through SignalR.
3. The server processes the action.
4. The server returns the HTML diff to the browser.
5. The browser updates the UI using that diff.

To make that diff (*step 4*), the server keeps a graph of the application state. It constructs that graph using components, which translates into Document Object Model (DOM) nodes.

Blazor Server makes stateful applications that must keep track of the current state of all visitors. It may be hard to scale up or would cost a lot of money in cloud hosting. I don't want you to discard the option just yet; the model may fit your application's needs. Moreover, paying more for hosting can save development costs, depending on many factors.

> **Disclaimer**
>
> I have not deployed any applications using Blazor Server yet. It makes me think of an improved remake of Web Forms too much, which I dread getting into. That might just be me, but a "magic" SignalR connection, latency, and everything processed in a stateful server does not sound good to me. I might be wrong. I recommend you do your experiments and research and judge for yourself. I may even change my mind in the future; the technology is still young.

To create a Blazor Server project, you can run the `dotnet new blazorserver` command. That's it for Blazor Server.

Next, we will look into Blazor WebAssembly, which is way more promising (once again, my opinion).

Overview of Blazor WebAssembly

Before getting into **Blazor WebAssembly**, let's look at **WebAssembly** itself. WebAssembly (Wasm) allows browsers to run code that is not JavaScript (such as C# and C++). Wasm is an open standard, so it is not a Microsoft-only thing. Wasm runs in a sandboxed environment close to native speed (that's the goal) on the client machine, enforcing browser security policies. Wasm binaries can interact with JavaScript.

As you may have "foreseen" from that last paragraph, Blazor WebAssembly is all about running .NET in the browser! And the coolest part is that it follows standards. It's not like running VBScript in Internet Explorer (oh, I don't miss that time). I think Microsoft's new vision to embrace open standards, open source, and the rest of the world will be very beneficial for us developers in the long run.

But how does that work? Like Blazor Server and other SPAs out there, we compose the application using **components**. A component is a piece of UI that can be as small as a button or as big as a page. Then, when a client requests our application, the following happens:

1. The server sends a more or less empty shell (HTML).

2. The browser downloads external resources (JS, CSS, and images).

3. The browser displays the application.

It is the same experience as any other web page so far. The difference is when a user carries out an action, such as clicking a button, the action is executed by the client. Of course, the client can call a remote resource, as you would using JavaScript in React, Angular, or Vue. However, the important part here is that you don't have to. You can control your user interface on the client using C# and .NET.

A significant advantage of Blazor Wasm is hosting: the compiled Blazor Wasm artifacts are only **static resources**, so you can host your web application in the cloud almost for free (provisioning an Azure Blob storage and a Content Delivery Network (CDN), for example).

That leads to another advantage: scaling. Since each client runs the frontend, you don't need to scale that part—only the delivery of static assets.

On the other hand, you can also use a server-side ASP.NET application to prerender your Blazor Wasm app if you prefer. That leads to a faster initial load time for the clients at an increased hosting cost.

Nevertheless, there is one significant disadvantage: it runs on .NET. But why would I say that? That's blasphemy, right? Well, the browser must download the Wasm version of the .NET runtime, which is massive. Fortunately, the people at Microsoft worked on a way to trim unused parts, so browsers only download the required bits. Blazor also supports lazy-loading Wasm assemblies, so a client doesn't need to download everything at once. That said, all in all, the minimum download size is still around 2 MB. With high-speed internet, 2 MB is small and fast to download, but it can take a bit longer for people living in a remote area. So, think about your audience before making a choice.

To create a Blazor Wasm project, you can run the `dotnet new blazorwasm` command.

Next, we'll explore Razor components and look at what Blazor has to offer.

Getting familiar with Razor components

Everything is a **Razor component** in Blazor Wasm, including the application itself, which is defined as a **root component**. In the `Program.cs` file, that root component is registered as follows:

```
builder.RootComponents.Add<App>("#app");
```

The `App` type is from the `App.razor` component (we cover how components work later), and the string `"#app"` is a CSS selector. The `wwwroot/index.html` file contains a `<div id="app">Loading...</div>` element that is replaced by the Blazor `App` component once the application is initialized. `#app` is the CSS selector identifying an element that has an `id="app"` attribute. The `wwwroot/index.html` static file is the default page served to clients; it is your Blazor app's starting point. It contains the basic HTML structure of the page, including scripts and CSS. And that's how a Blazor application is loaded.

The `App.razor` file defines a `Router` component that routes the requests to the right page. When the page exists, the `Router` component renders the `Found` child component. It displays the `NotFound` child component when the page does not exist. Here is the default content of the `App.razor` file:

```
<Router AppAssembly="@typeof(Program).Assembly">
    <Found Context="routeData">
        <RouteView RouteData="@routeData" DefaultLayout="@typeof(MainLayout)" />
    </Found>
    <NotFound>
        <LayoutView Layout="@typeof(MainLayout)">
            <p>Sorry, there's nothing at this address.</p>
        </LayoutView>
    </NotFound>
</Router>
```

Pages are **Razor components**, with a `@page "/some-uri"` directive at the top, similar to Razor Pages. You can use most, if not all, of the same things as you can with Razor Pages to compose those routes.

A **Razor component** is a C# class that implements the `IComponent` interface. You can also inherit from `ComponentBase`, which implements the following interfaces for you: `IComponent`, `IHandleEvent`, and `IHandleAfterRender`. All of these live in the `Microsoft.AspNetCore.Components` namespace.

Next, we'll take a look at how to create Razor components.

Creating Razor components

You can create your components anywhere in your project, unlike Razor Pages and view components. I like to create my pages under the `Pages` directory, so it is easier to find pages. Then you can create the non-page components wherever you see fit.

There are three ways to create a component:

- Using only C#.
- Using only Razor.
- Using a mix of C# (code-behind) and Razor.

You don't have to pick only one way for the whole application; you can choose on a per-component basis. All three approaches end up compiled into a single C# class anyway. Let's take a look at those three ways of organizing components.

C#-only

C#-only components are as simple as creating a class. In the following example, we inherit from `ComponentBase`, but we could implement only the interfaces we need.

Here is our first component:

CSharpOnlyComponent.cs

```csharp
namespace WASM
{
    public class CSharpOnlyComponent : ComponentBase
    {
        [Parameter]
        public string Text { get; set; }
```

The `Parameter` attribute allows setting the value of the `Text` property when consuming the component. Officially, it becomes a **component parameter**. We'll see this in action once we are done with this class.

The `BuildRenderTree` method, next, is responsible for rendering our component:

```csharp
        protected override void
BuildRenderTree(RenderTreeBuilder builder)
```

```
        {
            builder.OpenElement(0, "h1");
            builder.AddAttribute(1, "class", "hello-world");
            builder.AddContent(2, Text);
            builder.CloseElement();
        }
    }
}
```

By overriding this method, we control the render tree. Those changes are eventually translated into DOM changes. Here, we are creating an H1 element with a `hello-world` class. In it is a text node that contains the value of the `Text` property.

> **Sequence numbers**
>
> The sequence numbers (0, 1, and 2 in the `BuildRenderTree` method) are used internally to generate the diff tree that .NET uses to update the DOM. It is recommended to write those manually to avoid performance degradation in more complex code such as conditional logic blocks. See the *ASP.NET Core Blazor advanced scenarios* link in the *Further reading* section for more info.

Now, in the `Pages/Index.razor` page, we can use that component like this:

Pages/Index.razor

```
@page "/"
<CSharpOnlyComponent Text="Hello World from C#" />
```

The name of the class becomes the name of its tag. That's automatic; we have nothing to do to make it happen. We can set the value of the properties identified with the `Parameter` attribute as HTML attributes. In this case, we set the value of the `Text` property to `Hello World from C#`. We could mark more than one property with that attribute and use them as we would any normal HTML attribute.

When rendering the page, our component is rendered to the following HTML:

```
<h1 class="hello-world">Hello World from C#</h1>
```

With those few lines of code, we created our first Razor component. Next, we will create a similar component using the Razor-only syntax.

Razor-only

Razor-only components are created in `.razor` files. They are compiled into a C# class. The default namespace of that class depends on the directory structure where it is created. For example, a component created in the `./Dir/Dir2/MyComponent.razor` file generates the `MyComponent` class in the `[Root Namespace].Dir.Dir2` namespace. Let's look at some code:

RazorOnlyComponent.razor

```razor
<h2 class="hello-world">@Text</h2>
@code{
    [Parameter]
    public string Text { get; set; }
}
```

If you like Razor, you probably prefer this one already. That listing is straightforward and allows us to code the same component as the previous one, but leaner. In the `@code{ }` block, we can add properties, fields, methods, and pretty much anything we would in a normal class, including other classes. We can also override `ComponentBase` methods there if we need to. We can use the component the same way we used the other; the same goes for parameters.

Next is the page consuming the `RazorOnlyComponent`:

Pages/Index.razor

```razor
@page "/"
<CSharpOnlyComponent Text="Hello World from C#" />
<RazorOnlyComponent Text="Hello World from Razor" />
```

The rendering is also very similar, but we went for an H2 instead of an H1:

```html
<h2 class="hello-world">Hello World from Razor</h2>
```

And with those few lines of code, we created our second component. Next, we'll create a hybrid of the two styles.

Code-behind

This third model can separate the C# code (known as code-behind) from the Razor code. This hybrid counterpart leverages **partial classes** to achieve the same as the others and generate a C# class.

For this, we need two files:

- `[component name].razor`
- `[component name].razor.cs`

Let's remake our previous component for the third time, but rendering an H3 this time. Let's begin with the Razor code:

CodeBehindComponent.razor

```
<h3 class="hello-world">@Text</h3>
```

This code could barely be leaner; we have an H3 tag with the `Text` property as its content. The `.razor` file in this model replaces the `BuildRenderTree` method. The compiler translates the Razor code into C#, generating the `BuildRenderTree` method's content for us.

The `Text` parameter is defined in the following code-behind file:

CodeBehindComponent.razor.cs

```
public partial class CodeBehindComponent
{
    [Parameter]
    public string Text { get; set; }
}
```

It's the same code as the previous two samples – we just divided it into two files. The key is the `partial class`. It allows compiling a single `class` from multiple files. In this case, there is our `partial class` and the autogenerated one, from the `CodeBehindComponent.razor` file. We can use the `CodeBehindComponent` in the same way as the other two.

Next is the page that consumes the `CodeBehindComponent`:

Pages/Index.razor

```
@page "/"
<CSharpOnlyComponent Text="Hello World from C#" />
<RazorOnlyComponent Text="Hello World from Razor" />
<CodeBehindComponent Text="Hello World from Code-Behind" />
```

That renders the same way as the others but as an H3 with different content:

```
<h3 class="hello-world">Hello World from Code-Behind</h3>
```

Using code-behind can be very useful for two things:

- Keeping your `.razor` file clean of C# code.
- Getting better tooling support.

The tooling for `.razor` files tends to explode on us from time to time, includes weird bugs, or provides half-support. It seems that handling HTML, C#, and Razor in a single file is not as easy as it sounds. On a more positive note, it is getting better, so I can only see more stable tooling in the future. I could see myself write all the code of a component in a single `.razor` file if the tooling was on par with the C# tooling (in many scenarios). That would lead to less files and a closer proximity of all parts of the component (leading to better maintainability).

Next, we'll take a look at skinning our components with CSS, but with a twist…

CSS isolation

Like other SPAs, Blazor allows us to create CSS styles scoped to a component. That means that we don't have to worry about naming conflicts.

Unfortunately, this does not seem to work with C#-only components, so we will skin only two of the three components. Each of them has the same CSS class (`hello-world`). We are about to change their text's color by defining only simple `.hello-world` CSS selectors, for both.

To achieve that, we must create a `.razor.css` file named after our component. The following two files represent one CSS file for the RazorOnlyComponent and one for the CodeBehindComponent that we just built:

RazorOnlyComponent.razor.css

```
.hello-world {
    color: red;
}
```

CodeBehindComponent.razor.css

```
.hello-world {
    color: aqua;
}
```

As you can see from those two files, they define the same `.hello-world` selector, with a different color.

In the `wwwroot/index.html` file, the `dotnet new blazorwasm` template added the following line:

```
<link href="[name of the project].styles.css" rel="stylesheet" />
```

That line links the bundled component-specific styles into the page. Yes, you did read **bundled**. The Blazor CSS isolation feature also bundles all of those styles into a single `.css` file, so the browser only loads one file.

If we load the page, we see this (without the layout):

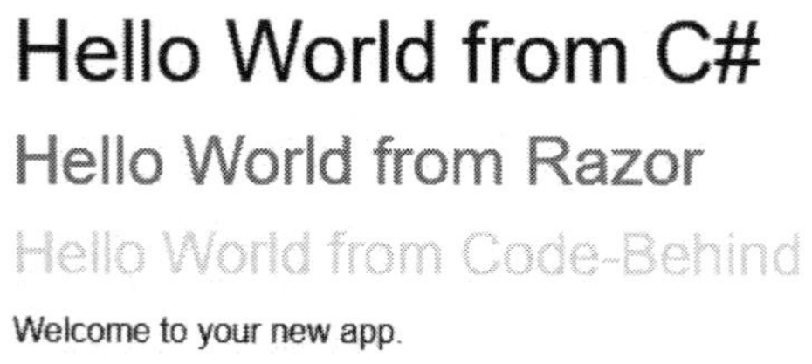

Hello World from C#

Hello World from Razor

Hello World from Code-Behind

Welcome to your new app.

Figure 18.1 – Output after loading the page

So it worked! But how? Blazor autogenerated random attributes on each HTML element and used those in the generated CSS. Let's first look at the HTML output:

```
<h1 class="hello-world">Hello World from C#</h1>
<h2 class="hello-world" b-cjkj1dpci4>Hello World from Razor</h2>
<h3 class="hello-world" b-0gygcymdih>Hello World from Code-Behind</h3>
```

Those two highlighted attributes are the "magic" links. Now, with the following CSS code, you should understand their usage and why they have been generated:

```
/* /CodeBehindComponent.razor.rz.scp.css */
.hello-world[b-0gygcymdih] {
    color: aqua;
}
/* /RazorOnlyComponent.razor.rz.scp.css */
.hello-world[b-cjkj1dpci4] {
    color: red;
}
```

If you are not too familiar with CSS, [. . .] is an **attribute selector**. It allows you to do all kinds of things, including selecting an element that has the specified attribute (as in this case). That's what we need here. The first selector means that all elements with the hello-world class and an attribute named b-0gygcymdih should have their color updated to aqua. The second selector is the same, but for elements with an attribute named b-cjkj1dpci4 instead.

With that pattern in place, we can define component-scoped styles with a high level of confidence that they won't conflict with other components' styles.

Next, let's explore the life cycle of those components.

Component life cycle

The components, including the root components, must be rendered as DOM elements for the browser to display them. The same goes for any changes that subsequently occur. Two distinct phases compose the components' life cycle:

1. Initial rendering, when a component is rendered for the first time.
2. Re-rendering, when a component needs to be rendered because it changed.

During the first rendering, if we get rid of the duplicated sync/async methods, the life cycle of a Razor component looks like this:

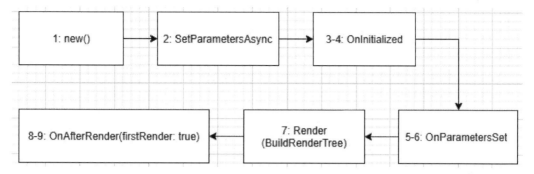

Figure 18.2 – Lifecycle of a Razor component

1. An instance of the component is created.

2. The SetParametersAsync method is called.

3. The OnInitialized method is called.

4. The OnInitializedAsync method is called.

5. The OnParametersSet method is called.

6. The OnParametersSetAsync method is called.

7. The BuildRenderTree method is called (the component is rendered).

8. The OnAfterRender(firstRender: true) method is called.

9. The OnAfterRenderAsync(firstRender: true) method is called.

During re-rendering, if we get rid of the duplicated sync/async methods, the life cycle of a Razor component is leaner and looks like this:

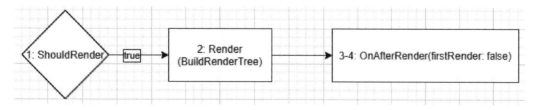

Figure 18.3 – Re-rendered version of a Razor component life cycle

1. The ShouldRender method is called. If it returns false, the process stops here. If it is true, the cycle continues.

2. The `BuildRenderTree` method is called (the component is re-rendered).

3. The `OnAfterRender(firstRender: false)` method is called.

4. The `OnAfterRenderAsync(firstRender: false)` method is called.

> **Note**
>
> If you worked with Web Forms before and dreaded Blazor life cycle's complexity, don't worry. It is leaner and doesn't contain any postback. They are two different technologies. Microsoft tries to push Blazor as the next logical step to migrate from Web Forms (which makes sense based on the actual state of .NET), but the only significant similarity that I see is the component-model of Blazor, which is close to the control-model of Web Forms. So if you moved away from Web Forms, don't be afraid to look into Blazor; they are not the same – Blazor > Web Forms.

I created a component named `LifeCycleObserver` in the WASM project. That component outputs its life cycle information to the console. That leads me to the following trick: `Console.WriteLine` writes in the browser console, like this:

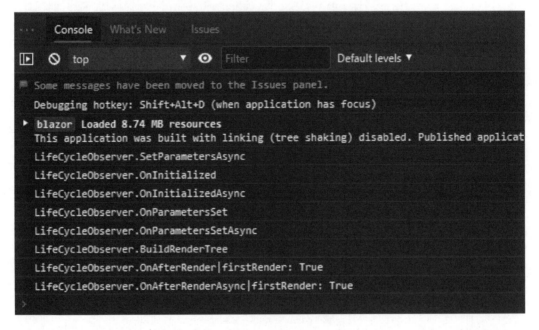

Figure 18.4 – The browser debug console displaying the life cycle of the LifeCycleObserver component

Next, we'll take a look at event handling and how to interact with our components.

Event handling

So far, we've displayed the same component built using three different techniques. Now it is time to interact with a component and see how it works. There are multiple events in HTML that can be handled using JavaScript. In Blazor, we can handle most of them using C# instead.

I slightly modified the `FetchData.razor` page component that comes with the generated project to show you two different event handler patterns:

- Without passing an argument.

- With an argument.

Both ways call `async` methods, but the same can be done with synchronous methods as well. Let's now explore that code. I'll skip some irrelevant markup, such as `H1` and `P` tags, to focus only on the real code, that starts with this:

```
@page "/fetchdata"
@inject HttpClient Http
```

At the top of the file, I left the injection of the `HttpClient` and the `@page` directive. These allow us to reach the page when navigating to the `/fetchdata` URL and to query resources over HTTP, respectively. The `HttpClient` is configured in the `Program.cs` file (the composition root). Then, I added a few buttons to interact with. Here is the first:

```
<button class="btn btn-primary mb-4"
@onclick="RefreshAsync">Refresh</button>
```

All buttons of this code example have an `@onclick` attribute. That attribute is used to react to click events, like the HTML `onclick` attribute and the JavaScript `"click"` `EventListener`. That button delegates the click event to the `RefreshAsync` method:

```
private Task RefreshAsync() => LoadWeatherAsync();
private async Task LoadWeatherAsync(int? index = null)
{
    var uri = index == null ? _uriList.Next() : _uriList[index.Value];
    forecasts = await Http.GetFromJsonAsync<WeatherForecast[]>(uri);
}
```

The refresh method then calls the `LoadWeatherAsync(index: null)` method, which in turn queries a resource returning an array of `WeatherForecast`. The forecasts are three static JSON files located in the `wwwroot/sample-data` directory. `_uriList` is an instance of the `Cycle` class that cycles through a series of strings. Its code is simple but helps simplify the rest of the page in an OOP manner:

```
private class Cycle
{
    private int _currentIndex = -1;
    private string[] _uris;
    public Cycle(params string[] uris) => _uris = uris;
    public string Next() => _uris[++_currentIndex % _uris.
Length];
}
```

When the forecasts change (when we click on the **Refresh** button), the component is reloaded automatically, leading to an updated weather forecast table.

We can also access the event argument like we would in JavaScript. In case of a click, we have access to the `MouseEventArgs` instance associated with the event. Here is a quick sample displaying possible usage:

```
<button class="btn btn-primary mb-4"
@onclick="DisplayXY">Display (X, Y)</button>
public void DisplayXY(MouseEventArgs e)
{
    Console.WriteLine($"DOM(x, y): ({e.ClientX}, {e.ClientY})
| Button(x, y): ({e.OffsetX}, {e.OffsetY}) | Screen(x, y): ({e.
ScreenX}, {e.ScreenY})");
}
```

In that code, the `@onclick` attribute is used the same way as before, but the `DisplayXY` method expects a `MouseEventArgs` as a parameter. The `MouseEventArgs` argument is provided automatically by Blazor. Then, the method will output the mouse position in the browser's DevTools Console (*F12* on Chromium-based browsers), which looks like this:

```
DOM(x, y): (921, 175) | Button(x, y): (119, 4) | Screen(x, y):
(-999, 246)
DOM(x, y): (809, 197) | Button(x, y): (7, 26) | Screen(x, y):
(-1111, 268)
```

To generate those coordinates, I clicked the top-right corner of the button, then the bottom-left corner. As we can deduce from the negative screen-x position, my browser was on my left monitor.

Another possibility is to use lambda expressions as inline event handlers. Those lambda expressions can also call a method. Here is an example:

```
<button class="btn btn-primary mb-4" @onclick="@(e => Console.
WriteLine($"DOM(x, y): ({e.ClientX}, {e.ClientY})"))">Lamdba
(X, Y)</button>
```

That button output only the client (x, y) coordinate to improve readability.

That's it for our overview of event handling. Next, we'll look into another way to manage the component's state other than each component doing its own thing.

The Model-View-Update pattern

Unless you've never heard of React, you've most likely heard of Redux. Redux is a library that follows the **Model-View-Update** (**MVU**) pattern. MVU comes from the Elm Architecture. If you don't know Elm, here is a quote from their documentation:

Elm is a functional language that compiles to JavaScript.

Next, let's see what the goal behind MVU is. No matter what we call it, it is the same pattern.

Goal

The goal of MVU is to simplify the **state management** of applications. If you built a stateful UI in the past, you probably know it can become hard to manage an application's state. MVU takes the two-way binding complexity out of the equation and replaces it with a linear one-way flow. It also takes mutations out of the picture by replacing them with immutable states, where state updates are moved to pure functions.

Design

The MVU pattern is a **unidirectional data flow** that routes an **action** to an **update function**. An update function must be **pure**. A pure function is **deterministic** and has **no side effects**. A model is a **state**. A state is **immutable**. A state must have an **initial state**. A **view** is the code that knows how to display a state.

Depending on the technology, there are many synonyms. Let's get into more details. It may sound confusing at first, but don't worry, it's not that bad.

An **action** is called a **command** or a **request** in MediatR. It is called an **action** in Redux, and a **message** in Elm. I will use **action**. An **action** is the equivalent of the commands that we used in our CQRS examples. There is no notion of query in MVU because a view always renders the current state.

Terminology	MediatR	Redux	Elm
Action	Command	Action	Message
	Request		

An **update function** is called a **handler** in MediatR. It is called a **reducer** in Redux and an **update** in Elm. I will use **reducer**. The **reducer** is a pure function that always returns the same output for any given input (it's deterministic). The pure function must have no impact on external actors (having no side effects). So, no mutation of external variables, no mutation of the input value: no side effect. One significant advantage of a pure function is testing. It is easy to assert the value of their output based on a given input since they are deterministic.

Terminology	MediatR	Redux	Elm
Reducer	Handler	Reducer	Update

A **view** is a **component** in React and Blazor and is a **view function** in Elm. I will use mostly **view** because **component** can be ambiguous and easily confused with Razor components, or view components, or the plain notion of a UI component.

Terminology	React (Redux)	Blazor	Elm
View	Component	Component	View function

A model or **state** cannot be altered and must be immutable. Every time a state changes, an altered copy of the state is created. The current state then becomes that copy. Elm calls the **state** a **model**; it is a **state** in Redux. We are using the term **state** as I found it defines the intent better.

Terminology	Redux	Elm
State	State	Model

Here is a diagram that represents this **unidirectional data flow:**

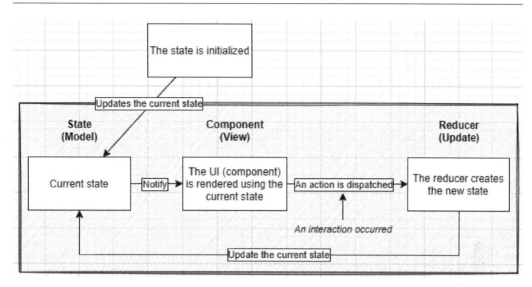

Figure 18.5 – Unidirectional data flow chart

1. When the application starts, the state is initialized. That initial state becomes the current state.

2. The current state change triggers the UI to render.

3. When an interaction occurs, such as the user clicking a button, then an **action** is dispatched to a **reducer**.

4. The reducer *creates an instance* of the updated state.

5. That new state *replaces* the current state.

6. Go back to *step 2* of the current list when an event occurs.

It may be hard to wrap your head around this at first. Like all new things, we must take the time to create new paths in our brains to get something fully. Don't worry; we are about to see that in action.

All in all, it is straightforward; the flow goes only one way. Whenever the state changes, the component is re-rendered. Since states are immutable, we cannot alter them directly, so we must pass by reducers.

Project: Counter

For this project, we will use an open source library that I created in 2020 while experimenting with C# 9 record classes. Since a record is immutable, it is a perfect candidate to represent an MVU state. Moreover, it allows streamlining our example in a limited amount of space.

> **Note**
> There are multiple similar libraries, but they were all created before C# 9, so there's no direct record support.

Context: We are building a counter page to increment and decrement a value.

I know it does not sound very exciting, but since many MVU libraries showcase one as well as Blazor itself, I believe this will be a good way to compare it with the others.

First, we need to install the library by loading the `StateR.Blazor` NuGet package. In this case, we are using a prerelease version.

> **Redux DevTools**
> I also installed the `StateR.Blazor.Experiments` NuGet package in the project. That project has a few experimental features, including a Redux DevTools connector. Redux DevTools is a browser extension that allows tracking states and actions. It also allows time-traveling between states.

Next, let's code the `Counter` feature:

Features/Counter.cs

```csharp
using StateR;
using StateR.Reducers;
namespace WASM.Features
{
    public class Counter
    {
        public record State(int Count) : StateBase;
```

The `State` record is our **state**. It exposes one `init-only` property. It inherits from `StateBase`, which is an empty record. `StateBase` serves as a generic constraint until C# supports that. States in StateR must be records; it is mandatory.

```csharp
        public class InitialState : IInitialState<State>
        {
            public State Value => new(0);
        }
```

The `InitialState` class represents the **initial state** of the `State` record. It tells StateR that by implementing the `IInitialState<State>` interface.

```
public record Increment : IAction;
public record Decrement : IAction;
```

Here, we declare two **actions**. They are records, but they could have been classes instead. Being a record is not a requirement but a shortcut to writing less code. In StateR, an action must implement the `IAction` interface.

```
public class Reducers : IReducer<Increment, State>,
    IReducer<Decrement, State>
```

The `Reducers` class implements the **pure functions** that handle the **actions**. In StateR, a reducer must implement the `IReducer<TAction, TState>` interface. `TAction` must be an `IAction`, and `TState` must be a `StateBase`. The interface defines only a `Reduce` method that input a `TAction` and `TState` and that output the updated `TState`:

```
{
    public State Reduce(Increment action, State state)
        => state with { Count = state.Count + 1 };
```

The `Increment` **reducer** returns a copy of `State` with its `Count` incremented by 1.

```
    public State Reduce(Decrement action, State state)
        => state with { Count = state.Count - 1 };
    }
}
}
```

Finally, the `Decrement` **reducer** returns a copy of `State` with its `Count` decremented by 1.

I find that using a **with expression** like that makes very clean code, especially if the `State` record has more than one property. Moreover, the record classes enforce the immutability of the states, which is in line with the MVU pattern.

That is all that we need to cover the model (state) and the update (actions/reducers). Now to the view (component) portion. The view is the following Razor component:

Features/CounterView.razor

```
@page "/mvu-counter"
@inherits StatorComponent
@inject IState<Counter.State> State


<h1>MVU Counter</h1>
<p>Current count: @State.Current.Count</p>
<button class="btn btn-primary" @onclick="() =>
DispatchAsync(new Counter.Increment())">+</button>
<button class="btn btn-primary" @onclick="() =>
DispatchAsync(new Counter.Decrement())">-</button>
```

There are only a few lines but quite a lot of things to discuss here. First, the Razor component is accessible at the /mvu-counter URL.

Then, it inherits from StatorComponent. This is not required, but it is convenient. The StatorComponent class implements a few things for us, including managing the component's re-rendering when an IState<TState> property changes.

That leads to the next line, the injection of an IState<Counter.State> interface implementation accessible through the State property. That interface wraps the TState instance and gives access to the current state through its Current property. The @inject directive enables **property injection** in Razor components.

Next, we display the page. @State.Current.Count represents the current count. Following that are two buttons. Both have an @onclick attribute that calls a lambda expression. The DispatchAsync method comes from StatorComponent. As its name implies, it **dispatches actions** through the StateR pipeline. It is similar to the MediatR Send and Publish methods.

Each button dispatches a different action; one is Counter.Increment and the other is Counter.Decrement. StateR knows the reducers and sends the action to the appropriate reducers.

That code creates a centralized state and uses the MVU pattern to manage it. If we need Counter.State elsewhere, we only need to inject it, as we did here, and the same state would be shared between multiple components or classes. In this example, we injected the state in a Razor component, but we could also use the same pattern in any code.

One more thing: we need to initialize StateR. To do that, in the `Program.cs` file, we need to register it like this:

```
using StateR;
using StateR.Blazor.ReduxDevTools; // Optional
// ...
builder.Services
    .AddStateR(typeof(Program).Assembly)
    .AddReduxDevTools() // Optional
    .Apply()
;
```

The `builder.Services` property is an `IServiceCollection`. The `AddStateR` method creates an `IStatorBuilder` and registers StateR's static dependencies.

Then the optional `AddReduxDevTools` method call links StateR to the *Redux DevTools* browser plugin that I mentioned previously. That helps to debug applications from the browser. Other optional mechanisms can be added here. A developer could also code their own extensions to add missing or project-specific features. StateR is DI-based.

Finally, the `Apply` method initializes StateR by scanning the specified assemblies for every type that it can handle. In this case, we are scanning only the Wasm application assembly (highlighted). The initialization is a two-stage process, completed with the `Apply` method call.

With that in place, we can run the application and play with our counter. I hope that you liked this little piece of Redux/MVU with StateR. If you did, feel free to use it. If you find missing features, bugs, performance issues, or want to share your ideas, please open an issue on GitHub (`https://net5.link/Z7Ej`).

Conclusion

The MVU pattern uses a **model** to represent the current **state** of the application. The **view** renders that **model**. To **update** the **model**, an **action** is dispatched to a **pure function** (a **reducer**) that returns the new **state**. That change triggers the **view** to re-render.

The **unidirectional flow** of MVU reduces state management's complexity.

Now let's see how the MVU pattern can help us follow the **SOLID** principles:

- **S**: Each part of the pattern (states, views, and reducers) has its own responsibility.

- **O**: We can add new elements without impact on existing ones. For example, adding a new action does not impact existing reducers.

- **L**: N/A

- **I**: By segregating responsibilities, each part of the pattern implicitly has a smaller surface (interface).

- **D**: This depends on how you implement it. Based on what we did using StateR, we depended only on interfaces and DTOs (state and actions).

Next, we'll take a quick peek at other Blazor information to give you an idea of what is available if you want to get started.

A medley of Blazor features

Your Blazor journey has just begun, and there are so many more features to Blazor than what we covered. Here are a few more possibilities to give you a glimpse of the options.

You can integrate Razor components with MVC and Razor Pages using the `Component Tag Helper`. When doing so, you can also prerender your applications (the `App` component) by setting the `render-mode` attribute to `Static`, leading to a faster initial render time. Prerendering can also be used to improve search engine optimization (SEO). The "drawback" is the need for an ASP.NET Core server to execute the prerendering logic.

Another lovely thing about full-stack C# is sharing code between the client and the server. Say we have a web API and a Blazor Wasm application; we could create a third project, a class library, and share the DTOs (API contracts) between the two.

In our component, we can also allow arbitrary HTML between the opening and closing tags by adding a `RenderFragment` parameter named `ChildContent` to that component. We can also catch arbitrary parameters and splat them on an HTML element of the component. Here is an example combining those two features:

Card.razor

```
<div class="@($"card {Class}")" @attributes="Attributes">
    <div class="card-body">
        @ChildContent
    </div>
```

```
</div>
@code{
    [Parameter]
    public RenderFragment ChildContent { get; set; }

    [Parameter(CaptureUnmatchedValues = true)]
    public Dictionary<string, object> Attributes { get; set; }

    [Parameter]
    public string Class { get; set; }
}
```

The Card component renders a Bootstrap card and allows consumers to set any attributes they want on it. The content between the `<Card>` and `</Card>` tags can be anything. That content is rendered inside the `div.card-body`. The highlighted lines represent that child content.

The Class parameter is a workaround to allow consumers to add CSS classes while enforcing the `card` class's presence. The Attributes parameter becomes a catch-all by setting the CaptureUnmatchedValues property of the Parameter attribute to true.

Next is an example that consumes the Card component:

Pages/Index.razor

```
<Card style="width: 25%;" class="mt-4">
    <h5 class="card-title">Card title</h5>
    <h6 class="card-subtitle mb-2 text-muted">Card subtitle</h6>
    <p class="card-text">Some quick example text to build on the card title and make up the bulk of the card's content.</p>
    <a href="#" class="card-link">Card link</a>
    <a href="#" class="card-link">Another link</a>
</Card>
```

We can see that the Card component (the highlighted lines) is filled with arbitrary HTML (from the official Bootstrap documentation). There are two attributes specified as well, a `style` and a `class`.

Here is the rendered result:

```
<div class="card mt-4" style="width: 25%;">
    <div class="card-body">
        <h5 class="card-title">Card title</h5>
        <h6 class="card-subtitle mb-2 text-muted">Card
subtitle</h6>
        <p class="card-text">Some quick example text to build
on the card title and make up the bulk of the card's content.</
p>
        <a href="#" class="card-link">Card link</a>
        <a href="#" class="card-link">Another link</a>
    </div>
</div>
```

The highlighted lines represent the Card component. Everything else is the ChildContent. We can also notice the attributes splatting added the style attribute. The Class attribute appended the mt-4 class to card. Here is what it looks like in a browser:

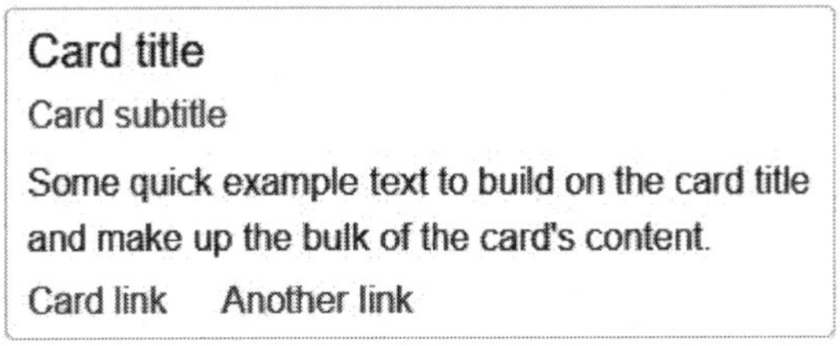

Card title

Card subtitle

Some quick example text to build on the card title and make up the bulk of the card's content.

Card link   Another link

Figure 18.6 – The Card component rendered in a browser

Another built-in component is the Virtualize component. It allows reducing the amount of rendered items to only those visible on the screen. You can also control the number of offscreen elements that are rendered to reduce the frequency at which elements are rendered while scrolling.

As we saw in the counter project, Blazor has full support for dependency injection. For me, that's a requirement. That's also why I learned Angular 2 when it came out and not React or Vue. Blazor's DI support is way better than all of the JavaScript IoC containers that I have seen so far, so this is a major benefit.

There are many other built-in features in Blazor, including an EditForm component, validation support, and a ValidationSummary component, as you'd expect in any MVC or Razor Pages application, but client-side.

As a quick tip, should you ever need to force the rendering of a component, you can call the `StateHasChanged` method from `ComponentBase`.

As mentioned earlier in this chapter, .NET code can interact with JavaScript and vice versa. To execute JavaScript code from C#, inject and use the `IJSRuntime` interface. To execute C# code from JavaScript, use the `DotNet.invokeMethod` or `DotNet.invokeMethodAsync` functions. The C# method must be `public static` and decorated with the `JSInvokable` attribute. There are multiple other ways C# and JavaScript can interact, including non-static methods. By supporting this, people can build wrappers around JavaScript libraries or use JavaScript libraries as is. It also means that we can implement features that Blazor does not support in JavaScript or even write browser-optimized code in JavaScript if Blazor is slower in one area or another.

You can even write 2D and 3D games using a JavaScript wrapper around a canvas (such as *BlazorCanvas*) or a full-fledged game engine such as *WaveEngine*.

The last bit of additional information that I can think of is an experimental project named *Blazor Mobile Bindings*. That project is a Microsoft experiment that allows Blazor to run in a phone app. It allows native performance by wrapping Xamarin Form Controls with Razor components. It also supports loading Blazor Wasm in a `WebView` control, allowing for better reusability between mobile and web apps, but at a performance cost.

I've left a long list of links in the *Further reading* section to complement this chapter's information.

Summary

Blazor is a great new piece of technology that could bring C# and .NET to a whole new level. In its present state, it is good enough to develop apps with. There are two main models; Server and WebAssembly.

Blazor Server links the client with the server over a SignalR connection allowing the server to push updates to the client whenever needed (such as when a user carries out an action). Blazor WebAssembly (Wasm) is a .NET SPA framework that compiles C# to WebAssembly. It allows .NET code to run in the browser. We can interact with JavaScript using `IJSRuntime` and vice versa.

Blazor is component-based, meaning that every piece of UI in Blazor is a component, including pages. We explored three ways to create components: C#-only, Razor-only, and a hybrid that combines C# and Razor in two different files. A component can also have its own isolated CSS without the need to worry about conflicts.

We explored the life cycle of a Razor component, which is very simple yet powerful. We also took a look at handling events and how to react to them.

We then dug into the MVU pattern, which is very well suited for stateful user interfaces like Blazor. We used an open source library and leveraged C# 9.0 record classes to implement a basic example.

Finally, we took a look at other possibilities that Blazor has to offer.

I will close this chapter with a personal opinion. I would like to see a Blazor-like model become the unified way to build user interfaces in .NET. I appreciate writing Razor way more than writing XAML, to name only one other way of writing UI code.

Questions

Let's take a look at a few practice questions:

1. Is it true that Blazor Wasm is compiled to JavaScript?
2. Out of the three methods explored to create a Razor component, which one is the best way to do so?
3. What are the three parts of the MVU pattern?
4. In the MVU pattern, is it true that it is recommended to use two-way binding?
5. Can Blazor interact with JavaScript?

Further reading

Here are a few links to build upon what we have learned in the chapter:

*   WebAssembly:

    a) WebAssembly.org: `https://net5.link/mRMf`

    b) Mozilla Developer Network (MDN): `https://net5.link/PDh5`
*   ASP.NET Core Blazor hosting models `https://net5.link/N8Do`
*   Component Tag Helper in ASP.NET Core `https://net5.link/mjqL`
*   Create and use ASP.NET Core Razor components `https://net5.link/iDVh`
*   How to deploy and host a Jekyll website in Azure Blob storage using a VSTS continuous deployment pipeline `https://net5.link/qCCZ`
*   ASP.NET Core Blazor WebAssembly performance best practices `https://net5.link/HrLJ`
*   ASP.NET Core Blazor advanced scenarios `https://net5.link/nBRc`

- ASP.NET Core Blazor component virtualization `https://net5.link/6DTq`

- Prerendering a Client-side Blazor Application (by Chris Sainty) `https://net5.link/Lwhj`

- Blazor Mobile Bindings:

  a) Documentation: `https://net5.link/yj6T`

  b) Source Code (GitHub): `https://net5.link/shFz`

- Call JavaScript functions from .NET methods in ASP.NET Core Blazor `https://net5.link/Wk9z`

- Call .NET methods from JavaScript functions in ASP.NET Core Blazor `https://net5.link/93CZ`

The last time I did 2D/3D development was back when XNA was a thing. I also used Ogre3D in C++ for a school project. That said, I talked about 2D and 3D games in the chapter, so here are a few resources that I found for those of you that are interested:

- Here are the resources that I found about using HTML5 Canvas in C#:

  a) David Guida (GitHub) `https://net5.link/3ksk`

  b) Stefan Lörwald (GitHub) `https://net5.link/zJep`

  c) Blazor Extensions (GitHub) `https://net5.link/XRAe`

- For games, WaveEngine supports 2D, 3D, VR, and AR. It is totally free and multiplatform:

  a) WaveEngine on GitHub: `https://net5.link/5qtW`

  b) Official website: `https://net5.link/fQZj`

An end is simply a new beginning

This may be the end of the book, but it is also the beginning of your journey into software architecture and design. No matter who you are, I hope you found this to be a refreshing view of design patterns and how to design SOLID web apps. Depending on your goal and current situation, you may want to explore one or more application-scale design patterns in more depth, start your next personal project, start a business, apply for a new job, or all of those at the same time. No matter your goal, keep in mind that designing software is technical but also art. There is rarely one right way of implementing a feature but multiple acceptable ways of doing so. Experience is your best friend, so keep programming, learn from your mistakes, and move forward. Remember that we are all born knowing next to nothing, so not knowing something is expected; we need to learn. Please ask questions to your teammates, learn from them, and share your knowledge with others.

Now that this book is complete, I'll get back to writing blog posts, so you can always learn new things there (`https://net5.link/blog`). Feel free to hit me up on social media, such as Twitter `@CarlHugoM` (`https://net5.link/twit`). I hope you found the book educative and approachable, and that you learned many things. I wish you success in your career.

Assessment Answers

The answers to the practice questions for each chapter:

Chapter 1

1. No.
2. Long methods are indicators that a method handles too many responsibilities and should be split.
3. Yes; by targeting .NET Standard, you can reach multiple runtime versions, including .NET Core and .NET Framework.
4. A code smell represents a potential design flaw that could benefit from being rewritten.

Chapter 2

1. Yes, it is true.
2. To test a unit of code, such as the logical code path of a method.
3. 3. As small as possible. A unit test aims at testing the smallest possible unit of code in isolation.
4. Integration tests are usually used for that kind of task.
5. No, there are multiple ways of writing code, TDD being only one of them.

Chapter 3

1. Five: S.O.L.I.D. (SRP, OCP, LSP, ISP, and DIP).
2. No, the idea is the opposite: create smaller components.
3. No, you want to encapsulate similar logic, not similar-looking blocks of code.

4. Yes, it is easier to reuse smaller pieces than adapt enormous ones.

5. It is the SRP, but the separation of concern principle states that too.

Chapter 4

1. The **controller** manipulates the **model** and chooses what **view** to render.

2. The @model directive.

3. A **view model** should have a one-to-one relationship with a **view**.

4. Yes.

5. Yes.

Chapter 5

1. 201 CREATED.

2. 2. The [FromBody] attribute.

3. The GET method.

4. Yes, those are precisely the objectives of a DTO: decoupling the *ins* and *outs* from the **model**.

5. Yes.

Chapter 6

1. It helps manage behaviors at runtime, such as changing an algorithm in the middle of a program.

2. The creational patterns are responsible for creating objects.

3. v1 and v2 are two different instances. The code next to the arrow operator is executed every time you call the getter of the property.

4. Yes, it is true. That's the primary goal of the pattern, as we demonstrated in the MiddleEndVehicleFactor code sample.

5. The Singleton pattern violates the SOLID principles and encourages the use of global (static) variables.

Chapter 7

1. Transient, Scoped, Singleton.

2. The composition root holds the code that describes how to compose the program–all the registrations and bindings between abstractions and implementations.

3. Yes, it is true. Volatile dependencies should be injected instead of instantiated.

4. The Strategy pattern.

5. The Service Locator pattern is all three. It is a design pattern used by DI libraries, internally, but becomes a code smell in application code. If misused, it is an anti-pattern that brings the same drawbacks as using the new keyword directly.

Chapter 8

1. Singleton.

2. Scoped.

3. Transient.

4. Yes, you can configure as many providers as you want. One could be for the console and another could be used to append entries to a file.

5. No, you should not log trace-level entries in production. You should only log debug-level entries when debugging a problem.

Chapter 9

1. Yes, we can decorate decorators by depending only on interfaces because they are just another implementation of the interface, nothing more.

2. The Composite pattern adds simplicity when it comes to managing complexity.

3. Yes, we could use an adapter for this.

4. We usually use façades to simplify the use of one or more subsystems, creating a wall in front of them.

5. The Adapter and Façade design patterns are almost the same but are applied to different scenarios. The Adapter pattern adapts an API to another API, while the Façade pattern exposes a unified or simplified API, hiding one or more complex subsystems.

Chapter 10

1. False; you can create as many `abstract` (required) or `virtual` (optional) extension points as long as the class is cohesive with a single responsibility.

2. Yes, there is no reason not to.

3. No, there is no greater limit than with any other code.

4. Yes, you can have one handler per message or multiple handlers per message. It is up to you and your requirements.

5. It helps divide responsibilities between classes.

Chapter 11

1. Yes. Actually, the `HttpResponseMessage` instance that is returned by the `HttpMessageInvoker`.Send method is an operation result. `HttpClient` inherits from `HttpMessageInvoker` and exposes other different methods that also return an instance of `HttpResponseMessage`.

2. We implemented two **static factory methods**.

3. Yes, returning an object is faster than throwing an exception.

Chapter 12

1. No, you can have as many layers as you need, and you can name and organize them as you want.

2. No, both have their place, their pros, and their cons.

3. Yes. A `DbContext` is an implementation of the Unit of Work pattern. `DbSet<T>` is an implementation of the Repository pattern.

4. No, you can query any system, any way you want. For example, you could use ADO.NET to query a relational database, manually create the objects using a `DataReader`, track changes using a `DataSet`, or do anything else that fits your needs. Nonetheless, ORMs can be very convenient.

5. Yes. A layer can never access outward layers, only inward ones.

Chapter 13

1. Yes, it can, but not necessarily. Moving dependencies around does not fix design flaws; it just moves those flaws elsewhere.

2. Yes, mappers should help us follow the SRP.

3. No, it may not be suitable for every scenario. For example, when the mapping logic becomes complex, think about not using AutoMapper.

4. Yes, use profiles to organize your mapping rules cohesively.

5. Four or more. Once again, this is just a guideline; injecting four services into a class could be acceptable.

Chapter 14

1. Yes, you can. That's the goal of the Mediator pattern: to mediate communication between colleagues.

2. In the original sense of CQRS: no, a command can't return a value. The idea is that a query reads data while commands mutate data. In a looser sense of CQRS, yes, a command could return a value. For example, nothing stops a create command from returning the created entity partially or totally. You can always trade a bit of modularity for a bit of performance.

3. MediatR is a free, open source project licensed under Apache License 2.0.

4. Yes, you should; using Marker Interfaces to add metadata is generally wrong. Nevertheless, you should analyze each use case individually, taking the pros and cons into consideration before jumping to a conclusion.

Chapter 15

1. Any pattern and technique that you know that can help you implement your solution. That's the beauty of it: you are not limited; only by yourself.

2. No, you can pick the best tool for the job inside each vertical slice; you don't even need layers.

3. The application will most likely become a Big Ball of Mud and be very hard to maintain, which is not good for your stress level.

4. We can create MVC filters in any ASP.NET MVC application. We can augment the MediatR pipeline using behavior in any application that uses MediatR. We can also implement ASP.NET middlewares in non-MVC applications or to execute code before getting into the MVC pipeline.

5. Cohesion means elements that should work together as a united whole.

6. Tight coupling describes elements that cannot change independently; that directly depend on one another.

Chapter 16

1. The message queue gets a message and has a single subscriber dequeue it. If nothing dequeues a message, it stays in the queue indefinitely (FIFO model). The pub-sub model gets a message and sends it to zero or more subscribers.

2. Event sourcing is the process of chronologically accumulating events that happened in a system. It allows you to recreate the state of the application by replaying those events.

3. Yes, you can mix Gateway patterns (or sub-patterns).

4. No, you can deploy micro-applications (microservices) on-premises if you want to. Moreover, in *Chapter 14, Mediator and CQRS Design Patterns*, we saw that we could use CQRS even inside a single application.

5. No, you can deploy microservices without containers if you want to. In any case, containers will most likely save you many headaches (and create new ones).

Chapter 17

1. Razor Pages is best at creating web page-oriented applications.

2. Yes, we have access to mostly the same things as with MVC.

3. Technically, yes, you could, but you should use partial views only to render part of the UI and UI logic, not domain logic and database queries.

4. Yes, you can. You can also create new tags.

5. Yes, you can. View components are like component-based, single-action controllers rendering one or more views.

6. Yes, it compiles. It uses the **target-typed** new **expressions**, introduced in C# 9.

7. No, it does not. If we replace the `class` keyword by the `record` keyword it will compile, like this: `public record MyDTO(int Id, string Name);`.

8. A class can have as many display templates as there are levels in the views/pages hierarchy.

9. Display and editor templates are directly related to a type.

Chapter 18

1. No, it is compiled to WebAssembly.

2. None. All three are acceptable options—it depends on what you are building and with whom.

3. Model (State) – View (Component) – Update (Reducer).

4. No. The MVU pattern is all about a unidirectional flow of data to simplify state management.

5. Yes. Blazor can interact with JavaScript and vice versa.

Acronyms Lexicon

Here is the list of all the acronyms used throughout the book:

- ACI: Azure Container Instances
- AKS: Azure Kubernetes Service
- AOP: Aspect-Oriented Programming
- API: Application Programming Interface
- ATDD: Acceptance Test-Driven Development
- BDD: Behavior-Driven Development
- BLL: Business Logic Layer
- CDN: Content Delivery Network
- CI: Continuous Integration
- CLI: Command-Line Interface
- CQS: Command Query Separation
- CQRS: Command Query Responsibility Segregation
- CRUD: Create, Read, Update Delete
- CSRF (or XSRF): Cross-site Request Forgery
- DAL: Data Access Layer
- DDD: Domain-Driven Design
- DI: Dependency Injection
- DIP: Dependency Inversion Principle
- DOM: Document Object Model
- DRY: Don't Repeat Yourself
- DTO: Data Transfer Object
- EF Core: Entity Framework Core

- FIFO: First in, First Out
- GOF: Gang of Four
- Grpc: gRPC Remote Procedure Calls
- GUI: Graphical User Interface
- IOC: Inversion of Control
- IOT: Internet of Things
- ISP: Interface Segregation Principle
- K8s: Kubernetes
- LSP: Liskov Substitution Principle
- MQTT: MQ Telemetry Transport
- MVC: Model View Controller
- MVU: Model -View-Update
- MVVM: Model-View-ViewModel
- NFS: Network File System
- OCP: Open/Closed principle
- OOP: Object-Oriented Programming
- ORM: Object-Relational-Mapper
- PoEAA: Patterns of Enterprise Application Architecture
- PV: Persistent Volume
- E2E: End-to-End
- REST: Representational State Transfer
- RPC: Remote Procedure Call
- SEO: Search Engine Optimization
- SME: Small-to-Medium-sized-Enterprise
- SOLID: SRP, OCP, LSP, ISP, DIP
- SPA: Single-Page Application
- SQL: Structured Query Language
- SRP: Single Responsibility Principle
- TDD: Test-Driven Development

- TLD: Top-Level Domain
- UML: Unified Modeling Language
- URI: Uniform Resource Identifier
- URL: Uniform Resource Locator
- VM: Virtual machine
- Wasm: WebAssembly
- Yagni: You aren't gonna need it

Other Books You May Enjoy

If you enjoyed this book, you may be interested in these other books by Packt:

ASP.NET Core 3 and React

Carl Rippon

ISBN: 978-1-78995-022-9

- Build RESTful APIs with .NET Core using API controllers
- Create strongly typed, interactive, and function-based React components using Hooks
- Build forms efficiently using reusable React components
- Perform client-side state management with Redux and the React Context API
- Secure REST APIs with ASP.NET identity and authorization policies
- Run a range of automated tests on the frontend and backend

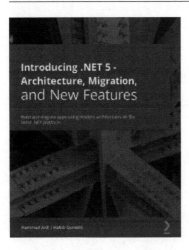

Introducing .NET 5 - Architecture, Migration, and New Features

Hammad Arif, Habib Qureshi

ISBN: 978-1-80056-056-7

- Find all of .NET 5's features and capabilities in one place

- Get to grips with application design and development using .NET 5

- Discover how to shift from legacy to modern application design using microservices and cloud-native architecture

- Explore common migration pitfalls and make the right decisions in situations where multiple options are available

- Understand container orchestration options for legacy applications

Leave a review - let other readers know what you think

Please share your thoughts on this book with others by leaving a review on the site that you bought it from. If you purchased the book from Amazon, please leave us an honest review on this book's Amazon page. This is vital so that other potential readers can see and use your unbiased opinion to make purchasing decisions, we can understand what our customers think about our products, and our authors can see your feedback on the title that they have worked with Packt to create. It will only take a few minutes of your time, but is valuable to other potential customers, our authors, and Packt. Thank you!

Index

Made in the USA
Monee, IL
12 September 2021